CASES AND MATERIALS

SALES

FIFTH EDITION

by

MARION W. BENFIELD, JR.
University Professor of Law Emeritus
Wake Forest University School of Law
and Albert E. Jenner Professor Emeritus
University of Illinois College of Law

MICHAEL M. GREENFIELD
Walter D. Coles Professor of Law
Washington University School of Law

FOUNDATION PRESS

2007

© 1980, 1986, 1992, 2004 FOUNDATION PRESS
© 2007 By FOUNDATION PRESS
        395 Hudson Street
        New York, NY 10014
        Phone Toll Free 1–877–888–1330
        Fax (212) 367–6799
        foundation–press.com
Printed in the United States of America

ISBN–13: 978–1–58778–986–1
ISBN–10: 1–58778–986–8

TEXT IS PRINTED ON 10% POST CONSUMER RECYCLED PAPER

To Dalida and Claire

*

PREFACE

This book originated in 1936 as Bogert and Britton, Sales, and in 1962 became Bogert, Britton and Hawkland, Sales and Security. After widespread enactment of the Uniform Commercial Code, in 1980 the book became Benfield and Hawkland, Sales, and enjoyed four editions. This version continues the basic structure of its immediate predecessor and will be familiar to users of the last edition. The main difference is a shift to the heavier use of problems. Twenty principal cases have been dropped or converted into notes, and there are nine new principal cases, many new and revised textual passages, and numerous new and revised problems. The primary substantive focus is Article 2 of the Uniform Commercial Code, but the book also considers Article 2A and enlarges the treatment of the Convention on Contracts for the International Sale of Goods. It also addresses UCC Articles 5, 6, 7, and 9 insofar as those Articles affect the rights of buyers and sellers of goods.

The prior editions of this book were designed primarily for use in upper-level courses on Sales, but the book also has been used successfully in first-year Sales courses. With its reliance on the use of problems and its emphasis on developing the skills of dealing with a comprehensive statute, the book continues to be suitable for both first-year and upper-level courses.

The primary criterion for selection of materials to be included in the book is effectiveness as teaching materials. Some are included for their description of the underlying business transaction; some are included for their exposition of the law; but all are included for the platform they create for exploring the rules and, especially, the methodology of the Code.

In the course of editing the judicial opinions, I have omitted numerous citations and footnotes without any notation of the omissions. The footnotes that remain bear their original numbers, and footnotes designated by superscript letters are explanatory footnotes that I have added to the opinions. I have corrected obvious typographical and grammatical errors in reprinted materials without using the conventional "sic." In view of the currently dim prospects for enactment of the 2003 amendments to Articles 2 and 2A, all unadorned references to those Articles are to the pre-amendment versions. References to the amended provisions are clearly labeled.

In preparing this edition, I am extremely grateful for the broad shoulders of Professors Benfield and Hawkland, two of the preeminent commercial law scholars of the twentieth century. Their work has provided a most solid foundation for me to build on, and Professor Benfield has reviewed the copy and provided suggestions for this edition.

MICHAEL M. GREENFIELD

St. Louis, Missouri
December 2006

SUMMARY OF CONTENTS

PREFACE v
TABLE OF CASES xv

CHAPTER 1 INTRODUCTION 1

A. Organization of the Book and Goals of the Course 1
B. Background and History of the UCC 2
C. The Code as "Code" 7
D. Scope of Article 2 11

CHAPTER 2 FORMATION OF THE SALES CONTRACT 39

A. Introduction 39
B. Offer and Acceptance 39
C. Statute of Frauds 49
D. The Battle of the Forms 69
E. Articles 2 and 2A and Electronic Commerce 96
F. Contract Modification 98
G. Options Without Consideration (Firm Offers) 117

CHAPTER 3 TERMS OF THE SALES CONTRACT 121

A. Terms of the Agreement 122
B. Terms Outside the Agreement: The "Statutory Terms" 159

CHAPTER 4 EXPRESS AND IMPLIED WARRANTIES 215

A. Introduction 215
B. Express Warranties 216
C. The Implied Warranties of Merchantability and Fitness 228
D. Warranty of Title 274

**CHAPTER 5 DISCLAIMERS AND OTHER LIMITATIONS
ON WARRANTIES** 279

A. Disclaimers 279
B. Privity and Warranty 295
C. Contributory Negligence and Assumption of Risk 325
D. Federal and State Statutes Applying Special Rules to Consumer
Transactions 338

CHAPTER 6   BUYER'S REMEDIES FOR BREACH BY THE SELLER 351

A. Introduction 351
B. Rejection, Cure, and Revocation of Acceptance 351
C. Remedies When the Buyer Does Not Have the Goods 408
D. Remedies When the Buyer Gets and Keeps the Goods 431
E. Contractual Limitations of Remedies 438

CHAPTER 7   SELLER'S REMEDIES FOR BREACH BY THE BUYER 450

A. Introduction 450
B. Remedies on Wrongful Rejection or Repudiation 450

CHAPTER 8   REPUDIATION AND THE PROSPECT OF BREACH 491

A. The Prospect of Breach 491
B. Repudiation 497

CHAPTER 9   DISCHARGE BY IMPOSSIBILITY OR FRUS-TRATION OF PURPOSE 514

CHAPTER 10   RIGHTS AND LIABILITIES OF THIRD PAR-TIES 534

A. Title 534
B. Situations in Which the Buyer Gets Better Title Than the Seller Had 538
C. Situations in Which the Buyer Gets Worse Title Than the Seller Had 555
D. Right of the Seller, As Against Creditors of the Buyer, to Recover Goods from a Buyer Who Is Insolvent 571

CHAPTER 11   DOCUMENTARY TRANSACTIONS 587

A. Introduction 587
B. Obligations of Carriers 588
C. Shipments Under Reservation 609
D. Letters of Credit 611

Index 625

TABLE OF CONTENTS

PREFACE v
TABLE OF CASES xv

CHAPTER 1 INTRODUCTION 1

A. Organization of the Book and Goals of the Course 1
B. Background and History of the UCC 2
   1. Sponsors 2
     a. The National Conference of Commissioners on Uniform
       State Laws 2
     b. The American Law Institute 3
   2. The Initial Drafting History 4
   3. Scope of the Uniform Commercial Code 5
   4. Permanent Editorial Board 7
C. The Code as "Code" 7
D. Scope of Article 2 11
   1. The Sales–Service Hybrid 11
     Anthony Pools v. Sheehan 11
   2. Computer Software 20
     Advent Systems Ltd. v. Unisys Corp. 20
     Architectronics, Inc. v. Control Systems, Inc. 22
   3. Application of Article 2 Rules in Non–Goods Transactions 29
     Hoffman v. Horton 29
   4. Effect of Article 2 on Other Statutes Applicable to Sale of
      Goods 33
     *Pet Dealers Association of New Jersey, Inc. v. Division of
     Consumer Affairs, Dept. of Law and Public Safety, State of
     New Jersey* 33
   5. Territorial and Temporal Limitations and Choice of Law 35
     a. Choice of Law 35
     b. Transitional Provisions 38

CHAPTER 2 FORMATION OF THE SALES CONTRACT 39

A. Introduction 39
B. Offer and Acceptance 39
   Unique Designs, Inc. v. Pittard Machinery Company 39
   Bacou Dalloz USA, Inc. v. Continental Polymers, Inc. 42
C. Statute of Frauds 49
   Southwest Engineering Co., Inc. v. Martin Tractor Co., Inc. 50
   Decatur Cooperative Association v. Urban 57
   Lige Dickson Co. v. Union Oil Co. of California 63
D. The Battle of the Forms 69
   C. Itoh & Co. (America), Inc. v. Jordan International Co. 69
   Northrop Corporation v. Litronic Industries 78

Hill v. Gateway 2000, Inc. 86
Klocek v. Gateway, Inc. 90
E. Articles 2 and 2A and Electronic Commerce 96
F. Contract Modification 98
Wisconsin Knife Works v. National Metal Crafters 98
BMC Industries, Inc. v. Barth Industries, Inc. 109
G. Options Without Consideration (Firm Offers) 117
Friedman v. Sommer 117

CHAPTER 3 TERMS OF THE SALES CONTRACT 121

A. Terms of the Agreement 122
   1. The Concept of Agreement 122
   2. Express Terms and the Limitations on Them 122
      Campbell Soup Co. v. Wentz 123
      A & M Produce Co. v. FMC Corp. 125
   3. The Hierarchy of the Various Components of Agreement 140
      a. The Parol Evidence Rule 141
         ARB, Inc. v. E–Systems, Inc. 141
         Noble v. Logan–Dees Chevrolet–Buick, Inc. 145
      b. Trade Usage, Course of Dealing, Good Faith 148
         Nanakuli Paving & Rock Co. v. Shell Oil Co., Inc. 148
B. Terms Outside the Agreement: The "Statutory Terms" 159
   1. Price 161
      a. Background 161
      b. Variable–Price Terms 162
      c. Drafting Open–Price Terms 162
      d. Mutuality of Obligation 163
      James Mathis v. Exxon Corporation 164
   2. Quantity 172
      Riegel Fiber Corp. v. Anderson Gin Co. 172
   3. Payment 180
   4. Delivery 181
      Luedtke Engineering Co., Inc. v. Indiana Limestone Co., Inc. 182
   5. Risk of Loss 186
      A.M. Knitwear Corp. v. All America Export–Import Corp. 188
      Silver v. Wycombe, Meyer & Co., Inc. 198
      Jakowski v. Carole Chevrolet, Inc. 201
   6. Choice of Law 206
      Wright-Moore Corporation v. Ricoh Corporation 206
   7. Special Arrangements 211
      a. Sale or Return; Sale on Approval 211
      b. Auctions 211
      Drew v. John Deere Co. of Syracuse, Inc. 211

CHAPTER 4 EXPRESS AND IMPLIED WARRANTIES 215

A. Introduction 215
B. Express Warranties 216
   Doug Connor, Inc. v. Proto–Grind, Inc. 216
   Royal Business Machines, Inc. v. Lorraine Corp. 219

C. The Implied Warranties of Merchantability and Fitness 228
  1. Historical Background 228
  2. The Standards 231
    Ambassador Steel Co. v. Ewald Steel Co. 232
    Bethlehem Steel Corp. v. Chicago Eastern Corp. 235
  3. Warranty and Strict Liability 246
    Denny v. Ford Motor Company 247
    Tyson v. Ciba–Geigy Corp. 262
    A. S. Leavitt v. Monaco Coach Corporation 264
  4. Leases 268
    All–States Leasing Co. v. Bass 268
D. Warranty of Title 274
  1. The Obligation to Provide Good Title 274
  2. Disclaimer of the Warranty 277
  3. Leases 278
  4. CISG 278

CHAPTER 5 DISCLAIMERS AND OTHER LIMITATIONS ON WARRANTIES 279

A. Disclaimers 279
  Sierra Diesel Injection Service, Inc. v. Burroughs Corporation 279
  Gindy Manufacturing Corp. v. Cardinale Trucking Corp. 285
B. Privity and Warranty 295
  Randy Knitwear, Inc. v. American Cyanamid Co. 295
  Tex Enterprises, Inc. v. Brockway Standard, Inc. 307
  Morrow v. New Moon Homes, Inc. 311
  Patty Precision Products Co. v. Brown & Sharpe Manufacturing Co. 321
C. Contributory Negligence and Assumption of Risk 325
  Correia v. Firestone Tire & Rubber Co. 329
  Fiske v. MacGregor, Div. of Brunswick 333
D. Federal and State Statutes Applying Special Rules to Consumer Transactions 338
  1. The Magnuson–Moss Consumer Warranty Act 338
    a. Introduction 338
    b. Invalidation of Disclaimers 339
    c. Impact on the Requirement of Privity 340
    d. Leases 345
  2. State Statutes Modifying Article 2 for Consumer Transactions ... 347

CHAPTER 6 BUYER'S REMEDIES FOR BREACH BY THE SELLER 351

A. Introduction 351
B. Rejection, Cure, and Revocation of Acceptance 351
  1. Single–Delivery Contracts 351
    D.P. Technology Corp. v. Sherwood Tool, Inc. 353

2. Installment Contracts -- 359
Midwest Mobile Diagnostic Imaging, L.L.C. v. Dynamics Corporation of America --- 361
3. Procedure for Effective Rejection and Duties After Rejection ---- 370
Miron v. Yonkers Raceway, Inc. -------------------------------- 370
4. Cure -- 383
Zabriskie Chevrolet, Inc. v. Smith ---------------------------- 384
5. Revocation of Acceptance -------------------------------------- 396
Jorgensen v. Pressnall -- 396
Gappelberg v. Landrum --- 402
Gappelberg v. Landrum --- 404
C. Remedies When the Buyer Does Not Have the Goods ---------------- 408
1. The Right to Get The Goods----------------------------------- 408
Sedmak v. Charlie's Chevrolet, Inc. -------------------------- 409
Hilmor Sales Co. v. Helen Neushaefer Div. of Supronics Corp.---- 412
2. The Right to Damages -- 415
Valley Die Cast Corp. v. A.C.W. Inc. ------------------------- 416
Allied Canners & Packers, Inc. v. Victor Packing Co. -------- 422
TexPar Energy Inc. v. Murphy Oil USA, Inc. ------------------ 427
D. Remedies When the Buyer Gets and Keeps the Goods --------------- 431
Jay V. Zimmerman Co. v. General Mills, Inc. ------------------- 433
Eastern Air Lines, Inc. v. McDonnell Douglas Corp. ----------- 436
E. Contractual Limitations of Remedies --------------------------- 438
Smith v. Navistar International Transportation Corporation -------- 441

CHAPTER 7 SELLER'S REMEDIES FOR BREACH BY THE BUYER --- 450

A. Introduction -- 450
B. Remedies on Wrongful Rejection or Repudiation ----------------- 450
1. Action for the Price--- 450
Industrial Molded Plastic Products, Inc. v. J. Gross & Son, Inc. 450
2. Action for Damages--- 456
Tesoro Petroleum Corp. v. Holborn Oil Co., Ltd. -------------- 458
Neri v. Retail Marine Corp. ---------------------------------- 465
3. Contracted-for Damages -------------------------------------- 475
Kvassay v. Murray -- 475
Superfos Investments Limited v. FirstMiss Fertilizer, Inc. --------- 477
Martin v. Sheffer -- 484

CHAPTER 8 REPUDIATION AND THE PROSPECT OF BREACH -- 491

A. The Prospect of Breach -- 491
Clem Perrin Marine Towing, Inc. v. Panama Canal Co. -------------- 492
B. Repudiation -- 497
1. Definition -- 497
2. Damages --- 504
Oloffson v. Coomer --- 505

**CHAPTER 9 DISCHARGE BY IMPOSSIBILITY OR FRUS-
TRATION OF PURPOSE** 514

United States v. Wegematic Corp. 514
Chase Precast Corporation v. John J. Paonessa Company, Inc. 518
Waldinger Corp. v. CRS Group Engineers, Inc. 522

**CHAPTER 10 RIGHTS AND LIABILITIES OF THIRD PAR-
TIES** 534

A. Title 534
   Home Indemnity Co. v. Twin City Fire Insurance Co. 534
B. Situations in Which the Buyer Gets Better Title Than the Seller
   Had 538
   1. Rights of the Buyer Against a Secured Creditor of the Seller 538
      Snap–On Tools Corporation v. Rice 539
      General Electric Credit Corporation v. Humble 543
   2. Rights of the Buyer when the Seller Does Not Own the Goods:
      Entrustment 550
      Atlas Auto Rental Corp. v. Weisberg 550
C. Situations in Which the Buyer Gets Worse Title Than the Seller
   Had 555
   1. Fraudulent Conveyances 555
      a. Seller's Retention of Possession After the Sale 555
      Lefever v. Mires 556
      Blumenstein v. Phillips Insurance Center, Inc. 557
      b. Sales Made with Actual Intent to Defraud Creditors 566
      c. Sales for Less than Fair Value by Sellers Who Are Insolvent
         or Who Are Left with Insufficient Capital 567
   2. Bulk Sales 568
      a. Transactions Covered 569
      b. Transfers Excepted 569
      c. Compliance with the Act 570
         (1) Compliance Procedures 570
         (2) Effect of Failure to Comply 570
D. Right of the Seller, As Against Creditors of the Buyer, to Recover
   Goods from a Buyer Who Is Insolvent 571
   1. Rights Against Lien Creditors and the Trustee in Bankruptcy 571
      In re Mel Golde Shoes, Inc. 571
   2. Rights Against Secured Creditors 579
      In re Emery Corp. 580
      Lavonia Manufacturing Co. v. Emery Corp. 583

CHAPTER 11 DOCUMENTARY TRANSACTIONS 587

A. Introduction 587
B. Obligations of Carriers 588
   Fine Foliage of Florida, Inc. v. Bowman Transportation, Inc. 594
   G.A.C. Commercial Corp. v. Wilson 600
   Rountree v. Lydick–Barmann Co. 606

C. Shipments Under Reservation ---------------------------------- 609
D. Letters of Credit -- 611
    Courtaulds North America, Inc. v. North Carolina National Bank   613
    United Bank Ltd. v. Cambridge Sporting Goods Corp. ---------------- 619

INDEX -- 625

TABLE OF CASES

Principal cases are in bold type. Non-principal cases are in roman type. References are to Pages.

Admiral Oasis Hotel Corp. v. Home Gas Industries, Inc., 68 Ill.App.2d 297, 216 N.E.2d 282 (Ill.App. 1 Dist.1965), 95

Advent Systems Ltd. v. Unisys Corp., 925 F.2d 670 (3rd Cir.1991), **20**

Air Heaters, Inc. v. Johnson Elec., Inc., 258 N.W.2d 649 (N.D.1977), 274

Alice v. Robett Mfg. Co., 328 F.Supp. 1377 (N.D.Ga.1970), 56

Allied Canners & Packers, Inc. v. Victor Packing Co., 162 Cal.App.3d 905, 209 Cal.Rptr. 60 (Cal.App. 1 Dist.1984), **422,** 430

Allied Grape Growers v. Bronco Wine Co., 203 Cal.App.3d 432, 249 Cal.Rptr. 872 (Cal.App. 5 Dist.1988), 66

All–States Leasing Co. v. Bass, 96 Idaho 873, 538 P.2d 1177 (Idaho 1975), **268,** 271, 272, 320

Ambassador Steel Co. v. Ewald Steel Co., 33 Mich.App. 495, 190 N.W.2d 275 (Mich.App.1971), **232,** 246

A. M. Knitwear Corp. v. All America Export–Import Corp., 390 N.Y.S.2d 832, 359 N.E.2d 342 (N.Y.1976), **188,** 193, 194

A & M Produce Co. v. FMC Corp., 135 Cal.App.3d 473, 186 Cal.Rptr. 114 (Cal. App. 4 Dist.1982), **125,** 135, 136, 293

Anthony Pools v. Sheehan, 295 Md. 285, 455 A.2d 434 (Md.1983), **11,** 17, 27, 29, 262, 293

Appeal of (see name of party)

ARB, Inc. v. E–Systems, Inc., 663 F.2d 189 (D.C.Cir.1980), **141,** 144, 145, 147, 159, 495

Architectronics, Inc. v. Control Systems, Inc., 935 F.Supp. 425 (S.D.N.Y.1996), **22,** 27

Atlas Auto Rental Corp. v. Weisberg, 54 Misc.2d 168, 281 N.Y.S.2d 400 (N.Y.City Civ.Ct.1967), **550,** 554, 586

Bacou Dalloz United StatesA, Inc. v. Continental Polymers, Inc., 344 F.3d 22 (1st Cir.2003), **42**

Baird v. Elliott, 63 N.D. 738, 249 N.W. 894 (N.D.1933), 32

Barrett v. Brian Bemis Auto World, 408 F.Supp.2d 539 (N.D.Ill.2005), 400

Bay State–Spray & Provincetown S.S., Inc. v. Caterpillar Tractor Co., 404 Mass. 103, 533 N.E.2d 1350 (Mass.1989), 319

Beal v. General Motors Corp., 354 F.Supp. 423 (D.Del.1973), 447

Beckman v. Brickley, 144 Wash. 558, 258 P. 488 (Wash.1927), 32

Bethlehem Steel Corp. v. Chicago Eastern Corp., 863 F.2d 508 (7th Cir.1988), **235,** 240, 242

Bethlehem Steel Corp. v. Litton Industries, Inc., 321 Pa.Super. 357, 468 A.2d 748 (Pa.Super.1983), 42

Beyond the Garden Gate, Inc. v. Northstar Freeze–Dry Mfg., Inc., 526 N.W.2d 305 (Iowa 1995), 300, 302

Big Knob Volunteer Fire Co. v. Lowe & Moyer Garage, Inc., 338 Pa.Super. 257, 487 A.2d 953 (Pa.Super.1985), 548

Blumenstein v. Phillips Ins. Center, Inc., 490 P.2d 1213 (Alaska 1971), **557,** 564

BMC Industries, Inc. v. Barth Industries, Inc., 160 F.3d 1322 (11th Cir. 1998), **109**

Bornstein v. Somerson, 341 So.2d 1043 (Fla. App. 2 Dist.1977), 49

Bowen v. Young, 507 S.W.2d 600 (Tex.Civ. App.-El Paso 1974), 380, 400

Bowes v. Shand, LR 2 App. Cas. 455 (H.L. 1877), 352

Brooks v. Federal Surety Co., 24 F.2d 884 (D.C.Cir.1928), 161

Brunswick Box Co. v. Coutinho, Caro & Co., 617 F.2d 355 (4th Cir.1980), 194

Campbell Soup Co. v. Wentz, 172 F.2d 80 (3rd Cir.1948), **123,** 136

Capitol Dodge Sales v. Northern Concrete Pipe, Inc., 131 Mich.App. 149, 346 N.W.2d 535 (Mich.App.1983), 328

Cardozo v. True, 342 So.2d 1053 (Fla.App. 2 Dist.1977), 22

Cervadoro v. First Nat. Bank and Trust Co., 267 A.D. 314, 45 N.Y.S.2d 738 (N.Y.A.D. 2 Dept.1944), 32

Chase Precast Corp. v. John J. Paonessa Co., 409 Mass. 371, 566 N.E.2d 603 (Mass.1991), **518,** 533

Chatlos Systems, Inc. v. National Cash Register Corp., 670 F.2d 1304 (3rd Cir.1982), 431

Chatlos Systems, Inc. v. National Cash Register Corp., 635 F.2d 1081 (3rd Cir.1980), 440

Chicago Prime Packers, Inc. v. Northam Food Trading Co., 408 F.3d 894 (7th Cir. 2005), 382

C. Itoh & Co. (America) Inc. v. Jordan Intern. Co., 552 F.2d 1228 (7th Cir. 1977), **69,** 77, 84

Clem Perrin Marine Towing, Inc. v. Panama Canal Co., 730 F.2d 186 (5th Cir. 1984), **492**

Cleveland Wrecking Co. v. Federal Deposit Ins. Corp., 66 F.Supp. 921 (E.D.Pa.1946), 32

Cline v. Prowler Industries of Maryland, Inc., 418 A.2d 968 (Del.Supr.1980), 320

Collins Co., Ltd. v. Carboline Co., 125 Ill.2d 498, 127 Ill.Dec. 5, 532 N.E.2d 834 (Ill. 1988), 320

Continental Concrete Pipe Corp. v. Century Road Builders, Inc., 195 Ill.App.3d 1, 142 Ill.Dec. 291, 552 N.E.2d 1032 (Ill.App. 1 Dist.1990), 378

Cook Specialty Co. v. Schrlock, 772 F.Supp. 1532 (E.D.Pa.1991), 194

Cooley v. Big Horn Harvestore Systems, Inc., 767 P.2d 740 (Colo.App.1988), 115

Copiers Typewriters Calculators, Inc. v. Toshiba Corp., 576 F.Supp. 312 (D.Md.1983), 302

Correia v. Firestone Tire & Rubber Co., 388 Mass. 342, 446 N.E.2d 1033 (Mass. 1983), **329,** 337

Courtaulds North America, Inc. v. North Carolina Nat. Bank, 528 F.2d 802 (4th Cir.1975), **613**

Cundy v. International Trencher Service, Inc., 358 N.W.2d 233 (S.D.1984), 320

Day v. Tenneco, Inc., 696 F.Supp. 233 (S.D.Miss.1988), 481

Decatur Co-op. Ass'n v. Urban, 219 Kan. 171, 547 P.2d 323 (Kan.1976), **57,** 63, 115

Dehahn v. Innes, 356 A.2d 711 (Me.1976), 27

DeJesus v. Cat Auto Tech Corp., 161 Misc.2d 723, 615 N.Y.S.2d 236 (N.Y.City Civ.Ct. 1994), 379

Denny v. Ford Motor Co., 639 N.Y.S.2d 250, 662 N.E.2d 730 (N.Y.1995), **247,** 262, 264, 306

Diskmakers, Inc. v. DeWitt Equipment Corp., 555 F.2d 1177 (3rd Cir.1977), 495

Dixie Lime & Stone Co. v. Wiggins Scale Co., 144 Ga.App. 145, 240 S.E.2d 323 (Ga.App. 1977), 18

Doug Connor, Inc. v. Proto–Grind, Inc., 761 So.2d 426 (Fla.App. 5 Dist.2000), **216**

D.P. Technology Corp. v. Sherwood Tool, Inc., 751 F.Supp. 1038 (D.Conn. 1990), **353,** 356

Drew v. John Deere Co. of Syracuse, Inc., 19 A.D.2d 308, 241 N.Y.S.2d 267 (N.Y.A.D. 4 Dept.1963), **211**

Durfee v. Rod Baxter Imports, Inc., 262 N.W.2d 349 (Minn.1977), 401

E. A. Coronis Associates v. M. Gordon Const. Co., 90 N.J.Super. 69, 216 A.2d 246 (N.J.Super.A.D.1966), 119

Eastern Air Lines, Inc. v. McDonnell Douglas Corp., 532 F.2d 957 (5th Cir. 1976), **436**

Eastern Rolling Mill Co. v. Michlovitz, 157 Md. 51, 145 A. 378 (Md.1929), 413

East River Steamship Corp. v. Transamerica Delaval, Inc., 476 U.S. 858, 106 S.Ct. 2295, 90 L.Ed.2d 865 (1986), 261

Eggl v. Letvin Equipment Co., 632 N.W.2d 435 (N.D.2001), 328

Ellis Canning Co. v. Bernstein, 348 F.Supp. 1212 (D.Colo.1972), 68, 96

Emery Corp., In re, 38 B.R. 489 (Bkrtcy. E.D.Pa.1984), **580**

Epprecht v. IBM Corp., 36 UCC Rep.Serv. 391 (E.D.Pa.1983), 68

Equitable Gas Light Co. of Baltimore City v. Baltimore Coal Tar & Mfg. Co., 63 Md. 285 (Md.1885), 413

Everett v. TK–Taito, L.L.C., 178 S.W.3d 844 (Tex.App.-Fort Worth 2005), 243

Ewanchuk v. Mitchell, 154 S.W.3d 476 (Mo. App. S.D.2005), 498

Fablok Mills, Inc. v. Cocker Mach. & Foundry Co., 125 N.J.Super. 251, 310 A.2d 491 (N.J.Super.A.D.1973), 378, 400

Fargo Mach. & Tool Co. v. Kearney & Trecker Corp., 428 F.Supp. 364 (E.D.Mich. 1977), 239, 358

Farrell v. Paulus, 309 Mich. 441, 15 N.W.2d 700 (Mich.1944), 567

Feary v. Aaron Burglar Alarm, Inc., 32 Cal. App.3d 553, 108 Cal.Rptr. 242 (Cal.App. 2 Dist.1973), 34

Federal's, Inc., In re, 12 UCC Rep.Serv. 1142 (Bkrtcy.E.D.Mich.1973), 574

Ferguson v. Sturm, Ruger & Co., 524 F.Supp. 1042 (D.Conn.1981), 302

Filley v. Pope, 115 U.S. 213, 6 S.Ct. 19, 29 L.Ed. 372 (1885), 352

Financial Federated Title & Trust, In re, 309 F.3d 1325 (11th Cir.2002), 566

Fine Foliage of Florida, Inc. v. Bowman Transp., Inc., 901 F.2d 1034 (11th Cir. 1990), **594,** 600

First Nat. Bank of Chicago v. Jefferson Mortg. Co., 576 F.2d 479 (3rd Cir.1978), 509

Fiske v. MacGregor, Div. of Brunswick, 464 A.2d 719 (R.I.1983), **333,** 337

Franklin v. Northwest Drilling Co., Inc., 215 Kan. 304, 524 P.2d 1194 (Kan.1974), 274

Frederick Raff Co. v. Murphy, 110 Conn. 234, 147 A. 709 (Conn.1929), 32

Friedman v. Sommer, 481 N.Y.S.2d 326, 471 N.E.2d 139 (N.Y.1984), **117,** 118

G. A. C. Commercial Corp. v. Wilson, 271 F.Supp. 242 (S.D.N.Y.1967), **600**

Gappelberg v. Landrum, 666 S.W.2d 88 (Tex.1984), **404**

Gappelberg v. Landrum, 654 S.W.2d 549 (Tex.App.-Dallas 1983), **402,** 407

Gasque v. Mooers Motor Car Co., Inc., 227 Va. 154, 313 S.E.2d 384 (Va.1984), 401

General Elec. Credit Corp. v. Humble, 532 F.Supp. 703 (M.D.Ala.1982), **543,** 547

Gicinto v. Credithrift of America, No. 3, Inc., 219 Kan. 766, 549 P.2d 870 (Kan.1976), 554

Gindy Mfg. Corp. v. Cardinale Trucking Corp., 111 N.J.Super. 383, 268 A.2d 345 (N.J.Super.L.1970), 245, **285,** 294

Graulich Caterer Inc. v. Hans Holterbosch, Inc., 101 N.J.Super. 61, 243 A.2d 253 (N.J.Super.A.D.1968), 359, 368

Green v. Armstrong, 1 Denio 550 (N.Y.Sup. 1845), 32

Green Chevrolet Co. v. Kemp, 241 Ark. 62, 406 S.W.2d 142 (Ark.1966), 400

Hamilton v. O'Connor Chevrolet, Inc., 399 F.Supp.2d 860 (N.D.Ill.2005), 283, 284

Hannover Corp., In re, 310 F.3d 796 (5th Cir.2002), 566

Heil v. Standard Chemical Mfg. Co., 301 Minn. 315, 223 N.W.2d 37 (Minn.1974), 325

Henningsen v. Bloomfield Motors, Inc., 32 N.J. 358, 161 A.2d 69 (N.J.1960), 292, 388

H. Hirschfield Sons Co. v. Colt Industries, 107 Mich.App. 720, 309 N.W.2d 714 (Mich.App.1981), 18

Hill v. Gateway 2000, Inc., 105 F.3d 1147 (7th Cir.1997), **86,** 95, 136

Hilmor Sales Co. v. Helen Neushaefer Div. of Supronics Corp., 1969 WL 11054 (N.Y.Sup.1969), **412**

Hoffman v. Horton, 212 Va. 565, 186 S.E.2d 79 (Va.1972), **29,** 32, 211

Hoffman Motors, Inc. v. Enockson, 240 N.W.2d 353 (N.D.1976), 34

Holiday Mfg. Co. v. B.A.S.F. Systems, Inc., 380 F.Supp. 1096 (D.Neb.1974), 369

Home Indem. Co. v. Twin City Fire Ins. Co., 474 F.2d 1081 (7th Cir.1973), **534**

Howard Const. Co. v. Jeff–Cole Quarries, Inc., 669 S.W.2d 221 (Mo.App. W.D.1983), 56

Hurricane Lumber Co. v. Lowe, 110 Va. 380, 66 S.E. 66 (Va.1909), 32

H–W–H Cattle Co. v. Schroeder, 767 F.2d 437 (8th Cir.1985), 430

Impossible Electronic Techniques, Inc. v. Wackenhut Protective Systems, Inc., 669 F.2d 1026 (5th Cir.1982), 68

Industrial Molded Plastic Products, Inc. v. J. Gross & Son, Inc., 263 Pa.Super. 515, 398 A.2d 695 (Pa.Super.1979), **450,** 454

In re (see name of party)

Insul–Mark Midwest, Inc. v. Modern Materials, Inc., 612 N.E.2d 550 (Ind.1993), 18

Insurance Co. of North America v. Radiant Elec. Co., 55 Mich.App. 410, 222 N.W.2d 323 (Mich.App.1974), 274

Jakowski v. Carole Chevrolet, Inc., 180 N.J.Super. 122, 433 A.2d 841 (N.J.Super.L.1981), **201,** 204, 396

Jay V. Zimmerman Co. v. General Mills, Inc., 327 F.Supp. 1198 (E.D.Mo.1971), **433,** 438

Jefferson v. Jones, 286 Md. 544, 408 A.2d 1036 (Md.1979), 275

Johannsen v. Minnesota Valley Ford Tractor Co., Inc., 304 N.W.2d 654 (Minn.1981), 395

Jones v. Star Credit Corp., 59 Misc.2d 189, 298 N.Y.S.2d 264 (N.Y.Sup.1969), 136

Jorgensen v. Pressnall, 274 Or. 285, 545 P.2d 1382 (Or.1976), **396,** 399, 400

Keystone Aeronautics Corp. v. R. J. Enstrom Corp., 499 F.2d 146 (3rd Cir.1974), 135

KKO, Inc. v. Honeywell, Inc., 517 F.Supp. 892 (N.D.Ill.1981), 135

Klocek v. Gateway, Inc., 104 F.Supp.2d 1332 (D.Kan.2000), **90,** 95

Koch Supplies, Inc. v. Farm Fresh Meats, Inc., 630 F.2d 282 (5th Cir.1980), 378

Krell v. Henry, 2 K.B. 740 (C.A. 1903), 514

Kvassay v. Murray, 15 Kan.App.2d 426, 808 P.2d 896 (Kan.App.1991), **475,** 477

Lamb v. Georgia–Pacific Corp., 194 Ga.App. 848, 392 S.E.2d 307 (Ga.App.1990), 302

Larry J. Soldinger Asso., Ltd. v. Aston Martin Lagonda of No. Amer., Inc., 1999 WL 756174 (N.D.Ill.1999), 343

Lavonia Mfg. Co. v. Emery Corp., 52 B.R. 944 (E.D.Pa.1985), **583**

Leavitt v. Monaco Coach Corp., 241 Mich. App. 288, 616 N.W.2d 175 (Mich.App. 2000), **264**

Lee Oldsmobile, Inc. v. Kaiden, 32 Md.App. 556, 363 A.2d 270 (Md.App.1976), 474

Lefever v. Mires, 81 Ill. 456 (Ill.1876), **556,** 557, 564

Lemley v. J & B Tire Co., 426 F.Supp. 1378 (W.D.Pa.1977), 274

Levy v. Radkay, 233 Mass. 29, 123 N.E. 97 (Mass.1919), 600

Lewis v. Big Powderhorn Mountain Ski Corp., 69 Mich.App. 437, 245 N.W.2d 81 (Mich.App.1976), 274

Lewis v. Hughes, 276 Md. 247, 346 A.2d 231 (Md.1975), 67, 68

Lige Dickson Co. v. Union Oil Co. of California, 96 Wash.2d 291, 635 P.2d 103 (Wash.1981), **63**

Lockheed Electronics Co. v. Keronix, Inc., 114 Cal.App.3d 304, 170 Cal.Rptr. 591 (Cal.App. 2 Dist.1981), 432

Luedtke Engineering Co., Inc. v. Indiana Limestone Co., Inc., 740 F.2d 598 (7th Cir.1984), **182**

Mahon v. Stowers, 416 U.S. 100, 94 S.Ct. 1626, 40 L.Ed.2d 79 (1974), 586

Martin v. Joseph Harris Co., 767 F.2d 296 (6th Cir.1985), 293

Martin v. Sheffer, 102 N.C.App. 802, 403 S.E.2d 555 (N.C.App.1991), **484,** 486, 487

Mathis v. Exxon Corp., 302 F.3d 448 (5th Cir.2002), **164,** 171

Mattek v. Malofsky, 42 Wis.2d 16, 165 N.W.2d 406 (Wis.1969), 554

Matter of (see name of party)

Max Bauer Meat Packer, Inc. v. United States, 198 Ct.Cl. 97, 458 F.2d 88 (Ct.Cl. 1972), 378

Mazur Bros. & Jaffe Fish Co., Inc., Appeal of, 3 UCC Rep.Serv. 419 (V.A.B.C.A.1965), 378

McCoy v. Mitsuboshi Cutlery, Inc., 67 F.3d 917 (Fed.Cir.1995), 455

Medico Leasing Co. v. Smith, 457 P.2d 548 (Okla.1969), 554

Mel Golde Shoes, Inc., In re, 403 F.2d 658 (6th Cir.1968), **571,** 574, 577

Menard & Holmberg Rambler, Inc. v. Shea, 44 Mass.App.Dec. 204 (Mass.App.Div. 1970), 379

Mercedes–Benz Credit Corp. v. Lotito, 306 N.J.Super. 25, 703 A.2d 288 (N.J.Super.A.D.1997), 273

Michael M. Berlin & Co., Inc. v. T. Whiting Mfg., Inc., 5 UCC Rep.Serv. 357 (N.Y.Sup. 1968), 378

Midwest Mobile Diagnostic Imaging, L.L.C. v. Dynamics Corp. of America, 965 F.Supp. 1003 (W.D.Mich.1997), **361**

Milau Associates v. North Ave. Development Corp., 398 N.Y.S.2d 882, 368 N.E.2d 1247 (N.Y.1977), 274

Milgard Tempering, Inc. v. Selas Corp., 902 F.2d 703 (9th Cir.1990), 446

Minnesota Min. & Mfg. Co. v. Nishika Ltd., 565 N.W.2d 16 (Minn.1997), 302

Miron v. Yonkers Raceway, Inc., 400 F.2d 112 (2nd Cir.1968), **370,** 378, 379

Morris Plan Co. of Cal. v. Moody, 266 Cal. App.2d 28, 72 Cal.Rptr. 123 (Cal.App. 4 Dist.1968), 34

Morrow v. New Moon Homes, Inc., 548 P.2d 279 (Alaska 1976), **311,** 319, 323, 324

Multiplastics, Inc. v. Arch Industries, Inc., 166 Conn. 280, 348 A.2d 618 (Conn.1974), 204

Murray v. D & J Motor Co., Inc., 958 P.2d 823 (Okla.Civ.App. Div. 4 1998), 292

Murray v. Holiday Rambler, Inc., 83 Wis.2d 406, 265 N.W.2d 513 (Wis.1978), 440

M & W Farm Service Co. v. Callison, 285 N.W.2d 271 (Iowa 1979), 67

Nanakuli Paving & Rock Co. v. Shell Oil Co., Inc., 664 F.2d 772 (9th Cir.1981), **148,** 159

National Historic Shrines Foundation, Inc. v. Dali, 4 UCC Rep.Serv. 71 (N.Y.Sup.1967), 17

National Importing & Trading Co. v. E.A. Bear & Co., 324 Ill. 346, 155 N.E. 343 (Ill.1927), 352

N. Bloom & Son (Antiques) Ltd. v. Skelly, 673 F.Supp. 1260 (S.D.N.Y.1987), 453, 454, 487

Neal v. Clark, 75 Ariz. 91, 251 P.2d 903 (Ariz.1952), 567

Nelson v. International Harvester Corp., 394 N.W.2d 578 (Minn.App.1986), 320

Nelson v. Wilkins Dodge, Inc., 256 N.W.2d 472 (Minn.1977), 240

Neri v. Retail Marine Corp., 334 N.Y.S.2d 165, 285 N.E.2d 311 (N.Y.1972), **465,** 468, 469, 472, 473

Nevada Contract Services, Inc. v. Squirrel Companies, Inc., 119 Nev. 157, 68 P.3d 896 (Nev.2003), 327

Nevada National Leasing Co. v. Hereford, 203 Cal.Rptr. 118, 680 P.2d 1077 (Cal. 1984), 213

Neville Chemical Co. v. Union Carbide Corp., 422 F.2d 1205 (3rd Cir.1970), 138, 378

Nisky v. Childs Co., 135 A. 805 (N.J.Err. & App.1927), 19

Noble v. Logan–Dees Chevrolet–Buick, Inc., 293 So.2d 14 (Miss.1974), **145,** 147

Nobs Chemical, United StatesA., Inc. v. Koppers Co., Inc., 616 F.2d 212 (5th Cir. 1980), 462

Norrington v. Wright, 115 U.S. 188, 6 S.Ct. 12, 29 L.Ed. 366 (1885), 352

Northern Indiana Public Service Co. v. Carbon County Coal Co., 799 F.2d 265 (7th Cir.1986), 533

Northrop Corp. v. Litronic Industries, 29 F.3d 1173 (7th Cir.1994), **78,** 83, 86

Northwest Acceptance Corp. v. Hesco Const., Inc., 26 Wash.App. 823, 614 P.2d 1302 (Wash.App. Div. 3 1980), 487, 490

O'Laughlin v. Minnesota Natural Gas Co., 253 N.W.2d 826 (Minn.1977), 274

Oloffson v. Coomer, 11 Ill.App.3d 918, 296 N.E.2d 871 (Ill.App. 3 Dist.1973), **505,** 509, 512

Olson v. Molacek Bros., 341 N.W.2d 375 (N.D.1983), 34

Patton v. Lucy, 285 Ky. 694, 148 S.W.2d 1039 (Ky.1940), 32

Patty Precision Products Co. v. Brown & Sharpe Mfg. Co., 846 F.2d 1247 (10th Cir.1988), **321,** 323, 324

Paullus v. Yarbrough, 219 Or. 611, 347 P.2d 620 (Or.1959), 413

Perlmutter v. Beth David Hospital, 308 N.Y. 100, 123 N.E.2d 792 (N.Y.1954), 19

Pet Dealers Ass'n of New Jersey, Inc. v. Division of Consumer Affairs, Dept. of Law and Public Safety, State of New Jersey, 149 N.J.Super. 235, 373 A.2d 688 (N.J.Super.A.D.1977), **33**

Peter Pan Seafoods, Inc. v. Olympic Foundry Co., 17 Wash.App. 761, 565 P.2d 819 (Wash.App. Div. 1 1977), 394

Pittsburgh Provision & Packing Co. v. Cudahy Packing Co., 260 Pa. 135, 103 A. 548 (Pa.1918), 195

Polycarbon Industries, Inc. v. Advantage Engineering, Inc., 260 F.Supp.2d 296 (D.Mass.2003), 350

Potomac Elec. Power Co. v. Westinghouse Elec. Corp., 385 F.Supp. 572 (D.D.C.1974), 135

Potter v. Tyndall, 22 N.C.App. 129, 205 S.E.2d 808 (N.C.App.1974), 34

Prairie Production, Inc. v. Agchem Division–Pennwalt Corp., 514 N.E.2d 1299 (Ind. App. 1 Dist.1987), 302

Prompt Elec. Supply Co., Inc. v. Allen–Bradley Co., 492 F.Supp. 344 (E.D.N.Y.1980), 138

Radloff v. Bragmus, 214 Minn. 130, 7 N.W.2d 491 (Minn.1943), 187

Randy Knitwear, Inc. v. American Cyanamid Co., 226 N.Y.S.2d 363, 181 N.E.2d 399 (N.Y.1962), **295**, 300, 302

Recold, S.A. de C.V. v. Monfort of Colorado, Inc., 893 F.2d 195 (8th Cir.1990), 324

R.E. Davis Chemical Corp. v. Diasonics, Inc., 826 F.2d 678 (7th Cir.1987), 469

Reeves Soundcraft Corp., Appeal of, 2 UCC Rep.Serv. 210 (A.S.B.C.A.1964), 31

Reliance Cooperage Corp. v. Treat, 195 F.2d 977 (8th Cir.1952), 508, 509

Rester v. Morrow, 491 So.2d 204 (Miss.1986), 369

Riegel Fiber Corp. v. Anderson Gin Co., 512 F.2d 784 (5th Cir.1975), **172**

Robbins v. Farwell, 193 Pa. 37, 44 A. 260 (Pa.1899), 32

Rogath v. Siebenmann, 129 F.3d 261 (2nd Cir.1997), 224

Rountree v. Lydick–Barmann Co., 150 S.W.2d 173 (Tex.Civ.App.-Fort Worth 1941), **606**

Royal Business Machines, Inc. v. Lorraine Corp., 633 F.2d 34 (7th Cir.1980), **219**, 224

Royal Store Fixture Co. v. Bucci, 48 Pa. D. & C.2d 696 (Pa.Co.Ct.1969), 171

Sabine Corp. v. ONG Western, Inc., 725 F.Supp. 1157 (W.D.Okla.1989), 483, 484

Samuels & Co., Matter of, 526 F.2d 1238 (5th Cir.1976), 586

Sandford v. Chevrolet Division of General Motors, 292 Or. 590, 642 P.2d 624 (Or. 1982), 338

Sarnecki v. Al Johns Pontiac, 3 UCC Rep. Serv. 1121 (Pa.Com.Pl.1966), 379

Scholes v. Lehmann, 56 F.3d 750 (7th Cir. 1995), 567

Sedmak v. Charlie's Chevrolet, Inc., 622 S.W.2d 694 (Mo.App. E.D.1981), **409**

Sierra Diesel Injection Service, Inc. v. Burroughs Corp., Inc., 874 F.2d 653 (9th Cir.1989), **279**, 283, 284, 294

Silver v. Wycombe, Meyer & Co., Inc., 124 Misc.2d 717, 477 N.Y.S.2d 288 (N.Y.City Civ.Ct.1984), **198**, 201

Simmons Oil Corp. v. Bulk Sales Corp., 498 F.Supp. 457 (D.N.J.1980), 67

Sinco, Inc. v. Metro–North Commuter Railroad Co., 133 F.Supp.2d 308 (S.D.N.Y. 2001), 389, 392

Skinner v. James Griffiths & Sons, 80 Wash. 291, 141 P. 693 (Wash.1914), 600

Smith v. Navistar Intern. Transp. Corp., 957 F.2d 1439 (7th Cir.1992), **441**

Smith v. Thomas, 224 Ala. 41, 138 So. 542 (Ala.1931), 32

Smith v. Zimbalist, 2 Cal.App.2d 324, 38 P.2d 170 (Cal.App. 2 Dist.1934), 215

Snap–On Tools Corp. v. Rice, 162 Ariz. 99, 781 P.2d 76 (Ariz.App. Div. 2 1989), **539**, 542, 547

Societé Nouvelle Vaskene v. Lehman Saunders, Ltd., 14 UCC Rep.Serv. 692 (N.Y.Sup.1974), 378

Southwest Engineering Co. v. Martin Tractor Co., 205 Kan. 684, 473 P.2d 18 (Kan.1970), **50,** 56, 181

Spagnol Enterprises v. Digital Equipment Corp., 390 Pa.Super. 372, 568 A.2d 948 (Pa.Super.1989), 324

Specht v. Netscape, 150 F.Supp.2d 585 (S.D.N.Y.2001), 25, 26

Spring Motors Distributors, Inc. v. Ford Motor Co., 98 N.J. 555, 489 A.2d 660 (N.J. 1985), 320

Starr v. Freeport Dodge, 54 Misc.2d 271, 282 N.Y.S.2d 58 (N.Y.Dist.Ct.1967), 67

Strause v. Berger, 220 Pa. 367, 69 A. 818 (Pa.1908), 413

Strong v. Retail Credit Co., 38 Colo.App. 125, 552 P.2d 1025 (Colo.App.1976), 274

Superfos Investments Ltd. v. FirstMiss Fertilizer, Inc., 821 F.Supp. 432 (S.D.Miss.1993), **477,** 484

Szajna v. General Motors Corp., 115 Ill.2d 294, 104 Ill.Dec. 898, 503 N.E.2d 760 (Ill. 1986), 341, 343

Taterka v. Ford Motor Co., 86 Wis.2d 140, 271 N.W.2d 653 (Wis.1978), 240

Taylor v. Caldwell, 3 B. & S. 826 (K.B. 1863), 514

Tennessee Carolina Transp., Inc. v. Strick Corp., 283 N.C. 423, 196 S.E.2d 711 (N.C. 1973), 266, 267

Tesoro Petroleum Corp. v. Holborn Oil Co., Ltd., 145 Misc.2d 715, 547 N.Y.S.2d 1012 (N.Y.Sup.1989), **458,** 462, 463, 464

Tex Enterprises, Inc. v. Brockway Standard, Inc., 149 Wash.2d 204, 66 P.3d 625 (Wash.2003), **307,** 309

TexPar Energy, Inc. v. Murphy Oil United StatesA, Inc., 45 F.3d 1111 (7th Cir. 1995), **427,** 430

Tiger Motor Co. v. McMurtry, 284 Ala. 283, 224 So.2d 638 (Ala.1969), 399

Tongish v. Thomas, 16 Kan.App.2d 809, 829 P.2d 916 (Kan.App.1992), 430

Toshiba Machine Co. v. SPM Flow Control, Inc., 180 S.W.3d 761 (Tex.App.-Fort Worth 2005), 400

Touchet Valley Grain Growers, Inc. v. Opp & Seibold General Const., Inc., 119 Wash.2d 334, 831 P.2d 724 (Wash.1992), 309

Trailmobile Division of Pullman, Inc. v. Jones, 118 Ga.App. 472, 164 S.E.2d 346 (Ga.App.1968), 378

Trans World Metals, Inc. v. Southwire Co., 769 F.2d 902 (2nd Cir.1985), 463

Twyne's Case, 76 Eng. Rep. 809 (K.B.D. 1601), 565

Tyson v. Ciba–Geigy Corp., 82 N.C.App. 626, 347 S.E.2d 473 (N.C.App.1986), **262,** 263

Underwood v. Sterner, 63 Wash.2d 360, 387 P.2d 366 (Wash.1963), 490

Unico v. Owen, 50 N.J. 101, 232 A.2d 405 (N.J.1967), 273

Union Carbide Corp. v. Consumers Power Co., 636 F.Supp. 1498 (E.D.Mich.1986), 464, 468

Unique Designs v. Pittard Machinery Co., 200 Ga.App. 647, 409 S.E.2d 241 (Ga.App.1991), **39,** 172

United Bank Ltd. v. Cambridge Sporting Goods Corp., 392 N.Y.S.2d 265, 360 N.E.2d 943 (N.Y.1976), **619,** 623

United States v. _____ (see opposing party)

United States Tire–Tech, Inc. v. Boeran, 110 S.W.3d 194 (Tex.App.-Hous. (1 Dist.) 2003), 302

Universal Resources Corp. v. Panhandle Eastern Pipe Line Co., 813 F.2d 77 (5th Cir.1987), 480

Valley Datsun v. Martinez, 578 S.W.2d 485 (TexCivApp.-Corpus Christi 1979), 223

Valley Die Cast Corp. v. A.C.W. Inc., 25 Mich.App. 321, 181 N.W.2d 303 (Mich. App.1970), **416**

Veik v. Tilden Bank, 200 Neb. 705, 265 N.W.2d 214 (Neb.1978), 57

Ventura v. Ford Motor Corp., 180 N.J.Super. 45, 433 A.2d 801 (N.J.Super.A.D.1981), 339, 340

Voelker v. Porsche Cars North America, Inc., 353 F.3d 516 (7th Cir.2003), 345

Waldinger Corp. v. CRS Group Engineers, Inc., 775 F.2d 781 (7th Cir.1985), **522**

Walsh v. Ford Motor Co., 588 F.Supp. 1513 (D.D.C.1984), 341

Wegematic Corp., United States v., 360 F.2d 674 (2nd Cir.1966), **514,** 517

Wenner Petroleum Corp. v. Mitsui & Co. (United StatesA.), Inc., 748 P.2d 356 (Colo.App.1987), 324

Wetopsky v. New Haven Gas Light Co., 88 Conn. 1, 90 A. 30 (Conn.1914), 32

Wilhelm Lubrication Co. v. Brattrud, 197 Minn. 626, 268 N.W. 634 (Minn.1936), 161

Wille v. Southwestern Bell Tel. Co., 219 Kan. 755, 549 P.2d 903 (Kan.1976), 31

Williams v. Walker–Thomas Furniture Co., 350 F.2d 445, 121 U.S.App.D.C. 315 (D.C.Cir.1965), 135

Wilson v. Massey–Ferguson, Inc., 21 Ill. App.3d 867, 315 N.E.2d 580 (Ill.App. 4 Dist.1974), 266, 267

Wilson v. M & W Gear, 110 Ill.App.3d 538, 66 Ill.Dec. 244, 442 N.E.2d 670 (Ill.App. 3 Dist.1982), 548

Wilson v. Scampoli, 228 A.2d 848 (D.C.App. 1967), 392, 395, 407

Windows, Inc. v. Jordan Panel Systems Corp., 177 F.3d 114 (2nd Cir.1999), 194

Winter v. Welker, 174 F.Supp. 836 (E.D.Pa. 1959), 567

Wisconsin Knife Works v. National Metal Crafters, 781 F.2d 1280 (7th Cir. 1986), **98,** 115

Worrell v. Barnes, 87 Nev. 204, 484 P.2d 573 (Nev.1971), 274

Wright v. Hart, 18 Wend. 449 (N.Y.1837), 231

Wright–Moore Corp. v. Ricoh Corp., 908 F.2d 128 (7th Cir.1990), **206,** 210

Zabriskie Chevrolet, Inc. v. Smith, 99 N.J.Super. 441, 240 A.2d 195 (N.J.Super.L.1968), **384,** 389, 394

Zapatha v. Dairy Mart, Inc., 381 Mass. 284, 408 N.E.2d 1370 (Mass.1980), 26, 31

CASES AND MATERIALS

SALES

*

CHAPTER 1

INTRODUCTION

A. ORGANIZATION OF THE BOOK AND GOALS OF THE COURSE

This book deals with the sale and leasing of goods, an area of the law that ranges from simple transactions that sometimes involve unsuspecting consumers to multi-million dollar deals between commercial giants; from face-to-face arrangements to complicated documentary agreements bringing together a seller, buyer, carrier, insurance company, bank, and, perhaps, others. One focus of this book is the substantive law governing these various contracts: a close and hard look at the substantive law set forth in Articles 2 and 2A of the Uniform Commercial Code ("UCC" or "Code") as clarified by Article 1 and augmented by Articles 5, 7, and 9 of the UCC.

The book has a second, and equally important, focus: to develop the skills of understanding and using the UCC, a sophisticated and far-ranging statute that may govern as much as twenty-five percent of the matters commonly associated with private law. The methodological emphasis in the first-year Contracts course typically is primarily on case law, on developing the important skills of reading cases carefully for their full factual and legal meanings, of synthesizing them, of distinguishing them, and of seeing their total importance and impact in a social and economic setting. In this study you may have considered, incidentally, some of the provisions of Article 2 of the UCC, such as, for example, section 2–207 dealing with the "battle of the forms." These exercises were important studies of some aspects of substantive law but they seldom were aimed at developing your skill in handling the legislative materials that make up the UCC. That is one of the missions of this book.

The goals of this book—to impart the substantive law of sales and leasing, including knowledge of the commercial background necessary to a full understanding of the operation of that law, and to teach the methodology of the UCC—involve a curious paradox. The substantive law of sales and leasing probably best can be taught by concentrating on the rules of law announced by the UCC, its Official Comments, and the cases decided under it, supplemented by expository text to assure full coverage. Such a concentration, however, disserves the effort to teach the student how to use the UCC specifically and handle a complicated statute generally, because this assignment is best carried out by wrestling with statutory language in the resolution of problems without the aid of cases or commentary. But, just as an excessive emphasis on substantive law and commercial background can defeat the goal of learning UCC methodology, a too-rigid concentration on methodology can leave the student with insufficient knowledge of the

1

substantive law and the basic facts underlying sales and leasing transactions to put that methodology to its most effective use. The authors have tried to resolve this paradox by selecting principal cases in which judges reveal the commercial background and articulate the competing interests underlying the rules of law used in the cases, supplemented by expository text to fill gaps, all toward the end of developing competence in the applicable substantive law, and by using these same cases, plus numerous problems and thought-provoking questions to develop skills in handling the UCC.

The organization of the book is based on a logical consideration of the applicable law broken down into its component parts. The law of sales and leasing must answer four basic contract questions and one property question: (1) How are contracts formed? (2) Once formed, what are their terms? (3) How are those terms performed—i.e. what things must the parties do in the proper performance of those terms? (4) What happens if they are not properly performed—i.e. what remedies are available upon breach? The property question is, who has title to the goods and what are the rights of bona fide purchasers and creditors? The book follows this structure, departing from it only by a special treatment of documentary sales in its concluding chapter.

In 1986 the United States ratified the Convention on Contracts for the International Sale of Goods, which had been promulgated by the United Nations in 1980. That Convention often will apply to sale of goods contracts entered into between a party in the United States and a party in one of the other countries (at present approximately 70) that also have ratified the Convention. We will frequently refer to the Convention.

B.   BACKGROUND AND HISTORY OF THE UCC

1.   SPONSORS

The Uniform Commercial Code is the most successful product of the uniform state law movement, which began in the 1890s. The Code is the joint product of two organizations, the National Conference of Commissioners on Uniform State Laws and the American Law Institute. Following is a brief description of the two bodies.

a.   THE NATIONAL CONFERENCE OF COMMISSIONERS ON UNIFORM STATE LAWS

In 1890 a committee of the American Bar Association proposed that the states set up a national organization to prepare legislation on matters as to which uniform laws would be desirable which could then be adopted by all states. By 1892 New York had adopted legislation authorizing the appointment of commissioners to work with commissioners from other states to prepare uniform laws to be offered for adoption in the various states. In that year the first meeting of the National Conference of

Commissioners on Uniform State Laws (NCCUSL) was held in Saratoga, New York. Commissioners from seven states attended that meeting.

In 1896 the Commissioners offered their first act, the Uniform Negotiable Instruments Act, which was ultimately adopted in all jurisdictions. Thereafter, many other uniform acts followed, including the Uniform Sales Act and the Revised Uniform Sales Act, the Uniform Conditional Sales Act, the Uniform Trust Receipts Act, and many other acts both in the commercial area and in other areas.

The NCCUSL is a government-supported organization. Each state appoints Commissioners to the Conference. The primary financial support for the Conference comes from assessments levied against the states based on population. Acts of the Conference are drafted by committees of the Conference, often with the help of a paid reporter-drafter. The drafting committees seek advice from persons and organizations knowledgeable and interested in the area and invite the American Bar Association to send advisors to committee meetings. The entire Conference, composed now of more than 300 commissioners representing all states, the District of Columbia, Puerto Rico, and the Virgin Islands, meets annually for seven or eight days to discuss drafts of proposed acts. Under Conference rules each act must be read line by line at two annual meetings before promulgation. Often acts are before the Conference for four or five years, and sometimes longer, before they finally are approved. After approval, the Conference submits them to the House of Delegates of the American Bar Association for approval. Occasionally, concerns expressed by the ABA lead to redrafting of Conference Acts. The Conference headquarters are in Chicago.

b. THE AMERICAN LAW INSTITUTE

The American Law Institute (ALI) was created in 1923 as the result of a proposal by a committee of the Association of American Law Schools that a "juristic center" be set up to "promote the clarification and simplification of the law and its better adaption to social needs, to secure the better administration of justice, and to encourage and carry on scholarly and scientific work." The first work of the ALI was preparation of restatements of the law in such areas as contracts, torts, property, trusts, and so on. As you already know from your other law school courses, the Restatements have been very influential.

The ALI is a private, non-profit, self-perpetuating body composed of lawyers, judges, and law professors from all over the country. New members are nominated by present members of the ALI and then approved by a membership committee and by the Council of the ALI. There are about 2500 elected members of ALI and a number of ex officio members such as the deans of all American Bar Association approved law schools, the chief justices of all state supreme courts, and the presidents of the state bar associations, and some others.

The ALI does its drafting work through reporters who work with a group of advisors and members of the ALI who join consultative groups. It, like NCCUSL, meets annually to discuss proposed drafts of Restatements. The ALI has done little statutory drafting, but it has occasionally drafted acts other than the Uniform Commercial Code. The ALI headquarters are in Philadelphia. In addition to activities related to the drafting activities of the ALI, it provides organizational and staff support for a substantial continuing legal education program in cooperation with the American Bar Association.

---

2. THE INITIAL DRAFTING HISTORY

The following excerpt from an article by Walter Malcolm describes the initial drafting of the Code in the 1940s and 50s.*

BACKGROUND AND HISTORY OF THE UNIFORM COMMERCIAL CODE—PERIOD 1938–52

In 1938, a proposal was sponsored by the Merchants Association of New York City for a federal sales Act to govern all interstate sales transactions. In response to this indication of the inadequacies in the Uniform Sales Act, the National Conference of Commissioners on Uniform State Laws undertook revision of the Uniform Sales Act which it had prepared in 1906. A revision of the Uniform Negotiable Instruments Law, prepared in 1896, was then also under consideration. In 1940, the National Conference adopted a proposal to prepare a uniform commercial code embracing a modernisation and co-ordination of the Uniform Sales Act, the Uniform Negotiable Instruments Law, the Uniform Bills of Lading Act, the Uniform Warehouse Receipts Act, and all other Uniform Acts in the field of commercial law, with new provisions where no uniform Acts existed on important and closely related commercial problems. The American Law Institute joined in the undertaking the following year and participated in 1942 in discussion of the draft Revised Sales Act as a proposed sales chapter of the prospective Code. In 1945, work on the enlarged project was begun. The project was financed to the extent of approximately $400,000 by a grant from the Maurice and Laura Falk Foundation, Pittsburgh, Pennsylvania and contributions by the Beaumont Foundation of Cleveland, Ohio and ninety-eight business and financial concerns and law firms.

Between 1945 and 1952 a great number of drafts and re-drafts of parts of the proposed code were prepared by a reportorial staff supervised by an Editorial Board.[8] They were considered successively by advisory groups of judges, lawyers and law teachers; by the Council of the American Law Institute and special Sections of the National Conference of Commissioners

---

* Malcolm, The Uniform Commercial Code in the United States, 12 Inter. & Comp. L.Q. 226 (1963).

8. The Chief Reporter for the Code was the late Professor Karl N. Llewellyn of the University of Chicago Law School and the Associate Chief Reporter was Professor Soia Mentschikoff of the same Law School.

on Uniform State Laws; and then by the general membership of the two organisations. In preparing the several drafts and re-drafts, the reporting and advisory groups also consulted with individuals and organisations in business and banking circles in many parts of the country who had come forward with criticisms. The first complete draft of the Code was released in May 1949.

While the Code was in preparation, the successive drafts available to the public were extensively commented on in legal periodicals and subsequent drafts reflect much of this criticism. In addition, many of the drafts and problems arising in the drafting were studied by bar associations and other groups in many parts of the country. In 1946, a committee on the Uniform Commercial Code of the Section of Corporation, Banking and Business Law of the American Bar Association was organised and the members of this Committee followed the development of the Code from that time to the present time. Many of the members of this Committee also have served either on the Editorial Board of the Sponsoring Organisations or on sub-committees of the Editorial Board and in this way played active roles in the drafting process, the consideration of comments and criticisms from outside sources, the making of decisions with respect to policy and many other matters.

A final text of the proposed Code was completed in September 1951 and at that time was approved by the two Sponsoring Organisations and was also approved by the House of Delegates of the American Bar Association. During the next year a limited number of further amendments were made and in October 1952 an official edition of the Code with explanatory comments was published as the *1952 Official Text and Comments Editions.*

Pennsylvania adopted the Code in 1953 and by 1967 the District of Columbia and all the states except Louisiana had adopted the Code. Louisiana lawyers felt that the Code was incompatible with Louisiana's civil law system, but ultimately the state adopted all Articles of the Code except Articles 2 and 2A.

3.   SCOPE OF THE UNIFORM COMMERCIAL CODE

The Code as originally adopted contained nine Articles, which are briefly summarized below.

Article 1. General Provisions. The other Articles of the Code each applies to a particular type of transaction. Article 1, on the other hand, has no specific transactional coverage, but rather states definitions and general rules applicable to any transaction covered by any of the other Articles. Article 1 was revised in 2001, and the states are in the process of enacting it. Approximately 20 states have done so.

Article 2. Sales. This Article covers sales of goods and is the primary focus of this course. Article 2 was revised in 2003, but as of this writing no state has adopted the revision, and the prospects for enactment look bleak.

Article 3. Commercial Paper. Article 3 covers negotiable instruments, including negotiable notes and checks. Amendments in 1990 and 1991 were widely adopted, but further amendments in 2002 were not. Their prospects, too, look bleak.

Article 4. Bank Deposits and Collections. Article 4 covers bank handling of checks and other items. The emphasis in the Article is on the rights and duties of banks between themselves and as against their customers as they take checks for collection and pay checks drawn on the account of their customers. Article 4 was amended in 1990.

Article 5. Letters of Credit. This brief Article covers some of the rules applicable to letters of credit. Letters of credit guaranteeing sellers that the price of goods will be paid are used often in international sales transactions. Article 5 was amended in 1995 and has been adopted by every state. The last chapter of this casebook gives limited coverage to letters of credit.

Article 6. Bulk Transfers. This Article imposes an obligation on buyers of a major part of the inventory of certain types of business to notify creditors of the seller so that the creditors can take steps to see that the seller pays his debts. On the recommendation of NCCUSL and ALI in 1989, most states have repealed Article 6. Chapter 10 briefly addresses bulk sales.

Article 7. Documents of Title. Article 7 states rules applicable to the issuance and transfer of warehouse receipts and bills of lading. A revised Article 7 was promulgated in 2003 and has been adopted by approximately 20 states.

Article 8. Investment Securities. Article 8 covers the issuance and transfer of stocks, bonds, and other investment securities. It was amended in 1994 and has been adopted by all states.

Article 9. Secured Transactions. Article 9 covers security interests in personal property. A security interest is an interest in property which secures performance of an obligation. The Article states rules on creation of the interest and the rights of the debtor to foreclose on the property if the debtor defaults on the secured obligation. It also states priority rules as between secured parties and as between a secured party and buyers or lien creditors. Article 9 was substantially revised in 1999, and all states have enacted the revision.

Two additional articles have been added to the original nine: Articles 2A and 4A.

Article 2A. Personal Property Leases. In 1989 the Code sponsors promulgated Article 2A covering leases of personal property. Modeled on Article 2, many of its provisions are identical to the provisions in Article 2. This book covers many provisions of Article 2A. The 2003 revision of Article 2 also included corresponding changes in Article 2A. They have not yet been enacted in any state.

Article 4A. Funds Transfers. Also promulgated in 1989, Article 4A deals with systems for the transfer of funds in which the transferor directs its bank to transfer the funds to a third party (as opposed to transferring funds by sending a check to the third party). These systems usually involve transfers between banks by rapid electronic means.

4. PERMANENT EDITORIAL BOARD

When the Code was originally promulgated, the ALI and the NCCUSL decided that a permanent body should be created and charged with the duty of oversight over the Code. In 1962 they organized the Permanent Editorial Board (PEB) for the Uniform Commercial Code, and each appointed five members to serve on it. The Board's first function was to secure uniform adoption of the Code. In its early years, therefore, it spent much of its time fending off proposed amendments to the Code. But as the Code became widely adopted, the PEB was able to turn its attention to needed improvements in the Code. Today the PEB, now composed of six members each from the two sponsoring organizations, meets periodically to discuss Code issues and make recommendations to the ALI and NCCUSL as to possible drafting projects. The PEB itself does not engage in drafting, but from time to time it issues Commentaries on matters as to which the Code seems unclear or as to which some courts have taken positions that the Board believes to be inconsistent with the language or policy of the Code.

C. THE CODE AS "CODE"

A basic issue relative to interpretation of the Uniform Commercial Code is whether the Code is just another statute, bigger than most, but basically like all other statutes in a common-law jurisdiction, or whether, on the other hand, it is a code in the Continental sense of the word. Following are short excerpts from two writers on the point. Professor Hawkland's piece also suggests the practical result of the difference in viewpoint. Professor Homer Kripke, at the time he wrote the article excerpted here, was a lawyer for a large New York financing organization.

UNIFORM COMMERCIAL CODE METHODOLOGY*

THE CODE CONCEPT

Although American lawyers tend to treat them as synonyms, there is a vast difference between a "code" and a "statute." This terminological confusion did not exist in earlier times, because then the word "code" had no legal meaning. The leading legal dictionary failed to list it as a term as late as the year 1797. This omission, it is believed, was not due to the fact

* Hawkland, Uniform Commercial Code Methodology, 1962 U.Ill.L.Forum 291. The author's citations of authority are omitted.

that the word was completely missing from our legal nomenclature, but to the absence of the concept from our legal system. "The word was at hand, ready for use," reports Charles Hepburn, "but at this time, the beginnings of the nineteenth century, there was no one thing, actual or clearly designed, in the legal system of either England or the United States, to which 'code' was naturally and specifically applicable."

Several events occurred around 1800 to bring the term into general legal usage. The French substantially codified their law between the years 1804 and 1810, the same period during which Bentham was announcing a new jurisprudence proclaiming the merits of a "complete Code of Laws." Bentham's views were dramatically brought to the attention of the American bar when he offered to prepare for President Madison a complete code of laws for use by the American states. During this period, Edward Livingston was actually drafting Codes for Louisiana, and this too undoubtedly served to make lawyers aware of the new term.

While these developments brought the ancient word "code" into common legal usage, its meaning was rendered ambiguous by virtue of the fact that no American State, save Louisiana, had adopted the code concept as part of its jurisprudence. Thus the term was employed in different ways to mean "statute," "jurisprudence of a single subject," "commissioner's manuscript," "all the statutes of the state," and "large part of the general laws of the state." Lawyers still use the term loosely, but presently it seems to be employed most frequently to connote a statute which regulates an area previously left to decisional law.

There is a wide difference between such a statute and a true code. A "code" is a pre-emptive, systematic, and comprehensive enactment of a whole field of law. It is pre-emptive in that it displaces all other law in its subject area save only that which the code excepts. It is systematic in that all of its parts, arranged in an orderly fashion and stated with a consistent terminology, form an interlocking, integrated body, revealing its own plan and containing its own methodology. It is comprehensive in that it is sufficiently inclusive and independent to enable it to be administered in accordance with its own basic policies.

A mere statute, on the other hand, is neither pre-emptive, systematic, nor comprehensive, and, therefore, its methodology is different from that of a code.

SYSTEMATIC CONSIDERATIONS

Since a true code pre-empts a large body of law and comprehensively deals with all of its parts, it obviously must be constructed systematically. This requires: (1) That its provisions be logically presented and coordinated and stated in language employing a chosen and consistent terminology; (2) that means be made available to handle competing and conflicting rules; (3) that means be provided to fill the gaps; and (4) that supereminent provisions be present to mitigate harshness which might otherwise flow from rigid rules.

The Uniform Commercial Code meets these requirements. Its provisions, following the organizational plan of most European codes, are logically divided into interlocking "articles," each handling one major subdivision of the entire subject. The first and last articles do not cover any traditional field of law. Article 1, instead, sets forth principles and definitions of general application, and article 10 provides rules relating to uniform construction, saving clauses, repealers, and the effective date. Subject to these general provisions, all the rules on sales are collected in article 2; commercial paper in article 3; bank deposits and collections in article 4; letters of credit in article 5; bulk transfers in article 6; documents of title in article 7; investment securities in article 8; and secured transactions in article 9.

A chosen and consistent terminology runs through the Code, a matter made possible by the forty-six generally-applicable definitions presented in article 1. These definitions, by and large, are both "conventional" and "real" in the jurisprudential sense. That is, they communicate to others conventional meanings and state real or essential attributes of the things defined.

METHODOLOGICAL IMPLICATIONS

Because the Uniform Commercial Code is a true code and states its own aims, courts construing it should make three changes in their standard legal method. They should: (1) use analogy, rather than "outside" law, to fill code gaps; (2) rely somewhat more heavily on the decisions of other code states in making their own decisions; and (3) give their own decisions somewhat less permanent precedential value.

PRINCIPLES UNDERLYING THE DRAFTING OF THE UNIFORM COMMERCIAL CODE*

Whatever may have been in the academicians' desire for more thorough-going changes in the law, it was recognized that, in order to be promulgated by the sponsor organizations as their product, the Code had to be conceived as a fundamentally conservative piece of amendatory legislation. The Code was prepared as a joint enterprise of its sponsors, the American Law Institute (whose prior work had been in the field of restatement of the law) and the National Conference of Commissioners on Uniform State Laws (the principal thrust of whose labors had been toward *uniformity,* not radical revamping). The drafts had to be approved by the Joint Editorial Board, by a Section of the National Conference, and by the joint membership meetings of the two organizations. The final product then had to be approved by the House of Delegates of the American Bar Association. While these institutions contain a sprinkling of judges and law

---

* Kripke, Principles Underlying the 1962 U.Ill.L.Forum 321.
Drafting of the Uniform Commercial Code,

school professors, fundamentally their membership is drawn from lawyers who have the interest and the ability to devote time to legal matters beyond the making of a living, i.e., principally the successful partners of established law firms with a corporate or other monied practice. Needless to say, the overall social, economic, and legal bent of such persons is conservative. As was proved with issue after issue on the floor of the joint meetings and in the work of the committees or sections, these lawyers instinctively react in opposition to any fundamental reshaping of the relative strengths of debtor and creditor, of secured creditor and unsecured creditor, of buyer and seller, of warehouseman and depositor, of carrier and bailor, or of bank and depositor. While they are willing to rectify matters where the law had developed lack of uniformity, their natural bent was opposed to change where the existing law presented a clear pattern.

It is fair to say that the draftsmen of the Code had an anticodification or antistatute predilection. They did not want to codify the law, in the continental sense of codification. They wanted to correct some false starts, to point the law in the indicated directions, and to restore the law merchant as an institution for growth only lightly kept in bounds by statute. To the present writer, the express statutory injunctions to give effect to all of the nonstatutory influences for growth are so strong that continental codification is a misleading analogy. The drafters did not intend that the solution to problems within the ambit of the Code must be found in the confines of the statute. Indeed, the drafters found themselves able in the official comments to extrapolate additional rules from the statutory text by repeated reference to the nonstatutory principles of decision.**

––––––––

The debate as to whether the UCC is a true code or a mere statute has proved to be mainly important in determining the scope and meaning of 1–103, which provides that:

> Unless displaced by the particular provisions of this Act, the principles of law and equity, including the law merchant and the law relative to capacity to contract, principal and agent, estoppel, fraud, misrepresentation, duress, coercion, mistake, bankruptcy, or other validating or invalidating cause shall supplement its provisions.

Statutes (including the UCC), like cases, often fail to meet precise questions with precise answers. Many commercial disputes, of course, fit more or less easily under one or more sections of the UCC, and the courts have resolved them, by and large, by reference to these sections, with no

---

** For examples of instances where the comments seem to state rules going beyond anything found in the text, see § 2–305, comment 4; the comments to §§ 2–306, 2–604, 2–607, and § 2–716, comment 2. So strongly did some of the participants in the drafting process feel about the breadth of the comments that the final Code omitted an earlier provision referring to the official comments as legislative history available for interpretation. ALI & Nat'l Conference of Comm'rs on Uniform State Laws, Uniform Commercial Code 1952 Text and Comments § 1–102(3)(f), comment 2.

need to go outside the Code for answers. This process seems to be employed instinctively in most situations and not as the result of any explicit jurisprudential pondering. On the other hand, there are some commercial law situations for which the UCC intentionally provides no answer, and in these cases the courts quickly resort to the common law for solution or supplementation, justifying their approach by 1–103. In between these extremes a number of situations can be found where a case obviously falls within the scope of a Code article (e.g., it clearly involves the sale of goods and thus falls under Article 2 of the UCC) but does not fit easily under any particular Code section. An ultimate question of great importance is whether such a case is to be resolved by the Code or by the common law. As you study the materials in this book, you will see that the courts are divided on this matter. Those desiring to stay within the Code frequently utilize the technique of analogy in these cases, whereas other courts find justification in 1–103 to apply outside law. This division of opinion is not along any jurisdictional lines but tends to occur within each jurisdiction depending on the kind of case that is before the court and how it is argued. There are valuable lessons to be learned from these cases, not the least of which is that philosophical ideas *do* play a role at least on the fringes. A persistent question is what other factors are determinative in these cases.

D.   SCOPE OF ARTICLE 2

Like most of the other Articles making up the UCC, Article 2 has a "scope" section (2–102) that prescribes, to a considerable extent, its coverage. Of course this scope section cannot operate unless the UCC itself is applicable, and, in this connection, there are important territorial and transitional limitations. This section of the book deals with the factors that courts take into account in borderline cases in determining whether Article 2 is applicable.

1.   THE SALES–SERVICE HYBRID

Anthony Pools v. Sheehan

Maryland Court of Appeals, 1983.
295 Md. 285, 455 A.2d 434.

■ RODOWSKY, JUDGE.

This products liability case presents questions of implied warranty and of defense to strict liability in tort involving an inground, gunite swimming pool and its diving board. Analysis of whether there is any implied warranty and, if so, whether it can be excluded takes us into the problem of hybrid transactions and into Md.Code (1975), § 2–316.1(1) and (2) of the Commercial Law Article (CL).[1]

1. CL § 2–316.1 in relevant part provides:

(1) The provisions of § 2–316 do not apply to sales of consumer goods, as defined by § 9–109, services, or both.

Plaintiffs, John B. Sheehan (Sheehan) and his wife, Pilar E. Sheehan, of Potomac Woods, Maryland, sued Anthony Pools, a division of Anthony Industries, Inc. (Anthony) in the Circuit Court for Montgomery County. Sheehan sustained bodily injuries when he fell from the side of the diving board of the plaintiffs' new, backyard swimming pool. The swimming pool had been designed and built by Anthony. Anthony also designed and manufactured the diving board which it installed as part of the swimming pool transaction.

The swimming pool is 16 feet by 40 feet, with a depth from 3 feet to 8 feet. Its style is "Grecian," which means that there is a curved alcove in the center of each of the 16 foot sides. The 6 foot long diving board in question was installed over an imaginary centerline bisecting the alcove at the deep end of the pool. Anthony had completed its work by mid-June of 1976. On August 21, 1976 the plaintiffs entertained at a pool party. Sheehan testified that he had not previously used the diving board. He said that on that evening he emerged from swimming in the pool, stepped up onto the diving board, and, while walking toward the pool end of the diving board, slipped and fell from the right side of the diving board and struck the coping of the pool.

Plaintiffs advanced two theories of liability. First, skid resistant material built into the surface of the top of the diving board did not extend to the very edge of the board on each side. It stopped approximately one inch short of each edge. This condition, it was claimed, breached an implied warranty of merchantability. Plaintiffs also presented testimony directed toward proving that use of the "defective" diving board, particularly as positioned in the alcove, was unreasonably dangerous.

At the end of the plaintiffs' case, the trial court directed a verdict for Anthony as to liability founded on warranty, because the written contract between the parties conspicuously provided that the express warranties which it contained were in lieu of any other warranties, express or implied. The case went to the jury on a strict liability in tort theory. Verdict was in favor of the defendant, and judgment was so entered.

Plaintiffs appealed to the Court of Special Appeals which reversed and remanded for a new trial. That court said that "the swimming pool package purchased by the Sheehans constitute[d] 'consumer goods'" so that CL § 2–316.1 rendered ineffective Anthony's attempt to limit the implied warranty of merchantability. Sheehan v. Anthony Pools, 50 Md.App. 614, 619, 440 A.2d 1085, 1088 (1982). The granting of the directed verdict based on the contractual limitation was held to be error . . . .

(2) Any oral or written language used by a seller of consumer goods and services, which attempts to exclude or modify any implied warranties of merchantability and fitness for a particular purpose or to exclude or modify the consumer's remedies for breach of those warranties, is unenforceable. However, the seller may recover from the manufacturer any damages resulting from breach of the implied warranty of merchantability or fitness for a particular purpose.

(1)

. . . Anthony contends that the Sheehans' swimming pool is not "goods," that exclusion of implied warranties is allowed, and that a directed verdict on the plaintiffs' warranty count was proper. We agree with the Court of Special Appeals that the directed verdict was improper in this case, but we reach that conclusion by a somewhat different route.

Title 2 of the Commercial Law Article is the Maryland Uniform Commercial Code—Sales. CL § 2–101. Unless the context otherwise requires, that title "applies to transactions in goods * * *." CL § 2–102. For purposes of title 2, and with certain exclusions not here relevant, "goods" means "all things (including specially manufactured goods) which are movable at the time of identification to the contract for sale * * *." CL § 2–105(1). * * *

. . .

The subject contract presents a mixed or hybrid transaction. It is in part a contract for the rendering of services and in part a contract for the sale of goods.

Burton v. Artery Company, 279 Md. 94, 367 A.2d 935 (1977) addressed the applicability *vel non* of the Maryland U.C.C.—Sales to hybrid contracts. The issue presented was whether the four year statute of limitations under § 2–725(1), or the general three year statute, applied to a contract to landscape around a construction project of 13 buildings. The contract called for the furnishing and planting of hundreds of trees, of hundreds of shrubs, and of sod. We there adopted the test enunciated in Bonebrake v. Cox, 499 F.2d 951 (8th Cir.1974), a case holding that the sale and installation of bowling lanes, with associated equipment, is a contract of sale and not of services. That test is whether "the predominant factor * * *, the thrust, the purpose, reasonably stated, is a transaction of sale with labor incidentally involved," or vice versa. 279 Md. at 114–15, 367 A.2d at 946. Applying that test, the Court held the contract in *Burton* to be predominantly a transaction in goods. *See also* Snyder v. Herbert Greenbaum & Associates, 38 Md.App. 144, 380 A.2d 618 (1977) (contract to furnish and install over 17,000 yards of carpet in 228 apartments was predominantly a sale of goods).

G.   Wallach, The Law of Sales Under the Uniform Commercial Code (1981), § 11.05[3] at 11–28 describes the current state of the law concerning implied warranties in hybrid transactions to be as follows:

The general pre-Code approach to this issue was to examine the transaction to see whether the goods aspect or the service aspect of the transaction predominated. If the service aspect predominated, no warranties of quality were imposed in the transaction, not even if the defect or complaint related to the goods that were involved rather than to the services. This mechanical approach remains the most popular method of resolving the issue.[3]

* * *

3. Among decisions applying the predominant purpose test are: White v. Peabody Construction Co., Inc., 386 Mass. 121, 434 N.E.2d 1015 (1982) (contract for the con-

Were the predominant purpose test mechanically to be applied to the facts of this case, there would be no quality warranty implied as to the diving board. But here the contract expressly states that Anthony agrees not only to construct the swimming pool, but also to sell the related equipment selected by the Sheehans. The Sheehans are described as "Buyer." The diving board itself is not structurally integrated into the swimming pool. Anthony offered the board as an optional accessory, just as Anthony offered the options of purchasing a pool ladder or a sliding board. When identified to the contract, the diving board was movable. See CL § 2–105. The board itself remains detachable from its support, as reflected by a photograph in evidence. The diving board, considered alone, is goods. Had it been purchased by the Sheehans in a transaction distinct from the pool construction agreement with Anthony, there would have been an implied warranty of merchantability.

A number of commentators have advocated a more policy oriented approach to determining whether warranties of quality and fitness are implied with respect to goods sold as part of a hybrid transaction in which service predominates. See Farnsworth, Implied Warranties of Quality in Non–Sales Cases, 57 Colum.L.Rev. 653 (1957); Comment, Sale of Goods in Service–Predominated Transactions, 37 Fordham L.Rev. 115 (1968). To support their position, these commentators in general emphasize loss shifting, risk distribution, consumer reliance and difficulties in the proof of negligence. These concepts underlie strict liability in tort. See Phipps v. General Motors Corp., 278 Md. 337, 363 A.2d 955 (1976).

A leading case applying a policy approach in this problem area is Newmark v. Gimbel's Incorporated, 54 N.J. 585, 258 A.2d 697 (1969). There the patron of a beauty parlor sued for injury to her hair and scalp allegedly resulting from a lotion used in giving her a permanent wave. Because the transaction was viewed as the rendering of a service, the trial court had ruled that there could be no warranty liability. The intermediate appellate court's reversal was affirmed by the Supreme Court of New Jersey which reasoned in part as follows (id. at 593, 258 A.2d at 701):

> The transaction, in our judgment, is a hybrid partaking of incidents of a sale and a service. It is really partly the rendering of service, and partly the supplying of goods for a consideration. Accordingly, we agree with the Appellate Division that an implied warranty of fitness of the products used in giving the permanent wave exists with no less force than it would have in the case of a simple sale. Obviously in permanent

struction of a housing project was one for services so that there was no warranty implied under the U.C.C. on the windows or frames, which leaked); Milau Associates v. North Avenue Development Corp., 42 N.Y.2d 482, 368 N.E.2d 1247, 398 N.Y.S.2d 882 (1977) (there is no warranty of merchantability on a section of pipe which ruptured and which had been installed as part of a sprin-

kler system in the course of construction of a new building); Northwestern Equipment, Inc. v. Cudmore, 312 N.W.2d 347 (N.D.1981) (contract for the repair of the transmission in a used bulldozer is a contract for services and carries no implied warranty of fitness for a particular purpose, even though the charges for parts exceeded the charges for labor).

wave operations the product is taken into consideration in fixing the price of the service. The no-separate-charge argument puts excessive emphasis on form and downgrades the overall substance of the transaction. If the beauty parlor operator bought and applied the permanent wave solution to her own hair and suffered injury thereby, her action in warranty or strict liability in tort against the manufacturer-seller of the product clearly would be maintainable because the basic transaction would have arisen from a conventional type of sale. It does not accord with logic to deny a similar right to a patron against the beauty parlor operator or the manufacturer when the purchase and sale were made in anticipation of and for the purpose of use of the product on the patron who would be charged for its use. Common sense demands that such patron be deemed a customer as to both manufacturer and beauty parlor operator. [Citations omitted.]

The court was careful to limit its holding to commercial transactions, as opposed to those predominantly involving professional services. Id. at 596–97, 258 A.2d at 702–703.

1 R. Anderson, Uniform Commercial Code (1970), § 2–102:5 at 209 refers to *Newmark* as illustrative of a possible trend in the law and states:

It is probable that a goods-services transaction will come to be subjected to Article 2 of the Code insofar as the contractor's obligations with respect to the goods themselves are involved, at least where the goods involved could have been purchased in the general market and used by the plaintiff-customer.

A warranty of fitness for particular purpose under § 2–315 of the U.C.C. was implied in Worrell v. Barnes, 87 Nev. 204, 484 P.2d 573 (1971). In that case a contractor was engaged to do some carpentry work and to connect various appliances in the plaintiff's home to an existing liquefied petroleum gas system. The appliances were not supplied by the contractor. Suit was for damage to the plaintiff's home resulting from a fire. The plaintiff produced evidence that the fire was caused by a defective fitting installed by the contractor which had allowed propane to escape. Dismissal of the plaintiff's claims, based on the Nevada version of strict liability in tort and based on implied warranty, was reversed. The court reasoned that, because it had held that the contractor had sold a product so as to bring into operation the doctrine of strict liability, "so also must we deem this case to involve 'goods' within the purview of the Uniform Commercial Code." Id. at 208, 484 P.2d at 576.

1 W. Hawkland, Uniform Commercial Code Series (1982), § 2–102:04, at Art. 2, p. 12 has suggested what might be called a "gravamen" test in light of the decision in *Worrell*. He writes:

Unless uniformity would be impaired thereby, it might be more sensible and facilitate administration, at least in this gray area, to abandon the "predominant factor" test and focus instead on whether the gravamen of the action involves goods or services. For example, in Worrell v. Barnes, if the gas escaped because of a defective fitting or connector, the case might be characterized as one involving the sale of goods. On the other hand, if the gas escaped because of poor work by Barnes the case might be characterized as one involving services, outside the scope of the UCC.

In this State, the provisions of CL § 2–316.1(1) and (2) reflect an implicit policy judgment by the General Assembly which prevents the mechanical application of the predominant purpose test to cases like the one under consideration. Subsection (1) states that § 2–316, dealing in part with the manner in which an implied warranty of merchantability may be excluded or modified, does not apply to "consumer goods * * * services, or both." Under subsection (2) language "used by a seller of consumer goods and services" to exclude or modify implied warranties is unenforceable. The hybrid transaction is covered by, or at least embraced within, those terms.

Under the predominant purpose test, as applied by a majority of the courts, a hybrid transaction must first be classified as a sale of goods in order for there to be U.C.C. based, implied warranties on the goods included in the transaction. If goods predominate and they are consumer goods, § 2–316.1 would render contractual disclaimers of implied warranties ineffective because that section applies to a seller of consumer goods. In such cases the result of applying the predominant purpose test is consistent with § 2–316.1. If, however, the predominant purpose test results in classifying the transaction as a contract for services there would, under the majority approach, be no U.C.C. based, implied warranties on goods included in the transaction. But, § 2–316.1 declares that a seller of consumer services may not contractually disclaim implied warranties. In the hybrid transaction, at least one effect of § 2–316.1 is to render ineffective contractual disclaimers of implied warranties on consumer goods included in a consumer service transaction. Section 2–316.1 is at least partially predicated on a legislative understanding that warranties under the U.C.C. are implied as to the goods included in such transactions. An all or nothing classification of the instant transaction under the predominant purpose test would mean there could be no U.C.C. based, implied warranties on the diving board and would be contrary to the legislative policy implicit in § 2–316.1. Consequently, we cannot use that test in order to determine whether U.C.C. based warranties are implied as to consumer goods in a transaction that is predominantly for the rendering of consumer services.

The gravamen test of Dean Hawkland suggests the vehicle for satisfying the legislative policy. Accordingly, we hold that where, as part of a commercial transaction, consumer goods are sold which retain their character as consumer goods after completion of the performance promised to the consumer, and where monetary loss or personal injury is claimed to have resulted from a defect in the consumer goods, the provisions of the Maryland U.C.C. dealing with implied warranties apply to the consumer goods, even if the transaction is predominantly one for the rendering of consumer services. The facts of the instant case, however, make it unnecessary for us presently to decide whether § 2–316.1 would require that

U.C.C. based, implied warranties also extend to consumer goods which are used up in the course of rendering the consumer service to the consumer.[5]

Thus the diving board which Anthony sold to the Sheehans as part of the swimming pool construction contract carried an implied warranty of merchantability under CL § 2–314. Anthony's contractual disclaimer of that warranty was ineffective under CL § 2–316.1. As a result, the trial court erred in relying on the disclaimer as a basis for directing a verdict in favor of Anthony on the warranty count.

. . .

Judgment of the Court of Special Appeals affirmed. Costs to be paid by Anthony Industries, Inc.

QUESTIONS AND NOTES

1. Distinguishing sales from services. What is the justification under the language of 2–102 for the test used in *Anthony Pools* to distinguish sales from services? What is the justification for the "predominant factor" test, which is used by most decided cases to date? In other words, do you find any test stated explicitly or implicitly by any Code section or comment? If not, is a court absolutely free to develop its own criteria for distinguishing sales from services? If so, should the distinction be based on common sense, administrative convenience, or something else?

With regard to the administrative convenience of the "predominant factor" test, there are undoubtedly a number of cases in which it can be used easily and in which results are clearly predictable. National Historic Shrines Foundation, Inc. v. Dali, 4 UCC Rep.Serv. 71 (N.Y.Sup.Ct.1967), is an example of a situation in which services clearly predominated. In that case the plaintiff, a charitable organization, sued the well-known artist, Salvador Dali, for breach of an oral contract to appear on a television program designed to raise funds for the plaintiff. As part of the program Dali was to paint before the cameras a picture of the Statue of Liberty and present the completed painting at the end of the program to the plaintiff, to be sold for its charitable purposes. The plaintiff estimated that the value of the painting would be $25,000. Dali denied making the contract, set up the statute of frauds of 2–201 of the UCC, and moved for summary judgment. The court held that summary judgment should be denied. It found that 2–201 was not applicable because the alleged transaction between plaintiff and Dali was for the rendition of services and not the sale of goods.

---

5. The reference to "services" in § 2–316.1 has been said to pose "a source of confusion." Freeman and Dressel, Warranty Law in Maryland Product Liability Cases: Strict Liability Incognito?, 5 U.Balt.L.Rev. 47, 61 n. 97 (1975). We express no opinion as to whether today's holding, which is limited to certain consumer goods in a hybrid transaction, is co-extensive with the warranty imposing effect of § 2–316.1's reach into the area of consumer services.

Therefore, the plaintiff was given the opportunity to prove that it had made the alleged agreement with Dali.

Cases in which goods predominate over services easily can be imagined, such as, for example, the sale of an automobile under a contract in which the dealer is obliged to install the sound system from the buyer's trade-in in place of the system that comes as standard equipment. It is equally clear that a large grey area exists in which contracts involving mixed goods and services do not readily fall into one classification or the other when tested in terms of predominating factors. Often the courts seem unaware that they are in the grey area and conclude without much analysis that the case belongs in one category or the other. In these cases, which test is easier to administer? Which test gives the fairer result in your view?

If a court adopts the predominant purpose test, how is it to apply that test? What determines whether the predominant purpose is the sale of goods with services merely incidental, or the sale of services with goods only incidental? One court has stated:

> To determine whether the predominant thrust of a mixed contract is to provide services or goods, one looks first to the language of the contract, in light of the situation of the parties and the surrounding circumstances. Specifically one looks to the terms describing the performance of the parties, and the words used to describe the relationship between the parties.
>
> Beyond the contractual terms themselves, one looks to the circumstances of the parties, and the primary reason they entered into the contract. One also considers the final product the purchaser bargained to receive, and whether it may be described as a good or a service.
>
> Finally, one examines the costs involved for the goods and services, and whether the purchaser was charged only for a good, or a price based on both goods and services. If the cost of the goods is but a small portion of the overall contract price, such fact would increase the likelihood that the services portion predominates.

Insul–Mark Midwest, Inc. v. Modern Materials, Inc., 612 N.E.2d 550, 555 (Ind.1993).

Is the problem of classification avoided where the contract contains a separate price for its service aspect? Some courts have so held. See H. Hirschfield Sons Co. v. Colt Industries, 107 Mich.App. 720, 309 N.W.2d 714 (1981), in which plaintiff bought a large scale for $16,525 and the contract called for the defendant to install it for an additional price of $12,242. Plaintiff complained that the installation was defective. The court held that Article 2 was not applicable. Accord, Dixie Lime & Stone Co. v. Wiggins Scale Co., 144 Ga.App. 145, 240 S.E.2d 323 (1977).

2. Problem. A woman has a medical device surgically implanted to monitor her heart, glucose level, and white-blood-cell count. She is billed $20,000, which includes $7,000 for the device and $4,000 for the other "movable things" used in the course of the surgery. Shortly thereafter the manufacturer of the device withdraws it from the market because it has serious adverse side effects in a large percentage of patients. Within a few months the woman experiences these side effects and has the device surgically removed. She sues the hospital for breach of warranty. Does Article 2 apply?

3.   Dispensation of food in restaurants and blood in hospitals. Under the Uniform Sales Act some courts held that the dispensation of food in restaurants was not a "sale of goods" but an "utterance" or a service. Since there was no sale, these courts concluded that no warranty could be implied. See e.g., Nisky v. Childs Co., 103 N.J.L. 464, 135 A. 805, 50 A.L.R. 227 (1927). The UCC reverses this result by providing in 2–314(1) that "Under this section the serving for value of food or drink to be consumed either on the premises or elsewhere is a sale."

Under the Uniform Sales Act some courts held that a blood transfusion was not a sale by a hospital or doctor to a patient, but rather a service, and hence no warranty protection was available under the statute. See, e.g., Perlmutter v. Beth David Hospital, 308 N.Y. 100, 123 N.E.2d 792 (1954). Article 2 does not address this matter specifically. Do the warranty provisions of Article 2 apply to blood transfusions? How would you argue this question on behalf of the hospital? On behalf of the patient?

Chances are good that your arguments on behalf of the hospital and patient were based to some considerable extent on analogy. Analogies underlie much judicial thinking, and this fact is both good and bad. An analogy is always logically fallacious. It can be expressed as the argument that because X has the properties A and B which also belong to Y, it must also have the property C, which also belongs to Y. On the other hand, it should be remembered that scientific thinking to a great extent is based on analogy, a technique that has proved (subsequently by empirical evidence) to be an invaluable guide to the discovery of truth. Similarly, jurisprudence has been advanced immeasurably by the use of analogy.

A statute as extensive in its coverage as Article 2 of necessity must be drafted in rather general terms, because it would be impossible to list all the specific situations that might come to be decided under it. In this connection the experience of the Prussians in the 19th Century is edifying. The Prussians were convinced that they could cover every single situation in their code and they drafted one that had more than 28,000 sections. But there still were gaps, and ultimately the Germans resorted to commercial and civil codes drafted in very general language.

The UCC is generally drafted in broad language and should not be read the way one reads a conveyance of real property (i.e. if a matter is not specifically included, it is deemed to be excluded); still, some of the UCC sections are rather specific, and this fact solves some problems but creates others. No court would now find that the dispensation of food in a restaurant did not carry with it warranty protection under section 2–314, but it might find the inclusion of such a transaction under that section to have special (and confusing?) meaning in blood transfusion cases. Even though most states now have statutes specifically addressing the liability of persons who provide blood transfusions, it still is valuable to think about what arguments based on the language of Article 2 can be made for and against applying Article 2 to blood transfusions. The techniques you will use in thinking about that question are similar to the techniques often used in arguing whether as statute covers a situation similar to, but not the same, as a situation specifically covered by the statute.

————

2.　COMPUTER SOFTWARE

A major issue in recent years has been whether Article 2 of the Code applies to the sale or licensing of computer software. When a customer pays for software on a disk for installation on the customer's computer, that transaction usually is a license that gives the customer the right to use the software under terms of the license. The document embodying the license sometimes is inside the shrink-wrapped package containing the disk and cannot be read by the customer until the package is opened. Often the license appears only on the computer screen after the user has begun loading the software. Some have questioned whether these methods of calling the user's attention to the license document is sufficient to make the terms of the document binding under Article 2. Others (specifically, software suppliers) have questioned whether Article 2 contains appropriate substantive rules for software transactions. More fundamental, of course, is whether Article 2 applies at all.

Advent Systems Ltd. v. Unisys Corp.

United States Court of Appeals, Third Circuit, 1991.
925 F.2d 670.

[Plaintiff contracted with defendant to supply certain computer-related items, the major part of which was software. When a dispute arose, the court had to decide whether the contract was for the sale of goods, so that the Article 2 statute of frauds applied. The trial court held that the contract was not for the sale of goods.]

■ WEIS, CIRCUIT JUDGE. . . .

In support of the district court's ruling that the U.C.C. did not apply, Advent contends that the agreement's requirement of furnishing services did not come within the Code. Moreover, the argument continues, the "software" referred to in the agreement as a "product" was not a "good" but intellectual property outside the ambit of the Uniform Commercial Code.

. . .

The increasing frequency of computer products as subjects of commercial litigation has led to controversy over whether software is a "good" or intellectual property. The Code does not specifically mention software.

In the absence of express legislative guidance, courts interpret the Code in light of commercial and technological developments. The Code is designed "[t]o simplify, clarify and modernize the law governing commercial transactions" and "[t]o permit the continued expansion of commercial practices." 13 Pa.Cons.Stat.Ann. § 1102(b)(1) (Purdon 1984). As the Official Commentary makes clear:

> "This Act is drawn to provide flexibility so that, since it is intended to be a semi-permanent piece of legislation, it will provide its own machinery for expansion of commercial practices. It is intended to make it possible for the law embodied in this Act to be developed by the courts in the light of unforeseen and new circumstances and practices."

Id. comment 1.

The Code "applies to transactions in goods." 13 Pa.Cons.Stat.Ann. § 2102 (Purdon 1984). Goods are defined as "all things (including specially manufactured goods) which are moveable at the time of the identification for sale." Id. at § 2105. The Pennsylvania courts have recognized that " 'goods' has a very extensive meaning" under the U.C.C. . . .

Computer programs are the product of an intellectual process, but once implanted in a medium are widely distributed to computer owners. An analogy can be drawn to a compact disc recording of an orchestral rendition. The music is produced by the artistry of musicians and in itself is not a "good," but when transferred to a laser-readable disc becomes a readily merchantable commodity. Similarly, when a professor delivers a lecture, it is not a good, but, when transcribed as a book, it becomes a good.

That a computer program may be copyrightable as intellectual property does not alter the fact that once in the form of a floppy disc or other medium, the program is tangible, moveable and available in the marketplace. The fact that some programs may be tailored for specific purposes need not alter their status as "goods" because the Code definition includes "specially manufactured goods."

The topic has stimulated academic commentary with the majority espousing the view that software fits within the definition of a "good" in the U.C.C.

Applying the U.C.C. to computer software transactions offers substantial benefits to litigants and the courts. The Code offers a uniform body of law on a wide range of questions likely to arise in computer software disputes: implied warranties, consequential damages, disclaimers of liability, the statute of limitations, to name a few.

The importance of software to the commercial world and the advantages to be gained by the uniformity inherent in the U.C.C. are strong policy arguments favoring inclusion. The contrary arguments are not persuasive, and we hold that software is a "good" within the definition in the Code.

The relationship at issue here is a typical mixed goods and services arrangement. The services are not substantially different from those generally accompanying package sales of computer systems consisting of hardware and software. . . .

Although determining the applicability of the U.C.C. to a contract by examining the predominance of goods or services has been criticized, we see no reason to depart from that practice here. As we pointed out in De Filippo v. Ford Motor Co., 516 F.2d 1313, 1323 (3d Cir.), cert. denied, 423 U.S. 912 (1975), segregating goods from non-goods and insisting "that the Statute of Frauds apply only to a portion of the contract, would be to make the contract divisible and impossible of performance within the intention of the parties."

. . .

In this case the contract's main objective was to transfer "products." The specific provisions for training of Unisys personnel by Advent were but a small part of the parties' contemplated relationship.

. . .

We are persuaded that the transaction at issue here was within the scope of the Uniform Commercial Code and, therefore, the judgment in favor of the plaintiff must be reversed.

QUESTIONS

1.   On page 21 the court refers to the policy arguments favoring inclusion of software contracts in Article 2. What are they, and how strong are they? The court asserts that the contrary arguments are not persuasive, but it does not identify those arguments. Can you identify any?

2.   To support its conclusion, the court refers to musical recordings and books, sales of which it says are within the scope of Article 2. If a book contains instructions for building a swing set, is Barnes & Noble liable under Article 2 when a purchaser's child is injured because the instructions omitted a crucial step? Cardozo v. True, 342 So.2d 1053 (Fla.App.1977).

3.   If an attorney drafts a contract for a client but fails to include one of the terms that the parties to the contract agreed should be included, does the attorney's client have a claim under 2–314 for breach of the implied warranty of merchantability?

Architectronics, Inc. v. Control Systems, Inc.

United States District Court, Southern District of New York, 1996.
935 F.Supp. 425.

[Plaintiff and defendants entered into a licensing agreement under which defendants had the right to use plaintiff's software as one component of a computer-aided-design (CAD) system. Under the agreement defendants would pay plaintiff a royalty on any of the systems using plaintiff's design which defendants sold. Claiming that defendants breached the contract, plaintiff sued. The suit would have been barred by the four-year statute of limitations of UCC Article 2 (2–725), but not barred under New York's six-year general contract statute of limitations.]

■ MUKASEY, DISTRICT JUDGE.

. . .

Under the UCC as adopted in New York, a "transaction" need not involve a sale; "[t]he use of the term 'transaction' rather than sale in UCC § 2–102 makes it clear that Article 2 is not to be confined merely to those transactions in which there is . . . a transfer of title." 1 Ronald A. Anderson, *Uniform Commercial Code* § 2–102:4 (3d ed.1981) (citing *Hertz Commercial Leasing Corp. v. Transportation Credit Clearing House, Inc.,* 59 Misc.2d 226, 298 N.Y.S.2d 392, 395 (N.Y. City Civ.Ct.1969), *rev'd on other grounds,* 64 Misc.2d 910, 316 N.Y.S.2d 585 (1st Dep't 1970)). The applicability of Article Two to a transaction is not defeated by the use of a license in lieu of a sale if the license provides for transfer of some of the incidents of goods ownership.

Under the UCC, " '[g]oods' means all things (including specially manufactured goods) which are movable at the time of identification to the contract for sale other than the money in which the price is to be paid, investment securities . . . and things in action." *Id.* § 2–105. Generally, software is considered a "good," even though a finished software product may reflect a substantial investment of programming services. *Schroders, Inc. v. Hogan Sys., Inc.,* 137 Misc.2d 738, 522 N.Y.S.2d 404, 406 (Sup.Ct. New York County 1987). However, copyrights, patents, and trademarks are classified as "general intangibles" under the UCC and are distinguished from goods. N.Y. U.C.C. Law § 9–106 & New York Annotations (McKinney 1990).

The SDLA provided for two licenses. Under the first license, Architectronics granted CSI the right to use its DynaMenu software prototypes for joint venture-related purposes only. That license gave CSI a tool necessary for the development of the "Derivative Work," a new display driver. Under the second license, CSI granted Architectronics and CADSource the right to use, copy, and distribute the "Derivative Work." That license was the centerpiece of the transaction, because it provided Architectronics and CADSource with the valuable right to manufacture the new display driver and sell it to the public. Architectronics and CADSource bargained primarily for the right to mass-market the product, not for the right to install single copies of the display driver onto their own PCs. *See generally* Andrew Rodau, *Computer Software: Does Article 2 of the Uniform Commercial Code Apply?,* 35 Emory L.J. 853, 874–883 (1986) (distinguishing tangible software use rights from intangible intellectual property rights). CSI's upside in the deal also was linked to the rights to reproduce and distribute: the parties anticipated thousands of sales of the new product, and Architectronics and CADSource promised to pay CSI a $20–per–copy royalty on those sales. CSI stood to gain in royalties a sum that would dwarf the $2,000 development fee. Because the predominant feature of the SDLA was a transfer of intellectual property rights, the agreement is not subject to Article Two of the UCC.[5] Plaintiff's second contract claim therefore is timely because plaintiff filed suit within six years of CSI's first attempt to repudiate the SDLA.

QUESTIONS AND NOTES

1.   What is the relevance of the book analogy in footnote 5?

2.   Problem. General Motors wants to produce a car to compete with the $90,000 Mercedes SL500. To that end, GM contracts with a famous European auto designer for the designer to create and deliver a prototype, which GM then will put into production. Is the contract between GM and the designer within the scope of Article 2?

3.   What does the book analogy have to say about the applicability of Article 2 to the situation in which a shrink-wrapped disk is acquired in a store?

Software may be distributed in other ways as well. For example, the user may acquire the software on-line from the supplier's web site. Or the supplier may design a program specifically for a particular user and deliver it on a disk or electronically to the hard drive on the user's computer. Or the supplier may permit the user to access the supplier's mainframe computer to use the program. Are these transactions within the scope of Article 2?

4.   UCITA. In 1999 NCCUSL promulgated the Uniform Computer Information Transactions Act (UCITA). As its name states, UCITA covers transactions in computer information, including sales (licensing) of computer programs on disks.

UCITA had a difficult gestation and has not fared well since its birth. It began as a proposal for addition to the UCC, to be known as Article 2B. When the ALI, the co-sponsor of the UCC, became displeased with the direction in which Article 2B was going, it withdrew from participation in further development of the proposal. The withdrawal of ALI meant that the

---

5.   This conclusion may follow more obviously from the following hypothetical analogous set of facts: Suppose that the parties here are book publishers, that Architectronics gives CSI a written outline for a new novel, and that CSI agrees to write the novel. An agreement provides that CSI will own the copyright to the novel, but will grant Architectronics the exclusive right to reproduce and distribute the novel. When Architectronics sells copies of the book to consumers, the sale will be a "transaction in goods" under the UCC. But in the agreement between Architectronics and CSI, Architectronics is contracting for intangible intellectual property rights, even though it will receive a "hard" copy of the novel when CSI finishes the project. The agreement to write the novel would not be a "transaction in goods" under the UCC.

project could not continue as a part of the Uniform Commercial Code, so NCCUSL renamed the Act and continued with its development.

UCITA is a difficult statute technically. It has long, complex definitions and intricate substantive provisions. It has been criticized for its complexity, and there has been sharp disagreement about the wisdom of its substantive provisions. Software developers have generally been strong supporters of UCITA; many purchasers of software have opposed it. UCITA has been adopted in only two states (Virginia and Maryland), and at least four states (Iowa, North Carolina, Vermont, and West Virginia) have adopted "UCITA-shield" statutes providing that choice of law provisions applying UCITA to residents of those states are not effective. In August 2003 NCCUSL announced that it would not seek additional adoptions of UCITA.

Though widespread adoption of UCITA is unlikely, its scope provisions have had a substantial impact upon the discussions about the scope of a revised Article 2. As its title indicates, UCITA "applies to computer information transactions." (§ 103(a)). Section 102(a)(11) defines "computer information transaction" as "an agreement or the performance of it to create modify, transfer, or license computer information or informational rights in computer information." Section 102(a)(10) defines "computer information" as "information in electronic form which is obtained from or through the use of a computer or which is in a form capable of being processed by a computer. The term includes a copy of the information and any documentation or packaging associated with the copy."

As you see from the last sentence quoted, UCITA covers the purchase of a computer program on a disk including the licensing agreement and liability disclaimers that go along with the disk. Therefore, in states that adopt UCITA, these transactions would be removed from Article 2 (if indeed they are covered by Article 2 now.)

In the revision of Article 2, a strong attempt was made to draft a new scope provision that would reach an accommodation with (and possibly mirror) the scope provisions of UCITA. The result would have been to remove software transactions from Article 2, even though states were resisting the adoption of UCITA. The attempt was largely unsuccessful and ultimately, the only change to Article 2 related to scope is the addition of a sentence to the definition of goods which reads, "The term [goods] does not include information." (§ 2–103(1)(k)). The intent is to exclude from Article 2 transactions in which computer programs or other information is downloaded from an internet site. Official Comment 7 states that " . . . this article does not directly apply to electronic transfer of information such as the transaction involved in Specht v. Netscape, 150 F.Supp.2d 585 (S.D.N.Y.2001)." The Comment goes on to say: "However, transactions often involve both goods and information: some are transactions in goods as that term is used in Section 2–102, and some are not. For example, the sale of 'smart goods' such as an automobile is a transaction in goods fully within this article even though the automobile contains many computer programs. On the other hand, an architect's provision of architectural plans on a computer disk would not be a transaction in goods. When a transaction includes both the sale of goods and the transfer of rights in information, it is up to the courts to determine whether the transaction is entirely within or outside of this article, or whether or to what extent this article should be applied to a portion of the transaction. While this article may apply to a transaction including information, nothing in this article alters, creates, or diminishes intellectual property rights." (In the *Specht* case, which was affirmed at 306 F.3d 17 (2d Cir.2002), the court assumed that Article 2 applied to a transaction in which a purchaser of software downloaded it from the Internet.)

5. The Official Comment to revised 2–103(1)(k) states, "the sale of 'smart goods' such as an automobile is a transaction in goods fully within this article even though the automobile contains many computer programs." Presumably, this means that the seller breaches a warranty if the software controlling the engine has a flaw that causes the engine to die when the car is traveling at highway speeds. But what if the seller calls the buyer six months after the purchase and says, "The manufacturer has just issued an improved software program to control the engine in your new car. It's only $50. Bring the car in, and we'll install the new software." If a flaw in this program causes the engine to malfunction, are the purchaser's rights governed by Article 2?

6. Distributorship and franchise agreements. In a franchise relationship the franchisee acquires goods and intellectual property from the franchisor and sells goods and services under the franchisor's trademark. To what extent is the relationship governed by Article 2? In Zapatha v. Dairy Mart, Inc., 381 Mass. 284, 408 N.E.2d 1370 (1980), the franchisee, Zapatha, claimed that the franchisor, Dairy Mart, wrongfully terminated the franchise under which Zapatha operated a Dairy Mart store. Zapatha argued that the franchise agreement was subject to Article 2 and that the provision allowing termination was unconscionable and its exercise was in bad faith under the relevant provisions of Article 2. In the course of upholding Dairy Mart's termination of the franchise, the court stated:

> We need not pause long over the question whether the franchise agreement and the relationship of the parties involved a transaction in goods. Certainly, the agreement required the plaintiffs to purchase goods from Dairy Mart. . . . However, the franchise agreement dealt with many subjects unrelated to the sale of goods by Dairy Mart. About 70% of the goods the plaintiffs sold were not purchased from Dairy Mart. Dairy Mart's profit was intended to come from the franchise fee and not from the sale of items to its franchisees. Thus, the sale of goods by Dairy Mart to the Zapathas was, in a commercial sense, a minor aspect of the entire relationship. We would be disinclined to import automatically all the provisions of the sales article into a relationship involving a variety of subjects other than the sale of goods, merely because the contract dealt in part with the sale of goods. Similarly, we would not be inclined to apply the sales article only to aspects of the agreement that concerned goods. Different principles of

law might then govern separate portions of the same agreement with possibly inconsistent and unsatisfactory consequences.

> We view the legislative statements of policy concerning good faith and unconscionability as fairly applicable to all aspects of the franchise agreement, not by subjecting the franchise relationship to the provisions of the sales article but rather by applying the stated principles by analogy . . . . This basic common law approach, applied to statutory statements of policy, permits a selective application of those principles expressed in a statute that reasonably should govern situations to which the statute does not apply explicitly.

7. Contracts involving the sale of both goods and real estate. In Dehahn v. Innes, 356 A.2d 711 (Me.1976), Dehahn orally agreed to sell and Innes orally agreed to buy for a price of $35,000 a 52-acre gravel pit, a backhoe, a bulldozer, a loader, a dump truck with plow, and a second truck and trailer. It was found that Dehahn had agreed to deliver the equipment in "ready-to-go condition." After numerous complaints about Dehahn's failure to put the equipment in this kind of condition, Innes notified him that he was canceling the contract. No payments were ever made pursuant to the contract. Dehahn sued for breach of contract, basing his cause of action on Article 2. Innes denied the applicability of Article 2. How would you decide the case? Do you need more facts than are given above to make your decision? If so, what are they and why do you need them? See 2–107.

8. "Unless the context otherwise requires." While 2–101 gives Article 2 the official title "Uniform Commercial Code—Sales," 2–102 provides that "Unless the context otherwise requires, this Article applies to transactions in goods . . . ." See also 2–106(1). Is there any inconsistency between these sections?

In *Architectronics* the court said that since Article 2 applies to *transactions* in goods, its coverage is not limited to sales, and that, therefore, a licensing transaction could fall within Article 2.

9. Leases: the scope of Article 2A. Article 2A applies to "any transaction, regardless of form, that creates a lease" (2A–102). Presumably, if the contract involves a mix of services and goods, the same issues that arise in *Anthony Pools* will arise and will be resolved in the same ways as in sales cases. However, the major scope issue that arises in connection with leases is whether the transaction is a lease or instead is a sale in which the seller retains a security interest. There is some incentive for the supplier to structure the transaction as a lease rather than a sale with a security interest, because (1) no public filing is necessary to preserve the rights of the lessor as against creditors of, or buyers from, the lessee; and (2) on default by the lessee, the lessor can just take the goods back, without any obligation to go through the foreclosure proceedings that Article 9 of the UCC requires for a sale with a security interest. We leave further discussion of the substantive difference between leases and security interests to the course dealing with Article 9. However, since there are some differences between Articles 2A and Article 2, it will occasionally be important for Articles 2 and 2A purposes to decide whether the transaction is a sale with a retained security interest, or a lease. For example, 2–316(2) and (3) apparently permit oral disclaimers of implied warranties in certain cases, while 2A–214 requires that these disclaimers be in writing.

Section 1–201(37) (section 1–203 in revised Article 1) sets out standards for determining whether a transaction is a lease or a security agreement. Please examine those sections in connection with the following two problems.

a. Problem. Apex and Bestway enter into a transaction under which Apex leases to Bestway a new IBM computer at a rental of $1,000 per month for five years, at the end of which Bestway has the option to acquire the computer for an additional payment of $100. Apex claims that it orally disclaimed all warranties of merchantability. Is the transaction a lease or a sale?

b. Problem. Acme and Buildit enter into a transaction under which Acme leases to Buildit a used road-paving machine for three years at a rental of $2,000 per month, with an option to purchase the machine at the end of the three-year period for $10,000. Acme claims that it orally agreed with Buildit that the transaction was "as is." Is the transaction a sale or a lease? Is it relevant that the reasonably expectable value of the machine at the end of the term is $30,000?

10. International transactions: the scope of CISG. There are three aspects to the scope of the Convention on Contracts for the International Sale of Goods: (1) whether the transaction is international; (2) whether the transaction is a type excluded from coverage of the Convention; and (3) whether the preponderant part of the transaction consists in the supply of labor or other services. Also, of course, it is necessary that the country whose law would apply have ratified the Convention.* As of July 1, 2005, approximately 70 countries, including the United States, have ratified it.

First, the Convention applies only to sales of goods between parties whose places of business are in different countries (Article 1). Further, the Convention does not apply even though the parties have their places of business in different countries if that "fact does not appear from the contract or from dealings between, or from information disclosed by, the parties at any time before or at the conclusion, of the contract." (Article 1). The reason for the second limitation is that a seller or buyer who at the time of contracting has no reason to know that the Convention is applicable should not be bound by it. An example is a buyer who is buying for an undisclosed foreign principal. See Honnold § 41.

Second, Article 2 of the Convention provides that it does not apply to sales of electricity, ships, vessels, hovercraft, or aircraft. Nor does it apply

---

* Article 1(1) of the Convention provides that the Convention applies to contracts of sale between parties whose places of business are in different countries if (1) the countries have ratified the Convention, or (2) if the rules of international private law would lead to the application of the law of a country that has ratified the Convention. The United States has declared that it is not bound by the second ground for application of the Convention.

to sales by auction or sales on execution or otherwise by authority of law. Further, it does not apply to goods bought for personal, family, or household use unless the seller neither knew nor had reason to know that the goods were bought for that use. The exclusion for consumer goods preserves the consumer-protection laws of the various countries.

Third, Article 3 provides that the Convention applies to contracts for the manufacture or production of goods unless the buyer is to supply "a substantial part of the materials necessary for such manufacture or production" (Paragraph 1), but "does not apply to contracts in which the preponderant part of the obligations of the party who furnishes the goods consists in the supply of labour or other services" (Paragraph 2). Since the manufacture of goods entails the use of "labour or other services," do the two rules of Article 3 contradict each other? Would the Salvador Dali contract (Question 1, page 17 supra) be covered by the Convention?

In the sales-service hybrid transaction, what test does the Convention adopt? If the parties to the contract in *Anthony Pools* were a Canadian swimming-pool supplier and a United States country club, would the transaction be governed by the Convention?

In Problem 2, page 18, if the parties were a German seller and an American auto manufacturer, and the contract called for the seller to design and incorporate into the buyer's plant several pieces of robotic equipment, for $2 million, would the Convention apply? Would it be relevant that the cost of the movable things incorporated into the equipment is $1.1 million? $800,000?

---

3. APPLICATION OF ARTICLE 2 RULES IN NON-GOODS TRANSACTIONS

Hoffman v. Horton

Virginia Supreme Court, 1972.
212 Va. 565, 186 S.E.2d 79.

■ CARRICO, JUSTICE. The question involved in this case is whether an auctioneer at a foreclosure sale may reopen the bidding when an overbid is made immediately prior to or simultaneously with the falling of the hammer in acceptance of a lower bid.

The question arises from an auction sale conducted to foreclose a deed of trust in the sum of $100,000 upon the "Field Tract" in Arlington County, owned by the defendants Howard P. Horton and wife and Ralph R. Kaul and wife. At the sale and after spirited bidding, a bid of $177,000 was made by Hubert N. Hoffman, the plaintiff, and received by the auctioneer. When no other bids appeared to be forthcoming, the auctioneer asked, "Are you all through bidding, gentlemen?" After a pause, he stated, "Going once for $177,000.00, going twice for $177,000.00, sold for $177,000.00." Whereupon, he struck the palm of his left hand with his right fist.

Immediately, one of the trustees, who had been standing nearby, rushed up to the auctioneer and told him that he had missed a bid of $178,000. The auctioneer, who had neither seen nor heard the bid, stated, "If I missed a bid, you people had better speak up. I am going ahead with the sale." The plaintiff then stepped forward and said, "Gentlemen, I have purchased this property for $177,000.00." The auctioneer and the trustee both disagreed with the plaintiff, and the auctioneer announced to the crowd that he had a bid of $178,000. The bidding proceeded, and the property was finally knocked down to the plaintiff for $194,000.

The plaintiff paid the $5,000 deposit required by the terms of the foreclosure but insisted that he had purchased the property for $177,000. Later, he paid the balance of the $194,000 under protest and brought an action against the former owners and the trustees to recover the $17,000 difference between the two bids in dispute. The trial court denied the plaintiff's claim, and we granted a writ of error to review the judgment.

. . .

The trial court found as a matter of fact, and this finding is not questioned by the plaintiff, that the $178,000 bid was made "prior to or simultaneously with" the falling of the auctioneer's fist in acceptance of the plaintiff's bid of $177,000. Based upon its finding of fact, the court held that "the bid for $178,000.00 was made before the bid for $177,000.00 had been accepted" and that the auctioneer had "acted within the discretion permitted" him in reopening the bidding and continuing with the sale.

In holding that the auctioneer was vested with discretion to reopen the bidding, the trial court relied upon Code § 8.2–328(2), a part of the Uniform Commercial Code. The statutory language so relied upon reads as follows:

"A sale by auction is complete when the auctioneer so announces by the fall of the hammer or in other customary manner. Where a bid is made while the hammer is falling in acceptance of a prior bid the auctioneer may in his discretion reopen the bidding or declare the goods sold under the bid on which the hammer was falling."

We disagree with the trial court that the transaction in this case, involving the sale of land, is controlled by § 8.2–328(2) of the Uniform Commercial Code. Title 8.2 of the Commercial Code applies only to transactions relating to "goods." Code § 8.2–105, § 107.

However, while the Uniform Commercial Code is not controlling here, we think it appropriate to borrow from it to establish the rule applicable to the transaction at hand. To vest the auctioneer crying a sale of land with the same discretion to reopen bidding that he has in the sale of goods is to achieve uniformity and, of more importance, to recognize a rule which is both necessary and fair.

We hold, therefore, that the auctioneer in this case was vested with discretion to reopen the bidding for the land which was being sold. And we agree with the trial court that the auctioneer "acted within" his discretion in reopening the bidding and continuing with the sale when it was made apparent to him that a higher bid had been submitted "prior to or simultaneously with" the falling of his fist in acceptance of the plaintiff's lower bid.

Accordingly, the judgment of the trial court will be affirmed.

QUESTIONS AND NOTES

1. Extension of Article 2 to cases clearly beyond its scope. Note that the court in the instant case recognized that the matter at hand was clearly outside the scope of Article 2 of the UCC. Yet it applied a rule found in 2–328. Why? Recall Zapatha v. Dairy Mart, page 26 supra.

Some courts have extended Article 2 to cover cases clearly beyond its scope because Article 2 has a rule or rules not readily available at common law or under other statutes. For example, in Wille v. Southwestern Bell Tel. Co., 219 Kan. 755, 549 P.2d 903 (1976), the Kansas Supreme Court applied the doctrine of unconscionability found in 2–302 in a case including a contract claim against the telephone company by a Yellow Pages advertiser. He had sued the phone company for an omission in the Yellow Pages of a telephone directory. The contract entered into by the parties limited the telephone company's liability for errors and omissions to an amount equal to the cost of the advertisement. Although stating that the doctrine of unconscionability had been part of the common law at least since 1750, the court said that the doctrine "received its greatest impetus when it was enacted as part of the Uniform Commercial Code. . . . Although the UCC's application is primarily limited to contracts for the present or future sale of goods (citing sections 2–102 and 2–105) many courts have extended the statute by analogy into other areas of the law or have used the doctrine as an alternative basis for their holdings." The court then proceeded to discuss the meaning of 2–302 and to apply it to the case at hand.

Other courts have turned to the UCC in cases beyond its scope because it is superior law, the best commercial law that the best experts in the United States could develop. See, e.g., Appeals of Reeves Soundcraft Corp., 2 UCC Rep.Serv. 210 (ASB–CA 1964). In that case the Armed Services Board of Contract Appeals had before it a case involving the question of the warranty obligation of a seller of magnetic tape to the federal government. The federal government claimed that the matter should be controlled by federal common law. The Board agreed, but then held that the federal common law should be deemed to include relevant portions of the UCC, because there is little, if any, federal case law on the point involved, and, anyway, the UCC reflects "the best in modern decisions and discussion."

2. Distinguishing real estate from personal property for purposes of the application of the UCC. In the *Hoffman* case it is clear that the contract involved the sale of real estate. Sometimes, however, it is not so clear whether real or personal property is involved. The distinction has been particularly important for purposes of the statute of frauds since, typically, it is much easier to satisfy the statute of frauds relating to personal property than real property. The problem has arisen most frequently in the context of contracts to sell crops, timber, and structures that are to be severed from land and delivered to the buyer for relocation.

With respect to crops, the common-law distinction did not turn on whether the sale involved growing crops or harvested crops. Instead, the distinction usually turned on the difference between *fructus naturales* and *fructus industriales*. *Fructus naturales* consisted of those things which grow without cultivation, such as grass and trees. *Fructus industriales* consisted of crops that must be planted and cultivated. The courts held that *fructus industriales* was "goods" for purposes of the sales statute of frauds, even though it was not severed from the land or matured at the time of the sale. See, for example, Green v. Armstrong, 1 Denio (N.Y.) 550 (1845). On the other hand, *fructus naturales* was often treated as land, even though the contract contemplated immediate severance. Smith v. Thomas, 224 Ala. 41, 138 So. 542 (1931); Baird v. Elliott, 63 N.D. 738, 249 N.W. 894, 91 A.L.R. 1274 (1933); Beckman v. Brickley, 144 Wash. 558, 258 P. 488 (1927); contra, Patton v. Lucy, 285 Ky. 694, 148 S.W.2d 1039 (1940); Hurricane Lumber Co. v. Lowe, 110 Va. 380, 66 S.E. 66 (1909). In Robbins v. Farwell, 193 Pa. 37, 44, 44 A. 260, 261, 262 (1899), the court stated, "If the agreement does not contemplate the immediate severance of the timber, it is a contract for the sale or reservation of an interest in land. . . . But when the agreement is made with a view to the immediate severance of the timber from the soil it is regarded as personal property."

With respect to the sale of buildings and fixtures that were to be severed and removed immediately, at common law the courts were inclined to permit the parties to treat the contract as involving "goods" for purposes of the statute of frauds. E.g., Wetopsky v. New Haven Gas Light Co., 88 Conn. 1, 90 A. 30 (1914); Cleveland Wrecking Co. v. Federal Deposit Ins. Corp., 66 F.Supp. 921 (E.D.Pa.1946); Cervadoro v. First Nat. Bank and Trust Co., 267 App.Div. 314, 45 N.Y.S.2d 738 (1944).

Consider the converse situation in which one sells goods that are to be affixed to real estate, with the property interest passing from the seller to the buyer after the affixture. In Frederick Raff Co. v. Murphy, 110 Conn. 234, 147 A. 709 (1929), the court held that a contract to do plumbing work and add fixtures was not for the sale of "goods," since under the agreement "title to the articles was not to pass to the [buyer] as in articles of personal property but in articles which, by the very terms of the contract, were to be affixed to and become part of the realty."

In what respects does the UCC change this common law?

———

4. EFFECT OF ARTICLE 2 ON OTHER STATUTES APPLICABLE TO SALE OF GOODS

Pet Dealers Association of New Jersey, Inc. v. Division of Consumer Affairs, Dept. of Law and Public Safety, State of New Jersey

New Jersey Superior Court, Appellate Division, 1977.
149 N.J.Super. 235, 373 A.2d 688.

■ PER CURIAM. By this appeal Pet Dealers Association of New Jersey, Inc. challenges the validity of the Attorney General's regulations governing the sale of pet cats and dogs adopted pursuant to the Consumer Fraud Act, N.J.S.A. 56:8–4.

Pet Dealers first contends that the regulations in question conflict with Article 2 of the Uniform Commercial Code (N.J.S.A. 12A:2–101 et seq.) in that the regulations provide the consumer with broader remedies than are available under the Code. It is argued that since the regulations conflict with applicable statutory provisions, the regulations are invalid. A similar argument was recently made to and rejected by the Supreme Court in Jeselsohn, Inc. v. Atlantic City, 70 N.J. 238, 358 A.2d 797 (1976). There, auctioneers doing business in Atlantic City attacked a local ordinance which regulated auction sales. The ordinance required an auctioneer to refund, in full, the purchase price of an article when a demand for such is made within 72 hours after purchase. The basic contention as to the invalidity of the ordinance was that it conflicted with provisions of the Uniform Commercial Code regulating auction sales. In rejecting that argument the court said that the provisions of the Code dealing with sales, rescission and revocation of acceptance "are intended to give certainty and stability to the law of commercial transactions. In this sense they do not purport to limit the proper exercise of police power in the public interest." 70 N.J. at 244, 358 A.2d at 800. So here. The fact that the regulations are part of a statewide plan to combat consumer fraud rather than a local ordinance does not alter their legitimacy as a valid exercise of police power. In any event the Code expressly provides that it does not "impair or repeal any statute regulating sales to consumers * * *." N.J.S.A. 12A:2–102. Thus, there is no conflict between the Code and the Consumer Fraud Act, nor with the regulations adopted thereunder. . . .

For the foregoing reasons we conclude that the regulations challenged by "Pet Dealers" (N.J.A.C. 13:45A–12.1 et seq.) are valid.

QUESTIONS AND NOTES

1. Statutes regulating sales to consumers, farmers or other specified classes of buyers. Note that 2–102 does not purport to "impair or repeal any statute regulating sales to consumers, farmers or other specified classes of buyers.'' Is this the same as saying that 2–102 does not purport to impair or repeal any regulatory statute involving the sale of goods? In this connection consider also 1–104.

In most civil law countries there is both a civil and a commercial code. The latter is usually made applicable only when one (or both) of the parties is a merchant, and the civil code applies when this condition is not met. Lawyers from civil law countries often assume that this dichotomy exists in the United States now that we have a ''Commercial Code.'' They are surprised to learn that most of the UCC covers transactions involving both consumers and merchants and all combinations thereof.

In a sense, however, the United States has been moving toward the distinction between merchant and consumer transactions celebrated in civil law countries, first, by setting forth some nineteen special rules for merchant sellers in Article 2 of the UCC, and, second, by the enactment of special legislation designed to give particular protection to consumers and others, such as farmers. With regard to this kind of special legislation, the lawyer must be careful in his or her statutory research, for local pressure groups (e.g., the dog and cat lovers of New Jersey) may be successful in securing legislation dealing with subject matter that may not seem particularly appropriate for special treatment. Transactions involving automobiles, home improvement products (or the installation thereof), and agricultural products (e.g., pesticides, seed, livestock, etc.) should be scrutinized carefully in terms of special legislation, since the bulk of special legislation involves consumers and farmers. For some interesting cases involving the interaction of special legislation on these matters and the UCC see, Morris Plan Co. of California v. Moody, 266 Cal.App.2d 28, 72 Cal.Rptr. 123 (1968) (interaction between 2–403 and the California Motor Vehicle Code); Feary v. Aaron Burglar Alarm, Inc., 32 Cal.App.3d 553, 108 Cal.Rptr. 242 (1973) (interaction between the UCC and a California statute governing damages for breach of a contract for installation of a burglar alarm system); Potter v. Tyndall, 22 N.C.App. 129, 205 S.E.2d 808 (1974) (interaction between 2–315 and a North Carolina statute relating to the sale of agricultural fertilizer); Olson v. Molacek Bros., 341 N.W.2d 375 (N.D.1983) (impact of Article 2 on a North Dakota statute providing civil and criminal penalties for the sale of diseased cattle); Hoffman Motors, Inc. v. Enockson, 240 N.W.2d 353 (N.D.1976) (interaction between 2–316 and a North Dakota statute governing warranties on the sale of tractors to farmers).

Of course, a lawyer handling sales problems will be aware of the ''big'' statutes that have been adopted in some states in recent years to give consumers special protection. Among these are statutes governing unfair or deceptive acts or practices and the Uniform Consumer Credit Code, promulgated in 1968, and revised in 1974, by NCCUSL, one of the sponsors of the UCC. The UCCC has not enjoyed the success of the UCC (having been adopted in fewer than a dozen states), but every state has enacted a statute prohibiting deceptive practices in consumer sales transactions.

In spite of the promulgation of the UCCC and other local statutes aimed at giving consumers special protection, Congress has been impatient with the efforts of the states and has made incursions of its own in the sales area, a significant example of which is the Magnuson–Moss Warranty Act, to be considered in Chapter 5.

It should be noted that there is a great difference between impairment and displacement. The UCC does not impair most regulatory statutes, but most regulatory statutes, in turn, do not completely displace the UCC. Thus, the sale of a cat in New Jersey may carry with it special remedies governed by the special legislation, but routine matters such as the price term and delivery requirements are governed by the UCC.

Finally, it should be observed that the time may come when it will be advisable to enact a "Uniform Consumer Code" to parallel the UCC, which, of course, would have to be appropriately amended to delete any coverage of consumer transactions. It may surprise you to know that the impetus for this change has been from the commercial, and not the consumer, sector. What do you think small merchants or commercial giants have to gain by separating the statutory law of commercial and consumer transactions? Are their interests identical with regard to such a proposal?

5. Territorial and Temporal Limitations and Choice of Law

a. CHOICE OF LAW. The choice-of-law rules deal with two related questions: (1) To what extent can the parties choose the jurisdiction whose law will govern their transaction? and (2) Which jurisdiction's law applies if the parties do not choose a jurisdiction or if their choice is ineffective? Before turning to the Code rules on these issues, we should note that the court in which litigation is brought, called the forum, does not, and constitutionally cannot, apply its own substantive law to every matter that is brought before it. See Scoles, Hay, Borchers & Symeonides, Conflict of Laws §§ 3.20–3.25 (4th ed. 2004). An entire body of law has developed to determine what substantive law applies when a transaction has contacts in more than one state or country. For example, suppose a New York seller makes a contract to sell goods to a California buyer. Suppose, additionally, that the contract is valid under the laws of New York but invalid under the laws of California. If the law of the forum were applied automatically, the plaintiff (either buyer or seller) could control the result of any dispute by bringing the action in California or New York, depending on the outcome the plaintiff desired. The prevention of this phenomenon, called forum-shopping, is one of the main purposes of conflict-of-laws rules.

A related issue is whether the parties in the New York–California hypothetical can choose the law of either California or New York. Similarly suppose the contract is between two New York parties; can they choose the law of California as the law governing their transactions?

Section 1–105 is the first uniform legislation in the United States to contain choice-of-law rules, and, as a result, it has generated considerable interest among conflict-of-laws specialists who otherwise might have treated the UCC with indifference. Their contribution to the development of 1–105 has been considerable, as its history, briefly discussed below, indicates.

Basically, 1–105 mandates the application of the law of a particular state for a handful of transactions and gives the parties the competence to choose their own law for all others. This competence, however, is not absolute. The law chosen must bear a "reasonable" relation to the transaction. This limitation will be discussed at a subsequent point when we will consider the choice-of-law term of the sales contract.

If the parties fail to specify the law of a state that bears a reasonable relation to the transaction, or if they make no choice of law at all, then the law of the forum applies if it bears an "appropriate" relation to the transaction. Some understanding of these rules may be gained by looking at the history of 1–105.

In 1949 when the UCC was submitted to the American Law Institute for the first serious public discussion of the entire Act, its drafters had reached two conclusions that played a key part in their initial formulation of 1–105. They were convinced that the UCC represented a distinct improvement of commercial law. Notwithstanding this belief, they were also convinced that many years would elapse before all, or even most, states would adopt it. These two convictions pointed to the desirability of formulating a choice-of-law section that would almost certainly make the UCC operative for any case that was brought in a state that had enacted it. This goal was accomplished in the 1949 Code by two techniques. First, 1–105 of that Code did not give the parties the general competence to choose the applicable law for the transaction, but provided that this power to choose was limited to making the UCC applicable to the deal. This provision, stated in 1–105(j) of the 1949 Code, was designed to prevent parties in a Code state from selecting non-Code law, but to allow parties in a non-Code state to choose the UCC for their transaction. Secondly, it made the Code applicable where the forum state had enacted it and any one of a number of acts or happenings had occurred in that state with respect to the transaction. For example, the UCC was made applicable to a sales deal if "any contract or transaction within its terms: (a) is made, proposed or accepted, or occurs within this state; or (b) is to be performed or completed wholly within this state; or (c) relates to or involves goods which are to be or are in fact delivered, shipped or received within this state; or (d) involves a bill of lading, warehouse receipt or other document of title which is to be or is in fact issued, delivered, sent or received within this state." Additionally, the UCC would be made applicable if credit arrangements had any contacts with the forum state, or if the parties agreed that the transaction should be governed by the UCC.

Public discussion of the 1949 draft of section 1–105 was critical of the fact that the drafters had denied the contracting parties autonomy with regard to choice of law, thereby contradicting a basic philosophical tenet of freedom of contract articulated by 1–102. As we shall see subsequently, the drafters yielded to this criticism by an amendment to the section, but they continued to try to prevent the parties from circumventing the Code by choosing the law of a non-Code state bearing little relationship to the transaction.

The 1949 draft of 1–105 was also criticized for its chauvinistic effort to make the UCC applicable to every possible transaction, the specific charge being that this effort ran counter to the general purposes of conflict of laws rules, namely "(a) the application of the most appropriate law or laws to a transaction transcending state lines, and (b) the minimization of the role of the forum in the outcome of the case." See 1 Study of the Uniform Commercial Code, State of N.Y. Law Revision Commission 175 (1955). Moreover, some scholars suggested that the section might be unconstitutional on due process grounds. E.g., Rheinstein, Conflict of Laws in the Uniform Commercial Code, 16 Law & Cont.Prob. 114, 120 (1951).

These criticisms were partially accepted and accommodated by the 1956 Recommendations of the Permanent Editorial Board which ultimately found their way into the present 1962 and 1972 Official Codes. The 1952 Code had accepted the suggestion (begrudgingly) that freedom of contract with regard to choice of law be given, but it provided, "In the absence of an agreement which meets the requirements of this subsection, this Act governs." That provision was changed as a result of the suggestions made in 1956 to its present language: "Failing such agreement this Act applies to transactions bearing an appropriate relation to this state."

What is the significance, if any, of this change? Does it require the forum state to apply the law that is most appropriate to the transaction? In view of the fact that all the states (except Louisiana, in part) have adopted the UCC, one of the major premises underlying 1–105 no longer is valid. Should that influence a court in its handling of the section? For example, most conflict-of-laws experts opine that the state that has the most important contacts with a transaction is the one whose law bears the most appropriate relationship to the transaction and ought to govern it. What weight, if any, should a court give to this accepted viewpoint in the light of the language of 1–105 and its legislative history?

Note that the importance of 1–105 has waned with the widespread enactment of the Code, because in most cases it makes no difference whether the law of one state or another is applied, since both operate under an identical statute. In some cases, however, the choice of law is still important, because the UCC has been amended in minor respects in all states and it has not been construed uniformly in all respects. In international transactions, of course, choice of law is a matter of major concern and should be handled by an express term of the contract.

In 2001 NCCUSL and ALI promulgated revised Article 1, which contains a choice of law provision (1–301) that greatly expands the parties ability to chose their law. With exceptions for consumer transactions, in domestic transactions (i.e. those that do not bear a reasonable relationship to a foreign country) the parties can chose the law of any state, whether or not the state chosen has a reasonable relationship to the transaction. Similarly, in an international transaction, the parties can choose the law of any state or country whether or not the state or country has a reasonable relationship with the transaction. The limitation on the parties' ability to choose the law of, say the Sudan, or Libya, is that "An agreement otherwise effective . . . is not effective to the extent that application of the law of the State or country designated would be contrary to a fundamental policy of the State or country whose law would govern in the absence of agreement. . . ."

In consumer transactions, the state or country whose law is chosen must bear a reasonable relationship to the transaction, and the law chosen cannot deprive the consumer of the protection of any rule of law applicable in the state or country in which the consumer "principally" resides, or, if the consumer both makes a contract for the purchase of goods and takes delivery of the goods in a state or country other than that in which the consumer resides, then the consumer protection laws of that jurisdiction.

The new choice-of-law provision has been the subject of substantial attack and it is not certain that it will be widely adopted. As of 2006, none of the states adopting revised Article 1 has adopted the revised version. Instead, they have retained original 1–105.

b.   TRANSITIONAL PROVISIONS. When a new statute governing private contracting is adopted, the statute, if well drafted, will state the extent to which transactions entered into before the effective date of the new statute are subject to the new statute. Those transitional provisions applicable to original Article 2 and 2A, appear in Articles 10 and 11. Today it is unlikely that any of those pre-existing contracts exist or would call the transitional provisions into play. The 2003 amendments to Article 2 have a transitional provision, 2–803, which states that the amendments do not apply to transactions entered into, or causes of actions that accrued, before the effective date of the amendments.

CHAPTER 2

FORMATION OF THE SALES CONTRACT

A. INTRODUCTION

Prior to the enactment of the UCC, the formation of a sales contract with few exceptions was governed by the same rules as the formation of any other contract. Initially, the drafters strongly suspected that sales contracts needed different formation rules from those employed in, for example, contracts for construction, employment, or the sale of real estate. As a result of this suspicion, the drafters of the Code made a thorough investigation of how the formation rules were operating in the sales area. To their surprise, they found that in the main the common-law rules were working quite well. Their investigation revealed, however, a few situations that needed to be corrected by special rules applicable only to sales transactions. These rules appear in Part 2 to Article 2, specifically, in the ten sections beginning with 2–201, and they are the principal focus of this chapter. In reading this chapter, please remember that unless Article 2 specifically provides otherwise, the contract formation rules of the common law continue to operate with full vigor in the commercial arena of sales law. See 1–103 and Official Comment 3.

(Supp. General Principles)

1–103

B. OFFER AND ACCEPTANCE

Unique Designs, Inc. v. Pittard Machinery Company

Georgia Court of Appeals, 1991.
200 Ga.App. 647, 409 S.E.2d 241.

■ COOPER, JUDGE.

In January or February of 1988, Pittard Machinery Company ("Pittard,") a distributor of lathes, attempted to sell to Unique Designs, Inc. ("Unique") a "Mori Seiki" lathe; however, Unique instead purchased a less expensive "Mazak" lathe from one of Pittard's competitors. In June of 1988, Unique contacted Pittard and requested Pittard's assistance in disposing of the Mazak lathe because it had turned out to be incompatible with Unique's business. During the course of this conversation, Unique indicated that in return for Pittard's assistance in disposing of the Mazak lathe, Unique would replace the Mazak lathe by purchasing a Mori Seiki lathe from Pittard. Pittard proceeded to arrange for the resale of the Mazak lathe by putting Unique in contact with an international broker of machinery who quickly found a purchaser for the used lathe. Pittard never asked Unique to pay a commission on the sale of the Mazak lathe because of its expectation that Unique would be replacing the Mazak lathe with a Mori Seiki lathe purchased from Pittard. Thereafter, Unique and Pittard commenced negotiating the price of the Mori Seiki lathe and during the course of a telephone conversation, the parties finally agreed upon a price of either $104,000 or $104,850, and arrangements were made for the delivery of a lathe to Unique. It is undisputed that an oral agreement to purchase the lathe was made, although the amount of the purchase price is in dispute.

The day after the agreement was reached, Unique contacted Pittard and cancelled its order to purchase the lathe. Apparently, Unique had been negotiating all along with one of Pittard's competitors and had used its contract with Pittard as leverage to secure a reduced price on a different model lathe with the competitor. Shortly after Unique's repudiation of the contract, Pittard was able to resell the Mori Seiki lathe to one of its regular customers, Sieco, Inc. ("Sieco") for $110,000.

Pittard brought suit against Unique seeking general damages and attorney fees for Unique's breach of its agreement to purchase the lathe. The trial court granted Pittard's motion for summary judgment on the issue of liability, ruling that the oral contract between the parties was valid pursuant to OCGA § 11–2–201(3)(b), and Pittard was a "high volume dealer," entitled to recover its lost profits pursuant to OCGA § 11–2–708(2), without having to offset the proceeds it received from the sale of the lathe to Sieco. The case proceeded to trial on the issue of damages, and the jury awarded Pittard $18,000 in general damages and $18,000 in attorney fees. Following the jury verdict, the trial court entered judgment in favor of Pittard for $18,000 in general damages but set aside the jury's award of attorney fees. Unique appeals from the trial court's grant of partial summary judgment to Pittard and the final judgment entered on the jury verdict for general damages. Pittard cross-appeals from the trial court's order setting aside the jury's award of attorney fees.

. . .

. . . Unique argues that although the trial court in his grant of partial summary judgment to Pittard ruled that an oral contract to purchase the lathe existed, Unique was still entitled to present evidence to show that the oral contract was unenforceable because there had been no meeting of the minds. Relying on OCGA § 13–3–1 and OCGA § 13–3–2,* Unique argues that because certain essential terms of the agreement were in dispute—the

---

* These sections provide:

13–3–1. To constitute a valid contract, there must be parties able to contract, a consideration moving to the contract, the assent of the parties to the terms of the contract, and a subject matter on which the contract can operate.

13–3–2. The consent of the parties being essential to a contract, until each has assented to all the terms, there is no binding contract; until assented to, each party may withdraw his bid or proposition.—Ed.

purchase price of the lathe, the accessory packages to be included in the sale, the amount of the downpayment and the financing arrangements—the contract was rendered unenforceable. We disagree. "Even though one or more terms are left open a contract for sale does not fail for indefiniteness if the parties have intended to make a contract and there is a reasonably certain basis for giving an appropriate remedy." OCGA § 11–2–204. The record clearly indicates that Unique intended to purchase a "Mori Seiki" lathe from Pittard for either $104,000 or $104,850. The confusion over the purchase price and the open terms in the agreement were not sufficient to negate the clear intent of the parties to enter into an enforceable agreement.

Unique also attempted to admit into evidence testimony and documentary evidence pertaining to a transaction between Unique and Pittard that occurred two years earlier, also involving Unique's purchase of a lathe from Pittard. Unique contends that the document evidencing the prior transaction, which consisted of ten pages containing a description of the accessory package to be included in the sale, as well as downpayment and financing terms, should have been admissible as evidence of a course of dealing between the parties in accordance with the provisions of OCGA § 11–1–205(1). It is Unique's argument that this course of dealing between the parties would have established that there had been no meeting of the minds in the present transaction because certain key terms that had been described in great detail in the prior transaction had not been discussed or agreed upon in the present transaction.

"A course of dealing is a sequence of previous conduct between the parties to a particular transaction which is fairly to be regarded as establishing a common basis of understanding for interpreting their expressions and other conduct." OCGA § 11–1–205(1). " 'It is a fundamental rule of statutory construction that where the language of a statute is plain and unambiguous, the terms used therein should be given their common and ordinary meaning.' " Sledge v. Employee's Retirement System, 196 Ga.App. 597, 598, 396 S.E.2d 550 (1990). We can only conclude under the plain and unambiguous language of this statute that a sale of a single lathe from Pittard to Unique, which occurred more than two years prior to the transaction at issue in this action, cannot be deemed to be a "sequence of previous conduct" under OCGA § 11–1–205(1). Thus, the trial court did not err in refusing to allow evidence of the previous transaction at trial.

QUESTIONS AND NOTES

1. According to the court, the parties reached agreement on the approximate price and on delivery arrangements. What if the conversation ended with the seller's rep saying that he would stop by the buyer's business the next day with a written version for the parties to sign. When the seller's rep shows up, the buyer sees that the document calls for payment on delivery, and the following colloquy occurs:

> Buyer: "Oh, no, I can't sign that. We need to have 90 days credit."
>
> Seller's rep: "Sorry, we don't do that, but we could give you 30 days."
>
> Buyer: "That's not enough. Look, you helped us with the sale of our old lathe, so we didn't haggle as much on the price as we normally would. We can't pay top dollar and also pay on delivery. We need some leeway on credit terms."

The seller's rep refuses, the buyer refuses to sign the document, and the seller sues. Is there a contract?

2. Defendant relied on two sections of the Official Code of Georgia Annotated that govern the formation of contracts. Why does the court hold that this reliance is misplaced? Is the court correct? Under common-law principles did the buyer make an offer? If so, did plaintiff accept? Are these the questions to ask under 2–204? If so, does 2–204 change the common-law answers to these questions?

When the parties have actually come to an agreement, it is apparent that 2–204 seeks to make that agreement binding and to eschew the technicalities developed under the common law in some states that prevented formation of a contract. These technicalities often were expressed in pre-Code cases in terms of indefiniteness or lack of mutuality and were used, for example, to invalidate contracts that contained an open-price term, those that were more or less indefinite as to the respective obligations of the parties as to the particulars of performance, and those that were vague as to the precise moment that the agreement had been struck. Section 2–204 reverses this case law, and thus liberalizes some basic aspects of the law of contract formation.

Granting that this liberalization of the law is welcome, is it not still important to find that the parties did, in fact, come to an agreement before a contract between them is found to exist? In other words, it is possible to work out rules of law that determine the details of performance once they have agreed on a deal, albeit vaguely as to some terms and details, but, is it not another matter to find that vague interaction between them amounts to an agreement?

The "intent to contract" is a question of fact for the trier of fact. The trial judge's finding of fact cannot be disturbed on appeal if supported by competent evidence in the record. Bethlehem Steel Corp. v. Litton Industries, Inc., 321 Pa.Super. 357, 468 A.2d 748 (1983).

Bacou Dalloz USA, Inc. v. Continental Polymers, Inc.

United States Court of Appeals, First Circuit, 2003.
344 F.3d 22.

■ BALDOCK, SENIOR CIRCUIT JUDGE.

[Howard L. Leight & Assoc., Inc. (HLI) manufactured foam earplugs. Bacou Dalloz was a customer of HLI. Bacou sought to purchase HLI, but Leight, the president and sole shareholder of HLI, thought the price was

inadequate. In response, Bacou proposed three ways to sweeten the pot: Leight would be paid a consulting fee; Bacou would make royalty payments to Leight; and for five years Bacou would purchase from a company controlled by Leight all of its requirements of the principal raw material used in manufacturing the earplugs. (The original name of this company was Howard Leight Enterprises (HLE), but at the time of the litigation, it was known as Continental Polymers.) This proposal was agreeable to Leight.]

On January 12th, [1998,] Stepan and Barr [officials of Bacou] presented to Leight . . . a letter drafted by Barr and Bacou's outside counsel. The first paragraph of the letter references an asset purchase agreement between Bacou and HLI. Paragraphs three and four discuss Bacou's agreement to make Leight a Bacou director, as well as various stock options for Leight. The fourth paragraph provides:

> Finally, we understand that you recently formed a new company named Howard Leight Enterprises, Inc. ("HLE,") which will manufacture polyurethane prepolymer, the raw material used in the production of foam ear plugs by Howard S. Leight & Associates, Inc. ("HLI") and currently purchased from Hampshire Chemicals. This will confirm that Bacou USA Safety, Inc. will enter into a supply agreement with HLE pursuant to which Bacou USA Safety, Inc. agrees to purchase its requirements for polyurethane prepolymer from HLE for a period of five years provided that the quality and price of such raw material are equivalent to that which is then used by HLI and available from third-party suppliers.

Stepan, Barr, and Leight signed the letter.

In February, the parties met to sign the closing documents. Continental alleges that at the closing, [its representative] asked Stepan to incorporate the January 12th letter agreement in the asset purchase contract. Stepan allegedly responded that this was unnecessary because the January 12th letter would stand on its own and if it did not, then Bacou would not be completing the deal that day. The parties subsequently signed the asset purchase agreement without any further memorialization of a supply agreement.

Following the sale, Continental purchased property in Mexico on which it built a manufacturing plant and machinery needed to manufacture prepolymer. In January 1999, Continental informed Bacou it had completed construction and was prepared to begin shipment to Bacou. Continental and Bacou commenced negotiations for a supply agreement in February 1999. Thomas Klein, President of Bacou's HLI division, represented Bacou. John Dean represented Continental. The negotiations centered around the four principle issues of price, quality, volume, and confidentiality.

According to Continental, the price of prepolymer remained relatively stable, around $2 per pound both at the time of the January 12th letter and up until February 1999. In October 1998, Bacou requested a price reduction on prepolymer from its then-current supplier, Dow (formerly Hamp-

shire Chemicals). Dow was aware of the January 12th letter between Bacou and Continental. Within days of Dean informing Bacou that Continental was prepared to ship prepolymer, Dow agreed to reduce its prepolymer price to $1.56 per pound. According to Continental, Dow did not offer this price to other customers.

As a result of Dow's offer, Bacou took the position in negotiations with Continental that $1.56 was the price "then available" to Bacou under the January 12th letter. Continental disputed the $1.56 price. According to Continental, Bacou artificially reduced the price by telling Dow that if it could lower the price enough, Continental would not be able to match Dow's offer and Dow would remain Bacou's principal supplier.

The parties also had difficulty agreeing on the quality term. Bacou requested production of specifications and samples of Continental's prepolymer for testing to assure adequate quality. Continental refused, arguing Bacou was attempting to impose onerous testing and sampling requirements that Bacou did not require from other vendors. The volume of prepolymer which Bacou would purchase from Continental also became a disputed issue between the parties. Bacou wanted to purchase a small percentage of prepolymer from a second source to maintain a backup supplier. Continental insisted Bacou purchase one hundred percent of its requirements from Continental. Finally, Bacou insisted Continental enter into confidentiality agreements. Continental refused.

Based on a breakdown in negotiations between Klein and Dean, Bacou's Barr replaced Klein in negotiations. Barr submitted to Continental an initial purchase order for 10,000 pounds of prepolymer at $2 per pound. The order informed Continental that a portion of this lot would be used for testing and upon qualification the balance would be used in production. The purchase order proposed that after developing a working relationship, executives from both companies could meet to work out a long term supply agreement. Continental did not ship prepolymer to Bacou in response to this purchase order.

The parties thereafter went through a series of negotiations on the price, volume, quality, and confidentiality terms. Bacou sent Continental several draft supply agreements, all of which Continental rejected. As of May 12, however, Bacou apparently believed the only sticking point was the confidentiality agreements. Barr sent another purchase order to Continental for 10,000 pounds at $2 per pound. The order mentioned that the parties were still working out a confidentiality agreement, but that they would not share confidential information until that was completed. Continental declined to ship any product to Bacou pursuant to this purchase order. Bacou offered Continental one last supply agreement in August 1999, but Continental again refused.

II.

Based on this series of events, Bacou filed suit in Rhode Island state court seeking a declaratory judgment that Bacou had no obligations under the January 12th letter. Continental removed to federal court based on

diversity jurisdiction. Continental counterclaimed that Bacou (1) breached the January 12th agreement; (2) breached its duty of good faith and fair dealing under the January 12th agreement; and (3) falsely misrepresented its intention to enter into a supply agreement with Continental to induce Leight to sell HLI at a reduced price.

Bacou moved for summary judgment. The district court granted Bacou's motion as to the contract claim, holding that under Rhode Island law, the January 12th letter was an unenforceable "agreement to agree." The court also found the January 12th letter was not a binding contract because it did not set out all material terms, and no reasonable criteria existed for supplying the missing terms of quality and price. . . . The district court also concluded that because no enforceable contract existed, Bacou owed no duty of good faith and fair dealing. The district court denied summary judgment as to Continental's fraudulent misrepresentation counterclaim, however, concluding Continental presented sufficient evidence of fraud to proceed to trial.

At the conclusion of trial, the district court entered judgment in Bacou's favor. The district court found Bacou negotiated in good faith, and the only reason the parties did not enter into a supply agreement was because Continental's Dean thwarted negotiations. Continental now appeals, arguing . . . the January 12th letter was an enforceable contract. . . .

III.

. . .

We review de novo the district court's grant of summary judgment. Summary judgment is appropriate if the pleadings, affidavits, admissions, answers to interrogatories, and other materials, viewed in the light most favorable to the nonmoving party, reveal no genuine issue of material fact and the moving party is entitled to judgment as a matter of law. Fed. R.Civ.P. 56. Where, as here, federal jurisdiction is based on diversity, the court applies the substantive law of the forum state. Crellin Tech., Inc. v. Equipmentlease Corp., 18 F.3d 1, 4 (1st Cir.1994). The parties agree Rhode Island law controls.

A.

The district court concluded the parties did not manifest a present intent to be bound to a supply agreement in the January 12th letter. Rather, the district court held the January 12th letter was an "agreement to agree" to enter into a supply agreement in the future. The district court relied on Centerville Builders, Inc. v. Wynne, 683 A.2d 1340 (R.I. 1996), to conclude such agreements are unenforceable under Rhode Island law.

In *Centerville Builders,* a prospective buyer entered into an agreement with the seller for the sale of a tract of land. In a document captioned "Offer to Purchase," the buyer deposited $5,000 towards the purchase of the property with a total deposit of five percent of the sale price due upon signing the purchase and sales agreement. The seller signed the Offer to Purchase after deleting the ninth condition, which would have prohibited the seller from negotiating with any other parties for the sale of the property. The agreement's sixth provision provided: "SUBJECT TO SATISFACTORY PURCHASE & SALES AGREEMENT BETWEEN SELLER AND BUYER."

Subsequently, the seller sent the buyer an unsigned purchase-and-sales agreement form. The buyer signed the agreement and returned it to the seller. The seller later notified the buyer that the seller wanted to "get more money" for the property and would therefore put the property back on the market. The buyer filed an action for breach of contract. The Rhode Island Supreme Court held no enforceable contract existed because there was no mutuality of obligation. In reaching this conclusion, the Rhode Island Supreme Court stated that—

> [W]hen the promises of the parties depend on the occurrence of some future event within the unilateral control of the promisors, the promises are illusory and the agreement is nonbinding. . . . In the instant case, . . . their promises were illusory since each party reserved the unfettered discretion to thwart the purchase and sale by unilaterally invoking condition 6 of the offer-to-purchase agreement and rejecting any purchase-and-sale agreement as "unsatisfactory."

> Although it is true that the seller displayed an intent to be bound by the offer-to-purchase agreement when he signed the document and agreed to sell the property subject to the conditions specified, the inclusion of condition 6 made this an illusory promise because its occurrence depended solely on the subjective will of either party. . . . The seller's deletion (with the buyer's consent) of the ninth condition further evidenced the lack of mutuality of obligation. Because the seller was allowed to negotiate with other prospective buyers, the offer to purchase amounted to little more than an agreement to see if the parties could agree on a purchase-and-sale agreement at some point in the future. As such, it was not an enforceable bilateral contract.

Id. at 1341–42.

We believe the district court read *Centerville Builders* too broadly in ruling that all agreements to agree are unenforceable in Rhode Island. The Rhode Island Supreme Court's comment that the Offer to Purchase was nothing more than agreement to agree and as such was unenforceable must be viewed in the context in which it was made. The court's main concern was that the parties made illusory promises resulting in a lack of mutuality of obligation.

The January 12th letter contains no such infirmities. The letter does not condition the parties' obligations on the illusory promise that the future supply agreement be "satisfactory" to either party. The letter set forth reciprocal promises in the form of the supply agreement's material terms. Such promises are sufficient to establish mutuality of obligation. *Id.* at 1341 (noting that a bilateral contract requires mutuality of obligation which is achieved through the making of reciprocal promises). The actual supply agreement could and likely would contain payment terms, delivery terms, and other similar provisions not contained in the letter. But the fact that the parties were to negotiate these details at a future date does not render illusory the obligation incurred under the January 12th letter. The parties clearly agreed to enter into a supply agreement consistent with the terms outlined in the January 12th letter. As discussed below, those terms were not so indefinite as to preclude enforcement of the letter.

B.

The district court alternatively held the January 12th letter was unenforceable because it lacked sufficiently definite material terms of price and quality. The letter describes the price and quality as follows: "the quality and price of such raw material are equivalent to that which is then used by HLI and available from third-party suppliers." The district court found this terminology too vague to provide a reasonably certain basis for giving an appropriate remedy. *See* Restatement (Second) of Contracts § 33 (1981) (endorsing the view that where the parties have intended to make a contract and there is a reasonably certain basis for granting a remedy, the court should grant that remedy). The court contended Bacou unilaterally could control the raw material HLI was using at any particular time, thus making its promise illusory.

We disagree with the district court that the price term was too vague to form an enforceable contract. The letter describes the price term as the price then available from third-party suppliers. The price term thus is readily discernible by obtaining quotes from other vendors or other evidence of the prevailing market price. Indeed, Bacou's position in negotiations with Continental was not that the price term in the January 12th letter was too vague, but that the then-available price was $1.56 per pound, Dow's last price quote to Bacou. Whether this price was artificially deflated as Continental argues is a matter for the trier of fact. Simply because the parties disagree on the factual issue of what the then-available price actually was does not mean that the price term in the January 12th letter was vague as a matter of law. A term specifying market price or the currently available price provides a sufficiently definite basis to provide a remedy. . . .

Likewise, the quality term is not indefinite or illusory. The January 12th letter specifies that the quality must be as good as the prepolymer then used by HLI and available from third party vendors. The comparability to products available from third party vendors creates an objective and reasonably definite measure of quality. And to the extent the district court believed HLI could manipulate their prepolymer needs, under Rhode Island law, "virtually every contract contains an implied covenant of good faith and fair dealing between the parties." *Crellin*, 18 F.3d at 10. Because Bacou would have a contractual duty to determine in good faith the quality of Continental's product as compared to third party vendors, the quality term was not illusory. Consequently, we reverse the district court's grant of summary judgment in favor of Bacou on Continental's contract claim. . . .

[Reversed and remanded.]

QUESTIONS AND NOTES

1. Since Rhode Island has enacted the UCC, it is remarkable that the court did not cite Article 2. It does cite Restatement (Second) § 33, which states:

§ 33. Certainty

(1) Even though a manifestation of intention is intended to be understood as an offer, it cannot be accepted so as to form a contract unless the terms of the contract are reasonably certain.

(2) The terms of a contract are reasonably certain if they provide a basis for determining the existence of a breach and for giving an appropriate remedy.

(3) The fact that one or more terms of a proposed bargain are left open or uncertain may show that a manifestation of intention is not intended to be understood as an offer or as an acceptance.

To what extent is this different from 2–204(3)?

2. The law of contracts provides that an offer operates to create a power of acceptance in the offeree. Because the offeror is "the master of the offer," as many common law cases have stated, it is for the offeror to determine the nature and extent of the resultant power of acceptance, including the mode or form that the acceptance must take. As a consequence of these rules, it has generally been held at common law that an attempted acceptance made in a manner other than that prescribed by the offer is ineffective to form a contract. Does 2–206(1) of the UCC modify that position?

Suppose an offer is unclear as to the mode of acceptance, leaving the offeree in doubt as to how to bring a contract into being. This situation has happened with some frequency in commercial sales cases when telegrams and cablegrams were commonplace and economy of language was prevalent. Today a buyer might send an e-mail, "Want 200 Elvis Presley CD sets. Ship Tuesday." Suppose the seller e-mails back: "Will ship Tuesday, price $45." On Monday morning, before the seller has started his performance, he receives from the buyer an e-mail revoking the offer. If the buyer can prove that she had written "Ship Tuesday" because she did not intend to be bound until the seller actually shipped the goods, is there a contract? Carefully read 2–206. Also look again at 2–204, and consult 2–305.

3. Is it possible for the offeree of an offer to enter into a unilateral contract to be in breach? Consider the following hypothetical: A buyer e-mails a seller: "Want 200 Presley sets. To accept, ship Tuesday." On

[handwritten margin note: There is a contract 2-206 (b)]

Tuesday the seller ships 200 sets but most of them are defective. The buyer sues for breach of contract. How would you defend the seller at common law? under Article 2?

4.   Problem. Under the law of Florida, the sale of a fruit crop constructively severs it from the realty, even while the fruit remains on the tree, so that a mortgage of the real estate no longer reaches the fruit. In Bornstein v. Somerson, 341 So.2d 1043 (Fla.App.1977), a purported contract for the sale of oranges still on the tree stated that the seller "does hereby bargain, sell and transfer unto the buyer all the fruit that meets the standards for the use agreed upon or specified in this contract at the time of picking the fruit. . . . Price of fruit, harvesting and delivery charges and harvesting dates shall be mutually agreed upon before the fruit is harvested." The seller defaulted on his mortgage debt, and, before the oranges were harvested, the holder of the mortgage instituted foreclosure proceedings. Is the orange crop subject to the mortgage?

C.   Statute of Frauds

Parliament enacted the Statute of Frauds in 1677 to avoid unfair results that seemed to flow from allowing courts to hear cases based on allegations of oral contracts. It was thought that where significant amounts of money were involved, the temptation to allege fraudulently the existence of contracts or terms that had not been made ought to be resisted by requiring some strong evidence that the allegations were true. Hence, the Statute of Frauds required a written agreement or other writing proving the existence of the contract and its essential terms. Unfortunately, rigid enforcement of the Statute of Frauds by some courts provided a shield for a bad-faith party by allowing that party to avoid a fairly made contract because of a failure to satisfy the formal requisites of the Statute. Other courts avoided unjust results such as these by ignoring the Statute of Frauds in certain situations and narrowly construing it in others.

In 1954 Parliament repealed the Statute of Frauds for sales cases governed by English law. Individuals studying and drafting the UCC were divided on the question whether the Statute of Frauds had done more harm than good, and a substantial number of them wanted to follow the English approach by eliminating it entirely. They were defeated in their efforts when the drafters promised to write a statute of frauds that would eliminate the potential for injustice by those who might be tempted to assert non-existent oral contracts, on the one hand, and those who would try to defeat, on technical grounds, contracts that in fact had been made, on the other hand. The result is 2–201, which generally requires a writing for contracts for more than $500 ($5,000 in the 2003 amendments). Consider whether the drafters made good on their promise.

Southwest Engineering Co., Inc. v. Martin Tractor Co., Inc.

Kansas Supreme Court, 1970.
205 Kan. 684, 473 P.2d 18.

■ FONTRON, JUSTICE. This is an action to recover damages for breach of contract. Trial was had to the court which entered judgment in favor of the plaintiff. The defendant has appealed.

Southwest Engineering Company, Inc., the plaintiff, is a Missouri corporation engaged in general contracting work, while the defendant, Martin Tractor Company, Inc., is a Kansas corporation. The two parties will be referred to hereafter either as plaintiff, or Southwest, on the one hand and defendant, or Martin, on the other.

We glean from the record that in April, 1966, the plaintiff was interested in submitting a bid to the United States Corps of Engineers for the construction of certain runway lighting facilities at McConnell Air Force Base at Wichita. However, before submitting a bid, and on April 11, 1966, the plaintiff's construction superintendent, Mr. R.E. Cloepfil, called the manager of Martin's engine department, Mr. Ken Hurt, who at the time was at Colby, asking for a price on a standby generator and accessory equipment. Mr. Hurt replied that he would phone him back from Topeka, which he did the next day, quoting a price of $18,500. This quotation was re-confirmed by Hurt over the phone on April 13.

Southwest submitted its bid on April 14, 1966, using Hurt's figure of $18,500 for the generator equipment, and its bid was accepted. On April 20, Southwest notified Martin that its bid had been accepted. Hurt and Cloepfil thereafter agreed over the phone to meet in Springfield on April 28. On that date Hurt flew to Springfield, where the two men conferred at the airfield restaurant for about an hour. Hurt took to the meeting a copy of the job specifications which the government had supplied Martin prior to the letting.

At the Springfield meeting it developed that Martin had upped its price for the generator and accessory equipment from $18,500 to $21,500. Despite this change of position by Martin, concerning which Cloepfil was understandably amazed, the two men continued their conversation and, according to Cloepfil, they arrived at an agreement for the sale of a D353 generator and accessories for the sum of $21,500. In addition it was agreed that if the Corps of Engineers would accept a less expensive generator, a D343, the aggregate price to Southwest would be $15,000. The possibility of providing alternative equipment, the D343, was suggested by Mr. Hurt, apparently in an attempt to mollify Mr. Cloepfil when the latter learned that Martin had reneged on its price quotation of April 12. It later developed that the Corps of Engineers would not approve the cheaper generator and that Southwest eventually had to supply the more expensive D353 generator.

At the conference, Mr. Hurt separately listed the component parts of each of the two generators on the top half of a sheet of paper and set out the price after each item. The prices were then totaled. On the bottom half of the sheet Hurt set down the accessories common to both generators and their cost. This handwritten memorandum, as it was referred to during the trial, noted a 10 per cent discount on the aggregate cost of each generator, while the accessories were listed at Martin's cost. The price of the D353 was rounded off at $21,500 and D343 at $15,000. The memorandum was handed to Cloepfil while the two men were still at the airport. We will refer to this memorandum further during the course of this opinion.

On May 2, 1966, Cloepfil addressed a letter to the Martin Tractor Company, directing Martin to proceed with shop drawings and submittal documents for the McConnell lighting job and calling attention to the fact that applicable government regulations were required to be followed. Further reference to this communication will be made when necessary.

Some three weeks thereafter, on May 24, 1966, Hurt wrote Cloepfil, . . . "Due to restrictions placed on Caterpillar products, accessory suppliers, and other stipulations by the district governing agency, we cannot accept your letter to proceed dated May 2, 1966, and hereby withdraw all verbal quotations."

On receipt of this unwelcome missive, Cloepfil telephoned Mr. Hurt who stated they had some work underway for the Corps of Engineers in both the Kansas City and Tulsa districts and did not want to take on any other work for the Corps at that time. Hurt assured Cloepfil he could buy the equipment from anybody at the price Martin could sell it for. Later investigation showed, however, that such was not the case.

. . .

Southwest eventually secured the generator equipment from Foley Tractor Co. of Wichita, a company which Mr. Hurt had one time suggested, at a price of $27,541. The present action was then filed, seeking damages of $6,041 for breach of the contract and $9,000 for loss resulting from the delay caused by the breach. The trial court awarded damages of $6,041 for the breach but rejected damages allegedly due to delay. The defendant only, has appealed; there is no cross-appeal by plaintiff.

The basic disagreement centers on whether the meeting between Hurt and Cloepfil at Springfield resulted in an agreement which was enforceable under the provisions of the Uniform Commercial Code. . . .

Southwest takes the position that the memorandum prepared by Hurt at Springfield supplies the essential elements of a contract required by the foregoing statute, i.e., that it is (1) a writing signed by the party sought to be charged, (2) that it is for the sale of goods and (3) that quantity is shown. In addition, the reader will have noted that the memorandum sets forth the prices of the several items listed.

It cannot be gainsaid that the Uniform Commercial Code has effected a somewhat radical change in the law relating to the formation of enforceable contracts as such has been expounded by this and other courts. In the Kansas Comment to 84–2–201, which closely parallels the Official UCC Comment, the following explanation is given:

"Subsection (1) relaxes the interpretations of many courts in providing that the required writing need not contain all the material terms and that they need not be stated precisely. All that is required is that the writing afford a basis for believing that the offered oral evidence rests on a real transaction. Only three definite and invariable requirements as to the writing are made by this subsection. First, it must evidence a contract for the sale of goods; second, it must be 'signed,' a word which includes any authentication which identifies the party to be charged; and third, it must specify quantity. Terms relating to price, time, and place of payment or delivery, the general quality of goods, or any particular warranties may all be omitted."

From legal treatises, as well, we learn that the three invariable requirements of an enforceable written memorandum under 84–2–201 are that it evidence a sale of goods, that it be signed or authenticated and that it specify quantity. In Vernon's Kansas Statutes Annotated, Uniform Commercial Code, Howe and Navin, the writers make this clear:

"Under the Code the writing does not need to incorporate all the terms of the transaction, nor do the terms need to be stated precisely. The Code does require that the writing be broad enough to indicate a contract of sale between the parties; that the party against whom enforcement is sought, or his agent, must have signed the writing; and that the quantity dealt with must be stated. Any error concerning the quantity stated in the memorandum prevents enforcement of the agreement beyond the precise quantity stated." (p. 116.)

The defendant does not seriously question the interpretation accorded the statute by eminent scriveners and scholars, but maintains, nonetheless, that the writing in question does not measure up to the statute of a signed memorandum within the purview of the Code; that the instrument simply sets forth verbal quotations for future consideration in continuing negotiations.

But on this point the trial court found there *was* an agreement reached between Hurt and Cloepfil at Springfield; that the formal requirements of K.S.A. 84–2–201 *were* satisfied; and that the memorandum prepared by Hurt contains the three essentials of the statute in that it evidences a sale of goods, was authenticated by Hurt and specifies quantity. Beyond that, the court specifically found that Hurt had apparent authority to make the agreement; that both Southwest and Martin were "merchants" as defined in K.S.A. 84–2–104; that the agreement reached at Springfield included additional terms not noted in the writing: (1) Southwest was to install the equipment; (2) Martin was to deliver the equipment to Wichita and (3) Martin was to assemble and supply submittal documents within three weeks; and that Martin's letter of May 24, 1966, constituted an anticipatory breach of the contract.

We believe the record supports all the above findings. With particular reference to the preparation and sufficiency of the written memorandum, the following evidence is pertinent:

Mr. Cloepfil testified that he and Hurt sat down at a restaurant table and spread out the plans which Hurt had brought with him; that they went through the specifications item by item and Hurt wrote each item down, together with the price thereof; that while the specifications called for a D353 generator, Hurt thought the D343 model might be an acceptable substitute, so he gave prices on both of them and Southwest could take either one of the two which the Corps of Engineers would approve; that Hurt gave him (Cloepfil) the memorandum "as a record of what we had done, the agreement we had arrived at our meeting in the restaurant at the airport."

We digress at this point to note Martin's contention that the memorandum is not signed within the meaning of 84–2–201. The sole authentication appears in hand-printed form at the top left-hand corner in these words: "Ken Hurt, Martin Tractor, Topeka, Caterpillar." The court found this sufficient, and we believe correctly so. K.S.A. 84–1–201(39) provides as follows:

" 'Signed' includes any symbol executed or adopted by a party with present intention to authenticate a writing."

The official U.C.C. Comment states in part:

"The inclusion of authentication in the definition of 'signed' is to make clear that as the term is used in this Act a complete signature is not necessary. Authentication may be printed, stamped or written; * * * It may be on any part of the document and in appropriate cases may be found in a billhead or letterhead. * * * The question always is whether the symbol was executed or adopted by the party with present intention to authenticate the writing."

Hurt admittedly prepared the memorandum and has not denied affixing his name thereto. We believe the authentication sufficiently complies with the statute.

The evidence already cited would be ample to sustain the trial court's finding that an agreement was reached between Hurt and Cloepfil in Springfield. However, Cloepfil's testimony is not the only evidence in support of that finding. In a pretrial deposition, Mr. Hurt, himself, deposed that "we agreed on the section that I would be quoting on, and we came to some over-all general agreement on the major items." At the trial Hurt testified he did not wish to change that statement in any way.

Hurt further testified that in his opinion the thing which stood in the way of a firm deal was Martin's terms of payment—that had Southwest agreed with those terms of payment, so far as he was concerned, he would have considered a firm deal was made. Mr. Hurt acknowledged while on the stand that he penned the memorandum and that as disclosed therein a 10 per cent discount was given Southwest on the price of either of the generators listed (depending on which was approved by the Corps of Engineers), and that the accessories common to both generators were to be net—that is, sold without profit.

It is quite true, as the trial court found, that terms of payment were not agreed upon at the Springfield meeting. Hurt testified that as the memorandum was being made out, he said they wanted 10 per cent with the order, 50 per cent on delivery and the balance on acceptance, but he did not recall Cloepfil's response. Cloepfil's version was somewhat different. He stated that after the two had shaken hands in the lobby preparing to leave, Hurt said their terms usually were 20 per cent down and the balance on delivery; while he (Cloepfil) said the way they generally paid was 90 per cent on the tenth of the month following delivery and the balance on final acceptance. It is obvious the parties reached no agreement on this point.

However, a failure on the part of Messrs. Hurt and Cloepfil to agree on terms of payment would not, of itself, defeat an otherwise valid agreement reached by them. K.S.A. 84–2–204(3) reads:

"Even though one or more terms are left open a contract for sale does not fail for indefiniteness if the parties have intended to make a contract and there is a reasonably certain basis for giving an appropriate remedy."

The official U.C.C. Comment is enlightening:

"Subsection (3) states the principle as to 'open terms' underlying later sections of the Article. If the parties intend to enter into a binding agreement, this subsection recognizes that agreement as valid in law, despite missing terms, if there is any reasonably certain basis for granting a remedy. The test is not certainty as to what the parties were to do nor as to the exact amount of damages due the plaintiff. Nor is the fact that one or more terms are left to be agreed upon enough of itself to defeat an otherwise adequate agreement. Rather, commercial standards on the point of 'indefiniteness' are intended to be applied, this Act making provision elsewhere for missing terms needed for performance, open price, remedies and the like.

"The more terms the parties leave open, the less likely it is that they have intended to conclude a binding agreement, but their actions may be frequently conclusive on the matter despite the omissions."

. . .

So far as the present case is concerned, K.S.A. 84–2–310 supplies the omitted term. This statute provides in pertinent part:

"Unless otherwise agreed

"(a) payment is due at the time and place at which the buyer is to receive the goods even though the place of shipment is the place of delivery;"

In our view, the language of the two Code provisions is clear and positive. Considered together, we take the two sections to mean that where parties have reached an enforceable agreement for the sale of goods, but omit therefrom the terms of payment, the law will imply, as part of the agreement, that payment is to be made at time of delivery. . . .

We do not mean to infer that terms of payment are not of importance under many circumstances, or that parties may not condition an agreement on their being included. However, the facts before us hardly indicate that Hurt and Cloepfil considered the terms of payment to be significant, or of more than passing interest. Hurt testified that while he stated his terms he did not recall Cloepfil's response, while Cloepfil stated that as the two were on the point of leaving, each stated their usual terms and that was as far as it went. The trial court found that only a brief and casual conversation ensued as to payment, and we think that is a valid summation of what took place.

Moreover, it is worthy of note that Martin first mentioned the omission of the terms of payment, as justifying its breach, in a letter written by counsel on September 15, 1966, more than four months after the memorandum was prepared by Hurt. On prior occasions Martin attributed its cancellation of the Springfield understanding to other causes. In its May 24 letter, Martin ascribed its withdrawal of "all verbal quotations" to "restrictions placed on Caterpillar products, accessory suppliers, and other stipulations by the district governing agency." In explaining the meaning of the letter to Cloepfil, Hurt said that Martin was doing work for the Corps of Engineers in the Kansas City and Tulsa districts and did not want to take on additional work with them at this time.

The entire circumstances may well give rise to a suspicion that Martin's present insistence that future negotiations were contemplated concerning terms of payment, is primarily an afterthought, for use as an escape hatch. Doubtless the trial court so considered the excuse in arriving at its findings.

We are aware of Martin's argument that Southwest's letter of May 2, 1966, referring to the sale is evidence that no firm contract had been concluded. Granted that some of the language employed might be subject to that interpretation, the trial court found, on what we deem to be substantial, competent evidence, that an agreement of sale *was* concluded at Springfield. Under our invariable rule those findings are binding upon this court on appeal even though there may have been evidence to the contrary.

. . .

We find no error in this case and the judgment of the trial court is affirmed.

QUESTIONS AND NOTES

1. In light of the language of 2–204(3) that the omission of terms is not fatal to the existence of a contract, how could defendant argue that the absence of a payment term precluded the existence of a contract? Why does the court reject this argument?

2. One asserting an enforceable sales contract has two hurdles to jump: (1) to show that the statute of frauds is inapplicable or has been satisfied; and (2) to show that the formation-of-contract rules have been fulfilled. These two matters often become blurred in a practical situation, and thus tend to be confused, because the kinds of concrete factual matters that are deemed to satisfy the statute of frauds or make it inapplicable also are likely to convince the trier of fact that a contract, in fact, was formed, just as concrete factual evidence of the formation of the contract is apt to satisfy the statute of frauds. But the careful analyst always recognizes that the two matters are separate and that both hurdles must be jumped. Did the court in *Southwest Engineering* address both issues?

3. What does it take for a writing to evidence that a contract for sale has been made? Why does the court conclude that the standard was met? In another case, a seller claimed that the following writing satisfied the statute of frauds:

> "Confirming our telephone conversation, we are pleased to offer the 3500 shirts at $4.00 each and the trousers at $3.00 each with delivery approximately ninety days after receipt of order. We will try to cut this to sixty days if at all possible.
>
> "This is, of course, quoted f. o. b. Atlanta, and the order will not be subject to cancellation, domestic pack only.
>
> "Thanking you for the opportunity to offer these garments, ..."

The court held that the writing did not satisfy the statute of frauds. "It does not evidence a contract for the sale of goods, but very clearly is only an offer." Alice v. Robett Mfg. Co., 328 F.Supp. 1377 (N.D.Ga.1970), aff'd 445 F.2d 316 (5th Cir.1971). Similarly, in Howard Construction Co. v. Jeff–Cole Quarries, Inc., 669 S.W.2d 221, 228 (Mo.App.1983), the buyer relied on a writing of the seller, entitled "Proposal," that listed six items and the price for each. The parties met and, according to the buyer, agreed on the purchase and sale of the six items at modified prices, as marked by the buyer on the Proposal. The court criticized and rejected the reasoning of *Southwest Engineering*:

> The court's finding that the writing evidenced a contract has been severely criticized. See 84 Harv.L.Rev. 1737 (1971). That criticism stems from the fact that "[t]he memorandum before the court—on its face nothing more than a price list—was proof not of agreement, but, at most, only of negotiations." Id. at 1738. Finding such writing sufficient plants the seeds for allowing the statute of frauds to be satisfied by any evidence of mere negotiations.
>
> While U.C.C. § 2–201 was indeed designed to eliminate much of the rigidity produced by prior interpretations of the statute of frauds, it retained some safeguards against fraudulent commercial practices. The requirement that the writing indicate that a contract for sale has been made is one of those safeguards. The words "as per our agreement," "in confirmation of," or "sold to buyer," would indicate that the parties had reached an agreement. Even the terms of the writing

itself might be so specific and favorable to the party against whom the writing is offered that the court at least could draw the inference that an agreement had been reached. Such writings would deter fraudulent assertions that a contract had been agreed upon where in fact only negotiations had taken place. The price list which the Kansas Supreme Court found sufficient to indicate that a contract had been made, however, contained no such words or terms. . . .

Although the typewritten proposal was signed by an agent of Jeff–Cole (prior to the handwritten alterations made thereon by plaintiff's agent) and states specific quantity terms, no words on the writing allow for the inference that any agreement was reached between the parties and therefore it does not by itself meet the primary require-ment of either § 2–201(1) or (2). Viewed in the light most favorable to the plaintiff, the unaltered proposal could be no more than an offer by Jeff–Cole.

But see Veik v. Tilden Bank, 200 Neb. 705, 265 N.W.2d 214 (1978), in which a written offer was held to satisfy the statute ("all that is required is that the writing afford a basis for believing that the offered oral evidence rests on a real transaction.")

Decatur Cooperative Association v. Urban

Kansas Supreme Court, 1976.
219 Kan. 171, 547 P.2d 323.

■ HARMAN, COMMISSIONER. This action was brought to obtain possession of 10,000 bushels of wheat allegedly purchased under an oral contract, or alternatively, for damages for failure to deliver the wheat. The primary issue is whether the alleged seller, a farmer, was a "merchant" within the meaning of the uniform commercial code so as to remove the oral contract from operation of the statute of frauds. A secondary issue is whether the seller was equitably estopped from relying on the statute of frauds as a defense to an action on the oral contract.

Appellant, The Decatur Cooperative Association, commenced this ac-tion August 24, 1973, by filing its petition against appellee, Franklin Urban, alleging an oral purchase of 10,000 bushels of wheat from Urban on July 26, 1973, at $2.86 per bushel and a repudiation by him of the agreement on August 14, 1973. Other facts were alleged which will be noticed later. Urban answered, denying the alleged purchase and raising the defense of the statute of frauds. Urban also moved for summary judgment.

For the purpose of ruling on the request for summary judgment the parties stipulated to the facts, which we summarize.

Appellant is a corporation which has been in existence since 1953. It owns and operates a grain elevator and its principal business is the purchasing of wheat and other grains from area farmers which it markets to larger regional elevators and grain dealers. During the fiscal year ending

March 31, 1973, appellant purchased grain from about 500 farmers and sold grain to four regional elevators.

Appellant has a well-established policy of never speculating on the price of grain. Therefore, as soon as it purchases grain from a farmer or farmers amounting to one train carload or about 2000 bushels, it places a phone call to a terminal elevator and orally sells the grain to that elevator at the prevailing price. Thereafter, a written confirmation of sale is sent by the terminal elevator to the cooperative. This procedure is a well-established and well-known method of handling and marketing grain in Decatur county, Kansas. Appellant has a general manager and an assistant manager to run its daily operations, each of whom is authorized to enter into sales contracts on behalf of the cooperative.

Appellee Urban is a resident of Decatur county and was a member of the cooperative throughout the year 1973. He has been engaged in the wheat farming business for about twenty years. He owns about 2,000 acres of his total farmed acreage of 2,320 acres. About 1,200 acres are broken out and farmable while the remaining acreage is unbroken and devoted to pasture. In the year 1974 appellee had approximately 500 acres sown in wheat. Appellee also owns a cow herd of about 200 head. He is engaged solely in the farming business, although he has in the past done some custom harvesting of wheat and other grains. He has sold wheat and other grains, which he raises, to the appellant cooperative and to other elevators in the area since 1966 and has sold livestock through area sale barns.

On July 26, 1973, appellee was in St. Francis, Kansas, on his way to Colorado to do some custom wheat harvesting. While in St. Francis he placed two phone calls to the cooperative. On the first call he requested to speak to the assistant manager but was told he was not available. Later that afternoon appellee placed a second call to the cooperative office and did reach the assistant manager. As a result of this second call, appellant contends the parties entered into an oral contract whereby appellee agreed to sell to the cooperative 10,000 bushels of wheat at $2.86 per bushel, to be delivered on or before September 30, 1973. Appellee denies that any contract of sale was made during this phone call and he has never admitted by pleading, testimony or otherwise that a sale agreement was reached during the call. The total cash value of the wheat alleged to have been sold was $28,600.00.

During the phone conversation there was discussion of a written memorandum of sale to be prepared and sent to appellee later. It is appellant's practice to send a signed written confirmation of sale to the seller immediately after oral conversations and appellant did in fact send such a confirmation to appellee. This confirmation was signed by appellant's assistant manager and was binding as against appellant. Appellee received the confirmation within a reasonable time, read it, and gave no written notice of objection to its contents within ten days after it was received.

Early in the morning of July 27, 1973, in reliance on the alleged oral contract of sale, appellant placed a phone call to Far–Mar–Co., a regional terminal elevator in Kansas City, Missouri, and sold the wheat for $3.46 per bushel, the cooperative to pay freight and other charges. During the latter part of July and early part of August of 1973, the price of wheat rose substantially.

On August 13, 1973, appellee notified appellant that he would not deliver the wheat. The price of wheat at the cooperative on that date was $4.50 per bushel.

... [The trial court concluded "that a farmer, whether he be large, intermediate or small is not a merchant under the facts of this case and that by reason thereof the provisions of K.S.A. 84–2–201 are not applicable to this case in so far as the defendant is concerned." It] sustained Urban's motion for summary judgment and Decatur Cooperative has appealed.

...

Under K.S.A. 84–2–201(2) a "merchant" is deprived of the defense of the statute of frauds as against an oral contract with another merchant if he fails to object to the terms of a written confirmation within ten days of its receipt. The issue presently here is whether or not appellee is, under the facts, also a "merchant." If he is not, section 2–201 acts as a bar to the enforcement of the alleged contract. K.S.A. 84–2–104 contains the following definitions:

"(1) 'Merchant' means a person who deals in goods of the kind or otherwise by his occupation holds himself out as having knowledge or skill peculiar to the practices or goods involved in the transaction or to whom such knowledge or skill may be attributed by his employment of an agent or broker or other intermediary who by his occupation holds himself out as having such knowledge or skill.

merchant

* * *

"(3) 'Between merchants' means in any transaction with respect to which both parties are chargeable with the knowledge or skill of merchants."

The official UCC comment states:

"Purposes:

"1. This Article assumes that transactions between professionals in a given field require special and clear rules which may not apply to a casual or inexperienced seller or buyer. It thus adopts a policy of expressly stating rules applicable 'between merchants' and 'as against a merchant,' wherever they are needed instead of making them depend upon the circumstances of each case as in the statutes cited above. This section lays the foundation of this policy by defining those who are to be regarded as professionals or 'merchants' and by stating when a transaction is deemed to be 'between merchants.'

"2. The term 'merchant' as defined here roots in the 'law merchant' concept of a professional in business. The professional status under the definition may be based upon specialized knowledge as to the goods, specialized knowledge as to business practices, or specialized knowledge as to both and which kind of specialized knowledge may be sufficient to establish the merchant status is indicated by the nature of the provisions. * * * "

From the foregoing it appears there are three separate criteria for determining merchant status. A merchant is (1) a dealer who deals in the goods of the kind involved, or (2) one who by his occupation holds himself out as having knowledge or skill peculiar to the practices or goods involved in the transaction, even though he may not actually have such knowledge, or (3) a principal who employs an agent, broker or other intermediary who by his occupation holds himself out as having knowledge or skill peculiar to the practices or goods involved in the transaction (see 1 Anderson, UCC, 2d ed., § 2–104:4, p. 220). Professionalism, special knowledge and commercial experience are to be used in determining whether a person in a particular situation is to be held to the standards of a merchant.

The few courts which have considered the question whether a farmer, with experience similar to that in the case at bar, is a merchant under the statute of frauds provision in the UCC have divided on the issue.

In our opinion the facts here disclose that appellee neither "deals" in wheat, as that term is used in 2–104, nor does he by his occupation hold himself out as having knowledge or skill peculiar to the practices or goods involved in the transaction. The concept of professionalism is heavy in determining who is a merchant under the statute. The writers of the official UCC comment virtually equate professionals with merchants—the casual or inexperienced buyer or seller is not to be held to the standard set for the professional in business. The defined term "between merchants," used in the exception proviso to the statute of frauds, contemplates the knowledge and skill of professionals on each side of the transaction. The transaction in question here was the sale of wheat. Appellee as a farmer undoubtedly had special knowledge or skill in raising wheat but we do not think this factor, coupled with annual sales of a wheat crop and purchases of seed wheat, qualified him as a merchant in that field. The parties' stipulation states appellee has sold only the products he raised. There is no indication any of these sales were other than cash sales to local grain elevators, where conceivably an expertise reaching professional status could be said to be involved.

We think the trial court correctly ruled under the particular facts that appellee was not a merchant for the purpose of avoiding the operation of the statute of frauds pursuant to K.S.A. 84–2–201(1) and (2).

This brings us to the second point of the appeal—not ruled upon by the trial court—whether appellee is equitably estopped to assert the statute of frauds as a defense. K.S.A. 84–1–103 provides that certain principles of law and equity, including estoppel, unless displaced by the particular provisions of the uniform code, shall supplement its provisions.

Appellant pleaded in its petition, and the parties stipulated the facts pertinent thereto, its immediate disposition of the wheat it thought it had purchased from appellee and contends that because appellee knew, or reasonably should have known because of his special relationship as a member of appellant, that it would sell the wheat immediately, he is estopped to assert the statute of frauds as a defense to enforcement of the oral contract.

In discussing the issue a distinction should be made between the concepts of equitable estoppel and promissory estoppel. In Marker v. Preferred Fire Ins. Co., 211 Kan. 427, 506 P.2d 1163, we stated:

> "A promise which the promisor should reasonably expect to induce action or forbearance of a definite and substantial character on the part of the promisee and which does induce such action or forbearance is binding if injustice can be avoided only by enforcement of the promise. This is called the doctrine of promissory estoppel.

> "Promissory estoppel differs from ordinary 'equitable' estoppel in that the representation is promissory rather than to an existing fact."

Courts have taken differing positions as to whether a party may be equitably estopped to assert the statute of frauds as a defense (see anno.: Promissory Estoppel As Basis For Avoidance of Statute of Frauds, 56 A.L.R.3d 1037). One line of cases holds that to allow the concept of estoppel to preclude assertion of the statute of frauds as a defense to an oral contract would defeat the purpose of the statute. These decisions take the position that promissory estoppel may not be used to defeat the statute of frauds in any case, or at least in any situation where the policy of the statute would be frustrated (see anno., supra, § 4[a], p. 1052).

A substantial number of courts, however, hold that the doctrine of promissory estoppel may render enforceable any promise upon which the promisor intended, or should have known, that the promisee would act to his detriment, and which is indeed acted upon in such a manner by the promisee, where application of the statute of frauds to that promise would thus work a fraud or a gross injustice upon the promisee (anno., supra, § 6[a], pp. 1060–1063; 73 Am.Jur.2d, Statute of Frauds, § 565, pp. 202–204). Courts in this line of cases bottom their reasoning on the general equity principle that the statute of frauds was enacted to prevent fraud and injustice, not to foster or encourage it, and a court of equity will not ordinarily permit its use as a shield to protect fraud or to enable one to take advantage of his own wrong. This court has long been committed to the principles enunciated in the last sentence and on that basis has applied the doctrine of estoppel to cases wherein the statute of frauds would otherwise be applicable as a defense.

Before the doctrine of promissory estoppel can be invoked in a case involving the statute of frauds the promisee must first show by competent evidence that a valid and otherwise enforceable contract was entered into by the parties (3 Williston on Contracts [3d ed., Jaeger], § 533A, pp. 802–803). The conduct of the promisor must be something more than a mere refusal to perform the oral contract, since any party to an oral contract unenforceable under the statute of frauds has that right, and the exercise of the right of nonperformance is no more a fraud than a breach of any other contract (37 C.J.S. Frauds, Statute of § 247, p. 755). And the promisee must show the facts of the case and the conduct of the promisor justifying application of the doctrine. We further outlined the elements of promissory estoppel in *Marker* in this fashion:

> "In order for the doctrine of promissory estoppel to be invoked the evidence must show that the promise was made under circumstances where the promisor intended and reasonably expected that the promise would be relied upon by the promisee and further that the promisee acted reasonably in relying upon the promise. Furthermore promissory estoppel should be applied only if a refusal to enforce it would be virtually to sanction the perpetration of fraud or would result in other injustice."

> "The vital principle [of estoppel rendering the statute of frauds inoperative] is that he who by his language or conduct leads another to do, upon the faith of an oral agreement, what he would not otherwise have done, and changes his position to his prejudice, will not be allowed to subject such person to loss or injury, or to avail himself of that change to the prejudice of such other party" (Williston, supra, § 533A, p. 800).

Recapitulating, appellant's theory is it changed its position in reliance upon appellee's conduct; that appellee was or reasonably should have been aware of its practices in the particular type of situation; that appellant bound itself in the transaction and it would be unjust and a fraud upon appellant to permit appellee to speculate and profit on a risen market at appellant's expense. From the facts pleaded and placed before the trial court by stipulation it is clear appellant was entitled to invoke the doctrine of promissory estoppel so as to bar application of the statute of frauds and to have an evidentiary hearing upon disputed matters in connection with that issue. The summary judgment denying that right was improperly entered and it must be and is hereby reversed and the cause remanded for further proceedings accordingly.

Reversed and remanded.

QUESTIONS AND NOTES

1. Note the rationale for subsection (2): in the absence of that provision, a party who receives a writing in confirmation of an oral agreement could await the time for performance and then perform only if at that time it is to his or her advantage, with no liability for failing to perform if nonperformance is the advantageous course of action.

2. Problem. Buyer phones Seller, offering to buy a generator system. Seller says, "Let me see if we can meet your deadline, and I'll get back to you." Seller then sends a letter, "As you requested, we agree to sell you the following items at the following prices . . . ." In due course, Seller tenders the goods, Buyer refuses to accept delivery, and Seller sues. Does 2–201(2) make the agreement enforceable against Buyer?

3. The court in *Decatur Coop* holds that promissory estoppel may obviate the need for a writing. If the purpose of the statute of frauds is to keep oral evidence from the finder of fact because of fear that

> (1) the person claiming contract will either lie about or mis-remember the contract or its terms, and

> (2) the finder of fact will believe the mistaken evidence,

what justifies admitting the evidence if the party who claims that a contract exists also alleges its detrimental reliance on the oral contract? Will not that party lie in the same way about its reliance? Or do you think that the fact of reliance is more subject to proof by objective facts that are less likely to be manufactured or mis-remembered? *Were* there "objective" facts in *Decatur Coop* which tended to establish that the claimed contract was in fact made? Was the sending of the confirmation such an "objective" fact even though the court holds that 2–201(2) does not apply?

Lige Dickson Co. v. Union Oil Co. of California

Washington Supreme Court, 1981.
96 Wash.2d 291, 635 P.2d 103.

■ DORE, J. The Ninth Circuit Court of Appeals certified the following question to us:

> "Under the law of the State of Washington, may an oral promise otherwise within the statute of frauds, Wash Rev Code § 62.A.2–101, nevertheless be enforceable on the basis of promissory estoppel? See Restatement (Second) of Contracts [§ 139]. See generally Klinke v. Famous Recipe Fried Chicken, Inc., 94 Wash.2d 255, 616 P.2d 644 (1980)."

Our answer to this question is "no." Analysis and elaboration follow.

The business relationship between plaintiff Lige Dickson Company (or its predecessor partnership) and defendant Union Oil Company of California is long standing, dating from 1937. Plaintiff was a general contractor and purchased its oil-based products from defendant. In 1964, defendant encouraged and aided plaintiff in entering the asphalt paving business. From 1964 through 1973, with one exception, plaintiff purchased all its liquid asphalt from defendant. In the ordinary course of business, plaintiff telephoned orders to defendant, plaintiff was invoiced, and all bills were paid. Plaintiff and defendant never executed a written contract providing for the sale and purchase of liquid asphalt.

From 1964 until late 1970, the defendant's price for liquid asphalt remained constant. In December 1970, all of the suppliers of liquid asphalt in the Tacoma area raised their prices. Responding to this in May or June of 1971, plaintiff requested, and defendant provided, an oral guaranty against further increases insofar as would affect those contracts which committed the plaintiff to manufacture and sell asphalt paving at fixed, agreed sums. A list was made of the plaintiff's contracts and the parties computed the amount of liquid asphalt needed to fulfill them. At the same time, defendant promised plaintiff that any upward change in price would be applicable only to contracts which plaintiff entered into after the price increase.

. . .

Nevertheless, in November 1973, defendant wrote to plaintiff that the price of liquid asphalt was rising by $3 per ton and plaintiff was informed on December 6 and 13, 1973 of further increases. The new prices were to be applicable to all purchases made after December 31, 1973. This was plaintiff's first notification that defendant was abandoning the parties' price protection agreement. In addition, the new prices were on a "verbal, indefinite basis . . . subject to change" with or without notice.

Without a firm supplier, plaintiff was unable to seek new paving contracts during the first part of 1974. What liquid asphalt was available was used by plaintiff to complete existing contracts. Plaintiff incurred a total increased out-of-pocket cost of $39,006.50 in acquiring liquid asphalt to perform existing contracts.

Plaintiff brought suit against defendant in the United States District Court for Western Washington for breach of contract. The trial court found that there was an oral contract between the parties, but the statute of frauds, RCW 62A.2–201 rendered the contract unenforceable. The cause was appealed to the Ninth Circuit which certified the question quoted above to this court.

. . .

. . . The Ninth Circuit Court of Appeals has held, in interpreting and applying California law, that UCC § 2–201 cannot be overcome through the application of the doctrine of promissory estoppel. C.R. Fedrick, Inc. v. Borg–Warner Corp., 552 F.2d 852 (9th Cir.1977). The Kentucky [Court of Appeals] reached the same conclusion based upon the UCC's internal method of avoiding § 2–201's hardship. C.G. Campbell & Son, Inc. v. Comdeq Corp., 586 S.W.2d 40 (Ky.Ct.App.1979). It reasoned that the statutory avoidance of § 2–201 found in § 2–201(3) was as far as the legislature was willing to go and

> "any attempt by the courts to judicially amend this statute which is plain on its face would contravene the separation of powers mandated by the Constitution." Campbell, at 41.

On the other hand, the Iowa Supreme Court reached the opposite result in Warder & Lee Elevator, Inc. v. Britten, 274 N.W.2d 339 (Iowa 1979). . . .

. . .

From the limited record before us in the subject case, it appears that equitable estoppel is not available to the plaintiff. There seems to be neither allegation nor proof of fraud or deceit. Plaintiff's only remedy may be based upon breach of the oral contract. Nonetheless, we must hold that promissory estoppel cannot be used to overcome the statute of frauds in a case which involves the sale of goods.

The Uniform Commercial Code was adopted to regulate commercial dealings. Uniformity among different jurisdictions in decisions concerning commerce was a major motivation behind development of the UCC. By so doing, it was hoped that this area of the law would become clearer and disputes would be more readily resolved. These policies are enunciated in the UCC, in part, as follows:

> "62A.1–102 Purposes; rules of construction; variation by agreement . . .

> "(2) Underlying purposes and policies of this Title are

> "(a) to simplify, clarify and modernize the law governing commercial transactions;

> . . .

> "(c) to make uniform the law among the various jurisdictions." . . .

If we were to adopt [§ 139] as applicable in the context of the sale of goods, we would allow parties to circumvent the UCC. For example, to prove justifiable reliance (an element of promissory estoppel), the promisee may offer evidence of course of dealing between the parties, as plaintiff did in this case. The Official Comments to RCWA 62A.1–205(4) state that the statute of frauds

> "restrict[s] the actions of the parties, and . . . cannot be abrogated by agreement, or by a *usage of trade* . . ." (Italics ours.) RCWA 62A.1–205, at 71.

Notwithstanding our appreciation of plaintiff's dilemma, we cannot help but foresee increased litigation and confusion as being the necessary result of the eroding of the UCC if [§ 139] is adopted in this case. We join the other courts which limit the doctrine of promissory estoppel from overcoming a valid defense based on the statute of frauds contained within the Uniform Commercial Code. . . .

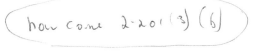

how come 2-201 (3) (b)

QUESTIONS AND NOTES

1. The court refers to Restatement (Second) of Contracts § 139, which states:

> § 139. Enforcement by Virtue of Action in Reliance

> (1) A promise which the promisor should reasonably expect to induce action or forbearance on the part of the promisee or a third person and which does induce the action or forbearance is enforceable notwithstanding the Statute of Frauds if injustice can be avoided only

by enforcement of the promise. The remedy granted for breach is to be limited as justice requires.

(2) In determining whether injustice can be avoided only by enforcement of the promise, the following circumstances are significant:

(a) the availability and adequacy of other remedies, particularly cancellation and restitution;

(b) the definite and substantial character of the action or forbearance in relation to the remedy sought;

(c) the extent to which the action or forbearance corroborates evidence of the making and terms of the promise, or the making and terms are otherwise established by clear and convincing evidence;

(d) the reasonableness of the action or forbearance;

(e) the extent to which the action or forbearance was foreseeable by the promisor.

In Allied Grape Growers v. Bronco Wine Co., 203 Cal.App.3d 432, 249 Cal.Rptr. 872 (1988), the court surveyed the cases and reported that jurisdictions are 14 to 4 in favor of applying estoppel principles to enforce contracts that would otherwise be unenforceable because of 2–201. In view of the judicial acceptance of the estoppel argument and Restatement § 139, at least one of the justifications given by the court for the result in Lige Dickson Co. seems weak. Since 1988, however, a few additional courts have rejected the use of promissory estoppel to enforce contracts subject to the statute of frauds.

In the revision process one of the contentious issues was whether to include a promissory estoppel exception in 2–201. The ultimate decision was to remain silent on the issue.

2. Part performance. Section 2–201(3)(c) provides that performance may make an oral agreement enforceable even if there is no writing. Please read that and consider the following problems.

Problem (a). Buyer claims that Buyer and Seller entered into an oral contract under which Seller would deliver 100 tons of grapes. Seller delivered 15 tons of grapes but denies that there was a contract for more than 15 tons. Does the partial delivery take the contract out of the statute of frauds so that Buyer can offer proof that there was a contract for 100 tons? See Allied Grape Growers v. Bronco Wine Co., 203 Cal.App.3d 432, 249 Cal.Rptr. 872 (1988). What result if Seller's pleading claims that the contract was for only 25 tons?

Problem (b). Buyer approaches Dealer about the purchase of a new car. After negotiations Dealer prepares a purchase order for the sale of a specified model, to be ordered from the factory, for $16,500, and Buyer signs it. Dealer, however, does not. As stated in the purchase order, Buyer gives $100 as a cash down payment. Six weeks later Dealer notifies Buyer that the automobile has arrived but that they had made a mistake as to the price and that the price would be $17,000 rather than the $16,500 stated on the purchase order. Does the down payment take the contract out of the statute of frauds so that Buyer can offer evidence that the sales manager orally accepted the order when Buyer signed it? See Starr v. Freeport Dodge, 54 Misc.2d 271, 282 N.Y.S.2d 58 (1967).

3. Admissions. If a party to an agreement admits in the context of judicial proceedings that a contract was made, 2–201(3)(b) makes that agreement enforceable even if there is no writing. In Lewis v. Hughes, 276 Md. 247, 346 A.2d 231 (Md. App. 1975), plaintiff offered to sell her mobile home to defendant for $5,000. No other terms were stated. Defendant accepted the offer. On trial, he stated that he did not intend to pay $5,000, except over period of time, and that he thought that the contract was still being negotiated. That is, he denied that a contract existed. The court stated:

> " . . . [I]t is apparent from . . . [Dr. Hughes'] testimony . . . that at the trial [he] admitted he told Mr. Baer [for communication to the plaintiff], without mention of any terms of payment, that he would purchase the mobile home for $5,000. Of course, it is legally irrelevant, in the face of Dr. Hughes' objective manifestation of unconditional assent to the offer, that [he] thought the contract was still being negotiated and had a subjective desire to impose certain conditions on the manner of payment. Consequently, when on May 9 the lawyer, in accordance with his agency authority, informed [plaintiff] of Dr. Hughes' assent, there was an acceptance of the offer and a contract, as a matter of law, came into existence.

> "We come then to the basic issue in this case, which is whether the Statute of Frauds is satisfied pursuant to § 2–201(3)(b) when the party denying the existence of the contract and relying on the statute takes the stand and, without admitting explicitly that a contract was made, testifies to facts which as a matter of law establish that a contract was formed. While we have found no case specifically deciding this question, numerous cases dealing with § 2–201(3)(b) seem to say that in such a situation the requirements of the statute have been fulfilled. . . . We hold that the Statute of Frauds does not bar enforcement of the contract involved in this case."

4. The possibility always exists, of course, that a defendant might inadvertently admit an oral contract during the course of a trial. Does this possibility mean that a court should never dismiss a case for failure to state a cause of action where the defendant has pleaded the statute of frauds? Compare Simmons Oil Corp. v. Bulk Sales Corp., 498 F.Supp. 457 (D.N.J. 1980) ("Plaintiff argues, in addition, that the defendant should be required to file an answer, before raising the statute of frauds as a defense, on the chance it will admit the existence of the alleged contract. . . . This contention is without merit,") with M & W Farm Service Co. v. Callison, 285 N.W.2d 271 (Iowa 1979) (the defense of the statute of frauds should not ordinarily be adjudicated on a motion to dismiss because, under the statute, the party asserting the claim is entitled to an opportunity to elicit an admission from the opposing party of the existence of a contract.) Which of these views does Lewis v. Hughes support? Which of these views makes the most sense to you?

5. Suppose the seller and buyer entered into an oral transaction in which the former agreed to sell and the latter to buy for $100 a new automobile worth $7,500.00. Suppose the seller denied ever making "such a ridiculous deal." Does 2–201 bar enforcement? If not, what protection does a seller have in situations in which he or she did not, in fact, make "such a ridiculous deal"? How can the buyer protect a "good" oral deal if the seller refuses to put it in writing? Would a tape recording, secretly made by the buyer and showing that the deal was made, satisfy the statute of frauds? Cf. Ellis Canning Co. v. Bernstein, 348 F.Supp. 1212 (D.Colo.1972).

6. Specially manufactured goods. Suppose a printer having a slack season prints calendars bearing the name and logo of a large department store. When the printer calls for delivery instructions, the department store denies that it had ever made a contract for the calendars. The printer, claiming that the department store had phoned in the order, sues for breach of contract. Can the department store rely on 2–201? See subsection (3)(a). If not, how can it protect itself against nonexistent deals?

Possibly because the special-manufacturing exception to the statute of frauds has the effect of leaving an area of sales law largely unprotected, at least one court has said it must be strictly construed. See Epprecht v. IBM Corp., 36 U.C.C. Rep. 391 (E.D.Pa.1983). How is this done? By finding the goods not to be specially manufactured after all? What is meant by "specially manufactured goods"? For an excellent case dealing with this question see Impossible Electronic Techniques, Inc. v. Wackenhut Protective Systems, Inc., 669 F.2d 1026 (5th Cir.1982) ("The crucial inquiry is whether the manufacturer could sell the goods in the ordinary course of his business to someone other than the original buyer. If with slight alterations the goods could be so sold, then they are not specially manufactured; if, however, essential changes are necessary to render the goods marketable by the seller to others, then the exception does apply.")

7. Noncompliance. Section 2–201 declares that contracts that fail to comply with its provisions are "unenforceable." This does not mean that they are "void" but only "voidable." Thus, failure to meet the requirements of 2–201 does not nullify a contract, but gives one of the parties an option to avoid it. As a result, a defense based 2–201 must be pleaded by the party seeking to use it, and only a party to the contract or a successor in interest can take advantage of it. In the absence of special pleading statutes or rules to the contrary, some courts have held that a defendant must plead 2–201 affirmatively and cannot raise it by a general denial.

8. Revised Article 2. Early in the drafting process, there was an attempt to delete the statute of frauds. Business lawyers strongly objected to deletion, and 2–201 is substantively unchanged except for (a) the increase from $500 to $5,000 in the amount that brings a contract within the section, and (b) the addition of subsection (4), which constricts the operation of any non-UCC statute of frauds requiring a writing for contracts not to be performed within a year of their formation.

9. Article 2A. Article 2A–201 is modeled on 2–201, though it raises the $500 of 2–201 to $1,000 (and the 2003 amendments increase this further, to the same $5,000 figure as revised 2–201).

Problem. Dealer delivers to User a large trenching machine. User retains the machine for one month and then demands that Dealer pick it up and refund $7,500 of the $10,000 that User has paid. Dealer picks up the machine (see 2A–529(1)(a)) and now sues User for damages claiming that User had accepted the machine under a two-year lease at a rental of $2,500 per month, with the first two months rental plus a security deposit of $5,000 to be paid in advance. User denies that there was a two-year lease, but says that the lease was for one month at a rental of $2,500, with a $7,500 security deposit. Can dealer prove a term longer than a month under 2A–201(4)(c)?

10. CISG and the statute of frauds. Article 11 of the Convention on Contracts for the International Sale of Goods rejects the Article 2 approach. It provides: "A contract of sale need not be concluded in or evidenced by writing and is not subject to any other requirement as to form. It may be proved by any means, including witnesses."

11. Problem. A sales rep calls on a business owner to discuss the sale of a generator. They talk about components, accessories, prices, warranty, delivery date, and payment terms. The business owner is not sure that she wants to buy the generator. So the sales rep fills out and signs Seller's standard sales form and says, "Think it over for a day or two. If you decide you want the generator, just sign this and send it in."

The sales form states, "Seller agrees to sell and Buyer agrees to buy and pay for the following equipment pursuant to the following terms ... ," and all the appropriate blanks are filled in. Buyer scans it and says, "OK, I'll let you know tomorrow." The sales rep leaves.

The business owner never calls, writes, signs, or returns the sales form. Not surprisingly, Seller never delivers the equipment. Meanwhile, the market price rises, and the business owner demands delivery. Seller of course refuses, and the alleged buyer sues. Pointing to 2–201, she argues that she is entitled to damages. Is she right?

D. THE BATTLE OF THE FORMS

C. Itoh & Co. (America), Inc. v. Jordan International Co.

United States Court of Appeals, Seventh Circuit, 1977.
552 F.2d 1228.

■ SPRECHER, CIRCUIT JUDGE. The sole issue on this appeal is whether the district court properly denied a stay of the proceedings pending arbitration under Section 3 of the Federal Arbitration Act, 9 U.S.C.A. § 3.

I.

C. Itoh & Co. (America) Inc. ("Itoh") submitted a purchase order dated August 15, 1974 for a certain quantity of steel coils to the Jordan International Company ("Jordan"). In response, Jordan sent its acknowledgment form dated August 19, 1974. On the face of Jordan's form, the following statement appears:

> Seller's acceptance is, however, expressly conditional on Buyer's assent to the additional or different terms and conditions set forth below and printed on the reverse side. If these terms and conditions are not acceptable, Buyer should notify seller at once.

One of the terms on the reverse side of Jordan's form was a broad provision for arbitration.[1] Itoh neither expressly assented nor objected to the additional arbitration term in Jordan's form until the instant litigation.

Itoh also entered into a contract to sell the steel coils that it purchased from Jordan to Riverview Steel Corporation, Inc. ("Riverview.") The contract between Itoh and Riverview contained an arbitration term which provided in pertinent part:

> Any and all controversies arising out of or relating to this contract, or any modification, breach or cancellation thereof, except as to *quality,* shall be settled by arbitration. * * *

After the steel had been delivered by Jordan and paid for by Itoh, Riverview advised Itoh that the steel coils were defective and did not conform to the standards set forth in the agreement between Itoh and Riverview; for these reasons, Riverview refused to pay Itoh for the steel. Consequently, Itoh brought the instant suit against Riverview and Jordan. Itoh alleged that Riverview had wrongfully refused to pay for the steel; as affirmative defenses, Riverview claimed that the steel was defective and that tender was improper since delivery was late. Itoh alleged that Jordan had sold Itoh defective steel and had made a late delivery of that steel.

Jordan then filed a motion in the district court requesting a stay of the proceedings pending arbitration under Section 3 of the Federal Arbitration Act, 9 U.S.C.A. § 3. The district court concluded that, as between Itoh and Riverview, the issue of whether the steel coils were defective was not referable to arbitration because of the "quality" exclusion in the arbitration provision of the contract between Itoh and Riverview. Since arbitration would not necessarily resolve all the issues raised by the parties, the district court, apparently assuming *arguendo* that there existed an agreement in writing between Jordan and Itoh to arbitrate their dispute, denied the stay pending arbitration. In the district court's opinion, sound judicial

---

1. The arbitration clause provides:

Any controversy arising under or in connection with the contract shall be submitted to arbitration in New York City in accordance with the rules then obtaining of the American Arbitration Association. Judgment on any award may be entered in any court hav-

ing jurisdiction. The parties hereto submit to the jurisdiction of the Federal and State courts in New York City, and notice of process in connection with arbitral or judicial proceedings may be served upon the parties by registered or certified mail, with the same effect as if personally served.

administration required that the entire litigation be resolved in a single forum; since some of the issues—those relating to quality between Itoh and Riverview—were not referable to arbitration, this goal could only be accomplished in the judicial forum.

It is from this denial of a stay pending arbitration that Jordan appeals.

. . .

III.

Having concluded that the district court had no discretion under Section 3 of the Federal Arbitration Act, 9 U.S.C.A. § 3, to deny Jordan's timely application for a stay of the action pending arbitration *if* there existed an agreement in writing for such arbitration between Jordan and Itoh, the remaining issue is whether there existed such an agreement.

The pertinent facts may be briefly restated. Itoh sent its purchase order for steel coils to Jordan which contained no provision for arbitration. Subsequently, Jordan sent Itoh its acknowledgment form which included, *inter alia,* a broad arbitration term on the reverse side of the form.[3] On the front of Jordan's form, the following statement also appears:

> Seller's acceptance is * * * expressly conditioned on Buyer's assent to the additional or different terms and conditions set forth below and printed on the reverse side. If these terms and conditions are not acceptable, Buyer should notify Seller at once.

After the exchange of documents, Jordan delivered and Itoh paid for the steel coils. Itoh never expressly assented or objected to the additional arbitration term in Jordan's form.

In support of its contention that there exists an agreement in writing to arbitrate, Jordan places some reliance on certain New York decisions interpreting Section 2–201 of the Uniform Commercial Code, the UCC Statute of Frauds provision. . . .

Several New York lower court decisions have apparently held that under Section 2–201, where there has been an oral offer or agreement followed by a written confirmation containing an additional arbitration term and where the merchant recipient of the confirmation has reason to expect that a provision for arbitration would be included in any written confirmation of an oral offer or agreement, the arbitration provision becomes a part of the parties' agreement unless notice of objection is given within the prescribed period.

These decisions are premised on a fundamental misconception of the purpose and effect of Section 2–201. See generally Duesenberg & King,

---

3. See note 1 supra. There is apparently no dispute that, if the arbitration provision is part of a written agreement between the parties, it is sufficiently broad to encompass the instant dispute. Therefore, under 9 U.S.C.A. § 3, if there was an "agreement in writing for * * * arbitration," arbitration should be directed since the underlying controversy is an "issue referable to arbitration" and there is no contention by Itoh that Jordan is "in default in proceeding with such arbitration."

Sales and Bulk Transfers Under the Uniform Commercial Code § 308[1] at 97–99 (1976). The *only* effect of a failure to object to a written confirmation of an oral offer or agreement under Section 2–201 is to take away from the receiving merchant the defense of the Statute of Frauds. See Official Comment 3 to Section 2–201. Although Section 2–201 may make *enforceable* an oral agreement which was in fact reached by the parties, it does not relieve the party seeking enforcement of the alleged oral agreement of the obligation to prove its existence. Official Comment 3 to Section 2–201. Section 2–201 obviously cannot be relied on to make a particular term, such as a provision for arbitration, binding on a party if that section does not even serve to establish the *existence* of an agreement.

The Official Comments make clear that, while under Section 2–201 the failure to object to a written confirmation of an oral agreement has the limited effect of removing the Statute of Frauds as a bar to the enforceability of an oral agreement, under Section 2–207 a failure to object to a term in a written confirmation may, *under the circumstances specified by that section,* have the effect of making that term a part of whatever agreement is proved to have been reached by the parties. Official Comment 3 to Section 2–201. Hence, once the existence and terms of an alleged oral agreement have been established, it is necessary to refer to Section 2–207, Additional Terms in Acceptance *or Confirmation,* not Section 2–201, to ascertain whether a term included in a written confirmation but not in the parties' oral agreement is binding on the recipient of the written confirmation. See, e.g., Dorton v. Collins & Aikman Corp., 453 F.2d 1161 (6th Cir.1972).

However, even if we assume that New York's highest court would adhere to those lower court decisions and their extremely questionable application of the Statute of Frauds to situations where a party has added an arbitration term to a written *confirmation* of an *oral* offer or agreement, this is not such a situation. Jordan does not suggest that its acknowledgment form was simply a *confirmation* of a prior *oral* offer or agreement. Rather, Jordan's argument is that *the exchange of forms* between itself and Itoh *created* a contract, which includes the additional arbitration term in Jordan's form.

The instant case, therefore, involves the classic "battle of the forms," and Section 2–207, not Section 2–201, furnishes the rules for resolving such a controversy. Hence, it is to Section 2–207 that we must look to determine whether a contract has been formed by the exchange of forms between Jordan and Itoh and, if so, whether the additional arbitration term in Jordan's form is to be included in that contract.

IV.

. . .

Under Section 2–207 it is necessary to first determine whether a contract has been formed under Section 2–207(1) as a result of the *exchange of forms* between Jordan and Itoh.

At common law, "an acceptance * * * which contained terms additional to * * * those of the offer * * * constituted a rejection of the offer * * * and thus became a counter-offer." *Dorton,* supra, at 1166. Thus, the mere presence of the additional arbitration term in Jordan's acknowledgment form would, at common law, have prevented the exchange of documents between Jordan and Itoh from creating a contract, and Jordan's form would have automatically become a counter-offer.

Section 2–207(1) was intended to alter this inflexible common law approach to offer and acceptance:

> This section of the Code recognizes that in current commercial transactions, the terms of the offer and those of the acceptance will seldom be identical. Rather, under the current "battle of the forms," each party typically has a printed form drafted by his attorney and containing as many terms as could be envisioned to favor that party in his sales transactions. Whereas under common law the disparity between the fine-print terms in the parties' forms would have prevented the consummation of a contract when these forms are exchanged, Section 2–207 recognizes that in many, but not all, cases the parties do not impart such significance to the terms on the printed forms. * * * Thus, under Subsection (1), a contract * * * [may be] recognized notwithstanding the fact that an acceptance * * * contains terms additional to * * * those of the offer * * *.

Id. at 1166. See also Comment 2 to Section 2–207. And it is now well-settled that the *mere presence* of an additional term, such as a provision for arbitration, in one of the parties' forms will not prevent the formation of a contract under Section 2–207(1).

However, while Section 2–207(1) constitutes a sharp departure from the common law "mirror image" rule, there remain situations where the inclusion of an additional term in one of the forms exchanged by the parties will prevent the consummation of a contract *under that section.* Section 2–207(1) contains a proviso which operates to prevent an exchange of forms from creating a contract where "acceptance is expressly made conditional on assent to the additional * * * terms." In the instant case, Jordan's acknowledgment form contained the following statement:

> Seller's acceptance is * * * *expressly conditional* on Buyer's *assent* to the additional or different terms and conditions set forth below and printed on the reverse side. If these terms and conditions are not acceptable, Buyer should notify Seller at once.

The arbitration provision at issue on this appeal is printed on the reverse side of Jordan's acknowledgment, and there is no dispute that Itoh never expressly assented to the challenged arbitration term.

The Court of Appeals for the Sixth Circuit has held that the proviso must be construed narrowly:

> Although * * * [seller's] use of the words "subject to" suggests that the acceptances were conditional to some extent, we do not believe the acceptances were "expressly made conditional on [the buyer's] assent

> to the additional or different terms,'' as specifically required under the Subsection 2–207(1) proviso. In order to fall within this proviso, it is not enough that an acceptance is expressly conditional on additional or different terms; rather, an acceptance must be expressly conditional on the offeror's *assent* to those terms (emphasis in original).

Dorton, supra, at 1168. In Construction Aggregates Corp. v. Hewitt–Robins, Inc., 404 F.2d 505 (7th Cir.1968), this court found that an acceptance came within the ambit of the Section 2–207(1) proviso even though the language employed in the acceptance did not precisely track that of the proviso. Under either *Construction Aggregates* or *Dorton,* however, it is clear that the statement contained in Jordan's acknowledgment form comes within the Section 2–207(1) proviso.

Hence, the exchange of forms between Jordan and Itoh did not result in the formation of a contract under Section 2–207(1), and Jordan's form became a counter offer. ''[T]he consequence of a clause conditioning acceptance on assent to the additional or different terms is that *as of the exchanged writings, there is no contract.* Either party may at this point in their dealings walk away from the transaction.'' Duesenberg & King, supra, § 3.06[3] at 73. However, neither Jordan nor Itoh elected to follow that course; instead, both parties proceeded to performance—Jordan by delivering and Itoh by paying for the steel coils.

At common law, the ''terms of the counter-offer were said to have been accepted by the original offeror when he proceeded to perform under the contract without objecting to the counter-offer.'' *Dorton,* supra, at 1166. Thus, under pre-Code law, Itoh's performance (i.e., payment for the steel coils) probably constituted acceptance of the Jordan counter-offer, including its provision for arbitration. However, a different approach is required under the Code.

Section 2–207(3) of the Code first provides that ''[c]onduct by both parties which recognizes the existence of a contract is sufficient to establish a contract for sale although the writings of the parties do not otherwise establish a contract.'' As the court noted in *Dorton,* supra, at 1166:

> [W]hen no contract is recognized under Subsection 2–207(1) * * * the entire transaction aborts at this point. If, however, the subsequent conduct of the parties—particularly, performance by both parties under what they apparently believe to be a contract—recognizes the existence of a contract, under Subsection 2–207(3) such conduct by both parties is sufficient to establish a contract, notwithstanding the fact that no contract would have been recognized on the basis of their writings alone.

Thus, ''[s]ince * * * [Itoh's] purchase order and * * * [Jordan's] counter-offer did not in themselves create a contract, Section 2–207(3) would operate to create one because the subsequent performance by both parties constituted 'conduct by both parties which recognizes the existence of a contract.' '' *Construction Aggregates,* supra, at 509.

issue

What are the terms of a contract created by conduct under Section 2–207(3) rather than by an exchange of forms under Section 2–207(1)?[7] As noted above, at common law the terms of the contract between Jordan and Itoh would be the terms of the Jordan counter-offer. However, the Code has effectuated a radical departure from the common law rule. The second sentence of Section 2–207(3) provides that where, as here, a contract has been consummated by the conduct of the parties, "the terms of the particular contract consist of those terms on which the writings of the parties agree, together with any supplementary terms incorporated under any other provisions of this Act." Since it is clear that the Jordan and Itoh forms do not "agree" on arbitration, the only question which remains *under the Code* is whether arbitration may be considered a supplementary term incorporated under some other provision of the Code.

We have been unable to find any case authority shedding light on the question of what constitutes "supplementary terms" within the meaning of Section 2–207(3)[9] and the Official Comments to Section 2–207 provide no guidance in this regard. We are persuaded, however, that the disputed additional terms (i.e., those terms on which the writings of the parties do not agree) which are necessarily excluded from a Subsection (3) contract by the language, "terms on which the writings of the parties agree," cannot be brought back into the contract under the guise of "supplementary terms." This conclusion has substantial support among the commentators who have addressed themselves to the issue. As two noted authorities on Article Two of the Code have stated:

> It will usually happen that an offeree-seller who returns an acknowledgment form will also concurrently or shortly thereafter ship the goods. If the responsive document [sent by the seller] contains a printed assent clause, and the goods are shipped and accepted, Subsection (3) of Section 2–207 comes into play. * * * [T]he terms on which the exchanged communications do not agree drop out of the transaction, and reference to the Code is made to supply necessary terms. * * * Rather than choosing the terms of one party over those of the other * * * it compels supplying missing terms by reference to the Code. * * *

Duesenberg & King, supra, § 3.06[4] at 73–74. Similarly, Professors White and Summers have concluded that "contract formation under subsection

---

7. If a contract had been formed by the exchange of forms between Jordan and Itoh, it would have been necessary to look to Section 2–207(2) to ascertain the terms of that contract.

9. In *Construction Aggregates,* supra, this court found it unnecessary to reach this issue since it found that there was conduct on the part of the buyer, other than mere acceptance of and payment for the goods without objection to the additional terms in seller's form, which manifested assent to the disputed additional terms. In that case, the buyer had expressly objected to some of the additional terms, without raising any objection to the others, and the seller agreed to the requested changes. It was held that such further action by the negotiating parties took the case out of Section 2–207(3) for purposes of ascertaining the terms of the parties' contract. It has not been suggested that any such additional conduct is involved in the instant case.

(3) gives neither party the relevant terms of his document, but fills out the contract with the standardized provisions of Article Two." White & Summers, supra, at 29.

Accordingly, we find that the "supplementary terms" contemplated by Section 2–207(3) are limited to those supplied by the standardized "gap-filler" provisions of Article Two. See, e.g., Section 2–308(a) ("Unless otherwise agreed * * * the place for delivery of goods is the seller's place of business or if he has none his residence"); Section 2–309(1) ("The time for shipment or delivery or any other action under a contract if not * * * agreed upon shall be a reasonable time"); Section 2–310(a) ("Unless otherwise agreed * * * payment is due at the time and place at which the buyer is to receive the goods even though the place of shipment is the place of delivery.") Since provision for arbitration is not a necessary or missing term which would be supplied by one of the Code's "gap-filler" provisions unless agreed upon by the contracting parties, there is no arbitration term in the Section 2–207(3) contract which was created by the conduct of Jordan and Itoh in proceeding to perform even though no contract had been established by their exchange of writings.

We are convinced that this conclusion does not result in any unfair prejudice to a seller who elects to insert in his standard sales acknowledgement form the statement that acceptance is expressly conditional on buyer's assent to additional terms contained therein. Such a seller obtains a substantial benefit *under Section 2–207(1)* through the inclusion of an "expressly conditional" clause. If he decides after the exchange of forms that the particular transaction is not in his best interest, Subsection (1) permits him to walk away from the transaction without incurring any liability so long as the buyer has not in the interim expressly assented to the additional terms. Moreover, whether or not a seller will be disadvantaged *under Subsection (3)* as a consequence of inserting an "expressly conditional" clause in his standard form is within his control. If the seller in fact does not intend to close a particular deal unless the additional terms are assented to, he can protect himself by not delivering the goods until such assent is forthcoming. If the seller does intend to close a deal irrespective of whether or not the buyer assents to the additional terms, he can hardly complain when the contract formed under Subsection (3) as a result of the parties' conduct is held not to include those terms. Although a seller who employs such an "expressly conditional" clause in his acknowledgement form would undoubtedly appreciate the dual advantage of not being bound to a contract under Subsection (1) if he elects not to perform and of having his additional terms imposed on the buyer under Subsection (3) in the event that performance is in his best interest, we do not believe such a result is contemplated by Section 2–207. Rather, while a seller may take advantage of an "expressly conditional" clause under Subsection (1) when he elects not to perform, he must accept the potential risk under Subsection (3) of not getting his additional terms when he elects to proceed with performance without first obtaining buyer's assent to those terms. Since the seller injected ambiguity into the transaction by inserting the "expressly conditional" clause in his form, he, and not the buyer, should bear the consequence of that ambiguity under Subsection (3).

. . .

Accordingly, for the reasons stated in this opinion, the decision of the district court is affirmed.

QUESTIONS AND NOTES

1. Section 2–207 is perhaps the most criticized section in Article 2. It is the subject of more law review articles than any other section, and it poses many difficult interpretive issues. Some of the difficulty results from confusion about the role of each subsection. A careful reading reveals that each subsection has a distinct role. Subsection (1) answers a single question, viz., do the writings of the parties form a contract? That is its only role, and subsections (2) and (3) have nothing to contribute to answering that question. Subsection (2) addresses the single question, if the writings do form a contract, what are the terms of that contract? Subsections (1) and (3) have nothing to contribute to answering that question. Finally, subsection (3) addresses two questions: if the writings do not form a contract, does the conduct of the parties form a contract? If so, what are the terms of that contract?

Which of these questions are involved in *Itoh*?

2. The court holds that Jordan's acknowledgment form did not operate as an acceptance because it stated that "Seller's acceptance . . . is expressly conditional on Buyer's assent to the additional or different terms and conditions set forth below and printed on the reverse side." Instead, it amounted to a counteroffer. The court then proceeded to apply subsection (3) of 2–207. Should the court instead have looked to 2–206(1)(b)?

3. Problem. Seller sends buyer a written offer offering to sell used steel pipe, delivery date to be October 15th. Buyer responds with a written acceptance that changes the delivery date to December 15th. The December 15th date is clearly typed in on the front of the acceptance form. If this is a material change from Seller's offer, does that prevent Buyer's response from operating as an acceptance?

no

If a contract is formed by the exchange of correspondence, what is the delivery term?

oct 15

Suppose that the variation between the offer and the acceptance is a 20% reduction in price. Do the parties have a contract?

yes

4. Problem. Buyer sends Seller a purchase order for a turbine. Seller responds with its standard acknowledgement form, which has 16 clauses on the reverse side, one of which states, "This acceptance is expressly made conditional upon offeror's assent to all the terms of this acceptance." Do the parties have a contract?

———

Northrop Corporation v. Litronic Industries

United States Court of Appeals, Seventh Circuit, 1994.
29 F.3d 1173.

■ POSNER, CHIEF JUDGE.*

. . .

The battle of the forms in this case takes the form of something very like a badminton game, but we can simplify it a bit without distorting the issues. The players are Northrop, the giant defense firm, and Litronic, which manufactures electronic components, including "printed wire boards" that are incorporated into defense weapon systems. In 1987 Northrop sent several manufacturers, including Litronic, a request to submit offers to sell Northrop customized printed wire board designated by Northrop as a "1714 Board." The request stated that any purchase would be made by means of a purchase order that would set forth terms and conditions that would override any inconsistent terms in the offer. In response, Litronic mailed an offer to sell Northrop four boards for $19,000 apiece, to be delivered within six weeks. The offer contained a 90–day warranty stated to be in lieu of any other warranties, and provided that the terms of the offer would take precedence over any terms proposed by the buyer. Lynch, a purchasing officer of Northrop, responded to the offer in a phone conversation in which he told Litronic's man, Lair, that he was accepting the offer up to the limit of his authority, which was $24,999, and that a formal purchase order for all four boards would follow. Litronic was familiar with Northrop's purchase order form, having previously done business with Northrop, which had been using the same form for some time. Had Lair referred to any of the previous orders, he would have discovered that Northrop's order form provided for a warranty that contained no time limit.

Lynch followed up the phone conversation a month later with a "turn on" letter, authorizing Litronic to begin production of all four boards (it had done so already) and repeating that a purchase order would follow. The record is unclear when the actual purchase order was mailed; it may have been as much as four months after the phone conversation and three months after the turn-on letter. The purchase order required the seller to send a written acknowledgment to Northrop. Litronic never did so, however, and Northrop did not complain; it does not bother to follow up on its requirement of a signed acknowledgment.

*Some paragraphs of the opinion have been reordered to locate the statement of facts at the beginning of the excerpt.—Ed.

Although Litronic had begun manufacturing the boards immediately after the telephone call from Lynch, for reasons that are unknown but that Northrop does not contend are culpable, Litronic did not deliver the first three boards until more than a year later, in July of 1988. Northrop tested the boards for conformity to its specifications. The testing was protracted, either because the boards were highly complex or because Northrop's inspectors were busy, or perhaps for both reasons. At all events it was not until December and January, five or six months after delivery, that Northrop returned the three boards (the fourth had not been delivered), claiming that they were defective. Litronic refused to accept the return of the boards, on the ground that its 90–day warranty had lapsed. Northrop's position of course is that it had an unlimited warranty, as stated in the purchase order.

As an original matter one might suppose that this dispute is not over the terms of the warranty but over whether Northrop waited more than the "reasonable time" that the Uniform Commercial Code allows the buyer of nonconforming goods to reject them. UCC § 2–602(1). That in fact is how the magistrate judge framed the issue, as we shall see. But the parties continue to treat it as a "warranty" case. Their implicit view is that Litronic's 90–day warranty, if a term of the contract, not only barred Northrop from complaining about defects that showed up more than 90 days after the delivery of the boards but also limited to 90 days the time within which Northrop was permitted to reject the boards because of defects that rendered them nonconforming. We accept this view for purposes of deciding these appeals.

. . . The magistrate judge gave judgment for Northrop in the amount of $58,000, representing the money it had paid for the three No. 1714 boards that it had taken delivery of. Both parties appeal.

. . .

Litronic's appeal concerns the breach of its warranty on the No. 1714 boards. It wins if the warranty really did expire after only 90 days. The parties agree that Litronic's offer to sell the No. 1714 boards to Northrop, the offer made in response to Northrop's request for bids, was the offer. So far, so good. If Northrop's Mr. Lynch accepted the offer over the phone, the parties had a contract then and there, but the question would still be on what terms. Regarding the first question, whether there was a contract, we may assume to begin with that the acceptance was sufficiently "definite" to satisfy the requirement of definiteness in section 2–207(1); after all, it impelled Litronic to begin production immediately, and there is no suggestion that it acted precipitately in doing so. We do not know whether Lynch in his conversation with Lair made acceptance of the complete contract expressly conditional on approval by Lynch's superiors at Northrop. We know that he had authority to contract only up to $24,999, but we do not know whether he told Lair what the exact limitation on his authority was or whether Litronic knew it without being told. It does not matter. The condition, if it was a condition, was satisfied and so drops out.

We do not think that Northrop's acceptance, via Lynch, of Litronic's offer could be thought conditional on Litronic's yielding to Northrop's demand for an open-ended warranty. For while Lynch's reference to the purchase order might have alerted Litronic to Northrop's desire for a warranty not limited to 90 days, Lynch did not purport to make the more extensive warranty a condition of acceptance. So the condition, if there was one, was not an express condition, as the cases insist it be.

There was a contract, therefore; further, and, as we shall note, decisive, evidence being that the parties acted as if they had a contract—the boards were shipped and paid for. The question is then what the terms of the warranty in the contract were. Lynch's reference in the phone conversation to the forthcoming purchase order shows that Northrop's acceptance contained different terms from the offer, namely the discrepant terms in the purchase order, in particular the warranty—for it is plain that the Northrop warranty was intended to be indefinite in length, so that, at least in the absence of some industry custom setting a limit on warranties that do not specify a duration (cf. UCC Sec. 2–207, comments 4 and 5), a point not raised, any limitation on the length of the warranty in the offer would be a materially different term. Of course the fact that Northrop preferred a longer warranty than Litronic was offering does not by itself establish that Northrop's acceptance contained different terms. But Lynch did not accept Litronic's offer and leave it at that. He said that he would issue a Northrop purchase order, and both he and Lair knew (or at least should have known) that the Northrop purchase order form contained a different warranty from Litronic's sale order form. And we have already said that Lynch did not, by his oral reference to the purchase order, condition Northrop's purchase on Litronic's agreeing to comply with all the terms in the purchase order form, given the courts' insistence that any such condition be explicit. (Judges are skeptical that even businesspeople read boilerplate, so they are reluctant, rightly or wrongly, to make a contract fail on the basis of a printed condition in a form contract.) But Lynch said enough to make clear to Lair that the acceptance contained different terms from the offer.

Mischief lurks in the words "additional to or different from" [as they appear in 2–207]. The next subsection of 2–207 provides that if additional terms in the acceptance are not materially different from those in the offer, then, subject to certain other qualifications, they become part of the contract, § 2–207(2), while if the additional terms are materially different they operate as proposals and so have no effect unless the offeror agrees to them, UCC § 2–207, comment 3; if the offeror does not agree to them, therefore, the terms of the contract are those in the offer. A clause providing for interest at normal rates on overdue invoices, or limiting the right to reject goods because of defects falling within customary trade tolerances for acceptance with adjustment, would be the sort of additional term that is not deemed material, and hence it would become a part of the contract even if the offeror never signified acceptance of it. *Id.,* comment 5.

The Code does not explain, however, what happens if the offeree's response contains *different* terms (rather than additional ones) within the meaning of section 2–207(1). There is no consensus on that question. See James J. White & Robert S. Summers, *Uniform Commercial Code* 33–36 (3d ed. 1988); John E. Murray, Jr., "The Chaos of the 'Battle of the Forms': Solutions," 39 *Vand.L.Rev.* 1307, 1354–65 (1986). We know there is a contract because an acceptance is effective even though it contains different terms; but what are the terms of the contract that is brought into being by the offer and acceptance? One view is that the discrepant terms in both the nonidentical offer and the acceptance drop out, and default terms found elsewhere in the Code fill the resulting gap. Another view is that the offeree's discrepant terms drop out and the offeror's become part of the contract. A third view, possibly the most sensible, equates "different" with "additional" and makes the outcome turn on whether the new terms in the acceptance are materially different from the terms in the offer—in which event they operate as proposals, so that the offeror's terms prevail unless he agrees to the variant terms in the acceptance—or not materially different from the terms in the offer, in which event they become part of the contract. This interpretation equating "different" to "additional," bolstered by drafting history which shows that the omission of "or different" from section 2–207(2) was a drafting error,* substitutes a manageable inquiry into materiality for a hair-splitting inquiry into the difference between "different" and "additional." It is hair-splitting ("metaphysical," "casuistic," "semantic," in the pejorative senses of these words) because all different terms are additional and all additional terms are different.

Unfortunately, the Illinois courts—whose understanding of Article 2 of the UCC is binding on us because this is a diversity suit governed, all agree, by Illinois law—have had no occasion to choose among the different positions on the consequences of an acceptance that contains "different" terms from the offer. We shall have to choose.

The Uniform Commercial Code, as we have said, does not say what the terms of the contract are if the offer and acceptance contain different terms, as distinct from cases in which the acceptance merely contains additional terms to those in the offer. The majority view is that the discrepant terms fall out and are replaced by a suitable UCC gap-filler. The magistrate judge followed this approach and proceeded to section 2–309, which provides that nonconforming goods may be rejected within a "reasonable" time (see also § 2–601(1)), and she held that the six months that Northrop took to reject Litronic's boards was a reasonable time because of the complexity of the required testing. The leading minority view is that the discrepant terms *in the acceptance* are to be ignored, and that would give the palm to Litronic. Our own preferred view—the view that assimilates "different" to "additional," so that the terms in the offer prevail over the different terms in the acceptance only if the latter are materially different, has as yet been adopted by only one state, California. *Steiner v. Mobil Oil Corp.*, 20 Cal.3d 90, 141 Cal.Rptr. 157, 569 P.2d 751, 759 n. 5

---

* See John L. Utz, "More on the Battle of the Forms: The Treatment of 'Different' Terms Under the Uniform Commercial Code," 16 *U.C.C.L.J.* 103, 110–12 (1983).—Ed.

(1977). Under that view, as under what we are calling the "leading" minority view, the warranty in Litronic's offer, the 90–day warranty, was the contractual warranty, because the unlimited warranty contained in Northrop's acceptance was materially different.

Because Illinois in other UCC cases has tended to adopt majority rules, e.g., *Rebaque v. Forsythe Racing, Inc.,* 134 Ill.App.3d 778, 89 Ill.Dec. 595, 598, 480 N.E.2d 1338, 1341 (1985), and because the interest in the uniform nationwide application of the Code—an interest asserted in the Code itself (see § 1–102)—argues for nudging majority views, even if imperfect (but not downright bad), toward unanimity, we start with a presumption that Illinois, whose position we are trying to predict, would adopt the majority view. We do not find the presumption rebutted. The idea behind the majority view is that the presence of different terms in the acceptance suggests that the offeree didn't *really* accede to the offeror's terms, yet both parties wanted to contract, so why not find a neutral term to govern the dispute that has arisen between them? Of course the offeree may not have had any serious objection to the terms in the offer at the time of contracting; he may have mailed a boilerplated form without giving any thought to its contents or to its suitability for the particular contract in question. But it is just as likely that the discrepant terms *in the offer* itself were the product of a thoughtless use of a boilerplate form rather than a considered condition of contracting. And if the offeror doesn't want to do business other than on the terms in the offer, he can protect himself by specifying that the offeree must accept all those terms for the parties to have a contract. UCC Sec. 2–207(2)(a); *Tecumseh International Corp. v. City of Springfield,* 70 Ill.App.3d 101, 26 Ill.Dec. 745, 748, 388 N.E.2d 460, 463 (1979). Now as it happens Litronic did state in its offer that the terms in the offer "take precedence over terms and conditions of the buyer, unless specifically negotiated otherwise." But, for reasons that we do not and need not fathom, Litronic does not argue that this language conditioned the existence of the contract on Northrop's acceding to the 90–day warranty in the offer; any such argument is therefore waived.

It is true that the offeree likewise can protect himself by making his acceptance of the offer conditional on the offeror's acceding to any different terms in the acceptance. But so many acceptances are made over the phone by relatively junior employees, as in this case, that it may be unrealistic to expect offerees to protect themselves in this way. The offeror goes first and therefore has a little more time for careful specification of the terms on which he is willing to make a contract. What we are calling the leading minority view may tempt the offeror to spring a surprise on the offeree, hoping the latter won't read the fine print. Under the majority view, if the offeree tries to spring a surprise (the offeror can't, since his terms won't prevail if the acceptance contains different terms), the parties move to neutral ground; and the offeror can, we have suggested, more easily protect himself against being surprised than the offeree can protect *himself* against being surprised. The California rule dissolves all these problems, but has too little support to make it a plausible candidate for Illinois, or at least a plausible candidate for our guess as to Illinois's position.

There is a further wrinkle, however. The third subsection of section 2–207 provides that even if no contract is established under either of the first two subsections, it may be established by the "conduct of the parties," and in that event (as subsection (3) expressly provides) the discrepant terms vanish and are replaced by UCC gap fillers. This may seem to make it impossible for the offeror to protect himself from being contractually bound by specifying that the acceptance must mirror his offer. But subsection (3) comes into play only when the parties have by their conduct manifested the existence of a contract, as where the offeror, having specified that the acceptance must mirror the offer yet having received an acceptance that deviates from the offer, nonetheless goes ahead and performs as if there were a contract. That is one way to interpret what happened here but it leads to the same result as applying subsection (2) interpreted as the majority of states do, so we need not consider it separately.

Given the intricacy of the No. 1714 boards, it is unlikely that Northrop would have acceded to a 90–day limitation on its warranty protection. Litronic at argument stressed that it is a much smaller firm, hence presumably unwilling to assume burdensome warranty obligations; but it is a curious suggestion that little fellows are more likely than big ones to get their way in negotiations between firms of disparate size. And Northrop actually got only half its way, though enough for victory here; for by virtue of accepting Litronic's offer without expressly conditioning its acceptance on Litronic's acceding to Northrop's terms, Northrop got not a warranty unlimited in duration, as its purchase order provides, but (pursuant to the majority understanding of UCC § 2–207(2)) a warranty of "reasonable" duration, courtesy the court. If special circumstances made a 90–day warranty reasonable, Litronic was free to argue for it in the district court.

On the view we take, the purchase order has no significance beyond showing that Northrop's acceptance contained (albeit by reference) different terms. The fact that Litronic never signed the order, and the fact that Northrop never called this omission to Litronic's attention, also drop out of the case, along with Northrop's argument that to enforce the 90–day limitation in Litronic's warranty would be unconscionable. But for future reference we remind Northrop and companies like it that the defense of unconscionability was not invented to protect multi-billion dollar corporations against mistakes committed by their employees, and indeed has rarely succeeded outside the area of consumer contracts.

Affirmed.

QUESTIONS AND NOTES

1. *Northrup* concerns the application of subsection (2), which determines the terms of the contract when it is clear that the writings (or the oral interactions of the parties) form a contract. Its apparent "first-shot" rule making the terms of the offer binding, rather than the terms of the "acceptance" is seen as being only marginally better, if at all, than the traditional "last-shot" rule of the common law under which an "acceptance" that states additional or different terms becomes a counter-offer, which is accepted if the original offeror then accepts performance by the counter-offeror. Therefore, when the offeree's acceptance contains a term that conflicts with a term in the offer, most courts have adopted the so-called "knockout" rule under subsection (2). Under this approach neither party gets its way by virtue of including the disputed term in its form, and the court looks elsewhere to supply the term.

What language in 2–207 authorizes use of the knockout rule?

If the offeree adds a term on a matter on which the offer is silent, then the dispute typically centers on subsection (2)(b): is the offeree's term a material alteration of the offer? In *Itoh*, if Jordan's acknowledgement had not contained the "expressly made conditional" clause, would the arbitration provision have been part of the contract?

2. Problem. Buyer sends Seller a purchase order for a preservative to be used in the wood doors and windows that Buyer manufactures. Seller responds with its Acknowledgement, which directs the buyer to sign and return it, and which states, "In no event shall Seller's liability for damages in respect to products sold hereunder exceed the purchase price of the products as to which a claim is made." Buyer does not sign or return the Acknowledgment. The preservative proves to be defective, causing Buyer's doors and windows to rot. Buyer's customers complain and seek compensation, which Buyer pays. Now Buyer sues Seller, seeking recovery under 2–713, including the amounts it paid to its customers. As we will see later, 2–713 authorizes recovery of these damages, but 2–719 permits the parties to agree to limitations on damages. If the limitation in Seller's Acknowledgement is part of the contract, Buyer loses. Is it part of the contract?

3. Problem. Following a telephone conversation discussing a potential transaction in general terms, Seller sends Buyer a letter, "We will be pleased to sell you 1,000 polo shirts, assortment of stripes and solid colors, at $20/shirt, transportation prepaid, payment due on delivery."

Buyer responds by sending a purchase order that repeats the quantity, price, payment, and shipping terms, but describes the goods as "1,000 polo shirts, assorted solid colors."

Seller ships 1,000 shirts, half solid colors and half striped. Buyer opens the shipping cartons, sees that half the shirts are striped, and sends all 1,000 back to Seller. Seller sues, alleging that Buyer has breached the contract by refusing to accept the shirts. Buyer counterclaims, alleging that Seller has breached the contract by not delivering all solid colors. Which party prevails?

4. Problem. Following a telephone conversation, Buyer sends Seller a purchase order for certain equipment, at prices and other terms discussed on the phone. Buyer's purchase order contains the provision, "Payment will be made 30 days after delivery of the goods."

Seller receives the purchase order, and, after glancing just at the provisions dealing with quantity, description, and price, sends Buyer its standard sales acknowledgment form. This form contains several boiler-plate provisions, including, (1) "Our assent to this transaction is expressly conditional on your assent to the terms on this acknowledgment form, including any terms that are additional to or different from the terms on any purchase order you may have sent us," and (2) "Payment is due in full on delivery of the goods." Neither party communicates further.

In due course, Seller's truck driver shows up at Buyer's dock and leaves the goods without demanding payment. Upon learning of this, Seller fires the driver and phones Buyer to inform Buyer that payment is due on delivery and to request immediate payment. Buyer refuses, but says Seller will receive payment in 30 days. Buyer pays 30 days after delivery, and ultimately, for other reasons, the parties wind up in litigation, and Seller asserts a claim for interest on the purchase price for 30 days. If the contract includes the term on Seller's acknowledgment, Seller is entitled to the interest. Is Seller's payment term part of the contract?

5. CISG and varying acceptances. The Convention on Contracts for the International Sale of Goods accepted only a part of 2–207. Article 19 reads as follows:

> (1) A reply to an offer which purports to be an acceptance but contains additions, limitations or other modifications is a rejection of the offer and constitutes a counter-offer.

> (2) However, a reply to an offer which purports to be an acceptance but contains additional or different terms which do not materially alter the terms of the offer constitutes an acceptance, unless the offeror, without undue delay, objects orally to the discrepancy or dispatches a notice to that effect. If he does not so object, the terms of the contract are the terms of the offer with the modifications contained in the acceptance.

> (3) Additional or different terms relating, among other things, to the price, payment, quality and quantity of the goods, place and time of delivery, extent of one party's liability to the other or the settlement of disputes are considered to alter the terms of the offer materially.

Article 18(1) of CISG provides that "A statement made by or other conduct of the offeree indicating assent to an offer is an acceptance . . . ."

Problem. Sprint sends Toshiba a purchase order for 10,000 cell phones, which includes the terms, "goods must be warranted to be mer-chantable." Toshiba sends Sprint an acknowledgement, which contains a disclaimer of all warranties. Neither party signs or returns the other party's form. In due course, Toshiba ships the cell phones, and Sprint pays for them. After distributing the phones to its customers, Sprint learns that many of the phones are defective. Sprint sues Toshiba. What result under CISG?

Professor Honnold argues that under CISG sections 18(1) and 19, in cases where buyer and seller exchange order and acknowledgement forms with conflicting terms and then both perform, it would be permissible for a court to conclude that neither had accepted the "offer" of the other and that the contract was formed only by acceptance of performance. In that case, it would be appropriate to find that the contract consists of those terms on which the exchanged writings agree with supplementary terms filled in from CISG. J. Honnold, Uniform Law for International Sales § 170.4 (3rd ed. 1999). That, of course, sounds very much like 2–207(3). Do Articles 18–19 support this analysis?

4. Leases. You will recall that Article 2A was drafted and adopted decades after Article 2. Because of the difficulties of 2–207 and because leases usually are not formed by an exchange of purchase order and acknowledgement forms, there is no provision like 2–207 in Article 2A.

5. Revised Article 2. The 2003 amendments completely rewrite 2–207.

The first phrase of 2–207(1) is relocated to 2–206(3), which states, "a definite and seasonable expression of acceptance operates as an acceptance even if it contains terms additional to or different from the offer." The last phrase of 2–207(1), "unless acceptance is expressly made conditional on assent to the additional or different terms," is omitted. Presumably, however, if the offeror is aware, or should have been aware, of the conditional nature of an "acceptance," it is not "a definite and seasonable expression of acceptance."

Section 2–207 itself has been substantially revised. Please read it and answer the following questions.

(a) How would the *Northrop* case be decided under revised 2–207? (Recall that Northrop's purchase order form specifically provided for a warranty that contained no time limit.)

Could Northrop successfully argue that Lair knew (or should have known?) from prior dealings that Northrop would not agree to the 90–day limitation on the warranty? If so, what then is the result?

(b) When will additional or different terms in a confirmation become part of the contract under revised 2–207? (You will recall that the common law permits parties to a contract to modify it at any time. This remains true under Article 2, and 2–209 liberalizes the common law by providing that consideration is not required for the enforceability of a modification.)

Hill v. Gateway 2000, Inc.

United States Court of Appeals, Seventh Circuit, 1997.
105 F.3d 1147.

■ EASTERBROOK, CIRCUIT JUDGE.

A customer picks up the phone, orders a computer, and gives a credit card number. Presently a box arrives, containing the computer and a list of terms, said to govern unless the customer returns the computer within 30 days. Are these terms effective as the parties' contract, or is the contract term-free because the order-taker did not read any terms over the phone and elicit the customer's assent?

One of the terms in the box containing a Gateway 2000 system was an arbitration clause. Rich and Enza Hill, the customers, kept the computer more than 30 days before complaining about its components and performance. They filed suit in federal court arguing, among other things, that the product's shortcomings make Gateway a racketeer (mail and wire fraud are said to be the predicate offenses), leading to treble damages under RICO for the Hills and a class of all other purchasers. Gateway asked the district court to enforce the arbitration clause; the judge refused, writing that "[t]he present record is insufficient to support a finding of a valid arbitration agreement between the parties or that the plaintiffs were given adequate notice of the arbitration clause." Gateway took an immediate appeal, as is its right. 9 USC. § 16(a)(1)(A).

The Hills say that the arbitration clause did not stand out: they concede noticing the statement of terms but deny reading it closely enough to discover the agreement to arbitrate, and they ask us to conclude that they therefore may go to court. Yet an agreement to arbitrate must be enforced "save upon such grounds as exist at law or in equity for the revocation of any contract." 9 U.S.C. § 2. *Doctor's Associates, Inc. v. Casarotto,* 517 U.S. 681, 116 S.Ct. 1652, 134 L.Ed.2d 902 (1996), holds that this provision of the Federal Arbitration Act is inconsistent with any requirement that an arbitration clause be prominent. A contract need not be read to be effective; people who accept take the risk that the unread terms may in retrospect prove unwelcome. Terms inside Gateway's box stand or fall together. If they constitute the parties' contract because the Hills had an opportunity to return the computer after reading them, then all must be enforced.

ProCD, Inc. v. Zeidenberg, 86 F.3d 1447 (7th Cir.1996), holds that terms inside a box of software bind consumers who use the software after an opportunity to read the terms and to reject them by returning the product. Likewise, *Carnival Cruise Lines, Inc. v. Shute,* 499 U.S. 585, 111 S.Ct. 1522, 113 L.Ed.2d 622 (1991), enforces a forum-selection clause that was included among three pages of terms attached to a cruise ship ticket. *ProCD* and *Carnival Cruise Lines* exemplify the many commercial transactions in which people pay for products with terms to follow; *ProCD* discusses others. 86 F.3d at 1451–52. The district court concluded in *ProCD* that the contract is formed when the consumer pays for the software; as a result, the court held, only terms known to the consumer at that moment are part of the contract, and provisos inside the box do not count. Although this is one way a contract could be formed, it is not the only way: "A vendor, as master of the offer, may invite acceptance by conduct, and may propose limitations on the kind of conduct that constitutes acceptance. A buyer may accept by performing the acts the vendor proposes to treat as acceptance." *Id.* at 1452. Gateway shipped computers with the same sort of accept-or-return offer ProCD made to users of its software. *ProCD* relied on the Uniform Commercial Code rather than any peculiarities of Wisconsin law; both Illinois and South Dakota, the two states whose law might govern relations between Gateway and the Hills, have adopted the UCC; neither side has pointed us to any atypical doctrines in those states that might be pertinent; *ProCD* therefore applies to this dispute.

Plaintiffs ask us to limit *ProCD* to software, but where's the sense in that? *ProCD* is about the law of contract, not the law of software. Payment preceding the revelation of full terms is common for air transportation, insurance, and many other endeavors. Practical considerations support allowing vendors to enclose the full legal terms with their products. Cashiers cannot be expected to read legal documents to customers before ringing up sales. If the staff at the other end of the phone for direct-sales operations such as Gateway's had to read the four-page statement of terms before taking the buyer's credit card number, the droning voice would anesthetize rather than enlighten many potential buyers. Others would hang up in a rage over the waste of their time. And oral recitation would not avoid customers' assertions (whether true or feigned) that the clerk did not read term X to them, or that they did not remember or understand it. Writing provides benefits for both sides of commercial transactions. Customers as a group are better off when vendors skip costly and ineffectual steps such as telephonic recitation, and use instead a simple approve-or-return device. Competent adults are bound by such documents, read or unread. For what little it is worth, we add that the box from Gateway was crammed with software. The computer came with an operating system, without which it was useful only as a boat anchor. Gateway also included many application programs. So the Hills' effort to limit *ProCD* to software would not avail them factually, even if it were sound legally—which it is not.

For their second sally, the Hills contend that ProCD should be limited to executory contracts (to licenses in particular), and therefore does not apply because both parties' performance of this contract was complete when the box arrived at their home. This is legally and factually wrong: legally because the question at hand concerns the *formation* of the contract rather than its *performance*, and factually because both contracts were incompletely performed. *ProCD* did not depend on the fact that the seller characterized the transaction as a license rather than as a contract; we treated it as a contract for the sale of goods and reserved the question whether for other purposes a "license" characterization might be preferable. 86 F.3d at 1450. All debates about characterization to one side, the transaction in *ProCD* was no more executory than the one here: Zeidenberg paid for the software and walked out of the store with a box under his arm, so if arrival of the box with the product ends the time for revelation of contractual terms, then the time ended in *ProCD* before Zeidenberg opened the box. But of course ProCD had not completed performance with delivery of the box, and neither had Gateway. One element of the transaction was the warranty, which obliges sellers to fix defects in their products. The Hills have invoked Gateway's warranty and are not satisfied with its response, so they are not well positioned to say that Gateway's obligations were fulfilled when the motor carrier unloaded the box. What is more, both ProCD and Gateway promised to help customers to use their products. Long-term service and information obligations are common in the computer business, on both hardware and software sides. Gateway offers "lifetime service" and has a round-the-clock telephone hotline to fulfill this promise. Some vendors spend more money helping customers use their products than on developing and manufacturing them. The document in Gateway's box includes promises of future performance that some consumers value highly; these promises bind Gateway just as the arbitration clause binds the Hills.

Next the Hills insist that *ProCD* is irrelevant because Zeidenberg was a "merchant" and they are not. Section 2–207(2) of the UCC, the infamous battle-of-the-forms section, states that "additional terms [following acceptance of an offer] are to be construed as proposals for addition to a contract. Between merchants such terms become part of the contract unless. . . ." Plaintiffs tell us that *ProCD* came out as it did only because Zeidenberg was a "merchant" and the terms inside ProCD's box were not excluded by the "unless" clause. This argument pays scant attention to the opinion in *ProCD,* which concluded that, when there is only one form, "sec. 2–207 is irrelevant." 86 F.3d at 1452. The question in *ProCD* was not whether terms were added to a contract after its formation, but how and when the contract was formed—in particular, whether a vendor may propose that a contract of sale be formed, not in the store (or over the phone) with the payment of money or a general "send me the product," but after the customer has had a chance to inspect both the item and the terms. *ProCD* answers "yes," for merchants and consumers alike. Yet again, for what little it is worth we observe that the Hills misunderstand the setting of *ProCD.* A "merchant" under the UCC "means a person who deals in goods of the kind or otherwise by his occupation holds himself out as having knowledge or skill peculiar to the practices or goods involved in the transaction," § 2–104(1). Zeidenberg bought the product at a retail store, an uncommon place for merchants to acquire inventory. His corporation put ProCD's database on the Internet for anyone to browse, which led to the litigation but did not make Zeidenberg a software merchant.

At oral argument the Hills propounded still another distinction: the box containing ProCD's software displayed a notice that additional terms were within, while the box containing Gateway's computer did not. The difference is functional, not legal. Consumers browsing the aisles of a store can look at the box, and if they are unwilling to deal with the prospect of additional terms can leave the box alone, avoiding the transactions costs of returning the package after reviewing its contents. Gateway's box, by contrast, is just a shipping carton; it is not on display anywhere. Its function is to protect the product during transit, and the information on its sides is for the use of handlers rather than would be purchasers.

. . .

Perhaps the Hills would have had a better argument if they were first alerted to the bundling of hardware and legal-ware after opening the box and wanted to return the computer in order to avoid disagreeable terms, but were dissuaded by the expense of shipping. What the remedy would be in such a case—could it exceed the shipping charges?—is an interesting question, but one that need not detain us because the Hills knew before they ordered the computer that the carton would include *some* important terms, and they did not seek to discover these in advance. Gateway's ads state that their products come with limited warranties and lifetime support. How limited was the warranty—30 days, with service contingent on shipping the computer back, or five years, with free onsite service? What sort of support was offered? Shoppers have three principal ways to discover these things. First, they can ask the vendor to send a copy before deciding whether to buy. The Magnuson–Moss Warranty Act requires firms to distribute their warranty terms on request, 15 U.S.C. § 2302(b)(1)(A); the Hills do not contend that Gateway would have refused to enclose the remaining terms too. Concealment would be bad for business, scaring some customers away and leading to excess returns from others. Second, shoppers can consult public sources (computer magazines, the Web sites of vendors) that may contain this information. Third, they may inspect the documents after the product's delivery. Like Zeidenberg, the Hills took the third option. By keeping the computer beyond 30 days, the Hills accepted Gateway's offer, including the arbitration clause.

The Hills' remaining arguments, including a contention that the arbitration clause is unenforceable as part of a scheme to defraud, do not require more than a citation to *Prima Paint Corp. v. Flood & Conklin Mfg. Co.,* 388 U.S. 395, 87 S.Ct. 1801, 18 L.Ed.2d 1270 (1967). Whatever may be said pro and con about the cost and efficacy of arbitration (which the Hills disparage) is for Congress and the contracting parties to consider. Claims based on RICO are no less arbitrable than those founded on the contract or the law of torts. The decision of the district court is vacated, and this case is remanded with instructions to compel the Hills to submit their dispute to arbitration.

Klocek v. Gateway, Inc.

United States District Court, District of Kansas, 2000.
104 F.Supp.2d 1332.

[Plaintiff purchased a computer and scanner from defendant. The parties disagree about the way in which plaintiff secured the computer from Gateway. He either purchased it in a store and took it home in the box, or Gateway shipped it to him in a box. Either way, in the box with the computer was a statement of terms of the sale, including an arbitration clause. This statement provided that by keeping the computer for five days, the buyer accepted the terms. Plaintiff set up the equipment, but the scanner would not work. Plaintiff sued for breach of warranty and breach of an agreement that the computer would work with certain peripherals. Defendant moved for dismissal of the suit on the ground that the in-the-box arbitration clause was binding. Only the portion of the opinion reject-ing Gateway's claim is set out below.]

■ VRATIL, DISTRICT JUDGE.

Gateway asserts that plaintiff must arbitrate his claims under Gate-way's Standard Terms and Conditions Agreement ("Standard Terms.") Whenever it sells a computer, Gateway includes a copy of the Standard Terms in the box which contains the computer battery power cables and instruction manuals. At the top of the first page, the Standard Terms include the following notice:

NOTE TO THE CUSTOMER

This document contains Gateway 2000's Standard Terms and Conditions. By retaining your Gateway 2000 computer system beyond five (5) days after the date of delivery, you accept these Terms and Conditions.

The notice is in emphasized type and is located inside a printed box which sets it apart from other provisions of the document. The Standard Terms are four pages long and contain 16 numbered paragraphs. Para-graph 10 provides

DISPUTE RESOLUTION. Any dispute or controversy arising out of or relating to this Agreement or its interpretation shall be settled exclusively and finally by arbitration. The arbitration shall be conducted in accordance with the Rules of Conciliation and Arbitration of the International Chamber of Commerce. The arbi-tration shall be conducted in Chicago, Illinois, U.S.A. before a sole arbitrator. Any award rendered in any such arbitration proceeding shall be final and binding on each of the parties, and judgment may be entered thereon in a court of competent jurisdiction.[1]

Gateway urges the Court to dismiss plaintiff's claims under the Feder-al Arbitration Act ("FAA,") 9 U.S.C. Sec. 1 *et seq*. . . .

. . .

When deciding whether the parties have agreed to arbitrate, the Court applies ordinary state law principles that govern the formation of contracts. *First Options of Chicago, Inc. v. Kaplan*, 514 U.S. 938, 944, 115 S.Ct. 1920, 131 L.Ed.2d 985 (1995). The existence of an arbitration agreement "is simply a matter of contract between the parties; [arbitration] is a way to

---

1. Gateway states that after it sold plaintiff's computer, it mailed all existing customers in the United States a copy of its quarterly magazine, which contained notice of a change in the arbitration policy set forth in the Standard Terms. The new arbitration policy afforded customers the option of arbi-trating before the International Chamber of Commerce ("ICC,") the American Arbitra-tion Association ("AAA,") or the National Arbitration Forum ("NAF") in Chicago, Illi-nois, or any other location agreed upon by the parties. Plaintiff denies receiving notice of the amended arbitration policy. Neither party explains why—if the arbitration agree-ment was an enforceable contract—Gateway was entitled to unilaterally amend it by send-ing a magazine to computer customers.

resolve those disputes—but only those disputes—that the parties have agreed to submit to arbitration.''

. . .

[In an omitted part of the opinion, the court concludes that it is not sure whether the law of Kansas or Missouri applies to the transaction, but] [t]he Uniform Commercial Code (''UCC'') governs the parties' transaction under both Kansas and Missouri law. *See* K.S.A. § 84–2–102; V.A.M.S. § 400.2–102 (UCC applies to ''transactions in goods.''); Kansas Comment 1 (main thrust of Article 2 is limited to sales); K.S.A. § 84–2–105(1) V.A.M.S. § 400.2–105(1) ('' 'Goods' means all things . . . which are movable at the time of identification to the contract for sale . . . .'') Regardless whether plaintiff purchased the computer in person or placed an order and received shipment of the computer, the parties agree that plaintiff paid for and received a computer from Gateway.

This conduct clearly demonstrates a contract for the sale of a computer. *See, e.g., Step–Saver Data Sys., Inc. v. Wyse Techn.,* 939 F.2d 91, 98 (3d Cir.1991). Thus the issue is whether the contract of sale includes the Standard Terms as part of the agreement.

State courts in Kansas and Missouri apparently have not decided whether terms received with a product become part of the parties' agreement. Authority from other courts is split. *Compare Step–Saver,* 939 F.2d 91 (printed terms on computer software package not part of agreement); *Arizona Retail Sys., Inc. v. Software Link, Inc.,* 831 F.Supp. 759 (D.Ariz. 1993) (license agreement shipped with computer software not part of agreement); *and U.S. Surgical Corp. v. Orris, Inc.,* 5 F.Supp.2d 1201 (D.Kan.1998) (single-use restriction on product package not binding agreement); *with Hill v. Gateway 2000, Inc.,* 105 F.3d 1147 (7th Cir.), *cert. denied,* 522 U.S. 808, 118 S.Ct. 47, 139 L.Ed.2d 13 (1997) (arbitration provision shipped with computer binding on buyer); *ProCD, Inc. v. Zeidenberg,* 86 F.3d 1447 (7th Cir.1996) (shrinkwrap license binding on buyer); *and M.A. Mortenson Co., Inc. v. Timberline Software Corp.,* 140 Wash.2d 568, 998 P.2d 305 (2000) (following *Hill* and *ProCD* on license agreement supplied with software). It appears that at least in part, the cases turn on whether the court finds that he parties formed their contract *before* or *after* the vendor communicated its terms to the purchaser. *Compare Step–Saver,* 939 F.2d at 98 (parties' conduct in shipping, receiving and paying for product demonstrates existence of contract; box top license constitutes proposal for additional terms under § 2–207 which requires express agreement by purchaser); *Arizona Retail,* 831 F.Supp. at 765 (vendor entered into contract by agreeing to ship goods, or at latest by shipping goods to buyer; license agreement constitutes proposal to modify agreement under § 2–209 which requires express assent by buyer); *and Orris,* 5 F.Supp.2d at 1206 (sales contract concluded when vendor received consumer orders; single-use language on product's label was proposed modification under § 2–209 which requires express assent by purchaser); *with ProCD,* 86 F.3d at 1452 (under § 2–204 vendor, as master of offer, may propose limitations on kind of conduct that constitutes acceptance; § 2–207 does not apply in case with only one form); *Hill,* 105 F.3d at 1148–49 (same); *and Mortenson,* 998 P.2d at 311–314 (where vendor and purchaser utilized license agreement in prior course of dealing, shrinkwrap license agreement constituted issue of contract formation under § 2–204, not contract alteration under § 2–207).

Gateway urges the Court to follow the Seventh Circuit decision in *Hill.* That case involved the shipment of a Gateway computer with terms similar to the Standard Terms in this case, except that Gateway gave the customer 30 days—instead of 5 days—to return the computer. In enforcing the arbitration clause, the Seventh Circuit relied on its decision in *ProCD,* where it enforced a software license which was contained inside a product box. *See Hill,* 105 F.3d at 1148–50. In *ProCD,* the Seventh Circuit noted that the exchange of money frequently precedes the communication of detailed terms in a commercial transaction. *See ProCD,* 86 F.3d at 1451. Citing UCC § 2–204, the court reasoned that by including the license with the software, the vendor proposed a contract that the buyer could accept by using the software after having an opportunity to read the license. *ProCD,* 86 F.3d at 1452. Specifically, the court stated:

A vendor, as master of the offer, may invite acceptance by conduct, and may propose limitations on the kind of conduct that constitutes acceptance. A buyer may accept by performing the acts the vendor proposes to treat as acceptance. *ProCD,* 86 F.3d at 1452. The *Hill* court followed the *ProCD* analysis, noting that "[p]ractical considerations support allowing vendors to enclose the full legal terms with their products." *Hill,* 105 F.3d at 1149.

The Court is not persuaded that Kansas or Missouri courts would follow the Seventh Circuit reasoning in *Hill* and *ProCD.* In each case the Seventh Circuit concluded without support that UCC § 2–207 was irrelevant because the cases involved only one written form. *See ProCD,* 86 F.3d at 1452 (citing no authority); *Hill,* 105 F.3d at 1150 (citing *ProCD*). This conclusion is not supported by the statute or by Kansas or Missouri law. Disputes under § 2–207 often arise in the context of a "battle of forms," *see, e.g., Diatom, Inc. v. Pennwalt Corp.,* 741 F.2d 1569, 1574 (10th Cir.1984), but nothing in its language precludes application in a case which involves only one form. . . . By its terms, § 2–207 applies to an acceptance or written confirmation. It states nothing which requires another form before the provision becomes effective. In fact, the official comment to the section specifically provides that §§ 2–207(1) and (2) apply "where an agreement has been reached orally . . . and is followed by one or both of the parties sending formal memoranda embodying the terms so far agreed and adding terms not discussed." Official Comment 1 of UCC § 2–207. . . .

In addition, the Seventh Circuit provided no explanation for its conclusion that "the vendor is the master of the offer." *See ProCD,* 86 F.3d at 1452 (citing nothing in support of proposition); *Hill,* 105 F.3d at 1149 (citing *ProCD*). In typical consumer transactions, the purchaser is the offeror, and the vendor is the offeree. *See Brown Mach., Div. of John Brown, Inc. v. Hercules, Inc.,* 770 S.W.2d 416, 419 (Mo.App.1989) (as general rule orders are considered offers to purchase); *Rich Prods. Corp. v.*

Kemutec, Inc., 66 F.Supp.2d 937, 956 (E.D.Wis.1999) (generally price quotation is invitation to make offer and purchase order is offer). While it is possible for the vendor to be the offeror, *see Brown Machine,* 770 S.W.2d at 419 (price quote can amount to offer if it reasonably appears from quote that assent to quote is all that is needed to ripen offer into contract), Gateway provides no factual evidence which would support such a finding in this case. The Court therefore assumes for purposes of the motion to dismiss that plaintiff offered to purchase the computer (either in person or through catalog order) and that Gateway accepted plaintiff's offer (either by completing the sales transaction in person or by agreeing to ship and/or shipping the computer to plaintiff).

Under § 2–207, the Standard Terms constitute either an expression of acceptance or written confirmation. As an expression of acceptance, the Standard Terms would constitute a counter-offer only if Gateway expressly made its acceptance conditional on plaintiff's assent to the additional or different terms. K.S.A. § 84–2–207(1); V.A.M.S. § 400.2–207(1). "[T]he conditional nature of the acceptance must be clearly expressed in a manner sufficient to notify the offeror that the offeree is unwilling to proceed with the transaction unless the additional or different terms are included in the contract." *Brown Machine,* 770 S.W.2d at 420. Gateway provides no evidence that at the time of the sales transaction, it informed plaintiff that the transaction was conditioned on plaintiff's acceptance of the Standard Terms. Moreover, the mere fact that Gateway shipped the goods with the terms attached did not communicate to plaintiff any unwillingness to proceed without plaintiff's agreement to the Standard Terms.

Because plaintiff is not a merchant, additional or different terms contained in the Standard Terms did not become part of the parties' agreement unless plaintiff expressly agreed to them. *See* K.S.A. § 84–2–207, Kansas Comment 2 (if either party is not a merchant, additional terms are proposals for addition to the contract that do not become part of the contract unless the original offeror expressly agrees). Gateway argues that plaintiff demonstrated acceptance of the arbitration provision by keeping the computer more than five days after the date of delivery. Although the Standard Terms purport to work that result, Gateway has not presented evidence that plaintiff expressly agreed to those Standard Terms. Gateway states only that it enclosed the Standard Terms inside the computer box for plaintiff to read afterwards. It provides no evidence that it informed plaintiff of the five-day review-and-return period as a condition of the sales transaction, or that the parties contemplated additional terms to the agreement. *See Step–Saver,* 939 F.2d at 99 (during negotiations leading to purchase, vendor never mentioned box-top license or obtained buyer's express assent thereto). The Court finds that the act of keeping the computer past five days was not sufficient to demonstrate that plaintiff expressly agreed to the Standard Terms. *Accord Brown Machine,* 770 S.W.2d at 421 (express assent cannot be presumed by silence or mere failure to object). Thus, because Gateway has not provided evidence sufficient to support a finding under Kansas or Missouri law that plaintiff agreed to the arbitration provision contained in Gateway's Standard Terms, the Court overrules Gateway's motion to dismiss.

. . .

QUESTIONS AND NOTES

1. What legal significance does the court in *Hill* give the phone call? Why does the court conclude that no contract was formed during that phone call? What significance does the court in *Klocek* give the initial interaction between the parties? Which court is right?

2. The court in *Hill* does not apply 2–207. *Klocek* criticizes *Hill* for this. Which court is right?

3. With respect to terms delivered with the goods only after a contract is formed, is there any basis in common sense for treating an express warranty differently from a disclaimer of warranties, an exclusion of damages, a forum-selection clause, or an arbitration clause?

Is there any basis in the law for treating them differently?

4. Problem. Buyer walks into Frank's Appliance Store and purchases a Cool–Aid window air conditioner. The entire transaction consists of the Buyer's saying, "I'll take one of those 13,000 BTU models that are on sale at $199.95," and the saleswoman's taking Buyer's check and helping Buyer load the unit into Buyer's automobile. When Buyer arrives home and opens the box in which the unit is packed, he discovers a warranty card that conspicuously disclaims the warranties of merchantability and fitness. Is the disclaimer effective? See Admiral Oasis Hotel Corp. v. Home Gas Industries, Inc., 68 Ill.App.2d 297, 216 N.E.2d 282 (1965). Should it be? What is the substantive difference between the facts in the problem and the facts in the two preceding cases in the casebook?

5. With which opinion do you agree, *Hill* or *Klocek*? Do you think that the Hills and Mr. Klocek knew when they ordered from Gateway that there would be some additional written material in the boxes in which the computers were packaged? If so, do you think that they knew that some of that material would contain limitations on their contract rights? Should they have known that written material in the boxes would contain limitations on their contract rights?

6. What if the Standard Terms document in *Klocek* stated, "This contract is expressly conditional on your assent to the additional terms herein." Would the arbitration term be part of the contract?

7. In *Hill* the court points to practical considerations that favor disclosure of terms only after delivery of the goods: it is not feasible for the sales representative to read a four-page document before taking the customer's credit-card information (page 88). How infeasible would it be for the sales rep to disclose those terms that restrict the customer's legal rights?

E. ARTICLES 2 AND 2A AND ELECTRONIC COMMERCE

Buyer sits down at a computer, goes to the website of an Internet seller, and finds a camera being offered for sale. Buyer decides to purchase that camera. Buyer clicks on the "order now" icon appearing adjacent to the picture of the camera on the computer screen. The price and shipping costs then appear on buyer's screen. At the bottom of the screen there is a "continue" button. Buyer clicks on that button and another screen appears on which Buyer enters shipping address information. At the bottom of that screen there is another "continue" button. Buyer clicks that button and another screen appears asking for credit-card information. The requested information will include at least Buyer's name as it appears on the card, the card number, and its expiration date. Buyer enters that information and clicks a button that says, "Submit order." A screen then appears which says, "Credit card accepted. Thank you for your order."

Transactions similar to the one above occur thousands of times a day. Do they present any special legal issues?

One possible answer might be no. There is no statute of frauds problem. And there is no formation problem because obviously the seller intends to sell, and buyer intends to buy.

As to the statute of frauds issue, nothing in Article 2 requires that the signature be by pen on paper, and nothing in Article 1 requires that the writing be on a piece of paper. Buyer's name appears on the order, at least in connection with the credit card information, and by submitting the order, Buyer has shown an intent to authenticate the order. Therefore, the buyer has signed since under 2–201(39) "signed" includes any symbol executed or adopted by a party with present intention to authenticate a writing. Further, 1–201(48) defines a writing as including any "intentional reduction to tangible form." If an intentional recording on tape of a spoken agreement satisfies the requirement that there be an intentional reduction to tangible form, as held in Ellis Canning v. Bernstein, 348 F.Supp. 1212 (D.Colo.1972), then the contract information on some hard-drive or disk in the buyer's and seller's computers should also be tangible. Even if the image on a computer screen is not tangible, it is tangible once it is printed out.

As to the formation issue, it seems obvious that both seller and buyer intend to contract through the on-screen process.

But a careful lawyer might question both of these assertions. As to the statute of frauds: "Hold on. Are you really sure that a click on a computer screen is a 'signing'? When Article 2 was being drafted in the 1940s and '50s no one was thinking of computer screens. If neither the buyer nor the seller ever prints out the information that appears on their respective computer screens, does the mere image on the screen satisfy 2–201 any more so than a skywriter in an airplane?" Are the zeros and ones on a disk or hard drive "tangible" and therefore a writing under the Article 1 definition?

As to formation: "How can a contract be formed if no human being at the seller's place of business knows that a contract has been made? If the seller's operation is highly automated, this may not occur for days. And if the seller is not bound until some human knows of and assents to the transaction, the buyer is not bound until that indefinite later time either." Can a contract exist if the seller is unaware of the interaction?

Other questions abound. For example, is the buyer bound by terms that he or she has not seen? If the buyer must click through screens that contain the terms desired by the seller, there is some basis for saying that those terms are part of the contract, even if the buyer has not actually read them. But what if the terms are accessible to the buyer only by clicking on a button labeled, "Terms and Conditions of Sale": if the buyer does not click on the button, are the terms and conditions part of the contract?

Further, is a computer printout admissible evidence of the existence of the agreement that it appears to show? Does a record kept only in electronic form satisfy record retention requirements applicable to some types of contracts?

Congress and the National Conference of Commissioners on Uniform State Laws both were concerned that the legal status of electronic transactions like the one described above be made clear. Hence, in 1999 NCCUSL promulgated the Uniform Electronic Transactions Act (UETA), and in 2000 Congress adopted the Electronic Signatures in Global and National Commerce Act, 15 U.S.C.A. 7001ff (popularly known as "E–Sign.")

E–Sign and UETA cover the same issues in very similar language, and E–Sign provides that it does not apply in states that have adopted UETA. More than 40 states have adopted UETA and thus are exempted from the federal law.

The 2003 amendments to Article 2 include provisions identical to those in UETA relating to contract formation. The relevant provisions appear in revised 2–204, 2–211, 2–212, and 2–213. Please read those sections and consider the following problem.

Problem. Buyer goes to Seller's website to purchase a digital camera. The website invites prospective buyers to place orders and indicates that an order will be shipped to the address provided by the buyer within five business days after it is placed. Buyer provides credit-card and shipping information and clicks through the screens necessary to place the order.

(1) If there is nothing on the website to indicate when a contract is formed, is the contract formed as soon as Buyer has clicked on the button showing that the order has been submitted?

(2) If Buyer types on an otherwise blank address line, "offer contingent on shipment by noon tomorrow," will that provision bind the seller or prevent the formation of a contract?

(3) If Seller charges $2,000 to Buyer's credit card, asserting that the price of the camera was $2,000, how can Buyer prove that the price stated on the website was $1,000? See also UETA section 13.

(4) If the order actually is placed by Buyer's 14–year-old son, who took the credit card from Buyer's purse without her knowledge or permission, is Buyer bound by a contract?

F.   CONTRACT MODIFICATION

Wisconsin Knife Works v. National Metal Crafters

United States Court of Appeals, Seventh Circuit, 1986.
781 F.2d 1280.

■ POSNER, CIRCUIT JUDGE.

. . . Wisconsin Knife Works, having some unused manufacturing capacity, decided to try to manufacture spade bits for sale to its parent, Black & Decker, a large producer of tools, including drills. A spade bit is made out of a chunk of metal called a spade bit blank; and Wisconsin Knife Works had to find a source of supply for these blanks. National Metal Crafters was eager to be that source. After some negotiating, Wisconsin Knife Works sent National Metal Crafters a series of purchase orders on the back of each of which was printed, "Acceptance of this Order, either by acknowledgment or performance, constitutes an unqualified agreement to the following." A list of "Conditions of Purchase" follows, of which the first is, "No modification of this contract, shall be binding upon Buyer [Wisconsin Knife Works] unless made in writing and signed by Buyer's authorized representative. Buyer shall have the right to make changes in the Order by a notice, in writing, to Seller." There were six purchase orders in all, each with the identical conditions. National Metal Crafters acknowledged the first two orders (which had been placed on August 21, 1981) by letters that said, "Please accept this as our acknowledgment covering the above subject order," followed by a list of delivery dates. The purchase orders had left those dates blank. Wisconsin Knife Works filled them in, after receiving the acknowledgments, with the dates that National Metal Crafters had supplied in the acknowledgments. There were no written acknowledgments of the last four orders (placed several weeks later, on September 10, 1981). Wisconsin Knife Works wrote in the delivery dates that National Metal Crafters orally supplied after receiving purchase orders in which the space for the date of delivery had again been left blank.

Delivery was due in October and November 1981. National Metal Crafters missed the deadlines. But Wisconsin Knife Works did not immediately declare a breach, cancel the contract, or seek damages for late delivery. Indeed, on July 1, 1982, it issued a new batch of purchase orders (later rescinded). By December 1982 National Metal Crafters was producing spade bit blanks for Wisconsin Knife Works under the original set of purchase orders in adequate quantities, though this was more than a year after the delivery dates in the orders. But on January 13, 1983, Wisconsin Knife Works notified National Metal Crafters that the contract was terminated. By that date only 144,000 of the more than 281,000 spade bit blanks that Wisconsin Knife Works had ordered in the six purchase orders had been delivered.

Wisconsin Knife Works brought this breach of contract suit, charging that National Metal Crafters had violated the terms of delivery in the contract that was formed by the acceptance of the six purchase orders. National Metal Crafters replied that the delivery dates had not been intended as firm dates. It also counterclaimed for damages for (among other things) the breach of an alleged oral agreement by Wisconsin Knife Works to pay the expenses of maintaining machinery used by National Metal Crafters to fulfill the contract. The parties later stipulated that the amount of these damages was $30,000.

The judge ruled that there had been a contract but left to the jury to decide whether the contract had been modified and, if so, whether the modified contract had been broken. The jury found that the contract had been modified and not broken. Judgment was entered dismissing Wisconsin Knife Works' suit and awarding National Metal Crafters $30,000 on its counterclaim. Wisconsin Knife Works has appealed from the dismissal of its suit. . . .

The principal issue is the effect of the provision in the purchase orders that forbids the contract to be modified other than by a writing signed by an authorized representative of the buyer. The theory on which the judge sent the issue of modification to the jury was that the contract could be modified orally or by conduct as well as by a signed writing. National Metal Crafters had presented evidence that Wisconsin Knife Works had accepted late delivery of the spade bit blanks and had cancelled the contract not because of the delays in delivery but because it could not produce spade bits at a price acceptable to Black & Decker.

Section 2–209(2) of the Uniform Commercial Code provides that "a signed agreement which excludes modification or rescission except by a signed writing cannot be otherwise modified or rescinded, but except as between merchants such a requirement on a form supplied by the merchant must be separately signed by the other party." . . . The meaning of this provision and its proviso is not crystalline and there is little pertinent case law.

. . .

We conclude that the clause forbidding modifications other than in writing was valid and applicable and that the jury should not have been allowed to consider whether the contract had been modified in some other way. This may, however, have been a harmless error. Section 2–209(4) of the Uniform Commercial Code provides that an "attempt at modification" which does not satisfy a contractual requirement that modifications be in writing nevertheless "can operate as a waiver." Although in instructing the jury on modification the judge did not use the word "waiver," maybe he gave the substance of a waiver instruction and maybe therefore the jury found waiver but called it modification. Here is the relevant instruction:

> Did the parties modify the contract? The defendant bears the burden of proof on this one. You shall answer this question yes only if you are convinced to a reasonable certainty that the parties modified the contract.
>
> If you determine that the defendant had performed in a manner different from the strict obligations imposed on it by the contract, and the plaintiff by conduct or other means of expression induced a reasonable belief by the defendant that strict enforcement was not insisted upon, but that the modified performance was satisfactory and acceptable as equivalent, then you may conclude that the parties have assented to a modification of the original terms of the contract and that the parties have agreed that the different mode of performance will satisfy the obligations imposed on the parties by the contract.

To determine whether this was in substance an instruction on waiver we shall have to consider the background of section 2–209, the Code provision on modification and waiver.

Because the performance of the parties to a contract is typically not simultaneous, one party may find himself at the mercy of the other unless the law of contracts protects him. Indeed, the most important thing which that law does is to facilitate exchanges that are not simultaneous by preventing either party from taking advantage of the vulnerabilities to which sequential performance may give rise. If A contracts to build a highly idiosyncratic gazebo for B, payment due on completion, and when A completes the gazebo B refuses to pay, A may be in a bind—since the resale value of the gazebo may be much less than A's cost—except for his right to sue B for the price. Even then, a right to sue for breach of contract, being costly to enforce, is not a completely adequate remedy. B might therefore go to A and say, "If you don't reduce your price I'll refuse to pay and put you to the expense of suit"; and A might knuckle under. If such modifications are allowed, people in B's position will find it harder to make such contracts in the future, and everyone will be worse off.

The common law dealt with this problem by refusing to enforce modifications unsupported by fresh consideration. Thus in the hypothetical case just put B could not have enforced A's promise to accept a lower price. But this solution is at once overinclusive and underinclusive—the former because most modifications are not coercive and should be enforceable whether or not there is fresh consideration, the latter because, since common law courts inquire only into the existence and not the adequacy of consideration, a requirement of fresh consideration has little bite. B might give A a peppercorn, a kitten, or a robe in exchange for A's agreeing to reduce the contract price, and then the modification would be enforceable and A could no longer sue for the original price.

The drafters of the Uniform Commercial Code took a fresh approach, by making modifications enforceable even if not supported by consideration (see section 2–209(1)) and looking to the doctrines of duress and bad faith for the main protection against exploitive or opportunistic attempts at modification, as in our hypothetical case. See UCC 2–209, official comment 2. But they did another thing as well. In section 2–209(2) they allowed the parties to exclude oral modifications. National Metal Crafters argues that two subsections later they took back this grant of power by allowing an unwritten modification to operate as a waiver.

The common law did not enforce agreements such as section 2–209(2) authorizes. The "reasoning" was that the parties were always free to agree orally to cancel their contract and the clause forbidding modifications not in writing would disappear with the rest of the contract when it was cancelled. . . . But the framers of the Uniform Commercial Code, as part and parcel of rejecting the requirement of consideration for modifications, must have rejected the traditional view; must have believed that the protection which the doctrines of duress and bad faith give against extortionate modifications might need reinforcement not from a requirement of consideration, which had proved ineffective, then from a grant of power to include a clause requiring modifications to be in writing and signed. An equally important point is that with consideration no longer required for modification, it was natural to give the parties some means of providing a substitute for the cautionary and evidentiary function that the requirement of consideration provides; and the means chosen was to allow them to exclude oral modifications.

If section 2–209(4), which as we said provides that an attempted modification which does not comply with subsection (2) can nevertheless operate as a "waiver," is interpreted so broadly that any oral modification is effective as a waiver notwithstanding section 2–209(2), both provisions become superfluous and we are back in the common law—only with not even a requirement of consideration to reduce the likelihood of fabricated or unintended oral modifications. . . . National Metal Crafters, while claiming that Wisconsin Knife Works broke their contract as orally modified to extend the delivery date, is not seeking damages for that breach. But this is small comfort to Wisconsin Knife Works, which thought it had a binding contract with fixed delivery dates. Whether called modification or waiver, what National Metal Crafters is seeking to do is to nullify a key term other than by a signed writing. If it can get away with this merely by testimony about an oral modification, section 2–209(2) becomes very nearly a dead letter.

The path of reconciliation with subsection (4) is found by attending to the precise wording of (4). It does not say that an attempted modification "is" a waiver; it says that "it can operate as a waiver." It does not say in what circumstances it can operate as a waiver; but if an attempted modification is effective as a waiver only if there is reliance, then both sections 2–209(2) and 2–209(4) can be given effect. Reliance, if reasonably induced and reasonable in extent, is a common substitute for consideration in making a promise legally enforceable, in part because it adds something in the way of credibility to the mere say-so of one party. The main purpose of forbidding oral modifications is to prevent the promisor from fabricating a modification that will let him escape his obligations under the contract; and the danger of successful fabrication is less if the promisor has actually incurred a cost, has relied. There is of course a danger of bootstrapping—of incurring a cost in order to make the case for a modification. But it is a risky course and is therefore less likely to be attempted than merely testifying to a conversation; it makes one put one's money where one's mouth is.

We find support for our proposed reconciliation of subsections (2) and (4) in the secondary literature. . . . 2 Hawkland, Uniform Commercial Code Series § 2–209:05, at p. 138 (1985), remarks, "if clear factual evidence other than mere parol points to that conclusion [that an oral agreement was made altering a term of the contract], a waiver may be found. In the normal case, however, courts should be careful not to allow the protective features of sections 2–209(2) and (3) to be nullified by contested parol evidence." (Footnote omitted.) The instruction given by the judge in this case did not comply with this test, but in any event we think a requirement of reliance is clearer than a requirement of "clear factual evidence other than mere parol."

Our approach is not inconsistent with section 2–209(5), which allows a waiver to be withdrawn while the contract is executory, provided there is no "material change of position in reliance on the waiver." Granted, in (5) there can be no tincture of reliance; the whole point of the section is that a waiver may be withdrawn unless there is reliance. But the section has a different domain from section 2–209(4). It is not limited to attempted modifications invalid under subsections (2) or (3); it applies, for example, to an express written and signed waiver, provided only that the contract is still executory. Suppose that while the contract is still executory the buyer writes the seller a signed letter waiving some term in the contract and then, the next day, before the seller has relied, retracts it in writing; we have no reason to think that such a retraction would not satisfy section 2–209(5), though this is not an issue we need definitively resolve today. In any event we are not suggesting that "waiver" means different things in (4) and (5); it means the same thing; but the effect of an attempted modification as a waiver under (4) depends in part on (2), which (4) (but not 5) qualifies. Waiver and estoppel (which requires reliance to be effective) are frequently bracketed. . . .

We know that the drafters of section 2–209 wanted to make it possible for parties to exclude oral modifications. They did not just want to give "modification" another name "waiver." Our interpretation gives effect to this purpose. It is also consistent with though not compelled by the case law. There are no Wisconsin cases on point. Cases from other jurisdictions are diverse in outlook. Some take a very hard line against allowing an oral waiver to undo a clause forbidding oral modification. See, e.g., South Hampton Co. v. Stinnes Corp., 733 F.2d 1108, 1117–18 (5th Cir.1984)

(Texas law); U.S. Fibres, Inc. v. Proctor & Schwartz, Inc., 358 F.Supp. 449, 460 (E.D.Mich.1972), aff'd, 509 F.2d 1043 (6th Cir.1975) (Pennsylvania law). Others allow oral waivers to override such clauses, but in most of these cases it is clear that the party claiming waiver had relied to his detriment. See, e.g., Gold Kist, Inc. v. Pillow, 582 S.W.2d 77, 79–80 (Tenn.App.1979) (where this feature of the case is emphasized); Linear Corp. v. Standard Hardware Co., 423 So.2d 966 (Fla.App.1982) . . . .

Missing from the jury instruction on "modification" in this case is any reference to reliance, that is, to the incurring of costs by National Metal Crafters in reasonable reliance on assurances by Wisconsin Knife Works that late delivery would be acceptable. And although there is evidence of such reliance, it naturally was not a focus of the case, since the issue was cast as one of completed (not attempted) modification, which does not require reliance to be enforceable. National Metal Crafters must have incurred expenses in producing spade bit blanks after the original delivery dates, but whether these were reliance expenses is a separate question. Maybe National Metal Crafters would have continued to manufacture spade bit blanks anyway, in the hope of selling them to someone else. It may be significant that the stipulated counterclaim damages seem limited to the damages from the breach of a separate oral agreement regarding the maintenance of equipment used by National Metal Crafters in fulfilling the contract. The question of reliance cannot be considered so open and shut as to justify our concluding that the judge would have had to direct a verdict for National Metal Crafters, the party with the burden of proof on the issue. Nor, indeed, does National Metal Crafters argue that reliance was shown as a matter of law.

. . .

When a jury instruction is erroneous there must be a new trial unless the error is harmless. On the basis of the record before us we cannot say that the error in allowing the jury to find that the contract had been modified was harmless; but we do not want to exclude the possibility that it might be found to be so, on motion for summary judgment or otherwise, without the need for a new trial. Obviously National Metal Crafters has a strong case both that it relied on the waiver of the delivery deadlines and that there was no causal relationship between its late deliveries and the cancellation of the contract. We just are not prepared to say on the record before us that it is such a strong case as not to require submission to a jury.

Reversed and remanded.

■ EASTERBROOK, CIRCUIT JUDGE, dissenting.

The majority demonstrates that the clause of the contract requiring all modifications to be in writing is enforceable against National Metal Crafters. There was no modification by a "signed writing." Yet § 2–209(4) of the Uniform Commercial Code, which Wisconsin has adopted, provides that "an attempt at modification" that is ineffective because of a modification-only-in-writing clause "can operate as a waiver." The majority holds that no "attempt at modification" may be a "waiver" within the meaning of

§ 2–209(4) unless the party seeking to enforce the waiver has relied to its detriment. I do not think that detrimental reliance is an essential element of waiver under § 2–209(4).

"Waiver" is not a term the UCC defines. At common law "waiver" means an intentional relinquishment of a known right. A person may relinquish a right by engaging in conduct inconsistent with the right or by a verbal or written declaration. I do not know of any branch of the law—common, statutory, or constitutional—in which a renunciation of a legal entitlement is effective only if the other party relies to his detriment. True, the law of "consideration" imposed something like a reliance rule; payment of a pine nut (the peppercorn of nouvelle cuisine) is a tiny bit of detriment, and often the law of consideration is expressed in terms of detriment. But § 2–209(1) of the UCC provides that consideration is unnecessary to make a modification effective. The introduction of a reliance requirement into a body of law from which the doctrine of consideration has been excised is novel.

Neither party suggested that reliance is essential to waiver. The parties did not even mention the question in their briefs, which concentrated on the meaning of "signed agreement." So far as I can tell, no court has held that reliance is an essential element of waiver under § 2–209(4). One has intimated that reliance is not essential. Double–E Sportswear Corp. v. Girard Trust Bank, 488 F.2d 292, 295–296 (3d Cir.1973), citing 1 Anderson, Uniform Commercial Code § 2–209:8 (2d ed.). The third edition of Anderson, like the second, states that reliance is unnecessary. Id. at § 2–209:42 (3d ed. 1982). See also Hawkland, Uniform Commercial Code Series § 2–209:05 (suggesting that reliance on a waiver by course of performance is unnecessary).*

Not all novel things are wrong, although legal novelties, like biological mutations, usually die out quickly. This novelty encounters an obstacle within § 2–209. Section 2–209(5) states that a person who "has made a waiver affecting an executory portion of the contract may retract the

---

* The sources the majority cites for the contrary position do not offer much support. Corbin's treatise on contracts views § 2–209(2) as a regrettable inroad on the flexible construction of contracts. 6 Corbin, Contracts § 1295 at 211–12 (1962). The word "reliance" does appear in Corbin's discussion, but I read it as a reference to § 2–209(5). Corbin's position is that § 2–209(4) and (5) should prevent § 2–209(2) from doing "serious damage"; the majority inserts a reliance requirement in § 2–209(4) to prevent what it sees as potentially serious damage to § 2–209(2). Farnsworth, like Corbin, is hostile to § 2–209(2). He opines: "It would be possible to give an expansive meaning to the term waiver in these provisions and thereby reach results similar to those reached in cases decided under the common law rule. The clause, then, would be effective only if there had been no reliance." Contracts 476–77 (1982) (emphasis in original). This does not look like a proposal to make waiver depend on reliance; it is a proposal to make "the clause"—the modification-only-in-writing clause—effective only if there has been reliance. Eisler would like to use reliance as part of a waiver because she wants to change § 2–209. She thinks that oral modifications of any contract should require consideration, despite § 2–209(1), and a reliance rule is a step in that direction. [Eisler, Oral Modification of Sales Contracts Under the Uniform Commercial Code: The Statute of Frauds Problem,] 58 Wash.U.L.Q. [277,] 280–81, 300–01 [(1980)].

waiver" on reasonable notice "unless the retraction would be unjust in view of a material change of position in reliance on the waiver." Section 2–209 therefore treats "waiver" and "reliance" as different. Under § 2–209(4) a waiver may be effective; under § 2–209(5) a waiver may be effective prospectively only if there was also detrimental reliance.

The majority tries to reconcile the two subsections by stating that they have different domains. Section 2–209(4) deals with oral waivers, while § 2–209(5) "is not limited to attempted modifications invalid under subsections (2) or (3); it applies, for example, to express written waivers, provided only that the contract is executory." This distinction implies that subsection (4) applies to a subset of the subjects of subsection (5). Things are the other way around. Subsection (4) says that an attempt at modification may be a "waiver," and subsection (5) qualifies the effectiveness of "waivers" in the absence of reliance. See comment 4 to § 2–209. The two have the same domain—all attempts at modification, be they oral, written, or implied from conduct, that do not satisfy the Statute of Frauds, § 2–209(3), or a "signed writing" requirement of a clause permitted under § 2–209(2). The majority suggests that § 2–209(5) also applies to signed waivers, but this gets things backward. A "signed writing" is binding as a modification under § 2–209(2) without the need for "waiver." Section 2–209(1) lifts the requirement of consideration, so a signed pledge not to enforce a term of a contract may not be revoked under § 2–209(5) unless the pledge reserves the power of revocation. Because "waiver" is some subset of failed efforts to modify, it cannot be a right to treat a successful effort to modify (a signed writing) as a "waiver" governed by subsection (5).

"Waiver" therefore ought to mean the same in subsections (4) and (5). Unsuccessful attempts at modification may be waivers under § 2–209(4). Then § 2–209(5) deals with a subset of these "waivers," the subset that affects the executory portion of the contract. Waivers affecting executory provisions are enforceable or not depending on reliance. We know from the language and structure of § 2–209 that there is a difference between waivers that affect the executory portions of contracts and waivers that do not. Under the majority's reading, however, there is no difference. No waiver is effective without detrimental reliance. It is as if the majority has eliminated § 2–209(4) from the UCC and rewritten § 2–209(5) to begin: "A party who has made [an ineffectual attempt at modification] affecting [any] portion of the contract may retract. . . ."

Repair work of this kind sometimes is necessary. A legislature has many minds, and as years pass these different people may use the same word in different ways; so, too, the shifting coalitions that create a complex statute may contribute to it multiple meanings of a single word, the more so because amendments may be added to a statute after other portions have been bargained out. Section 2–209 of the UCC is not a slapdash production or the work of competing committees unaware of each other's words, however. The UCC is one of the most carefully assembled statutes in American history. It was written under the guidance of a few people, all careful drafters, debated for a decade by the American Law Institute and committees of commercial practitioners, and adopted en bloc by the states. Vague and uncertain in places the Code is; no one could see all of the problems that would come within its terms, and in some cases foreseen problems were finessed rather than solved. But "waiver" did not call for finesses, and § 2–209 was drafted and discussed as a single unit. "Waiver" in § 2–209(4) and "waiver" in § 2–209(5) are six words apart, which is not so great a gap that the mind loses track of meaning.

The subsections read well together if waiver means "intentional relinquishment of a known right" in both. Section 2–209(4) says that a failed attempt at modification may be a waiver and so relinquish a legal entitlement (such as the entitlement to timely delivery); § 2–209(5) adds that a waiver cannot affect the executory portion of the contract (the time of future deliveries, for example) if the waiving party retracts, unless there is also detrimental reliance. But for § 2–209(2) the oral waiver could affect the executory portion of the contract even without reliance. It is not necessary to vary the meaning of the word to make sense of each portion of the statute.

The majority makes reliance an ingredient of waiver not because the structure of the UCC demands this reading, but because it believes that otherwise the UCC would not deal adequately with the threat of opportunistic conduct. The drafters of the UCC chose to deal with opportunism not through a strict reading of waiver, however, but through a statutory requirement of commercial good faith. See § 1–203 and comment 2 to § 2–209. The modification-only-in-writing clause has nothing to do with opportunism. A person who has his contracting partner over a barrel, and therefore is able to obtain a concession, can get the concession in writing. The writing will be the least of his worries. In almost all of the famous cases of modification the parties reduced the new agreement to writing.

A modification-only-in-writing clause may permit the parties to strengthen the requirement of commercial good faith against the careless opportunist, but its principal function is to make it easier for business to protect their agreement against casual subsequent remarks and manufactured assertions of alteration. It strengthens the Statute of Frauds. Even so, the Code does not allow the clause to be airtight. Comment 4 to § 2–209 states: "Subsection (4) is intended, despite the provisions of subsections (2) and (3), to prevent contractual provisions excluding modification except by a signed writing from limiting in other respects the legal effect of the parties' actual later conduct. The effect of such conduct as a waiver is further regulated in subsection (5)." In other words, the UCC made modification-only-in-writing clauses effective for the first time, but the drafters meant to leave loopholes. The majority's observation that waiver under § 2–209(4) could nullify some benefits of clauses permitted under § 2–209(2) is true, but it is not a reason for adding novel elements to "waiver." It might be sensible to treat claims of oral waiver with suspicion and insist on waiver by course of performance—for example, accepting belated deliveries without protest, or issuing new orders (or changing the specifications of old orders) while existing ones are in default. Waiver implied from performance is less prone to manipulation. This method of protecting modification-only-in-writing clauses gives waiver the same meaning throughout the statute, but it does not help Wisconsin Knife, for the claim of waiver here is largely based on the course of performance.

The reading I give to waiver also affords substantial effect to modification-only-in-writing clauses. To see this, consider three characterizations of the dealings between Wisconsin Knife Works and National Metal Crafters. The first, which Wisconsin Knife Works presses on us, is that there was no modification and no "attempt at modification" within the meaning of § 2–209(4). National Metal Crafters promised to deliver the blanks in the fall of 1981. When it fell behind, Wisconsin Knife Works had to decide whether to give up on National Metal Crafters (and collect any damages to which it may have been entitled) or ask National Metal Crafters to keep trying. National Metal Crafters may have been slow, but it had a head start on anyone else Wisconsin Knife Works might have asked to make the blanks. Wisconsin Knife Works wanted both to preserve its rights and to minimize its damages, and it did not surrender its legal remedies by trying to mitigate. It was entitled to throw up its hands in January 1983 and collect damages from National Metal Crafters for nonperformance.

The second characterization is that when National Metal Crafters ran into trouble producing on schedule, National Metal Crafters and Wisconsin Knife Works discussed the problem and agreed that National Metal Crafters could have more time in order to get the job done right. On this story, Wisconsin Knife Works valued a high quality product and a successful business relation more than it valued its legal right to prompt performance. Perhaps Wisconsin Knife Works did not even want performance so soon, for it was not ready to turn the blanks into spade bits and did not want blanks piling up in warehouses. So Wisconsin Knife Works told National Metal Crafters to take the time to do it right. On my view this would be a waiver under § 2–209(4). When National Metal Crafters took more time than Wisconsin Knife Works could stomach, Wisconsin Knife Works announced that too much is enough, and it retracted the waiver. Section 2–209(5) allowed it to do just this unless National Metal Crafters had relied to its detriment on Wisconsin Knife Work's words and conduct. Having retracted the waiver, Wisconsin Knife Works could declare National Metal Crafters in breach—but because the waiver excused National Metal Crafter's performance until January 1983, Wisconsin Knife Works could not collect damages for delay. The parties would simply walk away from the contract. See Dangerfield v. Markel, 252 N.W.2d 184, 191–93 (N.D.1977).

The third characterization is the one National Metal Crafters presses here. National Metal Crafters tells us that the purchase orders never were the "real" contract. Instead Wisconsin Knife Works and National Metal Crafters embarked on joint operations to find a new way to make spade bits. The purchase orders were parts of a larger joint venture, which did not have formal terms. As the parties went along they modified their understandings and accommodated each other's needs. The latest modification occurred when National Metal Crafters gave Wisconsin Knife Works a "pert chart" indicating realistic dates for quantity shipments, and people at Wisconsin Knife Works said that these dates and quantities were acceptable. The dates ran into April 1983. This implies that when Wisconsin Knife Works declared the relationship at an end in January 1983, it breached the contract (as modified), and National Metal Crafters is entitled to damages—at a minimum profits lost on blanks scheduled for delivery through April 1983, perhaps even profits National Metal Crafters anticipated through continuation of this relationship for a longer run.

Section 2–209(2) puts this third position out of court. The third story would be a thoroughgoing reshaping of the obligations, which could not occur unless reflected in a "signed writing." The "pert chart" is not such a writing because Wisconsin Knife Works, the party sought to be bound, did not sign it. The discussions could be at most "an attempt at modification" under § 2–209(4), and therefore could be a waiver. Under § 2–209(5) Wisconsin Knife Works could rescind its waiver prospectively unless that "would be unjust in view of a material change of position in reliance on the waiver"—here, for example, proof that National Metal Crafters had already manufactured the blanks scheduled for delivery in April 1983, or had bought equipment with no alternative use. National Metal Crafters has not argued that it had the sort of reliance that would enable it to enforce the executory portion of any modification, and therefore Wisconsin Knife Works was entitled to cancel the contract and walk away in January 1983 free from liability save for goods furnished or expenses incurred in reliance before January 1983. This treatment of § 2–209(5) solves, for the most part, the problem of fabricated claims of modification. "Attempts at modification" generally are not enforceable prospectively—and if there is commercial bad faith (that is, opportunistic conduct), they are not enforceable at all. There is no serious remaining problem to which a reliance element in the definition of waiver is a solution.

Because § 2–209(2) and (5) eliminate National Metal Crafters' principal position, we are left with the first two—either Wisconsin Knife Works stood on its entitlement to timely delivery but stuck with National Metal Crafters to mitigate damages, or Wisconsin Knife Works waived the requirement of timely delivery but in January 1983 rescinded the waiver. The jury's finding that Wisconsin Knife Works and National Metal Crafters "modified" their contract, though an answer to a legally erroneous question, resolves this dispute. Wisconsin Knife Works vigorously argued at trial that at all times it stood on its rights but went along with delayed delivery as a second-best solution. The jury's finding that Wisconsin Knife Works and National Metal Crafters modified their contract—in the words of the instruction, that Wisconsin Knife Works "by conduct or other means of expression induced a reasonable belief by [National Metal Crafters] that strict enforcement was not insisted upon, but that the modified performance was satisfactory and acceptable as equivalent"—necessarily rejects Wisconsin Knife Works's version of events. The evidence was sufficient to permit the jury to reject this version. We are left with "an attempt at modification" that may operate as a waiver, which Wisconsin Knife Works may and did revoke. See also Chemetron Corp. v. McLouth Steel Corp., 522

F.2d 469, 472 (7th Cir.1975), which defines the elements of waiver much as the district court's instruction defined modification.

If National Metal Crafters were claiming damages for lost profits, it would be necessary to determine whether National Metal Crafters detrimentally relied on Wisconsin Knife Works's waiver. But National Metal Crafters does not want damages for work to be performed after January 1983. It simply wants to defeat Wisconsin Knife Works's claim for damages for belated delivery. (It also sought and received $30,000 for reliance expenditures before January 1983, which is not problematic under my construction of § 2–209.) The jury, although improperly instructed, has found enough to support a judgment discharging National Metal Crafters from liability to Wisconsin Knife Works. This requires us to affirm the judgment.

A requirement of reliance will not make a difference very often—certainly not in this case. Any waiver that is more than a condonation of an existing default will induce some reliance. The buyer who asks a seller of fungible goods to defer delivery induces reliance even though the waiver of timely delivery will not affect the production of the goods. When the goods have a custom design, as the spade bit blanks do, some reliance is close to a certainty. I doubt that National Metal Crafters would have produced the same goods in the same quantity but for a belief that Wisconsin Knife Works wanted to have them. A change of position in reliance on the frequent discussions is all the majority requires. Summary judgment cannot be far away. Still, it is better not to ask unnecessary questions even when the questions have ready answers.

BMC Industries, Inc. v. Barth Industries, Inc.

United States Court of Appeals, Eleventh Circuit, 1998.
160 F.3d 1322.

[Plaintiff, BMC Industries, manufactured eyeglass lenses. It decided to become the first company to automate production of the lenses and entered into a contract with defendant under which defendant would develop and install an automated production line. The contract required all modifications to be in writing. The original delivery date under the contract was June 1987. Subsequent written modifications extended the delivery date to October, 1987. However, the defendant encountered a number of difficulties and notified plaintiff that delivery would be delayed. First, defendant said it would deliver in December, 1987. Then, experiencing further problems, defendant moved the delivery date to April, 1988. That date, too, was missed. In August, 1988, plaintiff was concerned that defendant would not perform and asked for assurances. It received a promise from Nesco, the parent company of defendant, that defendant would perform. Defendant finally tendered the production line in May or June of 1989, but plaintiff rejected delivery and brought suit. The trial court held that the transaction was not governed by Article 2 and that under Florida common law a waiver is not effective unless there is consideration or detrimental reliance. The court gave judgment for plaintiff on the jury verdict of three million dollars against Barth and two million dollars against Nesco, and it rejected defendant's counterclaim. Defendant appealed.

On appeal, the court held that the transaction was governed by Article 2 of the Code and discussed waiver under 2–209.]

■ TJOFLAT, CIRCUIT JUDGE:

. . .

1.

Although the UCC does not specifically lay out the elements of waiver, we have stated that waiver requires "(1) the existence at the time of the waiver a right, privilege, advantage, or benefit which may be waived; (2) the actual constructive knowledge thereof; and (3) an intention to relinquish such right, privilege, advantage, or benefit." *Dooley v. Weil (In re Garfinkle)*, 672 F.2d 1340, 1347 (11th Cir.1982). Conduct may constitute waiver of a contract term, but such an implied waiver must be demonstrated by clear evidence. Waiver may be implied when a party's actions are inconsistent with continued retention of the right.

As an initial matter, we must determine whether, under the UCC, waiver must be accompanied by detrimental reliance. Although it is settled that waiver under Florida common law must be supported by valid consideration or detrimental reliance, courts disagree on whether the UCC retains this requirement. We conclude, however, that the UCC does not require consideration or detrimental reliance for waiver of a contract term.

Our conclusion follows from the plain language of subsections 672.209(4) and (5). While subsection (4) states that an attempted modification that fails may still constitute a waiver, subsection (5) provides that the waiver may be retracted *unless* the non-waiving party relies on the waiver. Consequently, the statute recognizes that waivers may exist in the absence of detrimental reliance—these are the retractable waivers referred to in subsection (5). Only this interpretation renders meaning to subsection (5), because reading subsection (4) to require detrimental reliance for all waivers means that waivers would *never* be retractable. *See Wisconsin Knife Works v. National Metal Crafters*, 781 F.2d 1280, 1291 (7th Cir.1986) (Easterbrook, J., dissenting) (noting that reading a detrimental reliance requirement into the UCC would eliminate the distinction between subsections (4) and (5)). Subsection (5) would therefore be meaningless.

At least one Florida court implicitly agrees with this conclusion; in *Linear Corp. v. Standard Hardware Co.*, 423 So.2d 966 (Fla. 1st DCA 1982), the court held that a contract term had been waived despite the absence of any facts showing detrimental reliance. The court in *Linear* addressed a contract between a manufacturer and a retailer for the sale of electronic security devices. The contract included a provision stating that the manufacturer would not repurchase any devices the retailer was unable to sell, and another term providing that contract modifications must be in writing. Despite this contractual language, the retailer filed suit claiming that the manufacturer subsequently made an oral agreement to repurchase unsold devices, but failed to adhere to this oral agreement.

Citing chapter 672.209(4), the court concluded that the parties' conduct demonstrated that they had waived the requirement that modifications be in writing, and therefore gave effect to the oral modification. The court recognized this waiver despite the apparent absence of any detrimental reliance by the retailer—in fact the court never even mentioned any reliance requirement for waiver under the UCC. Consequently, the court implicitly held that a contract term could be waived without the existence of detrimental reliance by the non-waiving party.

. . . The leading case espousing [the view that waiver requires reliance] is *Wisconsin Knife Works v. National Metal Crafters,* 781 F.2d 1280 (7th Cir.1986) . . . . Writing for the majority, Judge Posner concluded that the UCC's subsection (2), which gives effect to "no oral modification" provisions, would become superfluous if contract terms could be waived without detrimental reliance. Judge Posner reasoned that if attempted oral modifications that were unenforceable because of subsection (2) were nevertheless enforced as waivers under subsection (4), then subsection (2) is "very nearly a dead letter." *Id.* at 1286. According to Judge Posner, there must be some difference between modification and waiver in order for both subsections (2) and (4) to have meaning. This difference is waiver's detrimental reliance requirement.

Judge Posner, however, ignores a fundamental difference between modifications and waivers: while a party that has agreed to a contract modification cannot cancel the modification without giving consideration for the cancellation, a party may unilaterally retract its waiver of a contract term provided it gives reasonable notice. The fact that waivers may unilaterally be retracted provides the difference between subsections (2) and (4) that allows both to have meaning. We therefore conclude that waiver under the UCC does not require detrimental reliance. Consequently, without reaching the issue of detrimental reliance, we consider whether BMC waived the Contract's October 1987 delivery date.

2.

Applying the elements of waiver to the facts before us, we hold as a matter of law that BMC waived the October 1987 delivery date. The October 1987 delivery date was a waivable contract right, of which BMC had actual knowledge. We also conclude that BMC's conduct impliedly demonstrated an intent to relinquish that right.

The most cogent evidence of this waiver is BMC's own representation of its relationship with Nesco. Throughout this litigation, BMC has maintained that Nesco, beginning in August 1988, "stepped in and promised to complete the project. In doing so, Nesco expressly represented that all of its resources were committed to the project, and instructed BMC to deal solely with Nesco." According to BMC, therefore, Nesco voluntarily became liable, in the fall of 1988, for Barth's completion of the project. By that time, however, the October 1987 delivery date had already passed. If, as BMC claims, the contract was already breached, then Nesco could never have performed its obligations; Nesco was in breach of its promise as soon as that promise was made, and could have been sued by BMC the next day. For Nesco's promise to have meaning, BMC must have given Barth and Nesco additional time to perform—in other words, BMC must have waived the October 1987 delivery date.

BMC argues, however, that while it agreed to *delay* enforcing its rights against Barth in return for Nesco's promise, it did not *waive* those rights. BMC's argument defies logic. According to this theory, BMC could sue Barth and Nesco at its whim. Consequently, Nesco miraculously could have completed the project the day after its promise, and still have been fully liable to BMC for Barth's breach of contract. Nesco had nothing to gain and everything to lose from such an agreement.

BMC's own complaint buttresses our conclusion that BMC waived the October 1987 delivery date. According to BMC's complaint, Nesco promised "that Barth would *meet dates,* performance and reliability criteria under the agreement, as amended," and that Nesco "ensure[d] that the equipment was *timely* completed and delivered to BMC in Florida" (emphasis added). Because the October 1987 delivery date had already passed, however, Barth could not "meet dates" or "timely" complete the equipment unless the delivery date had been extended.

Furthermore, BMC's course of dealing with Barth evidenced BMC's waiver of the October 1987 delivery date, because BMC failed timely to demand compliance with that contract term or terminate the Contract and file suit. When a delivery date passes without the seller's delivery, the buyer must object within a reasonable time and warn the seller that it is in breach. *See KLT Indus., Inc. v. Eaton Corp.,* 505 F.Supp. 1072, 1079 (E.D.Mich.1981); *see also Harrison v. City of Tampa,* 247 F. 569, 572 (S.D.Fla.1918) ("I do not recognize any principle by which one party to a contract, after a breach by the other party, may continue acting under such contract to some future time, and then abrogate the contract by reason of such former breach").

Although BMC maintained at trial that Barth breached the contract as of October 1987, BMC did not tell Barth it intended to terminate the contract and hold Barth liable for the breach until May 1989. In fact, the earliest indication from BMC that it was considering termination was August 1988, when BMC executives met with [Barth's representative] to seek assurance that Barth would perform. As we have already stated, however, the result of that meeting was a waiver of the October 1987 delivery date, not a timely exercise of BMC's right to terminate the Contract. BMC did not warn Barth in earnest of its intent to terminate until February 1989, when BMC sent Barth a letter along with $100,000 of the $250,000 payment [Barth's representative] had requested at the August 1988 meeting. This letter warned Barth that BMC was not waiving its rights and remedies for Barth's failure to meet contractual delivery dates.

BMC warned Barth again in March when it sent a letter advising of its intent to "hold [Barth] responsible, both for the initial breach and for all failures to meet subsequently promised dates."

Until 1989, however, BMC continued to act as though both parties were bound by the Contract and that Barth was not in default of its obligations: the October 1987 delivery date passed without comment from BMC; engineers from BMC frequently provided advice or assistance to help Barth personnel overcome technical problems; BMC executives frequently visited Barth's production facilities and encouraged Barth to continue working to complete the equipment; BMC even continued to spend money on the project—in December 1987, over one month after the October 1987 delivery date had passed, BMC purchased an additional $71,075 worth of springs and tooling for the machines. In sum, rather than terminating the Contract, or at least warning Barth that it was in breach after the October 1987 delivery date had passed, BMC continued to act as though the Contract remained in effect.

This is not to say that BMC never complained that Barth had missed deadlines; BMC executives frequently expressed their concern and disappointment that the project was so far behind schedule. On April 5, 1988, for example, the Chairman, President, and CEO of BMC sent a letter to Barth in which he stated: "[T]he project is well behind schedule, and each day of delay represents lost savings for Vision–Ease. I hope that Barth will exert every effort to ensure the speedy completion and installation of the equipment and avoid any further delay." But while BMC complained of delays, it never declared Barth in default or terminated the contract—instead, BMC told Barth to keep working. After Barth had spent an additional eighteen months of time and money and, according to Barth, was prepared to deliver the machines, however, BMC suddenly decided to terminate the Contract. This BMC could not do.

The UCC states that when a contractual delivery date is waived, delivery must be made within a reasonable time. *See* Fla. Stat. ch. 672.309(1) (1997). Consequently, because BMC waived the October 1987 delivery date, Barth was only obligated to deliver the machines within a reasonable time period. We remand this case to the district court for a new trial on the question of whether Barth tendered the machines within a reasonable time period.

. . .

QUESTIONS AND NOTES

1. In the first paragraph on page 102 Judge Posner says, "The main purpose of forbidding oral modifications is to prevent the promisor from fabricating a modification that will let him escape his obligations under the contract . . . ." He concludes that a modification is effective as a waiver only if there is reliance by the person offering to prove the modification.

Judge Posner realizes that under that rule, there is "a danger of bootstrapping—of incurring a cost in order to make the case for a modification." But, he says, that course is risky and is less likely to happen than merely testifying to a conversation.

Judge Easterbrook rejects reliance as a requirement for proof, and, at the bottom of page 106, says, "It might be sensible to treat claims of oral waiver with suspicion and insist on waiver by course of performance—for example accepting belated deliveries without protest."

In the following problem, which of the two tests for admissibility of the evidence do you prefer?

Problem. Seller and Buyer entered into a written contract in which Seller agreed to sell Buyer 10,000 pounds of sugar at 20 cents per pound, delivery on July 1st. The contract contained a "no-oral-modification" clause. Seller claims that on June 30th she called Buyer and told him that, while performance was possible, it would involve some difficulties. "I told him on the phone," Seller testified, "that I could get the sugar to him the next day, but that would involve working my crew overtime and far into the night. I asked him if he really needed the sugar on July 1st, saying that if he did I would have it there. He said, 'No, I really don't need it July 1st. I don't want your crew to work all night. If you get the sugar to me by the 3rd (of July) it will be ok.' I thanked him." When Seller tendered delivery on July 2nd, Buyer rejected on the ground that the sugar had been delivered too late and denied ever having participated in the alleged phone conversation. Seller sues.

(a) How would Judge Posner decide this case?

(b) How would Judge Easterbrook decide it?

(c) Would it make a difference if the price of sugar had dropped to 12 cents per pound on July 1st? What if the price drop occurred on June 25th? What if, conversely, the price of sugar had risen during this period?

2. CISG and oral modification of contract. Article 29(2) of the Convention on Contracts for the International Sale of Goods reads: "A contract in writing which contains a provision requiring any modification or termination by agreement to be in writing may not be otherwise modified or terminated by agreement. However, a party may be precluded by his conduct from asserting such a provision to the extent that the other party has relied on that conduct." That language sounds as if it might require some conduct by the party against whom the modification is offered other than the oral agreement itself as a condition of proof. However, Professor Honnold offers this gloss on the section:

The role of the second sentence of Article 29(2) may be illustrated as follows:

Example 29A. A written contract called for Seller to manufacture 10,000 units of a product according to specifications that were supplied by Buyer and set forth in the contract. The contract provided: "This contract may only be modified by a writing signed by the parties."

Before Seller started production, the parties by telephone agreed on a change in the specifications. Seller produces 2,000 units in accordance with the new specifications; Buyer refused to accept these units on the ground that they did not conform to the specifications in the written contract.

Because of the contract provisions, under Article 20(2) the oral agreement to the change in specifications, by itself, was ineffective to modify the contract. However, Buyer's oral agreement could be held to constitute "conduct" that would preclude him from invoking the contract clause "to the extent that the other party has relied on that conduct"; Seller's production of the 2,000 units in accordance with the oral agreement could constitute such reliance. However, Buyer is precluded only "to the extent" of the reliance; he should be able to insist on the original specifications for further production.

J. Honnold, Uniform Law for International Sales § 204, at 230–31 (3rd ed. 1999). Under this view, Article 29(2) really adopts a position like the one advanced by Judge Posner under 2–209(5).

3. Section 2–209 and the statute of frauds. Would the result in *Wisconsin Knife* have been different if the contract had not contained a no-oral-modification clause? Does 2–209(3) require that modifications like that claimed to have been made in *Wisconsin Knife* be in writing? If so, would "reliance" on an oral modification take it out of the statute of frauds? Under 2–201 itself, only specified forms of reliance take oral contracts out of the statute, viz., delivery and acceptance, payment, or commencing manufacture of specially manufactured goods. But cases like Decatur Cooperative Association v. Urban (page 57 supra) hold that detrimental reliance takes the case out of the statute.

It is possible to read 2–209(3) as requiring a writing for any modification of a contract for more than $500, but this reading creates an anomaly. Under 2–201 itself not all the terms of a contract have to be evidenced by a writing: the only essential term is a quantity term. Oral evidence can be offered showing all the other terms. Therefore, if the parties agree originally that delivery will be on July 5th, that term need not be evidenced by a writing. But if they later orally modify their agreement to require delivery on June 30, this reading of 2–209(3) would render the modification unenforceable. Therefore, perhaps 2–209(3) only states the obvious: that contracts for more than $500 must meet the requirements of 2–201. This would mean that any increase in the quantity term must be evidenced by a writing, since a contract is not enforceable beyond the quantity shown in the writing. And it would mean that if the price increases from less than $500 to more than $500, there must be a writing that satisfies 2–201(1).

In spite of the incongruity with 2–201, the casual reader of 2–209(3) is likely to conclude that if the contract is subject to 2–201, any modification of it has to be in writing. Several courts have held just that, though they often immediately go on to suggest that even though the statute has not been satisfied, the modification may be effective as a "waiver." See, e.g. Cooley v. Big Horn Harvestore Systems, Inc., 767 P.2d 740 (Colo.App.1988).

In Article 2A the section on modification (2A–208) does not mention the statute of frauds. The 2003 amendments make no changes to these parts of 2–209 and 2A–208, so this difference remains.

4. Problem. Buyer purchases an airplane to be used as an air taxi. The sales price is $45,000, to be paid $10,000 in cash and the balance at $1,000 per month for 35 months. Buyer, after making six monthly payments, tells Seller that she needs to buy some additional equipment if she is to stay in business, but cannot buy it unless the monthly payments are reduced to $600. Seller orally agrees to the reduction in payments. The parties' written contract, however, provides that oral modifications are ineffective. Seller accepts the reduced payments for six months and then notifies Buyer that future payments must be $1,000 per month and that the cumulative shortage in payment ($2,400, or $400 x 6) must be made up within 60 days. In the ensuing litigation, can Buyer show an oral modification? If so, what are the contract terms now? What additional facts do you need, if any?

Can Seller admit that the modification was made and nevertheless treat it as a "waiver" retractable under 2–209(5)? Or is the no-oral-modification provision treated like a private statute of frauds subject to the rule of 2–201 that an agreement is binding against a party who admits that the agreement was made?

On the facts of the problem, if Seller denies that a modification was made, he will say either, "No, I didn't agree to a modification of the contract, but I did accept reduced payments for a time" or "I didn't agree to a permanently binding modification, what I did agree to was to accept reduced payments for a limited time." Observe that if Seller makes the first assertion, and it is believed, it is a waiver situation to which 2–209(5) applies. See 2–208(3), which specifically refers to waivers by conduct, and to 2–209 as relevant to them.

5. Modifications of sales contract and consideration. Section 2–209 is considered by some to make a drastic change in the law of consideration as it applies to efforts to modify, rescind, or waive terms of a sales contract. Assuming this judgment is correct, were the changes desirable? In thinking about this question, consider how the common law and Article 2 would handle the two cases set out below.

Case One: The seller and buyer enter into a contract for the sale of 10,000 pounds of sugar to be delivered one year from the time of the execution of the contract, the price to be the market price at the time of delivery. At the time the contract is made, the market price is 60 cents per pound. During the year between the time of formation and the time of performance, the price of sugar rises to $5.00 per pound. Shortly before the date for performance the buyer approaches the seller and tells her that an insistence on strict performance of the contract will result in bankrupting him; that he can pay $3.00 a pound and remain solvent; that he is proposing that the parties tear up the original contract and make a new one calling for a price of $3.00.

The seller is unhappy with the proposition, but since she has plenty of sugar on hand which she had acquired at 50 cents a pound she tells the buyer she will go along with the proposed modification. The buyer pays $30,000 (i.e. $3.00 per pound), and takes delivery under an oral understanding that the original contract has been abrogated and replaced by a new one, with a price term of $3.00 per pound. Four months later the seller sues the buyer for $20,000, reflecting the excess of the original contract price over the amount the buyer actually paid for the sugar. Decide the case under the common law and Article 2.

Case Two: Same facts as above except that the price of sugar does not rise during the year between the formation and performance of the contract. The buyer informs the seller that he will pay only 40 cents per pound. Fearing difficulties with the buyer and the cost of litigating any dispute with him, the seller agrees to the 40–cent price, but persuades the buyer to purchase a $5 ticket for a raffle being held to raise money for the health care of sugar-cane workers. The seller delivers the sugar to the buyer, who pays $4,000 (i.e. 40 cents per pound) for it. The seller now sues for $2,000 (i.e. the 20–cent–per–pound excess of the original contract price over the modified contract price). Decide the case under the common law and Article 2.

G.   Options Without Consideration (Firm Offers)

Friedman v. Sommer

New York Court of Appeals, 1984.
63 N.Y.2d 788, 481 N.Y.S.2d 326, 471 N.E.2d 139.

Memorandum. . . .

Appellant and her late husband sponsored an offering plan to convert the 360–unit residential apartment building known as "The Sovereign" to cooperative ownership. By the terms of the sixteenth amendment to the plan dated April 14, 1981, the sponsor increased the purchase prices for all unsold apartments. That amendment also contained the following provision: "However, each tenant is granted the nonexclusive right to purchase his or her apartment at the price set forth in the Twelfth Amendment to the Offering Plan for a period of thirty (30) days from the presentation of this Sixteenth Amendment." Thereafter, but prior to May 12, 1981, the sponsor in oral communications to respondent tenant withdrew the offer to her with respect to her apartment 45G. Nevertheless, on May 12, 1981 the tenant undertook by a letter addressed to the sponsor to accept the offer contained in the sixteenth amendment and sought to purchase her apartment at the lower price. The determinative issue on this appeal is whether the sponsor's offer of April 14 was irrevocable. The tenant contends that it was and that she has an enforceable contract for the purchase of her apartment, and her position has been upheld by the lower courts. We, however, agree with the sponsor that the offer was revocable and that it was withdrawn prior to the tenant's purported acceptance.

It is conceded that there was no consideration for the offer and that it would therefore have been revocable at the common law. The tenant contends however that the offer was made irrevocable by statute.

A contract for the sale of a cooperative apartment, in reality a sale of securities in a cooperative corporation, is governed by the Uniform Commercial Code (Weiss v. Karch, 62 N.Y.2d 849, 850, 477 N.Y.S.2d 615, 466 N.E.2d 155). The applicable section of the Code is § 2–205 which provides in pertinent part: "An offer . . . in a signed writing which by its terms gives assurance that it will be held open is not revocable, for lack of consideration, during the time stated." The offer here gave no such assurance. Quite the contrary, it expressly provided that it was "non-exclusive." Thus, the sponsor explicitly reserved the right to sell the tenant's apartment to others at any time during the 30–day period—precisely the opposite of an assurance that the tenant would have the right at any time during that period to purchase the apartment for herself.

Inasmuch as the sponsor's offer was revocable, its withdrawal prior to acceptance by the tenant precluded the formation of a contract of purchase and requires dismissal of the tenant's complaint seeking specific performance or, in the alternative, damages for the breach of such contract.

QUESTIONS AND NOTES

1. By what reasoning does the court in *Friedman* conclude that Article 2 of the Code applies to the sale of a cooperative apartment? Does it apply?

Assuming that Article 2 does apply, is the court suggesting that if the offer had not contained the word "nonexclusive" it would have been a firm offer under 2–205? Do you think that if the offer had not stated that it was nonexclusive it should be treated as irrevocable during the 30 day period? Is there an alternative way of explaining the reference to 30 days in the offer?

2. Technical requirements of firm offers. It is a mistake to assume that all written offers, or even those that the parties have intended to be irrevocable, are firm without consideration. Note the technical requirements of 2–205.

How strictly should these requirements be construed? For example, is not the purpose behind the requirement that a firm offer be stated in a signed writing to insure that a merchant has deliberately intended such effectiveness? If so, is it possible to argue persuasively that a signed writing should not be needed if other kinds of conclusive evidence can be adduced to prove this deliberate intention? If a merchant, for example, admits that he made an oral promise not to revoke his offer, would the offer be firm under the rules of 2–205?

Is 2–205 limited to transactions involving the sale of goods? Suppose a merchant in writing offers to sell some shares of stock that are listed on the securities exchange and promises to keep the offer open for thirty days. Is this offer firm under 2–205? Would it make a difference if the shares were not listed on any exchange? If the offer was part of a "take over" bid or "proxy fight" in which the offeror was seeking to acquire control of a company?

What is the purpose of the "merchant" limitation in 2–205? Suppose a practicing lawyer makes a written promise to keep open for 30 days an offer to sell part of his law library. Suppose it can be shown that this lawyer knows more about these particular books, and more about the law of firm offers and the doctrine of consideration, than anyone in the publishing business. Is her offer firm under 2–205?

Would it matter if the lawyer practices in the area of trusts and estates and has forgotten everything she ever learned about the law of firm offers and the doctrine of consideration?

Suppose a merchant makes a written offer to sell goods and promises in writing to keep it open for six months. Is the offer firm under 2–205? If so, for how long? Suppose an offer that is firm under 2–205 for a three-month period contains an automatic renewal clause that provides, in effect, that it will be extended for an additional three months unless the offeror gives written notice prior to the ending of the first three-month period that no extension will be granted. If the offeror does not give the written notice-of-no-extension within the time limit, is the offer revocable at the four-month point?

3.   Many of the questions posed above have not been answered to date by judicial decisions. Some of them can be avoided by good drafting. There are other firm-offer difficulties, too, that can be handled by good drafting. Suppose, for example, a merchant in New York on April 1st mails a letter to a merchant in Los Angeles in which the offeror promises to keep the offer open for 30 days. Suppose the offeree in Los Angeles receives the letter on April 3rd and mails a purported acceptance on May 3rd at 11:59 P.M., P.S.T. (which is, of course 2:59 A.M., E.S.T., May 4th). Is there a contract?

If the offeree in Los Angeles mails the purported acceptance on May 5th, is it absolutely clear that there is no contract?

How would you draft a firm offer to avoid these problems?

4.   Section 2–205 and promissory estoppel. In E.A. Coronis Associates v. M. Gordon Construction Co., 90 N.J.Super. 69, 216 A.2d 246 (App.Div. 1966), the court rejected an argument by the offeree that the offeror had made a firm offer under 2–205. It then continued as follows:

> Defendant also argues that even if plaintiff's writing of April 22 is not a firm offer within the meaning of section 2–205, justice requires that we apply the doctrine of promissory estoppel to preclude its revocation. Restatement, Contracts, § 90 provides:

"A promise which the promisor should reasonably expect to induce action or forbearance of a definite and substantial character on the part of the promisee and which does induce such action or forbearance is binding if injustice can be avoided only by enforcement of the promise."

Defendant argues that it relied on plaintiff's bid in making its own bid and that injustice would result if plaintiff could now revoke. Thus, defendant contends that plaintiff's bid is made irrevocable by application of the doctrine of promissory estoppel.

. . .

To successfully establish a cause of action based on promissory estoppel Gordon must prove that (1) it received a clear and definite offer from Coronis; (2) Coronis could expect reliance of a substantial nature; (3) actual reasonable reliance on Gordon's part, and (4) detriment. Restatement, Contracts, § 90.

The Law Division did not think promissory estoppel would apply in the situation *sub judice.* Therefore we reverse. We also remand since it is necessary to determine if the elements of a promissory estoppel case are present. They are essentially factual and inappropriate to a summary judgment. Gordon must show the existence of an offer. The April 22 letter is subsequent in time to Gordon's bid to the Port Authority. It cannot furnish the basis for this suit since it would have been impossible for Gordon to have relied on it when making its bid. However, it is alleged that the letter merely confirmed prior oral agreements. The true facts must await a full hearing.

Similarly, Gordon must show that Coronis could reasonably expect Gordon to rely on the bid. This will depend on Coronis' actual knowledge or the custom and usage in the trade. Gordon must also show actual reliance.[2] And we note that if Coronis' bid was so low as to put Gordon on notice that it was erroneous it cannot claim reliance. Finally, of course, detriment must be shown.

Should promissory estoppel apply with respect to offers that fail to meet the standards of 2–205?

5. CISG and firm offers. Under Article 16 of the Convention on Contracts for the International Sale of Goods, an offer is irrevocable "if it indicates, whether by stating a fixed time for acceptance or otherwise, that it is irrevocable."

---

2. We do not consider whether the existence of section 2–205 of the Uniform Commercial Code precludes reliance on an offer not conforming to its provisions.

CHAPTER 3

TERMS OF THE SALES CONTRACT

If one had asked a lawyer of 150 years ago what the parties' obligations under a written contract were, he probably would have said: "Show me the contract and I'll show you the obligations." This response would correctly reflect the jurisprudence of the times: that the "courts should not make a contract for the parties." Arising out of that jurisprudence were the ideas that courts should avoid supplying missing terms and that the total contractual obligation should be set forth within the four corners of the written document and read as a conveyancer reads deeds—meaning that anything not included is deemed excluded. As stated by a contracts treatise of the time: "for whenever the contract is reduced into writing, nothing that is not found impressed upon it can be considered as forming part of the contract." C. Addison, Law of Contracts 159 (1847).

This jurisprudential position resulted in great certainty, but at the expense of penalizing the parties who had agreed on a matter, either explicitly or implicitly, but failed to write the term into the contract. It also resulted in the courts voiding a number of contracts on grounds of uncertainty, lack of mutuality of obligation, or illusory promise. Because of these drastic results, the courts gradually began to shift away from the early common law position described above, and this shift culminated in the enactment of the UCC. The philosophy of Article 2 concerning missing terms is almost diametrically opposed to the views of the past. Its drafters felt that a better result is achieved by supplying missing terms under some circumstances than by distorting the true meaning of the contract by enforcing it without making these additions or explanations, or by voiding it altogether. This change obviously improves the older law by giving greater effect to the actual agreement of the parties, but it has been made at the cost of certainty, and, accordingly, there is some hostility on the part of some of the bench and the bar with respect to some aspects of it.

In any case, a consideration of the terms of a contract governed by Article 2 involves much more than simply studying the ways in which explicit contractual provisions are interpreted. It does involve that, of course, but it is also concerned with the methodology for determining missing terms and the question of how these terms relate to express terms and to one another. These subjects are considered in this chapter.

As a starting point in determining the terms of the contract, note that 1–201(11) defines the word "contract" to mean "the total legal obligation which results from the parties' *agreement* as affected by this Act and any other applicable rules of law." (Emphasis added). What is meant by "agreement"? Are any and all kinds of agreements permissible? Suppose

121

the parties have not, in fact, agreed on a matter that later proves to be important. Does the UCC impose a term on the parties in that case, enforce the contract where possible without the term, or chuck the whole thing out as being too indefinite to permit enforcement? Finally, how do the parties protect their written contract against the contention that there are missing terms in it which should be supplied in one way or another? These questions are also considered in this chapter.

A.   TERMS OF THE AGREEMENT

1.   THE CONCEPT OF AGREEMENT

The term "agreement" is defined by 1–201(3) to mean "the bargain of the parties in fact as found in their language or by implication from other circumstances including course of dealing or usage of trade or course of performance as provided in this Act (1–205 and 2–208). Whether an agreement has legal consequences is determined by the provisions of this Act, if applicable; otherwise by the law of contracts (1–103). (Compare 'Contract')."

This definition makes it clear that not all agreements are effective and that the agreement itself consists of the express and implied terms constituting the actual bargain of the parties. But questions remain:

- Although a written term is an "express term," does "express term" mean "written term"?

- The definition makes it clear that implied terms may be developed by inference from course of dealing, usage of trade, and course of performance, but are implied terms limited to these sources?

In considering these questions, we start with express terms and then turn to course of dealing, usage of trade, and course of performance.

2.   EXPRESS TERMS AND THE LIMITATIONS ON THEM

When a contract is in writing, one should start with the writing in ascertaining the terms of the sales agreement. As will be seen below, the Code gives express terms preeminence over other terms, and written terms certainly are express terms. Moreover, as we shall see, written express terms displace any contradictory oral express terms that are made contemporaneously with or prior to the execution of the written contract. Thus it may be said that terms found in a written contract become the basic foundation on which the deal rests and that other express and implied terms, if admissible, become the superstructure on this foundation.

Article 2 adopts the general principle of freedom of contract, which means, among other things, that written terms in a sales contract are generally to be taken at face value and understood according to the normal techniques of legal interpretation. But there are limits on freedom of contract. In considering these limits, please start by reading 1–102(3), 2–302, and the Official Comments to those sections.

———

Campbell Soup Co. v. Wentz

United States Court of Appeals, Third Circuit, 1948.
172 F.2d 80.

■ Goodrich, Circuit Judge.

[The soup company had contracted with Wentz, a farmer, for the delivery of all his crop of carrots for $30/ton. At the time of delivery, the market price was $90/ton, and Wentz refused to deliver. Campbell Soup sought specific performance of this contract, which was denied by the District Court. The Court of Appeals concluded that since carrots of the variety under contract were not obtainable elsewhere, the remedy at law was not adequate. Nevertheless, the Court affirmed the District Court's denial of equitable relief.]

The reason that we shall affirm instead of reversing with an order for specific performance is found in the contract itself. We think it is too hard a bargain and too one-sided an agreement to entitle the plaintiff to relief in a court of conscience. For each individual grower the agreement is made by filling in names and quantity and price on a printed form furnished by the buyer. This form has quite obviously been drawn by skilful drafters with the buyer's interests in mind.

Paragraph 2 provides for the manner of delivery. Carrots are to have their stalks cut off and be in clean sanitary bags or other containers approved by Campbell. This paragraph concludes with a statement that Campbell's determination of conformance with specifications shall be conclusive.

The defendants attack this provision as unconscionable. We do not think that it is, standing by itself. We think that the provision is comparable to the promise to perform to the satisfaction of another[9] and that Campbell would be held liable if it refused carrots which did in fact conform to the specifications.[10]

The next paragraph allows Campbell to refuse carrots in excess of twelve tons to the acre. The next contains a covenant by the grower that he will not sell carrots to anyone else except the carrots rejected by Campbell nor will he permit anyone else to grow carrots on his land. Paragraph 10 provides liquidated damages to the extent of $50 per acre for any breach by

---

9. Restatement, Contracts § 265 (1932); 3 Williston, Contracts § 675A (Rev. ed.1937).

10. Griffin Mfg. Co. v. Boom Boiler & Welding Co., 6 Cir., 1937, 90 F.2d 209, certio-

rari denied 1937, 302 U.S. 741, 58 S.Ct. 143, 82 L.Ed. 573; Lord Co. v. Industrial Dyeing & Finishing Works, 1916, 252 Pa. 421, 97 A. 573; 3 Williston, Contracts § 675A, n. 11 (Rev. ed.1937).

the grower. There is no provision for liquidated or any other damages for breach of contract by Campbell.

The provision of the contract which we think is the hardest is paragraph 9, set out in the margin.[11] It will be noted that Campbell is excused from accepting carrots under certain circumstances. But even under such circumstances the grower, while he cannot say Campbell is liable for failure to take the carrots, is not permitted to sell them elsewhere unless Campbell agrees. This is the kind of provision which the late Francis H. Bohlen would call "carrying a good joke too far." What the grower may do with his product under the circumstances set out is not clear. He has covenanted not to store it anywhere except on his own farm and also not to sell to anybody else.

We are not suggesting that the contract is illegal. Nor are we suggesting any excuse for the grower in this case who has deliberately broken an agreement entered into with Campbell. We do think however, that a party who has offered and succeeded in getting an agreement as tough as this one is, should not come to a chancellor and ask court help in the enforcement of its terms. That equity does not enforce unconscionable bargains is too well established to require elaborate citation.[12]

The plaintiff argues that the provisions of the contract are separable. We agree that they are, but do not think that decisions separating out certain provisions from illegal contracts are in point here. As already said, we do not suggest that this contract is illegal. All we say is that the sum total of its provisions drives too hard a bargain for a court of conscience to assist.

While the doctrine of unconscionability was generally unknown in the courts of law prior to the passage of the UCC, courts of equity long have refused to enforce agreements that are so extreme in nature as to appear unconscionable in the light of business practices and mores. This refusal is illustrated by Campbell Soup Co. v. Wentz; by mortgage cases, in which an equity of redemption is found to exist in spite of express words to the

---

11. "Grower shall not be obligated to deliver any Carrots which he is unable to harvest or deliver, nor shall Campbell be obligated to receive or pay for any Carrots which it is unable to inspect, grade, receive, handle, use or pack at or ship in processed form from its plants in Camden (1) because of any circumstance beyond the control of Grower or Campbell, as the case may be, or (2) because of any labor disturbance, work stoppage, slow-down, or strike involving any of Campbell's employees. Campbell shall not be liable for any delay in receiving Carrots due to any of the above contingencies. During periods when Campbell is unable to receive Grower's Carrots, Grower may with Campbell's written consent, dispose of his Carrots elsewhere. Grower may not, however, sell or otherwise dispose of any Carrots which he is unable to deliver to Campbell."

12. Pomeroy, Equity Jurisprudence § 1405a (5th ed.1941); 5 Williston, Contracts § 1425 (Rev. ed.1937).

contrary in the contract; and by cases in which the courts refuse to enforce penalties and forfeitures provided by the contract.

Although the courts of law, as contrasted with courts of equity, had no well-formulated rules to police against outrageous contracts other than the concepts of fraud, duress, misrepresentation, etc., the fluidity of the rules of offer, acceptance, consideration, and conditions and the power of its courts to interpret contract language, often enabled them to avoid the enforcement of these contracts by manipulating these rules or the construction of the contract to get a "right" result. These techniques, however, had the bad effect of leaving twisted law on the books to perplex and mislead lawyers and judges considering subsequent cases in which the same "fireside equities" were not present.

The manipulation of the law and the adverse construction of contract language as covert devices to prevent unconscionable results had other bad effects as well. Three of these unfortunate consequences were emphasized by Professor Karl Llewellyn (the principal drafter of Article 2) as the primary justification for developing 2–302 and bringing the doctrine of unconscionability into the open. First, by avoiding a direct holding on unconscionability, the courts have implied that unconscionable contracts are not really bad, thereby encouraging drafters to reword these offensive contracts and try again. Second, by evading the real issues, the courts have failed to set minimum standards of decency for the commercial community. And, third, by disguising the methods of policing against these contracts, the courts have generated confusion respecting proper methods of contract interpretation. See K. Llewellyn, The Common Law Tradition 362–63 (1960).

Official Comment 1 to 2–302 reveals that the section is designed to correct these deficiencies, particularly the matter of adverse construction of contract and statutory language.

Official Comment 1 also attempts to give some meaning to the term "unconscionability" by listing some pre-Code cases designed to illustrate its meaning. Notice that these cases have to do with warranty disclaimers and efforts to limit the remedies of the parties. These are two of the principal matters to which the courts have applied 2–302.

———

A & M Produce Co. v. FMC Corp.

California Court of Appeal, 1982.
135 Cal.App.3d 473, 186 Cal.Rptr. 114.

■ WIENER, ASSOCIATE JUSTICE.

. . .

A & M, a farming company in the Imperial Valley, is solely owned by C. Alex Abatti who has been farming all of his life. In late 1973, after talking with two of his employees, Mario Vanoni and Bill Billingsley, he decided to grow tomatoes. Although they had grown produce before, they had never grown tomatoes or any other crop requiring a weight-sizer and were not familiar with weight-sizing equipment. At the suggestion of Billingsley, they first spoke with a salesman from Decco Equipment Company regarding the purchase of the necessary equipment. The salesman explained A & M would need a hydrocooler in addition to a weight-sizer and submitted a bid of $60,000 to $68,000 for the equipment. Abatti thought the Decco bid was high, and Billingsley suggested Abatti contact FMC for a competitive bid.

In January 1974, A & M called FMC whose representative, John Walker, met with them at A & M's office. Walker admitted he was not an expert on the capacity or specifics of weight-sizing equipment. Later he brought Edgar Isch of FMC into the negotiations to assist in making the determination on the proper type of equipment. Isch did not say a hydrocooler was required. According to Abatti, Isch recommended FMC equipment because it operated so fast that a hydrocooler was unnecessary thereby saving A & M about $25,000.

The parties discussed the capacity of the sizing equipment recommended by Isch. Walker and Isch proposed a preliminary bid of $15,299.55 for the weight-sizer. They obtained Abatti's signature to a "field order" for the equipment to "secure Abatti's consent" to order the equipment. The field order did not state the final price nor list all the necessary material and equipment. The order was on a standard form, printed on both sides, the terms of which were identical to the written contract which Abatti later received. Along with the order, Abatti delivered his $5,000 check as a deposit. Walker and Isch left a copy of the capacity chart for FMC weight-sizers which had been referred to in the negotiations.

The field order was sent to FMC where the proposed lay-out of the packing shed was analyzed by the engineering department, and a final list of essential materials was compiled. Abatti then received a copy of the form contract in the mail. It contained a list of all the equipment and materials being purchased, either typed in blanks on the front of the contract, or handwritten on an attached order sheet. The total bill was for $32,041.80. . . .

For our purposes the provisions of the agreement which are important are: paragraph 3, "Seller's Remedies" outlining the buyer's obligation to pay seller's reasonable attorney's fees in connection with any defaults by the seller; paragraph 4, "Warranty" containing a disclaimer of warranties, in bold print; and paragraph 5, "Disclaimer of Consequential Damages" stating in somewhat smaller print that "Seller in no event shall be liable for consequential damages arising out of or in connection with this agreement * * *."

Abatti signed the agreement and returned it to FMC with his check for an additional $5,680.60 as a down payment. He never paid the $21,361.20 due "on delivery of equipment." In April 1974 FMC delivered and installed the machinery. A 20-foot extension to A & M's packing house was required to house the equipment. A & M's problems with the FMC equipment began during the third week of May, when it started to pick the tomatoes. Tomatoes piled up in front of the singulator belt which separated the tomatoes for weight-sizing. Overflow tomatoes had to be sent through the machinery again, causing damage to the crop. The damage was aggravated because the tomatoes were not cooled by a hydrocooler, allowing a fungus to spread more quickly within the damaged fruit. Walker was called out and managed to control the overflow by starting and stopping the machine. This effort was counterproductive, however, because it significantly reduced the processing speed. Unlike the Decco machinery, the FMC equipment did not have a speed control.

Abatti unsuccessfully attempted to get additional equipment from FMC and/or Decco. There was insufficient time to set up a new packing shed to hand-pick the tomatoes. Moreover, a search for other packing operators to handle A & M's tomatoes was unavailing. On June 17, A & M closed its shed because the return on the fruit—some of which had been damaged—was inadequate to cover costs. Some tomatoes were sold to a canning plant; most were rejected because they were not cannery tomatoes.

Shortly thereafter, A & M offered to return the weight-sizer to FMC provided FMC would refund A & M's down payment and pay the freight charges. FMC rejected this offer and demanded full payment of the balance due.

A & M then filed this action for damages against FMC for breach of express warranties, breach of implied warranty for a particular use and misrepresentation. A & M dismissed the misrepresentation cause of action at trial. By stipulation the trial was bifurcated to permit the judge to decide FMC's cross-complaint for the balance due on the purchase price and the issue of attorney's fees after the jury returned its verdict on the complaint.

This appeal is the result of a third trial. In the earlier two cases special verdict forms were used. The first case resulted in a hung jury; a new trial was ordered in the second.

After hearing evidence presented to the jury, and additional evidence in the absence of the jury on the nature of the contract's formation and the bargaining position of the respective parties, the court ruled:

> "[I]t would be unconscionable to enforce [the waivers of warranties and waiver of consequential damage] provisions of the agreement, and further that they are not set out in a conspicuous fashion.

> "The Court's ruling is based on all of the circumstances in this case in connection with how the negotiations were conducted, the fact that initially a down payment of—a substantial down payment of $5,000 was made and later on the contract was signed."

Accordingly, the jury viewed only the front of the contract, not the reverse side with its lengthy provisions.

The jury returned a general verdict for $281,326 which the parties agreed to reduce by $12,090.70, the amount already paid to FMC for the machinery. The court found for FMC on its cross-complaint, but awarded plaintiff $45,000 in attorney's fees and prejudgment interest from September 18, 1976.

. . .

The major issues in this case involve the validity of FMC's purported disclaimer of warranties and limitation on the buyer's ability to recover consequential damages resulting from a breach of warranty. Resolution of both these issues turns largely on the proper application of the doctrine of unconscionability, which the trial court utilized in precluding enforcement of the warranty disclaimer and the consequential damage limitation. Although FMC concedes that California Uniform Commercial Code section 2719 allows a court under proper circumstances to declare a consequential damage limitation unconscionable, it argues that unconscionability is inapplicable to disclaimers of warranty, being supplanted by the more specific policing provisions of section 2316. We conclude otherwise, however, and turn our attention to the nature of this often-amorphous legal doctrine, outlining the analytic framework to be used in determining whether a particular contractual provision is unconscionable. That framework is then utilized in finding that the facts of this case, involving a preprinted form sales contract, support the trial court's conclusion that both the disclaimer of warranties and the limitation on consequential damages were unconscionable. We also reject FMC's argument that the consequential damages alleged by A & M were too speculative to be the basis for any damage award.

We then proceed to examine FMC's final contentions relating to the trial court's decision to award attorney's fees and prejudgment interest to A & M, concluding that the claimed breach of warranty is an "action on a contract" within the meaning of California's reciprocal attorney's fees statute, Civil Code section 1717, and that the trial court properly exercised its discretion under Civil Code section 3287, subdivision (b) in awarding prejudgment interest. Accordingly the judgment must be affirmed.

FMC's initial attack on the judgment alleges prejudicial error by the trial court in not allowing the jury to see the reverse side of the written agreement which contained both a disclaimer of all warranties as well as a provision stating that in the event a warranty was made, the buyer was precluded from recovering consequential damages resulting from a breach of the warranty. The trial court's decision to exclude evidence of the contents of the agreement's reverse side was based on its determination that the warranty disclaimer and the consequential damage exclusions were unconscionable and therefore unenforceable.[5] If this determination was

---

5. The court's ruling was also based on the inconspicuousness of the disclaimer and exclusion provisions. As to the disclaimer of warranty, we agree with FMC that a disclaimer printed in boldface type twice as large as the other terms of the agreement is conspicuous. Section 1201, subdivision (10), specifically provides:

"A term or clause is conspicuous when it is so written that a reasonable person against whom it is to operate ought to have noticed it. A printed heading in capitals (as: NON–NEGOTIABLE BILL OF LADING) is conspicuous. *Language in the body of a form is 'conspicuous' if it*

correct—that is, if the trial court properly applied the unconscionability doctrine to the facts of this case—then the reverse side of the contract was appropriately withheld from the jury.[6]

Acknowledging that a limitation on consequential damages may be unconscionable (§ 2719, subd. (3)), FMC asserts the trial court erred in applying that doctrine to the disclaimer of warranties. It contends unconscionability is irrelevant to warranty disclaimer provisions, having been eliminated by the specific statutory requirements of section 2316. (See J. White and R. Summers, [Uniform Commercial Code] 475–481 [2d ed. 1980]; Leff, Unconscionability and the Code—The Emperor's New Clause (1967) 115 U.Pa.L.Rev. 485, 516–528.) Alternatively, FMC suggests the California Legislature's failure to adopt the general Uniform Commercial Code section on unconscionability (§ 2–302) as part of California's Commercial Code precludes the trial court's reliance on the doctrine in this instance.

While FMC's argument is not without force, we conclude that an unconscionable disclaimer of warranty may be denied enforcement despite technical compliance with the requirements of section 2316. (See FMC Finance Corp. v. Murphree, supra, 632 F.2d at p. 420.) Unconscionability is a flexible doctrine designed to allow courts to directly consider numerous factors which may adulterate the contractual process. Uniform Commercial Code section 2–302 specifies that "any clause of the contract" may be unconscionable. The policing provisions of section 2316 are limited to problems involving the visibility of disclaimers and conflicts with express warranties. But oppression and unfair surprise, the principal targets of the unconscionability doctrine may result from other types of questionable commercial practices. Moreover, the subtle distinction between an "implied" warranty and an "express" warranty may do precious little to mitigate the exploitation of a party with inferior bargaining power. Yet as long as the warranty remains "implied," section 2316's policing provisions are ineffective.

. . .

We now turn to the principal question involved in this appeal: Whether the trial court erred in concluding that FMC's attempted disclaimer of warranties and exclusion of consequential damages was unconscionable and

---

is in larger or other contrasting type or color." (Italics added.)

This definition by its terms precludes the trial court's ruling on this issue.

In contrast to the provisions of section 2316, subdivision (2), which require that a warranty disclaimer be conspicuous, the Code imposes no similar requirement as to consequential damage limitations. This is not to say the conspicuousness of such a term is irrelevant; rather, it is one of several factors bearing on the procedural unconscionability of the limitation. It will therefore be considered in that context rather than as an inde-

pendent basis for denying enforcement to the consequential damage exclusion.

6. FMC has also argued that even if the disclaimer of warranty was unconscionable, evidence of the disclaimer clause's presence in the contract was admissible to suggest that no warranty was ever created by action of the parties. But assuming the unconscionability of the disclaimer, its value toward proving the factual proposition that no warranty was created is slight, and substantially outweighed by the disclaimer's tendency to unfairly prejudice and mislead the jury. (Evid. Code, § 352.)

therefore unenforceable. Before we can answer that question however, we must first concern ourselves with the nature of the unconscionability doctrine.

The Uniform Commercial Code does not attempt to precisely define what is or is not "unconscionable." Nevertheless, "[u]nconscionability has generally been recognized to include an absence of meaningful choice on the part of one of the parties together with contract terms which are unreasonably favorable to the other party." (Williams v. Walker–Thomas Furniture Company (D.C.Cir.1965) 350 F.2d 445, 449, fn. omitted.) Phrased another way, unconscionability has both a "procedural" and a "substantive" element.

The procedural element focuses on two factors: "oppression" and "surprise." "Oppression" arises from an inequality of bargaining power which results in no real negotiation and "an absence of meaningful choice." (Williams v. Walker–Thomas Furniture Company, supra, 350 F.2d at p. 449.) "Surprise" involves the extent to which the supposedly agreed-upon terms of the bargain are hidden in a prolix printed form drafted by the party seeking to enforce the disputed terms. Characteristically, the form contract is drafted by the party with the superior bargaining position.

Of course the mere fact that a contract term is not read or understood by the non-drafting party or that the drafting party occupies a superior bargaining position will not authorize a court to refuse to enforce the contract. Although an argument can be made that contract terms not actively negotiated between the parties fall outside the "circle of assent"[11] which constitutes the actual agreement, commercial practicalities dictate that unbargained-for terms only be denied enforcement where they are also *substantively* unreasonable. No precise definition of substantive unconscionability can be proffered. Cases have talked in terms of "overly-harsh" or "one-sided" results. (See, e.g., Schroeder v. Fageol Motors, Inc. (1975) 86 Wash.2d 256, 544 P.2d 20, 23; Weaver v. American Oil Company (1972) 257 Ind. 458, 276 N.E.2d 144, 146.) One commentator has pointed out, however, that " * * * unconscionability turns not only on a 'one-sided' result, but also on an absence of 'justification' for it." (Eddy, [On the "Essential" Purposes of Limited Remedies: The Metaphysics of UCC Section 2–719(2), 65 Cal.L.Rev. 28, 45 (1977)], which is only to say that substantive unconscionability must be evaluated as of the time the contract was made. (See U.Com.Code, § 2–302.) The most detailed and specific commentaries observe that a contract is largely an allocation of risks between the parties,

---

11. In the words of Professor Murray: "One of the fundamental concepts of contract law is the concept of *assent*. The basic idea that parties exercise their volition by committing themselves to future action and that the law provides their *circle of assent* with the status of a private law is fundamental to any discussion of contracts. The two basic questions raised are: (1) Did the parties agree to any future action or inaction? (2) If they did agree, what are the terms of their agreement (or, what is their circle of assent)?"

(Murray on Contracts (2d ed.1974) § 352, p. 743; first italics in original, second italics added.)

and therefore that a contractual term is substantively suspect if it reallocates the risks of the bargain in an objectively unreasonable or unexpected manner. (Murray, Unconscionability: Unconscionability (1969) 31 U.Pitt.L.Rev. 1, 12–23; see also Eddy, supra, 65 Cal.L.Rev. at pp. 45–51.) But not all unreasonable risk reallocations are unconscionable; rather, enforceability of the clause is tied to the procedural aspects of unconscionability such that the greater the unfair surprise or inequality of bargaining power, the less unreasonable the risk reallocation which will be tolerated.

... [We] must now determine whether the trial court in this case was correct in concluding that the clauses in the FMC form contract disclaiming all warranties and excluding consequential damages were unconscionable. In doing so, we keep in mind that while unconscionability is ultimately a question of law, numerous factual inquiries bear upon that question. The business conditions under which the contract was formed directly affect the parties' relative bargaining power, reasonable expectations, and the commercial reasonableness of the risk allocation as provided in the written agreement. To the extent there are conflicts in the evidence or in the factual inferences which may be drawn therefrom, we must assume a set of facts consistent with the court's finding of unconscionability if such an assumption is supported by substantial evidence.

Turning first to the procedural aspects of unconscionability, we note at the outset that this contract arises in a commercial context between an enormous diversified corporation (FMC) and a relatively small but experienced farming company (A & M). Generally, " * * * courts have not been solicitous of businessmen in the name of unconscionability." (White and Summers, supra, § 4–9 at p. 170.) This is probably because courts view businessmen as possessed of a greater degree of commercial understanding and substantially more economic muscle than the ordinary consumer. Hence, a businessman usually has a more difficult time establishing procedural unconscionability in the sense of either "unfair surprise" or "unequal bargaining power."

Nevertheless, generalizations are always subject to exceptions and categorization is rarely an adequate substitute for analysis. With increasing frequency, courts have begun to recognize that experienced but legally unsophisticated businessmen may be unfairly surprised by unconscionable contract terms (see, e.g., Weaver v. American Oil Company, supra, 257 Ind. 458, 276 N.E.2d 144; Schroeder v. Fageol Motors, Inc., supra, 544 P.2d at p. 24), and that even large business entities may have *relatively* little bargaining power, depending on the identity of the other contracting party and the commercial circumstances surrounding the agreement. (See, e.g., Graham v. Scissor–Tail, Inc., [1981)] 28 Cal.3d [807,] 818–819, 171 Cal.Rptr. 604, 623 P.2d 165; Allen v. Michigan Bell Telephone Company (1969) 18 Mich.App. 632, 171 N.W.2d 689, 693; Industralease Automated & Scientific Eq. Corp., Etc.,[(1977), 58 A.D.2d 482], 396 N.Y.S.2d [427,] 432.) This recognition rests on the conviction that the social benefits associated with freedom of contract are severely skewed where it appears that had the party actually been aware of the term to which he "agreed" or had he any real choice in the matter, he would never have assented to inclusion of the term.

Both aspects of procedural unconscionability appear to be present on the facts of this case. Although the printing used on the warranty disclaimer was conspicuous, the terms of the consequential damage exclusion are not particularly apparent, being only slightly larger than most of the other contract text. Both provisions appear in the middle of the back page of a long preprinted form contract which was only casually shown to Abatti. It was never suggested to him, either verbally or in writing, that he read the back of the form. Abatti testified he never read the reverse side terms. There was thus sufficient evidence before the trial court to conclude that Abatti was in fact surprised by the warranty disclaimer and the consequential damage exclusion. How "unfair" his surprise was is subject to some dispute. He certainly had the opportunity to read the back of the contract or to seek the advice of a lawyer. Yet as a factual matter, given the complexity of the terms and FMC's failure to direct his attention to them, Abatti's omission may not be totally unreasonable. In this regard, the comments of the Indiana Supreme Court in Weaver v. American Oil Company, supra, 276 N.E.2d at pp. 147–148 are apposite:

> "The burden should be on the party submitting [a standard contract] in printed form to show that the other party had knowledge of any unusual or unconscionable terms contained therein. The principle should be the same as that applicable to implied warranties, namely that a package of goods sold to a purchaser is fit for the purposes intended and contains no harmful materials other than that represented."

Here, FMC made no attempt to provide A & M with the requisite knowledge of the disclaimer or the exclusion. In fact, one suspects that the length, complexity and obtuseness of most form contracts may be due at least in part to the seller's preference that the buyer will be dissuaded from reading that to which he is supposedly agreeing. This process almost inevitably results in a one-sided "contract."

Even if we ignore any suggestion of unfair surprise, there is ample evidence of unequal bargaining power here and a lack of any real negotiation over the terms of the contract. Although it was conceded that A & M was a large-scale farming enterprise by Imperial Valley standards, employing five persons on a regular basis and up to fifty seasonal employees at harvest time, and that Abatti was farming some 8,000 acres in 1974, FMC Corporation is in an entirely different category. The 1974 gross sales of the Agriculture Machinery Division alone amounted to $40 million. More importantly, the terms on the FMC form contract were standard. FMC salesmen were not authorized to negotiate any of the terms appearing on the reverse side of the preprinted contract.[13] Although FMC contends that

---

13. The transcript of FMC salesman John Walker's testimony reads as follows:

"Q All right. Now do you negotiate the terms of those contracts, or are they

in some special instances, individual contracts are negotiated, A & M w
never made aware of that option. The sum total of these circumstances
leads to the conclusion that this contract was a "bargain" only in the most
general sense of the word.

Although the procedural aspects of unconscionability are present in
this case, we suspect the substantive unconscionability of the disclaimer
and exclusion provisions contributed equally to the trial court's ultimate
conclusion. As to the disclaimer of warranties, the facts of this case support
the trial court's conclusion that such disclaimer was commercially unreasonable. The warranty allegedly breached by FMC went to the basic
performance characteristics of the product. In attempting to disclaim this
and all other warranties, FMC was in essence guarantying nothing about
what the product would do. Since a product's performance forms the
fundamental basis for a sales contract, it is patently unreasonable to
assume that a buyer would purchase a standardized mass-produced product
from an industry seller without any enforceable performance standards.
From a social perspective, risk of loss is most appropriately borne by the
party best able to prevent its occurrence. (Escola v. Coca Cola Bottling Co.
(1944) 24 Cal.2d 453, 462, 150 P.2d 436 (conc. opn. of Traynor, J.); Rodgers
v. Kemper Constr. Co. (1975) 50 Cal.App.3d 608, 618, 124 Cal.Rptr. 143;
Holmes, The Common Law (1881) p. 117.) Rarely would the buyer be in a
better position than the manufacturer-seller to evaluate the performance
characteristics of a machine.

In this case, moreover, the evidence establishes that A & M had no
previous experience with weight-sizing machines and was forced to rely on
the expertise of FMC in recommending the necessary equipment. FMC was
abundantly aware of this fact. The jury here necessarily found that FMC
either expressly or impliedly guaranteed a performance level which the
machine was unable to meet. Especially where an inexperienced buyer is
concerned, the seller's performance representations are absolutely necessary to allow the buyer to make an intelligent choice among the competitive
options available. A seller's attempt, through the use of a disclaimer, to
prevent the buyer from reasonably relying on such representations calls
into question the commercial reasonableness of the agreement and may
well be substantively unconscionable. The trial court's conclusion to that
effect is amply supported by the record before us.

As to the exclusion of consequential damages, several factors combine
to suggest that the exclusion was unreasonable on the facts of this case.
Consequential damages are a commercially recognized type of damage
actually suffered by A & M due to FMC's breach.[14] A party " * * * should

preprinted and that's the way you use
them?

"A They are sent by our legal department, with the exception of payment
terms are negotiable, but not the 'Where-
ases' and Wherefores."

"Q So you don't separately negotiate the
terms on the back and the other terms,
other than payment terms?

"A I'm not empowered to do that, sir."

14.   In the absence of an exclusion, the
code provides that consequential damages are
generally recoverable. (§§ 2714, subd. (3) and

heir existence in the absence of being informed to the
chroeder v. Fageol Motors, Inc., supra, 544 P.2d at p.
particularly important given the commercial realities
ontract was executed. If the seller's warranty was
ntial damages were not merely "reasonably foresee-
plicitly obvious. All parties were aware that once the
ipen, they all had to be harvested and packed within a
od of time.

supporting the trial court's determination involves the
damages and relates directly to the allocation of risks
foundation of the contractual bargain. It has been
suggested that "risk shifting is socially expensive and should not be
undertaken in the absence of a good reason. An even better reason is
required when to so shift is contrary to a contract freely negotiated." (S.M.
Wilson & Co. v. Smith Intern., Inc. (9th Cir.1978) 587 F.2d 1363, 1375.)
But as we noted previously, FMC was the only party reasonably able to
prevent this loss by not selling A & M a machine inadequate to meet its
expressed needs. "If there is a type of risk allocation that should be
subjected to special scrutiny, it is probably the shifting to one party of a
risk that *only* the other party can avoid." (Eddy, supra, 65 Cal.L.Rev. at p.
47, italics in original.)

In summary, our review of the totality of circumstances in this case,
including the business environment within which the contract was executed, supports the trial court's determination that the disclaimer of warranties and the exclusion of consequential damages in FMC's form contract
were unconscionable and therefore unenforceable. When non-negotiable
terms on preprinted form agreements combine with disparate bargaining
power, resulting in the allocation of commercial risks in a socially or
economically unreasonable manner, the concept of unconscionability as
codified in Uniform Commercial Code sections 2–302 and 2–719, subdivision (3), furnishes legal justification for refusing enforcement of the offensive result. . . .

The Judgment is affirmed.

QUESTIONS AND NOTES

1. On page 130 the court states that unconscionability has both a procedural and a substantive element. This characterization of unconscionability

2715, subd. (2).) The general rule regarding
limitations on available remedies was stated
by the court in Chemetron Corporation v.
McLouth Steel Corporation (N.D.Ill.1974)
381 F.Supp. 245, 250:

"While parties may agree to limit the
remedies for breach of their contract, the

policy of the Uniform Commercial Code
disfavors limitations and specifically provides for their deletion if they would act
to deprive a contracting party of reasonable protection against breach." (Fn.
omitted.)

originated in Williams v. Walker–Thomas Furniture Co., 350 F.2d 445 (D.C.Cir.1965), and Leff, Unconscionability: The Emperor's New Clause, 115 U.Pa.L.Rev. 485 (1967). The characterization has proven very durable, and courts continue to rely on it.

2. With respect to the procedural element of unconscionability, the court mentions oppression and surprise. In what way was there oppression in *A & M Produce*? In what way was there surprise?

Would the reasoning or the result in *A & M Produce* have been affected if plaintiff had seen the disclaimer and objected to it, but assented when defendant replied, "Look, this is the way we do business. Once we install the equipment, we're finished. Fine tuning and maintenance are up to you. Do you still want it?"

3. Why does the court conclude that the substantive element of unconscionability is present? Since 2–316 explicitly permits the seller to disclaim implied warranties, how can the court reach this conclusion? In view of the court's conclusion, is it possible for a seller to disclaim implied warranties: notwithstanding 2–316, when will a disclaimer *not* be unconscionable?

4. Unconscionability in commercial transactions. A few other courts have held contracts between two business entities to be unconscionable, but in most commercial cases the courts have rejected claims of unconscionability. E.g., Keystone Aeronautics Corp. v. R.J. Enstrom Corp., 499 F.2d 146 (3d Cir.1974) ("A social policy aimed at protecting the average consumer by prohibiting blanket immunization of a manufacturer or seller through the use of standardized disclaimers engenders little resistance. But when the setting is changed and the buyer and seller are both business entities, in a position where there may be effective and fair bargaining, the social policy loses its raison d'etre"); Potomac Elec. Power Co. v. Westinghouse Electric Corp., 385 F.Supp. 572 (D.D.C.1974) ("The negotiated agreement between these parties was not a contract between two small unknowledgeable shopkeepers but between two sophisticated corporations each with comparable bargaining power and fully aware of what they were doing. The negotiations leading to the consummation of the contract were deliberate, detailed and consumed more than two years. [The buyer's] representatives were experienced and the final agreement was reviewed by their corporate legal staff. While the evidence shows that other than Westinghouse, there was only one other domestic manufacturer with the capability of marketing the turbine-generator, there is nothing to indicate that [the buyer] was precluded from contracting with that manufacturer or even foreign manufacturers. Nor is there any evidence in the record showing that [the buyer] was a reluctant and unwilling purchaser, overreached and forced to yield to onerous terms imposed by Westinghouse"); KKO, Inc. v. Honeywell, Inc., 517 F.Supp. 892 (N.D.Ill.1981) ("Although plaintiffs have argued vigorously that Honeywell's conduct in this matter was deceitful, fraudulent and in violation of its obligations under the warranty clause, they have all but ignored the factual issue critical to unconscionability claims: the relative bargaining positions of the parties and the consequences of those relative strengths when the contract was entered into . . . . Plaintiffs have been in the business of manufacturing and selling commercial cooking equipment for over forty years and are among the largest distributors of fryers in the country.'') Additional cases are collected in J. White & R. Summers, Uniform Commercial Code, 4th ed. (1995), § 4–9 n.2.

5. Campbell Soup v. Wentz revisited. In view of the text of section 2–302, the discussion in *A & M Produce* and the cases cited in note 4 supra, how do you think Campbell Soup v. Wentz would be decided today under the UCC?

Note that *Campbell Soup* involved a seller alleging that the buyer had made an unconscionable contract. Does 2–302 operate against buyers?

Assuming that paragraph 9 of the Campbell Soup–Wentz contract is unconscionable under 2–302, could it be redrafted to satisfy the requirements of that section and still give Campbell Soup all the protection it needs? Start by asking yourself why paragraph 9 is important to Campbell. Then try to accomplish that result in a way that will satisfy 2–302. This exercise may show you what Professor Llewellyn meant, and few understood, when he stated that the doctrine of unconscionability doesn't come into play unless one party tries to take "80% of the pie." Statement of Karl Llewellyn, Feb. 15, 1954, 1954 Hearings N.Y.L.Rev.Comm., 1 N.Y.L.Rev. Comm. Rep.U.C.C. 177 (1954).

6. Unconscionability in consumer transactions. Buyers in consumer transactions have had somewhat more success in arguing unconscionability. In one early case, the court held that the price term was unconscionable but had difficulty justifying its conclusion. Jones v. Star Credit Corp., 59 Misc.2d 189, 298 N.Y.S.2d 264 (Spec.Term 1969) ("Concededly, deciding the issue is substantially easier than explaining it.") For the most part, however, the courts have applied the two-part test articulated in *A & M Produce*.

In recent years the most frequently raised issues of unconscionability have concerned arbitration clauses like the one in Hill v. Gateway 2000, Inc., on page 86 supra. Was the procedural element of unconscionability present in *Hill*? Was the substantive element present? In considering unconscionability in the context of arbitration clauses, courts have focused on the extent to which the agreement

- imposes costs on the consumer that are higher than the costs to litigate
- specifies a situs of arbitration that forecloses participation by the consumer
- removes common-law or statutory remedies, including the right to attorney's fees, that would be available in litigation
- shortens the period for asserting a claim
- specifies an arbitration mechanism that is biased in favor of the merchant who has selected it
- obligates the consumer to arbitrate but leaves the merchant free to litigate
- precludes the consumer from proceeding by way of class action.

7. UCCC. An alternative approach to unconscionability in consumer transactions appears in the Uniform Consumer Credit Code (UCCC, or U3C), which was drafted 40 years ago during the period in which Article 2 was being widely enacted. Sections 5.108 and 6.111 of the UCCC authorize courts to grant relief from an unconscionable contract. Section 6.111(3) elaborates:

> (3) In applying this section, consideration shall be given to each of the following factors, among others:

> (a) belief by the creditor at the time consumer credit sales, consumer leases, or consumer loans are made that there was no reasonable probability of payment in full of the obligation by the debtor;

> (b) in the case of consumer credit sales or consumer leases, knowledge by the seller or lessor at the time of the sale or lease of the inability of the buyer or lessee to receive substantial benefits from the property or services sold or leased;

> (c) in the case of consumer credit sales or consumer leases, gross disparity between the price of the property or services sold or leased and the value of the property or services measured by the price at which similar property or services are readily obtainable in credit transactions by like buyers or lessees;

> (d) the fact that the creditor contracted for or received separate charges for insurance with respect to consumer credit sales or consumer loans with the effect of making the sales or loans, considered as a whole, unconscionable; and

> (e) the fact that the respondent has knowingly taken advantage of the inability of the debtor reasonably to protect his interests by reason of physical or mental infirmities, ignorance, illiteracy or inability to understand the language of the agreement, or similar factors.

The 2003 amendments to Article 2 do not elaborate on the elements of unconscionability in the text of 2–302.

8. Unconscionability in lease transactions. In 2A–108(1) Article 2A tracks 2–302. That section also, however, contains provisions that go further. Subsection (2) provides that, in a consumer lease, the court can grant appropriate relief if a lease contract or any provision of it has been induced by unconscionable conduct. In addition, it provides that relief can be granted for unconscionable conduct in the collection of a claim arising under a lease contract. Subsection (4) permits an award of attorney's fees to a consumer who successfully asserts an unconscionability claim under 2A–108. Presumably, there is no reason of principle for a different rule as to consumer leases than consumer sales, but the 2003 revisions preserve this difference between Article 2 and 2A.

9. CISG and unconscionability. The Convention on Contracts for the International Sale of Goods does not contain a provision like 2–302. However, Article 4 of the Convention provides that the Convention "is not concerned with: (a) the validity of the contract or of any of its provisions or of any usage." Unconscionability may be viewed as an issue of "validity." If a contract, under conflict-of-law rules, is subject to the law of a state of the United States, the court could appropriately apply 2–302 and find the contract or a clause thereof unconscionable, i.e. invalid.

10. Mandatory Code rules that cannot be varied by agreement. Section 1–102(3) (1–302(b) in revised Article 1) is clear in its provision that the parties are not competent to disclaim their "obligations of good faith, diligence, reasonableness and care as provided by the act." On the other hand, that same section empowers them to determine the standards by which the performance of these obligations is to be measured if those standards are not manifestly unreasonable. For example, a provision in a sales contract requiring a commercial buyer to give notice of any defect in goods within 15 days after their receipt on pain of losing all remedies for breach was held to be manifestly unreasonable and not permitted by section 1–102(3), even though the seller and buyer were commercial giants. See Neville Chemical Co. v. Union Carbide Corp., 422 F.2d 1205 (3d Cir.1970). Presumably, an agreement giving the buyer a longer period in which to discover defects but requiring it, then, to report them promptly by certified mail would satisfy 1–102(3). Compare Prompt Electrical Supply Co., Inc. v. Allen–Bradley Co., 492 F.Supp. 344 (E.D.N.Y.1980) (notice of breach required by 2–607 cannot be waived, but the parties are competent to agree that the notice must be given in writing so that oral notice of breach was not sufficient).

Note that 1–102(3) also limits variation by agreement of provisions of the UCC by its language "except as otherwise provided in this Act." (Revised 1–302(a) uses slightly different language, but the result is the same.) In other words, the provisions of the UCC can be varied by agreement unless the section or rules that the parties seek to vary provides otherwise. This means that some sections can be varied by agreement while others cannot. In this respect it is a difficult task to determine which provisions are mandatory and which are permissive, and the drafters have been criticized for not making this matter clear. Perhaps some clarity can be developed by looking at the history of the subsection.

The 1949 draft of the UCC, the first one seriously considered by the sponsors of the Code, contained a provision that was almost diametrically opposed to the thrust of present 1–102(3). Section 1–108 of the 1949 Code provided that "The rules enunciated in this Act are mandatory and may not be waived or modified by agreement unless the rule is qualified by the words 'unless otherwise agreed' or their equivalent."

This restrictive approach was justified on the ground of uniformity— that uniformity would be defeated if the parties were given the right to change the rules of the UCC, itself. On the other hand, it was recognized that many of the terms of Article 2 are really not rules of law but contractual terms to be imposed where the parties had failed to provide for the matter in their contract. These "gap-filling" rules could be varied or completely displaced by agreement. Explaining this, the official comment to the 1949 section stated that "This Act contains two types of rules: (1) Rules which are mandatory, that is, intended to govern the contract; (2) Rules which are intended merely to substitute for matters not expressed by the parties to the contract. The former may not be modified or waived by agreement. The latter may be waived or modified at will. The failure of the courts to distinguish between these two types of rules in interpreting prior Acts has led to complete lack of uniformity. Accordingly, great care has been used in specifying those rules which may be modified or waived by agreement. In all other cases, it is intended that the rules shall be mandatory."

This prohibitory approach ran into strong opposition, and it was substantially changed by the first official draft of the UCC in 1952. That draft (1–102(3)) provided that all provisions of the Code could be varied by agreement, except for matters falling within three categories, listed as subsections (a), (b) and (c) of 1–102(3) in the 1952 UCC: "(a) Definitions and formal requirements such as those determining what constitutes a negotiable instrument, a bona fide purchaser, a holder in due course, or due negotiation of documents of title are not subject to variation by agreement; (b) Except as otherwise provided by this Act the rights and duties of a third party may not be adversely varied by an agreement to which he is not a party or by which he is not otherwise bound; (and) (c) The general obligations prescribed by this Act such as good faith, due diligence, commercial reasonableness and reasonable care may not be disclaimed by agreement but the parties may by agreement determine the standards by which the performance of such obligations is to be measured if such standards are not manifestly unreasonable."

In implementing this change, the 1952 Code provided additionally that "Provisions of this Act which are qualified by the words 'unless otherwise agreed' or words of similar import may be waived or modified by agreement and the absence of such words contains no negative implication." 1–102(3)(d) (1952).

While the changes in 1952 were major steps away from a restrictive approach and toward the goal of freedom of contract, they did not go far enough to satisfy critics who were fearful of the language *"general obligations such as* good faith, due diligence ..." (emphasis added). These people thought there was a danger that an unduly wide range of provisions might be interpreted as "general obligations," thus preventing them from being varied by agreement. This criticism was accepted by the sponsors in 1955 and subsection 1–102(3) was amended to make clear that the matters of good faith, diligence, and care were not mere illustrations of general obligations that cannot be disclaimed by agreement but rather constitute the only general obligations that cannot be so disclaimed.

Even this change did not satisfy the New York Law Revision Commission which recommended that 1–102(3)(a) and (b) of the 1952 Code be deleted as unnecessary. This suggestion was accepted, the deletion was made in 1956, but the drafters of the Code prepared a new comment to section 1–102 to carry forward the ideas that formerly had been expressed in the text of subsection (3)(a) and (b).

Does this legislative history and Official Comment 2 to the present Code (the one formulated in 1956) help one identify mandatory terms? If in doubt, would you say that a Code provision should be construed as mandatory or permissive with regard to its variability by agreement, in view of the legislative history of the section? The answer to this question is important, because there is a large gray area between those sections which are clearly subject to variation and those which are clearly not subject to variation. Code sections prefaced by the words "unless otherwise agreed" or the like are definitely subject to variation. There are quite a few provisions having this prefatory language, a carry-over in most cases from the 1949 Code. There are far fewer clearly mandatory provisions on the other extreme. For an example of one, look at 2–725 which is mandatory in some, but not all, respects.

Is 2–201 mandatory? Could the parties orally agree that the statute of frauds would not apply to their deal? Is 2–302 mandatory? Could the parties agree that the doctrine of unconscionability had no role to play in their contract? If you answered that these sections are mandatory, how did you reach that conclusion? Consider whether that same process of reasoning will apply to the variability of other sections of the Code.

3.   THE HIERARCHY OF THE VARIOUS COMPONENTS OF AGREEMENT

Section 1–201(3) defines "agreement" as "the bargain of the parties in fact as found in their language or by implication from other circumstances including course of dealing or usage of trade or course of performance . . . . " To identify the agreement, then, one must consider several sources: oral interactions, written communications and documents, course of performance, course of dealing, usage of trade, and other circumstances. The definition goes on to state, "Whether an agreement has legal consequences is determined by the provisions of this Act, if applicable; otherwise by the law of contracts (Section 1–103)." In other words, some parts of the agreement may not count, that is to say, may not have legal consequences. Further, if a term supplied by one of these sources conflicts with a term supplied by one of the other sources, it becomes necessary to determine which term is part of the contract. The materials in this section examine how to make that determination.

In deciding what parts of the agreement count and do not count, particular attention is directed to 2–202, 1–205 (section 1–303 in revised Article 1), and 2–208. Please read these sections and the Official Comments to them. In the event of a conflict between terms supplied by the various components of an agreement, which term displaces which: what is the hierarchy of sources of terms under Article 2?

In your study of the law of contracts, you encountered the parol evidence rule, which limits the enforceability of agreements formed prior to or contemporaneously with the parties' adoption of a written agreement that they intend as the final expression of all or part of their deal. Article 2's version of this rule appears in 2–202. It addresses both partial integrations and complete integrations. If a writing is a complete integration, then the writing discharges all contemporaneous oral agreements and all prior oral *or written* agreements.

Problem. In a detailed, completely integrated agreement, Cartco contracts to deliver 50 golf carts to Country Club on February 1 for a specified price. The writing is silent on the time of payment (see 2–310(a)). Cartco tenders delivery on February 1 and demands payment. Country Club states that it will pay by March 1. Cartco insists that payment is due on delivery and refuses to leave the carts at the Club. In the ensuing litigation, Country Club wants to prove that it had purchased golf carts from Cartco four times over the preceding two years, that each time Cartco had delivered them without insisting on payment, and that each time Country Club had paid within 30 days. Should the court entertain Country Club's argument?

a. THE PAROL EVIDENCE RULE

ARB, Inc. v. E–Systems, Inc.

United States Court of Appeals, District of Columbia Circuit, 1980.
663 F.2d 189.

[ARB, a corporation engaged in television and radio research, brought suit against E–Systems, a designer of electronic systems, for breach of a negotiated contract that was more than fifty pages in length. During the negotiations ARB had submitted a draft contract containing the following term: "If, as a result of default of performance by the Seller (E–Systems), this contract is terminated in whole or in part and if it is necessary to procure any of the specified products or services elsewhere, then Seller will be liable for any re-procurement charges which exceed the amount which would have been due the Seller if he had satisfactorily completed this order." This proposed term, providing for "cover" damages, was deleted at E–Systems's request.

The case was tried to a special master, who found that E–Systems had breached the contract, but denied ARB cover damages on the ground that it had bargained them away. The District Court adopted the master's report.]

■ TAMM, CIRCUIT JUDGE.

. . .

Misapplication of Parol Evidence Rule

ARB challenges the district court's conclusion that it "bargained away" its right to cover under section 2–712. It contends primarily that the evidence relied upon by the master in reaching this conclusion should have been excluded under Md.Com. Law Code Ann. § 2–202 (1975), the statutory parol evidence rule. As discussed below, ARB's contention on this point is well-founded, and this case will be remanded to the district court for the calculation of "cover" damages.

. . .

Two issues are raised by the application of [section 2–202] to the present facts: first, was the written contract "intended * * * as a complete and exclusive statement of the terms of the agreement," such that no evidence is admissible to explain or supplement it? Second, if not, and the contract was the "final expression of their agreement with respect to such terms as are included therein," should the specific evidence considered by the master have been barred as "contradict[ory]" or as not constituting a "consistent additional term"?

We believe that the written contract was "intended * * * as a complete and exclusive statement of the terms of the agreement." Two factors support this conclusion: first and most important is that the written contract contains an integration clause, and integration clauses are generally to be given effect under section 2–202. See Franz Chemical Corp. v. Philadelphia Quartz Co., 594 F.2d 146, 149 (5th Cir.1979); United States v. Haas & Haynie Corp., 577 F.2d 568, 572 (9th Cir.1978).[12] The integration clause in question here is not susceptible of any other reasonable interpretation; it states: "This Contract * * * constitutes the entire agreement between Buyer and Seller." (Contract at 35, § 6.19.) When combined with two other clauses in the contract, explicitly preserving "other or further remedies provided in law or in equity" (Contract at 29, § 6.8; Contract at 33, § 6.13), and a clause reserving to ARB the power "to avail itself cumulatively of all remedies provided in law or in equity," (Contract at 31, § 6.11), it makes the addition of a non-written term eliminating an "other * * * remed[y] provided in law" an error.

This decision to give effect to the integration clause is consistent with non-U.C.C. Maryland law, which holds that integration clauses, although not "absolutely conclusive," are "indicative of the intention of the parties to finalize their complete understanding in the written contract * * * that there was no other prior or contemporaneous agreement not included in the written contract." Pumphrey v. Kehoe, 261 Md. 496, 505, 276 A.2d 194, 199 (1971). Maryland law further requires, however, that the circumstances surrounding the making of the contract be considered to discover whether the integration clause in question does, in fact, express the genuine intention of the parties to make the written contract the complete and exclusive statement of their agreement. Shoreham Developers, Inc. v.

---

12. See also the discussion by Professors White and Summers of the "special value" of the integration clause in the situation in which

> the parties negotiate over a period of time, making and withdrawing numerous proposals. They finally reach an agreement and reduce it to writing. Here

there is special need for a merger clause to protect against the risk that one party will, honestly or dishonestly, seek to resurrect some proposal that did not show up in the final writing.

J. White and R. Summers, Handbook of the Law of the Uniform Commercial Code 90 (2d ed.1980)

Randolph Hills, Inc., 248 Md. 267, 271–72, 235 A.2d 735, 739 (1967); Rinaudo v. Bloom, 209 Md. 1, 9, 120 A.2d 184, 190 (1956). Thus, the issue is not whether the deletion of a given sentence antecedent to the making of the written contract was an agreement as to the matter deleted, but whether the integration clause, at the time it was agreed upon, represented the intentions of the parties.[13] Here, the bulk of the evidence suggests that the parties intended the written contract to be the complete and exclusive statement of the terms of their agreement. The length of the contract, its exhaustive detail, and the prolonged period of negotiation preceding its signing, collectively considered, support this conclusion. At the same time, E–Systems has offered no persuasive evidence supporting a determination that the parties intended, at the time of contracting, that non-written terms be part of the overall agreement.

Even if the written contract had not been "intended * * * as a complete and exclusive statement of the terms of the agreement," however, we believe that section 2–202 would bar evidence of the deletion of the reprocurement provision on the grounds that this evidence is not a "consistent additional term" within the meaning of section 2–202(b). We reach this conclusion by applying the appropriate test of consistency under Maryland law. This test is based not on the standard of simple non-contradiction of an express term of the contract applied by the master, but on a stricter standard requiring a substantially greater agreement between the contract and the proffered additional terms. The Court of Special Appeals explained it this way in Snyder v. Herbert Greenbaum & Assoc., Inc., 38 Md.App. 144, 380 A.2d 618 (1977):

> we hold that the additional terms offered by appellants are inconsistent with the contract itself. In doing so we reject the narrow view of inconsistency * * * that to be inconsistent the "additional terms" must negate or contradict express terms of the agreement.

This interpretation of "inconsistent" is itself inconsistent with a reading of the whole of § 2–202. Direct contradiction of express terms is forbidden in the initial paragraph of § 2–202. The [narrow] interpretation renders that passage a nullity, a result which is to be avoided * * *.

---

13. Professor Corbin explained the effect of an integration clause in this way:

A provision that there are no previous understandings or agreements not contained in the writing is, on its face, a statement of fact; but it is more than such a statement. By limiting the contract to the provisions that are in writing, the parties are definitely expressing an intention to nullify antecedent understandings or agreements. They are making the document a complete integration.

Therefore, even if there had in fact been an antecedent warranty or other provision, it is discharged by the written agreement.

3 A. Corbin, Corbin on Contracts § 578 (1960). Professor Corbin suggests that the declaration of completeness contained in an integration clause is "conclusive as long as [the clause] has itself not been set aside by a court on grounds of fraud or mistake, or on some ground that is sufficient for setting aside other contracts." Id. (footnote omitted).

Rather we believe "inconsistency" as used in § 2–202(b) means the absence of reasonable harmony in terms of the language and respective obligations of the parties * * *.

380 A.2d at 623. We think that application of this test to the term here disputed indicates clearly that consideration of this "additional term"—the no-cover provision—would disrupt the delicate balance, the harmony, that the written contract establishes among the "respective obligations" of the parties.

Moreover, this conclusion is reinforced by application of the standard set out in Official Comment 3 to section 2–202 and expressly endorsed by the Maryland courts. See, e.g., Snyder v. Herbert Greenbaum & Assoc., Inc., 38 Md.App. 144, 380 A.2d 618, 623 (1977). It states in relevant part: "If the additional terms are such that, if agreed upon, they would certainly have been included in the document in the view of the court, then evidence of their alleged making must be kept from the trier of fact." We believe, for the reasons set out above in our discussion of the contract as a complete and exclusive statement of the agreement, that under all the circumstances of this case a term limiting the cover remedy, if agreed upon, would certainly have been included in the contract. In support, we note further that cover—referred to by White and Summers as "chief" among the general remedies of the buyer set out in section 2–711—occupies the central place in the U.C.C. remedy scheme.[16]

QUESTIONS

The court in *ARB* determines that the writing is a complete integration and therefore concludes that any agreement concerning the availability of cover damages is not enforceable. The court goes on to conclude that even if the writing is only a partial integration, the agreement is not enforceable. Under 2–202(b) the latter conclusion is correct only if the agreement concerning cover is not a "consistent additional term."

Why does the court conclude that the agreement concerning the availability of cover damages is not consistent with the writing? What test(s) does the court apply to determine if the agreement is consistent with the writing?

The relevant language of 2–202 is

16. Because ... we decide the "cover" question on the basis of the parol evidence rule, we ... do not consider [the master's] findings of fact as to the intentions of the parties on August 24, 1973, the day that the sentence upon which he based his decision was deleted from an earlier draft of the contract. We note, however, that were we to reach these fact findings, we would have res-ervations about the conclusion that the deletion "bargained away" cover, given the differences in scope—broader as to the kind of expenses included, narrower as to application (the deleted sentence applied only to a contract default)—between the reprocurement provision of the contract and the "cover" remedy under the U.C.C.

Terms ... set forth in a writing ... may not be contradicted by evidence of any prior agreement ... but may be explained or supplemented ... by evidence of consistent additional terms. . . .

Note that in the case of a partial integration, the statute excludes terms that "contradict" but enforces terms that are "consistent." If "consistent" means "does not contradict the writing," then the statute creates two categories, and we have to decide into which category the term in question falls. If "consistent" means something other than "does not contradict," e.g., is harmonious with, as the court in *ARB* holds, then the statute creates *three* categories: contradictory, harmonious, and non-contradictory but non-harmonious. Are terms in this third category enforceable? What basis for your answer is there in 2–202?

Is Official Comment 3 helpful? Does it address the question whether the additional term is consistent or whether the writing is completely integrated?

————

Noble v. Logan–Dees Chevrolet–Buick, Inc.

Mississippi Supreme Court, 1974.
293 So.2d 14.

■ SUGG, JUSTICE. . . .

Logan–Dees filed suit against Noble and alleged that it sold Noble a 1972 Buick Electra for the following consideration: trade-in of one 1970 wrecked Chevrolet El Camino, trade-in of one 1971 Dodge Charger and delivery to Logan–Dees of the proceeds of an insurance check covering the wrecked 1970 Chevrolet El Camino in the amount of $1,532.66 and payment of $2,150.00 cash. Logan–Dees further alleged that it delivered Noble the 1972 Buick, accepted delivery of the two automobiles traded in, accepted payment of $2,150 with the promise of Noble to deliver the insurance check as soon as he received it. [When Noble failed to turn over the insurance check, Logan–Dees sued and recovered $1,532.66. The intermediate appellate court affirmed.]

At the trial Logan–Dees introduced its contract with Noble entitled "Retail Buyer's Order" prepared by it showing that Noble agreed to purchase a new automobile which was described only by stock number, model and color and to pay the following consideration:

Total cash price		$6,615.00
Cash down payment	46.40	
Used car allowance	4,418.60	
		4,465.00
Balance payable		$2,150.00

The contract was duly executed by both parties and contained the following provision:

This order is not binding on dealer until accepted by dealer in writing. I have read the matter printed on the back hereof and agree to it as a part of this order the same as if it were printed above my signature. *The front and back of this order comprises the entire agreement pertaining to this purchase and no other agreement of any kind, verbal understanding or promise whatsoever, will be recognized.* Receipt of a copy of this order is hereby acknowledged. (Emphasis supplied.)

The contract was prepared and signed after oral negotiations between Noble and King, the salesman who handled the transaction for Logan–Dees. There is a conflict in the testimony as to when the contract was signed. King testified that it was signed at the time the 1972 Buick was delivered to Noble, but Noble testified that it was signed on a date previous to the delivery of the automobile. Regardless of the date the contract was signed, it is a writing expressing the contract between the parties.

Before delivery of the automobile, Noble paid Logan–Dees $46.40 and on the day of delivery gave the salesman a check for $2,150 and transferred title to the 1971 Charger and 1970 El Camino mentioned in the contract.

King testified that, when the Buick was delivered and the contract signed, Noble agreed to deliver the insurance check to Logan–Dees as part of the consideration. The insurance check is not mentioned in the contract and Noble objected on the ground that such testimony was an effort to alter the terms of a written agreement by parol evidence. The objection was overruled and judgment entered as aforesaid.

Noble contends that under the provisions of Miss.Code Ann. § 75–2–202 (1972) the court erred by permitting parol testimony contradicting the terms of the agreement of the parties as expressed in the contract. Logan–Dees contends that it was entitled to offer parol testimony under subsections (a) and (b) of the statute.

We hold that, under the facts as disclosed by the record, Logan–Dees was not entitled to offer parol testimony under subsection (a) because the evidence does not disclose a course of dealing and usage of trade as defined in Miss.Code Ann. § 75–1–205 neither does it disclose a course of performance as defined by Miss.Code Ann. § 75–2–208 (1972).

We hold that Logan–Dees was not entitled to introduce parol testimony under subsection (b) because the evidence offered was not of consistent additional terms, but the evidence offered would show a different consideration from that expressed in the writing. We also hold that parol evidence was not admissible under subsection (b) because the contract, by its own terms, was a complete and exclusive statement of the terms of the agreement of the parties.

If Logan–Dees expected to receive the proceeds of the insurance check as part of the consideration for the car sold to Noble, it would have been a very simple matter to include such a provision in the contract. Where parties, without any fraud or mistake, have deliberately put their contract in writing, the writing is not only the best, but the only, evidence of their agreement.

We hold that the court erred in receiving parol evidence to vary the terms of the written contract and that the parol evidence was not admissible either under Miss.Code Ann. § 75–2–202 (1972) or under the common-law parol evidence rule.

Reversed and rendered.

QUESTIONS

1. Would you characterize this decision as pro-consumer, pro-seller, or neutral?

2. The Retail Buyer's Order stated simply, "Used car allowance," evidently referring to the trade-ins. What if the transaction had fallen apart when Noble came to pick up his new Electra, tendering just the Charger and the $2,150 cash: would Logan–Dees be allowed to prove that "Used car allowance" means the Charger and the El Camino? If so, what are the implications of this conclusion on the actual case?

Does 2–202 permit evidence of the private understanding or agreement of the parties as to the meaning of a term if the term is found to be ambiguous? On what statutory language do you rely to support the conclusion you reach? Is it possible to argue that, under the Code, evidence of the private agreement or understanding of the parties is admissible without a prior finding of ambiguity?

3. Is the writing in *Noble* a complete integration or a partial integration? Compare the approach of the court in *ARB* to resolving this question.

4. The court states that if the writing is viewed as a partial integration, the alleged agreement concerning the insurance proceeds is not a "consistent additional term." What test does the court use to arrive at this conclusion. Is the conclusion consistent with the approach in *ARB*?

5. According to the court, the salesman testified that the Retail Buyer's Order was signed when Noble picked up his new car and dropped off the trade-ins. Noble, on the other hand, testified that they signed it when they struck the deal, some time before delivery of the new car. The court disregarded this difference, evidently believing it was irrelevant. Why was the court wrong?

6. CISG and the parol evidence rule. The Convention on Contracts for the International Sale of Goods does not contain a parol evidence rule. To the contrary, Article 8(3) states: "In determining the intent of a party or the understanding a reasonable person would have had, due consideration is to be given to all relevant circumstances of the case including the negotiations, any practices which the parties have established between themselves, usages and any subsequent conduct of the parties." This language specifically states that the court can take negotiations into account in determining the meaning of a contract provision.

b.   TRADE USAGE, COURSE OF DEALING, GOOD FAITH

Nanakuli Paving & Rock Co. v. Shell Oil Co., Inc.

United States Court of Appeals, Ninth Circuit, 1981.
664 F.2d 772.

■ HOFFMAN, DISTRICT JUDGE.

Appellant Nanakuli Paving and Rock Company (Nanakuli) initially filed this breach of contract action against appellee Shell Oil Company (Shell) in Hawaiian State Court in February, 1976. Nanakuli, the second largest asphaltic paving contractor in Hawaii, had bought all its asphalt requirements from 1963 to 1974 from Shell under two long-term supply contracts; its suit charged Shell with breach of the later 1969 contract. The jury returned a verdict of $220,800 for Nanakuli on its first claim, which is that Shell breached the 1969 contract in January, 1974, by failing to price protect Nanakuli on 7200 tons of asphalt at the time Shell raised the price for asphalt from $44 to $76. Nanakuli's theory is that price-protection, as a usage of the asphaltic paving trade in Hawaii, was incorporated into the 1969 agreement between the parties, as demonstrated by the routine use of price protection by suppliers to that trade, and reinforced by the way in which Shell actually performed the 1969 contract up until 1974. Price protection, appellant claims, required that Shell hold the price on the tonnage Nanakuli had already committed because Nanakuli had incorporated that price into bids put out to or contracts awarded by general contractors and government agencies. The District Judge set aside the verdict and granted Shell's motion for judgment n.o.v., which decision we vacate. We reinstate the jury verdict because we find that, viewing the evidence as a whole, there was substantial evidence to support a finding by reasonable jurors that Shell breached its contract by failing to provide protection for Nanakuli in 1974. . . .

Nanakuli offers two theories for why Shell's failure to offer price protection in 1974 was a breach of the 1969 contract. First, it argues, all material suppliers to the asphaltic paving trade in Hawaii followed the trade usage of price protection and thus it should be assumed, under the U.C.C., that the parties intended to incorporate price protection into their 1969 agreement. This is so, Nanakuli continues, even though the written contract provided for price to be "Shell's Posted Price at time of delivery," F.O.B. Honolulu. . . . Nanakuli points out that Shell had price protected it on the two occasions of price increases under the 1969 contract other than the 1974 increase. In 1970 and 1971 Shell extended the old price for four and three months, respectively, after an announced increase. This was done, in the words of Shell's agent in Hawaii, in order to permit Nanakuli to "chew up" tonnage already committed at Shell's old price.

Nanakuli's second theory for price protection is that Shell was obliged to price protect Nanakuli, even if price protection was not incorporated into their contract, because price protection was the commercially reasonable standard for fair dealing in the asphaltic paving trade in Hawaii in 1974.

Observance of those standards is part of the good-faith requirement that the Code imposes on merchants in performing a sales contract. Shell was obliged to price protect Nanakuli in order to act in good faith, Nanakuli argues, because such a practice was universal in that trade in that locality.

. . .

We hold that the judge did not abuse his discretion in defining the applicable trade, for purposes of trade usages, as the asphaltic paving trade in Hawaii, rather than the purchase and sale of asphalt alone . . . .

. . .

Lastly we hold that, although the express price terms of Shell's posted price of delivery may seem, at first glance, inconsistent with a trade usage of price protection at time of increases in price, a closer reading shows that the jury could have reasonably construed price protection as consistent with the express term. We reach this holding for several reasons. First, we are persuaded by a careful reading of the U.C.C., one of whose underlying purposes is to promote flexibility in the expansion of commercial practices and which rather drastically overhauls this particular area of the law. The Code would have us look beyond the printed pages of the contract to usages and the entire commercial context of the agreement in order to reach the "true understanding" of the parties. Second, decisions of other courts in similar situations have managed to reconcile such trade usages with seemingly contradictory express terms where the prior course of dealings between the parties, trade usages, and the actual performance of the contract by the parties showed a clear intent by the parties to incorporate those usages into the agreement or to give to the express term the particular meaning provided by those usages, even at times varying the apparent meaning of the express terms. Third, the delineation by thoughtful commentators of the degree of consistency demanded between express terms and usage is that a usage should be allowed to modify the apparent agreement, as seen in the written terms, as long as it does not totally negate it. We believe the usage here falls within the limits set forth by commentators and generally followed in the better reasoned decisions. The manner in which price protection was actually practiced in Hawaii was that it only came into play at times of price increases and only for work committed prior to those increases on non-escalating contracts. Thus, it formed an exception to, rather than a total negation of, the express price term of "Shell's Posted Price at time of delivery." Our decision is reinforced by the overwhelming nature of the evidence that price protection was routinely practiced by all suppliers in the small Oahu market of the asphaltic paving trade and therefore was known to Shell; that it was a realistic necessity to operate in that market and thus vital to Nanakuli's ability to get large government contracts and to Shell's continued business growth on Oahu; and that it therefore constituted an intended part of the agreement, as that term is broadly defined by the Code, between Shell and Nanakuli.

. . .

V. Scope of Trade Usage

The validity of the jury verdict in this case depends on four legal questions. First, how broad was the trade to whose usages Shell was bound under its 1969 agreement with Nanakuli: did it extend to the Hawaiian asphaltic paving trade or was it limited merely to the purchase and sale of asphalt, which would only include evidence of practices by Shell and Chevron.* Second, were the two instances of price protection of Nanakuli by Shell in 1970 and 1971 waivers of the 1969 contract as a matter of law or was the jury entitled to find that they constituted a course of performance of the contract? Third, could the jury have construed an express contract term of Shell's posted price at delivery as reasonably consistent with a trade usage and Shell's course of performance of the 1969 contract of price protection, which consisted of charging the old price at times of price increases, either for a period of time or for specific tonnage committed at a fixed price in non-escalating contracts? Fourth, could the jury have found that good faith obliged Shell to at least give advance notice of a $32 increase in 1974, that is, could they have found that the commercially reasonable standards of fair dealing in the trade in Hawaii in 1974 were to give some form of price protection?

We approach the first issue in this case mindful that an underlying purpose of the U.C.C. as enacted in Hawaii is to allow for liberal interpretation of commercial usages. . . .

The Code defines usage of trade as "any practice or method of dealing having such regularity of observance in a *place, vocation or trade* as to justify an expectation that it will be observed with respect to the transaction in question." Id. § 490:1–205(2) (emphasis supplied). We understand the use of the word "or" to mean that parties can be bound by a usage common to the *place* they are in business, even if it is not the usage of their particular vocation or trade. . . . The drafters' Comments say that trade usage is to be used to reach the " * * * commercial meaning of the agreement * * * " by interpreting the language "as meaning what it may fairly be expected to mean to parties involved in the particular transaction *in a given locality or* in a given *vocation or trade*." Id., Comment 4 (emphasis supplied). The inference . . . is that a usage need not necessarily be one practiced by members of the party's own trade or vocation to be binding *if* it is so commonly practiced in a locality that a party should be aware of it. . . . A party is always held to conduct generally observed by members of his chosen trade because the other party is justified in so assuming unless he indicates otherwise. He is held to more general business practices to the extent of his actual knowledge of those practices or to the degree his ignorance of those practices is not excusable: they were so generally practiced he should have been aware of them.

. . .

[E]ven if Shell did not "regularly deal" with aggregate supplies,** it did deal constantly and almost exclusively on Oahu with one asphalt paver.

---

* Only Chevron and Shell sold asphalt on Oahu.—Ed.

** Asphalt and aggregate are the two components of asphalt paving. There was evi-

It therefore should have been aware of the usage of Nanakuli and other asphaltic pavers to bid at fixed prices and therefore receive price protection from their materials suppliers due to the refusal by government agencies to accept escalation clauses. Therefore, we do not find the lower court abused its discretion or misread the Code as applied to the peculiar facts of this case in ruling that the applicable trade was the asphaltic paving trade in Hawaii. In so ruling, the judge undoubtedly took into account Shell's half-million dollar investment in Oahu strictly because of a long-term commitment by Nanakuli, its actions as partner in promoting Nanakuli's expansion on Oahu, and the fact that its sales on Oahu were almost exclusively to Nanakuli for use in asphaltic paving. The wisdom of the pre-trial ruling was demonstrated by evidence at trial that Shell's agent in Hawaii stayed in close contact with Nanakuli and was knowledgeable about both the asphaltic paving market in general and Nanakuli's bidding procedures and economics in particular.

Shell argued not only that the definition of trade was too broad, but also that the practice itself was not sufficiently regular to reach the level of a usage and that Nanakuli failed to show with enough precision how the usage was carried out in order for a jury to calculate damages. The extent of a usage is ultimately a jury question. The Code provides, "The existence and scope of such a usage are to be proved as facts." Haw.Rev.Stat. § 490:1–205(2).[27] The practice must have "such regularity of observance * * * as to justify an expectation that it will be observed * * *." A "regularly observed" practice of protection, of which Shell "should have been aware," was enough to constitute a usage that Nanakuli had reason to believe was incorporated into the agreement.[28]

Nanakuli went beyond proof of a regular observance. It proved and offered to prove[29] that price protection was probably a universal practice by suppliers to the asphaltic paving trade in 1969.[30] . . .

Shell next argues that, even if such a usage existed, its outlines were not precise enough to determine whether Shell would have extended the old price for Nanakuli for several months or would have charged the old price on the volume of tonnage committed at that price. The jury awarded Nanakuli damages based on the specific tonnage committed before the price

dence that aggregate suppliers also provided price protection in the same way that Chevron and Shell did.—Ed.

27. Written trade codes, however, are left to the court to interpret.

28. White and Summers write that Code requirements for proving a usage are "far less stringent" than the old ones for custom. "A usage of trade need not be *well known,* let alone 'universal.' It only needs to be regular enough that the parties expect it to be observed." White & Summers, supra § 3–3 at 87 (emphasis supplied). "Note particularly [in 1–205(1) & (2)] that it is not

necessary for both parties to be consciously aware of the trade usage. It is enough if the trade usage is such as to 'justify an expectation' of its observance." Id. at 84.

29. Nanakuli made an offer of proof, which the judge rejected as not sufficiently relevant to the asphaltic paving trade, that cement suppliers routinely price protected pavers for years.

30. All evidence was that trade usage continued to be universally practiced after 1969, even by Shell.

increase of 1974. Shell says the jury could not have ascertained with enough certainty how price protection was carried out to calculate such an award for Nanakuli. The argument is not persuasive. The Code provides, "The remedies provided by this chapter shall be liberally administered to the end that the aggrieved party may be put in as good a position as if the other party had fully performed * * *." Id. § 490:1–106(1). The Comments list as one of three purposes of this section "to reject any doctrine that damages must be calculable with mathematical accuracy. Compensatory damages are often at best approximate: they have to be proved with whatever definiteness and accuracy the facts permit, but no more." Id., Comment 1. Nanakuli got advance notices of each but the disputed increase by Shell, as well as an extension of several months at the old price in 1970, 1971, 1977, and 1978. Shell protests that in 1970 and 1971 Nanakuli's protected tonnage only amounted to 3,300 and 1,100 tons, respectively. Chevron's price protection of H.B.* in 1969 however, is also part of the trade usage; H.B.'s protection amounted to 12,000 tons. The increase in Nanakuli's tonnage by 1974 is explained by its growth since the 1970 and 1971 increases.

In addition, the scope of protection offered by a particular usage is left to the jury:

> In cases of a well established line of usage varying from the general rules of this Act where the precise amount of the variation has not been worked out into a single standard, the party relying on the usage is entitled, in any event, to the minimum variation demonstrated. The whole is not to be disregarded because no particular line of detail has been established. In case a dominant pattern [of usage] has been fairly evidenced, the party relying on the usage is entitled * * * to go to the trier of fact on the question of whether such dominant pattern has been incorporated into the agreement.

Id. § 490:1–205, Comment 9. . . .

VI. *Waiver or Course of Performance*

Course of performance under the Code is the action of the parties in carrying out the contract at issue, whereas course of dealing consists of relations between the parties *prior* to signing that contract. Evidence of the latter was excluded by the District Judge; evidence of the former consisted of Shell's price protection of Nanakuli in 1970 and 1971. Shell protested that the jury could not have found that those two instances of price protection amounted to a course of performance of its 1969 contract, relying on two Code comments. First, one instance does not constitute a course of performance. "A single occasion of conduct does not fall within the language of this section * * *." Haw.Rev.Stat. § 490:2–208, Comment 4. Although the Comment rules out one instance, it does not further delineate how many acts are needed to form a course of performance. The prior occasions here were only two, but they constituted the only occasions

---

* Nanakuli's major competitor.—Ed.

before 1974 that would call for such conduct. In addition, the language used by a top asphalt official of Shell in connection with the first price protection of Nanakuli indicated that Shell felt that Nanakuli was entitled to some form of price protection. On that occasion in 1970 Blee, who had negotiated the contract with Nanakuli and was familiar with exactly what terms Shell was bound to by that agreement, wrote of the need to "bargain" with Nanakuli over the extent of price protection to be given, indicating that some price protection was a legal right of Nanakuli's under the 1969 agreement.

Shell's second defense is that the Comment expresses a preference for an interpretation of waiver.

> 3.   Where it is difficult to determine whether a particular act merely sheds light on the meaning of the agreement or represents a waiver of a term of the agreement, the preference is in favor of "waiver" whenever such construction, plus the application of the provisions on the reinstatement of rights waived * * *, is needed to preserve the flexible character of commercial contracts and to prevent surprise or other hardship.

Id., Comment 3. The preference for waiver only applies, however, where acts are ambiguous. It was within the province of the jury to determine whether those acts were ambiguous, and if not, whether they constituted waivers or a course of performance of the contract. The jury's interpretation of those acts as a course of performance was bolstered by evidence offered by Shell that it again price protected Nanakuli on the only two occasions of post–1974 price increases, in 1977 and 1978.[31]

VII.   *Express Terms As Reasonably Consistent With Usage and Course of Performance*

Perhaps one of the most fundamental departures of the Code from prior contract law is found in the parol evidence rule and the definition of an agreement between two parties. Under the U.C.C., an agreement goes beyond the written words on a piece of paper. " 'Agreement' means the bargain of the parties in fact as found in their language or by implication from other circumstances including course of dealing or usage of trade or course of performance as provided in this chapter (sections 490:1–205 and 490:2–208)." Id. § 490:1–201(3). Express terms, then, do not constitute the entire agreement, which must be sought also in evidence of usages, dealings, and performance of the contract itself. The purpose of evidence of

---

31. Bohner testified on direct for Shell at the 1978 trial that the two later instances of price protection occurred "this" year and "last" year, by which he could have meant 1976 and 1977. Bohner's testimony was that on those later occasions Shell gave Nanakuli six and three or four months' notice of an increase to allow Nanakuli to buy tonnage it had committed at the old price. He defined Shell's actions as "in effect carryover pricing." The jury's finding was reasonable in light of the circumstances of universal price protection by asphalt and aggregate suppliers, as well as by Shell on all price increases except 1974.

usages, which are defined in the previous section, is to help to understand the entire agreement.

> [Usages are] a factor in reaching the commercial meaning of the agreement which the parties have made. The language used is to be interpreted as meaning what it may fairly be expected to mean to parties involved in the particular commercial transaction in a given locality or in a given vocation or trade * * *. Part of the agreement of the parties * * * is to be sought for in the usages of trade which furnish the background and give particular meaning to the language used, and are the framework of common understanding controlling any general rules of law which hold only when there is no such understanding.

Id. § 490:1–205, Comment 4. . . .

A commercial agreement, then, is broader than the written paper and its meaning is to be determined not just by the language used by them in the written contract but "by their action, read and interpreted in the light of commercial practices and other surrounding circumstances. The measure and background for interpretation are set by the commercial context, which may explain and supplement even the language of a formal or final writing." Id., Comment 1. Performance, usages, and prior dealings are important enough to be admitted always, even for a final and complete agreement; only if they cannot be reasonably reconciled with the express terms of the contract are they not binding on the parties. "The express terms of an agreement and an applicable course of dealing or usage of trade shall be construed wherever reasonable as consistent with each other; but when such construction is unreasonable express terms control both course of dealing and usage of trade and course of dealing controls usage of trade." Id. § 490:1–205(4).

. . .

Our study of the Code provisions and Comments, then, form the first basis of our holding that a trade usage to price protect pavers at times of price increases for work committed on nonescalating contracts could reasonably be construed as consistent with an express term of seller's posted price at delivery. Since the agreement of the parties is broader than the express terms and includes usages, which may even add terms to the agreement, and since the commercial background provided by those usages is vital to an understanding of the agreement, we follow the Code's mandate to proceed on the assumption that the parties have included those usages unless they cannot reasonably be construed as consistent with the express terms.

Federal courts usually have been lenient in not ruling out consistent additional terms or trade usage for apparent inconsistency with express terms. The leading case on the subject is Columbia Nitrogen Corp. v. Royster Co., 451 F.2d 3 (4th Cir.1971). Columbia, the buyer, had in the past primarily produced and sold nitrogen to Royster. When Royster opened a new plant that produced more phosphate than it needed, the parties reversed roles and signed a sales contract for Royster to sell excess phosphate to Columbia. The contract terms set out the price that would be charged by Royster and the amount to be sold. It provided for the price to go up if certain events occurred but did not provide for price declines. When the price of nitrogen fell precipitously, Columbia refused to accept the full amount of nitrogen specified in the contract after Royster refused to renegotiate the contract price. The District Judge's exclusion of usage of the trade and course of dealing to explain the express quantity term in the contract was reversed. Columbia had offered to prove that the quantity set out in the contract was a mere projection to be adjusted according to market forces. Ambiguity was not necessary for the admission of evidence of usage and prior dealings. Even though the lengthy contract was the result of long and careful negotiations and apparently covered every contingency, the appellate court ruled that "the test of admissibility is not whether the contract appears on its face to be complete in every detail, but whether the proffered evidence of course of dealing and trade usage reasonably can be construed as consistent with the express terms of the agreement." Id. at 9. The express quantity term could be reasonably construed as consistent with a usage that such terms would be mere projections for several reasons: (1) the contract did not expressly state that usage and dealings evidence would be excluded; (2) the contract was silent on the adjustment of price or quantities in a declining market; (3) the minimum tonnage was expressed in the contract as Products Supplied, not Products Purchased; (4) the default clause of the contract did not state a penalty for failure to take delivery; and (5) apparently most important in the court's view, the parties had deviated from similar express terms in earlier contracts in times of declining market. Id. at 9–10. As here, the contract's merger clause said that there were no oral agreements. The court explained that its ruling "reflects the reality of the marketplace and avoids the overly legalistic interpretations which the Code seeks to abolish." Id. at 10. The Code assigns dealing and usage evidence "unique and important roles" and therefore "overly simplistic and overly legalistic interpretation of a contract should be shunned." Id. at 11.

. . .

Probably the two leading cases that have rejected usage evidence as inconsistent with express terms are Southern Concrete Services, Inc. v. Mableton Contractors, Inc., 407 F.Supp. 581 (N.D.Ga.1975), aff'd, 569 F.2d 1154 (5th Cir.1978) (unpublished opinion), and Division of Triple T Service, Inc. v. Mobil Oil Corp., 60 Misc.2d 720, 304 N.Y.S.2d 191 (Sup.Ct.1969). In *Southern Concrete* the District Court, distinguishing its facts from those in *Columbia Nitrogen,* supra, held that evidence of a trade usage and an agreement to additional terms was not admissible. The usage allegedly was that contract quantity specifications were not mandatory on either buyer or seller. The court acknowledged that U.C.C. § 2–202 "was meant to liberalize the common law parol evidence rule to allow evidence of agreements outside the contract, without a prerequisite finding that the contract was ambiguous" and "requires that contracts be interpreted in light of the commercial context in which they were written and not by the rules on legal construction." *Southern Concrete,* supra, at 582–83. Nevertheless, the court held, the express quantity term in the contract and the usage could not be construed as reasonably consistent. "A construction which negates the express terms of the contract by allowing unilateral abandonment of its specifications is patently unreasonable." Id. at 585. The court's attempt to differentiate its facts from those in *Columbia Nitrogen* was unsuccessful; the distinctions discussed were very minor. The difference between the two results should depend less on such subtle variations in contract language and more on the strength of the usage evidence and whether the parties are or should be aware of the usage and thus should be bound by it. The court in *Southern Concrete* acknowledged that *Columbia Nitrogen* is not the only case at odds with its holding that a usage that quantities are projections cannot modify a seemingly unambiguous quantity term. *Southern Concrete,* supra, at 585–86.

The other leading case cited by Shell is a New York case, *Triple T,* supra. Because the express term of the franchise agreement gave either party the right to terminate [on] 90-days' notice, the court refused to find as reasonably consistent with that term a usage of the trade that a gasoline franchisor could only terminate a dealer for "cause." "[T]he express terms of the contract cover the entire area of termination and negate plaintiff's argument that the custom or usage in the trade implicitly adds the words 'with cause' in the termination clause. The contract is unambiguous and no sufficient basis appears for a construction which would insert words to limit the effect of the termination clause." Id. at 203. The court then held that only consistent usages are admissible, which is an incorrect reading of the Code. Usage is always admissible, even though the express term controls in the event of inconsistency, which is a jury question.

. . .

Directly in conflict with the holding in *Triple T* is that of Warrick Beverage Corp. v. Miller Brewing Co., 170 Ind.App. 114, 352 N.E.2d 496 (1976). The contract to establish a franchise for a beer dealership had no term binding the brewer as to the number of such dealerships, yet usage was admissible to establish that "it was customary in the beer industry to establish a single rather than dual distributorships." Id. at 501. That evidence of a single dealership limitation for each area was fully consistent with and "would in no way contradict the [express] terms,* * *" the court held. Id. That holding, in contrast to the holding in *Triple T,* is in keeping with the policy of allowing the introduction of such a usage if it is not a total negation of the contract term but simply a partial exception to it.

Some guidelines can be offered as to how usage evidence can be allowed to modify a contract. First, the court must allow a check on usage evidence by demanding that it be sufficiently definite and widespread to prevent unilateral post-hoc revision of contract terms by one party. The Code's intent is to put usage evidence on an objective basis. . . .

Evidence of a trade usage does not need to be protected against perjury because, as one commentator has written, "an outside standard does exist to help judge the truth of the assertion that the parties intended the usage to control the particular dispute: the existence and scope of the usage can be determined from other members of the trade." [R. Kirst, Usage of Trade and Course of Dealing: Subversion of UCC Theory, 1977 University of Ill. L.F. 811, 839.] . . . [Another author] writes, "Astonishing as it will seem to most practicing attorneys, under the Code it will be possible in some cases to use custom to contradict the written agreement * * *. Therefore usage may be used to 'qualify' the agreement, which presumably means to 'cut down' express terms although not to negate them entirely." [J. Levie, Trade Usage and Custom Under the Common Law and The Uniform Commercial Code, 40 N.Y.U. L.R. 1101, 1112 (1965).] Here, the express price term was "Shell's Posted Price at time of delivery." A total negation of that term would be that the buyer was to set the price. It is a less than complete negation of the term that an unstated exception exists at times of price increases, at which times the old price is to be charged, for a certain period or for a specified tonnage, on work already committed at the lower price on nonescalating contracts. Such a usage forms a broad and important exception to the express term, but does not swallow it entirely. Therefore, we hold that, under these particular facts, a reasonable jury could have found that price protection was incorporated into the 1969 agreement between Nanakuli and Shell and that price protection was reasonably consistent with the express term of seller's posted price at delivery.

VIII. *Good Faith in Setting Price*

Nanakuli offers an alternative theory why Shell should have offered price protection at the time of the price increases of 1974. Even if price protection was not a term of the agreement, Shell could not have exercised good faith in carrying out its 1969 contract with Nanakuli when it raised its price by $32 effective January 1 in a letter written December 31st and only received on January 4, given the universal practice of advance notice of such an increase in the asphaltic paving trade. The Code provides, "A price to be fixed by the seller or by the buyer means a price for him to fix in good faith," Haw.Rev.Stat. § 490:2–305(2). For a merchant good faith means "the observance of reasonable commercial standards of fair dealing in the trade." Id. § 490:2–103(1)(b). The comment to Section 2–305 explains, "[I]n the normal case a 'posted price' . . . satisfies the good faith requirement." Id., Comment 3. However, the words "in the normal case" mean that, although a posted price will usually be satisfactory, it will not be so under all circumstances. In addition, the dispute here was not over the amount of the increase—that is, the price that the seller fixed—but over the manner in which that increase was put into effect. It is true that Shell, in order to observe the good faith standards of the trade in 1974, was not bound by the practices of aggregate companies, which did not labor under the same disabilities as did asphalt suppliers in 1974. However, Nanakuli presented evidence that Chevron, in raising its price to $76, gave at least six weeks' advance notice, in accord with the long-time usage of the asphaltic paving trade. Shell, on the other hand, gave absolutely no notice, from which the jury could have concluded that Shell's manner of carrying out the price increase of 1974 did not conform to commercially reasonable standards. In both the timing of the announcement and its refusal to protect work already bid at the old price, Shell could be found to have breached the obligation of good faith imposed by the Code on all merchants. "Every contract or duty within this chapter imposes an obligation of good faith in its performance or enforcement," id. § 490:1–203, which for merchants entails the observance of commercially reasonable standards of fair dealing in the trade. The Comment to 1–203 reads:

> This section sets forth a basic principle running throughout this Act. The principle involved is that in commercial transactions good faith is required in the performance and enforcement of all agreements or duties. Particular applications of this general principle appear in specific provisions of the Act. . . . It is further implemented by Section 1–205 on course of dealing and usage of trade.

Chevron's conduct in 1974 offered enough relevant evidence of commercially reasonable standards of fair dealing in the asphalt trade in Hawaii in 1974 for the jury to find that Shell's failure to give sufficient advance notice and price protect Nanakuli after the imposition of the new price did not conform to good faith dealings in Hawaii at that time.

Because the jury could have found for Nanakuli on its price protection claim under either theory, we reverse the judgment of the District Court and reinstate the jury verdict for Nanakuli in the amount of $220,800, plus interest according to law.

Reversed and remanded with directions to enter final judgment.

■ KENNEDY, CIRCUIT JUDGE, concurring specially:

The case involves specific pricing practices, not an allegation of unfair dealing generally. Our opinion should not be interpreted to permit juries to import price protection or a similarly specific contract term from a concept of good faith that is not based on well-established custom and usage or other objective standards of which the parties had clear notice. Here, evidence of custom and usage regarding price protection in the asphaltic paving trade was not contradicted in major respects, and the jury could find that the parties knew or should have known of the practice at the time of making the contract. In my view, these are necessary predicates for either theory of the case, namely, interpretation of the contract based on the course of its performance or a finding that good faith required the seller to hold the price. With these observations, I concur.

QUESTIONS AND NOTES

1. Please look at 2–202. Under what circumstances does 2–202 provide that an oral agreement that is consistent with the writing is not part of the contract?

Under what circumstances does 2–202 provide that a trade usage is not part of the contract?

2. Note the difference in phrasing of 2–202(a) and 1–205(3). Does the difference have any significance?

3. Problem. Buyer phones Seller to inquire about purchasing its requirements of asphalt for the next three years. After extensive discussion, Buyer and Seller agree that Seller will supply Buyer with its requirements of asphalt, at Seller's posted price at the time of delivery, for three years.

a.   Assume there is a trade usage that when asphalt sellers raise their posted prices, they hold to the pre-raise price with respect to asphalt that the buyers already have committed to third parties. Is this trade usage part of the agreement between Buyer and Seller?

b.   During the phone call described above, Seller tells Buyer, "You're talking about a very large quantity of asphalt. Therefore, I can't give you the usual price protection." Buyer replies, "I understand." Under 2–202 is the trade usage part of the contract? under 1–205?

4. In what way does 1–205(4) qualify 1–205(3)? What is the price term in *Nanakuli*? The court holds that even though the writing is a complete integration, the price-protection trade usage is part of the contract, because it is not a "total negation" of the price term in the writing. Is this consistent with *ARB v. E–Systems*? See 2–202, Official Comment 2. Are both courts correct?

5. In revised Article 1, 1–205 and 2–208 have been consolidated in 1–303, and the language has been modified.

B.   Terms Outside the Agreement: The "Statutory Terms"

Article 2 provides, mainly (but not exclusively) in Part 3, a number of statutory terms to be used to fill gaps in the contract when missing terms cannot be supplied through resort to course of performance, course of dealing, or usage of trade. Parties may omit a term through inadvertence or ignorance, or they may omit it by design, planning to agree on it at a later time but then not being able to come to an agreement. By setting forth statutory terms, the Code supplies a commonly accepted term on the matter and perhaps prevents the contract from failing for lack of a reasonable basis for enforcement.

In case of conflict, it is clear that statutory terms are subordinated in rank to course of performance, course of dealing, and usage of trade, and this is sound because course of performance, course of dealing, and usage of trade are methods to find implied terms of the contract. Obviously, the implied terms are part of the agreement itself ("bargain of the parties in fact . . .), whereas the statutory terms are not. In this connection, it is essential to heed the statement of 1–205, Official Comment 4, which is narrowly concerned with usage of trade but is equally applicable to course of performance and course of dealing. Please read that Comment now.

Many statutory terms are signaled by the phrase, "Unless otherwise agreed . . . ." This language makes it clear that the provision that follows is to be used only in those cases where the parties have not expressly or impliedly agreed on the matter at hand. It would have been good drafts-manship to have flagged all the statutory terms in the UCC in this manner, but unfortunately this was not done. No negative inference is to be drawn, however, from the fact that some terms are prefaced with unless-otherwise-agreed language and others are not because 1–102(4) provides, "The presence in certain provisions of this Act of the words 'unless otherwise agreed' or words of similar import does not imply that the effect of other provisions may not be varied by agreement under subsection (3)." Indeed, the parties have the competence to displace most provisions of Article 2. Only mandatory provisions, like good faith, diligence, reasonableness, care, unconscionability, and others that are specifically made generally or par-tially binding irrespective of the expressed will of the parties (e.g., the parties have no competence under 2–725 to lower the period of the statute of limitations below one year), cannot be disclaimed by agreement. This indicates that all non-mandatory provisions are, basically, gap fillers to be used only when the parties have not come to a different express or implied agreement regarding a particular term.

For purposes of applying statutory terms, therefore, two propositions may be stated: (1) all unless-otherwise-agreed terms are optional and are deferred in ranking to express and implied terms; (2) most other provisions of Article 2 are optional and are similarly deferred unless the context of the section in which they appear or some strong social policy in favor of them makes it clear that they are to be imposed irrespective of the wishes of the parties. Mandatory provisions, such as the statute of frauds, unconsciona-bility, or the statute of limitations, displace express and implied terms of an agreement.

Assuming there is no express or implied agreement, not all missing terms may be filled by statutory terms. The rationale underlying the use of statutory terms is that they represent ordinary understanding about com-mon matters and therefore most likely would have been used by the parties had they considered the term when they made their agreement. In short, statutory terms presuppose that normally the parties have omitted, through haste, ignorance, or forgetfulness, a routine term that subsequent-ly has become important and that the fairest method to fill that missing term is to impose upon them the kind of term that normally is used by most parties in common, unexceptional deals. Clearly, therefore, exception-al terms will not be imposed in this manner. Thus, for example, a party who claims the contract calls for an arbitration of disputes would have to establish that contention by proving an express or implied term. In the absence of that proof, the party could not resort to a statutory term because Article 2 contains no provision calling for disputes to be resolved by arbitration.

The failure to establish an alleged missing term may mean that the contract cannot be enforced because of indefiniteness, but this is not necessarily the result. The court may enforce the contract despite the missing term if the total situation shows that the parties nevertheless intended to be contractually bound and if there is a reasonably certain basis for giving an appropriate remedy (2–204(3)). Parties fully aware of the importance of a term may omit it with the intention of adding it at a later time. This kind of missing term is often called an open term. If they can come to an agreement with respect to the open term at the later time, they will then add it in accordance with their agreement, and no problems result. But if they cannot come to an agreement, the contract is left with a missing term that almost always is one of great importance. To save these contracts, the Code drafters took the position that statutory terms should be provided to fill open terms when the parties themselves were unable or unwilling to do so. Open terms, however, will be filled only when the parties have indicated that they want to be contractually bound in spite of the fact that they were unable to come to an agreement on what the open term should specify.

The most common open terms involve price and details of performance.

1. PRICE

a. BACKGROUND. In most sales contracts a definite price is fixed, or course of dealing or usage of trade clearly indicates that a "reasonable" or "market" price is contemplated, as for example, where a homeowner phones a fuel company and asks to have her fuel tank filled with heating oil. In that case there is an implied term in the contract that the buyer will pay the going price charged by the seller. Cases in which the price is fixed in this way by an implied term have presented no difficulty for the courts.

Nevertheless, open-price contracts often have been troublesome. Since price is such an important term, the parties seldom will forget it completely. Why, then, do they leave the term open? One reason is suggested by the example above. Another common reason involves a conscious effort by both parties not to shift the risk of a possible fluctuating market. This risk is present whether the price is fixed or left open, but it may be shifted from one party to the other or retained, depending upon the agreement. Prior to entering into a fixed-price contract the seller has the risk that the price of his goods will decline before he can sell them, and the buyer has the risk that the price will increase before he can buy them. Once the contract is made with a fixed-price term these risks are shifted. Now the buyer has the risk that the value of the goods will decline, whereas the seller has the risk that their value will rise. In an open-price contract, the parties retain these risks. What might motivate the parties to agree that the price is the going price at the time of delivery?

The courts have not always understood the economics of open-price terms and the justifications for them. At common law the use of open-price terms frequently resulted in the avoidance of an otherwise valid contract on grounds of indefiniteness, illusory promise, or lack of mutuality of obligation. E.g., Wilhelm Lubrication Co. v. Brattrud, 197 Minn. 626, 268 N.W. 634 (1936); Brooks v. Federal Surety Co., 24 F.2d 884 (D.C.Cir.1928).

Article 2 acknowledges the usefulness of open-price contracts. Please read 2–305 (and the Official Comments to that section). Which part of 2–305 governs the price term in the heating oil example in the introductory paragraph to this section?

b. VARIABLE–PRICE TERMS. Variable prices that depend on the happening or non-happening of stated contingencies are sometimes described by courts as "open-price" terms, but they are open only in the sense that the parties do not know at the time the contract is executed what the ultimate price will be. Good examples of variable price terms are agreements to sell at the market price or at the price charged by a particular seller on the day in question. These terms become "open" in the true sense only if the external price standard becomes non-existent or otherwise fails to operate in the anticipated manner. In that case, a court is left with difficult decisions. First, it must determine whether the parties intended to be bound should their valuation scheme not operate. Secondly, if the court determines that the parties did intend to be bound (i.e. that the agreed-upon method of valuation is not a condition precedent to the existence of the obligation), what factors should it consider in setting the price? Of course, it would be better for the parties to agree in advance on these matters, but they do not always do so.

When the price is made to vary on the happening of a contingency that bears little or no relationship to the subject matter of the contract, a wager usually is involved, and it will not be enforced because of public policy. For example, suppose a barrel of flour usually sells for $50, that Black Beauty is running in the Kentucky Derby, and that the odds against Black Beauty winning the Derby are quoted at ten to one. Suppose, under these circumstances, the seller and buyer agree on the sale of a barrel of flour, the price to be $500 if Black Beauty wins the Derby but two cents if she loses. Is there any doubt that this "sale" is really a disguised wager?

Suppose, however, that before the Derby is run the owner of Black Beauty agrees to sell her to a buyer after the race, the price to be $5,000 if she loses, but $50,000 if she wins. Any "gambling" problem in that case?

In the second version of the hypothetical, what if Back Beauty is withdrawn from the race: is the agreement enforceable? If so, at what price?

c. DRAFTING OPEN–PRICE TERMS. Section 2–305 enables the parties to a sales contract to preserve flexibility with respect to establishing the price of the transaction. It goes a long way toward eliminating the common-law objections to a contract with an indeterminate price. But problems may remain, if there is doubt concerning the factual questions posed by subsections (1) and (4): do the parties intend for there to be a contract even though they have not agreed on the price and even though they ultimately do not agree on the price? To avoid the problems, it is wise for the parties to address these questions of intent in the contract. They should make it clear whether they consider themselves contractually bound in the event that the price is not fixed in accordance with their agreement. For example, suppose they have agreed that the price is to be fixed by the prices set by a designated market and no such prices are set. Is the contract to fail in that event, or is the court to fix a reasonable price?

Furthermore, it usually is a good idea for the parties to state the factors that should be used in determining a "reasonable price" in the event that a court is called on to make this determination. Unhappiness with open-price contracts in the commercial community often is the result of courts' setting prices without taking into account certain factors that are important to merchants. These factors ought to be stated in the agreement.

Finally, there may be minimum and maximum amounts beyond which the parties do not contemplate the price should be set. For example, the seller and buyer may not be able to agree on a precise price but both may be thinking in terms of a fairly limited range, such as some point between $8,000 and $10,000. If so, it is only common sense for them to state this range *in advance* of difficulties by placing the inside and outside limits in the contract itself. A court knowing from the contract itself that the parties intend to be bound even though they have not been able to agree on the price, that certain factors are critical in determining the price, and that the parties have set maximum and minimum limits, may arrive at a price different from that which the seller or buyer regard as proper, but working under these constraints it will seldom sorely disappoint either party.

d. MUTUALITY OF OBLIGATION. It should be noted that 2–305(2) permits the parties to agree that the price may be fixed in good faith by one party alone. Does this rule represent an exception to the basic contract concepts of mutuality of obligation or illusory promise?

The concept of bilateral contract includes the idea of mutual commitment, and this means that if one party has not really made any commitment, then there is no contract. In that case, the apparent but unreal commitment is illusory and is not consideration for the return promise. This idea has proved troublesome in sales law because often one of the parties to a sales agreement may wish to provide for "a way out" if certain contingencies occur or do not occur. For example, a buyer may wish to condition his obligation to buy upon obtaining satisfactory financing and a seller may want to reserve the right to cancel if certain events happen. Many courts were hostile to agreements that they thought left one of the parties free to perform or withdraw from the transaction at his own unfettered discretion, and their adverse decisions on these matters threatened the right of the parties to agree that one of them alone could determine such things as satisfaction, details of performance, price, cancellation, and good cause.

Section 2–305 does not allow the parties to agree effectively that the price may be set through the unfettered discretion of either. Discretion to set the price is limited by good faith. The drafters of the Code believed that this limitation was sufficient to satisfy the requirements of the concept of mutuality of obligation, and that any party giving the other the power to set the price should assume the risk that it will be set at an unexpectedly high or low point (from his point of view) so long as the power is exercised in good faith. Is this not a great risk for the party to undertake? How can the flexibility of such an open price term be preserved without so great an assumption of risk?

A common example of an open-price term to be set by one of the parties alone is found in the American steel industry where the standard contract gives the seller the right to set the price at the amount that is charged to all customers on the day of delivery. Under these contracts, the particular buyer is protected by the fact that it will get the same price other buyers got on the day in question. Is this enough to satisfy the requirements of mutuality of obligation? Is the buyer also protected by the seller's obligation to act in good faith? Any problem under 2–305(2)?

Specific attacks on the concept of mutuality of obligation can be found not only in 2–305 but in 2–306 (dealing with output and requirements contracts) and 2–311 (dealing with options and cooperation respecting details of performance). How far can these sections be used by way of analogy to resolve other mutuality problems, as, for example, the problem of "satisfaction"? For example, assume a seller and buyer enter into a contract in which a machine is sold and delivered on a "satisfaction-guaranteed" basis. Assume also that the buyer is not satisfied but the evidence establishes that the overwhelming number of people in the buyer's position would have been satisfied? If the buyer really is satisfied but wants to get out of the deal for other reasons and thus reports that he is dissatisfied, what result should the court reach? How can the fact finder determine whether the buyer really is dissatisfied with the machine?

———

James Mathis v. Exxon Corporation

United States Court of Appeals, Fifth Circuit, 2002.
302 F.3d 448.

■ JERRY E. SMITH, CIRCUIT JUDGE.

This is a breach of contract suit brought by fifty-four gasoline station franchisees against Exxon Corporation ("Exxon") for violating the Texas analogue of the Uniform Commercial Code's open price provision. We affirm.

Exxon markets its commercial gas bound for retailers primarily through three arrangements: franchisee contracts, jobber contracts, and company operated retail stores ("CORS.") A franchisee rents Exxon-branded gas stations and enters into a sales contract for the purchase of Exxon-brand gas. The contract sets the monthly quantity of gas the franchisee must purchase and allows Exxon to set the price he must pay. The franchisee pays the dealer tank wagon price ("DTW") and takes delivery of the gas at his station.

A jobber contract requires the purchaser to pay the "rack price," which usually is lower than the price charged to franchisees.* There is no sale of gas to CORS by Exxon, because the stores are owned by Exxon and

---

* A jobber is an intermediate distributor, in this case acquiring gasoline from Exxon   and, presumably, reselling it to independent service stations.—Ed.

staffed by its employees. Instead, an intra-company accounting is recorded that is equivalent to the price charged franchisees in the same price zone.

All the plaintiff franchisees operate stations in the greater Houston, Texas, and Corpus Christi, Texas, areas. The genesis of the dispute is the allegation that Exxon has violated the law and its contracts with these franchisees for the purpose of converting their stores to CORS by driving the franchisees out of business.

Since 1994, franchisees have been barred from purchasing their gas from jobbers, so all their purchases have been governed by the terms of the Retail Motor Fuel Store Sales Agreement, under which the "DEALER agrees to buy and receive directly from EXXON all of the EXXON-branded gasoline bought by DEALER, and at least seventy-five percent (75%) of the volume shown in [a specified schedule] . . . DEALER will pay EXXON for delivered products at EXXON's price in effect at the time of the loading of the delivery vehicle." This "price in effect," also known as the dealer tank wagon price ("DTW,") forms the heart of the present dispute. Exxon claims this arrangement is the industry standard and that almost all franchisor-franchisee sales of gasoline are governed by a similar price term. Plaintiffs respond that the DTW price charged under this clause is "consistently higher" than the rack price paid by jobbers plus transportation costs.

. . . The thrust of [plaintiffs'] testimony was that Exxon had set the DTW price at an uncompetitive level to drive them out of business (so as to replace their stores with CORS). Some of the plaintiffs testified that their franchises were unprofitable; they presented documents and witnesses to show that Exxon intended that result to drive them out of business.

The franchisees also submitted a market study showing that 62% of the franchisees in Corpus Christi were selling gas below the DTW price. The franchisees supported their theory of the case by calling Barry Pulliam as an expert witness on the economics of the gasoline market in Houston and Corpus Christi. [He] concluded that Exxon's DTW price was not commercially reasonable from an economic perspective because it was a price that, over time, put the purchaser at a competitive disadvantage. . . .

[His] conclusion rested on two main facts. First, he showed that 75% of the franchisee's competitors were able to purchase gasoline at a lower price. Second, he calculated a commercially reasonable DTW price by adding normal distribution charges to the average rack price of gasoline charged by Exxon and its competitors. He concluded that Exxon's DTW price exceeded the sum of these other prices by four or more cents per gallon.

Exxon countered with [its own expert], who testified that Exxon's DTW price was commercially reasonable because it reflected the company's investment in land, the store, transportation, and managers. [He] explained that Exxon recovers these costs through rent and the sale of gas.

The jury awarded $5,723,657 . . . . [Exxon appeals on the ground that the] court should have granted Exxon's motion for [judgment as a matter of law (j.m.l.)] . . . .

II.

Exxon contends that because it charged its franchisees a DTW price comparable to that charged by its competitors, the breach of contract claim is precluded as a matter of law.

A j.m.l. is appropriate where "a party has been fully heard on an issue and there is no legally sufficient evidentiary basis for a reasonable jury to find for that party on that issue." Fed.R.Civ.P. 50(a). We review the denial of j.m.l. *de novo.* . . .

III.

Texas law, which tracks the Uniform Commercial Code, implies a good faith component in any contract with an open price term. [§ 2.305]. The parties agree that the franchise agreement term governing the purchase of gasoline is an open price term.

. . .

The key disagreement is over what constitutes a breach of the duty of good faith. Exxon contends it has satisfied that duty because it has charged the plaintiffs a DTW price within the range of its competitors' DTW prices, thereby satisfying the "commercial reasonableness" meaning of good faith. Plaintiffs respond that good faith encompasses both objective and subjective duties. Even if Exxon is right, and its prices are within the range of its competitors', the argument runs, a subjective intent to drive the franchisees out of business would abridge the good faith duty of the open price term.

The pivotal provision is comment 3 to § 2.305. . . . In the absence of comment 3, there is no doubt Exxon would be subject to both the subjective "honesty in fact" good faith of § 1.201(19) and the objective "commercial reasonableness" good faith of § 2.103. The difficult question is whether comment 3 creates an exception to the normal principles of good faith governing the sale of goods.

The Code employs two standards of good faith. Section 1–201(19) states the generally applicable "subjective" ("white heart and empty head") standard which concentrates on the actual state of mind of the party rather than on the state of mind a reasonable man would have had under the same circumstances. Thus, the section defines good faith as "honesty in fact in the conduct or transaction concerned." In the case of merchants, however, or at least those merchants governed by Article 2 on Sales, an objective element is added to their good faith duties. Section 2–103(1)(b) provides that " '[g]ood faith' in the case of a merchant means honesty in fact and the observance of reasonable commercial standards of fair dealing in the trade." This definition imposes a duty on merchants to meet good faith requirements that are measured both subjectively and objectively.

No court in this circuit, and no Texas state court, has squarely addressed this question. Fortunately, because the Texas open price provision replicates that of the UCC, we can seek guidance from other courts.

To decide whether comment 3 creates an exception, we turn first to the text of the comment and the related sections of the Texas version of the UCC. In full, comment 3 reads,

> Subsection (2), dealing with the situation where the price is to be fixed by one party rejects the uncommercial idea that an agreement that the seller may fix the price means that he may fix any price he may wish by the express qualification that the price so fixed must be fixed in good faith. Good faith includes observance of reasonable commercial standards of fair dealing in the trade if the party is a merchant. (Section 2–103). But in the normal case a "posted price" or a future seller's or buyer's "given price," "price in effect," "market price," or the like satisfies the good faith requirement.

The bare text offers little to resolve the question. First, the comment notes that good faith "includes" reasonable commercial standards. This implies that the good faith required of a merchant setting an open price term encompasses both objective and subjective elements. The comment also creates a good faith safe harbor for such merchants when they use various sorts of fixed prices. But this safe harbor is applicable only in the "normal case." This suggests the safe harbor is not absolute, but it does nothing to define what takes a case out of the safe harbor.

As we will explain, we conclude that the "normal case" of comment 3 is coextensive with a merchant's residual "honesty in fact" duty embodied in §§ 1.201(19) and 2.103. Thus, the comment embraces both the objective (commercial reasonableness) and subjective (honesty in fact) senses of good faith; objective good faith is satisfied by a "price in effect" as long as there is honesty in fact (a "normal case"). This conclusion finds support in three sources: the structure of the UCC, its legislative history, and the caselaw.

Reading comment 3 to embody two different meanings of "good faith" tracks the general structure of the UCC. Courts and commentators have recognized that the meaning of "good faith" is not uniform throughout the code. The cases and commentary treat the "good faith" found in article 1 as subjective and the good faith found only in article 2 as objective. Thus, there is nothing inconsistent in comment 3's using "good faith" in both the objective and the subjective senses.

The history of comment 3 bolsters this conclusion. Some drafters of the UCC worried that for the "great many industries where sales are not made at fixed prices," such as the steel industry, where "practically every contract" is made at "the seller's price in effect," if § 2–305 "is to apply . . . it means that in every case the seller is going to be in a lawsuit . . . or he could be, because there isn't any outside standard at all." Proceedings of Enlarged Editorial Bd. of Am. Law Inst. (Sunday Morning Session, Jan. 28, 1951) (statement of Bernard Broeker). The drafters considered wholly exempting such contracts from § 2–305, or stating that for a price in effect, the only test is whether the merchant engaged in price discrimination. One drafter explained that the steel industry wanted to make "clear that we do not have to establish that we are fixing reasonable prices, because that gets you into the rate of return of profit, whether you are using borrowed money, and all those questions." *Id.*

The committee responded to these worries with the current comment 3: "[I]n the normal case a 'posted price' or a future seller's or buyer's 'given price,' 'price in effect,' 'market price,' or the like satisfies the good faith requirement." The drafter's solution was to avoid objective good faith challenges to prices set by reference to some "price in effect," while preserving challenges to discriminatory pricing. *See Hearing Before the Enlarged Editorial Board January 27–29, 1951,* 6 Business Lawyer 164, 186 (1951) (explaining this intent). Nothing in the proceedings leading to the addition of comment 3 suggests that the overall *subjective* good faith duty of §§ 1–201 and 2–103 was to be supplanted; the evidence is quite to the contrary.

The drafters ultimately rejected two suggested addendums to § 2–305:

> An agreement to the effect that the price shall be or be adjusted to, or be based upon, or determined by reference to the seller's going price, price in effect, regular price, market price, established price, or the like, at the time of the agreement or at any earlier or later time, is not an agreement to which this subsection is applicable.
>
> . . .
>
> An agreement such as this is an agreement under which the seller or the buyer does not have any burden of showing anything other than that he has not singled out the particular other party for discrimination. Proceedings of Enlarged Editorial Bd. (statement of Bernard Broeker).

Both of these recommendations are more sweeping than is the language ultimately adopted. The first would have omitted any mention of the good faith duty for open price provisions; the second would have limited the duty of the price-setter to that of avoiding discrimination.

The existing comment, however, avoids challenges to prices set according to an open price term unless that challenge is outside the normal type of case. Although price discrimination was the type of aberrant case on the minds of the drafters, price discrimination is merely a subset of what constitutes such an aberrant case. Any lack of subjective, honesty-in-fact good faith is abnormal; price discrimination is only the most obvious way a price-setter acts in bad faith—by treating similarly-situated buyers differently.

The caselaw supports this interpretation of comment 3. Courts that have addressed the normalcy question have consistently held that a lack of subjective good faith takes a challenge outside the bounds of what is normal.[11]

11. *See, e.g., Nanakuli Paving & Rock Co. v. Shell Oil Co.,* 664 F.2d 772, 806 (9th Cir.1981) (stating that "the dispute here was not over the amount of the increase—that is, the price that the seller fixed—but over the manner in which that increase was put into effect"); *Allapattah v. Exxon Corp.,* 61 F.Supp.2d 1308, 1322 (S.D.Fla.1999); ("Be-

Like the plaintiffs in *Nanakuli, Allapattah, and Wayman,* the franchisees here are alleging a breach of good faith grounded not in Exxon's failure to price in accord with an established schedule, but in its failure to set the price in good faith. Suits recognizing such a cause of action are rare, and with good reason: We would be ill-advised to consider a case to be outside the norm based only on an allegation of improper motive by the party setting the price.

Plaintiffs produced enough evidence to escape comment 3's "normal case" limitation. They showed, for example, that Exxon planned to replace a number of its franchises with CORS, that the DTW price was higher than the sum of the rack price and transportation, that Exxon prevented the franchisees from purchasing gas from jobbers after 1994, and that a number of franchisees were unprofitable or non-competitive.

For example, one Exxon document stated that the company's "Marketing Strategy for 1992–1997 is to reduce Dealer stores (est. 30%)." Another document set forth Exxon's plans to reduce dealer stations in Houston from 95 to 45, and to increase CORS from 83 to 150, between 1997 and 2003. James Carter, the Regional Director of the Exxon/Mobil Fuels Marketing Company, testified that Exxon made more of a profit from a CORS than from an independent lessee store. These plans and observations were validated by the fact that the number of dealer stations steadily declined.

An exhibit called the "Houston Screening Study" evaluated the strategy of "surplusing" (i.e., eliminating) 21 of 37 locations inside the Highway 610 loop. Of the 93 lessee-dealer stations, 69 would be done away with, but 73 of the 91 CORS would be kept.

Further indication of plans to shift from dealer-lessees to CORS is shown by Exxon's dissatisfaction with outlets featuring service bays. Exxon documents showed that service bays—generally associated with lessee-dealer locations—were becoming less profitable, while stations with convenience stores—generally associated with CORS—were the wave of the future. A document entitled "Retail Store Chain Outlook" revealed Exxon's plan to reduce stations with service bays from 2,506 to 190 from 1991 to 2005. That document included a plan to "[e]xpand CORS to improve profitability and to compete efficiently with private brands/distributors" and "[e]mphasize CORS operations in markets with high level of rack to retail competition."

Exxon's answer on appeal is that these documents "say nothing about *using pricing* to accomplish a 'plan' to eliminate dealers." Although that is so, there was sufficient evidence on this issue to go to the jury, which was

cause the parties' dispute is not over the actual amount of the purchase price Exxon charged for its wholesale gasoline to its dealers, but rather over the manner in which the wholesale price was calculated without considering the double charge for credit card processing, the instant action is not the 'normal' case."); *cf. Wayman v. Amoco Oil Co.,* 923 F.Supp. 1322, 1349 (D.Kan.1996), *aff'd,* 145 F.3d 1347 (10th Cir.1998) ("[T]his court believes the present case is a normal case. If there was evidence that Amoco had, for example, engaged in discriminatory pricing or tried to run plaintiffs out of business, then the court's decision might be different.").

free to, and apparently did, draw the inference connecting pricing to the elimination of dealer-lessees. The consequence of the jury's decision is that this case exceeds the "normal case" limit of § 2.305 comment 3. We still, however, must examine the content of the duty of subjective good faith. Although no Texas or Fifth Circuit case has squarely addressed the meaning of the good faith clause of § 2.305, Texas courts repeatedly have held that the "honesty in fact" definition of good faith found in § 1.201(19) is tied to the actual belief of the participant in the transaction. Thus, the same version of the facts accepted by the jury—that Exxon intended to drive the franchisees out of business—that takes this case out of the "normal" set of cases for purposes of comment 3 also satisfies the criteria for bad faith.

Exxon's bad faith, in this regard, is shown by the record. Facing the competition of self-service stations that were either selling food and other goods or had bare pumps with no overhead costs incurred in servicing vehicles, Exxon decided years ago that retail marketing through franchise dealers was becoming economically unsound. Although Exxon decided to move to CORS in Houston and jobbers in Corpus Christi, this decision was not communicated to its franchisees. Because of profit from their other sales, CORS could, and did, sell gas for less than the franchise dealers paid to Exxon for their gas. And the jobbers delivered Exxon gas to their dealers for less than Exxon franchisees were required to pay for their delivered gas, but Exxon prohibited its franchisees from buying at this lower price from the jobbers.

The loss of competitive position and profit to plaintiff franchisees was inevitable and foreseeable to Exxon. Although Exxon witnesses denied receiving complaints, its dealers testified that they had complained often and for years, without success, until the very eve of trial.

Accordingly, the jury's finding that Exxon breached its duty of good faith in setting the DTW price it charged the plaintiffs is not without foundation in the law or the evidence. As we have recounted, plaintiffs offered ample evidence tending to prove their version of price-setting. Accordingly, there is no error in the refusal to grant Exxon j.m.l. on the breach of contract claim.

. . .

QUESTIONS AND NOTES

1. The jury evidently concluded that Exxon lacked the good faith required by 2–305(2). As a practical matter, does this mean that Exxon may not charge more than its competitors charge their franchisees? more than it charges the jobbers who purchase its gasoline? If Exxon charges its franchisees the same price that it charges jobbers, but raises the franchise fee by an amount equal to 4¢ per gallon, would Exxon violate 2–305?

2. Revised Article 1. The court in *Mathis* notes that the Article 1 definition of good faith (1–201(19)) is "honesty in fact in the conduct or transaction concerned," while in Article 2, the definition of good faith, in the case of a merchant, is "honesty in fact *and the observance of reasonable commercial standards of fair dealing in the trade*" (2–103(1)(b)). Revised 1–201(20) and 2–103(j) extend the Article 2 definition to all persons, so that all parties, not just merchants, have an obligation to observe reasonable commercial standards of fair dealing. Of the states enacting revised Article 1, a small fraction has rejected this change, instead adhering to the original definition for Article 1.

3. Section 2–304 states that the price may be made payable in money, goods, realty, or otherwise. What is the purpose of this section? Is it really a scope section? If A agrees to trade his HDTV set to B in return for B's exercise equipment, does Article 2 govern the transaction? If so who is the seller and who is the buyer? (The answer to this question is important because many of the rules of Article 2 are directed to buyers or to sellers but not both). If A agrees to trade a small plot of land to B for $10,000 and a boat, is the transaction covered by Article 2? All of the transaction? Part of it?

4. Open-price problems compounded by other uncertain terms. The open-price contract may be the result of a decision by the buyer and seller as to allocation of market risks, or it may come about as part and parcel of a bigger problem involving uncertainty as to the description of the subject matter, the quantity of goods to be taken, or both. The problem may be further exacerbated when the open price is to be set by some standard other than "reasonable price" or "market price."

Consider Royal Store Fixture Co. v. Bucci, 48 Pa.D. & C.2d 696 (Pa. Co.1969). Defendant purchased real estate with the intention of erecting a restaurant on it. Plaintiff was an executive of the Royal Store Fixture Co. which specialized in selling restaurant equipment, and he had expertise as a planner of restaurants and stores. Plaintiff and defendant entered into a contract in which plaintiff agreed to work up the plans and specifications for the new restaurant and defendant promised to buy all his restaurant equipment from plaintiff "at prices competitive with other Manufacturers' equipment of equality and specifications." Plaintiff made the plans for defendant's restaurant and submitted a list of items of equipment that would be needed in it, but without specifications as to make and model. The first list totaled $29,004; the second list (different equipment) was $14,347; and third and fourth lists were in different amounts. Defendant rejected these bids and bought his equipment from another seller.

Plaintiff sued for breach of the sales contract, arguing that his prices were competitive for the items he had listed. He conceded that there were many items of equipment that could be used by defendant, and that he (plaintiff) had no way of knowing whether Royal's prices were competitive with prices that others would charge unless that equipment could be identified. He also indicated that he was willing to dicker the price. In explaining the overall price he testified that (referring to the second bid of

$14,347) ''this is normally only the beginning of a sale, because you then sit down with your customer, and then he starts to haggle, and before you know it, your fourteen thousand three forty five price might be down to thirteen thousand three hundred.'' The court said the parties had left the price open because it was to be agreed upon at a later time.

Was there a contract? Is *Unique Designs v. Pittard Machinery* (page 39 supra) relevant? Is 2–204(3) relevant? How about 2–306? How do these sections relate, if at all, to 2–305? Stated differently, assume a quantity term is vague in some respects but meets the standards of 2–306, and a price term is vague in some respects, but meets the standards of 2–305. If these two terms are combined in the same contract, is the contract too indefinite to be enforced? Do you add up the sum total of vagueness in determining whether the standard of 2–204(3) is met?

5.   CISG. Article 55 of the Convention on Contracts for the International Sale of Goods states

> Where a contract has been validly concluded but does not expressly or implicitly fix or make provision for determining the price, the parties are considered, in the absence of any indication to the contrary, to have impliedly made reference to the price generally charged at the time of the conclusion of the contract for such goods sold under comparable circumstances in the trade concerned.

Thus it substitutes ''the price generally charged at the time of the conclusion of the contract'' for the ''reasonable price'' of 2–305. Which formulation is preferable?

Consider Article 14, which states, in part, ''A proposal is sufficiently definite if it indicates the goods and expressly or implicitly fixes or makes provision for determining the quantity and the price.'' Under Article 14, if a proposal does not expressly or implicitly fix, or make provision for determining, the price, can its acceptance result in a contract? If not, then what is the effect of Article 55?

2.   QUANTITY

Riegel Fiber Corp. v. Anderson Gin Co.

United States Court of Appeals, Fifth Circuit, 1975.
512 F.2d 784.

■ THORNBERRY, CIRCUIT JUDGE. . . .

I.

In late March 1973 Riegel Fiber Company, whose headquarters are in Trion, Georgia, entered into certain ''forward'' contracts for the sale of cotton with the Alabama ginner-defendants, Ellis Brothers and Anderson Gin Company. After negotiations the parties agreed on a price of $.32 a pound. Contract cotton was to come from two sources. The owners of the ginning companies grow cotton as well as gin it, and they agreed to sell

Riegel a portion of their own contemplated production. To provide the major portion of the cotton called for by the contracts, however, the ginners had earlier entered into separate contracts with a number of individual Alabama cotton farmers, who promised to sell portions of their cotton production to Ellis and Anderson also at $.32 a pound. These contracts were executed on forms provided to the ginners by Riegel,[3] and it is undisputed that all the farmers knew that Riegel would be the ultimate buyer of their cotton. The commercial rationale for this sale and resale arrangement is not entirely clear, but nothing in the record contradicts Riegel's explanation that it allowed the company to take advantage of the ginners' familiarity with local farmers.

During the spring and summer of 1973 the price of cotton rose dramatically. By October 1973 the parties stipulated that the market price of the type of cotton called for by the contracts had reached $.81 a pound. As the Supreme Court has rather mildly put it, "This situation may generate a strong economic incentive for * * * [the farmer] to breach his contract and sell the cotton elsewhere." Allenberg Cotton Co., Inc. v. Pittman, supra, 419 U.S. 20, at 26 n.8, 95 S.Ct. 260, at 264 n.8, 42 L.Ed.2d 195, at 202 n.8. When Riegel's president first became aware of rumblings among the farmers he went to Alabama and told them that Riegel intended to enforce its contracts. Learning later, however, that this warning had fallen on less than receptive ears, Riegel brought suit against both Ellis and Anderson seeking to have the contracts declared valid and asking that they be specifically enforced. These suits named as additional defendants the individual farmers whose production Anderson and Ellis had agreed to purchase and then re-sell to Riegel.

Upon appellant's request, the district court entered a preliminary injunction directing the defendants to deliver to Riegel all cotton provided for by the contracts, conditioned upon Riegel's posting a $1,725,000 bond to secure payment of costs, damages, and attorney's fee in the event that the contracts were held invalid. Both sides concede that this injunction has been fully complied with. . . . Stating his conclusions orally from the bench, the district judge held ... that the Riegel-ginner contracts (the "master" contracts) did not contain a quantity term sufficient to satisfy the Alabama statute of frauds . . . .

II.

For the sake of clarity we will first consider Riegel's status with regard to the "individual" contracts [i.e. the contracts between the ginners and the farmers]. . . .

. . . [A]ppellant is entitled to enforce the individual contracts as a third party beneficiary thereof. The question remains, however, whether this right is of any value, since the district judge held that the master contracts failed to satisfy the Alabama statute of frauds and strongly implied that if

---

3. In fact, the forms used for the ginner-farmer contracts were identical to the forms used for the Riegel-ginner contracts.

necessary he would have reached the same conclusion concerning the individual contracts.

Our analysis begins, as did the district court's, with Code of Alabama Title 7A, § 2–201, the UCC's statute of frauds for the sale of goods. . . . As Official Comment 1 to § 2–201 notes:

> Only three definite and invariable requirements as to the memorandum are made by this subsection. First, it must evidence a contract for the sale of goods; second, it must be "signed," a word which includes any authentication which identifies the party to be charged; and third, it must specify a quantity.

Appellees do not question that the detailed and signed written contracts involved in this case satisfy the first two requirements set out in the comment. Nor can they well deny that the writings contain a quantity term, since they plainly do.[7] Instead, appellees apparently argue that because the quantity terms included in the written forms are allegedly too indefinite to support enforcement of the underlying agreement, the writings in legal effect have no quantity term at all. Accordingly, appellees contend, the district judge correctly held that § 2–201 barred enforcement of the contracts.

To the contrary, we think that the lower court erred in relying on § 2–201. The statute of frauds is only one of many potential barriers to the enforcement of agreements. As the language of § 2–201 reveals, the statute's overriding purpose is "to indicate that a contract for sale has been made between the parties." It is a device to prevent fraudulent and perjurious assertions of a contract where none in fact existed; the writing evidencing the parties' contractual status need not, and often does not, state all the terms of the agreement. In the instant case the evidence is overwhelming and uncontradicted that the parties intended to and did enter into a contract. They reduced their agreement—in fact, as the district judge found, they reduced their entire agreement—to written form: the writings were signed, attested, and contained a quantity term. Moreover, for the limited purposes of meeting the technical statute of frauds requirement embodied in § 2–201 the accuracy of the quantity term is immaterial.[11] Plainly, the real issue in this case is not whether these contracts

---

7. Typical is the Riegel–Ellis contract: 1. On the terms and conditions and at the prices set forth below, Buyer agrees to purchase and take delivery from Seller, and Seller agrees to sell and deliver to Buyer, all the acceptable cotton produced during the crop year 1973 on the following acreage, and none other:

No. of Acres	Farm No.	County	Allotment in Name of	Projected Yield 1973
4,222		Cherokee & Calhoun Counties, Alabama	Various	500 Lbs. Per Acre

11. "The only term which must appear is the quantity term which need not be accurately stated but recovery is limited to the amount stated." § 2–201, comment 1. That is, the litigant seeking to enforce the contract bears the risk if the writing entitles him to less than he and his opponent actually agreed upon, see White & Summers, Handbook of the Law Under the Uniform Commercial Code § 2–4, at 54 (1972), but such inaccuracy does not alone make the writing insufficient for purposes of the statute. White and Sum-

satisfy § 2–201, but whether the quantity term in the agreement the parties undeniably made—as reflected in the signed writings—is too indefinite to support judicial enforcement. Section 2–201 itself does not purport to address this question. The unspoken assumption in that section is that when court and litigants turn to the writing for the quantity term, no dispute will remain that the statute of frauds has been satisfied; hence, the agreement is no different from any other contract to which the Code applies. Thus, for the applicable standards of definiteness in contract provisions we must have recourse to Code sections other than § 2–201.

Appellant places principal reliance on U.C.C. § 2–306, which relates to output and requirements contracts and is the primary "gap-filler" in the Code for quantity terms. We need not reach the question whether these contracts fall within the reach of § 2–306, however, because we think appellant presented ample evidence that the quantity terms in the master and individual contracts—viewed as requiring delivery of various pounds of cotton[14]—meet the standards of definiteness required by the Code for enforceability.[15] Section 2–204(3) states the general rule:

mers plausibly suggest that the language of § 2–201 itself, as opposed to the comments, can be read to require no quantity term at all. Id. at 51 n. 44, 266 So.2d 896. Under this reading any quantity term in the writing would control, but if no such term were present the party seeking enforcement could establish it by parol along with all the other provisions of the agreement. Indeed, the quantity term requirement does appear to offer little in aid of the primary purpose of the statute, i.e. discouraging fraudulent oral assertions of nonexistent contracts. Once a party alleges that the agreement took place and proffers a signed writing to prove it, surely he is no more likely to lie about the agreed quantity term than about price, time of performance, or any other material term that § 2–201 expressly allows to be omitted from the writing. Nevertheless, the Code's authors apparently thought it necessary to protect parties against this one brand of perjury. Id. at 52–53. In any event, appellees do not contend that the "amount stated" in the writings is definite and that Riegel is attempting to force them to sell more than that amount.

14.   Riegel points out that simply by multiplying the number of acres stated in the contracts times the estimated yield, one derives a quantity term stated in pounds of cotton. Furthermore, citing U.C.C. § 2–306(1), the company contends that any slight variation in yield from acre to acre is immaterial, since in no event would the contract be enforceable beyond a quantity not unreason-

ably disproportionate to the estimated yield stated in the contract. Although § 2–306(1) concerns output and requirements contracts, we think that the Code's general good faith provision, U.C.C. § 1–203, accomplishes the same result here where a contractual quantity is subject to "natural" variations. Section 1–203 would also help obviate any difficulty with those individual contracts where no estimated yield is stated.

15.   We have already held that the two "levels" of contracts involved here can be viewed only as different parts of one contractual transaction. Any imprecision in the master contracts regarding which farmers have bound themselves through Anderson and Ellis to sell to Riegel was resolved by introduction of the individual contracts and by the testimony adduced at trial. This evidence was admissible both to explain the quantity terms in the master contracts and to allow Riegel to prove its interest in the individual contracts. Neither the parol evidence rule nor the so-called merger or integration clauses in the contracts affect the admissibility of the evidence. The parol evidence rule, except in certain circumstances, forbids the parties to supplement the terms stated in the writing evidencing the contract. It does not, however, forbid the admission of extrinsic evidence to explain the meaning of words contained in the writing. The line between explanation and supplementation is narrow and occasionally difficult to draw, but in this case it is clear that plaintiff offered its evidence for the former purpose and not for the latter. . . .

Even though one or more terms are left open a contract for sale does not fail for indefiniteness if the parties have intended to make a contract and there is a reasonably certain basis for giving an appropriate remedy.

The official comment to this section adds that "commercial standards on the point of 'indefiniteness' are intended to be applied." Thus, we view our inquiry as limited to the question whether these contracts contained quantity terms acceptable to the majority of buyers and sellers knowledgeable in the cotton trade.

Unfortunately, the parties directed their arguments more to technical contract doctrine than to the commercial reasonableness of the method used in these agreements to designate quantity. A review of the record, briefs, and argument of counsel convinces us, however, that the quantity terms as stated in the contracts can meet the Code's test for definiteness. Significantly, the record is clear that appellees themselves supplied the actual quantity provisions on the forms tendered by Riegel. The individual farmers provided the farm numbers and the acres to be covered by their contracts. The ginner defendants totalled the acreage in the individual contracts, added their personal acreage, and inserted the resulting total acreage into the master contracts. The evidence shows no objections made by any appellee to the forms at the time the contracts were entered into; likewise, it reveals no attempt by appellees to insert what they now argue would be more definite terms, even though they clearly had the opportunity to do so.[16] Moreover, although we do not give controlling weight to this factor, it cannot be ignored that appellees successfully identified and allocated contract and non-contract cotton when required to do so by the lower court's injunction.

The district court relied heavily on the impossibility of determining from the face of the master contracts the specific fields covered by the agreements. The judge likewise expressed doubt that the individual contracts would help much in locating this precise acreage. Yet we find no evidence that any of the parties believe that such specificity is *commercially* necessary or even desirable. For its part, Riegel is apparently willing to rely to a large extent on the farmers' good faith and commercial reasonableness in choosing which of their acres are to be used to grow contract cotton.[17] Likewise, the record contains no hint of why the individual farmers or the ginners might prefer as a normal practice to contract as to rigidly specified

---

16. As the Court of Claims recently noted, "The law rejects post facto claims that agreements are too indefinite for enforcement, where the parties knew what each of them was to do under the contract and some standard exists to measure performance." Saul Bass & Associates v. United States, Ct. Cl.1974, 505 F.2d 1386, 1394. Appellees' readiness to execute these agreements is strong evidence that they knew what they had to do to meet their contractual obligations.

17. There is little reason for them to do otherwise. Quality control is taken care of by the provision that Riegel will buy only "acceptable" cotton, as carefully defined in the contract. In addition, by stating quantity in terms of pounds or bales of acceptable cotton Riegel arguably avoids any hazards created by the varying productivity of specific fields.

fields.[18] We think Riegel's evidence clearly makes out a prima facie case that the quantity terms in the master contracts, as well as in the individual contracts, conform to acceptable practice in the cotton trade. Consequently, the district judge erred in granting appellees' motion for involuntary dismissal under Fed.R.Civ.P. 41(b).

. . .

QUESTIONS AND NOTES

1. Output and requirements contracts. Some common-law courts struck down sales contracts as illusory if they contained terms measuring the quantity of the goods by the seller's output or the buyer's requirements. These decisions were based on the assumption that an output or requirements agreement leaves one of the parties completely free to fix the

---

18. Appellees have pitched almost their entire argument on "unique" technical faults allegedly present in the particular arrangements chosen by Riegel here. They offer little to buttress their argument except hypotheticals showing a supposed lack of mutuality in the agreements. When asked directly at oral argument whether it is commercially important to know the specific fields covered by cotton contracts, counsel for the farmers responded only that it was important to *these* contracts. Significantly, the testimony of Mr. Ellis revealed with regard to his individual cotton acreage that (1) he had no specific fields in mind when he signed the contract; (2) he never designated any fields as "contract" acres; (3) his intent when contracting was to sell half of his production; and (4) when his production turned out to be less than he anticipated, he nevertheless delivered under the contract half of the cotton he did produce without protest on Riegel's part. Appendix at 169–71.

We admit to some confusion concerning why the column for farm numbers was inserted into the form contracts if Riegel intended only to obtain a given quantity of cotton; that object could have been achieved by specifying only the number of acres and the estimated yield. Although the record is not entirely clear, we think that one plausible explanation is that Riegel's forms were drawn to allow a stricter contract than Riegel in fact required of the farmers. That is, Riegel could have contracted as to specific farms but preferred a more flexible arrangement. See note 17, supra. This theory is bolstered,

we believe, by certain facts brought out at trial. Riegel obtained the completed individual contract forms from Ellis and Anderson only when preparing for this litigation. Presumably, then, if the ginners had delivered the quantity of cotton required by the master contracts, Riegel never would have known on which exact farms the cotton was produced. Second, the following testimony of Mr. Ellis, one of the ginner-defendants, suggests the possibility that the farmers may have provided the farm numbers only because they believed the forms required it of them:

> Q.: How was the information pertaining to each of the side [individual] contracts * * * that is the filling in of the blanks, how was that done?
>
> A.: You're referring to the farmer's name, the farm number, the acres?
>
> Q.: Yes, sir.
>
> A.: The individual farmer gave that information . . .
>
> Q.: All right, sir. Did you have any source of that information other than from the farmers themselves?
>
> A.: No, sir.

Appendix at 172. Of course, we need not decide whether the farmers could on these facts supply Riegel only with cotton grown on the farms specified in the individual contracts, but we do think it significant that appellees do not contend that the written contracts required them to sell more cotton to Riegel than they subjectively intended.

amount of goods to be sold, and thus completely free to avoid the contract altogether by fixing the amount at zero. Even adopting this assumption, however, some courts sustained these contracts on the ground that to set the quantity at zero would mean that the output seller would have to completely curtail manufacturing (thus having no output) and the requirements buyer to cease his selling activities (thus having no requirements for additional inventory), and that such cessation of activities, of itself, amounts to consideration for the return promise. Section 2–306 rejects both of these common law positions.

Output and requirements contracts are not considered one-sided in commercial circles. An output contract has obvious advantages for the seller, because it assures him that he will have a market for all the goods he produces. It is disadvantageous to the buyer in that he may end up buying more goods than he needs. What are the disadvantages to the seller, and what are the advantages to the buyer under this arrangement?

Consider the converse situation with requirements contracts. A requirements contract is advantageous to the buyer because it assures the buyer of having just the right amount of goods in inventory. The buyer does not have to guess at what the inventory needs will be, with the risk that too high an estimate will result in an unsold and unsalable supply of goods, and too low an estimate will result in the buyer's being unable to meet resale opportunities. The seller, on the other hand, suffers the disadvantage of not knowing the quantity to be sold and is likely to sell fewer goods to the buyer than would be the case under a contract that fixed the amount of quantity at a definite amount. What does the seller gain by such a contract, and what does the buyer lose? If the buyer is in fact "locked in" to the requirements seller, that fact (and its converse in output contracts) should provide the necessary facts to avoid consideration and mutuality problems.

Note that the good-faith limitation of 2–306 prevents the parties from arbitrarily increasing or decreasing their output or requirements for ulterior reasons. Is this safeguard sufficient? Prudent businessmen often feel that they are best safeguarded in output and requirements deals by including in the contract a stated estimate of what the output or requirements will be, or by a statement giving a range within which the output or requirements must fall. If either or both parties are new business enterprises, however, these safeguards may not be practicable. Can you think of other safeguards that might be used in this situation?

2. According to footnote 7, the contract called for "all the . . . cotton produced during . . . 1973 on the following acreage." This leaves open the precise number of pounds to be delivered, but 2–306(1) in effect provides that the agreement is sufficiently definite to be enforced. Why didn't the court rest its decision on 2–306? In what other way was the contract indefinite? See footnote 18.

Is 2–311 relevant?

3.   Problem. Buyer manufactures refrigerant, for which it needs chloroform. After difficult negotiations with Seller, in which Buyer has been unable to persuade Seller to reduce its price to less than $5 per pound, Buyer agrees to purchase its requirements of chloroform for five years at $5 per pound. After three years of performance, Buyer informs Seller that it has been losing money and will continue to do so unless Seller reduces the price to $3 per pound. Seller declines to lower the price of the chloroform. In response, Buyer closes its manufacturing facility and ceases manufacturing the refrigerant. To continue selling refrigerant, however, it arranges for another manufacturer to produce the refrigerant for it. Seller sues for breach of the requirements contract. What result?

4.   Exclusive-dealing contracts. Exclusive dealing contracts are a variant of requirements contracts, in which the buyer is given the exclusive right to sell the product produced by the seller in a given territory and the seller promises to supply the buyer's requirements of that product. Unless the contract provides to the contrary, the buyer is free to sell other products in that territory and to acquire those products from different sellers. Thus, a buyer may have an exclusive right to sell Prada shoes in a particular town, but may be free to sell other shoes as well. Are such contracts too one-sided (in favor of the buyer) to be enforceable? Section 2–306(2) answers this question in the negative. What does the seller gain by such an arrangement? If the buyer is selling several different products that compete with the seller's product, is there a conflict of interest? If so, does 2–306(2) adequately resolve the conflict?

5.   Open-quantity term. Can the quantity term of a sales contract be left open to the same extent as the price term? In many situations, of course, the presence of either term will provide a basis for finding the other. Thus, for example, a contract to sell "$1,000 worth of cotton" states the price term directly and the quantity term inferentially, and the converse is true if the contract calls for the sale of "100 bales of cotton at going prices."

If neither term is stated, is there "a reasonably certain basis for giving an appropriate remedy" within the meaning of 2–204(3)? Stated differently, could a court reasonably enforce a contract under which the seller agreed to sell and the buyer to buy "some of my cotton at a price to be worked out later" if they, in fact, could not come to an agreement subsequently as to these terms? If they later agreed on the quantity term, but not the price term, would the contract be saved? Or is it void *ab initio?* Read again 2–204(3). Suppose they could work out the price term (e.g. "$30 per bale") but not the quantity term. Would that save the contract?

6.   Problem. Jordan agrees to sell the entire production of cotton, estimated to be 500 pounds per acre, of 400 acres of her farm to Riegel Fiber Corp. at $1 per pound. Jordan's farm is much larger than 400 acres, and she actually plants and harvests 800 acres of cotton. In past years, the average yield of the 800-acre tract has been 500 pounds per acre. During this year, however, perhaps because of uneven application of fertilizers or irrigation, the actual yield on the 800 acres ranges from a low of 250 pounds per acre to a high of 900 pounds per acre. The poorest-yielding 400 acres yields an average of 400 pounds per acre; the highest-yielding 400 acres yields an average of 700 pounds per acre. The average yield for the entire tract of 800 acres is 550 pounds per acre. The following diagram of part of her farm illustrates the situation, with the stream dividing the land in half.

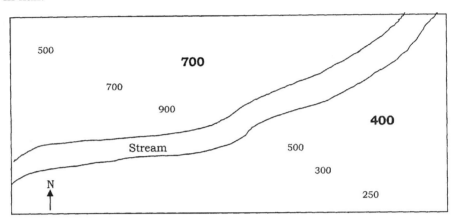

Does Jordan breach the contract by tendering delivery of 160,000 pounds of cotton, the output of the worst-yielding 400 acres? If you think so, what quantity must she tender in order for her not to be in breach?

Would it matter if, before she knows the yield for any part of the land, she contracts to sell to another buyer the output from the land to the northwest of the stream?

7. "More or less" quantity terms. Sometimes a contract of sale is made in which the quantity term is qualified by words such as "more or less" or "about" (e.g. "about 1000 bales of cotton.") Obviously, the purpose of the qualifying word or words is to protect the seller against variations in the number, measure, or weight of the described goods. Usually, when these qualifying words are used the variations will be slight, but suppose they are great: is there a contract in that case? If so, for what amount? Does it make a difference that the described goods can be identified by reference to independent circumstances? (E.g. "The entire lot of goods located in XYZ warehouse, more or less 10 tons." Suppose only two tons of goods comprise the entire lot in XYZ warehouse.) Compare: ("I will sell you all the goods I have, believed to be ten tons more or less." It turns out that the seller only has two tons) with ("I will sell you ten tons, more or less." The seller tenders two tons).

3. PAYMENT

The payment term should not be confused with the price term. The price term deals with "how much" must be paid. The payment term deals with "where, when, and how" that payment is to be made. Unlike the price term, which is usually stated in a sales contract, the payment term often is omitted. In that event, differences of opinion may result as to when the buyer is obliged to pay, where the payment is to be made, and in what manner (e.g. cash, check, certified check, etc.). These gaps, of course, can be filled in some cases by resort to course of performance, course of dealing, or usage of trade. In other cases statutory terms found in 2–310, 2–507, and 2–511 provide answers.

Sections 2–507(1) and 2–511(1) embrace the common-law doctrine of constructive conditions. The obligation of the seller to deliver the goods and the obligation of the buyer to pay for them are concurrently conditional. That is, the seller's obligation to deliver is conditional on the buyer's tender of payment, and the buyer's obligation to pay is conditional on the seller's tender of delivery. Section 2–310(a) reinforces this by requiring payment at the time and place of delivery even if the buyer takes delivery at the seller's place of business. Each of these rules, of course, may be varied by agreement of the parties.

Please reconsider Southwest Engineering v. Martin Tractor, page 50 supra. The seller argued that because the parties had never agreed on the time for payment, there was no contract. The court held that the parties did have a contract because they intended that a contract exist even though they had not settled on a payment term. The court observed that if the parties do not agree on the payment term, 2–310 supplies one. Since the deal collapsed before delivery of the goods, it was not necessary to determine when payment was due. But what if the seller had tendered delivery of the goods and refused to leave them unless the buyer paid the entire price: would it be appropriate to conclude that payment was due on delivery?

4.   Delivery

Delivery is an essential element in a sales contract, because if the transaction is really a sale the seller must at some time and some place and in some manner deliver the goods to the buyer. In well-written sales contracts these aspects of time, place, and manner are described. Unfortunately, not all contracts are well drafted, and some or all of these matters may be omitted.

Unlike open price and quantity terms, courts applying the common law did not take a dim view of open delivery terms. That is to say, they did not regard the delivery term as so material that its inclusion was deemed necessary to make the agreement enforceable. Rather, the courts used the same techniques for determining this missing term that Article 2 now adopts for many terms. The courts looked first to course of dealing, course of performance, and usage of trade to ascertain any implied understanding relating to delivery. If that produced no satisfactory answer, they used a set of rules, said to be based on common practices, to fill the gap. This approach, of course, is identical to the one employed by Article 2. With few exceptions, the statutory delivery terms of Article 2, found in 2–307, 2–308, and 2–309, carry forward the rules developed at common law.

Some of these rules, however, may seem strange to one not fully conversant with commercial practices. How would you handle this hypothetical: S in St. Louis agrees to sell to B in Chicago a large piece of equipment needed by B for manufacturing purposes. Nothing is said about place of delivery. At the proper time S calls B and says, "The machine is ready. Come down and get it." B refuses, "It is your duty to bring it to my plant." S refuses to deliver the machine to B's plant. Which party, if either, has breached the contract?

Suppose the hypothetical involved a large piece of furniture that a consumer bought from a retail furniture store. Any change in result? If so, where do you find that change in the UCC?

Luedtke Engineering Co., Inc. v. Indiana Limestone Co., Inc.

United States Court of Appeals, Seventh Circuit, 1984.
740 F.2d 598.

■ BAUER, CIRCUIT JUDGE. Plaintiff Luedtke Engineering Company brought this diversity action against defendant Indiana Limestone Company, alleging that Indiana Limestone breached its contract to sell breakwater stone to Luedtke. The district court held in favor of Indiana Limestone, and Luedtke appeals. We affirm.

I

In December 1977, the Army Corps of Engineers (the Corps) solicited bids for repair of the breakwater in the Milwaukee harbor. The Corps approved two sources from which bidders could purchase stone: Indiana Limestone and another quarry located in Indiana. The Corps earlier had given Indiana Limestone information about the repair project, including details of the Corps' time schedule. That schedule anticipated that work on the project would begin in March 1978 and be completed by November 1979.

The Corps also sent Indiana Limestone a list of the general contractors who planned to bid on the project; the list included Luedtke. Indiana Limestone and Luedtke had engaged in at least five other projects together. After receiving the list, Indiana Limestone sent Luedtke a letter containing a price quotation. Indiana Limestone's letter, dated February 20, 1978, contained the following proposals:

(1) Indiana Limestone would supply Luedtke with 70,000 tons of stone at $10.15 per net ton;

(2) The price would apply to shipments made during 1978 and 1979;

(3) Luedtke would be obligated to negotiate the freight rate for stone shipped in 1979 with the railroad company.

Luedtke relied on Indiana Limestone's quote to formulate its bid for the project. On April 12, 1978, the Corps awarded the contract to Luedtke.

After it received the Corps contract, Luedtke located a different quarry that offered to sell breakwater stone for $5.25 per ton. Because this quarry had not been approved by the Corps, Luedtke made several attempts to obtain permission from the Corps to buy stone from this quarry. When Indiana Limestone learned that Luedtke wanted to buy from another source, an Indiana Limestone official phoned Luedtke and offered to lower his company's price to $5.50 per ton. On the same day, the Corps denied Luedtke's request to purchase stone from the unapproved quarry.

On July 1, 1978, Luedtke issued, a purchase order to Indiana Limestone for 70,000 tons of stone at $5.50 per ton. The order stated that Indiana Limestone should "ship at 1500 tons/day starting 24 July 1978." At this rate, shipping would be completed by November 1978. For a variety of reasons, Indiana Limestone did not ship the stone at the specified rate; Luedtke instead received the last shipment in August 1979. Luedtke nevertheless finished the job in September 1979, seven weeks before the Corps' scheduled completion date of November 15.

Luedtke brought suit alleging that Indiana Limestone breached its contract by failing to ship the breakwater stone at the rate of 1,500 tons per day. Luedtke claimed that it incurred damages of $797,700 as a result of untimely and delayed deliveries. Indiana Limestone countered that it was unaware of Luedtke's intention to finish the project by November 1978, that it believed the shipping rate of 1,500 tons per day was merely an optimal goal, and that its delays in delivery were caused by factors beyond its control, including insufficient rail service, labor strikes, and bad weather.

The district court held in favor of Indiana Limestone. The court ruled that Indiana Limestone's February 20 quote letter was an offer to sell breakwater stone to Luedtke, and that Luedtke's purchase order was an acceptance of that offer. The court found that Luedtke's specific delivery requirement was a "material alteration" of the offer under Indiana law, and thus the parties had not agreed to a shipping rate. As a result, the court turned to the parties' course of dealing and trade usage in the industry to evaluate Indiana Limestone's performance. The court determined that Indiana Limestone delivered the stone in a reasonable time and thus did not breach the contract. Alternatively, the court held that even if Luedtke's shipping term was part of the contract, course of dealing and trade usage could help interpret the contract, and Indiana Limestone still would not be liable.

II

This case is governed by the Indiana Commercial Code, Ind. Code § 26–1–1–101 (1979), which is identical to the Uniform Commercial Code in all sections relevant to this dispute. Under § 2–207, an additional term in an acceptance to a contract between merchants becomes part of the contract unless the offer expressly limits acceptance to the offer's specific terms, the offeror objects to the additional term, or the additional term materially alters the contract. Luedtke argues that the district court erred in concluding that the delivery term in Luedtke's purchase order was a material alteration.

. . .

. . . Comment 4 to § 2–207 defines "material alteration" as a term that would "result in surprise or hardship if incorporated without express awareness by the other party." Determining this requires the trial court to make a factual evaluation of the parties' positions in each case. . . .

The evidence in the record supports the district court's conclusion that enforcing a delivery rate of 1,500 tons per day would have resulted in surprise and hardship for Indiana Limestone. The court based its finding on two factors. First, the court concluded that the delivery rate was based on Luedtke's intention to complete the Milwaukee breakwater project by November 1978, but that Indiana Limestone did not know of Luedtke's intention. The evidence amply supports this finding. In the summer of 1977, the Corps told Indiana Limestone that the completion date of the project was November 1979. Indiana Limestone made two references to 1979 prices in its offer to Luedtke and there is no evidence that Luedtke communicated to Indiana Limestone its desire to complete the project by November 1978. Indeed, in June 1978 Luedtke submitted a construction project chart to the Corps showing a July 1979 completion date.

. . . [T]he district court found that expecting Indiana Limestone to deliver stone at a consistent rate would have been contrary to the parties' other dealings. Evidence of prior dealings was admissible here to help supplement the terms of the contract under § 1–205. Again, the record supports the court's conclusion. Intervening factors such as railroad problems, bad weather, and labor disputes apparently prevented Luedtke from receiving prompt, consistent shipment of stone from this quarry in the past. Steven Zachmann, Luedtke's chief engineer, testified at trial that 1,500 tons per day was an "arbitrary in-between quantity" that he derived from the different rates proposed by the parties during negotiation. Both Zachmann and Luedtke's President, Karl Luedtke, admitted that they did not expect Indiana Limestone to meet the delivery rate. In addition, Indiana Limestone's sales representative, Robert New, and Indiana Limestone's quarry supervisor, Athol Bennett, both testified that they considered 1,500 tons per day to be the maximum rate up to which Indiana Limestone would ship stone to Luedtke.

Luedtke nevertheless argues that Indiana Limestone's conduct after receiving the purchase order shows that Indiana Limestone understood the delivery rate to be part of the contract. Luedtke notes that New wrote on the purchase order that twenty-five railroad cars would be needed to ship 1,500 tons per day, that New ordered twenty-five cars per day from the Milwaukee Railroad, and that he sent this information to the quarry. Luedtke also notes that during the contractual period Indiana Limestone never claimed that it had no responsibility to ship 1,500 tons per day as a justification for its sporadic deliveries. These arguments, however, challenge Indiana Limestone's motives and the credibility of its witnesses. The district court has broad discretion in making these factual determinations and we decline to re-try them on appellate review. As discussed, the district court's determinations are not clearly erroneous. (Incidentally, the factors Luedtke cites are entirely consistent with Indiana Limestone's contention that it considered the shipping rate to be a goal, not a requirement.)

Luedtke next argues that if we accept the district court's conclusion that the contract did not contain a shipping rate, then § 2–307 applied and Indiana Limestone was required to ship all the stone in a single delivery. Section 2–307 provides in part that "[u]nless otherwise agreed all goods called for by a contract for sale must be tendered in a single delivery." Yet § 2–307 contains an exception to the single delivery requirement "where the circumstances give either party the right to make or demand delivery in lots," and Comment 4 to § 2–307 states that the phrase "unless otherwise agreed" includes surrounding circumstances, usage of trade, course of dealing, and course of performance. The circumstances here indicate that both parties expected delivery in lots. Luedtke does not contend that Indiana Limestone could have delivered all 70,000 tons of stone in one shipment, and such delivery obviously was not contemplated or desired by either party.

The absence of a specific delivery term in the contract required Indiana Limestone to deliver the stone within a reasonable time. Ind.Code § 26–1–2–309 (1979). The district court found that Indiana Limestone's delivery rate was reasonable, both because Indiana Limestone delivered the stone in time for Luedtke to finish the project before the Corps' deadline, and because Indiana Limestone's delivery delays were caused by factors beyond its control and expected by both parties in light of their previous dealings and industry practice. These conclusions are not clearly erroneous, and thus we affirm the court's ruling that Indiana Limestone's delivery was reasonable under the circumstances.

III

In summary, Luedtke's delivery term was a material alteration of Indiana Limestone's offer, and thus the contract did not include an express delivery term. Because Indiana Limestone delivered the breakwater stone within a reasonable time under the circumstances, Indiana Limestone did not breach its contractual obligations. . . . The district court's order is affirmed.

QUESTIONS

1.   Problem. Seller, located in San Francisco, contracts to manufacture and sell to Buyer, located in Minneapolis, 10,000 printer cartridges at $50 per cartridge. Normal production time for this quantity is 30 days, but neither the negotiations nor the contract mentions a time of delivery. The day after forming this contract, Seller realizes it made a very bad deal, but that its loss from performing would be far less than its liability to Buyer if it (Seller) breaches. So Seller works its regular crew overtime and hires additional employees to get Buyer's order ready as soon as possible. When complete, Seller loads the goods on its trucks, send them on their way, and tenders delivery seven days after the contract is formed. Buyer phones Seller to say that she was not expecting the cartridges for another two weeks and that she has not yet talked to her banker about financing the transaction. She offers a post-dated check, which Seller refuses, and Seller instructs the truck drivers to bring the cartridges back to San Francisco. Who, if anyone, has breached the contract, and why?

2.   Problem. Seller, a manufacturer, agrees to sell printer cartridges to Buyer, a reseller, for $50 per cartridge. The first shipment is to be of 100 cartridges, to be delivered in 10 days and paid for on delivery. Buyer is to submit orders from time to time thereafter, but the agreement says nothing about the duration of the agreement, the time of shipment, or the time of payment. Buyer hires additional sales personnel to handle the new product. For how long does Buyer have the right to purchase cartridges from Seller?

A month after formation of the agreement, Seller's board of directors decides to change its method of distribution and open its own retail stores. Seller notifies Buyer that it will not deliver any more cartridges. Is this a breach?

3.   Problem. Seller, a manufacturer, agrees to sell printer cartridges to Buyer, for as long as Buyer wants to buy them, at $50 per cartridge, except that the price is to increase to the extent of any increase in Seller's direct costs. For how long does Buyer have the right to purchase cartridges from Seller?

What is the relevance of the price-adjustment clause?

Three years later Seller informs Buyer that it will deliver no more cartridges. Is this a breach?

5.   RISK OF LOSS

Who should have the risk of loss when goods are lost, damaged, or destroyed? The common law and Uniform Sales Act said the owner should have this risk, just as the owner stands to benefit if the goods appreciate in value. Losses and gains in the value of the goods were thought to be normal aspects of ownership. Since the seller owns goods that ultimately will be owned by the buyer, risk of loss passed from one to the other at the precise moment that title was transferred from the seller to the buyer, unless the contract otherwise provided. Because the parties seldom make express agreements as to either risk of loss or the time that title passes from the seller to the buyer, the pre-Code law had to develop rules to determine passage of title when the goods had been damaged or destroyed. It made the "intention of the parties" preeminent in determining when title passed, but since that intention was seldom expressed, a number of presumptive rules were developed to determine it. Thus, if the goods were specific and nothing remained to be done to put them into a deliverable state, the title passed when the bargain was struck. On the other hand, if the goods were unascertained (i.e. not yet identified as the goods constituting the subject matter of the contract), or if something remained to be done to them to make them deliverable, the passage of title was postponed until the goods were "appropriated" to the contract and made deliverable.

These presumptions had a ring of certainty about them, but results in particular cases were far from certain, and a great deal of unnecessary litigation resulted. Consider Radloff v. Bragmus, 214 Minn. 130, 7 N.W.2d 491 (1943), in which a farmer contracted to sell a poultry dealer a flock of "about 100 turkey hens and 600 Toms." The hens and toms were to be graded by the parties and characterized by them as #1 or #2; the #1 hens carried a price of 18½ cents per pound; the #1 toms a price of 13½ cents per pound; and the #2 birds were 3 cents less in each case. The contract was made on November 9th and the birds were to be delivered on November 13th. On November 11th a blizzard destroyed 330 of the turkeys involved and damaged the others. Who had the risk of loss? The court held that the risk passed to the buyer on November 9th, since the turkeys were sufficiently specific and nothing remained to be done to them to put them into deliverable condition. The weighing and grading process was described as merely ministerial, and not something "remaining to be done" so as to prevent the passage of title. The court was aided, of course, by the fact that the turkeys were frozen and thus still available for counting, grading, and weighing. What would have been the result if the turkeys had been destroyed by fire? How could the court have worked out the price? In that case, the court might well have found that the risk of loss remained with the seller since something important (i.e. price) remained to be done to make the birds deliverable.

Radloff v. Bragmus, and many common law and USA cases like it, also raised other policy problems that the title passage concept did not take into account. For example, the farmer was in a better position to prevent the loss of the turkeys than the poultry dealer, and the farmer was more likely to have insurance on the birds. These facts favor placing the risk of loss on the seller.

In one of its most significant changes, Article 2 scrapped the passage-of-title, or property, approach to risk of loss and replaced it with what its drafters called a contractual approach. See Official Comment 1 to 2–509. Obviously, the parties are free under the UCC, as they were at common law and under the USA, to agree as to risk of loss. Assuming no agreement on the matter, 2–509 and 2–510 state rules on where the risk will fall. What factors do these rules emphasize? Is it correct to say that these sections adopt a contract approach to the problem of risk of loss? If not, what is the approach and how does it differ from the common law and the USA? The following cases and notes should help you to answer these questions.

Under 2–509 the risk of loss depends in the first instance on whether the seller is required or authorized to ship the goods by carrier. If the seller is so required or authorized, then the risk of loss depends on where the seller is to deliver the goods. This is logical because the place of delivery normally is the point at which the seller's responsibilities for the goods end and the buyer's begin. Often the place of delivery is expressed by use of a mercantile term, such as "f.o.b.," "c.i.f.," "ex ship," etc. The most important mercantile terms are elaborately defined in 2–319 through 2–325. When the parties use one of these terms they are making an express contract, and in this respect 2–319 through 2–325 serve a different function from most of the other statutory terms found in Part 3 of Article 2. The definitions of mercantile terms found in 2–319 through 2–325 make it possible for the parties to express with a short symbol an entire range of rights and obligations that otherwise might take a full page to state. In this connection look at 2–319(1). It defines the "f.o.b." term in some twenty lines of type. Merely using that symbol creates an express term to do the things stated in those twenty lines, unless the parties choose to give the symbol a different meaning. The economy is obvious, and it accounts for the widespread use of the mercantile terms. Most of the other sections of Part 3 of Article 2 do not create express terms; they are gap fillers to be used in the absence of express or implied terms.

A.M. Knitwear Corp. v. All America Export–Import Corp.

New York Court of Appeals, 1976.
41 N.Y.2d 14, 390 N.Y.S.2d 832, 359 N.E.2d 342.

■ COOKE, JUDGE. . . .

In June of 1973, the buyer All America Export–Import Corp., placed an order with the seller, A.M. Knitwear Corp., for several thousand pounds of yarn. The buyer used its own purchase order form, dated June 4, 1973, and typed thereon a description of the goods, a statement that partial shipments would be accepted, a description of how to mark the cartons, the quantity in pounds, and the dollar amount of the order. In addition, at the place on the buyer's form where the words "Ship Via" are printed, the buyer typed the instructions: "Pick Up from your Plant to Moore–McCormack Pier for shipment to Santos, Brazil." Further, in the price column on the form, the buyer typed: "FOB PLANT PER LB. $1.35". . . . However, left blank by the buyer was the place on the form where the letters F.O.B. are printed and space is provided for the entry of F.O.B. terms.

In support of its contention that it had fully performed when the goods were loaded in the container, the seller quotes from an examination before trial of the buyer's vice-president, who stated:

"Q. What about the second order?

"A. After the first order was completed, Mr. Lubliner said he has more on hand.

"I said 'What do you mean by hand? Do you have again at the pier?'

"He says 'No. I have the same type of merchandise in my warehouse.' He says 'I could make you a similar offer, the same amount of cartons,

352 cartons. I do not know the weight. The weight may vary, at the same price.'

"I said, 'Okay,' We bought it. I accepted it.

"He asked me, what should I do.

"I said, 'As you know, most of the goods being shipped to South America is being containerized. I have to order a container or a trailer, whatever is the simplest expression. And then in turn you will have to put it into the container.'

"Mr. Lubliner said, 'This is no problem. Just send down the container. I will try to help you.' ' "

In preparation for shipping the goods to South America, the buyer phoned International Shipper's Co. of New York, a customs house broker and freight forwarder, and a third-party defendant in this action, to arrange for a local truckman to pick up and deliver the goods to the pier. International Shippers engaged a local truckman, Ability Carriers, Inc., another third-party defendant in this action, which as part of its services picked up an empty container from the Moore–McCormack Lines.

On Friday, June 22, 1973, the local truckman [delivered] the empty container . . . to the seller for loading.

On Monday, June 25, 1973, the seller had the goods loaded in the container and, on the same day, notified the buyer that the loading had been completed. The buyer then advised its freight forwarder to have the local truckman pick up the loaded container and deliver it to the Moore–McCormack pier. At around 8:00 p.m. that evening, prior to the arrival of the local truckman engaged by the buyer's freight forwarder, an individual driving a tractor arrived at the . . . premises where the container was located and hooked up the trailer containing the loaded container to his tractor. The tractor driven by this individual had no descriptive markings thereon or anything to identify its owner. Before leaving the premises, the driver signed a bill of lading, but the signature was indecipherable. It appears that this individual was a thief and had stolen the goods.

Sometime after June 25, the buyer delivered to the seller a check dated July 2, 1973 in the sum of $24,119.10 in payment for the goods loaded in the container. Payment on the check was thereafter stopped by the buyer, apparently when it was learned that the goods had not been received, and the seller brought an action against the buyer to recover payment for the goods.

At Special Term, both the seller and the buyer moved for summary judgment. That court found that the seller's undertaking was to load the goods in a deliverable condition into the carrier's container and that, by doing so and notifying the buyer, delivery was made in conformity with the agreement of the parties. Special Term thus determined that the risk of loss of the goods had passed to the buyer and granted the seller's motion for summary judgment.

The Appellate Division reversed Special Term and granted the buyer's motion for summary judgment, on the basis that there was neither physical delivery to the carrier nor delivery within the meaning of the Uniform Commercial Code. Both courts relied on subdivision (2) of section 2–401 and section 2–509, but the Appellate Division also relied on the holding in Avisun Corp. v. Mercer Motor Frgt., 37 A.D.2d 517, 321 N.Y.S.2d 658. We affirm the order of the Appellate Division which granted the buyer's motion for summary judgment.

Although the seller contends that the F.O.B. term on the buyer's form did not have its ordinary meaning, the Uniform Commercial Code provides that, unless otherwise agreed, the term F.O.B. at a named place "even though used only in connection with the stated price, is a delivery term" (Uniform Commercial Code, § 2–319, subd. [1]). Where the term F.O.B. the place of shipment is used, as in this case with the term F.O.B. plant, the code provides that the seller must ship the goods in the manner provided in section 2–504 of the Uniform Commercial Code and "bear the expense and risk of putting them into the possession of the carrier" (Uniform Commercial Code, § 2–319, subd. [1], par. [a]).

With respect to shipment by the seller, the code provides that where the seller is "required or authorized" to send the goods, but not required to deliver them to a particular destination, then "unless otherwise agreed" the seller must "put the goods into the possession of * * * a carrier" (Uniform Commercial Code, § 2–504, subd. [a]). Further, with respect to the risk of loss, the code provides that where the contract requires or authorizes the seller to ship the goods by carrier "if it does not require him to deliver them at a particular destination, the risk of loss passes to the buyer *when the goods are duly delivered to the carrier*" (Uniform Commercial Code, § 2–509, subd. [1], par. [a]; emphasis added). The risk of loss provision is, however, "subject to contrary agreement of the parties" (Uniform Commercial Code, § 2–509, subd. [4]). Although the seller contends that section 2–509 is not applicable because the agreement between the parties does not "require" the seller to "ship the goods by carrier," it should be noted that the section applies where the seller is "required or authorized" to ship the goods by carrier and is thus applicable here.

The effect of the provisions of the Uniform Commercial Code may be varied by agreement, with exceptions not applicable here (Uniform Commercial Code, § 1–102, subd. [3]). Furthermore, the provisions relevant to this action provide that the requirements set forth therein apply "unless otherwise agreed" or "subject to contrary agreement of the parties," though the absence of these words in the specific provisions was not intended to imply that the effect of such provisions may not be varied by agreement (Uniform Commercial Code, § 1–102, subd. [4]). In this respect, the Official Comment to one provision states that "[c]ontrary agreement can also be found in the circumstances of the case, a trade usage or practice, or a course of dealing or performance" (Official Comment 5, § 2–509; see, also, Uniform Commercial Code, § 1–205 ["Course of Dealing and Usage of Trade"].)

Despite the provisions of the code which place the risk of loss on the seller in the F.O.B. place of shipment contract until the goods are delivered to the carrier, here the seller contends that the parties "otherwise agreed" so that pursuant to its agreement, the risk of loss passed from the seller to the buyer at the time and place at which the seller completed physical delivery of the subject goods into the container supplied by the buyer for that purpose. In support of this contention, the seller alleges that the language of the purchase order "Pick Up from your Plant" is a specific delivery instruction and that the language "FOB PLANT PER LB. $1.35," which appears in the price column, is a price term and not a delivery term. Further support for the seller's contention is taken from the fact that the space provided in the buyer's own purchase order form for an F.O.B. delivery instruction was left blank by the buyer. Thus, the seller contends its agreement with the buyer imposed no obligation on it to make delivery of the loaded container to the carrier.

As often happens in commercial transactions, the parties to this action did not prepare an extensive written agreement, but merely made an arrangement that, under normal circumstances, would have been entirely satisfactory. The intervention of a wrongdoer who stole the goods that were the subject of the agreement forces the court to determine who should bear the loss resulting from the theft. In this respect, although the seller argues that only to the extent that the agreement is silent should the code apply, it should be noted that the underlying purpose and policy of the code is "to simplify, clarify and modernize the law governing commercial transactions" (Uniform Commercial Code, § 1–102, subd. [2], par. [a]). To this end, the code provides a framework for analyzing a variety of commercial transactions.

The seller's contention, that the parties intended the F.O.B. term as a price term and not a delivery term, conflicts with the code provision that states that the F.O.B. term is a delivery term "even though used *only* in connection with the stated price" (Uniform Commercial Code § 2–319, subd. [1]; emphasis added). That the F.O.B. term was not inserted in the space provided for such an expression in the buyer's own purchase order form does not require a determination that the F.O.B. term was intended as a price term, since the drafters of the code recognized that the term F.O.B. will often be used in connection with the stated price. Thus, the place where the term F.O.B. was typed on the buyer's form is not sufficient to suggest that the parties intended a price term, particularly when one considers that the relevant code provision was specifically intended to negate the decisions which treated this term as "merely a price term" (Official Comment 1, § 2–319.)

Since the term "FOB PLANT" was a delivery term, the risk of loss was on the seller until the goods were put into the possession of the carrier— unless the parties "otherwise agreed" or there was a "contrary agreement" with respect to the risk of loss. In this respect, the holding in Avisun v. Mercer Motor Frgt., cited by the Appellate Division, is illustrative. There, the question was whether the defendant carrier was liable as bailee for goods that were loaded in its trailer but were stolen before it arrived to pick them up. The Appellate Division there determined that until the acceptance of the goods by the defendant carrier, there was no bailment and that making available a vehicle for "possible temporary storage" was not an "acceptance." The seller contends that the *Avisun* case has no relevance to this case because it involves the issue as to when a bailment arises as a matter of law. The seller's interpretation is, however, too limited. The *Avisun* case is relevant here because, in the same sense that loading the trailer was not an "acceptance" of a bailment by the carrier, the loading of the container by the seller is not "delivery" to the carrier for purposes of the code, unless the parties so agree.

With respect to the agreement of the parties, the seller contends that the statements in the affidavits of the parties and a portion of an examination before trial of the buyer's vice-president manifest that the parties intended that the seller's performance would be complete when the goods were loaded into the container and the buyer was notified thereof. That this was the agreement of the parties is, according to the seller, further suggested by the fact the buyer issued a check, the payment of which was subsequently stopped, in payment for the goods.

The issuance of the check by the buyer gives little support to the seller's view. The making of payment is as consistent with the buyer's expectation that delivery had been made to the proper carrier as it is with the seller's contention that payment was made because the buyer considered the seller's performance to be completed upon loading the container.

With respect to the seller's contention as to the meaning of the statements of the buyer's vice-president, the seller has a formidable task in trying to prove that the parties did not intend the ordinary meaning of the term "FOB PLANT," i.e., delivery to the carrier. Although the only written expression in the transaction was the buyer's purchase order form on which the buyer typed the F.O.B. term, if the seller did not agree to this term, the seller should have expressed its disagreement after it received the purchase order form. For example, the seller should have indicated that the term "FOB PLANT" was merely a price term and not a delivery term or that the risk of loss was on the buyer after loading. The code anticipates that a written confirmation by a party may state terms additional to, or even different from, those offered and agreed upon, which terms, depending on certain factors, may become part of the contract (see Uniform Commercial Code, § 2–207). Yet here the seller did not seek to modify the F.O.B. term typed on the buyer's purchase order, but apparently relied on its own understanding of the agreement.

The provisions of the code with respect to risk of loss are subject to the "contrary agreement" of the parties (Uniform Commercial Code, § 2–509, subd. [4]). In this respect, the Official Comment states that " '[c]ontrary' is in no way used as a word of limitation and the buyer and seller are left free to readjust their rights and risks * * * in any manner agreeable to them" (Official Comment 5, § 2–509). It is, however, a recognized principle that "if the parties have made a memorial of their bargain * * * the law does not recognize * * * their intent, unless it is expressed in, or may fairly be implied from, their writing" (4 Williston, Contracts [3d ed.], § 600A, p. 286). It has also been established that when words have a well-understood meaning the courts are not permitted to search for the intent of the parties. The term "FOB PLANT" is well understood to require delivery to the carrier and does not imply any other meaning. If a contrary meaning was intended, an express statement varying the ordinary meaning is required. The statements made by an officer of the buyer and the other circumstances of this case are not enough to show that the term did not mean what it does in ordinary commercial transactions. One of the principal purposes of the code is to simplify, clarify and modernize the law governing commercial transactions (Uniform Commercial Code, § 1–102, subd. [2], par. [a]). To allow a commonly used term such as F.O.B. to be varied in meaning, without an express statement of the parties of an intent to do so, would not serve that purpose.

Accordingly, the order of the Appellate Division which granted the buyer's motion for summary judgment should be affirmed with costs.

QUESTIONS AND NOTES

1.   The seller contended that "FOB Plant per lb. $1.35," as used in the contract, was a price term, not a delivery term. In view of the language in 2–319(1) that specifies the meaning of FOB "even though used only in connection with the stated price," how can the seller make this argument?

Note that 2–319(1)(a) requires the seller to ship the goods in the manner required by 2–504. Please read subsection (a) of 2–504. Is that section relevant to the court's reasoning in *A.M. Knitwear*?

2.   Section 2–319 assigns a meaning to "f.o.b." but permits the parties to agree otherwise, i.e. to assign a different meaning to the term. Does that mean that any special understanding of the parties as to the meaning of a mercantile symbol must be expressed to overcome the force of the definitions found in 2–319 through 2–325? Suppose, for example, the course of dealing between a seller and a buyer indicates a special, and different, meaning for the symbol "f.o.b." from the definition given by 2–319(1). How would you interpret the meaning of the symbol "f.o.b." in their contract?

A contract for window units between seller in South Dakota and a buyer in New York provided, "All windows to be shipped properly crated/packaged/boxed suitable for cross-country motor-freight transit and delivered to New York City." The windows were damaged in transit. Holding that this loss fell on the buyer, the court stated, "We conclude that this was a shipment contract. To overcome the presumption favoring shipment contracts, the parties must have explicitly agreed to impose on [the seller] the obligation to effect delivery at a particular destination. The language of this contract did not do so. Nor did [the buyer] use any commonly recognized industry term indicating that a seller is obligated to deliver the goods to the buyer's specified destination." As between seller and buyer, therefore, under 2–509(1)(a) the buyer had the risk of loss. Windows, Inc. v. Jordan Panel Systems Corp., 177 F.3d 114, 117 (2d Cir.1999). In Brunswick Box Co. v. Coutinho, Caro & Co., 617 F.2d 355 (4th Cir.1980), however, the seller was able to establish by the parties' course of dealing that "F.A.S" meant in the dock area, rather than "alongside the vessel" as provided in 2–319(2)(a).

3. It is common for the seller to send goods to the buyer by common carrier, and one of the parties must bear the risk of loss or damage to the goods in transit. (Of course, the party who bears the risk may have a claim against the carrier, but that is a different question.) Under 2–503, 2–504, and 2–509, the risk ordinarily passes from the seller to the buyer when the goods are placed in the hands of the carrier. That position is exemplified by the court in the *Windows, Inc.* case. However, in order to shift the risk to the buyer, the seller must "put the goods in the hands of such a carrier and make such a contract for their transportation as may be reasonable having regard to the nature of the goods and other circumstances of the case." (2–504) In Cook Specialty Co. v. Schrlock, 772 F.Supp. 1532 (E.D.Pa.1991), the buyer argued that the seller had not made a reasonable contract with the carrier because the seller did not make sure that the carrier had insurance covering the full value of the shipment. (The carrier had shown the seller an insurance policy with a face-value coverage of $100,000 but in the particular circumstances, the policy covered only $5,000 of a $28,000 loss.) The court held that the seller had no responsibility to ascertain that the carrier's insurance would cover the full loss and that the seller had made a reasonable contract with the carrier.

4. Section 2–509(4) recognizes, perhaps redundantly, that the parties are competent to allocate the risk of loss by their agreement. Thus, the parties could agree to split any loss on a 50–50 basis or some other fractional division or cast the entire burden on one party or the other. In the last major paragraph of its opinion, the court in *AM Knitwear* rejects the seller's argument that the parties did so in that case. Was this proper?

5. If the court concluded that the parties had changed the meaning of "FOB Seller's Plant," what section would govern risk of loss, 2–319, 2–504, or 2–509?

6. C.I.F. and C & F terms and risk of loss. C.I.F. and C & F terms are frequently employed in marine shipments. In almost all cases the place named by the term is the destination point. Thus, if the seller is in London and the buyer in New York, the contract employing c.i.f. or c & f terms would almost always provide "c.i.f. New York." What do these terms mean? The answer is found in section 2–320. Subsection (1) states that c.i.f. "means that the price includes in a lump sum the cost of the goods and the insurance and freight to the named destination. The term C & F or C.F. means that the price so includes cost and freight to the named destination." Thus a contract between a London seller and New York buyer which provided "$50,000 c.i.f. New York" would mean that for a price of $50,000, the London seller agrees to sell the goods to the buyer, pay the freight (and other costs) to New York, and take out insurance on the goods in favor of the buyer. The c. & f. term is identical, except that the London seller has no obligation to take out insurance.

Who has the risk of loss under these terms? At common law and under the USA, the buyer was said to have the risk of loss during the transit period (i.e. after the goods had been loaded on board in London) even though the contract required delivery in New York and for the seller to pay the freight. The conclusion was derived from the insurance term. Since, it was argued, the seller is obliged to take out insurance in favor of the buyer, the parties must have agreed that the buyer had the risk of loss. Otherwise, it was questioned, why would he want insurance?

Apply this reasoning to the c. & f. contract, and a different result is reached. Here the seller is paying the freight; a destination point is named in the contract; and there is no duty on his part to provide insurance for the buyer. To some courts, at least, the "c. & f. New York" contract looked suspiciously like the "f.o.b. New York" contract and they, accordingly, put the risk of loss for the transit period on the seller. For an interesting case on this point, see Pittsburgh Provision & Packing Co. v. Cudahy Packing Co., 260 Pa. 135, 103 A. 548 (1918).

How does Article 2 assign risk of loss under c.i.f. and c & f contracts?

It makes no commercial sense to treat the c.f. contract the same as if it were an f.o.b. contract, because the various mercantile symbols are intended by merchants to be short-hand expressions of different kinds of contracts. Two important factors in sales contracts are expense of transportation (is it included in the price or does the buyer have to pay it in addition to the price?) and risk of loss. Risk of loss becomes unimportant if there is insurance against it. If a seller, for example, has insurance against loss in any shipment made by him, he is well advised to make c.i.f. contracts. On the other hand, if the buyer has insurance against loss in transit, the c.f. or f.o.b. origin contracts may be appealing to him. Note how the parties can allocate the risk of loss and cost of shipment by using f.o.b. and c.i.f. or c & f terms. Suppose the seller is in London and the buyer in New York. Which mercantile terms would you use to accomplish the following:

(1) Buyer is willing to take the transit risk and to pay the freight charges;

(2) Seller is willing to take the transit risk and pay the freight charges;

(3) Buyer is willing to take the risk (because he already has insurance), but he wants the seller's price to include the transit charges;

(4) Buyer is willing to take the risk if the seller will take out insurance for him, but he wants the seller to assume (as part of the price) the transit charges;

(5) Buyer is willing to pay the transit charges but wants seller to assume the risk of loss.

A little reflection will indicate that the price will vary depending on which of the five contracts stated above is selected by the parties. In this connection the use of *pro forma* invoices is common, particularly in international trading. After coming to an agreement as to the basic price of goods at the factory in London, the London seller may be requested by the New York buyer to supply *pro forma* invoices showing what the price will be under some mercantile symbols. For example, the buyer may ask the seller to give him a *pro forma* invoice on "f.o.b. London" and "c.f. New York." These invoices are usually considered to be offers, and the buyer is free to accept the one that best suits its needs.

7. Sharpening the risk and expense points. London and New York are large cities. What happens when a term reads "f.o.b. London" or "c.i.f. New York" and the loss occurs in those cities themselves. Suppose, for example, the contract reads "f.o.b. London" and the goods are destroyed as they are being moved from the seller's plant in London to a ship anchored in the harbor? Suppose the goods are delivered to the shipowner at his dock, but they are destroyed as he tries to load them on board. Suppose they are put on board but are destroyed before the ship hoists its anchor or leaves the harbor. Similar hypotheticals easily can be developed for any mercantile term. Answers are of great importance, because many losses occur as goods are being loaded or unloaded from carriers, transported to and from carriers, and the like. How does Article 2 handle these problems?

The parties can better assure themselves as to where the risk will be placed by sharpening the points used in conjunction with mercantile terms. Thus, for example, instead of using a term "f.o.b. London," the parties might prefer to use a term such as "f.o.b. seller's plant London" or "f.o.b. dock London." Note also the additional mercantile terms that are available (because defined) for easy use where the parties want to pinpoint the risk of loss.

In terms of the London seller and the New York buyer, notice the continuum of risk points from the seller's plant in London to the buyer's plant in New York, and how the parties may make these points the ones at which the risk of loss will pass, through the use of mercantile terms:

(1) There is a risk that the goods will be damaged or destroyed in loading them on a truck at the seller's plant. If the buyer is to take the risk after this point the contract might specify "f.o.b. truck seller's plant London";

(2) there is a risk that the truck will be involved in an accident between the seller's plant and the loading dock. If the buyer is to take the risk after this point, the contract might specify "f.o.b. dock London";

(3) there is a risk that the goods will be destroyed moving them from the dock onto a lighter to be used to transport them to the ship in the river. If the buyer is to take the risk after this point, the contract might specify "f.o.b. lighter London";

(4) there is a risk that the lighter will be involved in an accident before it gets to the ship. If the buyer is to take the risk after this point, the

contract might provide "f.a.s. Jolly Jack London" (see 2–319(2) for the meaning of "f.a.s.");

(5) there is a risk that the goods will be destroyed loading them onto the ship from the lighter. If the buyer is to have the risk after this point, the contract might read "f.o.b. Jolly Jack London."

By the same token, the various risk points thereafter (i.e. transit; unloading onto lighter in New York; unloading from lighter to dock; loading from dock onto truck; unloading from truck and loading onto boxcar; train transit; unloading from boxcar; loading onto truck in buyer's city; truck transit; unloading from truck at buyer's plant, etc.) can be identified in the contract as the risk-passing point. Obviously the price will vary depending on the risk assumed by the parties.

8.   Mercantile terms under revised Article 2. The revisions to Article 2 delete sections 2–319 through 2–324, which set out seller's obligations under the mercantile terms F.O.B, F.A.S, C.I.F, C & F, and Delivery "Ex–Ship." The provisions were deleted because of concern that they do not accurately reflect the current understanding as to the meaning of those terms. This rationale seems to assume that the definitions would prevent a court from using the current understanding. But this reasoning ignores that if trade usage or course of dealing gives the terms some meaning other than the meaning specified in those sections, the other meaning controls. Thus, even under current Article 2, the terms in 2–319 through 2–324 may not have the effect that those sections seem to give them. With the deletion of 2–319 through 2–324, there will be no default definitions, so when there is no trade usage or common understanding, the meaning of the terms may be uncertain.

In lieu of the definitions in 2–319 through 2–324, the courts may look to a set of terms developed by the International Chamber of Commerce (ICC), known as Incoterms. The ICC first adopted the Incoterms in 1936 to establish a common worldwide understanding of the meanings of certain trade terms such as "F.O.B." and the obligations of the seller and buyer thereunder. The most recent version of the Incoterms was promulgated in 2000 and contains 13 terms, including some that appear in Article 2, but also a number of additional ones. As to terms used in Article 2, the Incoterms 2000 defines them differently than Article 2 does. (For example, 2–323 provides that in an "F.O.B. vessel" contract, the seller must furnish a negotiable bill of lading. Under Incoterms 2000, however, "F.O.B. vessel" merely requires that the seller assist the buyer in procuring a bill of lading.) The Incoterms 2000 are intended for international, rather than domestic, trade, and the definitions reflect this difference.

Under current Article 2, of course, the Incoterms 2000 may, for the reason stated above, displace the definitions and rules of 2–319 through 2–324.

———

Silver v. Wycombe, Meyer & Co., Inc.

City of New York, City Court, 1984.
124 Misc.2d 717, 477 N.Y.S.2d 288.

■ David B. Saxe, Judge. . . .

Plaintiff, through his agent, Elsie Simpson, an interior decorator, ordered custom furniture from defendant Wycombe, Meyer & Co., Inc. (Wycombe). The furniture was manufactured by codefendant Jackson–Allen Upholstery Corp. (Jackson–Allen), a subsidiary of defendant Wycombe, at its factory in Catasauqua, Pennsylvania. On or about February 23, 1982, Wycombe sent invoices to plaintiff advising that the furniture was ready for shipment. Plaintiff thereupon tendered payment in full and directed Wycombe to ship one room of furniture but to hold the other until instructed further. Accordingly, one room of furniture was shipped to plaintiff. But before any instructions were received as to the second room of furniture, it was destroyed in a fire which was not due to any negligence on the part of defendants. Fireman's Fund Insurance Co. paid plaintiff for the loss and seeks to recover the proceeds from defendants on the theory that the risk of loss never passed to the buyer, its insured.

In the absence of contrary agreement by the parties, risk of loss under the Uniform Commercial Code is determined by the manner in which delivery is to be made (U.C.C. 2–509). The original order, documented by defendant Wycombe's order form, indicates a price of $7053 "+ del'y," and all invoices provide for shipment to plaintiff's home "Truck prepaid." It is clear that the provisions of U.C.C. 2–509 Subdiv. (1) govern the issue of when risk of loss passes to the buyer "where the contract requires or authorizes the seller to ship the goods by carrier * * *" Where the contract requires the seller to deliver the merchandise at a particular location, risk of loss passes upon tender of the goods at that location (U.C.C. 2–509(1)(b)) and where the contract does not require the seller to deliver the goods to a particular destination, it passes upon their delivery to the carrier (par. (a)). Where the contract provides for delivery at the seller's place of business or at the situs of the goods, risk of loss passes upon actual receipt by the buyer, if seller is a merchant, and otherwise upon tender of delivery (U.C.C. 2–509(3)).

Under the facts of the case at bar, the terms of the contract as it regards delivery are not stated. It is apparent, however, that regardless of the particular agreement between buyer and seller, defendants have set forth no facts sufficient to place the risk of loss upon plaintiff under any of the cited U.C.C. provisions. Indeed, the Official Comment 3 to U.C.C. 2–509 makes it clear that "a merchant seller cannot transfer risk of loss and it remains upon him until actual receipt by the buyer, even though full payment has been made and the buyer has been notified that the goods are at his disposal."

Defendants, however, advance the novel theory that, because of plaintiff's request that they hold the furniture subject to further instruction, they became mere bailees of the goods and that the provisions of U.C.C. 2–

509(2) should govern this case. They argue that the invoices informing plaintiff that the furniture was ready for shipment constitute acknowledgment of the buyer's right to possession, transferring the risk of loss pursuant to U.C.C. 2–509(2)(b) to the buyer.

This position is entirely without merit. The provisions of U.C.C. 2–509(2) contemplate a situation in which goods are in the physical possession of a third party who will continue to hold them after consummation of the sale. Therefore, this is not a provision appropriately applied to the circumstances at bar which anticipate the passing of title *and* physical possession more or less simultaneously. Furthermore, bailment requires *delivery* of the goods to the bailee (see Black's Law Dictionary, 4th ed., p. 179, 1968). Having concluded that defendants failed to establish delivery of the furniture to plaintiff, by no stretch of the imagination may plaintiff be said to have redelivered it to defendants for safe-keeping.

Defendants cannot transform what is clearly a sale of goods into a bailment simply because they acceded to the buyer's request to postpone delivery. The agreement between buyer and seller clearly contemplates delivery at the buyer's home and, under the Uniform Commercial Code, risk of loss remains upon a merchant seller until he completes his performance with reference to the physical delivery of the goods (U.C.C. 2–401(2); U.C.C. 2–509(3) and [Official Comment] 3 to U.C.C. 2–509; Ramos v. Wheel Sports Center, 96 Misc.2d 646, 409 N.Y.S.2d 505, Civ.Ct., Bx.) It may be that defendant Jackson–Allen is a bailee for defendant Wycombe, but this Court is not required to rule on and makes no determination of this question.

Accordingly, judgment for plaintiff in the amount demanded in the complaint together with costs, disbursements and interest from April 13, 1982.

QUESTIONS AND NOTES

1. In the third paragraph of the opinion, the court cites subsections (1) and (3) of 2–509. Which of the two subsections governs this dispute? See 2–308.

2. Would the outcome or the analysis be different if Wycombe, Meyer were to use its own truck to deliver the furniture to Silver's home?

3. The receipt-tender rules of 2–509(3). Under 2–509(3) if a consumer purchases goods from a merchant, risk of loss does not pass to the buyer until the buyer receives the goods. On the other hand, if a consumer purchases from another consumer, risk of loss passes upon tender of delivery. Often tender occurs an instant before the buyer receives the goods. But sometimes the buyer may not receive the goods until some time after the seller tenders delivery. For example, the buyer may leave the goods with the seller for a time, as when a car dealer calls a buyer to set up a time for the buyer to pick up her newly arrived car, or when a buyer of furniture at a garage sale promises to return the next day with a truck. Is the distinction between merchants and non-merchants made by 2–509(3) justified? Are non-merchant sellers less likely to insure than merchant sellers? Are buyers from non-merchants more likely to insure goods tendered but not "received" by the buyer? Revised 2–509(3) abolishes the distinction between merchants and non-merchants. It provides : "In any case not within subsection (1) or (2), the risk of loss passes to the buyer on the buyer's receipt of the goods."

4.   Risk of loss on bailed goods. The UCC does not define the word "bailment," though the term is used in 7–204(3) and the word bailee is found in 1–201(15), defining "document of title." The dictionary defines it as "A delivery of personal property by one person (the bailor) to another person (the bailee) who holds the property for a certain purpose under an express or implied-in-fact contract." Black's Law Dictionary (8th ed. 2004). In commercial transactions, the most common and useful kinds of bailments involve the shipment or storage of goods. The shipper or storer is the bailor; the carrier or the warehouse is the bailee. Usually when goods are shipped or stored, the bailee issues a document of title covering them. In the case of shipment this document is called a "bill of lading"; in the case of storage it is called a "warehouse receipt." These documents have three aspects. They are receipts for the goods; they are contracts describing the bailee's duty of care and the bailor's obligations to pay for that care; and they are "documents," meaning pieces of paper that control the goods. The documentary aspect is derived from the fact that the warehouse or carrier promises to deliver the goods only to the person who is in possession of the warehouse receipt or bill of lading under circumstances in which the promise runs to that person either directly, or through indorsement over to that person.

Not all bills of lading and warehouse receipts are documents. Usually they may be said to have documentary aspects only when they are negotiable, because the paper does not necessarily control the goods if it is nonnegotiable. This distinction is considered in greater detail in Chapter 11 in conjunction with documentary sales.

One who has stored goods with a warehouse may want to sell them to a buyer who wants to leave them in the warehouse. This can be accomplished very easily if a negotiable warehouse receipt has been issued. In that case, the bailor "negotiates," i.e. transfers, the warehouse receipt to the buyer by indorsing and delivering it to the buyer. Thereafter, the buyer is entitled to take possession of the goods by surrendering the receipt to the bailee-warehouse. Under 2–509(2) the risk of loss passes from the seller to the buyer when the seller delivers the warehouse receipt.

When the warehouse receipt or bill of lading is nonnegotiable, the transfer of the paper does not necessarily mean that the buyer will be able to get the goods, and thus this transfer, in and of itself, does not pass the risk of loss. The acknowledgment of the bailee that it will hold the goods for the buyer, rather than for the original bailor-seller, is the kind of assurance needed by the buyer of a nonnegotiable warehouse receipt or bill of lading. Under 2–509(3)(b) this acknowledgment is the risk-passing event. But the rule is qualified. The buyer must obtain the acknowledgment or dishonor of the bailee within a reasonable time. If the buyer delays and waits more than a reasonable time before attempting to get the acknowledgment, the risk of loss passes as of the moment that the reasonable time period expires. This qualification is stated in 2–509(2)(c), which incorporates by reference 2–503(4)(b).

None of these rules, of course, has any relevance to *Silver v. Wycombe–Meyer*. The bailment situation contemplated by 2–509 is one in which the bailee is neither the seller nor the buyer, but rather is a third party. Subsection (2) applies when goods in possession of that third party are sold under circumstances in which the goods themselves are not to be moved but are to remain in the hands of the bailee.

5. Organization of the sections on risk of loss. In the absence of contrary agreement, 2–509 states rules that apply depending on which of four categories is applicable to the transaction in question: Category one covers transactions in which the contract requires or authorizes the seller to ship the goods by carrier. Rules for this category are found in 2–509(1). Category two applies to transactions in which goods are held by a bailee to be delivered without being moved. Rules for this category are found in 2–509(2). Category three is residual. All transactions not covered by categories one and two are governed by category three. Rules for this category are found in 2–509(3). Category four is transactions in which one of the parties has breached the contract before the loss or destruction of the goods, and the rules for these transactions are in 2–510.

Jakowski v. Carole Chevrolet, Inc.

New Jersey Superior Court, Law Division, 1981.
180 N.J.Super. 122, 433 A.2d 841.

■ Newman, J.S.C.

Plaintiff seeks summary judgment on count I of the complaint alleging breach of a new car sales contract by defendant Carole Chevrolet, Inc.

The essential facts are not in dispute. On March 8, 1980 plaintiff Jakowski (hereinafter "buyer") entered into a contract of sale with defendant Carole Chevrolet, Inc. (hereinafter "seller,") calling for the purchase of one new 1980 Chevrolet Camaro. The parties also agreed that the car would be undercoated and that its finish would have a polymer coating. While there is some disagreement as to exactly when the buyer ordered the coatings, it is undisputed that prior to delivery the seller agreed to deliver the car with the coatings applied. Likewise, it is undisputed that the car in question was delivered to the buyer without the required coatings on May 19, 1980.

The next day, May 20, 1980, the seller contacted the buyer and informed him that the car delivered to him lacked the coatings in question and seller instructed buyer to return the car so that the coatings could be applied. On May 22, 1980 the buyer returned the auto to the seller for application of the coatings. Sometime during the evening of May 22 or the morning of May 23 the car was stolen from the seller's premises and it was never recovered. Seller has refused to either provide a replacement auto to buyer or to refund the purchase price. Buyer remains accountable on the loan, provided through GMAC, for the purchase of the car.

The narrow question thus presented is upon whom, as between buyer and seller, this loss should fall. In U.C.C. terminology, on May 22, 1980, which party bore the risk of the car's loss.

Seller argues that the risk of loss passed to the buyer upon his receipt of the auto. This is consistent with U.C.C. § 2–509(3) pursuant to which the risk of loss passes to the buyer upon his receipt of the goods. Section 2–509(4), however, expressly provides that the general rules of § 2–509 are subject to the more specific provisions of § 2–510 which deals with the effect of breach upon risk of loss.

Buyer relies upon § 2–510(1) which provides:

Where a tender or delivery of goods so fails to conform to the contract as to give a right of rejection the risk of their loss remains on the seller until cure or acceptance.

Application of this section to the instant facts requires that three questions be answered. First, did the car "so fail to conform" as to give this buyer a right to reject it? If so, did the buyer "accept" the car despite the nonconformity? Finally, did the seller cure the defect prior to the theft of the auto?

The first question must be answered in the affirmative. The contract[1] provided that the car would be delivered with undercoating and a polymer finish, and it is undisputed that it was delivered without these coatings. The goods were thus clearly nonconforming and, despite seller's assertion to the contrary, the degree of their nonconformity is irrelevant in assessing the buyer's concomitant right to reject them. N.J.S.A. 12A:2–106 is clear in its intent to preserve the rule of strict compliance, that is, the "perfect tender" rule:

Goods * * * are "conforming" or conform to the contract when they are in accordance with the obligations under the contract. [N.J.S.A. 12A:2–106(2), emphasis supplied. See also, Comment 2 to § 2–106].

The language of § 2–510(1), "so fails to conform," is misleading in this respect: no particular quantum of nonconformity is required where a single delivery is contemplated. The allusion is to § 2–612 which substitutes a rule of substantial compliance where, *and only where,* an installment deal is contemplated. White & Summers, Uniform Commercial Code (2nd ed.1980), § 5.5 at 187–188.

---

1. Seller makes much of the fact that the original sales order failed to specify the coatings in question. It is undisputed, however, that seller, subsequent to execution of the order, agreed to supply the coatings prior to delivery. As such, the coatings were clearly part of the "contract," as that term is defined by the Code. N.J.S.A. 12A:1–201(11).

Secondly, did buyer "accept" the auto by taking possession of it? This question was presented in Zabriskie Chevrolet, Inc. v. Smith, 99 N.J.Super. 441, 240 A.2d 195 (Law Div.1968). In *Zabriskie* it was held that the mere taking of possession by the purchaser is not equivalent to acceptance. Before he can be held to have accepted, a buyer must be afforded a "reasonable opportunity to inspect" the goods. N.J.S.A. 12A:2–606.

Seller's actions in this matter preclude analysis in conventional "acceptance" terms. Buyer had no opportunity, indeed no reason, to reject, given seller's own communication to buyer shortly after delivery, to the effect that the goods did not conform and that the seller was exercising its right to cure said nonconformity. See N.J.S.A. 12A:2–508 (seller's right to cure). This communication, in effect an acknowledgment of nonconformity, obviated the need for a formal rejection on buyer's part, if, indeed, § 2–510(1) imposes such an obligation. Put another way, it precluded the buyer from rejecting the car. Consistent with this analysis, I find as a matter of law that there was no acceptance by buyer of this nonconforming auto.

As to the final question of whether the seller effected a cure, there is no evidence—in fact defendant does not even contend—that cure was ever effected.

Given the undisputed facts, the operation of § 2–510(1) is inescapable. The goods failed to conform, the buyer never accepted them and the defect was never cured. Accordingly, the risk of loss remained on the seller and judgment is granted for plaintiff.

A further note on the law is in order. It is possible to conjure up a host of hypotheticals leading to seemingly perverse results under § 2–510. The section has been the subject of some scholarly criticism. See e.g., White & Summers, supra, § 5.5 at 187. Williston, "The Law of Sales in the Proposed Uniform Commercial Code," 63 Harv.L.Rev. 561, 583 (1950).

The fact is, however, that those courts considering it have had little difficulty in applying it as written. See, e.g., United Air Lines, Inc. v. Conductron Corp., 69 Ill.App.3d 847, 26 Ill.Dec. 344, 387 N.E.2d 1272 (Ill.App.1979) (flight trainer destroyed in fire after delivery to buyer); Southland Mobile Home v. Chyrchel, 255 Ark. 366, 500 S.W.2d 778 (Sup.Ct. 1973) (mobile home destroyed in fire after delivery to buyer); Graybar Elec. Co. v. Shook, 283 N.C. 213, 195 S.E.2d 514 (Sup.Ct.1973) (nonconforming cable stolen while in buyer's possession); Wilke v. Cummins Diesel Eng'g, Inc., 252 Md. 611, 250 A.2d 886 (Ct.App.1969) (engine block frozen while in buyer's possession).

The rule is simple enough: under N.J.S.A. 12A:2–510(1), where goods fail to conform to the contract of sale the risk of loss remains on the seller until the buyer accepts the goods or until the seller cures the defect. Such was the result in the aforecited cases, even though in all of them the goods were still in the *buyer's* possession at the time of their destruction.

For present purposes it is adequate to hold simply that where a seller obtains possession of the goods in an effort to cure defects in them so as to comply with his end of the bargain, he is under a contractual duty to redeliver them to the buyer. In failing to do so, he has breached the contract.

Pursuant to N.J.S.A. 12A:2–711 buyer is entitled to a refund of so much of the purchase price as has been paid to seller. Included in the cost of the automobile are the finance charges incurred by the buyer, who secured financing from GMAC pursuant to a retail installment sales contract entered into with the seller. There is no dispute about including these charges in the purchase cost, and the buyer, as of March 30, 1981, indicated the total amount due on any judgment to be $9,398.75. However, since this case was first heard some additional time has passed and a current pay-off figure should be obtained for inclusion in this judgment.

QUESTIONS AND NOTES

1.   Problem. Buyer contracts to purchase a new car from Seller, to be ordered from the manufacturer. When it arrives, Seller prepares it for delivery in accordance with the manufacturer's protocol and phones Buyer to come pick it up. Before Buyer can get there, the car is severely damaged by hail. Who bears the risk of this casualty?

2.   In *Jakowski* the seller phoned the buyer on May 20 to bring the car back so that the seller could apply the coatings, and the car was stolen on May 22 after the buyer had returned it. What if the car had been stolen from the buyer's garage on May 21st: who would have had the risk of loss?

3.   Problem. Buyer contracts to purchase a new car from Seller, to be ordered from the factory. In due course, Seller phones Buyer to say that the car has arrived. Buyer goes to pick it up and sees that the car has a racing stripe, which Buyer did not order and does not want. Seller says, "I won't charge you for it; or, if you like, I can order in another car. It'll only be 6–8 weeks." Buyer does not want to wait that long and says, "Oh, I'll take it that way." Seller then persuades Buyer to add undercoating, for another $250, and tells Buyer to return the next day after 5:00 to pick it up. Late that night the car is stolen. Who has the risk of loss?

4.   Problem. Buyer and Seller enter into a contract under which Buyer is to accept delivery of plastic pellets at the rate of 1,000 pounds per day for 120 days, beginning July 1. Before July 1st, Seller produces the full quantity of 120,000 pounds, places it in his warehouse, and identifies it to the particular contract. Buyer declines to accept delivery of the first installment on July 1, but says she will be able to begin taking deliveries on July 10th. On July 7th, Seller's warehouse burns and the entire stock of pellets is destroyed. Seller has no insurance on the pellets. To what extent is Buyer liable to Seller for the price of the goods? See 2–709. Cf. Multiplastics, Inc. v. Arch Industries, Inc., 166 Conn. 280, 348 A.2d 618 (1974).

What if Buyer took delivery of the pellets on July 1–7, but the remainder of the pellets were destroyed by fire during the early morning hours on July 8? Buyer must pay for the pellets it received (see 2–607(1)), but must Buyer pay the rest of the price, i.e. who has the risk of loss?

5. The court's statement in the last paragraph on page 202, that the "language of § 2–510(1), 'so fails to conform,' is misleading," is itself misleading, as we will see when we consider the buyer's right to reject nonconforming goods.

6.   CISG and risk of loss. Article 69 of the Convention on Contracts for the International Sale of Goods reads as follows:

> (1) ... [In cases in which the contract of sale does not involve carriage of the goods or sale of goods in transit], the risk passes to the buyer when he takes over the goods, or, if he does not do so in due time, from the time when the goods are placed at his disposal and he commits a breach by failing to take delivery.
>
> (2) However, if the buyer is bound to take over the goods at a place other than a place of business of the seller, the risk passes when delivery is due and the buyer is aware of the fact that the goods are placed at his disposal at that place.
>
> (3) If the contract relates to goods not then identified, the goods are not considered to be placed at the disposal of the buyer until they are clearly identified to the contract.

What result under the Convention in Problem 4 above?

See Articles 67 and 68 of the Convention as to passage of risk in carriage contracts. Article 67 contains rules like those of 2–509 on carriage contracts. The Convention does not state a rule as to goods being held by bailees.

Article 70 of the Convention deals with the effect of seller's breach on risk of loss. It provides: "If the seller had committed a fundamental breach of contract, Articles 67, 68 and 69 do not impair the remedies available to the buyer on account of the breach."

7.   Problem. Buyer in the United States and Seller in China have entered into a contract for the purchase and sale of 4000 bicycles. Seller's delivery obligation is to put the bicycles on board a ship at Canton, and it does so. When the goods arrive in San Francisco, Buyer discovers that 1,000 of the bicycles are unusable because of warped wheels. Also, another 500 of the bicycles have been soaked by seawater on the voyage and are essentially worthless. The warped wheels were in that condition when loaded on the vessel. Can Buyer reject the entire shipment of bicycles? See CISG Articles 49, 51 and 82.

Can Buyer accept the bicycles and shift the risk of loss as to the seawater-damaged bicycles to the seller? Assume that there are no relevant sections other than those already cited here and in Note 6? Compare UCC 2–510.

8.   Ultimate risk of loss. The concept of "risk of loss" does not refer to ultimate loss. Rather, it is used to determine which party takes the initial loss. Often the initial loss can be shifted to the other party to the sales contract or to a carrier, warehouseman, or insurance company. For example, if the buyer has the risk and a loss occurs because of the seller's negligence, the seller is liable for its negligence and will suffer the ultimate loss. The initial loss is put on the buyer, but, on straight tort principles, the buyer can recover from the seller. Consideration of the liability of the carrier appears in Chapter 11.

6.   CHOICE OF LAW

Wright-Moore Corporation v. Ricoh Corporation

United States Court of Appeals, Seventh Circuit, 1990.
908 F.2d 128.

■ FLAUM, CIRCUIT JUDGE.

[Plaintiff had a one year distributorship agreement with defendant under which it had a right to distribute certain Ricoh copiers nation wide. Plaintiff was an Indiana corporation headquartered in Fort Wayne Indiana. Defendant was incorporated in New York and had its principal place of business in New Jersey. Under the agreement, plaintiff, at its expense, had to train employees of retailers to whom it sold Ricoh copiers to service the copiers. At the end of the year, defendant notified plaintiff that it would not renew the arrangement because it had decided to undertake itself all national distribution of the copiers. Plaintiff claimed that it had been assured that the distributorship arrangement would be long term as long as plaintiff performed its obligations under the agreement and that it had performed those obligations during the year.

Plaintiff alleged violation of the Indiana franchise law, breach of contract, fraud, misrepresentation, and estoppel. The contract contained a provision that the courts of Manhattan had exclusive jurisdiction over any dispute arising out of the agreement and that the law of New York would govern any dispute. The trial court, among other things, held that application of New York law would be inconsistent with the public policy of Indiana as reflected in its franchise law. It applied Indiana law but held that under the Indiana franchise law the distributorship had been cancelled in good faith and that, therefore, defendant had no liability under the franchise law. It also held that all other claims were groundless and gave summary judgment for defendant. Plaintiff appealed.]

      . . .

A.   *Indiana Franchise Law Claims*

Wright–Moore's appeal raises several significant issues under the Indiana franchise laws. Ind.Code §§ 23–2–2.5–1, *et seq.,* 23–2–2.7–1, *et seq.* Wright–Moore argues that the district court erred as a matter of law in holding that non-renewal for the economic purposes of the franchisor constitutes good cause under Ind.Code § 23–2–2.7–1(7). In addition, Wright–Moore claims that summary judgment was improper because there were material issues of fact with respect to Ricoh's good faith during termination and with respect to the claim of discrimination. Ricoh supports the district court's holding but argues in the alternative that the contractually chosen New York law applies rather than Indiana law and, in addition, that Wright–Moore was not a franchise.

1.   Choice of Law

We begin with the choice of law question. Wright–Moore claims Indiana franchise law applies, despite the choice of New York law in the agreement, on the ground that the Indiana franchise statutes prohibit waiver of its protections and prohibit "limiting litigation brought for breach of the [franchise] agreement in any manner whatsoever." Ind.Code § 23–2–2.7–1(10). Ricoh argues that the express choice of law provision of the contract should govern. The district court held that Indiana has articulated a strong public policy against allowing parties to contract out of the protections of its franchise law and that this public policy overrides the choice of law provided for in the agreement.

Indiana has long adhered to the "most intimate contacts" test for choice of law. *W.H. Barber v. Hughes,* 223 Ind. 570, 63 N.E.2d 417 (1945). This approach has since been elaborated in the Restatement (Second) Conflict of Laws § 188 (the "Restatement"). Under this approach, "the court will consider all acts of the parties touching the transaction in relation to the several states involved and will apply as the law governing the transaction the law of that state with which the facts are in most intimate contact." *W.H. Barber,* 63 N.E.2d at 423. This approach also recognizes that parties may expressly choose the applicable law through a contract. "The law of the state chosen by the parties to govern their contractual rights and duties will be applied if the particular issue is one which the parties could have resolved by an explicit provision in their agreement directed to that issue." Restatement § 187(1). Typical issues that cannot be determined by explicit agreement include capacity, formalities, substantial validity, and illegality, but the set issues which cannot be contractually chosen is determined by local law. *Id.* at comment d. If the issue is one which could not have been explicitly resolved by the contract, the choice of law provisions of the contract will still apply unless the "chosen state has no substantial interest" in the litigation or "application of the law of the chosen state would be contrary to a fundamental policy of a state which has a materially greater interest than the chosen state in the determination of the particular issue and which, under the rule of § 188, would be the state of applicable law in the absence of an effective choice of law by the parties." *Id.* at § 187(2).

We agree with the district court that enforcement of the choice of law provision in the distributorship agreement would be contrary to Indiana's express public policy. Indiana has made it unlawful to enter into a franchise agreement "requiring the franchisee to prospectively assent to a release ... [or] waiver ... which purports to relieve any person from liability to be imposed by this chapter" or to enter into an agreement "limiting litigation brought for breach of the agreement in any manner whatsoever." Ind.Code § 23–2–2.7–1(10). We owe deference to the district judge's interpretation of the law of the state in which the judge sits, and the district judge here found that these provisions articulated a strong state policy against allowing contractual choice of law provisions to control the applicability of these provisions to Indiana franchises. The public policy, articulated in the nonwaiver provisions of the statute is clear: a franchisor, through its superior bargaining power, should not be permitted to force the franchisee to waive the legislatively provided protections, whether directly through waiver provisions or indirectly through choice of law. This public policy is sufficient to render the choice to opt out of Indiana's franchise law one that cannot be made by agreement.

Indiana law, following the Restatement, however, permits state public policy to override the contractual choice of law only if the state has a materially greater interest in the litigation than the contractually chosen state. Thus, for the Indiana public policy to control the choice of law, Indiana must have a materially greater interest in the litigation than does New York. We conclude that this is the case here. Wright–Moore is potentially a franchisee and is incorporated and located in the state of Indiana; its witnesses and documents are there; the contract negotiations occurred there; and the contract was, in part, performed there. New York's only connection to this litigation is that the defendant is incorporated in New York. The defendant's principal place of business is New Jersey. Indiana, therefore, has a materially greater interest in the litigation than New York. Since Indiana has a materially greater interest than New York and application of New York law would be contrary to a fundamental Indiana policy, Indiana franchise law governs this case.

. . .

3.　*Nonrenewal of the Distributorship Agreement*

Ind.Code §§ 23–2–2.7–1(7) and (8) declare unlawful any provision in a franchise agreement which permits the franchisee to be terminated or not renewed "without good cause or in bad faith." The district court found that Wright–Moore did not put forth sufficient evidence to show that its nonrenewal was in bad faith. The court found instead that Wright–Moore's nonrenewal was based on economic reasons internal to Ricoh, which the court held was good cause in compliance with Ind.Code § 23–2–2.7–1(7). The district court also found that Wright–Moore was not discriminated against in violation of Ind.Code § 23–2–2.7–2(5) because none of Ricoh's national distributors were renewed and consequently Wright–Moore cannot show treatment different from similarly situated franchises.

. . .

[As to the lack of good cause,] Wright–Moore also argues that the district court erred in holding that termination for the franchisor's own economic reasons constitutes good cause. The statute defines good cause to "include[ ] any material violation of the franchise agreement." Ind.Code § 23–2–2.7–1(7). There is no evidence that Wright–Moore breached the franchise agreement, so Ricoh's actions did not fall within the plain terms of the statute. Good cause, however is defined to *include* breach of the franchise agreement. The language of the statute does not indicate that it is limited to breach. The question is whether good cause also includes termination for the benefit of the franchisor's balance sheet.

Indiana courts have not yet considered this issue. We believe, however, that the language and structure of the Indiana law, along with the guidance provided by interpretation of franchise laws in other states, compel a conclusion that the internal economic reasons of the franchisor are not, by themselves, good cause for termination or nonrenewal of a franchise. Primarily, Ricoh's suggested conclusion that the franchisor's economic reasons would constitute good cause directly contravenes the very purpose of franchise statutes and would render the statutes ineffective. As noted above, franchise statutes are designed to prevent franchisors from extracting quasi-rents from franchisees. They are designed to ensure fair dealing between the parties. If the business reasons of the franchisor were sufficient, the protections of the statute would be meaningless since it is in the franchisor's short term business interest (and therefore good cause) to act opportunistically. (While this may not be effective in the long term as the franchisor may lose reputation or good will, a court is unlikely to make this determination.) Even absent opportunistic behavior, a franchisor could virtually always claim a plausible business reason for termination. Without a smoking gun, it would be difficult, if not impossible, for a franchisee to prove that a particular action is not in the business interests of the franchisor. Ricoh's suggested reading would, therefore, allow franchisors to extract rents from franchisees, the very behavior the statutes are designed to prevent.

This reasoning is supported by the decisions of several courts. In *Kealey Pharmacy & Home Care Services, Inc. v. Walgreen Co.,* 761 F.2d 345 (7th Cir.1985), we held that Walgreen's termination of all its Wisconsin franchises and replacement with Walgreen-owned stores was not supported by good cause. Walgreen had valid business reasons to make this change. Nevertheless, we held that because Walgreen intended to appropriate the good will established by the franchisees, Walgreen's behavior was opportunistic and therefore, economic justifications alone were not sufficient. *See also Remus v. Amoco Oil Co.,* 794 F.2d 1238, 1241 (7th Cir.1986) (good cause is limited to faults with the franchisee).

In addition, the structure of the Indiana statute indicates that good cause refers only to problems with the performance of the franchisee.

Sections 23–2–2.7–1(7) and (8) prohibit termination or nonrenewal without good cause and list material violations of the franchise agreement as an example of good cause. The language of the statute is inclusive; the statute does not say material violations of the agreement are the sole legal cause for termination. The statute simply says that good cause *includes* material violations of the agreement. But as an example of the type of cause that the legislature had in mind, this indicates that the statute may be limited to other problems with the performance of the franchisee. Economic reasons internal to the franchisor do not fit this pattern; they generally have nothing to do with the performance of the franchisee.

. . .

[The court remanded the case to the district court for further consideration of the good faith termination issue.]

QUESTIONS AND NOTES

1. You will observe that the court does not mention the UCC. The reason is that Article 2 does not apply to franchise contracts. See page 26 supra. Nevertheless, the court's discussion of the choice-of-law issue is apropos of the rule of the UCC, found in 1–105.

2. Revised Article 1. A passage on pages 37–38 supra introduced the provisions of revised 1–301, which greatly relax the rules regarding the effectiveness of contractual choice of law clauses. Unlike the rule of 1–105, revised 1–301(b) authorizes commercial parties to a domestic transaction to choose the law of any state to govern their transaction, whether or not the state whose law is chosen bears a reasonable relationship to the transaction. Similarly, commercial parties to an international transaction can choose the law of any country to govern their transaction, whether or not the country whose law is chosen bears a reasonable relation to the transaction.

The states that have enacted revised Article 1 have rejected this relaxation and have retained the rule of original 1–105. Under the revised rule, subsection (e) substantially limits choice-of-law provisions as against a consumer, and subsection (f) provides, "An agreement otherwise effective under subsection (c) is not effective to the extent that application of the law of the State or country designated would be contrary to a fundamental policy of the State or country whose law would govern in the absence of agreement . . . ." Under revised 1–301 the analysis used in the *Wright* opinion will be relevant in many contractual choice-of-law cases. Presumably, the strong public policy of a jurisdiction could be found in its case law as well as in its statutes. Official Comment 6, however, suggests that the fundamental-public-policy limitation on the ability of the parties to choose applicable law should be sparingly applied.

7. Special Arrangements

a. SALE OR RETURN; SALE ON APPROVAL. Buyers of goods for their own use will frequently want a trial period before deciding whether to purchase. Sections 2–326 and 2–327(1) define and describe the incidents of such "sales on approval." Notice particularly that title and risk of loss do not shift to the buyer until acceptance of the goods (which is not the same thing as acceptance of the seller's offer to sell). If the buyer does not accept the goods, their return is at the expense and risk of the seller. Also, goods on approval are not subject to the claims of buyer's creditors until the buyer accepts them. Therefore, for example, if a judgment creditor of the buyer has the sheriff seize goods that the buyer has "on approval" and has not accepted, the seller would be able to reclaim the goods from the sheriff.

A buyer who purchases goods for resale often will want the right to return the goods to the seller for credit if the buyer is unable to sell them. Sections 2–326 and 2–327(2) also define and describe the incidents of such "sale or return" transactions. In a sale or return, title to the goods passes to the buyer under the ordinary rules of 2–401 (which we will study later), and the goods are subject to claims of the buyer's creditors while the goods are in the hands of the buyer. Therefore, the seller runs the risk of losing the goods to the buyer's creditors who get an interest in them while the goods are in the possession of the buyer. Also, in a sale or return transaction, return is at the buyer's risk and expense.

Note 2–326(4), which seeks to discourage buyers from falsely claiming that they have the right to return unsold goods.

b. AUCTIONS. Please reread Hoffman v. Horton, page 29 supra.

Drew v. John Deere Co. of Syracuse, Inc.

New York Supreme Court, Appellate Division, 1963.
19 A.D.2d 308, 241 N.Y.S.2d 267.

■ Halpern, Justice. . . . [The defendant repossessed a tractor because the owner defaulted in his obligation to pay for it. State law requires a repossessing creditor to resell the tractor] at public auction (Personal Property Law, § 79). The defendant advertised the auction sale, stating that the property would be sold to the highest bidder at the sale. The plaintiff bid $1500 at the sale but the auctioneer did not accept the bid; instead he announced that the defendant itself had bid $1600 and accordingly the property was struck down to the defendant.

The plaintiff claims that the defendant was disqualified to bid because it had not announced in advance that it intended to bid pursuant to section 102, subdivision 4, of the Personal Property Law. Hence, the plaintiff argues, his bid was the highest lawful bid and therefore a contract of sale came into existence between the plaintiff and the defendant for the sale of the tractor at the price bid.

The plaintiff's whole case rests upon the theory that the auction was one "without reserve." At such an auction, the owner of the property has no right to withdraw the property after bidding has commenced. It is also necessarily implicit in an auction "without reserve," that the owner of the property may not himself bid in the property, as this would be equivalent to withdrawing it from sale (Restatement of Contracts, § 27). Various legal theories have been advanced for the holding that the announcement that the auction would be "without reserve" imposes a binding legal obligation upon the owner, but the best view seems to be that the owner, by making such an announcement, enters into a collateral contract with all persons bidding at the auction that he will not withdraw the property from sale, regardless of how low the highest bid might be (Gower, "Auction Sales of Goods Without Reserve," 68 Law Quarterly Review 457; Warlow v. Harrison (1859) 1 E. and E. 295, 309). Therefore, the highest bona fide bidder at an auction "without reserve" may insist that the property be sold to him or that the owner answer to him in damages.

On the other hand, in an auction sale not expressly announced to be "without reserve," the owner may withdraw the property at any time before it is actually "knocked down" to a bidder by the auctioneer. There is no contract until the offer made by the bidder is accepted by the auctioneer's "knocking down" the property to him (Personal Property Law, § 102, subd. 2). "An auction 'with reserve' is the normal procedure" (Comment 2 to section 2–328, Uniform Commercial Code).

In our case, there was no express statement that the auction would be "without reserve." The statement that the sale would be made to the highest bidder is not the equivalent of an announcement that the auction would be "without reserve" (cf. Personal Property Law, § 102(2); Uniform Commercial Code, § 2–328, subd. 3). "An announcement that a person will sell his property at public auction to the highest bidder is a mere declaration of intention to hold an auction at which bids will be received" (7 C.J.S. Auctions and Auctioneers § 1a, p. 1240).

Corbin writes that the auctioneer at an auction sale in asking for bids, does not make an operative offer. "This is true even though the seller or his representative has issued advertisements or made other statements that the article will be sold to the highest bidder, or is offered for sale to the highest bidder. Such statements are merely preliminary negotiation, not intended and not reasonably understood to be intended to affect legal relations. When such is the case, the seller or his representative is as free to reject the bids, highest to lowest, as are the bidders to withdraw them. The seller may at any time withdraw the article from sale, if he has not already accepted a bid. He need give no reasons; indeed, he rejects all bids by merely failing to accept them—by doing nothing at all. It is not necessary for him to say that 'the privilege is reserved to reject any and all bids.' Such a statement is merely evidence that the goods are not being offered 'without reserve'" (1 Corbin on Contracts, § 108, pp. 338–40).

Since, upon the present record, the auction sale appears to have been "with reserve," no contract of sale came into existence, even if we assume that the plaintiff was the highest lawful bidder. Concededly, the plaintiff's bid was never accepted. Therefore, the plaintiff's papers upon his motion for summary judgment fail to make out a cause of action for breach of contract.

. . .

The plaintiff's motion for summary judgment was therefore properly denied. The defendant asks us to go further and to grant a summary judgment in favor of the defendant. We do not believe that this should be done. The plaintiff relied upon the announcement that the sale would be to the highest bidder as showing that the auction sale was to be "without reserve." As we have seen, the announcement was insufficient of itself for that purpose but the plaintiff should be given an opportunity to produce any other evidence he may have on that subject. For that reason, summary judgment for the defendant should be denied.

QUESTIONS AND NOTES

1. Shill bidding or puffing. Secret bidding at auctions by the seller or one acting on his behalf is known as "shill bidding" or "puffing," a practice that is considered fraudulent because it creates a misleading impression that there is greater competition for the goods than actually exists. The practice also may violate the obligations of one conducting an auction without reserve, for it permits the shill to overbid the highest bona fide bidder and deprive that bidder of the goods. Further, it enables the seller to convert an auction "without reserve" into one "with reserve," by purporting to sell the goods to the shill and by that subterfuge in effect withdraw them from the sale. How does the UCC police against this practice?

2. Problem. S, through A, an auctioneer, puts up goods at auction announced to be "without reserve." B attends the auction and bids $100 for a particular item. Shill, a puffer employed by S "to keep the bidding going unless otherwise signaled by A," bids $110. A, knowing Shill's true role, accepts the bid. B then bids $120. Seeing the great interest manifested in the goods by B and Shill, C becomes interested in the goods and bids $130. Shill then bids $140, and B tops that with a bid of $150. At that point Shill declines to make another bid, having received a signal from A to stop bidding. The goods are knocked down to B at $150. Does B have to pay? If so, or if B elects to take the goods, how much must B pay for them?

Would it make any difference if the auction were announced to be "with reserve"?

In Nevada National Leasing Co. v. Hereford, 36 Cal.3d 146, 203 Cal.Rptr. 118, 680 P.2d 1077 (1984), the owner's agent bid without the knowledge of others at the auction. Hereford bought three items of equipment at bid prices of $10,000, $6,100 and $8,600 respectively. His last bids before the agent started bidding were $6,000, $3,500 and $500 respectively. Hereford was given a judgment for the excess of the prices he paid over his last bid before the agent started bidding. Hereford was also awarded $10,000 in punitive damages for the fraud of owner. The court did not state whether other bidders bid between the agent's first bid and Hereford's accepted bid. However, the awarding of punitive damages indicates that the court would not have accepted an argument that recovery under 2–328 should be limited to the excess of Hereford's high bid over the next highest bid of a third party "good faith" bidder.

3.   Revised 2–328. Revised 2–328 modernizes the language of 2–328, at some expense to colorfulness, but with no change in substance.

CHAPTER 4

EXPRESS AND IMPLIED WARRANTIES

A. INTRODUCTION

Caveat emptor—literally "buyer beware"—means that the buyer takes all risk concerning the quality of the goods being purchased, even including the risk that the goods are not as described. At one time the doctrine of caveat emptor was the law. For more than a century, however, the doctrine has not applied to the law of sales. For a judicial description of the evolution and abandonment of the doctrine at common law, see the 1934 case, Smith v. Zimbalist, 2 Cal.App.2d 324, 38 P.2d 170 (Cal.App.1934).

Today, of course, the matter is governed by Article 2, under which a merchant seller who deals in goods of the kind has an obligation that, unless the parties otherwise agree, the goods be of a certain quality. This obligation, a "warranty of merchantability," arises independently of any overt representations by the seller concerning the goods. Since it does not depend upon any affirmative statements or acts by the seller, it is referred to as an "implied warranty." Article 2 also provides for another implied warranty, the warranty of fitness for particular purpose, which arises if the seller has reason to know that the buyer is relying on the seller to select for the buyer goods that are suitable for the buyer's purposes. Also, another warranty, an "express warranty" arises if the seller makes promises or representations as to the goods in such a manner as to become a part of "the basis of the bargain."

The core idea underlying these provisions is that the buyer is entitled to have the quality that the buyer reasonably expects under the contract. While it has sometimes been suggested that the Code warranty scheme is too complicated and could better have provided merely that a buyer is entitled to the quality that the buyer reasonably expects (the approach later taken by the CISG), the Code division of warranties of quality into three categories does rest on relatively easily distinguishable core factual differences. The following examples show the differences:

(a) Express warranty (2–313). Seller says to Buyer: "This pick-up truck is a 2005 model." It actually is a 2004 model. Seller has breached an express warranty.

(b) Implied warranty of merchantability (2–314). The truck in the above example is a 2005 model as represented but it has three cracked pistons, a differential ring gear with 10% of its teeth missing, and an inoperative automatic transmission pump (to those of you who don't know, these are fairly serious problems). If Seller is a dealer in motor vehicles, Seller undoubtedly has breached the warranty of merchantability, even if Seller said nothing at all about the quality of the vehicle. We can view the merchant seller as impliedly representing that any goods it sells are of usual or normal quality. A person who is not a dealer in goods of the kind, on the other hand, does not impliedly warrant the merchantable quality of the goods. (If, however, a seller— merchant or non-merchant—does not disclose defects of which the seller is aware, the seller may be liable for that failure to disclose.)

(c) Implied warranty of fitness for particular purpose (2–315). Buyer tells Seller that she needs a truck capable of towing her sailboat from her home to the various lakes in the region. Seller directs her to the truck in question. If the strain of towing the sailboat causes the truck's transmission to seize, there probably is a breach of the warranty of fitness for particular purpose.

The foregoing warranties relate primarily to the quality of the goods being sold. In addition to these warranties, Article 2 also provides a warranty of title (2–312), to protect a buyer's expectation that third parties may not disturb the buyer's possession of the goods.

Warranty is one of the areas of the law where tort and contract overlap. The same facts may require analysis under both bodies of law. The focus of this book, of course, is contract. But you should be aware of the need to consider tort doctrine as well. For example, a false representation of fact (such as, "This is a 2005 model") gives rise to an express warranty. It also may be actionable as deceit, negligent misrepresentation, or innocent misrepresentation (if the other elements of those torts are present). Similarly, if goods are defective and cause personal injuries, the seller may be subject to strict liability in tort as well as liability in contract for breach of the implied warranty of merchantability.

B. EXPRESS WARRANTIES

Before reading the next case, please read 2–313(1)(a) and identify the facts that must exist in order for there to be an express warranty.

———

Doug Connor, Inc. v. Proto–Grind, Inc.

Florida District Court of Appeal, 2000.
761 So.2d 426.

■ PETERSON, J. . . .

Connor is in the land clearing business. In 1997, Doug Connor ("Doug"), the president of Connor, Inc., became interested in acquiring a large commercial grinding machine called a Proto–Grind 1200 manufactured by Proto–Grind, Inc. ("Proto–Grind"). Proto–Grind's brochure describes the machine as the toughest grinder on the market and capable of grinding "trouble free" a wide variety of debris. The brochure specifically lists timber, stumps, and railroad ties as items capable of being reduced to mulch and contains pictures of a large log being processed by the grinder. The brochure does not describe any type of timber or stumps as being incapable of being reduced to mulch.

Doug attended a demonstration of the machine in Atlanta, Georgia, during which a large log was reduced to mulch. During the demonstration, Doug told George Protos, the president of Proto–Grind, that he would need "a machine that would handle my land clearing operation . . . in Melbourne, Florida. . . . I told him that I needed it to grind, be able to grind palmettos, palm trees, oak trees, pine trees, pepper trees, whatever type of land clearing that's out there, that's what I needed the machine to do." Doug testified that he explained to Protos that he mainly conducted large land clearing in his business, approximately 15 acres to up to 100 acres, and that Protos assured him that "the machine would do what I needed it to do, large jobs, small jobs, whatever I needed."

In April 1997, Connor contracted to purchase a Proto–Grind 1200 for $226,000. Upon delivery, Connor employed it in a land clearing job which consisted of pepper and oak trees, but not palm trees or palmettos. The contract for the purchase of the grinder provided for a two-week trial period in which Connor could use the machine and, only if satisfied with its performance during the trial run, would he be irrevocably committed to purchasing the grinder. However, Doug could not resist the incentive offered by Protos only three days after the delivery that eliminated Connor's first installment payment of $5,500 in exchange for the elimination of the trial period.

Unfortunately, the grinder proved not to be as tough as advertised or represented. Connor experienced repeated mechanical difficulty but the most serious problem was the inability of the machine to discharge the mulch from cabbage palm trees and palmettos.

Connor's mechanic talked to representatives of Proto–Grind about the problem and was advised that some new grates, "demo grates," would perform better with not only the cabbage palms but other land clearing debris. The mechanic ordered the demo grates. The new grates "worked a little better as far as the land clearing debris, with the exception of cabbage palms." The mechanic testified that when grinding cabbage palms the mulch would simply not pass through the grates. During this period, from April to June, Connor wrote several letters to Protos complaining about the deficiencies.

In July 1997, Connor filed its complaint and alleged in Count III, that Proto–Grind breached an express oral warranty that the machine purchased would grind organic materials effectively, including palmettos, and that the machine "would be free from defects for a period of six months upon delivery and that should service be necessary, that defendant would promptly come to Florida to fix the machine at plaintiff's location."

The matter proceeded to a jury trial, but the trial court granted Proto–Grind's motion for directed verdict at the conclusion of Connor's case-in-chief. . . .

Connor alleged in Count III, that "at the time of sale . . . as an inducement to cause plaintiff to purchase the Proto–Grind 1200, defendant . . . through its agents, expressly, orally warranted to plaintiff that the Proto–Grind 1200 would grind, in an efficient and effective manner, organic waste materials from Florida land clearing operations, including the grinding and disposition of palmettos." At trial, Doug testified that the agents of Proto–Grind "all assured me all day long that the machine would do what I needed it to do here in Florida." Doug, during his meeting with Protos, informed Protos that he typically cleared large tracts of land—anywhere from 15 to 100 acres. Doug also told him that he needed to grind palmettos, palm trees, oak trees, pine trees and pepper trees. Doug's mechanic testified that during his inspection of a Proto–Grind machine in Tampa, company officials "had assured us that the machine would grind cabbages, because they had already done it."

Proto–Grind argues that the oral affirmations made by the Proto–Grind agents merely constituted puffing, sales talk, or otherwise non-actionable opinion and that in order to satisfy the threshold of an affirmation of fact, the statement must be detailed and specific. *See Miles v. Kavanaugh,* 350 So.2d 1090 (Fla. 3d DCA 1977). In *Miles,* the court found that a seller of an airplane, by reference to his logbook, had warranted the accuracy of the information contained in the book. Proto–Grind states that the principle of that case is that the threshold of making a factual affirmation is that the statement be specific and detailed. Contrarily, *Miles* seems to support the opposite conclusion by providing a broad definition of an express warranty. The court wrote:

> [A]n express warranty need not be by words, but can be by conduct as well, such as, the showing of a blueprint or other description of the goods sold to the buyer. Moreover, fraud is not an essential ingredient. . . . It is sufficient that the warranty was made which formed part of the basis of the bargain. *Id.* at 1093.

We believe that the statements made by Proto–Grind could amount to more than puffing or sales talk. Proto–Grind specifically understood the buyer's needs and represented to Connor that the Proto–Grind 1200 would meet those needs. The trier of fact should have had the opportunity to consider whether Proto–Grind made the express warranty that the Proto–Grind 1200 could, without modification of its basic components, reduce palmettos and palm trees to mulch on a regular basis. Connor's evidence that an unmodified Proto–Grind 1200 would only mulch palm trees 50% of the time without jamming, presented a jury question as to whether Proto–Grind's pre-purchase representations regarding mulching palm trees and palmetto brush were met.

Proto–Grind further argues that an express warranty generally arises only where the seller asserts a fact of which the buyer is ignorant prior to the beginning of the transaction, and on which the buyer reasonably relies on as part of the basis of the bargain. It is not clear from the record, however, that when Connor purchased the Proto–Grind 1200 he was aware that it was ill-equipped to mulch palm trees and palmetto brush.

On a similar note, Proto–Grind argues that because Doug knew that a competitor was, at times, quite dissatisfied with his Proto–Grind 1200, Connor was on equal footing with Proto–Grind with respect to knowledge of the machine's capability. Doug testified that the Proto–Grind was the first grinder that Connor ever purchased. Even if Doug was more savvy than he acknowledged, the manufacturer of an expensive product should be well aware of the product's attributes and deficiencies before it offers it to the public. We conclude that the relative knowledge of the parties is a matter for the jury to consider, not a complete bar to recovery by Connor.

We conclude that the trial court erred in dismissing Connor's count alleging a breach of an express warranty. . . . [T]he finder of fact could reasonably conclude that the alleged oral promises made were more than mere puffing, that the product failed to meet the promise that it would sufficiently grind palm trees and palmettos, that Connor relied on these affirmations, and that because the deficiency of the product was not cured, Proto–Grind breached this express warranty.

The directed verdict in favor of Proto–Grind on Count III is vacated and the matter is remanded to the trial court for further proceedings.

QUESTIONS AND NOTES

1.   Defendant argued that it had not made the affirmation of fact required by 2–313(1)(a) for there to be an express warranty. In view of subsection (2) and Official Comment 8, why does the court reject that argument?

2.   In the first full paragraph on this page, the court suggests that the relative knowledge of the parties is relevant. To what is it relevant?

Royal Business Machines, Inc. v. Lorraine Corp.

United States Court of Appeals, Seventh Circuit, 1980.
633 F.2d 34.

■ BAKER, DISTRICT JUDGE.

[Plaintiff purchased 128 photocopiers from defendant. Dissatisfied with the performance of the copiers, plaintiff sued and won. Defendant appealed.]

We first address the question whether substantial evidence on the record supports the district court's findings that Royal made and breached express warranties to Booher [the plaintiff]. The trial judge found that Royal Business Machines made and breached the following express warranties:

(1) that the [copiers] and their component parts were of high quality;

(2) that experience and testing had shown that frequency of repairs was very low on such machines and would remain so;

(3) that replacement parts were readily available;

(4) that the cost of maintenance for each RBC machine and cost of supplies was and would remain low, no more than 1/2 cent per copy;

(5) that the RBC machines had been extensively tested and were ready to be marketed;

(6) that experience and reasonable projections had shown that the purchase of the RBC machines by Mr. Booher and Lorraine Corporation and the leasing of the same to customers would return substantial profits to Booher and Lorraine;

(7) that the machines were safe and could not cause fires; and

(8) that service calls were and would be required . . . on the average of every 7,000 to 9,000 copies, including preventive maintenance calls.

. . .

The decisive test for whether a given representation is a warranty or merely an expression of the seller's opinion is whether the seller asserts a fact of which the buyer is ignorant or merely states an opinion or judgment on a matter of which the seller has no special knowledge and on which the buyer may be expected also to have an opinion and to exercise his judgment. General statements to the effect that goods are "the best," Thompson Farms, Inc. v. Corno Feed Products, 173 Ind.App. 682, 366 N.E.2d 3 (1977), or are "of good quality," Olin–Mathieson Chemical Corp. v. Moushon, 93 Ill.App.2d 280, 235 N.E.2d 263 (1968), or will "last a lifetime" and be "in perfect condition," Performance Motors, Inc. v. Allen, 280 N.C. 385, 186 S.E.2d 161 (1972), are generally regarded as expressions of the seller's opinion or "the puffing of his wares" and do not create an express warranty.

No express warranty was created by Royal's affirmation that [the copiers] and their component parts were of high quality. This was a statement of the seller's opinion, the kind of "puffing" to be expected in any sales transaction, rather than a positive averment of fact describing a product's capabilities to which an express warranty could attach.

Similarly, the representations by Royal that experience and testing had shown that the frequency of repair was "very low" and would remain so lack the specificity of an affirmation of fact upon which a warranty could be predicated. These representations were statements of the seller's opinion.

The statement that replacement parts were readily available is an assertion of fact, but it is not a fact that relates to the goods sold as required by Ind.Code § 26–1–2–313(1)(a) and is not an express warranty to which the goods were to conform. Neither is the statement about the future costs of supplies being 1/2 cent per copy an assertion of fact that relates to the goods sold, so the statement cannot constitute the basis of an express warranty.

It was also erroneous to find that an express warranty was created by Royal's assurances to Booher that purchase of the RBC machines would bring him substantial profits. Such a representation does not describe the goods within the meaning of U.C.C. § 2–313(1)(b), nor is the representation an affirmation of fact relating to the goods under U.C.C. § 2–313(1)(a). It is merely sales talk and the expression of the seller's opinion. See Regal Motor Products v. Bender, 102 Ohio App. 447, 139 N.E.2d 463, 465 (1956) (representation that goods were "readily saleable" and that the demand for them would create a market was not a warranty).

On the other hand, the assertion that the machines could not cause fires is an assertion of fact relating to the goods, and substantial evidence in the record supports the trial judge's findings that the assertion was made by Royal to Booher. The same may be said for the assertion that the machines were tested and ready to be marketed. See Bemidji Sales Barn v. Chatfield, 312 Minn. 11, 250 N.W.2d 185 (1977) (seller's representation that cattle "had been vaccinated for shipping fever and were ready for the farm" constituted an express warranty). See generally R. Anderson, Uniform Commercial Code § 2–313:36 (2d ed. 1970) (author asserts that seller who sells with seal of approval of a third person, e. g., a testing laboratory, makes an express warranty that the product has been tested and approved and is liable if the product was in fact not approved). The record supports the district court's finding that Royal represented that the machines had been tested.

As for findings 8 and the maintenance portion of Number 4, Royal's argument that those statements relate to predictions for the future and cannot qualify as warranties is unpersuasive. An expression of future capacity or performance can constitute an express warranty. In Teter v. Schultz, 110 Ind.App. 541, 39 N.E.2d 802, 804 (1942), the Indiana courts held that a seller's statement that dairy cows would give six gallons of milk per day was an affirmation of fact by the seller relating to the goods. It was not a statement of value nor was it merely a statement of the seller's opinion. The Indiana courts have also found that an express warranty was created by a seller's representation that a windmill was capable of furnishing power to grind 20 to 30 bushels of grain per hour in a moderate wind and with a very light wind would pump an abundance of water. Smith v. Borden, 160 Ind. 223, 66 N.E. 681 (1903). . . .

Whether a seller affirmed a fact or made a promise amounting to a warranty is a question of fact reserved for the trier of fact. Substantial evidence in the record supports the finding that Royal made the assertion to Booher that maintenance cost for the machine would run 1/2 cent per copy and that this assertion was not an estimate but an assertion of a fact of performance capability.

Finding Number 8, that service calls on the RBC II would be required every 7,000 to 9,000 copies, relates to performance capability and could constitute the basis of an express warranty. There is substantial evidence in the record to support the finding that this assertion was also made.

While substantial evidence supports the trial court's findings as to the making of those four affirmations of fact or promises, the district court failed to make the further finding that they became part of the basis of the bargain. Ind.Code § 26–1–2–313(1) (1976). While Royal may have made such affirmations to Booher, the question of his knowledge or reliance is another matter.[7]

This case is complicated by the fact that it involved a series of sales transactions between the same parties over approximately an 18–month period and concerned two different machines. The situations of the parties, their knowledge and reliance, may be expected to change in light of their experience during that time. An affirmation of fact which the buyer from his experience knows to be untrue cannot form a part of the basis of the bargain. City Machine & Mfg. Co. v. A. & A. Machinery Corp., 4 UCCRS 461 (E.D.N.Y.1967). See generally R. Anderson, Uniform Commercial Code, § 2–313:18 (2d ed.1970). Therefore, as to each purchase, Booher's expanding knowledge of the capacities of the copying machines would have to be considered in deciding whether Royal's representations were part of the basis of the bargain. The same representations that could have constituted an express warranty early in the series of transactions might not have qualified as an express warranty in a later transaction if the buyer had acquired independent knowledge as to the fact asserted.

The trial court did not indicate that it considered whether the warranties could exist and apply to each transaction in the series. Such an analysis is crucial to a just determination. Its absence renders the district court's findings insufficient on the issue of the breach of express warranties.

Since a retrial on the questions of the breach of express warranties and the extent of damages is necessary, we offer the following observations. The court must consider whether the machines were defective upon delivery. Breach occurs only if the goods are defective upon delivery and not if the goods later become defective through abuse or neglect.

In considering the promise relating to the cost of maintenance, the district court should determine at what stage Booher's own knowledge and experience prevented him from blindly relying on the representations of Royal. A similar analysis is needed in examining the representation concerning fire hazard . . . . The court also should determine when that

---

7. The requirement that a statement be part of the basis of the bargain in order to constitute an express warranty "is essentially a reliance requirement and is inextricably intertwined with the initial determination as to whether given language may constitute an express warranty since affirmations, promises and descriptions tend to become a part of the basis of the bargain. It was the intention of the drafters of the U.C.C. not to require a strong showing of reliance. In fact, they envisioned that all statements of the seller become part of the basis of the bargain unless clear affirmative proof is shown to the contrary. See Official Comments 3 and 8 to U.C.C. § 2–313." Sessa v. Riegle, 427 F. Supp. 760, 766 (E.D.Pa.1977), aff'd without op. 568 F.2d 770 (3d Cir.1978).

representation was made. If not made until February 1975, the representation could not have been the basis for sales made prior to that date. . . .

QUESTIONS AND NOTES

1.   Why does the court conclude that the statements concerning availability of replacement parts and the future cost of supplies do not relate to the goods? How is the statement concerning the cost of maintenance different?

2.   At the end of the excerpt, the court asserts that the representation concerning fire hazard could not give rise to an express warranty in those sales made before the seller made the representation. Intuitively this seems correct. In view of Official Comment 7, however, is it actually correct?

3.   The court states, "General statements to the effect that goods are 'the best,' or are 'of good quality,' or will 'last a lifetime' and 'be in perfect condition' are generally regarded as expressions of the seller's opinion and do not create an express warranty." Do not overlook the word "generally" in this sentence.

Consider Valley Datsun v. Martinez, 578 S.W.2d 485 (Tex.Civ.App. 1979), in which plaintiff in 1977 purchased a 6–year–old Volkswagen camper from defendant. When the clutch failed and the engine threw a rod two days after delivery, plaintiff sued. Addressing the question whether defendant made an express warranty, the court stated:

> Special issues 1, 2 and 3 basically presented the question of whether plaintiff was adversely affected by the representation made by defendant's salesman that the camper, at the time of purchase, was in good mechanical condition, as found by the jury. Both plaintiff and his wife testified that the salesman stated to them that the vehicle in question was "in excellent condition." Plaintiff further testified that after he drove the vehicle for a short distance, he asked the salesman "about a noise that I thought I heard in the engine * * * a knocking or slapping noise," and that the salesman told him "that was just a typical Volkswagen noise," and that the engine noise "was probably the muffler." The salesman based his representation on the fact that he had driven the camper "about three miles"; he assumed that plaintiff relied on his representation. It was undisputed that after only 120 miles of driving by plaintiff, the camper sustained a burned-out clutch and thrown rod, which occurred only two days after the camper was picked up from the defendant's lot.
>
> . . .
>
> The test of whether a salesman's statement constituted "affirmations of fact" going to the very "basis of the bargain" is whether the salesman was asserting a fact of which the buyer was ignorant, or whether he was merely declaring his belief with reference to a matter of which he had no special knowledge and of which the buyer may also

have been expected to have an opinion. Here, the salesman, when he told plaintiff that the camper was in "excellent condition," was obviously asserting a fact of which plaintiff was ignorant. Under the circumstances existing, this statement was more than mere "dealer's talk" because knowledge of the seller, in conjunction with the buyer's relative ignorance, operates to make the slightest divergence from mere praise into representations of fact, which become effective as a warranty. The statement constituted an express oral warranty.

The jury found that the defendant's representation (through its salesman), was untrue, which was tantamount to a finding that the express warranty was breached. This is because a breach of an express warranty is essentially the failure of a product to comply with a definite warranty established by competent evidence.

4. Under the Uniform Sales Act, the predecessor to Article 2, the buyer's reliance on the seller's statement was an essential element of express warranty. The drafters of Article 2 specifically departed from expressing the requirement in terms of reliance. Instead, they created the phrase, "basis of the bargain." What does it take for an affirmation of fact to become part of the basis of the bargain? The court in *Royal Business Machines* addresses this briefly in footnote 7. Please reread that footnote and the Official Comments cited there.

5. In Rogath v. Siebenmann, 129 F.3d 261 (2d Cir.1997), plaintiff purchased a painting from defendant for $570,000. After the exchange, the authenticity of the painting was questioned, and plaintiff sued. The trial court granted plaintiff's motion for summary judgment, holding that defendant breached express warranties. Defendant appealed, acknowledging that he made the affirmations but claiming that at the time of the purchase plaintiff knew that the affirmations were false. The court wrote:

The Bill of Sale provides:

In order to induce David Rogath to make the purchase, Seller . . . makes the following warranties, representations and covenants to and with the Buyer.

1. That the Seller is the sole and absolute owner of the painting and has full right and authority to sell and transfer same; having acquired title as described in a copy of the Statement of Provenance signed by Seller annexed hereto and incorporated herein; [and] that the Seller has no knowledge of any challenge to Seller's title and authenticity of the Painting . . . .

Because the Bill of Sale was a contract for the sale of goods, Rogath's breach of warranty claims are governed by Article Two of the Uniform Commercial Code ("UCC"). Section 2–313 of the UCC provides that "any description of the goods which is made part of the basis of the bargain creates an express warranty that the goods shall conform to the description."

Whether the "basis of the bargain" requirement implies that the buyer must rely on the seller's statements to recover and what the nature of that reliance requirement is are unsettled questions. See Note, "Express Warranties under the Uniform Commercial Code: Is There a Reliance Requirement?" 66 N.Y.U. L. Rev. 468, 469 (1991); see also Annotation, "Purchaser's Disbelief in, or Nonreliance upon, Express Warranties Made by Seller in Contract for Sale of Business as Precluding Action for Breach of Express Warranties," 7 A.L.R. 5th 841 (1992). Not surprisingly, this same confusion haunted the New York courts for a time.

Some courts reasoned that the buyer must have relied upon the accuracy of the seller's affirmations or promises in order to recover.

Other courts paid lip service to a "reliance" requirement, but found that the requirement was met if the buyer relied on the seller's promise as part of "the basis of the bargain" in entering into the contract; the buyer need not show that he relied on the truthfulness of the warranties.

Finally, some courts reasoned that there is a "reliance" requirement only when there is a dispute as to whether a warranty was in fact given by the seller. These courts concluded that no reliance of any kind is required "where the existence of an express warranty in a contract is conceded by both parties." CPC Int'l Inc. v. McKesson Corp., 134 Misc.2d 834, 513 N.Y.S.2d 319, 322 (Sup.Ct.1987). In these cases, the buyer need establish only a breach of the warranty.

In 1990 New York's Court of Appeals dispelled much of the confusion when it squarely adopted the "basis of the bargain" description of the reliance required to recover for breach of an express warranty. In CBS Inc. v. Ziff–Davis Publishing Co., 75 N.Y.2d 496, 553 N.E.2d 997, 554 N.Y.S.2d 449 (N.Y.1990), the court concluded that "this view of 'reliance'—i.e., as requiring no more than reliance on the express warranty as being a part of the bargain between the parties— reflects the prevailing perception of an action for breach of express warranty as one that is no longer grounded in tort, but essentially in contract." 553 N.E.2d at 1001. The court reasoned that "the critical question is not whether the buyer believed in the truth of the warranted information ... but whether [he] believed [he] was purchasing the [seller's] promise [as to its truth]." Id. 1000–01 (quotations omitted and some insertions altered).

CBS was not decided on the basis of the UCC, probably because the sale of the magazine business at issue did not constitute the sale of goods. Nevertheless, the court relied heavily on UCC authorities, expressly noting that "analogy to the Uniform Commercial Code is 'instructive.' " Id. at 1002 n.4.

In 1992, in a case also involving the sale of a business, we followed the New York Court of Appeals and delineated fine factual distinctions in the law of warranties: a court must evaluate both the extent and the source of the buyer's knowledge about the truth of what the seller is warranting. "Where a buyer closes on a contract in the full knowledge and acceptance of facts disclosed by the seller which would constitute a breach of warranty under the terms of the contract, the buyer should be foreclosed from later asserting the breach. In that situation, unless the buyer expressly preserves his rights under the warranties ..., we think the buyer has waived the breach." Galli v. Metz, 973 F.2d 145, 151 (2d Cir.1992) (emphasis added). The buyer may preserve his rights by expressly stating that disputes regarding the accuracy of the seller's warranties are unresolved, and that by signing the agreement the buyer does not waive any rights to enforce the terms of the agreement. See Galli, 973 F.2d at 150.

On the other hand, if the seller is not the source of the buyer's knowledge, e.g., if it is merely "common knowledge" that the facts warranted are false, or the buyer has been informed of the falsity of the facts by some third party, the buyer may prevail in his claim for breach of warranty. In these cases, it is not unrealistic to assume that the buyer purchased the seller's warranty "as insurance against any future claims," and that is why he insisted on the inclusion of the warranties in the bill of sale. Galli, 973 F.2d at 151.

In short, where the seller discloses up front the inaccuracy of certain of his warranties, it cannot be said that the buyer—absent the express preservation of his rights—believed he was purchasing the seller's promise as to the truth of the warranties. Accordingly, what the buyer knew and, most importantly, whether he got that knowledge from the seller are the critical questions.

The court held that the granting of plaintiff's motion for summary judgment was improper because the affidavits of the parties in connection with that motion raised genuine questions of fact concerning what defendant told plaintiff about challenges to the authenticity of the painting.

6. Problem. After taking it for a test drive, Buyers purchased a ten-year-old car with 96,000 miles from a used-car dealer for $800. The dealer told them that the car was "mechanically sound," was "in good condition," and had "no problems." On Buyers' way home after the purchase, the car did not seem to operate properly. They took it to a mechanic, who said that it needed $1,500 in repairs to be made safe to drive. Buyers sued, claiming breach of express warranty. What result?

7. Problem. To sell a used crane, Seller ran the following advertisement:

"CRANE–Railroad 30 ton. McMyler Cummins diesel engine; 55 ft. hvy. duty boom; complete with generator for magnet work. Good condition."

(a) Buyer looked at the crane and was told by one of the seller's employees that it was "in very good condition." Buyer purchased the crane and, when delivered, it was inoperable. Did Seller make an express warranty as to condition?

(b) Assume that the advertisement and oral statement as to good condition created an express warranty. Assume also that at the time of sale, Buyer and Seller signed a document that reads as follows:

Contract of Sale

Seller agrees to sell and Buyer agrees to buy the following equipment:

> 1 Used Locomotive Crane, Manufactured by McMyler, 30–ton capacity, 55–ft. boom, complete with Cummins Diesel Engine and Generator.

Price F.O.T. Chicago–$4,000

Buyer understands that the contract between the parties hereto consists solely and completely of the terms found in this instrument.

s/Buyer

s/Seller

Does this document affect Buyer's ability to prove the earlier statements as express warranties?

(c) Assume that the last paragraph of the document also states, "Furthermore, Buyer hereby waives all warranties, express or implied, including the implied warranty of merchantability, or any warranty given by operation of law, statutory or otherwise, regarding the subject matter of this contract." Now what result?

(d) Assuming the same contract of sale, what result if the boom turns out to be only 45 feet long? (Assume that Buyer was reasonable in not noticing that fact)? See 2–316(1).

If Buyer had noticed that the boom was only 45 feet long but had said nothing to Seller about that fact before entering the contract, what result?

(e) Suppose that the crane was as described above in problem (b), but a conspicuous clause in the body of the contract states: "All equipment is subject to inspection and the descriptions are approximate and intended to serve as a guide." If the crane will lift only seven tons, is there a breach of express warranty?

8. Leases. Except for stylistic improvements, 2A–210 is identical to Article 2's provision on express warranties. Consequently, the foregoing materials on sales transactions are equally applicable to lease transactions.

9. CISG. The Convention on Contracts for the International Sale of Goods uses different terminology than Article 2. Section (1) of Article 35 declares, "The seller must deliver goods which are of the quantity, quality and description required by the contract and which are contained or packaged in the manner required by the contract." To what extent does this cover the same ground as 2–313(1)?

Section (2) proceeds to articulate several gap-filling quality terms, using some of the terminology used in Article 2, mostly in the sections on *implied* warranties. At this time, note subsection (2)(c), which resembles 2–313(1)(c). We will return to this section in connection with implied warranties.

C.   THE IMPLIED WARRANTIES OF MERCHANTABILITY AND FITNESS

1.   HISTORICAL BACKGROUND

By 1830 the courts of England had recognized an implied warranty of merchantability in contracts for the sale of goods. The courts of this country had not. For example, in 1833 a merchant sold a large quantity of flour. When the flour proved to be of unsatisfactory quality, the buyer sued, and lost. Three members of New York's highest court wrote opinions; one is excerpted here:

> I have been accustomed to suppose that the rules as to the liability of vendors, on sales of personal property, were clearly defined and firmly settled, at least in this State; but I am getting to learn that the spirit of the age, which is disposed to consider nothing settled that it imagines susceptible of improvement—a spirit which regards nothing as too ancient to be attacked—nothing as too new to be attempted, is extending its influences to the oldest and deepest rooted principles of the common law. This event might not be so much regretted, if it were proposed to be brought about only through the open and responsible agency of legislation; but when pursued through the devious and occult process of judicial exceptions and qualifications, it becomes a subject of some solicitude and apprehension. Ld. Eldon wisely remarked, that instead of struggling by little circumstances to take cases out of a general rule, it is more wholesome to struggle not to let little circumstances prevent the application of the general rule. But this principle, in modern times, has been so poorly maintained, that the profession of the law, it seems to me, is fast becoming a matter of memory rather than of reason and judgment; and the study of it is already so much more the study of the exceptions and evasions of general principles, than of general principles themselves, that I am sometimes induced to think that as a science, the law would be better understood, and as a rule of right, more justly administered, if the reports of judicial decisions for the last half century were struck out of existence. We see continually that the qualification or relaxation of a general principle, established by one reported case, is made the place of departure for ascertaining a new position in another, and this again in a third, and so on, until the original rule, the natural standard of the law, is obscured and utterly lost sight of, by means of intervening artificial measures of supposed particular justice. The consequence to be feared is that judicial reports, instead of being what, no doubt it is intended they should be, beacons and landmarks to guide the public into quiet havens of security and repose, may become false lights to decoy into the whirls and shoals of litigation. In speaking of the new and refined distinctions upon general principles, which in his day were multiplying, though in no degree as rapidly as since, Ld. Mansfield remarked, that

"If our rules are too incumbered with all the exceptions which ingenious minds can imagine, there is no certain principle to direct us, and
it were better to apply the principles of justice to every case, and not to
proceed to more fixed rules." And much more may we say, in looking
at the ponderous volumes of reported cases which flood the country,
and are multiplying with a rapidity that no diligence can keep pace
with, that rather than that the science of the law should have to be
sought in the exceptions, qualifications and ingenious evasions of
general rules, made and to be made by innumerable judges, the records
of which are to be spread through thousands of volumes, it were better
to abandon all attempts to preserve a written system of jurisprudence,
and to revert at once to that species of administrative justice com-
mended by Cicero, when *"Amissis auctoritatibus, ipsa re et ratione
exquirere possumus veritatem."**

In the earliest history of the common law, the distinction between
its rules and those of the civil law in respect to the liability of vendors,
was marked and acknowledged. More than 200 years ago, Ld. Coke, in
speaking of it, says: "The civil law binds every man to warrant the
thing he selleth, albeit there be no express warranty; but the common
law bindeth him not, unless there be a warranty in deed or in law."
And Popham, who, in the language of Ch. J. Eyre, was "a very able
judge," says Dyer, 75: "If I have an article which is defective, whether
victuals or anything else, and I, knowing it to be defective, sell it as
sound, and so represent or affirm it, an action upon the case lies for
the deceit; but although it be defective, if that is unknown to me,
although I represent or affirm it to be sound, no action lies unless I
warrant it to be sound."

Originally, the only implied warranty or warranty in law, as
distinguished from a warranty in fact on the sale of personal property,
was that of ownership by the vendor. Afterwards the sale of goods by
sample was held to imply a warranty that the bulk of the goods
corresponded in quality with the specimen exhibited; then, in case of
goods not present at the sale, and consequently not susceptible of
inspection by the buyer, a warranty was implied that they were of the
general denomination or nature represented; then, though the goods
were present and susceptible of inspection by the buyer, yet if not
actually inspected, a warranty was implied that they were of the
description and quality represented in the invoice or sale bill, this,
however, is rather on the ground that the writing amounts to an
express warranty in fact. Then, where goods are sold by the manufacturer of them, a warranty has been implied that they are of a
merchantable quality; then, where goods are sold for a particular
purpose, a warranty that they are fit for that purpose. Finally, in Jones
v. Bright, 5 Bing., 533, Ch.J. Best is disposed to consider the law as
resolving itself into this: "that if a man sells generally, he undertakes
[warrants] that the article is fit for some purpose, viz.: that it is

---

* Authority being absent, we are able to
find the truth by reason.—Ed.

merchantable; and if he sells for a particular purpose, he undertakes [warrants] that it is fit for that particular purpose." Thus the English courts, in a circle of about 200 years, by the process of finding a new principle in each departure from the old one, by extending each case a little beyond the rule of the case immediately preceding it, instead of measuring it by the original standard principle, have gradually but completely subverted the common law maxim of *caveat emptor,* and effectually, though perhaps undesignedly, substituted for it the repudiated principle of the civil law, which, as Ld. Coke quaintly but correctly states it "binds every man to warrant the thing he selleth, albeit there be no express warranty." Some cases with us, and especially some propositions in the case of Gallagher v. Waring, 9 Wend., 20, would seem to indicate that our courts are upon the same pilgrimage; but the qualification of those propositions, in the opinion of the Supreme Court in the present case, and especially the decisive and enlightened views expressed upon the whole subject, I am happy to say, afford satisfactory assurance that there is no disposition to adopt further changes, which, it is well remarked, "would at best unsettle inveterate habits of business, and introduce a vast amount of litigation." In this connection, I will add, in the words of a distinguished jurist: "The common law affords to every one reasonable protection against fraud in dealings; but it does not go to the romantic length of giving indemnity against the consequences of indolence and folly, or a careless indifference to the ordinary and accessible means of information."

For one, I am not disposed to go beyond what the courts of this State have heretofore gone in furtherance of the doctrine of implied warranty; and, indeed, am constrained to think that in some instances, even they have allowed the hardship of the case to outweigh considerations of public policy, and in the pursuit of particular justice, have confused a little the certainty and simplicity of a rule, which, if firmly adhered to by courts, would soon come to be universally heeded by contracting parties. . . . [T]o imply a warranty of anything whatever except title in the vendor, much more to imply a warranty that the article is merchantable; or if the purchaser happens to signify the purpose for which he wishes the article, to imply a warranty that it is fit for that particular purpose, is necessarily to subvert the common law principle, that the risk of the sale is with the purchaser, and to substitute for it the loose and litigious principle of the civil law, that the quality of the article must correspond with the price given for it. And here I will say, that if as a judge I possessed, what no judge does possess, the power of determining which of the two rules should hereafter prevail in this State, I should not hesitate to prefer the rule of the common law, as exceedingly better fitted both for its certainty and general justice to the transactions of a commercial community, than that of the civil law. . . . In short, I am satisfied with the rule of the common law, notwithstanding the occasional hardships, which, under it, as under all fixed rules, may occur; and I am disposed to adhere to it closely, not only because of the solemn obligation upon us as judges to administer the law as we shall find it to be, but also because I am firmly persuaded that it is the most honest and salutary general rule that can be established on the subject.

Wright v. Hart, 18 Wend. 449 (N.Y.Ct. Errors 1837) (Tracy, Sen.).

———

This eloquent opinion did not stem the tide: courts continued to find new principles in departures from the old and in sales of goods by merchants implication of warranties of merchantability became the rule rather than the exception. Why were the arguments made by Senator Tracy in Wright v. Hart ultimately not persuasive? What reasons occur to you for accepting or rejecting his arguments on the issue whether a warranty of quality should be implied in sales contracts?

The Uniform Sales Act, drafted by Professor Samuel Williston and approved by NCCUSL in 1906, provided: "Where goods are bought by description from a seller who deals in goods of that description (whether he be the grower or manufacturer or not), there is an implied warranty that the goods shall be of a merchantable quality." [§ 15(2)]. Williston had lifted that language from section 14 of the British Sale of Goods Act, adopted in England in 1894.

Under the Uniform Sales Act, an implied warranty of merchantability would arise in a fact situation like that in Wright v. Hart, but might not arise in a case in which a buyer purchased specific barrels of flour that were on hand at the time of the purchase: there it might be concluded that the sale was not "by description." See generally, Williston on Sales, Revised Edition, §§ 227–32 (1948).

2.   THE STANDARDS

The Uniform Commercial Code dropped the sale-by-description limitation on the warranty of merchantability: now the warranty arises under 2–314 against any merchant who deals in goods of the kind in any sales transaction unless there is an effective disclaimer. In addition, the Code provides in 2–315 for an implied warranty of fitness for particular purpose. Please review these sections now.

1.   Problem. To promote sales of its high-end Viking stoves, Seller advertises that it will give anyone who purchases a Viking stove a free cordless telephone with a built-in answering machine. Buyer purchases one of the stoves, installing it and the telephone in his kitchen. The answering machine short circuits and causes a small fire, quickly extinguished. Has Seller breached an implied warranty?

2.   Problem. Needing to replace some of the windows in her house, Buyer purchases six double-paned thermal windows from Seller. After installation Buyer discovers that the seal is defective, water has gotten between the panes, and the glass is foggy. Seller replaces the six windows with new ones. The replacement windows have a sound seal, but the insulating gas between the panes is defective, causing the glass to appear cloudy. Can Buyer recover for breach of the implied warranty of merchantability?

3.   Problem. Seller, a new-car dealership, is renovating its mechanical and body repair shops. To make room for a new spray-paint machine, Seller sells its current machine to an independent body-repair shop, for $6,000. Buyer installs the sprayer in its shop, but when operated at full speed the machine sprays unevenly. To perform in an acceptable manner, it must be used at 50% of its capacity. Buyer sues for breach of the implied warranty of merchantability. What result?

Ambassador Steel Co. v. Ewald Steel Co.

Michigan Court of Appeals, 1971.
33 Mich.App. 495, 190 N.W.2d 275.

■ Fitzgerald, Judge. . . .

Plaintiff and defendant are both merchants in the business of the sale of steel. On or about October 4 and 5, 1966, plaintiff sold a certain amount of steel to defendant. The purchase price of the steel was $9,856.44, of which defendant paid $4,107.60, leaving an unpaid balance of $5,748.84. Plaintiff brought an action in the common pleas court to recover the balance due, waiving all amounts over $5,000 so as to bring the matter within the jurisdiction of that court.

Defendant admitted the purchase price of the steel, but claimed a set-off, alleging that plaintiff breached its implied warranty of merchantability in that plaintiff failed to supply defendant with "commercial quality" steel, that is, steel with a carbon content of 1010 to 1020. The defect came to light when the company to whom the defendant in turn sold the steel informed defendant that the steel cracked after being welded on to railroad cars. As a result of this, defendant's customer charged back its losses to defendant. Defendant thus claimed the set-off against plaintiff.

The trial court allowed defendant to set off the entire amount of the charge-back, with the exception of a claim for overhead, and entered a judgment for plaintiff in the amount of $1,055.78. Plaintiff appealed to the circuit court, contending the judgment was inadequate. The circuit court affirmed, plaintiff applied for leave to appeal to this court and we granted it.

Plaintiff on appeal raises four issues which will be dealt with *seriatim.*

The first issue can be stated in the following form:

As between dealers in steel, is there an implied warranty that the steel is merchantable for the purpose for which it is used, where plaintiff was not advised by defendant of the use to which the steel was to be put?

Plaintiff contends on appeal that because defendant did not inform plaintiff of the purposes for which the steel was to be used, defendant cannot claim that it was not fit for the purpose for which it was used. Defendant, however, appears to be relying on a different implied warranty, that of merchantability, and not that of particular fitness.

Section 2–314 of the Uniform Commercial Code provides, in part:

"(1) Unless excluded or modified * * *, a warranty that the goods shall be merchantable is implied in a contract for their sale if the seller is a merchant with respect to goods of that kind. * * *

"(2) Goods to be merchantable must be at least such as

"(a) pass without objection in the trade under the contract description; and . . .

"(c) are fit for the ordinary purposes for which such goods are used; and

"(d) run, within the variations permitted by the agreement, of even kind, quality and quantity within each unit and among all units involved; . . . .

"(3) Unless excluded or modified * * *, other implied warranties may arise from course of dealing or usage of trade." (M.C.L.A. § 440.2314).

This section is further explained in the Comments of National Conference of Commissioners following the section, which states:

"2. The question when the warranty is imposed turns basically on the meaning of the terms of the agreement as recognized in the trade. Goods delivered under an agreement made by a merchant in a given line of trade must be of a quality comparable to that generally acceptable in that line of trade under the description or other designation of the goods used in the agreement."

Thus, unless there is an exclusion or modification, when, as here, a merchant sells such goods, an implied warranty arises that the goods would pass without objection in the trade under the contract description; also, that they are fit for the ordinary purposes for which the goods are used.

The implied warranty of merchantability is decidedly different from the implied warranty for a particular purpose that arises under M.C.L.A. § 440.2315. The particular purpose warranty is defined by the official UCC comment as:

"2. A 'particular purpose' differs from the ordinary purpose for which the goods are used in that it envisages a specific use by the buyer which is peculiar to the nature of his business whereas the ordinary purposes for which goods are used are those envisaged in the concept of merchantability and go to uses which are customarily made of the goods in question. For example, shoes are generally used for the purpose of walking upon ordinary ground, but a seller may know that a particular pair was selected to be used for climbing mountains."

It appears, then, that the warranty of merchantability warrants that the goods sold are of average quality within the industry, whereas a warranty of fitness for a particular purpose warrants that the goods sold are fit for the purposes for which they are intended. The latter is also further qualified by the requirement that the seller must know, at the time of sale, the particular purpose for which the goods are required and also that the buyer is relying on the seller to select or furnish suitable goods.

In the instant case, it is undisputed that the plaintiff was not made aware of the purpose for which the steel was to be used. Therefore, the implied warranty of fitness for a particular purpose did not arise under M.C.L.A. § 440.2315.

The question then becomes whether or not the steel sold by plaintiff to defendant was subject to the implied warranty of merchantability under M.C.L.A. § 440.2314. Although defendant sold the goods to a third party, M.C.L.A. § 440.2314 Comment 1 states that the warranty of merchantability applies to goods sold for resale as well as those for sale. And, as we previously stated, Comment 2 of the same section states that the question of when the warranty is imposed turns basically on the meaning of the terms as recognized in the trade.

M.C.L.A. § 440.1205(2) defines a usage of trade as "any practice or method of dealing having such regularity of observance in a place, vocation or trade as to justify an expectation that it will be observed with respect to the transaction in question."

M.C.L.A. § 440.1205(3) provides, "A course of dealing between parties and any usage of trade in the vocation in which they are engaged or of which they are or should be aware give particular meaning to and supplement or qualify terms of an agreement."

Testimony in the transcript indicates that defendant made no specific request concerning the particular quality of steel they ordered. However, there was also ample testimony below to the effect that when an order is placed without specification as to the particular quality desired, custom and usage of the steel business is that a "commercial quality" steel, that is, steel with a carbon content between 1010 and 1020, is to be used. Further testimony was to the effect that if one desired steel other than "commercial quality" it must be specified in the order, according to local custom and usage. The testimony indicated that the steel sold by plaintiff to defendant was not within the commercial range, thus the steel cracked after being welded. Therefore, plaintiff breached the implied warranty of merchantability in selling to defendant steel of a different quality than ordinarily sold in the custom and usage of the steel business, and not fit for the ordinary purposes for which such goods are used. M.C.L.A. § 440.2314.

Plaintiff raises the point that they were not notified of the purpose to which the steel was to be put. Apparently plaintiff implies that the use made of the steel was a particular purpose and thus not an ordinary purpose. We have already held that plaintiff is not liable for any implied warranty for fitness for a particular purpose. Furthermore, we need not decide whether this was a particular purpose, because the quality of steel that should have been delivered under the general warranty of merchantability, but was not, was sufficient to satisfy the use in the instant case.

. . .

Plaintiff next raises the issue that defendant did not sustain the burden of proving that plaintiff had breached the contract. We agree; defendant did not sustain the burden of proving plaintiff had breached the contract. However, defendant did not need to do so. What defendant needed to do, and what the record shows he did do, was prove that plaintiff had breached its implied warranty of merchantability. Defendant proved below that plaintiff impliedly warranted the steel sold as being of "commercial quality," that the plaintiff did not, in fact, sell to defendant steel that was of "commercial quality," and that if the steel had been of "commercial quality" it would not have cracked after being welded on to the railroad cars. This is sufficient to sustain an action for breach of warranty. See U.C.C., Sec. 2–314, Official Comment 13.

. . .

Therefore, the lower court should be, and hereby is, affirmed. Costs to appellees.

QUESTIONS AND NOTES

1. Section 2–314 articulates six examples of merchantability standards. Which of them did the steel fail to meet?

2. In the last paragraph of its opinion, the court says that buyer did not prove that seller breached the contract, but did prove that seller had breached the implied warranty of merchantability. Is it appropriate to say that breach of warranty is not breach of contract? See 1–201(11). What difference would it make whether the court views a breach of warranty as a breach of contract?

3. Non-uniform amendments regarding livestock. At least 24 states in the Midwest, South, and West have limited the existence or scope of implied warranties in the sale of livestock, either by amending 2–316 or by enacting a separate statute for that purpose. The statutes vary as to the animals included in the amendment, but cattle and hogs are always included. Most include horses, and some include sheep and poultry, and at least one includes rabbits. Most say there is no warranty as to freedom from disease, but a few exclude any implied warranties. Many condition the exclusion on compliance with any applicable state and federal regulations.

———

Bethlehem Steel Corp. v. Chicago Eastern Corp.

United States Court of Appeals, Seventh Circuit, 1988.
863 F.2d 508.

■ FLAUM, CIRCUIT JUDGE.

[Plaintiff sued for the price of two orders of steel sold to defendant. Defendant counterclaimed that the warranty of merchantability had been breached. The trial court gave judgment on a verdict for plaintiff, and defendant appealed.]

. . .

The second issue on appeal is whether the district court properly granted Bethlehem's motion for a directed verdict on Chicago Eastern's claim that Bethlehem breached the implied warranty of merchantability applicable to the steel acquired in the first purchase. . . .

Under Illinois law, if the seller of goods is a merchant of goods of the kind being sold, a warranty that the goods are "merchantable" is implied into a contract for their sale as a matter of law, unless otherwise expressly excluded or modified. Ill.Rev.Stat. ch. 26, para. 2–314(1) and 2–316. Chicago Eastern and Bethlehem agree that the first purchase included an implied warranty that the steel sold by Bethlehem would be "merchantable." The minimum criteria for determining merchantability are set forth in paragraph 2–314(2)(a)-(f). Chicago Eastern claims that the factors particularly relevant to the present dispute are those enumerated "(b)" and "(c)" in the statute. Paragraph 2–314(2)(b) requires that goods, if fungible, be of "fair average quality within the [contract] description," while 2–314(2)(c) states that goods must be "fit for the ordinary purposes for which such goods are used." Chicago Eastern contends that it introduced evidence at trial from which a reasonable juror could conclude that the steel acquired from Bethlehem in the first purchase failed to satisfy these two requirements and that the district court therefore erred in granting Bethlehem's motion for a directed verdict.

Prior to trial, Bethlehem and Chicago Eastern stipulated to a number of facts. The parties agreed that Chicago Eastern submitted an order for steel sheets to be manufactured by Bethlehem and that confirmation of the first purchase was memorialized on two Chicago Eastern purchase orders. The first purchase order, dated February 4, 1976, states that Chicago Eastern ordered sheet steel of a type designated by the American Society of Testing Materials (ASTM) as "446 Grade C." The second confirmation, a supplement to the first confirmation, did not use the ASTM designation; rather it specified a certain chemical composition and maximum yield strength: ".14–.20 carbon yield to 40,000 PSI after roll forming."

Chicago Eastern acknowledges that it received steel that complied with the requirements necessary to qualify as ASTM 446 Grade C and the requirements specified in the second purchase order. Chicago Eastern also acknowledged at oral argument that the steel would pass without objection in the trade under the contract description. It argues, however, that the steel was not merchantable because the steel was subjected to a renitrogenization process—a process not traditionally used with steel of this designation. Under this process, the nitrogen content of the steel was substantially increased. This increased the yield strength of the steel, but also made the steel more brittle and more susceptible to fracturing upon sudden impact. In other words, Chicago Eastern admits that the steel it received from

Bethlehem did indeed possess the properties necessary to comply with the ASTM designation it ordered, but argues that the steel also possessed additional properties as a result of the renitrogenization process that made the steel unmerchantable. In the procedural posture of this case, the specific inquiry is whether Chicago Eastern introduced evidence from which a reasonable juror could conclude that steel which admittedly was ASTM 446 Grade C steel, was also less than "fair average quality within the [contract] description" and not "fit for the ordinary purposes for which such goods are used."

Chicago Eastern points to the testimony of its expert, Professor David W. Levinson, as evidence introduced at trial from which a reasonable juror could conclude that the steel acquired from Bethlehem in the first purchase was not merchantable. Levinson testified that although there was no specific prohibition against using the renitrogenization process in the production of ASTM 446 Grade C steel, the amount of nitrogen was 25 to 50 times higher than the level found in typical steel of this designation and that this amount of nitrogen "is added to very few steels." He further testified that this amount of nitrogen increased the yield strength of the steel, but also raised the "transition temperature" of the steel. Levinson explained that the transition temperature is the temperature below which fractures in a steel are substantially brittle and above which they are substantially ductile. This distinction is important because steel above the transition temperature stretches before it fractures. More pressure is therefore required to cause a ductile fracture than a brittle fracture.

Levinson testified that after examining samples of the fractured steel from the grain bins that it was his opinion that the fractures were brittle and not ductile. He also noted that tests conducted by third parties indicated that the transition temperature of the fractured steel was substantially higher because of the renitrogenization process than it otherwise would have been. Chicago Eastern's direct examination of Levinson culminated with his agreement that the renitrogenized steel was unsuitable "for use as a wall sheet in a grain tank which could be erected anywhere in the United States." Chicago Eastern contends that this was evidence which indicated that the steel acquired from Bethlehem was not of fair-average quality under the contract description and that the steel was not fit for the ordinary purposes for which such steel is used. In Chicago Eastern's view, Levinson's testimony provided sufficient evidence that the Bethlehem steel was not merchantable and therefore the warranty of merchantability issue should have been presented to the jury.

Even viewing the evidence presented at trial in the light most favorable to Chicago Eastern, we hold that no reasonable juror could conclude that the steel acquired from Bethlehem was not merchantable. All the evidence introduced by Chicago Eastern, including Levinson's testimony, was directed towards showing that the steel acquired in the first purchase was unfit for use as wall sheets in grain storage bins. Merchantability, however, does not look only at the particular use to which the buyer puts the goods. Rather, Uniform Commercial Code Comment 7 states that paragraph 2–314(2)(a) and (b) are to be read together and refer "to the standards of that line of the trade which fits the transaction and the seller's business." Ill.Rev.Stat. ch. 26, para. 2–314 comment 7. It is therefore appropriate to analyze the transaction from the selling merchant's perspective. Bethlehem is in the business of selling unfinished steel products, including ASTM 446 Grade C steel. Chicago Eastern was required to show the ordinary purposes for which this type of steel is used and that the renitrogenization made the steel acquired from Bethlehem unfit for these purposes. This Chicago Eastern did not do.

Chicago Eastern has not pointed to any evidence presented at trial on the ordinary uses of this type of steel or how the renitrogenization affected these uses, nor has Chicago Eastern directed us to any place in the record where it introduced evidence showing that use as wall sheets in grain bins was in fact an ordinary use of this type of steel. In addition, Chicago Eastern did not introduce evidence that the increased nitrogen made the steel below fair-average quality. Levinson's testimony indicated that the nitrogen increased the transition temperature and made the steel more brittle, but that it also increased the yield strength of the steel. The steel was therefore not defective in the typical warranty of merchantability sense because the nitrogen that allegedly made the product defective by making the steel too brittle also had the seemingly desirable effect of making the steel stronger. It seems possible that different uses of steel require a different balancing of the apparent tradeoff between strength and brittleness. We do not hold that steel subjected to this process is merchantable under the ASTM 446 Grade C description, rather we hold only that Chicago Eastern failed to offer evidence that it was not. Chicago Eastern was required to introduce evidence that the brittleness of the steel, regardless of the improved strength, made this steel unfit for the ordinary uses of ASTM 446 Grade C steel; no such evidence was introduced.[9]

QUESTIONS AND NOTES

1. In the penultimate paragraph of its opinion, the court quotes Official Comment 7 and asserts that it therefore is appropriate to analyze the transaction from the seller's perspective. Official Comment 7 addresses subsections (2)(a) and (b). Is this the proper perspective from which to analyze a transaction involving subsection (2)(c)? the other provisions of subsection (2)?

2. What level of quality is required by the standard "merchantability"? Subsection (2) lists several translations. Notably, the word "defective" does not appear among them. Is a showing that the goods contain some defect

---

9. Indeed, Chicago Eastern conceded at oral argument that the steel it acquired would pass without objection under the contract description of ASTM 446 Grade C steel. Although this designation does not speak to brittleness or provide for a particular level of nitrogen, if the steel was in fact too brittle to be used for ordinary purposes it is difficult to understand how it would pass without objection in the trade.

tantamount to a showing that they are not fit for their ordinary purposes or will not pass without objection in the trade? Consider *Fargo Machine & Tool Co. v. Kearney & Trecker Corp.*, 428 F.Supp. 364 (E.D.Mich.1977), in which Fargo purchased a complex milling machine from Kearney & Trecker for approximately $150,000. During the first two years of the machine's operation, a large number of service calls were made by seller in response to complaints by buyer. The court stated:

> Fargo's complaint alleges that the H–100 is "defective in material and workmanship" and "has required numerous and repetitive repairs, including some thirty-seven separate repair jobs." Certainly, however, every mechanical failure in a new and complex machine does not constitute a breach of warranty. *N.C.R. v. Adell*, 57 Mich.App. 413, 225 N.W.2d 785 (1975). At the outset then, it is necessary to distinguish and segregate those defects which merely required that work be performed and those legally significant defects which either remained uncured after reasonable opportunity to correct them or which are otherwise related to plaintiff's damage claims. Fargo does not contend that it was entitled to a perfect machine, nor that the installation and break-in period should have been completely service free. Exactly what Fargo was entitled to is governed by the Uniform Commercial Code unless permissibly modified by agreement between the parties.

> . . .

> . . . Fargo's complaints must be read in terms of their significance in the machining trade and relative to what would normally pass in the trade without objection under the contract description. Notably, with regard to repairs, Fargo's expert, Fassey, testified not only that Fargo's $850.00 total expenditures through 1976 were remarkably low, but in addition, that a high degree of debugging is required on such machines and that normally the first five years of a machine of this nature often generate $5,000 to $10,000 in maintenance costs. As noted earlier, case law recognizes that such mechanical failures in new and complex machines are expected, and to the extent that deficiencies and corrective service performed were routine for so sophisticated a machine, no breach occurs. Indeed, McCaffrey conceded from the stand that, although numerous problems developed at one time or another, most were of a minor nature, almost all were fixed by Kearney & Trecker promptly, and Fargo is left with relatively few defects which have any operational impact. Both the service reports and the lists of defects prepared by McCaffrey for payment conferences with Kearney & Trecker support this conclusion. Nearly all of the service reports, bearing McCaffrey's signature as chief engineer of Fargo, indicate the precise problems for which the service call was made and whether or not the job was completed. An uncompleted job was indicated only seven times after installation had been finished and four of these jobs were satisfactorily completed on follow-up calls. . . .

The court concluded, however, that there were three remaining serious problems with the machine which the seller had been unable to correct and which did constitute breaches of warranty.

To similar effect is Taterka v. Ford Motor Co., 86 Wis.2d 140, 271 N.W.2d 653 (1978), in which the taillight assembly gaskets in plaintiff's new 1972 Mustang had been installed in a manner that allowed water to enter. The problem was common to all Mustangs of that year. The presence of water in the taillight assembly caused rust. Plaintiff sued for breach of the implied warranty of merchantability:

> Where automobiles are concerned the term "unmerchantable" has only been applied where a single defect poses a substantial safety hazard or numerous defects classify the car as a "lemon." *See e.g., Zabriskie Chevrolet, Inc. v. Smith*, 99 N.J.Super. 441, 240 A.2d 195 (1968); *Henningsen v. Bloomfield Motors, Inc.*, 32 N.J. 358, 161 A.2d 69 (1960). The ordinary purpose for which a car is intended is to provide transportation. Where a car can provide safe, reliable transportation it is generally considered merchantable.
>
> . . .
>
> The automobile here involved had been driven for 33 months and in excess of 75,000 miles without a serious misadventure. In fact, it had been driven 90,000 miles at the time of the hearing on the motion for summary judgment in 1976. The only inference that can reasonably be drawn from the undisputed facts is that the rust problem described in this case did not render the car unfit for the purpose of driving and therefore unmerchantable. Since conflicting inferences did not arise from the undisputed facts, summary judgment was appropriate.

Would the result in *Taterka* be different if the problem had been with the paint, so that the rust appeared on the hood (the panel covering the engine compartment) of the car?

3. *Bethlehem Steel* illustrates the importance—and the difficulty—of establishing not only the quality standard envisioned by a particular subsection of 2–314(2), but also the failure of the goods to meet that standard. Use of expert witnesses is one way, but it is not the only way. A buyer may be able to establish by circumstantial evidence that goods are not fit for their ordinary purposes. Consider these excerpts from Nelson v. Wilkins Dodge, Inc., 256 N.W.2d 472 (Minn. 1977):

> The elemental facts are not in dispute. On August 16, 1972, plaintiffs, William and Cheryl Nelson, bought a new 1972 Toyota Hilux 4–cylinder half-ton pickup truck from Wilkins Dodge, Inc. (Wilkins), a Toyota dealer in St. Paul. Before making this purchase, Mr. Nelson, concerned about the size of a 4–cylinder engine, told a salesman at Wilkins that he needed a vehicle that could withstand constant freeway speeds. Plaintiff needed a sturdy vehicle because as an ironworker he was required to travel long distances to and from various jobs. The salesman replied that the pickup was fine for freeway driving and that it could be driven at 65 miles per hour all the time.

After purchasing the pickup, plaintiffs experienced numerous difficulties with it in its use as the family car. The difficulties included the following:

(1) Within a month of purchase and within its first 2,000 miles of use, bubbles appeared in the paint covering the seam on the back part of the pickup.

(2) Within the same period of time, the taillights failed to function. Mr. Nelson noticed that the taillight covers had been installed upside down, enabling rain to enter the assembly and short out the lights. He inverted the covers himself and experienced no problem with the lights thereafter.

(3) In the middle of October 1972, with approximately 7,500 miles on the pickup, as Mr. Nelson was driving through Wisconsin during a rainstorm the windshield-wiper blade and arm flew off into the night, forcing him to negotiate the last 100 miles of his journey at a slow speed keeping watch from the side window. The next day he discovered that the bolts from the windshield-wiper motor were loose and tightened them; he later had a new wiper blade and arm installed.

(4) In February 1973, with approximately 12,000 miles on the pickup, Mr. Nelson noticed oil leakage from the front and rear of the pickup. . . .

(5) In March of 1973 . . . the horn bracket broke causing the horn to fall out, and the shift lever became loose preventing engagement of the transmission.

. . .

Defendant asserts that the evidence supported inconsistent inferences as to the causes of the condition of the pickup. If the state of the evidence was such that the jury would have had to speculate among possible causes of the pickup's condition, then plaintiffs would have failed to sustain their burden of production, and the court's ruling would be correct. In Heil v. Standard Chemical Mfg. Co., 301 Minn. 315, 324, 223 N.W.2d 37, 42 (1974), we quoted approvingly the following language . . . . :

> Where the record shows that there are several possible causes of an injury, for one or more of which the defendant was not responsible, and it is just as reasonable and probable that the injury was the result of the latter, the plaintiff may not recover, since he has failed to prove that the defendant's breach caused the injury.

Plaintiffs assert that there can be no question that proximate cause has been demonstrated with respect to the paint bubbles, the inverted taillight covers, and the loosened windshield-wiper blade and arm and shift lever. Defendant suggests that the paint bubbles and the loosened windshield wiper, horn bracket, and shift lever just as probably resulted from the continuous and hard use to which plaintiffs put the pickup as from any defect inhering in the vehicle when plaintiffs purchased it. Although liability for breach of warranty attaches only when a defect existing in the goods causes a breakdown in quality, generally no specific defect need be alleged, and a defective condition can be proved by circumstantial evidence. No direct evidence was introduced as to the causes of the conditions in question. It is reasonable to suppose, however, that vehicles that are fit for ordinary purposes probably do not display these defects this early, even if they are driven a great deal within a short period of time. Thus, the causes of the faulty paint, windshield wiper, horn bracket, and shift lever were questions that should have been decided by the jury. A fortiori, the cause of the inverted taillight covers was a jury question.

Plaintiffs have also cited antifreeze and oil leaks as being further defects of the pickup. Defendant correctly asserts that there was no probative evidence of an antifreeze leak and thus there could be no breach in that respect. The question of the oil loss is less clear. Although defendant contends that the jury might reasonably have inferred that the oil leakage was caused by an earlier improper oil change, this contention is unavailing because the record does not indicate that anyone other than defendant performed an earlier oil change. Therefore, the cause of the oil loss was also a question for the jury.

4. Would the buyer in *Bethlehem Steel* have had better luck arguing that the warranty of fitness for particular purpose had been breached? What factual inquiries would you make if you were trying to determine the buyer's chances of successfully asserting a breach of that warranty in *Bethlehem Steel*? Should there be any obligation on the part of the seller to notify the buyer that this steel was more brittle at lower temperatures than most steel of the designated grade?

5. Problem. Buyer purchases from Seller, a used car dealer, two 2000 Ford Mustang GT Coupes, one at a price of $12,000 and the other at a price of $7,000. Seller makes no express warranties other than that the automobiles are 2000 Mustangs, as they are. A few weeks after purchase, Buyer discovers that both cars require a $500 valve job. Buyer demands that Seller bear the cost of the valve job for both automobiles. Seller agrees to pay for the repair of the auto for which Buyer paid $12,000, but it refuses to bear the cost of repairing the $7,000 car. Buyer consults you as to whether Seller has, in fact, conceded warranty liability as to both autos by agreeing to pay for repair of the $12,000 one. What do you advise?

6. Problem. Buyer orders a plate of chicken enchiladas at a Mexican restaurant. As she is chewing on a forkful of enchilada, she bites down on a chicken bone and chips a tooth. Is the restaurant liable for breach of the implied warranty of merchantability?

Would it matter if she had ordered vegetarian enchiladas?

7. Problem. Buyer is preparing a dish pursuant to a recipe in a cookbook. The recipe calls for an ingredient known as elephant's ear plant root.

It is common for consumers to snack on or taste ingredients while they cook. Buyer casually eats a small piece of the uncooked ingredient. She becomes violently ill because, in its raw form, the elephant's ear plant root is highly toxic. Is the cookbook merchantable?

In connection with this problem, you may be interested to know that in 1978, "Random House recalled some 3,000 copies of 'Woman's Day Crockery Cuisine' by Sylvia Vaughn Thompson and mounted a media campaign to warn purchasers of approximately 10,000 additional copies of the book. That action came after it was discovered that the recipe for Silky Caramel Slices, if followed exactly as printed in the book, could cause an explosion . . . ." N.Y. Times, p. 19, Dec. 14, 1983. Is this relevant to determining the answer to the problem?

8.   Problem. Buyer purchases a used 2004 Honda Accord from Seller, a used-car dealer, for $18,000. Unknown to Seller, the car had been in a serious accident and had been declared a total loss by the company that had insured it. The car wound up in the hands of a rebuilder, who made enough cosmetic and mechanical repairs to be able to sell it. Structurally, however, the car is not safe to drive. Seller knows nothing of this prior history of the car. When Buyer experiences excessive tire wear, she investigates and discovers that the car had been declared a total loss by its insurer and sold as salvage. Has Seller breached the implied warranty of merchantability?

9.   The car in Problem 8 has manifested a condition—tire wear—that is not normal. It has not yet manifested another defect, viz., collapse of the frame in the event of a collision. Under what circumstances should a flaw in the goods which has not yet—and may never—become apparent constitute a breach of the implied warranty of merchantability? Consider Everett v. TK–Taito, L.L.C., 178 S.W.3d 844 (Tex.App.2005), in which plaintiffs sued because their 10–year–old vehicles were equipped with seat belt buckles that the buckle manufacturer admitted had a propensity to engage only partially and therefore to release during a collision. This propensity had not yet manifested itself in plaintiffs' vehicles.

> We begin our analysis by drawing a distinction between manifested product defects and unmanifested product defects—like the one alleged by the Everetts—because most of the cases relied upon by the Everetts involve manifested defects, not unmanifested defects; therefore, those cases are not controlling.

> The Texas Supreme Court has not yet addressed which claims, if any, a plaintiff possesses standing to assert based on an unmanifested product defect that causes only economic damages. Our sister courts, as well as out-of-state courts, have reached different conclusions concerning which, if any, theories of recovery are available to a plaintiff seeking economic benefit-of-the-bargain or cost-of-replacement damages based on an unmanifested product defect.

> . . . Because this is a statutory cause of action, we apply statutory standing principles. The statutory elements of the Everetts' breach of implied warranty of merchantability are (1) that their vehicles' seat

belt buckles are defective as unfit for their purpose because of a lack of what was required for adequacy, (2) that the alleged defect existed when the buckles left the manufacturer's and the seller's possession, and (3) that the alleged defect proximately caused the injuries for which the Everetts seek damages. See id. §§ 2.314 & cmt. 13, 2.607(c)(1), 2.714–.715 . . . .

In determining whether the allegations show that the defect caused injury, we recognize that the defect in an implied warranty of merchantability case may not be the same as the defect in a strict products liability case. In the context of an implied warranty of merchantability case, the word "defect" means a condition of the goods that renders them unfit for the ordinary purposes for which they are used because of a lack of something necessary for adequacy. In the area of strict products liability, however, the word "defect" means a condition of the product that renders it unreasonably dangerous. A defective design may render a product unreasonably dangerous for strict liability purposes, but may not render a product unfit for the ordinary purposes for which it is used if the product works properly when used for its ordinary purpose. [E.g.,] Sears, Roebuck & Co. v. Kunze, 996 S.W.2d 416, 422 (Tex. App. 1999) (involving products liability suit based on unreasonably dangerous radial saw—defective for lack of a lower blade guard—but obviously fit for sawing, the ordinary purpose for which it was used).

The Everetts pleaded a breach of the implied warranty of merchantability cause of action, but they pleaded a products liability defect—a defective design of the buckle giving it a *propensity* to partially latch and *potentially* provide insufficient restraint during a crash." [Emphasis added.] A product that performs its ordinary function adequately is not defective in the implied warranty of merchantability context simply because it does not function as well as the buyer would like, or even as well as it could. That is, for a defect to cause redressable damages in a breach of the implied warranty of merchantability action, it must cause the product not to function adequately in the performance of its ordinary function for the plaintiff. Compare Microsoft Corp., 914 S.W.2d 602, 610 (holding software that could not successfully perform data compression—regardless of whether plaintiff attempted to use this feature—did not or would not perform adequately in its ordinary function so that a "defect" existed causing injury and loss of benefit-of-the-bargain damages) . . . .

Here, the Everetts' vehicles are many years old; Pete's Nissan truck is a 1994 model and Marcella's Isuzu Rodeo is a 1991 model. Although the vehicles are over a decade old, the Everetts do not allege that the TK–52 buckles in their vehicles have ever only partially latched when they latched them or have ever provided them with insufficient restraint. They instead seek economic damages based on the "buckles' *propensity* to partially latch and *potentially* provide insufficient restraint during a crash." [Emphasis added.] To cause redressable injuries in the breach of the implied warranty of merchantability context, a "defect" must either have manifested during the product's normal use or such manifestation must be inevitable when the defective feature of the product is used—such as the software data compression feature in Manning. Although the Everetts' vehicles are over a decade old, the defect that they allege has caused them economic injuries has not manifested itself, nor do the Everetts claim that it will inevitably manifest itself.

Instead, the Everetts have pleaded for contract-based damages from the alleged breach of the implied warranty of merchantability while alleging a tort-based products liability defect. This mixing of liability and damage theories does not establish an injury. Consequently, we hold that the Everetts have not pleaded facts demonstrating the type of injury that is redressable within the context of their breach of the implied warranty of merchantability claim.

. . . The statute implicitly defines a buyer's injury as the product's defect, that is, the condition of the product or good that renders it unfit for the ordinary purposes for which it is used because of a lack of something necessary for adequacy. See § 2.314 & cmt. 13. An actual malfunction of the product or good is not required to establish an injury; what is required is an allegation that the alleged defect will inevitably manifest itself in the ordinary use of the product and that the defect renders the product unfit for the ordinary purposes for which the product is used. Such an allegation would make the plaintiff's injury personal and nonspeculative, establishing the plaintiff's statutory standing to assert a claim for breach of the implied warranty of merchantability. Here, as discussed above, the Everetts have pleaded only an unmanifested defect. They have not pleaded or established that the alleged defective design of the TK–52 buckles will inevitably cause the buckle to malfunction; they have pleaded that the buckles have a propensity to partially latch and to potentially provide insufficient restraint during a crash. Because the buckles' alleged propensity to partially latch and their potential to ineffectively restrain have not occurred—despite over a decade of ordinary use of the TK–52 buckles—we cannot agree that the Everetts have pleaded the existence of a defect that renders their seat belt buckles unfit for the ordinary purposes for which they were intended. The TK–52 buckles in the Everetts' vehicles, by performing as they were supposed to for over ten years have lived up to that "minimum level of quality" implied by section 2.314(b),(c). For the reasons stated, we . . . hold that the Everetts do not possess statutory standing to assert a claim for breach of the implied warranty of merchantability.

10. Subsection (3) of 2–314 provides that implied warranties also may arise by virtue of usage of trade or course of dealing. Thus in Gindy Mfg. Corp. v. Cardinale Trucking Corp. (page 285 infra), in a contract for the sale of new trucks, the court points to 2–314(3) to find an implied warranty that the seller will repair all defects, no matter how trivial.

3. WARRANTY AND STRICT LIABILITY

As *Ambassador Steel* establishes, if goods fail to meet applicable industry standards, the goods are not merchantable. But what if the goods do meet industry standards: can they still be unmerchantable? In most states the answer is "yes." If the goods cause personal injury or property damage, they may be found to be not merchantable even though they meet industry standards. Often the courts analyze the issue under the rubric of products liability or strict liability in tort. Traditionally sellers were liable in tort for defective products only if they were negligent. But the law evolved, as it did with respect to implied warranty (pages 228–31 supra), culminating in 1960 with promulgation of the Restatement (Second) of Torts § 402A, which imposed liability on sellers for personal injuries caused by defects in the products they sell regardless of the absence of negligence. The test for whether a product was defective was whether the product failed to meet the reasonable expectations of the consumer. And the courts applied this test without regard to the kind of defect, whether it be an alleged defect in manufacturing or an alleged defect in design. Over the years, however, some courts became dissatisfied with this test as applied to design defects, because it places liability on manufacturers for injuries that they could not have foreseen and could not have avoided or prevented. In 1998 the American Law Institute promulgated the Restatement (Third) of Torts—Products Liability. It provides:

§ 1. Liability of Commercial Seller or Distributor for Harm Caused by Defective Products.

One engaged in the business of selling or otherwise distributing products who sells or distributes a defective product is subject to liability for harm to persons or property caused by the defect.

§ 2. Categories of Product Defect.

A product is defective when, at the time of sale or distribution, it contains a manufacturing defect, is defective in design, or is defective because of inadequate instructions or warnings. A product:

(a) contains a manufacturing defect when the product departs from its intended design even though all possible care was exercised in the preparation and marketing of the product;

(b) is defective in design when the foreseeable risks of harm posed by the product could have been reduced or avoided by the adoption of a reasonable alternative design by the seller or other distributor, or a predecessor in the commercial chain of distribution, and the omission of the alternative design renders the product not reasonably safe;

(c) is defective because of inadequate instructions or warnings when the foreseeable risks of harm posed by the product could have been reduced or avoided by the provision of reasonable instructions or warnings by the seller or other distributor, or a predecessor in the commercial chain of distribution, and the omission of the instructions or warnings renders the product not reasonably safe.

These provisions, unlike their predecessor in the Restatement (Second), distinguish between production defects and design defects. Under the Restatement (Second), one looks to the reasonable expectations of the buyer to determine whether the product is defective. This is still the test for production defects under the Restatement (Third), but the test for design defects under that Restatement turns on the availability of a reasonable alternative design that would have made the product reasonably safe.

At the beginning of this chapter, we pointed out that the basic purpose of warranty law is to give the buyer the quality of goods that the buyer reasonably expects under the contract. The next case points out the difference between the "consumer-expectations" test of sales law and the "reasonable-alternative-design" test adopted in the Restatement (Third) to determine whether a product design is defective.

Denny v. Ford Motor Company

New York Court of Appeals, 1995.
87 N.Y.2d 248, 639 N.Y.S.2d 250, 662 N.E.2d 730.

■ TITONE, JUDGE.

Are the elements of New York's causes of action for strict products liability and breach of implied warranty always coextensive? If not, can the latter be broader than the former? These are the core issues presented by the questions that the United States Court of Appeals for the Second Circuit has certified to us in this diversity action involving an allegedly defective vehicle. On the facts set forth by the Second Circuit, we hold that the causes of action are not identical and that, under the circumstances presented here, it is possible to be liable for breach of implied warranty even though a claim of strict products liability has not been satisfactorily established.

I.

As stated by the Second Circuit, this action arises out of a June 9, 1986 accident in which plaintiff Nancy Denny was severely injured when the Ford Bronco II that she was driving rolled over. The rollover accident occurred when Denny slammed on her brakes in an effort to avoid a deer that had walked directly into her motor vehicle's path. Denny and her spouse sued Ford Motor Co., the vehicle's manufacturer, asserting claims for negligence, strict products liability and breach of implied warranty of merchantability (*see* UCC 2–314[2][c]; 2–318). The case went to trial in the District Court for the Northern District of New York in October of 1992.

The trial evidence centered on the particular characteristics of utility vehicles, which are generally made for off-road use on unpaved and often rugged terrain. Such use sometimes necessitates climbing over obstacles such as fallen logs and rocks. While utility vehicles are traditionally considerably larger than passenger cars, some manufacturers have created a category of down-sized "small" utility vehicles, which are designed to be lighter, to achieve better fuel economy and, presumably, to appeal to a wider consumer market. The Bronco II in which Denny was injured falls into this category.

Plaintiffs introduced evidence at trial to show that small utility vehicles in general, and the Bronco II in particular, present a significantly higher risk of rollover accidents than do ordinary passenger automobiles. Plaintiffs' evidence also showed that the Bronco II had a low stability index attributable to its high center of gravity and relatively narrow track width. The vehicle's shorter wheel base and suspension system were additional factors contributing to its instability. Ford had made minor design changes in an effort to achieve a higher stability index, but, according to plaintiffs' proof, none of the changes produced a significant improvement in the vehicle's stability.

Ford argued at trial that the design features of which plaintiffs complained were necessary to the vehicle's off-road capabilities. According to Ford, the vehicle had been intended to be used as an off-road vehicle and had not been designed to be sold as a conventional passenger automobile. Ford's own engineer stated that he would not recommend the Bronco II to someone whose primary interest was to use it as a passenger car, since the features of a four-wheel-drive utility vehicle were not helpful for that purpose and the vehicle's design made it inherently less stable.

Despite the engineer's testimony, plaintiffs introduced a Ford marketing manual which predicted that many buyers would be attracted to the Bronco II because utility vehicles were "suitable to contemporary life styles" and were "considered fashionable" in some suburban areas. According to this manual, the sales presentation of the Bronco II should take into account the vehicle's "suitability for commuting and for suburban and city driving." Additionally, the vehicle's ability to switch between two-wheel and four-wheel drive would "be particularly appealing to women who may be concerned about driving in snow and ice with their children." Plaintiffs both testified that the perceived safety benefits of its four-wheel-drive capacity were what attracted them to the Bronco II. They were not at all interested in its off-road use.

At the close of the evidence, the District Court Judge submitted both the strict products liability claim and the breach of implied warranty claim, despite Ford's objection that the two causes of action were identical. With respect to the strict products liability claim the court told the jury that "[a] manufacturer who places a product on the market in a defective condition is liable for injury which results from use of the product when the product is used for its intended or reasonably foreseeable purpose." Further, the court stated:

> "A product is defective if it is not reasonably safe. * * * It is not necessary for the plaintiffs to prove that the defendant knew or should

have known of the product's potential for causing injury to establish that the product was not reasonably safe. Rather, the plaintiffs must prove by a preponderance of the evidence that a reasonable person * * * who knew of the product's potential for causing injury and the existence of available alternative designs * * * would have concluded that such a product should not have been marketed in that condition. Such a conclusion should be reached after balancing the risks involved in using the product against the product's usefulness and its costs against the risks, usefulness and costs of the alternative design as compared to the product defendant did market.''

With respect to the breach of implied warranty claim, the court told the jury:

"The law implies a warranty by a manufacturer which places its product on the market that the product is reasonably fit for the ordinary purpose for which it was intended. If it is, in fact, defective and not reasonably fit to be used for its intended purpose, the warranty is breached.

"The plaintiffs claim that the Bronco II was not fit for its ordinary purpose because of its alleged propensity to rollover and lack of warnings to the consumer of this propensity."

Neither party objected to the content of these charges.

In response to interrogatories, the jury found that the Bronco II was not "defective" and that defendant was therefore not liable under plaintiffs' strict products liability cause of action. However, the jury also found that defendant had breached its implied warranty of merchantability and that the breach was the proximate cause of Nancy Denny's injuries. Following apportionment of damages, plaintiff was awarded judgment in the amount of $1.2 million.

Ford subsequently moved for a new trial ... arguing that the jury's finding on the breach of implied warranty cause of action was irreconcilable with its finding on the strict products liability claim. The trial court rejected this argument, holding that it had been waived and that, in any event, the verdict was not inconsistent.

On defendant's appeal, a majority at the Second Circuit held that defendant's trial conduct had not resulted in a waiver of the inconsistency issue. Reasoning that the outcome of the appeal depended upon the proper application of New York law, the court certified the following questions for consideration by this Court (1) whether the strict products liability claim and the breach of implied warranty claim are identical; (2) whether, if the claims are different, the strict products liability claim is broader than the implied warranty claim and encompasses the latter; and (3) whether, if the claims are different and a strict liability claim may fail while an implied warranty claim succeeds, the jury's finding of no product defect is reconcilable with its finding of a breach of warranty.

II.

In this proceeding, Ford's sole argument is that plaintiffs' strict products liability and breach of implied warranty causes of action were identical and that, accordingly, a defendant's verdict on the former cannot be reconciled with a plaintiff's verdict on the latter. This argument is, in turn, premised on both the intertwined history of the two doctrines and the close similarity in their elements and legal functions. Although Ford recognizes that New York has previously permitted personal injury plaintiffs to simultaneously assert different products liability theories in support of their claims, it contends that the breach of implied warranty cause of action, which sounds in contract, has been subsumed by the more recently adopted, and more highly evolved, strict products liability theory, which sounds in tort. Ford's argument has much to commend it. However, in the final analysis, the argument is flawed because it overlooks the continued existence of a separate *statutory* predicate for the breach of warranty theory and the subtle but important distinction between the two theories that arises from their different historical and doctrinal root.

When products liability litigation was in its infancy, the courts relied upon contractual warranty theories as the only existing means of facilitating economic recovery for personal injuries arising from the use of defective goods . . . . [T]he courts posited the existence of an implied warranty arising as an incident of the product's sale and premised a cause of action for consequential personal injuries based on breaches of that warranty.

Eventually, the contractually based implied warranty theory came to be perceived as inadequate in an economic universe that was dominated by mass-produced products and an impersonal marketplace. Its primary weakness was, of course, its rigid requirement of a relationship of privity between the seller and the injured consumer—a requirement that often could not be satisfied (*see, Martin v. Dierck Equip. Co.*, 43 N.Y.2d 583, 589–590, 403 N.Y.S.2d 185, 374 N.E.2d 97). Some courts (including ours) recognized certain narrow exceptions to the privity requirement in an effort to avoid the doctrine's harsher effects. (Prosser and Keeton, Torts § 96, at 682 [5th ed.1984]). However, the warranty approach remained unsatisfactory, and the courts shifted their focus to the development of a new, more flexible tort cause of action: the doctrine of strict products liability.

The establishment of this tort remedy has, as this Court has recognized, significantly diminished the need to rely on the contractually based breach of implied warranty remedy as a means of compensating individuals injured because of defective products. Further, although the available defenses and applicable limitations principles may differ, there is a high degree of overlap between the substantive aspects of the two causes of action . . . .

Nonetheless, it would not be correct to infer that the tort cause of action has completely subsumed the older breach of implied warranty cause of action or that the two doctrines are now identical in every respect. The continued vitality of the warranty approach is evidenced by its retention and expansion in New York's version of the Uniform Commercial Code (UCC 2–314[2] [c]; 2–318). The existence of this statutory authority belies any argument that the breach of implied warranty remedy is a dead letter.[2]

Although the products liability theory sounding in tort and the breach of implied warranty theory authorized by the UCC coexist and are often invoked in tandem, the core element of "defect" is subtly different in the two causes of action. Under New York law, a design defect may be actionable under a strict products liability theory if the product is not reasonably safe. Since this Court's decision in *Voss v. Black & Decker Mfg. Co.,* 59 N.Y.2d 102, 108, 463 N.Y.S.2d 398, 450 N.E.2d 204, the New York standard for determining the existence of a design defect has required an assessment of whether "if the design defect were known at the time of manufacture, a reasonable person would conclude that the utility of the product did not outweigh the risk inherent in marketing a product designed in that manner." This standard demands an inquiry into such factors as (1) the product's utility to the public as a whole, (2) its utility to the individual user, (3) the likelihood that the product will cause injury, (4) the availability of a safer design, (5) the possibility of designing and manufacturing the product so that it is safer but remains functional and reasonably priced, (6) the degree of awareness of the product's potential danger that can reasonably be attributed to the injured user, and (7) the manufacturer's ability to spread the cost of any safety-related design changes. The above-described analysis is rooted in a recognition that there are both risks and benefits associated with many products and that there are instances in which a product's inherent dangers cannot be eliminated without simultaneously compromising or completely nullifying its benefits (*see,* Prosser and Keeton, *op. cit.,* § 99, at 699). In such circumstances, a weighing of the product's benefits against its risks is an appropriate and necessary component of the liability assessment under the policy-based principles associated with tort law.

The adoption of this risk/utility balance as a component of the "defectiveness" element has brought the inquiry in design defect cases closer to that used in traditional negligence cases, where the reasonableness of an actor's conduct is considered in light of a number of situational and policy-driven factors.[3] While efforts have been made to steer away from the fault-oriented negligence principles by characterizing the design defect cause of action in terms of a product-based rather than a conduct-based analysis, the reality is that the risk/utility balancing test is a "negligence-inspired"

---

2. Indeed, the statutory provision for personal injury recovery as an element of "consequential damages" (UCC 2–715[2][b]) makes it illogical to conclude, as the *amicus* Product Liability Advisory Council suggests, that the breach of implied warranty theory should be confined to recovery for economic loss.

3. In design defect cases, the alleged product flaw arises from an intentional deci-

sion by the manufacturer to configure the product in a particular way. In contrast, in strict products liability cases involving manufacturing defects, the harm arises from the product's failure to perform in the intended manner due to some flaw in the fabrication process. In the latter class of cases, the flaw alone is a sufficient basis to hold the manufacturer liable without regard to fault.

approach, since it invites the parties to adduce proof about the manufacturer's choices and ultimately requires the fact finder to make "a judgment about [the manufacturer's] judgment" (Birnbaum, *Unmasking the Test for Design Defect: From Negligence [to Warranty] to Strict Liability to Negligence*, 33 Vand.L.Rev. 593, 610, 648). In other words, an assessment of the manufacturer's conduct is virtually inevitable, and, as one commentator observed, "[i]n general, * * * the strict liability concept of 'defective design' [is] functionally synonymous with the earlier negligence concept of unreasonable designing" (Schwartz, *New Products, Old Products, Evolving Law, Retroactive Law*).

It is this negligence-like risk/benefit component of the defect element that differentiates strict products liability claims from UCC-based breach of implied warranty claims in cases involving design defects. While the strict products concept of a product that is "not reasonably safe" requires a weighing of the product's dangers against its over-all advantages, the UCC's concept of a "defective" product requires an inquiry only into whether the product in question was "fit for the ordinary purposes for which such goods are used" (UCC 2–314[2][c]). The latter inquiry focuses on the expectations for the performance of the product when used in the customary, usual and reasonably foreseeable manners. The cause of action is one involving true "strict" liability, since recovery may be had upon a showing that the product was not minimally safe for its expected purpose—without regard to the feasibility of alternative designs or the manufacturer's "reasonableness" in marketing it in that unsafe condition.

This distinction between the "defect" analysis in breach of implied warranty actions and the "defect" analysis in strict products liability actions is explained by the differing etiology and doctrinal underpinnings of the two distinct theories. The former class of actions originates in contract law, which directs its attention to the purchaser's disappointed expectations; the latter originates in tort law, which traditionally has concerned itself with social policy and risk allocation by means other than those dictated by the marketplace.

The dissent takes issue with the foregoing conclusion, arguing, in essence, that any residual distinction that exists between the two causes of action should be eliminated and that the analysis for "defect" in implied warranty claims should be deemed to encompass the risk/utility analysis that has previously been incorporated in tort causes of action. This argument is predicated on the dissent's view that the common history of the two causes of action and the perceived advantages of risk/utility analysis counsel in favor of the use of a unitary standard. The dissent has even gone so far as to suggest that the breach of implied warranty cause of action should be treated like a tort claim despite the fact that it is based on the provisions of the Uniform Commercial Code.

What the dissent overlooks is that, as long as that legislative source of authority exists, we are not free to merge the warranty cause of action with its tort-based sibling regardless of whether, as a matter of policy, the contract-based warranty claim may fairly be regarded as a historical relic that no longer has any independent substantive value. Rather, we must construe and apply this separate remedy in a manner that remains consistent with its *current* roots in contract law (*see, Codling v. Paglia,* [32 N.Y. 2d 330, 345 N.Y.S.2d 461, 298 N.E. 2d 622] [recognizing a tort cause of action to avoid stretching the breach of implied warranty theory to the point where it no longer reflects its origin as part of the bargain between the consumer and seller]).

. . .

Contrary to the dissent's suggestion, the current version of UCC 2–318 . . . [does not] manifest an intention by our State's Legislature to engraft a tort cause of action onto a UCC article that concerns itself principally with the contract-based obligations (*see,* dissenting opn., at [258]). Indeed, the Law Revision Commission Staff Notes, which the dissent cites, clearly state that the proposed amendments to UCC 2–318 "would * * * allow recovery by the [strict products liability] plaintiffs *on a different cause of action* "(Bill Jacket, L.1975, ch. 774, Mem of N.Y.Law Rev.Commn, Staff Notes relating to A–3070 [emphasis supplied]). Similarly, the Sponsoring Memorandum on which the dissent relies states that the bill's purpose was to "extend more intelligently the warranty provided to a purchaser of goods under the UCC" (Mem of Assemblyman Silverman, reprinted in 1975 NY Legis Ann, at 110). In fact, it is evident from the legislative materials accompanying the bill's passage that its purpose was to expand the class of plaintiffs who can avail themselves of the Code's warranty remedies and not to transform those remedies into a new tort cause of action (*see,* 1A U.L.A. 558 [Master ed.], UCC 2–318, Official Comment).

. . .

. . . [W]hile the commentators on which the dissent relies criticize the consumer-expectation-based tests for product defect and argue instead for the use of a risk/utility approach, their arguments are addressed to tort causes of action alone. One of the cited commentators, for example, argues that the consumer expectation test is a "blunt instrument" "when it comes to recognizing and maximizing the * * * goals, objectives, interests and values *important to modern tort law* "(Kennedy, *The Role of the Consumer Expectation Test under Louisiana's Products Liability Tort Doctrine,* 69 Tul.L.Rev. 117, 152 [emphasis supplied]). The same commentator also acknowledges that different standards might be appropriate for different theories of recovery where other objectives and values are pertinent (*id.*). Another commentator cited by the dissent contends that the risk/utility analysis should be used in place of a consumer-expectation test, but the argument is, once again, premised on the assumption that the latter "is *not a tort way* of looking at the problem of product defect" (Birnbaum, *op. cit.,* at 646 [emphasis supplied]). This commentator also affirmatively criticizes courts that have failed "to separate conceptually the notions of strict liability, negligence, warranty, and absolute liability" (*id.* at 601).

. . .

In any event, while the critics and commentators may debate the relative merits of the consumer-expectation and risk/utility tests, there is no existing authority for the proposition that the risk/utility analysis is appropriate when the plaintiff's claim rests on a claimed breach of implied warranty under UCC 2–314(2)(c) and 2–318. Further, the absence of authority for the dissent's position is not surprising since the negligence-like risk/utility approach is foreign to the realm of contract law.

As a practical matter, the distinction between the defect concepts in tort law and in implied warranty theory may have little or no effect in most cases. In this case, however, the nature of the proof and the way in which the fact issues were litigated demonstrates how the two causes of action can diverge. In the trial court, Ford took the position that the design features of which plaintiffs complain, i.e., the Bronco II's high center of gravity, narrow track width, short wheel base and specially tailored suspension system, were important to preserving the vehicle's ability to drive over the highly irregular terrain that typifies off-road travel. Ford's proof in this regard was relevant to the strict products liability risk/utility equation, which required the fact finder to determine whether the Bronco II's value as an off-road vehicle outweighed the risk of the rollover accidents that could occur when the vehicle was used for other driving tasks.

On the other hand, plaintiffs' proof focused, in part, on the sale of the Bronco II for suburban driving and everyday road travel. Plaintiffs also adduced proof that the Bronco II's design characteristics made it unusually susceptible to rollover accidents when used on paved roads. All of this evidence was useful in showing that routine highway and street driving was the "ordinary purpose" for which the Bronco II was sold and that it was not "fit"—or safe—for that purpose.

Thus, under the evidence in this case, a rational fact finder could have simultaneously concluded that the Bronco II's utility as an off-road vehicle outweighed the risk of injury resulting from rollover accidents *and* that the vehicle was not safe for the "ordinary purpose" of daily driving for which it was marketed and sold. Under the law of this State such a set of factual judgments would lead to the concomitant legal conclusion that plaintiffs' strict products liability cause of action was not viable but that defendant should nevertheless be held liable for breach of its implied promise that the Bronco II was "merchantable" or "fit" for its "ordinary purpose." Importantly, what makes this case distinctive is that the "ordinary purpose" for which the product was marketed and sold to the plaintiff was *not* the same as the utility against which the risk was to be weighed. It is these unusual circumstances that give practical significance to the ordinarily theoretical difference between the defect concepts in tort and statutory breach of implied warranty causes of action.

From the foregoing it is apparent that the causes of action for strict products liability and breach of implied warranty of merchantability are not identical in New York and that the latter is not necessarily subsumed by the former. It follows that, under the circumstances presented, a verdict such as the one occurring here—in which the manufacturer was found liable under an implied warranty cause of action and not liable under a strict products cause of action—is theoretically reconcilable under New York law.

Accordingly, certified question No. 1 should be answered in the negative, certified question No. 2 in the negative and certified question No. 3 in the affirmative.

■ Simons, Judge (dissenting).

I agree with the majority that causes of action in strict products liability and breach of implied warranty are not identical. In my view, however, the strict products liability claim is substantively broader than and encompasses the implied warranty claim and, thus, the jury's verdict of no defect in the products liability cause of action is not reconcilable with its finding of breach of implied warranty. Accordingly, I would answer the first two questions certified to the Court no and yes and find it unnecessary to answer the third question.

I

Liability without fault may be imposed against a manufacturer or supplier of a defective product and in favor of one injured by the product. The product may be defective because it is improperly made, because its design is defective or because the manufacturer's warnings against foreseeable risks in using it are inadequate. The members of the Court agree that strict products liability and implied warranty are similar in the sense that both causes of action require that, before plaintiff may recover, the product be defective, i.e., there must be something wrong with it. We disagree, however, over how defectiveness is determined. The question does not appear to have been previously addressed by the Court in the context of personal injury litigation.

The majority concludes that the implied warranty and strict products liability causes of action are different because the existence of an actionable defect is determined by two different analyses. Viewing implied warranty from a contract perspective, it would define defectiveness by whether the product lived up to the consumer's expectations whereas defectiveness, for strict products liability purposes, is determined by application of the risk/utility standard. In my judgment, the consumer expectation standard, appropriate to commercial sales transactions, has no place in personal injury litigation alleging a design defect and may result in imposing absolute liability on marketers of consumers' products. Whether a product has been defectively designed should be determined in a personal injury action by a risk/utility analysis.

. . .

. . . Breach of implied warranty and strict liability in tort developed from separate legal doctrines but are not materially different when applied to personal injury claims involving design defects. While breach of implied warranty retains its contractual law characteristics when applied to commercial transactions, it has been consistently recognized that it is a tort when applied to personal injury litigation and that tort principles should apply. To introduce a new test of defectiveness into tort litigation—one based on contract principles—can only destabilize the well-settled law in this area. Both causes of action are torts and defectiveness for both should be determined by the same standard.

. . .

Nevertheless, the idea that contractual principles inhere in breach of implied warranty claims for personal injuries has persisted, producing conceptual difficulties and anomalies when the courts tried to apply the cause of action in a tort setting (*see,* Prosser and Keeton, Torts § 97, at 692 [5th ed.1984]). In *Codling v. Paglia,* 32 N.Y.2d 330, 345 N.Y.S.2d 461, 298 N.E.2d 622, we were confronted with a claim in implied warranty seeking to impose liability against a manufacturer in favor of a nonuser bystander injured by a defective automobile. We had long since abandoned the privity requirement in many personal injury claims based on implied warranty and incrementally extended the duty of manufacturers and suppliers not only to purchasers and users, but to users' family members, to remote purchasers, to an airline passenger suing the manufacturer of a defective component part of an airplane, and to rescuers suing the manufacturer of a defective oxygen mask. In *Codling* we recognized the difficulties in adopting implied warranty principles in personal injury claims and, abandoning privity entirely, recognized a new cause of action under the broad principle of strict products liability, as other courts before us had done, to hold the manufacturer liable to the bystander.

This new cause of action was not separate from implied warranty but an amalgam which had been constructed by the courts to establish a cause of action for liability without fault by merging warranty concepts (to avoid fault analysis) with negligence concepts (to avoid privity) . . . . It makes little sense, therefore, to perpetuate a legal distinction between them based upon the method for determining defectiveness, particularly when the flaws in the consumer expectation standard for measuring defectiveness are recognized.

II

The majority has not attempted to define the consumer expectation standard, nor did the District Court use the phrase in its charge. Under one formulation, however, the standard provides that a product is defective, i.e., it is unreasonably dangerous, if it is "dangerous to an extent beyond that which would be contemplated by the ordinary consumer who purchases it, with the ordinary knowledge common to the community as to its characteristics" (*see,* Restatement [Second] of Torts § 402A, comment i; *see also,* Kennedy, *The Role of the Consumer Expectation Test under Louisiana's Products Liability Tort Doctrine,* 69 Tul.L.Rev. 117, 120 [1994]). The consumer expectation standard originated from the sales notion that a seller could agree, expressly or impliedly, to indemnify a buyer if the purchased product did not satisfy the buyer's purposes. The obligation to "indemnify" applied only to the parties to the sale, those in privity, and did not "run with the goods" (*see*, 5 Harper, James and Gray, *op. cit.*, § 28.16, at 454). As evolving social policy sought to hold manufacturers and sellers liable for personal injuries caused by defective products, however, the requirement of privity was narrowed and then eliminated, and the courts extended liability as far as social policy required (*id.*). With these developments, it made little sense to think in terms of the buyer's bargain or expectations. In many, if not most, cases the buyer was not litigating.

By contrast, the standard usually employed to determine design defectiveness in strict products liability claims requires a balancing of the risks attendant on using the product with the utility of the product when used as intended. As we stated in *Robinson v. Reed–Prentice Div. of Package Mach. Co.*, 49 N.Y.2d 471, 479, 426 N.Y.S.2d 717, 403 N.E.2d 440: "Where a product presents an unreasonable risk of harm, notwithstanding that it was meticulously made according to detailed plans and specifications, it is said to be defectively designed. This rule, however, is tempered by the realization that some products, for example knives, must by their very nature be dangerous in order to be functional. Thus, a defectively designed product is one which, at the time it leaves the seller's hands, is in a condition not reasonably contemplated by the ultimate consumer and is unreasonably dangerous for its intended use; that is one whose utility does not outweigh the danger inherent in its introduction into the stream of commerce."

. . .

If the [consumer expectations] test is applied to determine the actual buyer's expectations, as in contract law, it can result in imposing absolute liability upon manufacturers and sellers making them insurers of the product's safety merely because the product did not live up to the consumer's subjective expectations. If the test is used objectively, it is beyond the experience of most lay jurors to determine what an "ordinary consumer" expects or "how safe" a sophisticated modern product could or should be made to satisfy those expectations unless the jury is allowed to consider the cost or impracticality of alternative designs or, indeed whether any alternative design for the product was available.

The test can also produce bad results. For example, if the risk is one that is easily understood and appreciated by the average consumer, the manufacturer might not be liable even if the defect could be eliminated by available and inexpensive design changes. Conversely, if the defect was not apparent, liability might attach even if the product was in fact state of the art.

. . .

No New York court has recognized the consumer expectation standard to determine defectiveness in personal injury actions grounded on implied warranty—at least the parties and the majority have not cited any decision doing so—and I can see no persuasive policy reasons why we should do so now. If the test is unworkable when applied in tort causes of action grounded on strict products liability, it is equally unworkable when applied in tort causes of action grounded on breach of implied warranty. The correct standard in strict liability claims, according to the Third Restatement, should include a balancing of the risk of danger against the utility of the product as designed. In its words, "consumer expectations do not constitute an independent standard for judging the defectiveness of product designs" (Restatement [Third] of Torts: Products Liability [Tent Draft No. 2] § 2, comment *f*, at 29). They are "not determinative of defectiveness" because they do not take into account "whether the proposed alternative design could be implemented at reasonable cost, or whether an alternative design would provide greater overall safety," i.e., the test does not take into consideration risk/utility factors (*id.*). Consumer expectations' only value is when used as a factor in determining the reasonableness of alternative designs or how the product is portrayed and perceived by the public, i.e., whether the risk was foreseeable. As we stated in *Robinson v. Reed–Prentice Div. of Package Mach. Co., supra,* the conditions contemplated by "the ultimate consumer" must be taken into account, but the risk/utility analysis remains a necessary part of the equation for determining defectiveness in products liability cases (Restatement [Third] of Torts, *op. cit.*).

III

The majority maintains, however, that the consumer expectation standard must be applied because breach of implied warranty is a statutory cause of action and the Court is not free to ignore the statute's provisions or draw a distinction between its application to commercial claims and personal injury claims.

Implied warranties have been a part of our statutory law since at least 1911, long before any serious attempt was made to base tort liability on them (*see,* former Personal Property Law § 96; now UCC 2–314). Section 96, and its successor provisions in the Uniform Commercial Code, were enacted to address problems arising in commercial transactions. For many years they had no significant impact upon personal injury litigation because of the rules of privity. However, in 1975, shortly after *Codling v. Paglia, supra,* was decided, *section 2–318* of the Uniform Commercial Code was amended to harmonize it with existing case law by eliminating the requirement of privity in personal injury claims. The amendment had no relevance to commercial claims; it was proposed by the Legislature, and widely supported, because it acknowledged and encouraged the judicial development of a separate category of warranty providing a tort remedy for personal injuries (*see,* 1975 N.Y.Legis.Ann., at 110; *see also,* Bill Jacket, L.1975, ch. 774, Mem of State Consumer Protection Board, July 14, 1975; Mem of NY Law Rev Commn, Staff Notes Relating to A–3070; Mem of New York State Trial Lawyers Assn, May 12, 1975). The Legislature's recognition of a distinction between the statutory cause of action for personal injury claims and commercial claims based on implied warranty is further manifested by the Legislature's decision to adopt alternative B of the three formulations proposed by the National Conference of the Commissioners on Uniform State Laws, the alternative which removed the requirement of privity in personal injury claims based upon implied warranty, rather than alternative C which extends the rule (abolishing privity) to warranty claims other than those dealing with injuries to the person (*see* UCC 2–318, Official Comment 3).

Moreover, no words in the statute either before or after the amendment, provide that the defectiveness of the product in tort claims, or commercial claims for that matter, is to be measured by the consumer's expectations. That standard has been developed by the courts. It may accurately assess the terms and conditions of the bargain between the parties to a sale but it can hardly extend beyond them to address defectiveness in the sense that something is "wrong" with the product. The thing "wrong" with the product in the consumer expectation test is that it has not lived up to the consumer's expectations and this is so even if the design of the product is perfection itself. The standard may retain some vitality when applied to commercial transactions but its individualized concept of injury is entirely foreign to tort doctrine underlying this area of law which is based upon the broad concept of enterprise responsibility to protect the public at large from harm.

. . .

. . . Nothing has prevented us in the past from construing and applying the provisions of the Uniform Commercial Code to supplement and advance the policy concerns underlying strict products liability generally, and we should not construe the statute now to establish a standard for determining defectiveness which is inconsistent with the present law in this area (*see generally,* UCC 1–103).

Accordingly, I dissent.

QUESTIONS AND NOTES

1. The Restatement differentiates between manufacturing defects and design defects. Comment *a* elaborates:

> In contrast to manufacturing defects, design defects and defects based on inadequate instructions or warnings are predicated on a different concept of responsibility. In the first place, such defects cannot be determined by reference to the manufacturer's own design or marketing standards because those standards are the very ones that plaintiffs attack as unreasonable. Some sort of independent assessment of advantages and disadvantages, to which some attach the label "risk-utility balancing," is necessary. Products are not generically defective merely because they are dangerous. Many product-related accident costs can be eliminated only by excessively sacrificing product features that make products useful and desirable. Thus, the various trade-offs need to be considered in determining whether accident costs are more fairly and efficiently borne by accident victims, on the one hand, or, on the other hand, by consumers generally through the mechanism of higher

product prices attributable to liability costs imposed by courts on product sellers.

2. Comment *n* addresses the relationship between warranty and tort liability:

> The rules in this Section and in other provisions of this Chapter define the bases of tort liability for harm caused by product defects existing at time of sale or other distribution. The rules are stated functionally rather than in terms of traditional doctrinal categories. Claims based on product defect at time of sale or other distribution must meet the requisites set forth in Subsection (a), (b), or (c), or the other provisions in this Chapter. As long as these requisites are met, doctrinal tort categories such as negligence or strict liability may be utilized in bringing the claim.
>
> Similarly, a product defect claim satisfying the requisites of Subsection (a), (b), or (c), or other provisions in this Chapter, may be brought under the implied warranty of merchantability provisions of the Uniform Commercial Code. It is recognized that some courts have adopted a consumer expectations definition for design and failure-to-warn defects in implied warranty cases involving harm to persons or property. This Restatement contemplates that a well-coordinated body of law governing liability for harm to persons or property arising out of the sale of defective products requires a consistent definition of defect, and that the definition properly should come from tort law, whether the claim carries a tort label or one of implied warranty of merchantability.

The comment goes on to say that since the factual predicate for a breach of the warranty of merchantability and strict-tort liability are the same in both manufacturing defect and design-defect cases, claims on both theories should not be submitted to a jury. However, according to the comments, the plaintiff can choose whether to assert a claim in strict tort or in contract for breach of the warranty of merchantability. One or the other causes of action may be more favorable for other reasons, such as the statute of limitations.

Express warranties and the warranty of fitness for particular purpose depend on specific representations by the seller and, therefore, a claim for breach of those warranties is not duplicative of strict-tort liability and can be asserted along with a claim for strict-tort liability.

The Restatement takes the position that the strict-liability tort rules adopted by the Restatement apply to personal injury and to injury to property other than the thing being sold (Restatement of Torts (Third) § 21). Defects that injure only the property being sold are left to the law of contract, including warranty law. Therefore, if the defect injures the product being sold and also injures persons or other property, the plaintiff's claim would be in warranty as to the product itself and could be in tort as to the injury to person or property. (The leading case holding that warranty law, not the strict-liability doctrine of tort law, applies to defects that injure the property itself is East River Steamship Corp. v. Transamerica Delaval, Inc., 476 U.S. 858, 106 S.Ct. 2295, 90 L.Ed.2d 865 (1986)). Under the Restatement (Third), then, if an SUV rolls over when the plaintiff attempts to avoid a deer on the road, the plaintiff may assert breach of the implied warranty of merchantability for the destruction of the vehicle, but may recover damages for the defective design that caused her personal injuries and the destruction of the new TV she had just purchased only if she establishes that the design is defective under the standard of Restatement (Third) section 2(b). Should different standards apply to the different kinds of injuries resulting from the same alleged design defect?

3. Problem. In early November Buyer sees a TV advertisement for the Jumbo Roaster, a large roasting pan shown being used to cook a 25–pound turkey. Buyer purchases the Jumbo Roaster and uses it to roast a large turkey on Thanksgiving. When the turkey is done, she dons insulated mittens to remove it from the oven. The handles on the pan are only large enough, however, for her to use two fingers of each hand to grip them. As she removes the pan from the oven, she loses control of it, and the pan tips toward her, spilling hot drippings on her feet and ankles. She sues, alleging both products liability and breach of implied warranty of merchantability. The trial court holds that the two claims are duplicative, and it submits only the products liability claim to the jury. Based on evidence that the pan functions well to cook lasagna, stuffed potatoes, casseroles, cutlets, cookies, cake, and other low-weight dishes, the jury returns a verdict for Seller. The trial court enters judgment on the verdict, and Buyer appeals, alleging that the trial court erred in refusing to submit the warranty claim to the jury. What should the appellate court do?

4. Revised Article 2. The ALI is responsible for the Restatements, and it also is responsible (along with NCCUSL) for the UCC. The drafting of the Restatement (Third) of Torts and revised Article 2 occurred at about the same time, but the Restatement project was finished first. The drafting committee on the Article 2 project (only a few of whose members were appointed by the ALI) resisted the idea that the definition of defect in tort law should control the meaning of merchantable in warranty law. The ALI was in a bind: having just approved the torts restatement, with comment *n* quoted above, how could it approve revisions to Article 2 that did not conform to the Restatement? It urged the drafting committee to change 2–314. The result, acceptable to both organizations, was the addition of language in the Official Comments that when personal injuries are involved, "defective" under tort law and "unmerchantable" under warranty law should have the same meaning. See Official Comment 7 to revised 2–314.

5. Under Official Comment 7 to revised 2–314, the reasonable expectations test continues to apply to determinations whether a seller has breached an express warranty or an implied warranty of fitness for particular purpose. What is the difference between the implied warranty of merchantability under 2–314(a) and (c) and an express warranty under 2–313(1)(b)?

Could plaintiff in *Denny* have sued under 2–313(1)(b)?

6. Recall *Anthony Pools*, page 11 supra, in which the trial court had submitted to the jury the buyer's tort claim that the diving board was defective, but directed a verdict for the seller on the buyer's breach-of-warranty claim. The appellate court held that the hybrid construction contract was within the scope of Article 2 and subject to the rules on disclaimers, which invalidated the disclaimer in this contract. Therefore, the case had to be retried on the breach-of-warranty claim, that the diving board was not fit for its ordinary purposes. The jury in that case had found that the seller was not liable in tort, presumably because it believed that the diving board was not unreasonably dangerous, i.e. not defective. According to the appellate court, this tort claim was not to be retried. Under the position of Official Comment 7 to revised 2–314, would any of this be changed? under *Denny*?

Tyson v. Ciba–Geigy Corp.

North Carolina Court of Appeals, 1986.
82 N.C.App. 626, 347 S.E.2d 473.

[Plaintiff, intending to plant no-till soybeans, approached defendant Farm Chemical to order the herbicides Lasso and Lorox. A Farm Chemical salesman, after plaintiff had described the characteristics of his land and indicated that he wanted to plant no-till soybeans, told plaintiff that Dual 8E, mixed with Paraquat would be as good as and cheaper than Lasso or Lorox. Plaintiff thereupon purchased Dual 8E. The mixture recommended by Farm Chemical did not kill crabgrass and, as a result, plaintiff had a very low yield of soybeans. Plaintiff sued Farm Chemical and Ciba–Geigy Corp., the manufacturer of Dual 8E. The trial court dismissed all counts against both defendants.]

■ HEDRICK, CHIEF JUDGE.

. . .

Plaintiff argues that he presented sufficient evidence for the jury to find that Farm Chemical breached express warranties relating to the effectiveness of Dual 8E, to kill crabgrass in the no-till cultivation of soybeans. Plaintiff contends that the statements of the sales representative of Farm Chemical that the Dual 8E, when mixed with Paraquat and a surfactant, would "do a good job" created an express warranty.

. . . A salesman's expression of his opinion in "the puffing of his wares" does not create an express warranty. Performance Motors, Inc. v. Allen, 280 N.C. 385, 186 S.E.2d 161 (1972). Thus, statements such as "supposed to last a lifetime" and "in perfect condition" do not create an express warranty. *Id*. Similarly, the statement made by the salesman in the present case that the Dual 8E would "do a good job" is a mere expression of opinion and did not create an express warranty.

Finally, plaintiff contends that the trial court erred in granting defendant Farm Chemical's motion for directed verdict on the issue of breach of implied warranty. We agree with this contention. . . .

The evidence in the present case, when considered in the light most favorable to plaintiff, tends to show that plaintiff contacted defendant Farm Chemical to order the herbicides Lasso and Lorox, for the no-till cultivation of soybeans. He spoke with Mr. Gregory, an employee of Farm Chemical, on the telephone and told him that he was planning the no-till cultivation of soybeans on 145 acres of his land and described the type of soil on the land. Mr. Gregory gave Dual 8E a good recommendation and told plaintiff that it would "do a good job," would be less expensive to use than the chemicals he had used the previous year and would also be less risky to use on plaintiff's type of land. He further told plaintiff that Dual 8E could be mixed with Paraquat and a surfactant to replace Lasso and Lorox. He also told plaintiff the amount of Dual 8E per acre that he should use. Plaintiff testified that based upon Mr. Gregory's recommendation and his past business dealings with Farm Chemical, he decided to use Dual 8E and ordered thirty-five gallons from Farm Chemical. Vance Tyson testified that he mixed the chemicals in accordance with Mr. Gregory's instructions, but that the Dual 8E was ineffective in killing crabgrass. Plaintiff also introduced evidence tending to show that Dual 8E must be mixed with Sencor, Lexone or Lorox and either Ortho Paraquat CL or Roundup. This evidence is sufficient to support a finding that the seller, Farm Chemical, had reason to know of the particular purpose, the no-till cultivation of soybeans, for which the product was required and that plaintiff was relying on its recommendation when he ordered the Dual 8E. There is no evidence in the record indicating that defendant Farm Chemical disclaimed any warranties relating to the Dual 8E. Thus, the evidence in the record is sufficient for a jury to find that Farm Chemical made an implied warranty relating to the fitness of the Dual 8E for plaintiff's purpose and that this warranty was breached. We hold, therefore, that the trial court erred in directing a verdict for defendant Farm Chemical on the issue of breach of an implied warranty of fitness for particular purpose.

. . .

QUESTIONS AND NOTES

1.   Why does the court in *Tyson* hold that the statement by the salesman did not create an express warranty? Do you agree? Characterization of the warranty as "express" would make a difference if the seller had effectively disclaimed the implied warranty of fitness for purpose. See 2–316(1).

2.   What are the elements of the implied warranty of fitness for a particular purpose? Was each present in *Tyson*?

3. Could plaintiff in *Denny* have asserted breach of the implied warranty of fitness for particular purpose?

———

A. S. Leavitt v. Monaco Coach Corporation

Michigan Court of Appeals, 2000.
241 Mich.App. 288, 616 N.W.2d 175.

■ METER, J.

. . .

In 1991, plaintiff purchased a 1992 Monaco Dynasty motor coach, with an engine upgraded to 230 horsepower. Plaintiff presented evidence that while shopping for his coach, he informed defendant of his plans to use the coach extensively for travel in mountainous areas and of his wish to avoid problems he had experienced with rented vehicles that lacked sufficient engine and braking power. Almost immediately upon receiving the vehicle, and for the years leading up to this lawsuit, plaintiff complained that his coach could not maintain ordinary highway speeds going up steep hills and that the brakes were prone to overheating while going down. Defendant performed many warranty repairs and other service, but plaintiff ultimately concluded that the engine and brakes, as a matter of design, simply were not suitable for his expressed needs, and he commenced this action.

. . . [T]he only claim that went to the jury was the allegation that Monaco had breached an implied warranty of fitness for a particular purpose. The jury returned a verdict in favor of plaintiff in the amount of $33,730.50.

. . .

. . . [T]o establish a valid warranty of fitness for a particular purpose, "the seller must know, at the time of sale, the particular purpose for which the goods are required and also that the buyer is relying on the seller to select or furnish suitable goods." *Ambassador Steel Co. v. Ewald Steel Co.*, 33 Mich.App. 495, 501, 190 N.W.2d 275 (1971).

In this case, plaintiff testified that in order to avoid risky situations such as he had experienced before, he described to defendant's sales manager his concerns for maintaining speed and having reliable brakes while traversing mountain roads, including those east of the Sierras, at Death Valley, through the Cascades, and through Mexico. Plaintiff further testified that he told the sales manager that he desired a vehicle that, while fully loaded and towing a fully loaded car, would keep up with commercial buses. According to plaintiff, the sales manager assured him that he would have no problem with the coach's engine and that the standard brakes would be fine with no supplementation.

Plaintiff also testified that (1) he explained to the sales manager that he had had no experience with diesel engines, and (2) defendant's representatives were instrumental in convincing him that he should obtain one.

Defendant argues that plaintiff did not explain his special needs for engine power with sufficient particularity to establish a warranty of fitness for a particular purpose. Defendant points out that the evidence indicates that plaintiff never negotiated for specific speed capabilities and that the coach in question could, in fact, negotiate the steepest mountain grades while fully loaded, albeit at slow speeds. However, the evidence that plaintiff communicated his wish to traverse mountain roads while keeping up with commercial buses was sufficiently specific to support a finding that plaintiff articulated to defendant his particular need for engine power. Likewise, plaintiff's testimony about having communicated his problems with brakes in the past while seeking defendant's advice in the matter, along with having described the mountainous areas in which he wished to drive the coach, was sufficient to support a finding that defendant articulated to defendant his particular braking needs.

Concerning plaintiff's reliance on defendant in selecting the coach for his special needs, defendant points to evidence that suggests that plaintiff relied primarily on his own judgment, not defendant's, in the matter. However, plaintiff's insistence that he relied mainly on defendant for the choice of engine, and for deciding against upgrading the brakes, is sufficient to support a finding that plaintiff relied on defendant's expertise in selecting a coach that suited his needs.

Because the evidence created genuine issues of material fact concerning whether defendant knew of plaintiff's particular needs and whether defendant knew that plaintiff was relying on defendant's expertise in making his selection, the trial court properly denied defendant's motion for a directed verdict.

[The court affirmed a verdict of approximately $33,000 based on the depreciation in value of the motor home during the period that the defendant was trying to bring it into compliance with the warranty.]

QUESTIONS AND NOTES

1. Problem. Buyer tells Seller that she needs a vehicle capable of towing her boat, which with its trailer weighs 6,500 pounds. Seller recommends a particular model pickup truck, and Buyer purchases it. Is there an implied warranty of fitness for the buyer's particular purpose? Is there an implied warranty of merchantability?

As Buyer is driving to her vacation destination 500 miles from her home, the transmission seizes. Is there a breach of the implied warranty of fitness? Is there a breach of the implied warranty of merchantability? What additional facts do you need?

Assume that further investigation reveals that the manufacturer ran out of one of the components used in fabricating the transmission. To keep its production line operating, it obtained substitutes from an alternate supplier, and these components were substandard and failed in most of the

100 transmissions in which they were used. Has Seller breached an implied warranty of merchantability? an implied warranty of fitness for the buyer's particular purpose? What does Official Comment 2 to 2–315 suggest?

2. In Wilson v. Massey–Ferguson, Inc., 21 Ill.App.3d 867, 315 N.E.2d 580 (1974), plaintiff purchased a farm tractor. Claiming that the tractor could not handle heavy duty plowing and that the engine failed earlier than it should have, he sued for breach of the warranty of merchantability and the warranty of fitness for particular purpose. The court responded:

> [T]here was no evidence to support a warranty for a particular purpose. The Illinois Code Comment to section 2–315 indicates that:
>
> > "Thus, where the goods are to be put to ordinary use, the concept of merchantability and not particular purpose is involved." (S.H.A., ch. 26, Sec. 2–315, p. 239.)

The Uniform Commercial Code Comment similarly indicates that:

> "2. A 'particular purpose' differs from the ordinary purpose for which the goods are used in that it envisages a specific use by the buyer which is peculiar to the nature of his business whereas the ordinary purposes for which goods are used are those envisaged in the concept of merchantability and go to uses which are customarily made of the goods in question. For example, shoes are generally used for the purpose of walking upon ordinary ground, but a seller may know that a particular pair was selected to be used for climbing mountains." (Id. at p. 240.)

In this case, the tractor was sold and used for ordinary farm work, which includes, without question, heavy duty plowing. Thus, section 2–315 is not relevant in this case, and the implied warranty of merchantability (Sec. 2–314), is the only relevant concept here.

Compare Tennessee Carolina Transportation, Inc. v. Strick Corp., 283 N.C. 423, 196 S.E.2d 711 (1973), in which plaintiff purchased truck trailers from defendant. When the trailers collapsed while carrying normal loads on normal roads, plaintiff sued for breach of warranty of fitness for particular purpose. Applying the law of Pennsylvania, the court stated:

> At trial, plaintiff stipulated that it was not relying on the implied warranty of merchantability, Pa.Stat.Ann. tit. 12A, Sec. 2–314 (1970). Therefore, the suit was only for breach of the implied warranty of fitness for a particular purpose, Pa.Stat.Ann. tit. 12A, Sec. 2–315 (1970). Defendant now contends that such a suit is tenable only where the goods were purchased for a *particular* purpose. It further contends that this term does not embrace purchases of goods for the *general* purpose for which goods of that kind are used. Thus, defendant urges that plaintiff has failed to make out a case for the jury since it bought the trailers not for a particular purpose but rather for the general or ordinary purpose of hauling cargo. For this reason defendant assigns as error the overruling of its motions for directed verdict.

We find no merit in this assignment. Although the primary purpose of Pa.Stat.Ann. tit. 12A, Sec. 2–315 (1970) is indeed to protect a buyer who purchases goods with the intention of using them in a "particular" manner, meaning a manner in which they would not normally be expected to be used, we do not think that section is limited exclusively to purchases of such a nature. That warranty also protects a buyer when his particular purpose *is* the general or ordinary purpose.

Although no cases have been found either expressly adopting or rejecting this construction of "particular purpose," Professor Nordstrom so construes that term. See Nordstrom Sales Sec. 78 (1970): "[I]f the buyer's use of the goods is the ordinary use of those goods, * * * the buyer's particular purpose coincides with the ordinary use of the goods, and *either section 2–314 or section 2–315* will give the buyer the protection he needs." (Emphasis added) Such was also the rule at common law. See 46 Am.Jur. Sales § 346 (1943).

Despite the lack of authority expressly adopting this interpretation of "particular purpose," several cases have done so impliedly, without discussion of the issue. *See* Annot. 17 A.L.R.3d 1010, 1071 (1968). Among these is Adams v. Scheib, 408 Pa. 452, 184 A.2d 700 (1962). There, the Pennsylvania Supreme Court held that where plaintiff bought pork sausage for the purpose of consumption—obviously the ordinary purpose—an implied warranty arose, citing *both* Pa.Stat.Ann. tit. 12A, Sec. 2–314 *and* Sec. 2–315. See also L & N Sales Co. v. Stuski, 188 Pa.Super. 117, 146 A.2d 154 (1958), where whiskey pourers were bought for the ordinary purpose of pouring drinks, and the Pennsylvania Superior Court, assuming that a warranty of fitness for a particular purpose arose under Pa.Stat.Ann. tit. 12A, Sec. 2–315, held that such warranty was not excluded by an express warranty of merchantability or by a disclaimer contained in the purchase money security agreement executed after the sale.

Therefore, we think it beyond dispute that in Pennsylvania the warranty of fitness does protect a buyer whose particular purpose *is* the general or ordinary one.

Which court is right, *Wilson* or *Tennessee–Carolina Transportation?* What is the relevance of 2–315, Official Comment 2: is it addressing the issue in these cases, or some other issue?

What difference does it make whether a warranty of fitness for particular purpose can arise where the buyer's purpose is the ordinary and normal purpose for which the goods are used?

3. CISG. The introduction to this chapter pointed out that the division of warranty into express warranties and implied warranties of merchantability and fitness for a particular purpose is somewhat artificial and that perhaps the Code should merely have said that the buyer is entitled to the quality he reasonably expected. The Convention on Contracts for the International Sale of Goods deals with seller's obligation as to quality of goods in Article 35. That article does not use the term warranty, and it does not distinguish between express and implied obligations. Please read Article 35.

Is the formulation in the Convention better than the one in Article 2? Why or why not?

Article 35, section 2(a) tracks 2–314, but section 2(b) does not exactly track 2–315. Exactly how does it differ?

4.   LEASES

Article 2A recognizes two kinds of leases. In one, the lessor typically maintains an inventory of the goods, retains the title to the goods, and gets them back at a time when they still have meaningful value. These might be characterized as true leases, and they are analogous to sales. Before the promulgation of Article 2A in 1989, when called upon to decide whether there were warranties in this kind of lease transaction, the courts held that Article 2 warranties apply to leases. In 2A–210 to –213, Article 2A confirms this result. Section 2A–212, for example, provides for an implied warranty of merchantability identical to the warranty for sales under 2–314. Both sales and this form of lease are mechanisms for putting goods into the possession of the user of the goods.

The other kind of lease is more a mechanism for financing a transaction than it is a mechanism for putting goods into the possession of the user. A finance lessor has no inventory of goods, knows nothing about the goods it leases, and provides no repair or other services with respect to those goods. Rather, it is purely a source of money for the user of the goods. A person who wants to acquire goods but does not have ready cash may borrow the needed funds, use them to purchase the goods, and repay the lender in monthly installments. Alternatively, the person may enter a lease arrangement in which the lessor purchases the goods specified by the lessee and is repaid in the form of monthly lease payments. The lessee may have tax, accounting, or other business reasons for preferring to structure the transaction this way.

This kind of lease is known as a finance lease. The following case arose before enactment of Article 2A and concerns the applicability of the implied warranty of merchantability to a finance lease.

All–States Leasing Co. v. Bass

Idaho Supreme Court, 1975.
96 Idaho 873, 538 P.2d 1177.

[Defendant Noah Bass, doing business as Bass Phillips "66" Service Station in Boise, Idaho, contacted Auto Laundry Manufacturing Company about the purchase of a coin-operated car wash machine. Two salesmen for the company contacted Bass and, when Bass said he wanted the machine, suggested that a lease arrangement be worked out. The salesmen filled out two forms for a leasing arrangement: a lease application form and the lease agreement itself. Both forms showed the name of plaintiff conspicuously on the front. Plaintiff approved the transaction, purchased the machine from Auto Laundry, and leased it to defendant.

The car wash system was delivered and Bass signed a completion certificate acknowledging that the system was properly installed and was in proper condition. Defendant made two payments but then refused to make any further payments: among the reasons given for this refusal was that there were breaches of warranty as to the machine. Plaintiff brought suit for rent due under the lease. Bass asserted as a defense that plaintiff had breached warranties of fitness and merchantability.

The trial court found that plaintiff had breached implied warranties "in the nature of fitness." It rescinded the agreement, but allowed plaintiff to retain payments already made as compensation for the use of the machine by defendant. Plaintiff appeals.]

■ McQuade, C.J.

. . .

Appellant contends that it is unsettled in Idaho whether the lease of personal property has the same legal effect with respect to implied warranties as does a sale of goods. Appellant concedes that there is authority in other jurisdictions to that effect, but maintains that even if this be the rule of law in this state, the trial court committed reversible error when it concluded that under the facts of this case there existed either an implied warranty of fitness for a particular purpose or an implied warranty of merchantability. In the alternative, appellant argues that any warranties which may have been applicable were effectively disclaimed by it.

Before answering appellant's contentions, we must first determine whether the trial court was correct in applying warranty doctrine to a lease transaction.

[In an omitted part of the opinion, the court held that implied warranty principles should apply to leases of goods.]

. . .

By analogy in a lease transaction, in order for such an implied warranty [of fitness] to arise it must be shown that: (1) the lessor was made aware of the lessee's need, (2) that the lessor recommended a product, and (3) that the lessee leased the product as recommended.

In the instant case, the record indicates that while appellant lessor may have been aware of respondent lessee's need, it made no suggestion or recommendation as to a choice of car wash system to meet this need. Furthermore there is no evidence that respondent made his selection on any basis other than his own inspection of the manufacturer's literature describing the equipment and his impressions of the equipment based upon the statements made by the manufacturer's salesmen which the trial court correctly found did not bind appellant lessor. This being the case, we conclude that no implied warranty of fitness for a particular purpose existed.

Turning our inquiry next to the question of whether appellant impliedly warranted that the car wash system would be of merchantable quality, we conclude that no such implied warranty existed in the instant case. . . .

In a lease transaction, in order for such an implied warranty of merchantability to exist it must be shown that the lessor is a "merchant" with respect to the goods which he leases.

. . .

The official comment following [section 2–104] notes:

> "On the other hand, in Section 2–314 on the warranty of merchantability, such warranty is implied only 'if the seller is a merchant with respect to goods of that kind.' Obviously this qualification restricts the implied warranty to a much smaller group than everyone who is engaged in business and requires a professional status as to particular kinds of goods."

It is true that prior to the execution of the lease in issue, appellant handled between forty to fifty transactions over a period of six to eight months, concerning the same Budg-O-Matic Car Wash System that is the subject of this dispute. However, this in our mind does not make All–States Leasing a "merchant" for purposes of the Code. The record discloses that appellant does not build, manufacture or sell any equipment or machines of any kind, but rather is in the business of purchasing or financing the purchase of equipment specifically selected and specified by an approved lessee. Mr. Lorenz, the Chairman of the Board of Directors and Vice President of appellant company testified:

> Q. "Now, what business—what is the business nature of All–States Leasing Company?
>
> A. "We are a capital equipment lessor. We provide equipment to people who make application to use for a lease, if we grant it, we buy the equipment that they specify from the people that they want us to buy if from and we lease it to them.
>
> Q. "Does All–States Leasing Company manufacture any kind of equipment?
>
> A. "No.
>
> Q. "Does All–States Leasing Company broker or distribute any kind of equipment?
>
> A. "No.
>
> Q. "Do you distribute any kind of merchandise at all?
>
> A. "None.
>
> Q. "Do you manufacture any kind of merchandise?
>
> A. "None.
>
> Q. "In other words, your business or All–States Leasing Company is strictly a company that leases or buys equipment that people specify and, then, lease that to them?

A. "That's correct."

. . .

[A]s one law journalist has noted:

> "Section 2–314 presents several obstacles to the imposition of liability on the finance lessor. First, the implied warranty of merchantability applies only to 'merchants.' The Code defines a merchant as one who deals in goods of the kind, or holds himself out as having knowledge peculiar to the goods, involved in the transaction. Since the finance lessor neither deals in goods of the kind being leased nor holds himself out as knowledgeable in the field, the finance lessor does not fit the Code definition of a merchant. Hence, it would appear at the outset that the UCC's implied warranty of merchantability cannot be applied by analogy to the finance lessor."[11]

In light of our conclusion that appellant was a finance lessor and not a merchant for purposes of IC § 28–2–314, it is unnecessary to pass upon the validity of the disclaimer clause, as it has no bearing on the merits of this appeal.

We do not have to decide whether respondent would have a cause of action against the manufacturer, as the manufacturer was not joined as a party to this action.

Judgment reversed. . . .

■ Shepard, J., dissenting. Scoggin, D.J. (retired) concurs in dissent.

I disagree with that portion of the majority opinion that holds that the lessor is not a "merchant." I cannot agree that the appellant who purchased and thereafter leased large numbers of car wash systems was not "a person who deals in goods of the kind." Although the appellant here did not build or manufacture such equipment, neither do most retailers. The sole distinction in this case is that appellant, being a lessor rather than a vendor, retained title to the equipment. The majority's purported change in rule permitting a lessor, in some circumstances, to be held to an implied warranty of merchantability is in reality no change at all. If a person must "sell" and divest himself of title to become a "merchant" and thus subject himself to implied warranty liability a lessor can never be subjected to such liability on implied warranty.

QUESTIONS AND NOTES

1. *All–States Leasing* was decided 3 to 2. If All–States Leasing had sold 40 of the machines over six to eight months, is there any doubt that it would have been a merchant for purposes of the warranty of merchantability?

---

11. Comment, Finance Lessor's Liability for Personal Injuries, Univ. of Ill. Law Forum, Vol. 1, 154, 158 (1974).

More specifically, suppose that Auto Laundry's method of doing business was to have its personnel handle all customer contacts and install the machines, and then transfer title to All–States Leasing, which then sold to the buyers of the machines. (Perhaps business might be handled this way to avoid having to comply with requirements for doing business in the state.) Could All–States Leasing argue that it was not a merchant in that case?

2. Idaho adopted Article 2A in 1993, two decades after the transaction in *All–States Leasing*. If the case arose today, how would it be decided? The applicable section is 2A–212. Ignoring for the moment the five introductory words of that section, would there be an implied warranty of merchantability?

3. The introductory words to 2A–212 mean that with respect to the implied warranty of merchantability, Article 2A puts a finance lessor in the same category as a lender: there is no implied warranty. In both kinds of transactions, the plaintiff who is acquiring the goods must look to the person that sold the goods, that is, sold to either the plaintiff or the lessor. "Finance lease" is defined in 2A–103(g).* Please read that definition now.

For a lease to be a finance lease, three elements must be present. It appears that the lease in *All–States Leasing* would not have qualified as a "finance lease" under the definition in Article 2A because the third element was not present: Bass did not receive a copy of the contract between Auto Laundry and All–States Leasing, the transaction was not conditional upon his approval of that contract, and he had not received a statement of the rights against Auto Laundry. If the case arose today, how strong an argument does All–States Leasing have that it still has no implied warranty of merchantability liability because it is not a merchant?

Even if a lessor is not a finance lessor under Article 2A, it can still avoid warranty liability by an effective disclaimer. See 2A–214.

4. Problem. When Atlas Construction Co.'s fifteen-year-old crane became unreliable, Atlas decided to replace it by leasing a new one. After identifying the crane it wanted to acquire, Atlas approached Worldbank Leasing, Inc., about financing the transaction. Worldbank was amenable, telling Atlas that its experience with leasing Craneco equipment had been excellent and that Craneco's equipment is the best on the market. Worldbank Leasing and Atlas Construction entered a ten-year lease contract for the crane, and Worldbank acquired the equipment from Craneco, pursuant to a contract containing several express warranties. Atlas took possession of the crane and made payments for six years, at which time the crane collapsed and could not be repaired. Does Atlas have a claim against Worldbank Leasing for breach of warranty? against Craneco?

The right of a remote buyer to recover for breach of warranty from a person with whom it has no contract is considered in Chapter 5, pages 295–324 infra. For the right of a *lessee* to recover from the person with whom it

---

* In revised Article 2A, it is in 2A–103(*l*).

has no contract, see 2A–209, which gives the lessee in a finance lease a direct cause of action against the "supplier" of the goods. For the definition of "supplier," see 2A–103(x).

5. Insulation of the financer. Finance leases frequently include so-called "hell or high water" clauses under which the lessee promises to pay the lessor even though the leased goods are defective. These clauses recognize that the finance lessor is really a supplier of money rather than a supplier of goods and provide that the lessor is entitled to be repaid, whether or not the leased goods are defective. Similar devices are available to sellers and lenders. For example, a sales contract may contain a waiver-of-defenses clause, by which the buyer agrees not to assert against an assignee of the contract those claims or defenses (e.g., breach of warranty) that it has against the seller. In the loan context, the holder-in-due-course doctrine achieves the same result. (A holder in due course takes a negotiable instrument—a promissory note—free of the claims and defenses that the promisor may have against the seller who received the instrument or its proceeds.)

For the Article 2A rule as to a lessee's right to assert defenses against a finance lessor, see 2A–407. What are the lessee's rights under that section as against a finance lessor prior to the lessee's acceptance of the goods? Observe that 2A–407 is a statutory "hell or high water" provision that is effective even though the contract itself does not contain a "hell or high water" provision. Should the section have merely validated contractual clauses?

In consumer transactions a number of courts have held that it may be unfair or contrary to public policy for the buyer to have to pay the assignee of a contract or promissory note for goods that were never delivered or that were grossly defective, when the assignee or note holder is little more than an extension of the seller. E.g., Unico v. Owen, 50 N.J. 101, 232 A.2d 405 (1967). After determining that it is inefficient to externalize the costs of the seller's breach from the consumer's obligation to pay, the Federal Trade Commission adopted the Trade Regulation Rule Concerning Preservation of Consumers' Claims and Defenses (often called the Holder Rule). This Rule requires sellers to include the following language in their contracts:

> Any holder of this consumer credit contract is subject to all claims and defenses which the debtor could assert against the seller of goods or services obtained pursuant hereto or with the proceeds hereof. . . .

With respect to loans directly from a lender to a consumer, if the lender is closely related to the seller, the Rule permits sellers to accept loan proceeds only if the loan contract contains that language. But the Rule does not apply to leases. In Mercedes–Benz Credit Corp. v. Lotito, 306 N.J.Super. 25, 703 A.2d 288 (App.Div.1997), however, the court extended the reasoning underlying Unico v. Owen and the Holder Rule to lease transactions.

6. Hybrid and services transactions. There are a number of conflicting cross-currents in the decisional law relating to liability for implied warranty in non-sales and non-lease situations.

One area of disagreement involves contracts for the fabrication of machines or buildings or parts of them. It frequently is difficult to categorize these transactions. A number of courts have held that, on the facts of the particular case, the transaction is not a sale of goods but instead is a sale of services and that no implied warranties arise in sales of services. E.g., Milau Associates, Inc. v. North Ave. Development Corp., 42 N.Y.2d 482, 398 N.Y.S.2d 882, 368 N.E.2d 1247 (1977). As we saw in Chapter 1, some courts have held that implied warranty liability does arise as to the goods components of hybrid transactions. E.g., Franklin v. Northwest Drilling Co., Inc., 215 Kan. 304, 524 P.2d 1194 (1974); Worrell v. Barnes, 87 Nev. 204, 484 P.2d 573 (1971). Some courts have held that there is warranty liability even as to the services component of fabrication or construction contracts. E.g., Insurance Co. of North America v. Radiant Electric Co., 55 Mich.App. 410, 222 N.W.2d 323 (1974); O'Laughlin v. Minnesota Natural Gas Co., 253 N.W.2d 826 (Minn.1977). Compare Franklin v. Northwest Drilling Co., supra (implied warranty that services will be performed in a workmanlike manner with the skill that ordinarily is expected in the profession) and Air Heaters, Inc. v. Johnson Electric, Inc., 258 N.W.2d 649 (N.D.1977) (warranty as to the total resulting structure whether the failure is based on a defect in the component materials or in the services involved in assembling the components).

In "pure" services transactions there is no implied-warranty liability for non-negligent mistakes or failures. E.g., Lemley v. J & B Tire Co., 426 F.Supp. 1378 (W.D.Pa.1977) (failure of brakes after defendant repaired them); Strong v. Retail Credit Co., 38 Colo.App. 125, 552 P.2d 1025 (1976) (credit report); Lewis v. Big Powderhorn Mountain Ski Corp., 69 Mich.App. 437, 245 N.W.2d 81 (1976) (ski tow-rope snapped).

D. WARRANTY OF TITLE

1. THE OBLIGATION TO PROVIDE GOOD TITLE

As in land transactions, personal property may be sold on a quit-claim basis, giving the buyer all the risks of ownership. Sales of goods on this basis, however, are rare, and thus, in the absence of an express agreement to the contrary, 2–312 requires the seller to give the buyer good title.

Subsection (1)(a) requires that the seller warrant "good title." Good title is not defined by the Code, but Official Comment 1 states that a good title is one that is not exposed to a lawsuit. Any non-spurious claim, asserted against the buyer by a third party as to the title to the goods will constitute a breach of the warranty of title, entitling the buyer to cancel the sale or to recover from the seller costs of defending the title. Merely because the buyer can defeat the third party in a lawsuit does not necessarily mean that the buyer has a "good" title. The fact that his title is unreasonably exposed to the claim of the third person is what constitutes the breach of the seller's warranty of good title, and that breach is not cured by the buyer's ability to defeat the third party. The operation of this subsection is illustrated by Jefferson v. Jones, 286 Md. 544, 408 A.2d 1036 (1979), in which plaintiff purchased a motorcycle from defendant. The vehicle identification number (VIN) on the title certificate did not match the VIN stamped on the motorcycle, and the police seized it. Plaintiff obtained return of the vehicle and then sued defendant, claiming breach of the warranty of title. The court agreed:

> ... [T]he U.C.C.'s warranty of title requirement is to protect a vendee from legal claims which may arise concerning his ownership of the purchased goods. The type or nature, however, of a third party's claim of title or right to possession giving rise to a breach of the warranty is not further delineated by the statute. Consequently, we will now proceed to determine the nature of the claims which the legislature intended should have the protection of the warranty of title provided for in section 2–312.

> The intermediate appellate and trial court's answer to this query was that a breach of section 2–312(1) (a) occurs only when a purchaser establishes the existence of a "superior or paramount" title in a third party. Their rulings are in accord with the showing that was required at common law before a breach of the implied warranty of title could be found. However, it is our view that the legislature intended, in accord with the design of the drafters, that the Code's warranty of title would provide a buyer with greater protection than its common law counterpart. Our determination in this regard here is amply supported by the statement in the comments that "[disturbance] of quiet possession, ... [which at common law required interference by a holder of a superior or paramount title before a breach was declared] is one way, among many, in which the breach of the warranty of title may be established." § 2–312, comment 1 (emphasis added). Again, finding nothing to the contrary, we therefore conclude that the General Assembly intended that section 2–312's protection, unless waived by the purchaser, applies to third party claims of title no matter whether eventually determined to be inferior or superior to the buyer's ownership. . . .

> Our holding here, that proof of a superior title is not necessary, does not mean, however, that all claims, no matter how unfounded, which may be made against the buyer's title should result in a breach of the warranty. "Good title" is "usually taken to mean that the title which the seller gives to the buyer is 'free from reasonable doubt, that is, not only a valid title in fact, but [also] one that can again be sold to a reasonable purchase or mortgaged to a person of reasonable prudence.' " [citation omitted] As such, "there is some point at which [a] third party's claim against the goods becomes so attenuated that we should not regard it as an interference against which the seller has warranted." [citation omitted] All that a purchaser should expect from a seller of property is that he be protected from colorable claims against his title and not from all claims. Spurious title claims can be made by anyone at any time. . . . Thus, before a third party's claim

against the title of another will result in a breach of the warranty of title, the claim must be colorable, nonspurious and of such a nature as to produce a reasonable doubt as to the title's validity. . . .

. . . When analyzing the legal questions presented, a court, in our opinion, may profitably draw upon the principles which this Court has developed over the years for deciding whether title to real property is marketable. Decisions of this Court, stretching back for over 100 years, have discussed the reasonable doubt concept in this regard as it pertains to real property. The criteria which have developed essentially require a determination of whether the claim is of such a substantial nature that it may reasonably subject the buyer to serious litigation. While such a standard may be considered vague, it is one which courts have successfully applied for many years. Furthermore, the public policy considerations underlying this standard concerning marketability of title to realty are similar to those which section 2–312 was designed to foster in the sales of personalty—to balance the needs of the purchaser concerning title with the litigious nature of our society and the seller's needs for a limit to his liability.

When we examine the facts of the case now before us, in light of the legal standard just mentioned, we conclude that, as a matter of law, there exists a warranty of title that has been breached here. . . . Whenever the title to personal property is evidenced by a document which is an aid to proving ownership, as is true in the case of motor vehicles, any substantial defect in that document necessarily creates a reasonable doubt as to that ownership. A certificate of title, which, with limited exceptions, all owners of motor vehicles must have in this State, is prima facie evidence of ownership. To be valid, such a certificate must include, among other things, the vehicle's identification number; and while the owner of the vehicle may prove his title by means other than the certificate, any seller of a motor vehicle who executes . . . an assignment of the vehicle's certificate of title that contains identifying information that is different from that on the vehicle itself, knows or should know that problems concerning the buyer's ownership would arise. Without a valid title certificate, the owner of a vehicle cannot register, drive or sell it, and if problems do arise, as in this case, the seller is responsible for any damages caused. In other words, a breach of the warranty of title occurs whenever a seller of a motor vehicle fails to provide his purchaser with adequate proof of ownership because of the reasonable doubts which faulty documentation raise as to the validity of the buyer's title.

Subsection 2–312(1)(b) requires that the goods be free from any security interest, lien, or encumbrance of which the buyer has no actual knowledge. If there is a security interest, then, the seller breaches the warranty of title, but only if the buyer does not know of the security interest. The knowledge limitation reflects the fact that a person buying goods with actual knowledge of a possible outstanding interest in them will pay less for them, in return for which it is fair for that person to assume the title risks. But the buyer is not charged with knowledge of a security interest merely because it is on the public record by virtue of a financing statement filed pursuant to Article 9 (which deals with security interests). Whether the buyer takes free of the perfected security interest, however, is determined by other law. This aspect of the transaction is addressed in Chapter 10.

Revised 2–312 makes no material change, other than incorporating in the text of subsection (1)(a) the "exposure-to-a-lawsuit" rule that appears now in the Official Comment. It provides that a transfer "shall not unreasonably expose the buyer to litigation because of any colorable claim to or interest in the goods."

2.   DISCLAIMER OF THE WARRANTY

Subsection (2) of 2–312 sets out requirements for disclaiming the warranty of title. A disclaimer of title can be only by specific language. The word "only" in subsection (2) means that the warranty of title cannot be disclaimed by using broad disclaimer language, which we will see is authorized by 2–316(2) and (3) to disclaim the implied warranties of merchantability and fitness for particular purpose. Rather, the seller must use specific language calling the buyer's attention to the fact that the warranty of title is being disclaimed. This requirement is for the protection of the buyer because general disclaiming language usually suggests only that the buyer assumes quality risks and not that the buyer assumes title risks as well.

Subsection (2) also provides that no warranty of title exists when the circumstances of the sale give the buyer reason to know that the seller does not claim to have title or purports to be selling only whatever ownership the seller may have. Sales by sheriffs, executors, and pawnbrokers, for example, are of such nature that a buyer is not entitled, by virtue of sale alone, to the personal obligation of the seller respecting good title to the merchandise. Article 9, however, provides that creditors foreclosing under Article 9 make title warranties that by operation of law accompany a voluntary disposition of collateral of the kind being sold (9–610(d)). Therefore, the warranties of 2–312 apply to foreclosure sales. Subsections 9–610(e) and (f) provide that the creditor may disclaim the warranty of title in the manner specified in 2–312 or by giving the buyer a statement that "there is no warranty relating to title, possession, quiet enjoyment, or the like in this disposition."

Subsection 3 provides that a merchant dealing in goods of the kind that are being sold warrants that the goods will be free from infringement claims by third persons which may arise out of violations of patents, trademarks, and the like. If, however, the buyer furnishes specifications for the goods that the seller is to deliver, the buyer does not get this infringement protection, but, on the contrary, must hold the seller harmless against any such claims that arise out of compliance with the specification. In other words, in this case it is the buyer who gives the warranty that no harm will come to the seller through compliance with the specification.

3. LEASES

Though modeled on 2–312, the warranty in 2A–211 reflects the fact that in lease transactions the title does not pass to the lessee. Therefore, 2A–211 imposes a warranty of quiet possession: that no person holds a claim or interest arising from an act or omission of the lessor which will interfere with the lessee's enjoyment of the leasehold interest. Further, except in a finance lease, the warranty also protects against claims of infringement. As with the warranty of title in sales transaction, this warranty may be excluded or modified. Unlike its analog in Article 2, however, the provision authorizing disclaimer of the warranty of quiet possession appears in the section authorizing disclaimers of other implied warranties (2A–214(4)).

Revised 2A–211 modifies the language and organization of the current law. For example, it contains the provision on disclaimers (2A–211(4)).

4. CISG

The Convention on Contracts for the International Sale of Goods requires the seller to hand over any documents relating to the goods, as required by the contract and the Convention (Articles 30, 34). Most often this refers to documents pertaining to possession of the goods, such as bills of lading, but it also encompasses certificates of title for goods that have them. Article 41 requires the seller, unless the parties have agreed otherwise, to deliver the goods free from any right or claim of a third party. Though not denominated a warranty, this imposes on the seller obligations similar to those imposed by Article 2.

CHAPTER 5

DISCLAIMERS AND OTHER LIMITATIONS ON WARRANTIES

A. DISCLAIMERS

Consistent with the underlying freedom-of-contract philosophy of Article 2, the provisions that create implied warranties (2–314 and 2–315) are simply default provisions. The parties are free to agree otherwise, that there will be no implied warranties in their particular transaction. Section 2–316 provides the mechanism for implementing this agreement. Please read that section, noting the different language dealing with express warranties, the implied warranty of merchantability, and the implied warranty of fitness for a particular purpose.

———

Sierra Diesel Injection Service, Inc. v. Burroughs Corporation

United States Court of Appeals, Ninth Circuit, 1989.
874 F.2d 653.

■ STEPHENS, SENIOR DISTRICT JUDGE.

Sierra Diesel Injection Service, Inc. (Sierra Diesel) is a family owned and operated business that services the fuel injection portions of diesel engines and sells related diesel engine parts. In September 1977, 19–year–old Caroline Cathey, the daughter-in-law of the Sierra Diesel's owner and operator James Cathey, worked as the company bookkeeper. She went to the Reno, Nevada branch office of the Burroughs Corporation (Burroughs) to purchase a posting machine to speed up Sierra Diesel's invoicing and accounting. The salespeople at Burroughs told Caroline Cathey that Sierra Diesel should buy a B–80 computer (B–80) instead of a posting machine. Caroline and James Cathey attended a demonstration of the B–80 at the Burroughs office. . . .

In October 1977, Mr. Cathey decided to purchase the B–80. Sierra Diesel and Burroughs signed various contracts for the sale of hardware and software and for maintenance service. Mr. Cathey's highest level of formal education was a high school degree. At the time he bought the B–80 he was not knowledgeable about computers. He had a general knowledge of warranties and their limitations from the warranty service work Sierra Diesel did for diesel component parts manufacturers, but he did not understand the meaning of "merchantability." He read the contracts from Burroughs to see that they contained the correct price information and product description and he glanced at the back of the contract to see, as he put it, that "I'm not actually signing away the deed to my home or something of this nature."

The B–80 computer did not perform the invoicing and accounting functions for which it had been purchased. It experienced basic equipment breakdowns and was unable to "multiprogram." Sierra Diesel personnel complained to the Burroughs service personnel. Burroughs responded to these complaints and its staff attempted to solve the problems and also attempted to repair the system during their regularly scheduled visits under the Maintenance Agreement. Eventually, the Burroughs staff recommended to Sierra Diesel that it purchase a different Burroughs computer (B–91) to remedy the problems. Sierra Diesel purchased the B–91 and took delivery in February 1981. The B–91 computer was no better able to perform the invoicing and accounting functions than the B–80. After additional unsuccessful attempts by Burroughs employees to correct the problems, Sierra Diesel employed an independent computer consultant who concluded that the Burroughs computers would never perform the functions for which they had been purchased. Sierra Diesel bought another computer from a different company. In 1984, Sierra Diesel initiated the present litigation.

Sierra Diesel sued Burroughs . . . . Burroughs moved for summary judgment on the grounds that . . . the warranties had been excluded . . . . After the trial, the court held that the exclusion of warranties clauses were not conspicuous . . . .

. . .

Warranty exclusions are permitted under the UCC § 2–316 to allow parties to bargain to allocate the risk of loss. However, exclusions of warranties are generally disfavored, and standardized take it or leave it form contracts such as the one in this case are construed against the drafter. They are subject to the general obligation of good faith and of not imposing unconscionable terms upon a party. Restatement (Second) of Contracts § 211. Nevada has adopted the UCC waiver of warranty language in NRS § 104.2316. According to official comment one the purpose of the warranty waiver section is to "protect a buyer from unexpected and unbargained language of disclaimer by denying effect to such language when inconsistent with language of express warranty and permitting the exclusion of implied warranties only by conspicuous language or other circumstances which protect the buyer from surprise."

Conspicuousness is defined by NRS § 104.1201(10): "A term or clause is conspicuous when it is so written that a reasonable person against whom it is to operate ought to have noticed it. . . . Language in the body of a form is 'conspicuous' if it is in larger or other contrasting type or color." Official comment 10 notes that "the test is whether attention can reasonably be expected to be called to it."

"Whether a term or clause is 'conspicuous' or not is for decision by the court." NRS § 104.1201(10). Review of the trial court's finding is de novo.

Both the hardware and software agreements contained the following warranty disclaimer, "EXCEPT AS SPECIFICALLY PROVIDED HEREIN, THERE ARE NO OTHER WARRANTIES, EXPRESS OR IMPLIED, IN-CLUDING, BUT NOT LIMITED TO, ANY IMPLIED WARRANTIES OF MERCHANTABILITY OR FITNESS FOR A PARTICULAR PURPOSE." In the hardware agreement the disclaimer appeared in the middle of the page at the left hand column in all capital bold type. It is one of the three paragraphs on the reverse side in all capital bold type. There are 15 separately numbered sections. The warranty exclusions clause is in section 4. There is no heading to identify it as a warranty section.

On the front of the software agreement a sentence standing alone in large capital bold letter directs the signor to read the warranty terms on the back, "THE TERMS AND CONDITIONS, INCLUDING THE WAR-RANTY AND LIMITATION OF LIABILITY, ON THE REVERSE SIDE ARE PART OF THE AGREEMENT." The back of the contract contains 14 separately numbered and titled sections, some of which are further divided into paragraphs. The ninth section, entitled **WARRANTY**, contains the exclusion clause in the fourth paragraph of the section. The clause is in all capital letters, but it is not bold type. The only words in bold on the back of the form are the title headings and the words **TERMS AND CONDI-TIONS** at the top of the page.

Whether a disclaimer is conspicuous is not simply a matter of measuring the type size or looking at the placement of the disclaimer within the contract. A reviewing court must ascertain that a reasonable person in the buyer's position would not have been surprised to find the warranty disclaimer in the contract. One factor to consider is the sophistication of the parties. See e.g., Collins Radio v. Bell, 623 P.2d [1039,] 1051 [(Okla.Civ. App.1980)] ("we note that the disclaimer [in capital letters] is of minimal compliance, and we do not venture to state what factors might alter this determination in future cases outside of the sophistication of the buyer") (emphasis in the original). Also relevant as to whether a reasonable person would have noticed a warranty disclaimer are the circumstances of the negotiation and signing.

The trial court found that Mr. Cathey was not familiar with computers or with contracts. Mr. Cathey read the front of the contracts, but did not notice the warranty disclaimer clauses on the back. Given Mr. Cathey's lack of sophistication in the field of contracts and the written and oral representations made by Burroughs, it is not surprising that it would require more than a collection of standardized form contracts on various subjects involved in a transaction to notify a reasonable person in Mr. Cathey's position that the B–80 came without any warranty of merchantability.

Burroughs faults the trial court for holding that all warranty disclaimers must be in capital letters and in bold type, but the trial court did not rule in so mechanistic a fashion. The trial court's rulings consider type size and boldness as factors in an overall analysis and also the fact that the disclaimers were on the back of the page. Cf. Sellman Auto, Inc. v. McCowan, 89 Nev. 353, 513 P.2d 1228, 1230 (1973) (Under Uniform Sales Act, a waiver of an express warranty printed on the back of a contract is not effective unless the buyer is actually aware of it.) The trial court also considered the relative sophistication of the parties.

Burroughs points to two Nevada cases interpreting NRS § 104.2316. In Bill Stremmel Motors, Inc. v. IDS Leasing Corp., 89 Nev. 414, 514 P.2d 654 (1973), the Nevada Supreme Court affirmed a trial court judgment holding that a warranty exclusion clause in all capital letters was conspicuous. In *Stremmel* the trial court found that both parties were sophisticated, that there was no evidence that the buyer had not read the contract, and that the disclaimer was conspicuous. There is a marked difference in the dispute between Burroughs and Sierra Diesel. The district court found that Mr. Cathey was not a sophisticated buyer, he had not read the contract, and the trial court found that the disclaimers were not conspicuous. In the second case, Sierra Creek Ranch v. J. I. Case, 97 Nev. 457, 634 P.2d 458 (1981), the Nevada Supreme Court again affirmed a trial court finding that an exclusion clause was conspicuous. Both *Stremmel* and *Sierra Creek* show that a disclaimer in capital letters that mentions merchantability can be effective to exclude warranties. They do not hold that capital letters as a matter of law will be effective in all cases.

In the circumstances of this case, the district court's finding that the warranty disclaimer clauses were not conspicuous is not erroneous.

. . .

■ CANBY, CIRCUIT JUDGE, concurring in part and dissenting in part: . . .

My disagreement with the majority concerns the question whether the disclaimers of implied warranties were conspicuous. On that issue, our standard of review is de novo. My own view of the contracts leads me to conclude that the clauses are conspicuous within the meaning of Nev.Rev. Stat. § 104.1201(10).

The software agreement is the clearest. In a separate paragraph, in large, capital bold type immediately above the signature line on the face page, there appears the following sentence: "THE TERMS AND CONDITIONS, INCLUDING THE WARRANTY AND LIMITATION OF LIABILITY, ON THE REVERSE SIDE ARE PART OF THIS AGREEMENT." That language is possibly the most conspicuous single item in the entire agreement. On the reverse side, under the section headed "WARRANTY" appears the disclaimer of implied warranties, in a separate paragraph, all in capital letters. These provisions, in my view, would call a reasonable buyer's attention to the disclaimer.

The disclaimer in the hardware agreement presents a closer question. There is no reference to warranties or limitation of liability on the front of the contract, but the last line, in capitals, before the signature states that the customer has agreed to all terms and conditions including those on the reverse side. The reverse side contains 15 numbered sections, in print of small size and low contrast that discourages reading. Nevertheless, in the middle of the left column, in much larger print and all capitals, there appears the separate paragraph stating: "EXCEPT AS SPECIFICALLY PROVIDED IN THIS AGREEMENT, THERE ARE NO OTHER WARRANTIES EXPRESS OR IMPLIED INCLUDING BUT NOT LIMITED TO ANY IMPLIED WARRANTIES OF MERCHANTABILITY OF FITNESS FOR A PARTICULAR PURPOSE." By location and prominence, this clause is probably the most conspicuous one on the page. I conclude that it would notify the reasonable buyer. . . . The fact that the disclaimer was on the back side of the contract ought not to render it ineffective, so long as the language on the front side prominently referred to the terms and conditions on the back. . . .

QUESTIONS AND NOTES

1.   To be effective under 2–316(2), a disclaimer of the implied warranty of merchantability must mention "merchantability." What is the rationale for this requirement. Compare revised 2–316(2).

2.   To be effective under 2–316(2), a disclaimer of the implied warranty of merchantability must be conspicuous, which is defined in 1–201(10). In *Sierra Diesel* the disclaimer was in capital letters. Given the definition in 1–201, by what reasoning can the court conclude that the disclaimer was not conspicuous? On page 281 the court asserts that "whether a disclaimer is conspicuous is not simply a matter of measuring the type size or looking at the placement of the disclaimer in the contract." Is this statement defensible?

3.   In Hamilton v. O'Connor Chevrolet, Inc., 399 F.Supp.2d 860 (N.D.Ill. 2005), a car dealer included language of disclaimer in its retail installment sales contract. When the purchasers sued for breach of warranty, the dealer argued that the disclaimer was effective. The court agreed:

> In the case *sub judice*, the disclaimer mentioned "merchantability" in writing that is conspicuous. The disclaimer specifically states, in bold: **"Warranties Seller Disclaims. You understand that the Seller is not offering any warranties and that there are no implied warranties of merchantability, or fitness for a particular purpose, or any other warranties, express or implied by the Seller . . . ."** The bold-faced writing is not hidden or obscured; in fact, it is free-standing and set forth in its own paragraph out from the remainder of the text. In addition, below the disclaimer, the Retail Contract provides a definition of implied warranty of merchantability. ("An implied warranty of merchantability generally means that the vehicle is fit for the ordinary purpose for which such vehicles are generally used.")
>
> The fact that the disclaimer is on the back side of the Retail Contract does not, in this case at least, alter the result of the analysis

about whether a reasonable person would be expected to notice it. *Accord, e.g., Larry J. Soldinger, Assocs., Ltd. v. Aston Martin Lagonda of N. Am., Inc., 1998 WL 151817 at *4 (N.D.Ill., 1998)* ("The fact that the disclaimer is on the back side of the bill of sale does not make it invalid."). Like the bill of sale in *Soldinger,* the front side of the Retail Contract directs the reader in bold-face type to the back side of the contract "for other important agreements." In addition, in at least three other places, the front side of the Retail Contract directs the reader to the back side of the agreement. The front side of the Retail Contract also states in bold-face type: "Notice to the buyer. 1. Do not sign this agreement before you read it or if it contains any blank spaces. 2. You are entitled to an exact copy of the agreement you sign . . . ." In short, with respect to the language directing the reader to the back side of the Retail Contract, a "reasonable person would have read the back side of the [agreement] and noticed the disclaimer."[8]

4. *Sierra Diesel* and *Hamilton v. O'Connor* present two very different attitudes toward contract formation. Which of the two more closely represents your view?

5. Problem. Consumer negotiates the purchase of a new automobile from Dealer. Upon completion of the negotiations, Dealer presents a standard-form retail sales contract. This document is two-sided and consists of four copies joined at the top by a perforated strip. On the back side of the document is a disclaimer, in red letters and larger than the other type on the back side. On the front side is the statement, "This sale is subject to the terms and conditions on the reverse side." Dealer puts this document in front of Consumer, points to the signature line, and says, "Sign here." Consumer signs where indicated. Is the disclaimer effective?

6. Problem. Buyer purchases a truck-tractor from Seller. The tractor requires repairs shortly after the purchase, and Buyer sues for breach of implied warranty. Seller claims that the warranty was disclaimed by language in the contract of sale executed by the parties. The disclaimer language is in the same size and kind of type as the rest of the contract. Buyer however, admits that she had read the disclaimer clause before signing the document. Can Buyer successfully argue that the disclaimer is not effective because it is not conspicuous?

7. Revised Article 2. The revisions modify 2–316, making it somewhat more likely that consumer buyers will understand disclaimers. Subsection (2) requires that disclaimers of the warranties of merchantability or fitness for particular purpose in a consumer contract be conspicuous and in a record. A disclaimer of the warranty of merchantability must state, "The seller undertakes no responsibility for the quality of the goods except as

---

8. Moreover, although not necessary to the result of the analysis, the Court notes that the contract at issue in this appears to be an oversized document—8.5 inches by perhaps as much as 22 inches—such that a read-er would naturally be curious about the document and be inclined to flip it over, even if it did not expressly and repeatedly direct the reader to do so, as this one did.

otherwise provided in this contract"; and a disclaimer of the warranty of fitness must state, "The seller assumes no responsibility that the goods will be fit for any particular purpose for which you may be buying these goods except as otherwise provided in this contract." To disclaim implied warranties in a consumer transaction, the seller *must* use this language. In a non-consumer transaction, the seller need not use the quoted language, but may use it, in which event it will be effective. In a consumer transaction, the disclaimers must be in a record, but in a commercial transaction, they may be oral.

Gindy Manufacturing Corp. v. Cardinale Trucking Corp.

New Jersey Superior Court, Law Division, 1970.
111 N.J.Super. 383, 268 A.2d 345.

■ BOTTER, J.S.C. This is an action by the seller (Gindy) of twenty-five 1967 semi-trailers for a deficiency of $13,052.37 after repossession and resale following defendant's default in payment under a conditional sales contract. The defense and counterclaim are based on the assertion that the trailers were delivered with faulty radius rods which caused premature tire wear and consequent monetary loss.

The matter is before the court on plaintiff's motion for summary judgment. Plaintiff contends that the installment sales contract expressly excluded all warranties. Accordingly, plaintiff seeks a judgment for the amount of the deficiency, with interest and costs, and a dismissal of the counterclaim.

On or about June 1, 1967, the parties entered into a written installment sales contract in the total sum of $141,756, inclusive of finance charges. The contract, provided by plaintiff, was a one-page form contract with considerable close print. The only additions were by typewriter to show the name and address of the buyer, the various charges and installment payments involved, and the due date of the first installment. Also, in prominent position, a description of the trailers was typed in under various headings in the printed form as shown below, with the typewritten portions indicated by my use of italics:

New Or Used	Make or Year	Manufacturer's Trade Name	Description	Model	Serial No.
New	*1967*	*Gindy*	*semi-trailer*	*C240AV9*	*38480 thru 38504*

The printed form also contained the following paragraph:

H. WARRANTIES. Buyer is buying the vehicle "as is" and no representations or statements have been made by Seller except as herein stated, so that no warranty, express or implied, arises apart from this writing. Buyer warrants that any property which is offered in trade for the vehicle is free from any lien, claim, encumbrance or security interest.

Plaintiff contends that the above clause, particularly the provision that the vehicles are sold "as is," excludes all warranties. Plaintiff further contends that the recital in the contract that the "writing contains the full, final and exclusive statement of the agreement of the parties" precludes any modification by oral agreement or otherwise of the specific provision excluding warranties. There was also a separately signed provision that: "No modification of this contract may be made except in writing signed by Seller." Since defendant failed to meet installment payments due for May, June, July and August of 1968, defendant was in default under the agreement, and plaintiff had the right to repossess and resell the trailers and sue for the deficiency. The only question, therefore, is whether defendant can assert as an offset or by way of counterclaim damages caused by the alleged defects in the vehicles furnished.

Defendant asserts that it has been doing business with Gindy for 20 years and had purchased hundreds of trailers, none of which were purchased "as is." Defendant asserts that in past dealings with Gindy and in accordance with the custom of the trade all defects in the manufacture of the trailers were the responsibility of Gindy. Defendant further asserts that in the past Gindy did correct at its own cost manufacturing defects whenever they appeared; that in the present transaction, when the defect caused by faulty radius rods appeared, Gindy agreed to replace them and ordered defendant to take the trailers to the Husky Trailer Company with whom Gindy contracted to have the repairs made at Gindy's expense; that Gindy sent new parts to be installed in the trailers in question in replacement of the defective parts; that every trailer which defendant purchased from Gindy was purchased brand new; that Gindy knew defendant's operation and, in fact, when Gindy started in business the founders of defendant corporation helped Gindy in designing the trailers; that defendant was not aware of the existence of the "as is" provision in the contract; that on June 12, 1967 another installment sales contract in an amount in excess of $200,000 entered into with Gindy by a corporation related to defendant did not have an "as is" clause; that the inclusion of the "as is" clause is contrary to the custom in the trade which provides implied warranties that all *new* equipment will perform as represented and will do the job for which it was purchased; that *used* equipment may be purchased "as is," and the absence of warranties in such case is reflected in the price of the equipment; and that at no time in the dealings between the parties during the period when defects arose on the trailers did Gindy ever take the position that the equipment had been purchased "as is." These assertions in the affidavit of defendant's president are uncontroverted in the record before me.

. . .

Defendant asserts without contradiction that it has always been the custom in the trade and in defendant's relationship with Gindy that all manufacturing defects were the responsibility of Gindy and that, when such defects appeared, Gindy in the past did make the necessary corrections or repairs at its own expense. In this transaction, too, Gindy undertook to correct the defects in the trailers. The express terms of an agreement should be construed where reasonable as consistent with the custom of the trade or a course of dealing evidenced by previous conduct of the parties. N.J.S.A. 12A:1–205. Moreover, a course of performance is relevant to the interpretation of an agreement. N.J.S.A. 12A:2–208. The express terms of an agreement and a course of performance, course of dealing and usage of trade "shall be construed whenever reasonable as consistent with each other * * *." N.J.S.A. 12A:2–208(2).

Defendant asserts that the trailers were delivered with faulty radius rods. In the answer and counterclaim defendant asserts that the defects caused premature tire wear and loss of use of the equipment, presumably while repairs were being made. From the facts at hand it is not clear whether the defects were so serious as to make the vehicles unmerchantable . . . . Repairs undertaken by plaintiff, the usage of trade and prior dealings of the parties offer strong evidence of plaintiff's obligation to make such repairs, whether in satisfaction of an implied warranty of merchantability or in satisfaction of a stricter implied warranty claimed by defendant under N.J.S.A. 12A:2–314(3), . . . namely, an implied warranty to repair all defects in manufacture regardless of their seriousness. Code Comment 12 has been interpreted to indicate that "other implied warranties" arising under section 2–314(3) by course of dealing or usage of trade are not limited to "what might ordinarily be regarded as warranties but also include collateral obligations related to a seller's performance." 1 Anderson Uniform Commercial Code, Sec. 2–314:10, p. 209 (1961). Accordingly, unless properly disclaimed pursuant to section 2–316, there arose in this transaction an implied warranty on the part of Gindy to accept responsibility for defects in manufacture, at least to the extent of repair or replacement.

Plaintiff contends that an appropriate disclaimer of all warranties was expressly provided by Paragraph H of the agreement quoted above. Plaintiff also relies upon the separately signed agreement that a modification of the contract cannot be made except in writing. N.J.S.A. 12A:2–209(2).

. . .

To disclaim an implied warranty of merchantability, section 2–316(2) of the Code requires the use of the word "merchantability," and requires, in a written contract, that such exclusion must be in "conspicuous" language. "Conspicuous" is defined by N.J.S.A. 12A:1–201(10) to include such writing "that a reasonable person against whom it is to operate ought to have noticed it." The definition provides that "a printed heading in capitals * * * is conspicuous," and that "conspicuous" writing includes larger print or other contrasting type or color. This section also provides that conspicuousness is to be determined by the court.

The definition also provides that "in a telegram any stated term is conspicuous." The definition of "conspicuous" is not exhaustive nor does it mean that in all circumstances ordinary print cannot be conspicuous. See Code Comment 10, Sec. 1–201 which says that "the test is whether attention can reasonably be expected to be called to it."

In the case at hand an implied warranty of merchantability has not been excluded in a manner that conforms to N.J.S.A. 12A:2–316(2). The word "merchantability" is not used and the exclusion is not conspicuous. Paragraph H does not contain larger or different type in the exclusionary provision; the only large type is the printed heading which reads, "WARRANTIES." The use of that heading did not make the *exclusion* conspicuous; if anything, it would suggest to a buyer who does not read the fine print that warranties are included, not excluded. In fact, there is an express warranty in the clause, but not by the seller. It is a warranty by the buyer as to clear title of a vehicle given in trade.

Plaintiff contends, however, that the "as is" provision is sufficient to disclaim all implied warranties. On the other hand, defendant contends that the "as is" clause is inoperative because it is not appropriate to the transaction, involving the sale of new vehicles, and because the clause is not in conspicuous language.

Subsection (3) does not use the term "conspicuous." Subsection (2), which requires the use of conspicuous language in written agreements to exclude or modify implied warranties of merchantability or fitness, is expressly made subject to subsection (3). The introductory language of subsection (3) also suggests the supremacy of its provisions over subsection (2). Thus, reading the two subsections literally would eliminate the requirement of "conspicuous" language as a condition for the exclusion of all implied warranties where expressions like "as is" are used. On the other hand, the intent may have been simply to provide in subsection (3) a qualification of subsection (2) so as to permit the use of commonly understood terms in substitution for the term "merchantability" or terms respecting fitness, without eliminating the requirement of conspicuous language where the agreement is in writing. . . . [T]he basic purpose of the Code [is] to protect the buyer from surprise. Code Comment 1, Sec. 2–316. See also Code Comment 11, Sec. 2–314, which says in part:

> The warranty of merchantability, wherever it is normal, is so commonly taken for granted that its exclusion from the contract is a matter threatening surprise and therefore requiring special precaution.

The original draft of section 2–316 contained a single paragraph (2) which provided for the exclusion of warranties with three exceptions comparable to sub-paragraphs (a), (b) and (c) now contained in subsection (3). U.C.C.Supp. No. 1 (1952), Sec. 2–316. The amendment of section 2–316 to its present form broke subsection (2) into two parts. One part remained section (2) and the exceptions became section (3). To section (2) was added the requirement of conspicuous language where a disclaimer is in writing. In addition, section (2) was amended to require that a disclaimer of an implied warranty of fitness must always be in writing, and the requirement of specific language to avoid a warranty of fitness was changed.

The drafters of the Code made the following comment upon the redrafting of subsection (2):

Reason: Former subsection (2) was rewritten and divided into subsections (2) and (3) in Supp. No. 1 to relieve the seller from the requirement of disclaiming the warranty of fitness in specific language and yet afford the buyer an adequate warning of such disclaimer. Subsequently, subsection (1) was rewritten and subsections (3)(a) and (3)(b) changed for clarification and to meet criticism by the New York Commission. U.C.C., 1956 Recommendations, at 40.

No comment was made regarding the applicability of the conspicuous language requirement to subsection (3), and no case has been found in New Jersey or elsewhere which deals with the problem. Nor is it dealt with in the Code Comments or in the New Jersey Study Comment. . . .

The metamorphosis of section 2–316 and the reason given in the legislative history mentioned above suggest that the use of expressions like "as is" was intended merely to give effect to common terms in addition to those specified in subsection (2) as a means for disclaiming certain warranties. There is no evidence of a legislative purpose to require conspicuous language in one case and not when expressions like "as is" are used.

It appears desirable to read into section 2–316(3) the requirement of conspicuousness when the attempted disclaimer is in writing. This would avoid surprise to a buyer and fulfill a fundamental purpose of the Code. However, one of the difficulties is that subsection (2) deals expressly with disclaiming the implied warranties of merchantability and fitness. It does not deal with disclaimer of other implied warranties arising from a course of dealing or usage of trade under N.J.S.A. 12A:2–314(3). While subsection (2) deals with two types of implied warranties and expressly imposes the requirement of conspicuous language in writings as to them, subsection (3)(a) specifically refers to "all implied warranties" and does not contain the requirement of conspicuous language. . . . If the requirement of "conspicuous" language had been intended, being a term defined by the Code itself in section 1–201(10), the draftsmen should have expressly included that term in subsection (3). Perhaps it is a matter of poor draftsmanship or oversight. But it always presents a problem for the court when the omission of a provision that could so easily have been included seems to conflict with an underlying purpose of the legislation.

It does not make sense to require conspicuous language when a warranty is disclaimed by use of the words "merchantability" or "fitness" and not when a term like "as is" is used to accomplish the same result. It serves no intelligible design to protect buyers by conspicuous language when the term "merchantability" is used, but to allow an effective disclaimer when the term "as is" is buried in fine print. Nor does it make sense to require conspicuous language to disclaim the implied warranties of merchantability and fitness and not impose a similar requirement to disclaim other implied warranties that arise by course of dealing or usage of trade. The expectations of the buyer need as much protection in one case as in another. My preference, therefore, is to find that there is a requirement of conspicuousness when terms like "as is" are used to exclude an implied warranty of merchantability or fitness. It seems reasonable to say that to avoid these implied warranties the requirements of subsection (2) must be met, except that expressions like "as is" will be given effect in addition to the expressions specified in subsection (2). This interpretation, nevertheless, would still leave intact the exclusion of implied warranties arising from a course of dealing or usage of trade by expressions like "as is," whether conspicuous or not. It would appear desirable, to eliminate all doubt in this area, for the legislature to amend N.J.S.A. 12A:2–316 so as to include an express requirement of conspicuous language when a writing is used to exclude or modify any and all implied warranties. In any case, an interpretation requiring conspicuousness to avoid the warranties of merchantability and fitness still leaves open the effect of the disclaimer clause here on the implied warranties arising under section 2–314(3). My holding below on this issue is dispositive of this motion.

The agreement in question is at least ambiguous as to the applicability of the "as is" clause in this transaction. Subsection (3)(a) of section 2–316 gives force to an "as is" clause "unless the circumstances indicate otherwise." Moreover, by the terms of that section the "as is" clause must call the buyer's attention to the exclusion of all warranties and make that result "plain." Ambiguity arises by virtue of the fact that at the beginning of the contract, before the description of the vehicles sold, there is a clause providing, "Buyer accepts delivery in good condition." (Defendant claims that this provision provides an express warranty of quality.) Moreover, the form contract provided by the seller by its terms was applicable to the sale of either a new vehicle or a used vehicle. Defendant's uncontradicted affidavit recites that an "as is" clause by custom of the trade may be expected in the sale of used vehicles but not in the sale of new vehicles. Accordingly, whether or not the provision for "delivery in good condition" was intended to create an express warranty of quality, that clause, together with the inappropriateness of the "as is" clause in the sale of new trailers, would not "make it plain" to a buyer that the "as is" clause was intended to disclaim all implied warranties in this transaction. A buyer could reasonably expect that the clause in question was to apply only when the form contract was employed in the sale of used vehicles. This interpretation would make the provisions of the contract consistent with prevailing usage of trade and the previous course of dealing between the parties. Also, Gindy's undertaking to supply replacement parts and to have the vehicles repaired at its own cost, without disclaiming responsibility, without reliance on the "as is" clause, shows an interpretation by Gindy of this contract consistent with defendant's position.

The "as is" clause employed in the contract, even augmented by language stating "that no warranty express or implied arises apart from this writing," appears inappropriate to this transaction, given the usage of the trade and the dealings of the parties. All of that language was not sufficient to call attention and make plain to defendant that there was no implied warranty intended by the seller with respect to the sale of new vehicles as distinguished from used vehicles. Significantly, almost without exception, "as is" and similar expressions construed by the courts are found in cases dealing with the sale of used vehicles, articles or equipment. . . .

The effectiveness of an "as is" clause as a disclaimer is conditioned by the preamble of Section 2–316(3), namely, "unless the circumstances indicate otherwise." In the case at hand the circumstances do indicate otherwise. One buying a new vehicle under a contract requiring acceptance of delivery "in good condition" could readily say that in these circumstances "as is" means new and in good mechanical condition. This is exactly the interpretation which the parties gave to this instrument.

Accordingly, the "as is" clause in this contract is not effective to disclaim an implied warranty of merchantability, nor an implied warranty arising by usage of trade or course of dealing. . . . [T]he buyer should be assured of reasonable performance and not be deprived thereof by unexpected terms in a form contract.

For the foregoing reasons plaintiff's motion for summary judgment is denied. An appropriate order shall be submitted.

QUESTIONS AND NOTES

1. What warranty did plaintiff allegedly breach?

2. Based in part on the legislative history, the court concludes that the conspicuousness requirement in subsection (2) also exists in subsection (3). Please reread the court's recitation of this legislative history. Can you construct another interpretation of it, one that does not necessarily lead to the conclusion that the conspicuousness requirement exists in subsection (3)?

3. The court states (page 289) that it does not make sense to require conspicuousness in subsection (2) and not require it in subsection (3). The court's assertion of that proposition does not necessarily make the proposition true. See if you can construct an argument for the opposite proposition, viz., that there is a reason to require conspicuousness under subsection (2) but not require it under subsection (3). Is your argument persuasive?

4. **Problem.** *Dealer* sells a used car to *Consumer*, using a bill of sale that provides, on its face, "This vehicle is sold as is." As it turns out, the car is not fit to drive and would not pass without objection in the trade. Is the disclaimer effective?

5. Should "as is" be sufficient to disclaim implied warranties in transactions with consumers? According to several surveys commissioned by the Federal Trade Commission in the 1970s, approximately 25–50% of consumers do not understand the legal effect of that phrase. Many believe the phrase applies to apparent or disclosed defects (e.g, dings and dents) but not to latent defects. FTC, Staff Report, Sale of Used Motor Vehicles 263–65 (1978).

6. In Murray v. D & J Motor Company, Inc., 958 P.2d 823 (Okla.App. 1998), plaintiff told defendant's salesman that she needed a reliable van so that she could transport her ailing, disabled daughter. When plaintiff noticed a rattling noise during a test drive, the salesman told her that the engine had been replaced, that it had been inspected by a mechanic, and that there was nothing wrong with it. Plaintiff purchased the van, pursuant to documents that stated the vehicle was sold "as is." Within a day of the purchase, the engine broke down. The court stated:

> [A]mong the circumstances that could render a purported "as is" or "with all faults" disclaimer unreasonable and ineffective are fraudulent representations or misrepresentations concerning the condition, value, quality, characteristics or fitness of the goods sold that are relied upon by the Buyer to the Buyer's detriment. Therefore if the disclaimer ... [is] tainted with, or by, such misrepresentations or false representations, that then is a "circumstance" that will preclude an effective disclaimer. To hold otherwise would allow a seller to profit from his fraud and to be effectively granted a license to mislead or conceal facts.

Id. at 830 (reversing the action of the trial court in upholding defendant's demurrer to the evidence).

7. Problem. Buyer calls at Seller's furniture warehouse for the purpose of purchasing a large number of tables and chairs. One entire floor of the warehouse is covered with tables and chairs, and Buyer selects several of them at random and inspects them. The parties agree on the terms, and Buyer purchases the entire floor of merchandise. After delivery of the merchandise, Buyer discovers that many of the tables and chairs are defective. Is there a breach of warranty? Are additional facts necessary to resolve this problem? If so, what facts?

8. Even if a disclaimer meets the requirements of 2–316, it may nevertheless not be effective, in which event the buyer may recover for breach of implied warranty.

a. Personal injuries. If the buyer seeks to recover for personal injuries, the action may be in tort or in contract (warranty). In either case, the buyer is likely to recover. E.g., Henningsen v. Bloomfield Motors, Inc., 32 N.J. 358, 161 A.2d 69 (1960).

The Restatement (Third) of Torts, section 18 states that disclaimers or limitations of remedies do not bar or limit liability claims for injury to persons. However, the comments to that section state that it takes no position on whether disclaimers are effective as to injury to property. That is left to developing case law. The comments also state that nothing prevents sellers in the distributive chain from contracting among themselves as to who bears the risk of product liability claims. One of the basic assumptions about the development of the strict tort rules is that they prevent effective contract disclaimers, at least as to personal injury. It is highly likely, therefore, that even if a claim for personal injury is brought in warranty, the court will hold that any warranty disclaimer is ineffective to bar the claim.

b. Economic loss. In a landmark article, Professor Arthur Leff argued that a court cannot find that a disclaimer meeting the requirements of 2–316 is unconscionable. Leff, Unconscionability and the Code: The Emperor's New Clause, 115 U.Pa.L.Rev. 485, 516–528 (1966). As we have seen, the courts disagree. *A & M Produce v. FMC*, page 125 supra. See also Martin v. Joseph Harris Co., 767 F.2d 296 (6th Cir.1985):

> A threshold problem in this context is whether under Michigan law warranty disclaimers which comply with U.C.C. § 2–316 are limited by U.C.C. § 2–302. In holding Harris Seed's disclaimer clause unconscionable under the facts of this case, the district court implicitly held that U.C.C. § 2–302 is a limitation on U.C.C. § 2–316. Harris Seed argues that by enacting § 2–316 the Michigan Legislature "unequivocally [authorized the] exclusion or modification of the implied warranty of merchantability by disclaimer." We have been presented with no Michigan cases resolving this issue; however, a number of arguments support the district court's conclusion that § 2–316 is not insulated from review under § 2–302. First, § 2–302 provides that "any clause" of a contract may be found unconscionable. Similarly, "section 2–316 does not state expressly that all disclaimers meeting its requirements are immune from general policing provisions like section 2–302. . . ." J. White & R. Summers, *Handbook of the Law Under the Uniform Commercial Code*, § 12–11, at 476 (2d Ed. 1980). Had the drafters of the Uniform Commercial Code or the Michigan Legislature chosen to limit the application of § 2–302, language expressly so stating could easily have been included. Furthermore, as pointed out by Professors White and Summers:

>> Comment 1 [to § 2–302] lists and describes ten cases which are presumably intended to illustrate the underlying basis of the section: In seven of those cases disclaimers of warranty were denied full effect. It is difficult to reconcile the intent on the part of the draftsman to immunize disclaimers from the effect of 2–302 with the fact that they used cases in which courts struck down disclaimers to illustrate the concept of unconscionability.

> *Id.* (footnotes omitted). Therefore, because this issue is unsettled under Michigan law and according the district court's conclusion "considerable weight," we hold that the district court correctly relied upon § 2–302 as a limitation on § 2–316.

9. Recall *Anthony Pools*, page 11 supra, which revealed a non-uniform amendment to 2–316, invalidating disclaimers of implied warranties in consumer transactions. The federal government and many other states also have adopted special rules governing warranties in consumer transactions. Section D, page 338 infra, addresses these statutes. In some states, non-uniform legislation modifies 2–316 for all contracts, commercial as well as consumer. For example, Mississippi has deleted 2–316 entirely. Implied warranties of merchantability and fitness for a particular purpose arise under 2–314 and 2–315, but the phrase "unless excluded or modified" has been deleted from both sections. In 1987 Mississippi added a provision (2–315.1) that specifically states that written or oral disclaimers of the warranties of merchantability or fitness or attempts to limit liability for breach of the warranties are unenforceable. There is an exception for the sale of motor vehicles that are six or more years old or that have been driven more than 75,000 miles. In those transactions the seller may disclaim warranties or limit remedies by using a form prescribed by the state attorney general.

South Carolina permits disclaimers of implied warranties, but its non-uniform 2–316(2) provides that language to exclude implied warranties must be specific. Expressions such as "as is" and "with all faults" are not effective to disclaim warranties.

10.   Revised Article 2. The revisions to Articles 1 and 2 include changes to the definition of "conspicuous." If a state adopts the revisions to Article 1 but not to Article 2, the definition of "conspicuous" appears in revised 1–201(b)(10). Please read that section, noting especially the last sentence of Official Comment 10.

If the state adopts the revisions to both Articles, the definition applicable to Article 2 appears in revised 2–103(b), which tracks the revisions to the definition in revised Article 1 but adds language addressing conspicuousness in electronic transactions. See revised 2–103(b)(ii). The revised definition embraces the common practice of Internet sellers of providing that the buyer cannot complete the transaction without clicking that the buyer has accepted a particular term. The section also recognizes that in some commercial transactions on the Internet, purchasers program computers to place orders on events triggered without any human intervention. Therefore, the new section contains provisions relating to making language conspicuous when it will not be seen by any human before the deal is closed. Please read revised Article 2's definition of conspicuous now.

Do you think that the "click here to proceed" provision is sufficient to call an Internet buyer's attention to a disclaimer? Do you think that a clause, "sign here only if you have read the terms on the back," in a face-to-face transaction is sufficient to make a disclaimer conspicuous if it is not otherwise conspicuous? Are the two situations analogous? See the last sentence of revised 2–103, Official Comment 1.

Would the language of revised Article 2 change the outcome of *Sierra Diesel*?

Is *Gindy Manufacturing* still good law under revised 2–316? What is the relevance, if any, of the fact that subsection (3) was amended to require that in consumer transactions a disclaimer of implied warranties in a record be conspicuous?

11.   Leases. Section 2A–214 is the analog of 2–316 for leasing contracts. Subsection (2) requires that any disclaimer of the warranty of merchantability be conspicuous and in writing, and subsection (3)(a) imposes those same requirements on "as is" or "other similar language" disclaimers.

12. Problem. In need of a new home, Buyer goes to Seller Mobile Home Sales. Of the mobile homes that she views there, one is much more appealing than the rest. She tells Seller that she wants to buy a mobile home just like that one. "Ah," the salesman says, "that's the Dreamland, we can order you one just like it." Buyer and Seller sign a retail installment sales contract, for the sale of a Dreamland for $46,000, to be set up by Seller on a lot to be designated by Buyer. On the reverse side is a provision, "Seller disclaims all warranties, express or implied, including the implied warranty of merchantability." On the front side, above the signature line, is a statement, "Please read this contract carefully. Do not sign it if it contains any blanks. This contract is the entire agreement of parties and there are no other representations, warranties, or agreements." The Dreamland arrives and is installed, but it lacks several features of the home viewed by Buyer at Seller's lot: the heating and air conditioning system is less efficient than the one on the lot, the bedroom is somewhat smaller, and shortly after set-up a wall separates from the ceiling, allowing cold air and rain to leak into the home. When Buyer complains to Seller, Seller tells her to take it up with the manufacturer of the mobile home. Buyer comes to you for assistance. Does Buyer have a claim against Seller for breach of warranty?

B. PRIVITY AND WARRANTY

A buyer contracts to purchase a computer from a seller. If the computer is not merchantable, the seller has breached a warranty, and the buyer may recover for the loss sustained as a result of the breach. If the buyer has permitted her daughter to use the computer, may the daughter recover from the seller for loss she sustained as a result of the seller's breach of warranty? Alternatively, if a manufacturer sells a computer to a retailer, who resells it to a consumer, may the consumer recover from the manufacturer? In neither of these situations does the person responsible for the injury have a contract with the injured person. They are not in privity of contract. This section considers the liability of a seller to persons who purchase or are affected by the goods but who are not in privity of contract with the seller. As we will see, the answer may depend on

(1) whether the plaintiff asserts breach of express warranty or breach of implied warranty; and

(2) whether the plaintiff seeks damages for personal injuries, other direct damages, or consequential damages.

Randy Knitwear, Inc. v. American Cyanamid Co.

New York Court of Appeals, 1962.
11 N.Y.2d 5, 226 N.Y.S.2d 363, 181 N.E.2d 399.

■ FULD, JUDGE. "The assault upon the citadel of privity," Chief Judge Cardozo wrote in 1931, "is proceeding in these days apace." (Ultramares

Corp. v. Touche, 255 N.Y. 170, 180, 174 N.E. 441, 445, 74 A.L.R. 1139.) In these days, too, for the present appeal, here by leave of the Appellate Division on a certified question, calls upon us to decide whether, under the facts disclosed, privity of contract is essential to maintenance of an action against a manufacturer for breach of express warranty.

American Cyanamid Company is the manufacturer of chemical resins, marketed under the registered trade-mark "Cyana," which are used by textile manufacturers and finishers to process fabrics in order to prevent them from shrinking. Apex Knitted Fabrics and Fairtex Mills are manufacturers of fabrics who were licensed or otherwise authorized by Cyanamid to treat their goods with "Cyana" and to sell such goods under the "Cyana" label and, with the guaranty that they were "Cyana" finished. Randy Knitwear, a manufacturer of children's knitted sportswear and play clothes, purchased large quantities of these "Cyana" treated fabrics from Apex and Fairtex. After most of such fabrics had been made up into garments and sold by Randy to customers, it was claimed that ordinary washing caused them to shrink and to lose their shape. This action for breach of express warranty followed . . . .

Insofar as relevant, the complaint alleges that Cyanamid "represented" and "warranted" that the "Cyana" finished fabrics sold by Fairtex and Apex to the plaintiff would not shrink or lose their shape when washed and that the plaintiff purchased the fabrics and agreed to pay the additional charge for the cost involved in rendering them shrink-proof "in reliance upon" Cyanamid's representations. However, the complaint continues, the fabrics were not as represented since, when manufactured into garments and subjected to ordinary washing, they shrank and failed to hold their shape. The damages suffered are alleged to be over $208,000.

According to the complaint and the affidavits submitted in opposition to Cyanamid's motion, the representations relied upon by the plaintiff took the form of written statements expressed not only in numerous advertisements appearing in trade journals and in direct mail pieces to clothing manufacturers, but also in labels or garment tags furnished by Cyanamid. These labels bore the legend,

"A

CYANA

FINISH

This Fabric Treated for

SHRINKAGE

CONTROL

Will Not Shrink or

Stretch Out of Fit

CYANAMID,"

and were issued to fabric manufacturers using the "Cyana Finish" only after Cyanamid had tested samples of the fabrics and approved them. Cyanamid delivered a large number of these labels to Fairtex and Apex and they, with Cyanamid's knowledge and approval, passed them on to garment manufacturers, including the plaintiff, so that they might attach them to the clothing which they manufactured from the fabrics purchased.

. . . Cyanamid moved for summary judgment dismissing the complaint against it on the ground that there was no privity of contract to support the plaintiff's action. The court at Special Term denied the motion and the Appellate Division unanimously affirmed the resulting order.

Thirty-nine years ago, in Chysky v. Drake Bros. Co., 235 N.Y. 468, 139 N.E. 576, 27 A.L.R. 1533, this court decided that an action for breach of implied warranty could not succeed, absent privity between plaintiff and defendant and, some time later, in Turner v. Edison Storage Battery Co., 248 N.Y. 73, 161 N.E. 423, we reached a similar conclusion with respect to express warranties, writing, "There can be no warranty where there is no privity of contract" (p. 74, 161 N.E. p. 424).[2] This traditional privity limitation on a seller's liability for damage resulting from breach of warranty has not, however, been adhered to with perfect logical consistency and, just a year ago, in Greenberg v. Lorenz, 9 N.Y.2d 195, 213 N.Y.S.2d 39, 173 N.E.2d 773, we noted the definite shift away from the technical privity requirement and recognized that it should be dispensed with in a proper case in the interest of justice and reason. More specifically, we held in Greenberg that, in cases involving foodstuffs and other household goods, the implied warranties of fitness and merchantability run from the retailer to the members of the purchaser's household, regardless of privity of contract. We are now confronted with the further but related question whether the traditional privity limitation shall also be dispensed with in an action for breach of express warranty by a remote purchaser against a manufacturer who induced the purchase by representing the quality of the goods in public advertising and on labels which accompanied the goods.

It was in this precise type of case, where express representations were made by a manufacturer to induce reliance by remote purchasers, that "the citadel of privity" was successfully breached in the State of Washington in 1932. (See Baxter v. Ford Motor Co., 168 Wash. 456, 12 P.2d 409, 15 P.2d 1118.) It was the holding in the Baxter case that the manufacturer was liable for breach of express warranty to one who purchased an automobile

---

2. These decisions proceed, manifestly, from a characterization of the breach of warranty action as one essentially *contractual* in nature. The soundness of this characterization becomes highly questionable, however, when the problem is seen against the backdrop of legal history. The action for breach of warranty "was, in its origin, a pure action of tort". (Ames, Lectures on Legal History [1913], p. 136, reprinted, with revisions, from 2 Harv.L.Rev. 1, 8). Indeed, the earliest reported case upon a warranty arose in 1383 (Fitz. Abr. Monst. de Faits, pl. 160), a century before special assumpsit found its place among the forms of action. And it was not until 1778 that the first decision was report- ed in which an action on a warranty was brought in assumpsit. (Stuart v. Wilkins, 1 Dougl. 18.) Accordingly, for some 400 years the action rested not on an enforceable promise but on a wrong or tort. In the historical development of the law of warranty, however, as so often happens in law and life in general, accident was evidently confused with essence: from the fact that the cases which arose involved contractual relationships and represented enforceable promises, the courts seem to have concluded that the contract was of the essence of the action. The occasion for the warranty was constituted a necessary condition of it.

from a retailer since such purchaser had a right to rely on representations made by the manufacturer in its sales literature, even though there was no privity of contract between them. And in the 30 years which have passed since that decision, not only have the courts throughout the country shown a marked, and almost uniform, tendency to discard the privity limitation and hold the manufacturer strictly accountable for the truthfulness of representations made to the public and relied upon by the plaintiff in making his purchase,[3] but the vast majority of the authoritative commentators have applauded the trend and approved the result.

The rationale underlying the decisions rejecting the privity requirement is easily understood in the light of present-day commercial practices. It may once have been true that the warranty which really induced the sale was normally an actual term of the contract of sale. Today, however, the significant warranty, the one which effectively induces the purchase, is frequently that given by the manufacturer through mass advertising and labeling to ultimate business users or to consumers with whom he has no direct contractual relationship.

The world of merchandising is, in brief, no longer a world of direct contract; it is, rather, a world of advertising and, when representations expressed and disseminated in the mass communications media and on labels (attached to the goods themselves) prove false and the user or consumer is damaged by reason of his reliance on those representations, it is difficult to justify the manufacturer's denial of liability on the sole ground of the absence of technical privity. Manufacturers make extensive use of newspapers, periodicals and other media to call attention, in glowing terms, to the qualities and virtues of their products, and this advertising is directed at the ultimate consumer or at some manufacturer or supplier who is not in privity with them. Equally sanguine representations on packages and labels frequently accompany the article throughout its journey to the ultimate consumer and, as intended, are relied upon by remote purchasers. Under these circumstances, it is highly unrealistic to limit a purchaser's protection to warranties made directly to him by his immediate seller. The protection he really needs is against the manufacturer whose published representations caused him to make the purchase.

The policy of protecting the public from injury, physical or pecuniary, resulting from misrepresentations outweighs allegiance to an old and outmoded technical rule of law which, if observed, might be productive of great injustice. The manufacturer places his product upon the market and, by advertising and labeling it, represents its quality to the public in such a way as to induce reliance upon his representations. He unquestionably intends and expects that the product will be purchased and used in reliance upon his express assurance of its quality and, in fact, it is so purchased and used. Having invited and solicited the use, the manufacturer should not be permitted to avoid responsibility, when the expected use leads to injury and loss, by claiming that he made no contract directly with the user.

---

3. See, e.g., Burr v. Sherwin Williams Co., 42 Cal.2d 682, 696–697, 268 P.2d 1041; Rogers v. Toni Home Permanent Co., 167 Ohio St. 244, 147 N.E.2d 612.

It is true that in many cases the manufacturer will ultimately be held accountable for the falsity of his representations, but only after an unduly wasteful process of litigation. Thus, if the consumer or ultimate business user sues and recovers, for breach of warranty, from his immediate seller and if the latter in turn, sues and recovers against his supplier in recoupment of his damages and costs, eventually, after several separate actions by those in the chain of distribution, the manufacturer may finally be obliged "to shoulder the responsibility which should have been his in the first instance." (Hamon v. Digliani, 148 Conn. 710, 717, 174 A.2d 294, 297; see Kasler & Cohen v. Slavouski [1928], 1 K.B. 78, where there was a series of 5 recoveries, the manufacturer ultimately paying the consumer's damages, plus a much larger sum covering the costs of the entire litigation.) As is manifest, and as Dean Prosser observes this circuity of action is "an expensive, time-consuming and wasteful process, and it may be interrupted by insolvency, lack of jurisdiction, disclaimers, or the statute of limitations." (Prosser, The Assault upon the Citadel [Strict Liability to the Consumer], 69 Yale L.J. 1099, 1124.)

Indeed, and it points up the injustice of the rule, insistence upon the privity requirement may well leave the aggrieved party, whether he be ultimate business user or consumer, without a remedy in a number of situations. For instance, he would be remediless either where his immediate seller's representations as to quality were less extravagant or enthusiastic than those of the manufacturer[5] or where—as is asserted by Fairfax in this very case—there has been an effective disclaimer of any and all warranties by the plaintiff's immediate seller. Turning to the case before us, even if the representations respecting "Cyana" treated fabric were false, the plaintiff would be foreclosed of all remedy against Fairtex, if it were to succeed on its defense of disclaimer, and against Cyanamid because of a lack of privity.

. . .

We perceive no warrant for holding—as the appellant urges—that strict liability should not here be imposed because the defect involved, fabric shrinkage, is not likely to cause personal harm or injury. Although there is language in some of the opinions which appears to support Cyanamid's contention, most of the courts which have dispensed with the requirement of privity in this sort of case have not limited their decisions in this manner. (See, e.g., Burr v. Sherwin Williams Co., 42 Cal.2d 682, 696–697, 268 P.2d 1041 [insecticide; damage to crops]; State Farm Mut. Auto Ins. Co. v. Anderson–Weber, Inc., 110 N.W.2d 449 [Iowa], [automobile; property damage]; [additional citations omitted].) And this makes sense.

---

5. Typical of this would be a case where the consumer, relying on representations contained on labels or in advertisements for which the manufacturer is responsible, purchases a brand-name article from the shelves of the retailer. In such a case, the retailer ordinarily makes no express warranty and the purchaser may not even invoke an implied warranty of fitness. Consequently, if privity were prerequisite to an action by the consumer against the manufacturer, whose representations induced his purchase, he would (absent proof of negligence) be denied all redress except, perhaps, for breach of the implied warranty of merchantability (Personal Property Law, § 96, subd. 2).

Since the basis of liability turns not upon the character of the product but upon the representation, there is no justification for a distinction on the basis of the type of injury suffered or the type of article or goods involved.

. . .

Nor may it be urged that section 93 of the Personal Property Law renders privity of contract necessary. The Legislature has there defined a warranty as an "affirmation" (or "promise") made by a seller, but the section nowhere states that liability for breach of express warranty extends only to the warranting seller's immediate buyer and cannot extend to a later buyer who made the purchase from an intermediate seller but in foreseeable and natural reliance on the original seller's affirmations. Indeed, we made the matter clear in Greenberg v. Lorenz when, after observing that the rule requiring a direct contractual relationship between the plaintiff and the defendant is of "judicial making", we went on to say, "our statutes say nothing at all about privity" (9 N.Y.2d 195, 200, 213 N.Y.S.2d 39, 42, 173 N.E.2d 773, 775).

In concluding that the old court-made rule should be modified to dispense with the requirement of privity, we are doing nothing more or less than carrying out an historic and necessary function of the court to bring the law into harmony "with modern-day needs and with concepts of justice and fair dealing." (Bing v. Thunig, 2 N.Y.2d 656, 667, 163 N.Y.S.2d 3, 11, 143 N.E.2d 3, 9.)

The order appealed from should be affirmed, with costs, and the question certified answered in the negative.

QUESTIONS AND NOTES

1. *Randy Knitwear* arose shortly before New York adopted the UCC, so the applicable law was the Uniform Sales Act. As originally enacted, 2–318 consisted of what is now labeled 2–318 (Alternative A). It answers the first question posed at the beginning of this section, viz., is the seller of goods liable for breach of warranty to a person who the buyer permits to use the goods. What answer does it provide?

2. In 1966 the sponsoring organizations revised 2–318 to add two additional versions of that section. Please read those alternatives and the Official Comments. By far the most states have adopted Alternative A, but several states have adopted one of the others.

3. If a seller breaches an express warranty, the ultimate user may suffer direct economic loss, in the form of paying the price of conforming goods but receiving only nonconforming goods. See 2–714(2). In addition, the user may sustain consequential loss. See 2–714(3) and 2–715(2). In *Randy Knitwear* plaintiff suffered both kinds of loss. And in denying defendant's motion for summary judgment, the court apparently believed that plaintiff can recover both. Compare Beyond the Garden Gate, Inc. v. Northstar

Freeze–Dry Manufacturing, Inc., 526 N.W.2d 305 (Iowa1995), in which a manufacturer of a machine for freeze-drying flowers made affirmations of fact concerning the machine to the plaintiff, who then purchased one of the machines from another person. When the machine failed to operate as represented, plaintiff asserted breach of express warranty against the manufacturer. The jury awarded no damages for direct loss, but awarded $40,000 for lost profits and other consequential loss. In holding that a nonprivity plaintiff may at most recover for direct loss, the court quoted extensively from the White and Summers treatise:

> "Courts allow a nonprivity buyer to recover for direct economic loss damages if the remote seller has breached an express warranty." [James J. White & Robert S. Summers, *Uniform Commercial Code* § 11–5, at 538 (3d ed. 1988)]. "On the other hand, courts are split on whether to allow a nonprivity buyer to recover consequential economic loss damages." *Id.* at 539. White and Summers make a good argument for siding with those courts that have refused to allow remote or nonprivity buyers from recovering consequential economic loss damages:

> "We agree with those courts that have refused to allow recovery of consequential economic loss by remote buyers. Even if relevant policies justify allowing nonprivity consumers to recover for direct economic loss, there can be no justification in the usual case for allowing nonprivity consumer buyers to recover for consequential economic losses they sustain. Remote buyers may use a seller's goods for unknown purposes from which enormous losses might ensue. Since the remote seller cannot predict the purposes for which the goods will be used he faces unknown liability and may not be able to insure himself. Insurers are hesitant to insure against risks they cannot measure. Moreover, here more than in personal injury and property damage cases, it is appropriate to recognize the traditional rights of parties to make their own contract. If a remote seller wishes to sell at a lower price and exclude liability for consequential economic loss to subpurchasers, why should we deny him that right? Why should we design a system that forces him to bear the unforeseeable consequential economic losses of remote purchasers? Indeed, by forcing the buyer to bear such losses we may save costly law suits and even some economic losses against which buyers, knowing they have the responsibility, may protect themselves. In short, we believe that a buyer should pick his seller with care and recover any economic loss from that seller and not from parties remote from the transaction. Put another way, we believe the user is often the 'least cost avoider.' By placing the loss on him or by forcing him to bargain with his immediate seller about the loss, we may minimize the total loss to society. If the manufacturer is not the least cost risk avoider, but must nevertheless bear the loss, we may cause him to spend more of society's resources than are optimal to avoid the loss and may unnecessarily increase the cost of the commodity sold." *Id.* at 539–40. We agree and now hold that nonprivity buyers

who rely on express warranties are limited to direct economic loss damages.

Are you persuaded by the argument lifted from *White & Summers*? Granted that a manufacturer that places a tag on its goods or circulates a brochure about its product cannot foresee all uses to which remote buyers may put the product, was that the case in *BGG*? Please read 2–715(2), defining "consequential damages." How, if at all, is this definition relevant to the court's reasoning?

4. There are surprisingly few cases imposing liability for breach of express warranty on remote sellers. There are, however, even fewer decisions refusing to impose that liability. For three cases holding remote sellers liable for breaching their express warranties, see U.S. Tire–Tech, Inc. v. Boeran, 110 S.W.3d 194 (Tex.App.2003); Prairie Production, Inc. v. Agchem Div.–Pennwalt Corp., 514 N.E.2d 1299 (Ind.App.1987); and Ferguson v. Sturm, Roger & Co., 524 F.Supp. 1042 (D.Conn.1981). Contra Copiers Typewriters Calculators, Inc. v. Toshiba Corp., 576 F.Supp. 312 (D.Md. 1983) (under Maryland law a remote seller is not liable for breach of express warranty). Georgia courts reject express-warranty liability to remote parties unless, through such facts as the manufacturer's authorization to the retailer to deliver written warranties to the buyer, it appears that the remote seller intends the remote buyer to be the beneficiary of its warranties. But see Lamb v. Georgia–Pacific Corp., 194 Ga.App. 848, 392 S.E.2d 307 (1990) (to the extent that the defective product damaged other property, a strict tort action would lie).

As *Randy Knitwear* suggests, it might be more rational to treat cases in which a buyer relies on representations by a remote seller, in advertising or otherwise, as involving the tort of misrepresentation. See Hill, Damages for Innocent Misrepresentation, 73 Colum.L.Rev. 679 (1973).

5. In Minnesota Mining & Manufacturing Co. v. Nishika Ltd., 565 N.W.2d 16 (Minn.1997), 3M, a manufacturer of photo-finishing emulsion, expressly warranted to two photo-processing companies that the emulsion would work well in their process for producing 3–dimensional images. In fact, it did not work well at all, and the purchasers went out of business. The manufacturer also communicated the express warranty to two camera companies whose business depended on the ability of the photo-processors to process the photographs taken by the cameras they produced. These camera companies also failed, and they sued 3M for the consequential damages (i.e. lost profits) they sustained. The dispute was governed by the law of Minnesota, which has adopted a variant of Alternative C of 2–318:

> A seller's warranty whether express or implied extends to any person who may reasonably be expected to use, consume or be affected by the goods and who is injured by breach of the warranty. A seller may not exclude or limit the operation of this section.

Denying recovery, the court stated:

> We agree with 3M that the statute is not so clear and free from ambiguity that we may disregard legislative intent, the aims of section

336.2–318 at the time of enactment, or the consequences of a particular construction. The unadorned term "injured" is not defined in the U.C.C., nor is it used elsewhere in the text of Article 2. As applied to [plaintiffs], the reach of section 336.2–318 is unclear. We must therefore interpret the statute consistent with legislative intent and in a sensible manner that avoids unreasonable, unjust, or absurd results.

Under section 336.2–318, this court has sanctioned the recovery of lost profits (one form of economic loss) by a third-party beneficiary whose damages arose from a remote seller's breach of warranty. We have also indicated that plaintiffs who never used, purchased, or otherwise acquired defective goods may qualify as third-party beneficiaries when they suffer property damage.

But this court has never gone so far as to hold that section 336.2–318 reaches a plaintiff who is seeking lost profits unaccompanied by physical injury or property damage and who never used, purchased, or otherwise acquired the goods in question. To do so, we believe, would expand warranty liability well beyond the limits contemplated by the legislature.

When placed in historical context, it seems clear that the primary motivation for the current version of section 336.2–318 was concern for injured consumers. A prevalent legal conflict at the time of enactment was how best to protect consumers from dangerous products. One route was to expand the doctrine of "warranty" to reach subpurchasers and others injured in person by defective products. During the 1960s, however, the preferred course was to recognize that the concept of "warranty" had been outgrown and to legitimize recovery in tort. See William L. Prosser, The Fall of the Citadel (Strict Liability to the Consumer), 50 Minn. L. Rev. 791, passim (1966) (recounting the legal battle to break down the barrier of "privity," which culminated in widespread adoption of strict products liability in tort). Despite the promulgation of Restatement of Torts (Second) § 402A in 1965 . . ., the drafters of the model U.C.C. presented states with Alternative C of the third-party beneficiaries provision, which was intended to follow the trend of strict products liability and extend warranty protection "beyond injuries to the person." U.C.C. § 2–318 cmt. 3. But the expansion of warranty protection to certain classes of noncontracting parties in the U.C.C. cannot be completely detached from the concerns that motivated our legislature in 1969.

Our understanding of the background and aims of section 336.2–318 leads us to conclude that the scope of a seller's liability for breach of warranty should recede as the relationship between a "beneficiary" of the warranty and the seller's goods becomes more remote. . . . [T]hose who purchase, use, or otherwise acquire warranted goods have standing to sue for purely economic losses. Those who lack any such connection to the warranted goods must demonstrate physical injury or property damage before economic losses are recoverable. This line comports with legislative intent, provides a clear rule of law, and identifies a sensible limit to liability without disrupting settled precedent.

Any other result implies almost unlimited liability for sellers of warranted goods. If section 336.2–318 were interpreted as the [plaintiffs] advocate, it seems that the [plaintiffs'] individual employees, or perhaps even their families, would have standing to sue 3M for causing the loss of their jobs or even a decline in their wages. The [plaintiffs'] reading also appears to allow recovery on the facts of Nebraska Innkeepers, Inc. v. Pittsburgh–Des Moines Corp., 345 N.W.2d 124 (Iowa 1984), in which plaintiffs connected with motel, restaurant, bar, and retail businesses invoked Iowa's third-party beneficiaries provision in an attempt to sue solely for economic losses arising from a bridge closing; the closing was allegedly caused by the defendant-seller's defective steel. That attempt to expand the scope of the U.C.C. was rejected. The [plaintiffs] appear to advocate warranty recovery as a catch-all alternative for [persons] with no viable legal basis for suit. The risk, however, is that the fortuitous existence of a warranty—between some seller and some buyer, somewhere—would allow remote yet foreseeable parties to recover for their hampered expectations, while others in similar circumstances—but who could not identify a warranty—would not. Cf. Cunningham v. Kartridg Pak Co., 332 N.W.2d 881, 885 (Iowa 1983) ("Plaintiff is not an injured consumer; he was a shareholder of a corporation whose expectations did not materialize. To allow a shareholder to use products liability law as the vehicle to a direct cause of action otherwise denied by general corporate law would be an injustice to both areas of the law.").

Confronted with liability of this magnitude, sellers would be encouraged to attempt to disclaim warranties or exclude consequential damages remedies—affecting both the immediate buyer and third-party beneficiaries alike.

We therefore reject the [plaintiffs'] reading of the statute—an interpretation that would likely lead to a variety of unreasonable, unjust, and absurd results that we cannot imagine were intended by the legislature. In light of the statute's language and purpose, and consistent with the legislature's apparent intent, the best reading of section 336.2–318 is that noncontracting parties who never used, purchased, or otherwise acquired the seller's warranted goods may not seek lost profits, unaccompanied by physical injury or property damage, for breach of warranty under the statute. [Plaintiffs] are simply not within the class of warranty "beneficiaries" protected by section 336.2–318.

6.   Revised Article 2. The extent of a seller's express warranty to remote purchasers was one of the hotly debated issues in the revision of Article 2. The result is a revision of 2–313 and the addition of two new sections, 2–313A and 2–313B. Revised section 2–313 is specifically limited to immediate buyers. Both new sections do not call the obligations created under their provisions warranties; rather, they are simply obligations.

Section 2–313A apples to information packaged with or accompanying the goods and which the seller reasonably expects to be given, and is given, to the remote purchaser. That section provides that the remote seller has an obligation that "the goods will conform to the affirmation of fact, promise or description in the supplied information unless a reasonable person in the position of the remote purchaser would not believe that the affirmation of fact, promise or description created an obligation." There is no requirement, as there is as to immediate buyers, that the affirmation of fact, promise, or description, become a part of the basis of the bargain.

2A–313B applies to an affirmation of fact, promise, or description of the goods in advertising or "a similar communication to the public." If a remote purchaser knows of, and expects the goods to conform to, the statement at the time of the purchase of the goods, the seller has an obligation that the goods will conform to the statement.

The remedies under both 2–313A and 2–313B can be modified or limited if the modification or limitation is made in the information given to the remote buyer or the advertising or if the modification is made at the time of purchase by the remote buyer. Liability for breach of the express warranty includes incidental and consequential damages, except that lost profits are not recoverable. Both sections protect only buyers of new goods.

Since the "obligations" under 2–313A and 2–313B are not "warranties," 2–316, which refers only to exclusion or modification of warranties, may not apply to disclaimers under those sections.

Please read 2–313A and 2–313B. Then consider the following questions.

a. If a remote buyer never opens or reads the record packaged with the goods, is the buyer nevertheless entitled to enforce any representations, promises, or descriptions if a reasonable person would believe that they created an obligation? If so, does the same rule apply as to a transaction between the seller and an immediate purchaser under revised 2–313?

Most courts have assumed that the "basis of the bargain" language of 2–313 requires reliance on the statements, representations, or models that create the warranty and that there cannot be reliance without knowledge. However, it has been argued that there are two kinds of express warranties. One arises from sales-pitch assertions about the quality of the goods. The other arises from specific terms of the sales contract under which the seller makes certain promises as to the characteristics of the goods. The second type of warranty, like any other contract term, should be binding on the seller, whether or not the buyer knows of it. It is a part of the deal. On the other hand, the sales-pitch statement about the quality of the goods is an inducement to the sale, but is not a term of the contract and, therefore, should create liability only if the buyer reasonably relies on it. Of course, 2–313 makes no such distinction between types of warranties.

Perhaps new 2–313A adopts the view that records packaged with or accompanying goods which the remote seller intends to be delivered to the remote purchaser should, like contract terms, be binding whether or not the remote buyer knows of them. The Official Comments to 2–313A lend some support to the idea that the obligation that arises under 2–313A is binding whether or not it is a part of the basis of the bargain. Official Comment 1 states: "Use of 'obligation' rather than 'express warranty' avoids any inference that the obligation arises as part of the basis of the bargain as would be required to create an express warranty section under 2–313."

b. Under 2–313B a seller has liability to a remote purchaser only if the remote purchaser knows of the representation, etc., at the time of the purchase and has the expectation that the goods will conform to the representation. How is that requirement different from the "basis of the bargain" requirement of revised 2–313?

c. Observe that both 2–313A and 2–313B contain provisions permitting the remote seller to modify or limit its liability for breach of its obligations arising under those sections. However, neither section discusses a disclaimer of liability (as distinguished from a modification or limitation of liability) for breach of obligations arising under those sections. Do you think that the provisions of revised 2–316(1) should apply to disclaimers of liability under 2–313A or 2–313B?

d. If a record packaged with goods is not read or called to the attention of the remote purchaser until after the purchase, are disclaimers of the implied warranty of merchantability or of fitness for particular purpose which appear in the record nevertheless binding on the remote purchaser? Would the disclaimer be effective if the immediate seller directs the remote purchaser to read the record before purchase even though the purchaser does not comply with the request? Would the disclaimer be effective if the remote purchaser asserts rights under the statements in the record which create express obligations? See the following cases on liability of remote sellers for breach of implied warranties. See also Denny v. Ford Motor Co., page 247 supra.

e.   Problem. As a regular part of her business, Distributor (a seller of diesel generators) periodically visits the dealers that purchase her products for resale. While visiting Retailer one day, Distributor overheard one of Retailer's sales reps interacting with a customer, Buyer. When the sales rep seemed unsure of the answer to a question posed by Buyer, Distributor intervened to say, "The model you're looking at will run for 36 hours with an emission level safe for infants." Buyer purchased the generator. During a power outage that lasted for three days, the generator ran out of fuel after 24 hours. The food in buyer's refrigerator and stand-alone freezer spoiled. Under revised Article 2, can Buyer recover from Distributor?

―――――

The foregoing materials concern primarily liability to nonprivity plaintiffs for breach of express warranty. Liability for breach of implied warranty presents additional considerations.

Tex Enterprises, Inc. v. Brockway Standard, Inc.

Washington Supreme Court, 2003.
149 Wn.2d 204, 66 P.3d 625.

■ EN BANC. OWENS, J. A commercial purchaser seeks to recover economic damages from a manufacturer for breach of implied warranties under Article 2 of the Uniform Commercial Code, Title 62A RCW (UCC). The plaintiff asserts that implied warranties arose out of the manufacturer's verbal assurances as to the quality of his product, made directly to the plaintiff. However, the plaintiff ultimately purchased the product from an intermediate distributor, not the manufacturer. Furthermore, an agreement between the manufacturer and the distributor contained a disclaimer of all warranties. Thus, absent privity between the plaintiff and the manufacturer, and without reliance on the contract between the manufacturer and the distributor as a third party beneficiary, we hold that such assurances do not give rise to implied warranties.

FACTS

Brockway Standard, Inc. (Brockway) is a Georgia corporation that manufactures three- and five-gallon unlined steel containers, treated only with a rust inhibitor. J.F. Shelton Company (Shelton) is a Washington distributor of Brockway products. Tex Enterprises, Inc. (Tex) is a Washington corporation that purchases three- and five-gallon containers in which it ships and stores Spantex, a liquid coating used to seal decks and other exterior surfaces. Brockway sells its containers to Shelton, who in turn sells them to Washington purchasers like Tex. [When Shelton placed an order with Brockway,] Brockway would ship the goods and mail an invoice. On the back of the invoice, terms and conditions were printed which warranted only that the goods would be free from defects in workmanship and materials. The terms explicitly disclaimed all other warranties, express or implied, and limited damages to refund of the purchase price and cost of return shipping. An additional clause required that Georgia law govern the agreement. Although Shelton had received multiple invoices over the course of its relationship with Brockway, these terms were never negotiated, and Shelton was unaware of their existence until the inception of this lawsuit.

Similarly, Tex's practice was to place verbal orders with Shelton for Brockway products. No party has referred to any written agreement between Tex and Shelton. Furthermore, because Tex never ordered directly from Brockway, Tex was unaware of the disclaimer, remedy limitation clause, and choice of law clause printed on Brockway's invoices. No similar disclaimers or limitations were printed anywhere on Brockway products or their packaging, and Shelton never notified Tex that the disclaimers existed.

Prior to September 1997, Tex used Brockway one-gallon tin cans to store and ship Spantex, but used another company's three- and five-gallon steel containers. In September 1997, [a Shelton representative and a Brockway representative visited Tex's president], with the objective of persuading him to switch to Brockway three- and five-gallon containers for storing and shipping Spantex. [They] toured the Tex facility and examined the containers that Tex was using. [The Brockway rep] told [Tex's president] that Brockway containers were "just as good" for storing Spantex as the containers Tex was using. . . . Relying on these representations, [Tex] agreed to switch to Brockway containers. Ultimately, Tex purchased 4,800 Brockway containers in which it stored and shipped more than 22,000 gallons of Spantex to its customers.

In the spring of 1998, Tex began to receive complaints from retail and consumer customers. The Spantex that was stored in the three- and five-gallon Brockway containers had begun to thicken and solidify, rendering it useless. Tex claims that the problem was caused by a reaction between the Spantex and the rust inhibitor with which the containers were treated. Tex expected that its costs for replacing the ruined Spantex would exceed $440,000.

Tex sued both Brockway and Shelton, claiming that it was entitled to recovery under a variety of theories including breach of express warranty, breach of implied warranty of merchantability, breach of implied warranty of fitness for a particular purpose, and breach of contract (against Shelton only). Tex sought to recover its costs for replacing the ruined product, incidental and consequential damages, disposal costs, and attorney fees. Shelton settled with Tex and is no longer a party to this lawsuit.

Brockway responded that the language on its invoices limited the claims and remedies available to Tex. . . . [T]he trial court . . . dismissed all claims based upon the disclaimers printed on the Brockway invoices and lack of privity.

The Court of Appeals agreed that any third party beneficiary claims would depend upon Shelton's agreement with Brockway, which was limited by the language on Brockway's invoices. Still, the court reversed and remanded, holding instead that "direct representations to the purchaser can create express *and implied* warranties that run to the purchaser independent of any contract between the manufacturer and distributor." (emphasis added).

. . .

ISSUE

Can an implied warranty arise from a manufacturer's direct representation to a remote commercial purchaser, absent a contract between the parties or reliance as a third party beneficiary on the contract between the manufacturer and its immediate buyer?

ANALYSIS

When reviewing an order of summary judgment, this court engages in the same inquiry as the trial court. Thus, we must affirm the trial court's summary judgment on this issue if we determine that there is no genuine issue of material fact and Brockway is entitled to judgment as a matter of law. The facts and reasonable inferences from the facts must be considered in the light most favorable to Tex as the nonmoving party.

Article 2 of the UCC, as adopted in Washington, governs . . . . [L]ack of privity has historically been a defense to claims of breach of warranty. There are two types of plaintiffs for whom lack of privity has been a concern. A " 'horizontal' non-privity plaintiff" is not a buyer of the product in question, but is one who consumes or is affected by the goods. The " 'vertical' non-privity plaintiff" is a buyer who is in the distributive chain, but who did not buy the product directly from the defendant. Tex is a vertical nonprivity plaintiff.

By adopting alternative A of section 2–318 . . . , the Washington Legislature chose to eliminate the privity requirement for horizontal non-privity plaintiffs under certain circumstances. . . . UCC comment 3 to section 2–318, as adopted in Washington, notes that this provision is silent with regard to vertical privity, but the section "is not intended to enlarge or restrict the developing case law on whether the seller's warranties, given to his buyer who resells, extend to other persons in the distributive chain." RCWA 62A.2–318 U.C.C. cmt. 3, at 207 (purpose); see also RCWA 62A.2–318 Wash. cmt. at 206 (noting comment 3 is emphatic that the section was intended to be neutral with regard to vertical privity). Thus, questions regarding the extension of warranties to vertical nonprivity plaintiffs are left to the courts.

In Baughn v. Honda Motor Co., 107 Wn.2d 127, 727 P.2d 655 (1986), this court upheld a trial court's summary judgment order in favor of a manufacturer, dismissing the remote purchasers' claims for breach of implied warranty. The *Baughn* court adopted the traditional rule that a plaintiff may not bring an implied warranty action under the UCC without contractual privity. It is important to note that the *Baughn* court would have allowed a plaintiff's express warranty claim to proceed because "[t]he privity requirement is relaxed . . . when a manufacturer makes express representations, in advertising or otherwise, to a plaintiff." Id. at 151–52

A few years later in [Touchet Valley Grain Growers, Inc. v. Opp & Seibold General Construction, Inc., 119 Wn.2d 334, 831 P.2d 724 (1992)], this court created an exception to the privity requirement for implied warranties. The *Touchet Valley* court allowed a vertical nonprivity plaintiff to recover where the plaintiff was the intended third party beneficiary of the implied warranty that the manufacturer gave to its intermediate dealer. Notably, the *Touchet Valley* court did not overturn *Baughn*. Instead, it distinguished *Baughn* based in part on the fact that "the analysis was not based on a third party beneficiary argument." Thus, we conclude that *Touchet Valley* carved a third party beneficiary exception out of the general rule that a vertical nonprivity plaintiff cannot recover from a remote manufacturer for breach of implied warranty.

The Court of Appeals in this case held that a manufacturer's direct verbal representations to a remote purchaser can create express and implied warranties that run to the remote purchaser, independent of any contract between the manufacturer and the intermediate distributor. However, allowing implied warranties to arise without reliance on an underlying contract is inconsistent with both the plain language of RCW 62A.2–314 and –315 and this court's prior approach to implied warranties.

First, the plain language of both RCW 62A.2–314 and –315 requires that implied warranties arise only out of contractual relationships. RCW 62A.2–314 states that the warranty that goods shall be merchantable is "implied in a contract for their sale." Similarly, RCW 62A.2–315 explains that the implied warranty of fitness for a particular purpose arises based on the seller's understanding "at the time of contracting." This language can be contrasted with RCW 62A.2–313 (express warranties), the language of which does not refer to an underlying "contract." Thus, the plain meaning of this statutory language forecloses application of implied warranties where there is no underlying contract to which the purchaser is a party or an intended third party beneficiary.

In addition, Tex has failed to cite to any case in which this court has allowed a vertical nonprivity plaintiff to recover economic damages for breach of implied warranty without reliance on some underlying contract. Such a restriction is justified because, to be enforceable, contractual relationships under the UCC must be formed according to the Code's safeguards, making contractual relationships comparatively formalized. See, e.g., RCW 62A.2–201 (statute of frauds). In contrast, express representations, made in advertisements or otherwise, require no formalities. Thus, we recognize that allowing implied warranties to arise out of express representations could leave a manufacturer unable to adequately predict when implied warranties will attach.

This court has also distinguished between express and implied warranties, restricting recovery for breach of implied warranty where it would have allowed recovery for breach of express warranty. See *Baughn*, 107 Wn.2d at 151–52. Because implied warranties arise by operation of law without specific adoption by the seller, we recognize that such warranties must be more closely guarded than express warranties, whose adoption requires some voluntary action.

The combination of the plain language of the statutory scheme and this court's prior treatment of implied warranties overcomes the reasoning of the Court of Appeals in this case. . . .

The Court of Appeals also adopted the reasoning of the Florida Court of Appeals in Cedars of Lebanon Hospital Corp. v. European X–Ray Distributors of America, Inc., 444 So. 2d 1068 (Fla. Ct. App. 1984), a case involving a fact pattern similar to this one. The Cedars court reasoned that it would be "fundamentally unfair . . . to allow the manufacturer to hide behind the doctrine of privity when the product, which it induced the purchaser to buy, turns out to be worthless." *Cedars*, 444 So. 2d at 1072. The *Cedars* court also hoped to avoid prolonged indemnity litigation, gradually advancing up the chain of privity. However, both of these concerns are easily alleviated where the plaintiff is allowed to pursue a claim under breach of express warranty, something that Washington law clearly allows in this case. Therefore, we find the *Cedars* reasoning unconvincing.

It is important to note that Tex and future vertical nonprivity plaintiffs are not left without recourse. We emphasize that this court has already clearly established that the privity requirement is relaxed where a manufacturer makes express representations to a plaintiff. In fact, the issue of whether an express warranty was made in this case still remains to be decided by the trial court. . . . Finally, where a commercial plaintiff can show that it is the intended third party beneficiary of a contract between the manufacturer and its direct purchaser, recovery may be available under a third party beneficiary analysis.

For all of the reasons discussed above, we hold that implied warranties do not arise out of express representations made by a manufacturer to a remote commercial purchaser absent privity or reliance on some underlying contract.

CONCLUSION

We reverse the Court of Appeals with regard to the implied warranty claim and hold that in cases where a commercial purchaser seeks to recover economic damages from a remote manufacturer, implied warranties do not arise absent privity or an underlying contract to which the remote commercial purchaser is a third party beneficiary.

———

Morrow v. New Moon Homes, Inc.

Alaska Supreme Court, 1976.
548 P.2d 279.

■ RABINOWITZ, CHIEF JUSTICE. . . .

In October of 1969, Joseph R. and Nikki Morrow bought a mobile home from Golden Heart Mobile Homes, a Fairbanks retailer of mobile homes. A plaque on the side of the mobile home disclosed that the home had been manufactured in Oregon by New Moon Homes, Inc. The Morrows made a down payment of $1,800, taking out a loan for the balance of the purchase price from the First National Bank of Fairbanks. The loan amount of $10,546.49, plus interest of 9 percent per year, was to be repaid by the Morrows in 72 monthly installments of $190.13 each.

At the time of the purchase, the Morrows inspected the mobile home and noticed that the carpeting had not been laid and that several windows were broken. Roy Miller, Golden Heart's salesman, assured them that these problems would be corrected and later made good his assurances. Miller also told the Morrows that the mobile home was a "good trailer," " * * * as warm as * * * any other trailer." After the sale, Miller moved the Morrows' mobile home to Lakeview Terrace, set it up on the space the

Morrows had rented, and made sure that the utilities were connected. Then the troubles started.

On the first night that the mobile home's furnace was in use, the motor went out and had to be replaced. The electric furnace installed by the manufacturer had been removed by someone who had replaced the original with an oil furnace. The furnace vent did not fit, and consequently the "stove pipe" vibrated when the furnace was running. Subsequent events showed the furnace malfunction was not the primary problem with the mobile home.

About four days after the mobile home had been set up, the Morrows noticed that the doors did not close all the way and that the windows were cracked. The bathtub leaked water into the middle of the bedroom. In March of 1970 when the snow on the roof began to melt, the roof leaked. Water came in through gaps between the ceiling and the wall panels, as well as along the bottom of the wallboard. A short circuit developed in the electrical system; the lights flickered at various times. When it rained, water came out of the light fixture in the hallway. Other problems with the mobile home included the following: the interior walls did not fit together at the corners; the paneling came off the walls; the windows and doors were out of square; the door frames on the bedroom doors fell off and the closet doors would not slide properly; the curtains had glue on them; and the finish came off the kitchen cabinet doors.

Despite all these problems, the Morrows continued to live in the mobile home and make the loan payments. Golden Heart Mobile Homes was notified many times of the difficulties the Morrows were having with their mobile home. Roy Miller, the Golden Heart salesman with whom the Morrows had dealt, did put some caulking around the bathtub, but otherwise he was of little assistance. Finally, sometime before April 1, 1970, Nikki Morrow informed Miller that if Golden Heart did not fix the mobile home the Morrows wanted to return it. Miller said the Morrows would "[h]ave to take it up with the bank." Subsequently Golden Heart went out of business.

The First National Bank of Fairbanks was more sensitive to the Morrows' plight. Upon being informed by the Morrows that they intended to make no further payments on the mobile home, bank personnel went out and inspected the home several times. In addition on May 27, 1970, the bank wrote to New Moon Homes, Inc. in Silverton, Oregon. Its letter informed New Moon of the problems the Morrows were having with their New Moon mobile home and asked whether New Moon expected to send a representative to Fairbanks since Golden Heart, the dealer, was no longer in business. Apparently, New Moon did not respond to the bank's letter.

A short time later the Morrows' counsel wrote a letter to New Moon Homes notifying New Moon that the Morrows intended to hold the company liable for damages for breach of implied warranties. About a month later the Morrows separated, with Nikki Morrow continuing to live in the mobile home. She continued to make payments to First National because she "couldn't afford Alaskan rents." Nikki Morrow eventually moved out of the mobile home but made no effort to sell or rent it because she considered it "not fit to live in." In October of 1971 the Morrows filed this action against both New Moon Homes and Golden Heart Mobile Homes, alleging that defendants had breached implied warranties of merchantability and fitness for particular purpose in manufacturing and selling an improperly constructed mobile home. . . .

. . . The superior court granted the Morrows a default judgment against Golden Heart, but dismissed their claim against New Moon "for both failure of jurisdiction and failure of privity of contract." The Morrows then appealed from that portion of the superior court's judgment which dismissed their claim against New Moon.

The heart of this appeal concerns the remedies which are available to a remote purchaser against the manufacturer of defective goods for direct economic loss. The superior court held that the Morrows had no legal claim against New Moon because they were not in privity of contract with New Moon. The first argument advanced here by the Morrows amounts to an end run around the requirement of privity. The Morrows contend that their complaint asserted a theory of strict liability in tort. They further argue that they should have prevailed irrespective of any lack of privity of contract between New Moon and themselves, because lack of privity of contract is not a defense to a strict tort liability claim. . . . [T]he Morrows argue that strict liability should . . . apply in the situation where a consumer sues a manufacturer solely for economic loss attributable to the manufacturer's defective product. This precise contention presents a question of first impression in Alaska.

The issue whether strict liability in tort should extend to economic loss has prompted no small amount of discussion in legal journals. . . .

. . . Under the Uniform Commercial Code the manufacturer is given the right to avail himself of certain affirmative defenses which can minimize his liability for a purely economic loss. Specifically, the manufacturer has the opportunity, pursuant to AS 45.05.100 [UCC 2–316], to disclaim liability and under AS 45.05.230 [UCC 2–719] to limit the consumer's remedies, although the Code further provides that such disclaimers and limitations cannot be so oppressive as to be unconscionable and thus violate AS 45.05.072 [UCC 2–302]. In addition, the manufacturer is entitled to reasonably prompt notice from the consumer of the claimed breach of warranties, pursuant to AS 45.05.174(c)(1) [UCC 2–607(3)(a)].

In our view, recognition of a doctrine of strict liability in tort for economic loss would seriously jeopardize the continued viability of these rights. The economically injured consumer would have a theory of redress not envisioned by our legislature when it enacted the U.C.C., since this strict liability remedy would be completely unrestrained by disclaimer, liability limitation and notice provisions. Further, manufacturers could no longer look to the Uniform Commercial Code provisions to provide a predictable definition of potential liability for direct economic loss. In short, adoption of the doctrine of strict liability for economic loss would be contrary to the legislature's intent when it authorized the aforementioned remedy limitations and risk allocation provisions of Article II of the Code. To extend strict tort liability to reach the Morrows' case would in effect be an assumption of legislative prerogative on our part and would vitiate clearly articulated statutory rights. This we decline to do. Thus, we hold that the theory of strict liability in tort ... does not extend to the consumer who suffers only economic loss because of defective goods.

The principal theory of liability advocated by the Morrows at trial was that New Moon had breached statutory warranties which arose by operation of law with the manufacture and distribution of this mobile home. Specifically, the Morrows rely upon AS 45.05.096 [UCC 2–314] and AS 45.05.098 [UCC 2–315] of the Uniform Commercial Code as enacted in Alaska. The former section provides for an implied warranty of "merchantability" in the sale of goods governed by the Code; the latter establishes an implied warranty that the goods are fit for the particular purpose for which they were purchased. The superior court was of the view that these Code warranties operated only for the benefit of those purchasing directly from a manufacturer or seller. Since the Morrows were not in privity of contract with New Moon, the superior court concluded that a warranty theory based on AS 45.05.096 and AS 45.05.098 could not serve as a basis for liability.

. . .

... The critical question in this case is whether the Morrows, as remote purchasers, can invoke the warranties attributable to the manufacturer which arose when New Moon passed title of the mobile home to the next party in the chain of distribution. In other words, do the implied warranties of merchantability and fitness run from a manufacturer only to those with whom the manufacturer is in privity of contract?

Although sometimes criticized, the distinction between horizontal and vertical privity is significant in this case. The issue of horizontal privity raises the question whether persons other than the buyer of defective goods can recover from the buyer's immediate seller on a warranty theory. The question of vertical privity is whether parties in the distributive chain prior to the immediate seller can be held liable to the ultimate purchaser for loss caused by the defective product. The Code addresses the matter of horizontal privity in AS 45.05.104 [UCC 2–318], extending the claim for relief in warranty to any " * * * person who is in the family or household of his buyer or who is a guest in his home if it is reasonable to expect that the person may use, consume, or be affected by the goods * * *." With regard to vertical privity, the Code is totally silent and strictly neutral, as Official Comment 3 to AS 45.05.104 makes eminently clear. The Code leaves to the courts the question of the extent to which vertical privity of contract will or will not be required.[25]

25. By this statement we do not mean to intimate that the matter of horizontal privity is exclusively controlled by AS 45.05.104. The fact that a given plaintiff is not expressly authorized to sue for breach of warranty under that provision will not preclude this court from possibly holding at some future date, as a matter of case law, that plaintiff is not barred by a requirement of horizontal privity.

This court has never previously confronted the question whether a requirement of privity of contract will preclude a purchaser from recovering against the original manufacturer on a theory of implied warranties. . . . [I]n Clary v. Fifth Avenue Chrysler Center, Inc., 454 P.2d 244 (Alaska 1969), [we expressly held] that a manufacturer is strictly liable in tort for personal injuries attributable to his defective goods. In approving a theory based on strict liability in tort, we stressed the efficacy, simplicity, and comprehensiveness of that theory. Appellees in *Clary* had urged this court to limit the consumer's source of redress to possible application of the statutory provisions governing sales warranties, particularly AS 45.05.096 [UCC 2–314]. This we declined to do. As we have noted, under the statutory scheme an injured consumer is required to give notice of the defect to the warrantor within a relatively short period of time, and potential liability may be circumscribed by express disclaimers from the manufacturer. The *Clary* court was concerned that such provisions might operate as a trap for the unwary, and it expressed a preference for a tort theory more solicitous of the needs of the consumer in the modern, prepackaged, mass merchandised market place. However, this preference was never intended to imply that reliance on the statutory warranty provisions was not available as an alternative vehicle for relief. There is nothing incompatible in affording parallel consumer remedies sounding in tort and in contract, and several jurisdictions which have adopted strict liability in tort also make available an implied warranty theory without regard to privity of contract.

The dispute here is whether the requirement of vertical privity of contract should be abolished in Alaska. This battle has already been waged in many jurisdictions, and the results are well known: the citadel of privity has largely toppled. The course of this modern development is familiar history and we need not recount it at length here. Contrived "exceptions" which paid deference to the hoary doctrine of privity while obviating its unjust results have given way in more recent years to an open frontal assault. The initial attack came in Spence v. Three Rivers Builders & Masonry Supply, Inc., 353 Mich. 120, 90 N.W.2d 873 (1958), but the leading case probably remains Henningsen v. Bloomfield Motors, Inc., 32 N.J. 358, 161 A.2d 69 (1960), in which the New Jersey Supreme Court held liable for personal injuries and property damages both the manufacturer of an automobile and the dealer who sold the vehicle. The rationale for the widespread abolition of the requirement of privity stems from the structure and operation of the free market economy in contemporary society; it was succinctly summed up not long ago by the Supreme Court of Pennsylvania:[31]

> Courts and scholars alike have recognized that the typical consumer
> does not deal at arms length with the party whose product he buys.
> Rather, he buys from a retail merchant who is usually little more than

---

31. Kassab v. Central Soya, 432 Pa. 217, 246 A.2d 848, 853 (1968) (footnote omitted).

an economic conduit. It is not the merchant who has defectively manufactured the product. Nor is it usually the merchant who advertises the product on such a large scale as to attract consumers. We have in our society literally scores of large, financially responsible manufacturers who place their wares in the stream of commerce not only with the realization but with the avowed purpose, that these goods will find their way into the hands of the consumer. Only the consumer will use these products; and only the consumer will be injured by them should they prove defective.

The policy considerations which dictate the abolition of privity are largely those which also warranted imposing strict tort liability on the manufacturer: the consumer's inability to protect himself adequately from defectively manufactured goods, the implied assurance of the maker when he puts his goods on the market that they are safe, and the superior risk bearing ability of the manufacturer. In addition, limiting a consumer under the Code to an implied warranty action against his immediate seller in those instances when the product defect is attributable to the manufacturer would effectively promote circularity of litigation and waste of judicial resources. Therefore, we decide that a manufacturer may be held liable for a breach of the implied warranties of AS 45.05.096 [UCC 2–314] and AS 45.05.098 [UCC 2–315] without regard to privity of contract between the manufacturer and the consumer.

The more difficult question before this court is whether we should extend this abolition of privity to embrace not only warranty actions for personal injuries and property damage but also those for economic loss. Contemporary courts have been more reticent to discard the privity requirement and to permit recovery in warranty by a remote consumer for purely economic losses. In considering this issue we note that economic loss may be categorized into direct economic loss and consequential economic loss, a distinction maintained in the Code's structure of damage remedies. One commentator has summarized the distinction:

> Direct economic loss may be said to encompass damage based on insufficient product value; thus, direct economic loss may be 'out of pocket'—the difference in value between what is given and received— or 'loss of bargain'—the difference between the value of what is received and its value as represented. Direct economic loss also may be measured by costs of replacement and repair. Consequential economic loss includes all indirect loss, such as loss of profits resulting from inability to make use of the defective product.

The claim of the Morrows in this case is one for direct economic loss.

A number of courts recently confronting this issue have declined to overturn the privity requirement in warranty actions for economic loss. One principal factor seems to be that these courts simply do not find the social and economic reasons which justify extending enterprise liability to the victims of personal injury or property damage equally compelling in the case of a disappointed buyer suffering "only" economic loss.[37] There is an apparent fear that economic losses may be of a far greater magnitude in value than personal injuries, and being somehow less foreseeable these losses would be less insurable, undermining the risk spreading theory of enterprise liability.

Several of the courts which have recently considered this aspect of the privity issue have found those arguments unpersuasive. We are in agreement and hold that there is no satisfactory justification for a remedial scheme which extends the warranty action to a consumer suffering personal injury or property damage but denies similar relief to the consumer "fortunate" enough to suffer only direct economic loss. Justice Peters' separate opinion in Seely v. White Motor Co., 63 Cal.2d 9, 45 Cal.Rptr. 17, 24, 403 P.2d 145, 152 (1965), persuasively establishes that the cleavage between economic loss and other types of harm is a false one, that each species of harm can constitute the "overwhelming misfortune" in one's life which warrants judicial redress. The Supreme Court of New Jersey is also in complete agreement with this view:

> From the standpoint of principle, we perceive no sound reason why the implication of reasonable fitness should be attached to the transaction and be actionable against the manufacturer where the defectively made product has caused personal injury and not actionable when inadequate manufacture has put a worthless article in the hands of an innocent purchaser who has paid the required price for it. In such situations considerations of justice require a court to interest itself in originating causes and to apply the principle of implied warranty on that basis, rather than to test its application by whether personal injury or simply loss of bargain resulted in the breach of the warranty. True, the rule of implied warranty had its gestative stirrings because of the greater appeal of the personal injury claim. But, once in existence, the field of operation of the remedy should not be fenced in by such a factor.[40]

The fear that if the implied warranty action is extended to direct economic loss, manufacturers will be subjected to liability for damages of unknown and unlimited scope would seem unfounded. The manufacturer may possibly delimit the scope of his potential liability by use of a

---

37. See, e.g., State ex rel. Western Seed Prod. Corp. v. Campbell, 250 Or. 262, 442 P.2d 215 (1968) and Price v. Gatlin, 241 Or. 315, 405 P.2d 502 (1965). In the latter case Justice Holman tried to elucidate the distinction in a concurring opinion at 504:

> In establishing liability in personal injury cases courts have been motivated to overlook any necessity for privity because the hazard to life and health is usually a personal disaster of major proportions to the individual both physically and financially and something of minor

importance to the manufacturer or wholesaler against which they can protect themselves by a distribution of risk through the price of the article sold. There has not been the same social necessity to motivate the recovery for strict economic losses where the damaged person's health, and therefore his basic earning capacity, has remained unimpaired.

40. Santor v. A. & M. Karagheusian, Inc., 44 N.J. 52, 60, 207 A.2d 305, 309 (1965).

disclaimer in compliance with AS 45.05.100 [UCC 2–316] or by resort to the limitations authorized in AS 45.05.230 [UCC 2–719]. These statutory rights not only preclude extending the theory of strict liability in tort, supra, but also make highly appropriate this extension of the theory of implied warranties. Further, by expanding warranty rights to redress this form of harm, we preserve " * * * the well developed notion that the law of contract should control actions for purely economic losses and that the law of tort should control actions for personal injuries."[41] We therefore hold that a manufacturer can be held liable for direct economic loss attributable to a breach of his implied warranties, without regard to privity of contract between the manufacturer and the ultimate purchaser.[42] It was therefore error for the trial court to dismiss the Morrows' action against New Moon for want of privity.

Our decision today preserves the statutory rights of the manufacturer to define his potential liability to the ultimate consumer, by means of express disclaimers and limitations, while protecting the legitimate expectation of the consumer that goods distributed on a wide scale by the use of conduit retailers are fit for their intended use. The manufacturer's rights are not, of course, unfettered. Disclaimers and limitations must comport with the relevant statutory prerequisites and cannot be so oppressive as to be unconscionable within the meaning of AS 45.05.072 [UCC 2–302]. On the other hand, under the Code the consumer has a number of responsibilities if he is to enjoy the right of action we recognize today, not the least of which is that he must give notice of the breach of warranty to the manufacturer pursuant to AS 45.05.174(c)(1) [UCC 2–607(3)(a)]. The warranty action brought under the Code must be brought within the statute of limitations period prescribed in AS 45.05.242 [UCC 2–725]. If the action is for breach of the implied warranty of fitness for particular purpose, created by AS 45.05.098 [UCC 2–315], the consumer must establish that the warrantor had reason to know the particular purpose for which the goods were required and that the consumer relied on the seller's skill or judgment to select or furnish suitable goods. In the case of litigation against a remote manufacturer, it would appear that often it will be quite difficult to establish this element of actual or constructive knowledge essential to this particular warranty.

. . .

Reversed and remanded for a new trial in accordance with this opinion.

41. Comment, The Vexing Problem of Purely Economic Loss in Products Liability: An Injury in Search of a Remedy, 4 Seton Hall L.Rev. 145, 175 (1972).

42. We recognize that the arguments against the abolition of privity are more compelling when the injury alleged is damages of a consequential nature many times the value of the manufacturer's product. See, e.g., Note, Economic Loss in Products Liability Jurisprudence, 66 Colum.L.Rev. 917, 965–66 (1965). We do not speak today to the issue of consequential economic loss, other than to note that AS 45.05.222 [UCC 2–715] governs the recovery of such damages and requires, among other things, that said damages must have been foreseeable by the manufacturer.

QUESTIONS AND NOTES

1. In discussing the rights of parties who did not contract with the defendant being sued, courts distinguish vertical privity from horizontal privity. Vertical privity, illustrated by *New Moon*, refers to a chain of sellers: e.g., Manufacturer–Distributor–Wholesaler–Retailer–Consumer, and raises the issue whether a buyer (in *New Moon*, a buyer from a retailer) can assert an implied warranty claim against a remote seller. Horizontal privity deals with the question whether a non-buyer can assert a claim against the immediate seller to a buyer. Examples of such a non-buyer include people who have relationships such as the following with the buyer: donee of goods, user of goods, person in the buyer's family or household, guest of the buyer, and bystander.

In *New Moon* the court holds that a buyer not in vertical privity with a remote seller may recover for direct loss caused by the remote seller's breach of implied warranty. Would the court permit recovery for consequential loss (e.g., rent paid for alternate housing while the mobile home was being repaired) caused by a remote seller's breach of implied warranty?

2. *Tex Enterprises* and *New Moon* reach different conclusions with respect to a seller's liability for economic loss for breach of implied warranty to a person not in privity of contract with the seller. What reason does each court give for its conclusion? Which opinion to you find more persuasive? Are the cases distinguishable?

3. In the absence of a specific statute, many courts have agreed with the result in *Tex Enterprises*. See J.White & R.Summers, Uniform Commercial Code §§ 11–5, 11–6 (4th ed. 1995). *White & Summers* concludes, however, that more and more courts are imposing liability for breach of the warranty of merchantability in favor of remote purchasers. The authors suggest that courts might reasonably distinguish between direct economic loss (diminution in value of the thing sold) and consequential damages, allowing recovery of direct loss but not consequential damages against remote sellers. It is not clear that courts have made this distinction. Do you think the distinction is justified? Remember that revised 2–313A and 2–313B impose liability for consequential damages, except for lost profits, in favor of remote purchasers for breach of the express warranty obligations arising under those sections.

At least 12 states (Hawaii, Iowa, Maine, Massachusetts, Minnesota, New Hampshire, North Dakota, Rhode Island, South Dakota, South Carolina, Utah, and Virginia) have adopted Alternative C of 2–318 or similar statutory language that specifically extends sellers' warranty liability to remote buyers. Alternative C seems literally to cover both vertical and horizontal privity and there is no limitation to personal injury or property damage. The Supreme Judicial Court of Massachusetts has held, however, that the statute was intended to apply only to actions that are in essence products liability actions. Bay State–Spray & Provincetown S.S., Inc. v. Caterpillar Tractor Co., 404 Mass. 103, 533 N.E.2d 1350 (1989). On the other hand, courts in Minnesota and South Dakota have held that under their state's adoption of Alternative C, remote buyers can recover for purely economic loss. Nelson v. International Harvester Corp., 394 N.W.2d 578 (Minn.App.1986); Cundy v. International Trencher Service, Inc., 358 N.W.2d 233 (S.D.1984).

In Collins Company, Ltd. v. Carboline Company, 125 Ill.2d 498, 127 Ill.Dec. 5, 532 N.E.2d 834 (1988), the court held that an assignee of a buyer's rights under a sales contract could assert the buyer's warranty claims against the seller. It is somewhat surprising that the rights of an assignee to assert the assignor's warranty claims against a seller have not been more fully developed in the cases. We are not sure of the extent to which warrantors try to preclude this possibility by limiting the warranty to the immediate buyer.

4. A number of states have adopted statutes that protect intermediate sellers in the distributive chain from actions for personal injury, death, or property damage that result from defective products or from failure to properly warn of the dangers of products. These statutes usually protect only sellers who had no reasonable opportunity to examine the product, as would be the case with goods that are intended to be delivered to a buyer in the original package. The statutes typically also permit buyers to sue manufacturers directly for personal injury, death, or property damage caused by a breach of warranty. The statutes do not protect sellers in the state if the manufacturer is not subject to the jurisdiction of courts of the state or if the manufacturer is insolvent. See, e.g., N.C.Gen.Stat. ch. 99B.

5. In spite of the fact that several writers have argued that Article 2's warranty provisions preempt the field and should prevent courts from adopting strict tort theories of liability for personal injuries, courts have embraced strict tort liability, which largely provides a remedy parallel to warranty liability. In 1980, however, the Delaware Supreme Court concluded that adoption of the Code precludes the application of strict tort liability to sales transactions, even for personal injuries. Cline v. Prowler Industries of Maryland, Inc., 418 A.2d 968 (Del.1980).

A few years later, in Spring Motors Distributors, Inc. v. Ford Motor Co., 98 N.J. 555, 489 A.2d 660 (1985), the New Jersey Supreme Court held that a commercial buyer seeking recovery only for economic loss was limited to its Article 2 remedies and could not assert an independent claim in tort for strict liability. It left open the question whether the same rule apples to a consumer buyer, but hinted that it does.

The Restatement (Third) of Torts extends the strict-liability rules only to personal injury and damage to property other than the defective product. Therefore, strict liability in tort is not available for recovery of purely economic loss.

6. Leases. For ordinary leases, Article 2A pretty much tracks Article 2. But for finance leases, 2A–209 explicitly gives the lessee a direct cause of action against the supplier of the goods. The "supplier" is the person from whom the lessor buys the goods (2A–103(x)). In *All-States Leasing v. Bass*, page 268 supra, the court held that the lessee had no claim against the lessor for breach of the implied warranty of merchantability. Under Article 2A, would the lessee have a claim against Auto Laundry Mfg. Co., the supplier?

Patty Precision Products Co. v. Brown & Sharpe Manufacturing Co.

United States Court of Appeals, Tenth Circuit, 1988.
846 F.2d 1247.

■ BARRETT, SENIOR CIRCUIT JUDGE. In these consolidated appeals, Patty Precision Products Company (Patty Precision) appeals from an order of the district court denying its motion for a new trial and an order of the district court awarding appellee (General Electric) attorney fees of $170,421.54.

During April, 1974, Patty Precision was awarded a contract by the United States for the manufacture of bomb racks. Subsequently, Patty Precision contacted appellee (Brown & Sharpe) relative to the purchase of a vertical hydrotape machining center capable of producing the side plates for the bomb racks. Following its meeting with Brown & Sharpe, Patty Precision purchased from Marsuco, Inc., a Brown & Sharpe hydrotape vertical machining center equipped with a General Electric "G.E. 550 Mark Century Numerical Control."

. . .

It is uncontested that during Patty Precision's initial meeting with Brown & Sharpe that a Brown & Sharpe employee specifically recommended General Electric controls, that the employee stated that Brown & Sharpe had bought over 700 controls from General Electric, and that they had a lot of confidence in the General Electric controls. It is also uncontested that after Patty Precision had ordered the machines, but prior to their delivery, that Brown & Sharpe notified General Electric of the scheduled shipment of each machine including the serial number of each General Electric control being shipped to Patty Precision, that after the machines were shipped to Patty Precision's plant General Electric employees participated in the installation and start up of each machine, and that because of the volume of controls that General Electric supplied to Brown & Sharpe, General Electric "had a service engineer basically full time at Brown & Sharpe whose job was to assist in the start up of machines and provide any feedback" from customers.

From the outset, the three machines failed to perform in accordance with Patty Precision's expectations:

"In fact, because the machines needed almost constant repairs, defendants voluntarily extended the warranty period on the machines until June, 1977. Despite the alleged poor performance of the machines, plaintiff continued to use them to meet the deadlines of a government contract. After the warranties expired in June, 1977, plaintiff attempted to resolve its grievances by meeting with defendants in November, 1977. Those attempts were unsuccessful and plaintiff filed this diversity suit in May, 1978, more than three years after the purchase of the first machine."

Patty Precision v. Brown & Sharpe Mfg. Co., et al., 742 F.2d 1260, 1262 (10th Cir. 1984) (*Patty Precision I*).

. . .

During the trial, General Electric was allowed, over Patty Precision's relevancy objection, to present evidence regarding the warranty between Brown & Sharpe and General Electric covering the General Electric numerical controls utilized in Machines No. 1, No. 2 and No. 3. A General Electric employee testified that General Electric's warranty on the controls extended only to Brown & Sharpe and that General Electric's "warranty policy has always excluded all consequential damages and has limited it to parts and repairs or replacement only." The employee also testified that, to his knowledge, there was never "any written document expressing a warranty given by the General Electric Company to the end user in this case, Patty Precision Products Company."

. . .

Patty Precision contends that the district court erred in permitting evidence of and instructing on any disclaimer from General Electric to Brown & Sharpe. We agree. Patty Precision argues that General Electric's disclaimer, as set forth in its Statement of Warranty (Appendix A herein), was disclosed only to Brown & Sharpe and could not, as a matter of law, be considered effective against Patty Precision. . . .

In response, General Electric argues that its disclaimer to Brown & Sharpe was effective as to Patty Precision as a subsequent purchaser and a valid defense as a matter of law. . . .

The parties agree that the dispositive issue is whether General Electric's disclaimer applies to Patty Precision. The disclaimer, according to General Electric's evidence, extended only to Brown & Sharpe. Patty Precision was not informed of the disclaimer prior to its purchases of the three machines, and the disclaimer was never expressed to Patty Precision in writing. The issue thus is whether the disclaimer of warranties can nonetheless be binding on Patty Precision and admissible herein. Based on our review of applicable Oklahoma law, we hold that General Electric's disclaimer to Brown & Sharpe was not binding on Patty Precision, that the disclaimer was irrelevant, and that the district court erred in admitting it in evidence and instructing on it.

. . .

The implied warranty of merchantability has been referred to as the most important warranty in the UCC. See, White & Summers, [Handbook of the Law under the Uniform Commercial Code, 2d Edition], § 9–6, p. 343 (1984). One of the prime goals of the Code was to do away with the requirement of privity of contract consistent with "402A of the Restatement which abolishes the privity requirement only in cases of property damage and personal injury." Id. at 407. In our view, the broad-sweeping language used by the Supreme Court of Oklahoma in Old Albany Estates v. Highland Carpet Mills, [604 P.2d 849 (Okla. 1979)], reiterated and enlarged upon in Elden v. Simmons, [631 P.2d 739 (Okla. 1981)], rejected the majority view that a "vertical" non-privity plaintiff, i.e., one who buys within the distributive chain but who does not buy directly from the defendant, cannot maintain an action for breach of implied warranty. In both *Old Albany* and *Elden v. Simmons*, the claimed economic losses were alleged to have resulted from a builder-vendor's breach of implied warranty of habitability and construction in a workmanlike manner.

. . .

Thus, an ultimate consumer in the distribution chain in Oklahoma can bring a direct breach of warranty action against a manufacturer, notwithstanding his lack of privity. Since there is an implied warranty of merchantability under Sec. 2–314 and fitness for particular use under Sec. 2–315 unless excluded in accordance with Sec. 2–316, we hold that General Electric's disclaimer to Brown & Sharpe, undisclosed to Patty Precision, was irrelevant and that the district court erred in admitting it into evidence and instructing on it. General Electric's evidence showed that the disclaimer extended only to Brown & Sharpe and that it was never expressed in writing to Patty Precision. Patty Precision also presented evidence that the disclaimer was not related or disclosed to it prior to its purchase of the machines.

Furthermore, General Electric was fully aware of the use to be made of the numerical controls it sold to Brown & Sharpe, which were, in turn, sold to Patty Precision as part of the machines. General Electric employees participated in the installation and start up of the machines at Patty Precision's plant. There is nothing in the record indicating that the numerical controls sold by General Electric were specially designed. Thus, the fact that they were components of a machining center used by Patty Precision does not distinguish them from any other "goods" insofar as implied warranty of merchantability is concerned. The record demonstrates that General Electric knew of the intended use of the machines by Patty Precision and the system for which the component was to be an integral part. Under these circumstances, the implied warranty of merchantability under Sec. 2–314 applied and it was not "excluded or modified" by a conspicuous writing under Sec. 2–316. We hold that district court erred in admitting evidence of and instructing on General Electric's Statement of Warranty.

. . .

Reversed and remanded for a new trial.

QUESTIONS AND NOTES

1. How do you think the Alaska court that decided *Morrow v. New Moon* would have decided *Patty Precision*?

2. After the decision in *Patty Precision*, Oklahoma amended its version of 2–318 (Alternative A) by adding two paragraphs partially excerpted below:

(2) This section does not displace principles of law and equity that extend a warranty to or for the benefit of a buyer to other persons.

(3) ... [A]n exclusion, modification, or limitation of the warranty, including any with respect to rights and remedies, effective against the buyer is also effective against any beneficiary designated under this section.

Presumably, paragraph 3 was intended to overrule the result in *Patty Precision*. What do you think about the policy issue? Should sellers be obligated to see that their purchasers pass along to their customers any limitations on warranties imposed by the first seller?

3. Other courts have held that warranty disclaimers effective against the immediate buyer are also effective against remote buyers. E.g., Wenner Petroleum Corp. v. Mitsui & Co. (U.S.A.), Inc., 748 P.2d 356 (Colo.App. 1987). Would a requirement that any warranty disputes be subject to arbitration bind a remote buyer who is entitled to the benefit of the warranty but does not know of the arbitration clause? See Recold, S.A. de C.V. v. Monfort of Colorado, Inc., 893 F.2d 195 (8th Cir.1990) (applying Colorado law). However, in Spagnol Enterprises v. Digital Equipment Corp., 390 Pa.Super. 372, 568 A.2d 948 (1989), the court held that a disclaimer by a seller to its immediate buyer was not effective against a remote purchaser.

We have seen that the doctrine of unconscionability operates as a limit on the enforceability of a disclaimer of implied warranties. If a disclaimer is unconscionable and therefore ineffective against an immediate purchaser, presumably it also is ineffective against a remote purchaser. But how about the converse: if a disclaimer is effective against the immediate purchaser, can it be unconscionable with respect to a remote purchaser?

4. In *Morrow v. New Moon* suppose Golden Heart (the immediate seller) had discovered substantial defects in the trailer when it was delivered and New Moon (the manufacturer) settled Golden Heart's warranty claim by deducting $6,000 from the price. How would that affect the right of the plaintiffs to recover from New Moon?

Or, suppose that New Moon had sold the mobile home to Golden Heart as "factory defective" at a discount of 50% off the ordinary price. How should that affect the manufacturer's liability to the Morrows?

5. Revised Article 2. Revised Article 2 makes no change in the provisions of 2–314 or 2–318 relevant to the issues whether implied warranties extend to remote purchasers and whether a seller's disclaimer is effective against a remote purchaser. With respect to the effectiveness of a disclaimer to foreclose strict liability in tort, recall that the Restatement of Torts takes the position that disclaimers as to personal injury are not effective, but that the effectiveness of disclaimers as to property damage is left to the courts (see page 292 supra).

C. CONTRIBUTORY NEGLIGENCE AND ASSUMPTION OF RISK

For a buyer to recover for breach of warranty, the buyer must prove:

- that there is a warranty with respect to the goods,
- that the seller breached the warranty,
- that the buyer suffered a loss or injury,
- that the breach of warranty is the factual and legal cause of the injury, and
- the amount of the loss.

See 2–314, Official Comment 13. Thus it is not enough for the buyer to establish a warranty and a loss. The buyer also must establish a breach of the warranty, and the mere fact of injury does not establish that the seller breached the warranty. For example, in Heil v. Standard Chemical Manufacturing Co., 301 Minn. 315, 223 N.W.2d 37 (1974), a seller of a cattle-feed supplement made an express warranty that proper use of the product would produce a weight gain of two pounds per day for the cattle in the buyer's herd. When the cattle gained less than half that amount, the buyer sued for breach of express warranty. The trial court gave judgment for the buyer, and defendant appealed. Reversing, the Supreme Court of Minnesota stated:

> It is necessary that the breach has proximately caused the damages complained of by the plaintiff. The burden is upon the buyer to establish the breach. Minn. St. 336.2–607(4). Further:

> "In an action based on breach of warranty, it is of course necessary to show not only the existence of the warranty but the fact that the warranty was broken and that the breach of the warranty was the proximate cause of the loss sustained." U.C.C. Comment 13 on U.C.C. § 2–314 (referring specifically to actions based upon implied warranties).

> The defendant-appellant essentially contends that inasmuch as plaintiff failed to introduce evidence that exemplified this causal connection, the jury verdict could have only been based upon pure speculation. . . .

> Several courts have indicated the importance of the element of causation. The result of this lack of proof is that an otherwise valid action for a breach of warranty will fail. In an action based upon the failure of a weed killer to perform as warranted, the Idaho Supreme Court stated:

> > " * * * Even if such a failure occurred, the plaintiffs still had to establish that the resulting weeds proximately caused the loss of their potato crop. * * *

* * *

"In an action based on breach of warranty, it is necessary to show that the breach of warranty was the proximate cause of the loss sustained. Where the record shows that there are several possible causes of an injury, for one or more of which the defendant was not responsible, and it is just as reasonable and probable that the injury was the result of the latter, the plaintiff may not recover, since he has failed to prove that the defendant's breach caused the injury." ... Chisholm v. J.B. Simplot Co., 94 Idaho 628, 631, 495 P.2d 1113, 1116 (1972).

Further, the following result was reached by the Illinois Court of Appeals when it was requested to find that the explosives the defendant quarry operator had purchased from the plaintiff were the cause of the inadequate results obtained by the use of the product:

"On this evidence, we are left to speculate. It could be that the poor results were caused by the powder failing to measure up to an implied warranty of fitness for the purpose intended. It could also be that the poor results were caused by failing to remove the broken rock from the toe and the loading to within five feet of the top. There is even a possibility that the shot holes were improperly drilled or that a difference in the rock formation was the cause.

"We have no evidence in this record that anything was wrong with the explosive except by reasoning backward, i.e., the result was poor; therefore, something must have been wrong with the explosive. In view of the other possibilities this is not enough." Olin Mathieson Chemical Corp. v. Moushon, 93 Ill.App.2d 280, 282, 235 N.E.2d 263, 264 (1968).

It appears that defendant has made a substantial argument for this court's determination. . . . It is a rather specious argument by plaintiff that the factors of weather, management, animal health, supervision of employees, and feeding procedures were not proven to have caused the failure, for that statement results in acceptance of the theory that since no other factor could have prevented realization of the expectations, the minimal results had to have been the product of the failure of the feed supplement. As shown above, proof of causation cannot be established through negative implication.

. . .

In the case before us, the factual disputes obviously open the door for many inferences to be drawn by a jury. However, the conclusion seems compelling that there was little evidence offered which would tend to allow the jury to conclude that defendant's feed supplement, and not one of the other factors which could adversely affect production of healthy animals, was the causation element. It cannot be doubted that causation should at least have been mentioned by the lower court in its instructions to the jury. Instead the jury instructions were the following: That it was the plaintiff's duty to follow the feeding instructions given by the defendant and to use reasonable skill and diligence in feeding and caring for the cattle; that the defendant would not be liable for any losses which were not the direct result of any failure of the defendant's product, but rather were the result of some failure on the part of the plaintiff to use this care and diligence; that the plaintiff could not recover unless he established by a fair preponderance of the evidence that there existed an express warranty that the feed supplement, if used as directed, would produce a 2–pound–per–day weight gain in the cattle; and finally, that the plaintiff could not recover unless there was a breach of this warranty. It appears that the statement to the jury that defendant's liability depends upon the damage being the direct result of its, and not plaintiff's, failure, is not sufficient without the more definite requirement of an affirmative finding under the special verdict that the breach of warranty proximately caused plaintiff's damages.

Without an affirmative finding by the jury on causation, the conclusion that the entire verdict is based upon speculation is well supported. For this reason, we therefore grant a new trial.

On the other hand, the burden is not insuperable, even if the buyer cannot establish the cause of the product's failure to do what it is supposed to do. In Nevada Contract Services, Inc. v. Squirrel Companies, 68 P.3d 896 (Nev.2003), the buyer, NCS, purchased an electronically controlled system for dispensing liquor in its bar. The system was designed to control the quantity and price of servings, provide inventory management, prevent theft, and manage the revenue generated by liquor sales. Shortly after installation, the system failed to do these things. NCS sued.

Prior to filing its complaint in the district court, NCS made numerous requests that the problems it was experiencing with the liquor-dispensing system be corrected. In response, service technicians from Vega, Squirrel, and BMS evaluated the liquor-dispensing system. Upon inspection, the technicians found a lack of dedicated power; water damage to the EasyBar system caused by a leaking water filter near the EasyBar system's control box; and employee misuse, namely the liquor-dispensing guns were submerged in water for cleaning and one of the pumps had a nail in it. The parties disputed whether these findings could have caused the liquor-dispensing system to malfunction. . . .

Following the inability [of NCS's expert witness] to opine as to the cause of the liquor-dispensing system's malfunction, respondents filed a motion for summary judgment, arguing that NCS could not sustain its causation burden. The district court expressed concern over the fact that NCS's own experts could not opine as to the probable cause of the liquor-dispensing system's malfunction. NCS responded that the experts were attempting to pinpoint the exact cause of the malfunction, not the probable cause, and argued that it did not have to prove the precise cause of the malfunction.

The district court disagreed [and] . . . granted summary judgment in favor of respondents. This appeal followed. . . .

In this appeal, we consider the degree of specificity required to meet the causation burden in a breach of warranty action. In Nelson v. Wilkins Dodge, Inc., [256 N.W.2d 472, 476 (Minn. 1977),] the Minnesota Supreme Court observed that in a breach of warranty case, "generally no specific defect need be alleged, and a defective condition can be proved by circumstantial evidence." Likewise, in Hershenson v. Lake Champlain Motors, Inc., [139 Vt. 219, 424 A.2d 1075, 1078 (1981),] the Vermont Supreme Court observed :

"Circumstantial evidence may be resorted to ... if there can be drawn therefrom a rational inference that [a defect in the defendant's product] was the source of the trouble. There must be created in the minds of the jurors something more, of course, than a possibility, suspicion or surmise, but the requirements of the law are satisfied if the existence of this fact is made the more probable hypothesis, when considered with reference to the possibility of other hypotheses."

We agree with those courts that hold that the specific cause of the malfunction need not be shown. Indeed, we reached a similar conclusion in Stackiewicz v. Nissan Motor Corp., [100 Nev. 443, 450–51, 686 P.2d 925, 929 (1984) (concluding that "evidence of a steering malfunction which resulted in the [plaintiff's] losing control of [her] vehicle might properly be accepted by the trier of fact as sufficient circumstantial proof of a defect ... without direct proof of the mechanical cause of the malfunction")]. Although *Stackiewicz* is a products liability case, we are adopting a similar causation burden in breach of warranty actions. In *Stackiewicz*, we stated that requiring a plaintiff to prove the specific cause of a product defect or to negate alternative causes in order to establish that a product is defective is far too restrictive. Applying this reasoning, we conclude that it is too burdensome to require a plaintiff to prove precisely why a product does not work in a breach of warranty action, specifically in instances such as the one presented here, where a product integrating electronic and mechanical components is involved. [Cf. Capitol Dodge Sales v. Northern Concrete Pipe, 131 Mich.App. 149, 346 N.W.2d 535, 539 n.11 (1983) (holding that a new car's inoperability establishes its failure to conform to the contract of sale without showing the specific technical cause of the overheating); Eggl v. Letvin Equipment Co., 2001 ND 144, 632 N.W.2d 435, 439 (2001) (holding that evidence that a farm tractor was not fit for the ordinary purposes for which such goods are used was sufficient when it was shown that the tractor could not be used to pull an implement).]

Based on the testimony of the various technicians, we conclude that there was sufficient evidence to support a reasonable inference that respondents breached the warranty and caused NCS's damages. We acknowledge that NCS's experts could not opine as to the precise cause of the liquor-dispensing system's malfunction and that there is evidence of alleged misuse of the liquor-dispensing system that may have contributed to the malfunction; however, such evidence affects the weight of NCS's case. Thus, we conclude that a genuine issue of material fact exists, thereby precluding summary judgment.

We hold that a plaintiff need not show the specific technical cause of a product's malfunction in order to sustain its causation burden in a breach of warranty cause of action. Because NCS produced evidence creating an inference that the newly acquired liquor-dispensing system's problems were not related to misuse and may have resulted from respondents' breach of warranty, we conclude that NCS is entitled to litigate its case before a jury.

————

Correia v. Firestone Tire & Rubber Co.

Massachusetts Supreme Judicial Court, 1983.
388 Mass. 342, 446 N.E.2d 1033.

■ NOLAN, JUSTICE.

This case comes before the court on certification from the United States District Court for the District of Massachusetts. The court has certified to us five questions involving Massachusetts tort and warranty law.

This is an action for wrongful death under G.L. c. 229, Sec.2, commenced in the United States District Court. Mildred R. Correia, as administratrix of the estate of her husband, Alfred R. Correia, brought suit against the Firestone Tire & Rubber Company (Firestone). Alfred Correia was killed on November 10, 1978, in an accident arising out of and in the course of his employment as a truck driver for Concord Steel Corporation (Concord Steel). Mrs. Correia filed a complaint in September, 1979 . . . .

Discovery has been completed and the case is ready for trial. Firestone requested certain jury instructions on negligence and warranty that presented issues of law for which the trial judge found no controlling precedent in the decisions of this court. He believed that an authoritative answer "would materially advance the ultimate termination of this litigation consistently with Massachusetts law." In certifying these questions to this court, he summarized the parties' allegations as follows: "The plaintiff alleges the following facts as to which there is no dispute: At the time of the accident, Mr. Correia was driving a tractor-trailer rig owned by Concord Steel from its plant in Everett to its plant in Methuen. The trailer was loaded with several large, one-inch thick, steel plates for ultimate delivery to Concord Steel's customers. While the truck was proceeding north on Route 93 in Andover, the right front tire of the tractor blew out. The rig, which was in the center lane at the time of the blowout, veered to the right, went across the right travel lane, then through the right guardrail and down an embankment. In the course of the accident, Mr. Correia was killed. His body was found on the ground approximately ten feet from the tractor.

"The plaintiff further alleges that the tire which blew out was a Firestone tire, and that the blowout was caused by negligence or breach of warranty by Firestone.

"Firestone denies any negligence or breach of warranty and alleges contributory negligence by Mr. Correia, particularly with respect to his failure to control the rig after the blowout, his failure to properly inspect and maintain the rig and its tires, and his failure to wear a seatbelt.

. . .

"Firestone has also requested this court to determine what effect, if any, should be given under the breach of warranty count to any negligence of Mr. Correia, or to any negligence of Concord Steel (other than negligence of Mr. Correia). In this regard, Firestone contends that this court should apply the comparative negligence statute to the breach of warranty count in the same manner that it applies that statute to the negligence count, i.e., that it should treat M.G.L. c. 231, § 85, as a comparative 'fault' statute, or, alternatively, that this court should apply common law contributory negligence principles to the breach of warranty count. . . ." [Section 85 provides, in pertinent part:

> Contributory negligence shall not bar recovery in any action by any person or legal representative to recover damages for negligence resulting in death or in injury to person or property, if such negligence was not greater than the total amount of negligence attributable to the person or persons against whom recovery is sought, but any damages allowed shall be diminished in proportion to the amount of negligence attributable to the person for whose injury, damage or death recovery is made. In determining by what amount the plaintiff's damages shall be diminished in such a case, the negligence of each plaintiff shall be compared to the total negligence of all persons against whom recovery is sought. The combined total of the plaintiff's negligence taken together with all of the negligence of all defendants shall equal one hundred per cent.]

. . .

The judge . . . certified the following questions to this court.

. . .

Question Three

"Does Massachusetts recognize contributory or comparative negligence or fault as a full or partial defense to an action for personal injury or wrongful death based on breach of warranty?" We answer, "No."

We have recognized on a number of occasions that claims based on breach of warranty sound essentially in tort. . . . Further, we have recognized that in this Commonwealth the theory of implied warranty provided by G.L. c. 106, §§ 2–314, 2–318, is "congruent in nearly all respects with the principles expressed in Restatement (Second) of Torts § 402A (1965)," which defines the strict liability of a seller for physical harm to a user or consumer of the seller's product. Back v. Wickes Corp., 375 Mass. [633,] 640, 378 N.E.2d 964 [1978].

Starting with Firestone's argument that G.L. c. 231, § 85, should be construed to apply to breach of warranty actions, we think that this argument is foreclosed by the language of § 85 itself. Section 85 is applicable only to actions "by any person or legal representative to recover damages for negligence resulting in death or in injury to person or property." Id. As Restatement (Second) of Torts § 402A, comment *n*, indicates, actions for strict liability are not actions in negligence. The defendant may be liable "even though he has exercised all possible care in the preparation and sale of the product." Restatement (Second) of Torts § 402A, comment a (1965).[11]

If the comparative negligence statute does not literally apply, the question remains whether its underlying principles should be given effect by judicial adoption. This is the course of action most strongly urged by Firestone. We decline to take such action. To do so would be to meld improperly the theory of negligence with the theory of warranty as expressed in G.L. c. 106, §§ 2–314–2–318, and thereby to undercut the policies supporting these statutes.

Simply stated, the policy of negligence liability presumes that people will, or at least should, take reasonable measures to protect themselves and others from harm. This presumption justifies the imposition of a duty on people to conduct themselves in this way. A person harmed by one whose conduct "falls below the standard established by law for the protection of others against unreasonable risk," Restatement (Second) of Torts § 282 (1965), may recover against the actor. However, if the injured person's unreasonable conduct also has been a cause of his injury, his conduct will be accounted for in apportioning liability or damages.

Strict liability is justified on a much different basis. "On whatever theory, the justification for the strict liability has been said to be that the seller, by marketing his product for use and consumption, has undertaken and assumed a special responsibility toward any member of the consuming public who may be injured by it; that the public has the right to and does expect, in the case of products which it needs and for which it is forced to rely upon the seller, that reputable sellers will stand behind their goods; that public policy demands that the burden of accidental injuries caused by products intended for consumption be placed upon those who market them, and be treated as a cost of production against which liability insurance can be obtained; and that the consumer of such products is entitled to the maximum of protection at the hands of someone, and the proper persons to afford it are those who market the products." Restatement (Second) of Torts § 402A, comment c (1965). Recognizing that the seller is in the best

---

11. We do not view strict liability as tantamount to negligence per se and we decline to follow those Wisconsin cases which do so. Powers v. Hunt–Wesson Foods, Inc., 64 Wis.2d 532, 219 N.W.2d 393 (1974); Dippel v. Sciano, 37 Wis.2d 443, 155 N.W.2d 55 (1967) (apparently the first case to apply a comparative negligence statute to a strict products liability case). Compare Murray v. Fairbanks Morse, 610 F.2d 149 (3d Cir.1979).

position to ensure product safety, the law of strict liability imposes on the seller a duty to prevent the release of "any product in a defective condition unreasonably dangerous to the user or consumer," into the stream of commerce. Restatement (Second) of Torts § 402A(1) (1965). This duty is unknown in the law of negligence and it is not fulfilled even if the seller takes all reasonable measures to make his product safe. The liability issue focuses on whether the product was defective and unreasonably dangerous and not on the conduct of the user or the seller. Given this focus, the only duty imposed on the user is to act reasonably with respect to a product which he knows to be defective and dangerous. When a user unreasonably proceeds to use a product which he knows to be defective and dangerous, he violates that duty and relinquishes the protection of the law. It is only then that it is appropriate to account for his conduct in determining liability. Since he has voluntarily relinquished the law's protection, it is further appropriate that he be barred from recovery. The absolute bar to the user for breach of his duty balances the strict liability placed on the seller.[12] Other than this instance, the parties are not presumed to be equally responsible for injuries caused by defective products, and the principles of contributory or comparative negligence have no part in the strict liability scheme. Given this focus, the user's negligence does not prevent recovery except when he unreasonably uses a product that he knows to be defective and dangerous. In such circumstances, the user's conduct alone is the proximate cause of his injuries, as a matter of law, and recovery is appropriately denied. In short, the user is denied recovery, not because of his contributory negligence or his assumption of the risk but rather because his conduct is the proximate cause of his injuries.

The policies of negligence and warranty liability will best be served by keeping the spheres in which they operate separate until such time as the Legislature indicates how and to what extent they should be melded.[13] The standards of care and the duties are well defined in each sphere. The comparative negligence statute defined no standard of behavior and imposed no duty not previously recognized under the traditional theories of contributory negligence. It merely adjusted the manner in which unreasonable conduct which caused injury would be treated in a negligence action. There is no reason to presume that by passage of the comparative negligence statute the Legislature intended to merge negligence liability with

12. Since G.L. c. 231, § 85, is limited to actions in negligence, it would not apply here to diminish damages for a product user found to be contributorily negligent in the manner described. Cf. Thibault v. Sears, Roebuck & Co., 118 N.H. 802, 395 A.2d 843 (1978) (adopting comparative concept to diminish plaintiff's recovery to the degree his "misconduct" caused his injury. If plaintiff's "misconduct," a term used to encompass the conduct previously recognized as assumption of the risk or abnormal use or mishandling of the product, is greater than fifty per cent, verdict for the defendant is required). Schwartz, Strict Liability & Comparative Negligence, 42 Tenn.L.Rev. 171, 174–176 (1974). For this reason, also, the use of the phrase "assumption of the risk" in Restatement (Second) of Torts § 402A, comment *n* (1965), is not incompatible with the abolition of assumption of the risk in § 85 as a defense in negligence actions.

13. At least one State legislature has specifically prohibited such a merger. See Conn.Gen.Stat. § 52–572n(a) (1981).

warranty liability. Even if we were convinced that some restructuring of the Massachusetts law of warranty was necessary, we ordinarily would leave that restructuring to the Legislature, given the wide variety of possible solutions it might reasonably adopt.[14]

Restatement (Second) of Torts § 402A, comment *n* (1965), states the essence of our position. To paraphrase and elaborate on that comment, we conclude that the plaintiff in a warranty action under G.L. c. 106, § 2–314, may not recover if it is found that, after discovering the product's defect and being made aware of its danger, he nevertheless proceeded unreasonably to make use of the product and was injured by it.[15] No recovery by the plaintiff shall be diminished on account of any other conduct which might be deemed contributorily negligent. . . .

———

Fiske v. MacGregor, Div. of Brunswick

Rhode Island Supreme Court, 1983.
464 A.2d 719.

[Plaintiff was injured when he attempted a tackle in a high school football game. He sued MacGregor in strict tort and for breach of warranty claiming that the football helmet manufactured by it was defective in design. The jury found that plaintiff had not assumed the risk and that MacGregor had breached its warranty of merchantability as to the helmet. The jury, applying the Rhode Island comparative negligence statute, found that plaintiff had been 40% at fault. The trial judge thereupon reduced the recovery by 40%, to $2,100,000. Defendant appealed the trial court's judgment holding it liable; plaintiff appealed the trial court's application of the comparative fault statute to reduce the recovery.]

IV

Application of Comparative Negligence Principles to
Strict Liability and Implied Warranty Theories

. . . [P]laintiff's cross-appeal . . . presents us with a question that has not yet been considered by this court. Essentially, we are asked to consider whether or not Rhode Island's comparative-negligence statute, G.L.1956

---

14. . . . We are not the first court to conclude that the principles of comparative negligence are fundamentally incompatible with strict liability. See, e.g., Melia v. Ford Motor Co., 534 F.2d 795 (8th Cir.1976) (applying Nebraska law); Kinard v. Coats Co., 37 Colo.App. 555, 553 P.2d 835 (1976). Smith v. Smith, 278 N.W.2d 155 (S.D.1979); Annot., 9 A.L.R. 4th 638–641 (1981 & Supp.1982).

15. The fact that a seller, manufacturer, or distributor is not liable if a plaintiff is injured as a consequence of his unforeseeable misuse of a product, see Back v. Wickes Corp., 375 Mass. 633, 640, 378 N.E.2d 964 (1978), is most properly analyzed as an element of the plaintiff's case, since he must prove that his injury was caused by a defect making the product unfit for its ordinary use. As such, it is distinct from the defendant's burden to prove contributory negligence, although the defendant may offer evidence tending to prove that the plaintiff's injury did not occur as the result of a foreseeable use.

(1969 Reenactment) § 9–20–4, as amended by P.L.1972, ch. 18, § 1, should be applied to breach-of-implied-warranty actions and to strict-liability actions.

To reiterate, the jury in the present case found against defendant on both the strict-liability and breach-of-implied-warranty counts. On the negligence count the jury found defendant to be 60 percent negligent and plaintiff to be 40 percent negligent. The jury awarded plaintiff $3,500,000 in damages, but the trial justice entered judgment in the amount of $2,100,000, plus interest, which amount represents the damages reduced by the jury's finding of 40 percent negligence on the part of plaintiff. On appeal, plaintiff contends that the Legislature did not intend that § 9–20–4 be applied to reduce damages based on strict liability and breach of implied warranty.

In construing a statute, we are bound to give effect to the literal meaning when the meaning of the text is plain or clear and unambiguous. The statute in question, § 9–20–4, reads as follows:

> "Comparative negligence.—In all actions hereafter brought for personal injuries, or where such injuries have resulted in death, or for injury to property, the fact that the person injured, or the owner of the property, or person having control over the property may not have been in the exercise of due care shall not bar a recovery, but damages shall be diminished by the finder of fact in proportion to the amount of negligence attributable to the person injured, or the owner of the property or the person having control over the property."

The defendant and the trial justice both interpret the language, "all actions hereafter brought for personal injuries," to clearly and unambiguously include actions brought on the theories of strict liability and implied warranty. In opposition, plaintiff vehemently asserts that such an interpretation is in stark contrast to the legislative history of the statute. Among other things, plaintiff contends that the title given a 1972 public law that amended § 9–20–4 limits the statute's application to negligence cases. In response to the obvious omission of the term "negligence" from the text of the statute, plaintiff maintains that "the statute by its terms calls for a comparison of *negligence* when the plaintiff was negligent. Necessarily his negligence must and can only be compared with the negligence of the defendants."

After a prolonged consideration and reading of this statute, we can only come to the conclusion that the language "all actions hereafter brought for personal injuries" includes actions brought on the theories of strict liability and breach of implied warranty as well as actions brought on a negligence theory. Because we find that the statutory language is clear and unambiguous on this matter, we do not need to utilize the title as an aid to construe the statute. Orthopedic Specialists, Inc. v. Great Atlantic & Pacific Tea Co., 120 R.I. 378, 388 A.2d 352 (1978). Our finding that the statute is clear and unambiguous would be more difficult had the drafters used more limited wording. However, the drafters deemed it necessary to use the language "in all actions," leaving no doubt in our minds that they intended to include actions in strict liability and implied warranty.[7]

Our decision today to apply comparative-negligence principles to strict liability and implied warranty is well supported by other jurisdictions [citing five cases]. The state of Mississippi, which has the same comparative-negligence statute as our own, has had that statute interpreted by a federal court to allow its application to strict-liability claims. Johnson v. William C. Ellis & Sons Iron Works, Inc., 604 F.2d 950, 960 (5th Cir.1979); Edwards v. Sears, Roebuck & Co., 512 F.2d 276, 290 (5th Cir.1975). Moreover, there are jurisdictions that have applied comparative-negligence principles to strict-liability claims despite the presence of comparative-negligence statutes that are limited by their terms to actions for negligence. Sun Valley Airlines, Inc. v. Avco–Lycoming Corp., 411 F.Supp. 598, 663 (D.Idaho 1976); Dippel v. Sciano, 37 Wis.2d 443, 462, 155 N.W.2d 55, 64 (1967) (held that strict liability in tort is the equivalent of negligence per se; therefore, application of comparative negligence in such cases would be appropriate). Contra Correia v. The Firestone Tire & Rubber Co., 388 Mass. 342, 446 N.E.2d 1033 (1983) (rejecting the negligence-per se analysis); see also Thibault v. Sears, Roebuck & Co., 118 N.H. 802, 813, 395 A.2d 843, 848 (1978) (held that the comparative negligence statute did not apply to strict-liability cases because it is confined by its term to actions for negligence; however, the court further held that strict liability is a judicially created doctrine to which the principal of comparative causation will apply.) Suter v. San Angelo Foundry & Machine Co., 81 N.J. 150, 160, 406 A.2d 140, 145 (1979) (held that phrase, "in an action * * * for negligence" should not be read literally so as to refer only to traditional negligence tort actions.) Fortunately, because of the broad language in our comparative negligence statute, we do not need to engage in any such creative analysis. Nonetheless, the existence of these cases can only lend support to our decision.

We think it important to note an unfair and inequitable result that would occur were we to decide differently. If the comparative-negligence statute only applied to negligence actions, a defendant manufacturer found liable in strict liability or implied warranty could not have the damages apportioned because of plaintiff's culpable conduct. Ironically, defendant manufacturers found liable in negligence would have the damages apportioned, despite the fact that their conduct was clearly more culpable than the conduct of those defendants found liable in strict liability or implied

---

7. A noted commentator has stated the following with respect to § 9–20–4:

> "It is important to remember that this problem of whether a court can utilize a comparative negligence statute on strict liability does not arise in states such as Arkansas, Maine, Mississippi, Nevada, or Rhode Island where statutes do not contain any words of limitation such as 'to recover damages for negli-

gence.'" Schwartz, Comparative Negligence § 12.1 at 196 (1974).

The following states have statutes that contain the term negligence: Connecticut, Colorado, Georgia, Hawaii, Idaho, Kansas, Massachusetts, Minnesota, Montana, New Hampshire, New Jersey, North Dakota, Ohio, Oklahoma, Pennsylvania, South Dakota, Texas, Utah, Vermont, Wisconsin and Wyoming.

warranty. We believe that the just outcome of a case should not be determined by adroit pleading or semantical distinctions. A defendant's culpability is the basis for an award of damages, whether that culpability is denominated negligence, strict liability, or breach of warranty. Similarly, a plaintiff's culpable conduct is the basis for an apportionment of those damages. In the present case there is a finding of fact by the jury in regard to plaintiff's culpability which cannot be dismissed by adverting to semantics.

In his brief, plaintiff relies on a variety of Rhode Island cases to support the position that comparative-negligence principles should not be applied to strict liability and implied-warranty actions. Our examination of these cases leads us to conclude that plaintiff's reliance is misplaced.

. . .

The plaintiff also relies on our decision in Kennedy v. Providence Hockey Club Inc., 119 R.I. 70, 376 A.2d 329 (1977). He correctly recites the law in this jurisdiction when he states that Rhode Island has refused to allow the doctrines of assumption of the risk and contributory negligence to become muddled. Id. In *Kennedy* we clearly distinguished the two doctrines:

> "As we have defined assumption of the risk, the concern is with *knowingly* encountering the danger. This is to be contrasted with *negligently* encountering a risk and falling victim, at one time in our legal history, to the defense of contributory negligence. It seems to us that one who 'sees, knows, understands and appreciates' what he is doing, D'Andrea v. Sears, Roebuck & Co., [109 R.I. 479, 287 A.2d 629 (1972),] is worlds apart from one who unwittingly and unsuspectingly falls prey to another's negligence. In the former instance the plaintiff can be said to have consented to the possibility of harm, whereas in the latter situation he has failed to assess accurately his situation and the ramifications of his own action." *Kennedy*, 119 R.I. at 76, 376 A.2d at 333.

The plaintiff is also correct when he states that the enactment of our comparative-negligence statute, § 9–20–4, did not dissolve the distinction. However, what plaintiff fails to realize is that the two doctrines can coexist despite the fact that they do not overlap. Each doctrine concerns a different type of culpable conduct on the part of a plaintiff, one being a knowing encounter with danger and the other a negligent encounter with a risk or danger. In *Kennedy*, both doctrines were applied to a negligence count, and it was found, through the granting of summary judgment, that the plaintiff's conduct more closely resembled a knowing encounter with danger and therefore assumption of the risk should apply.

In the present case we see no reason why the same type of application should not be made. The jury, in a strict-liability action or an implied-warranty action, should be able to consider a plaintiff's negligent encounter with danger if it decides that plaintiff's conduct does not reach that level of culpability that amounts to a knowing encounter with danger, that is, assumption of the risk. The damages should then be reduced by the percent the plaintiff was found to have been negligent. The contention that such a comparison amounts to mixing apples and oranges is nothing more than an argument based on semantics. Adhering to such artificial distinctions would result in a windfall for plaintiffs, in that their conduct, however culpable, could not be taken into account as long as it fell short of their assuming the risk. In light of the difficulty of proving that a plaintiff knowingly encountered a danger, and in consideration of the harsh result that occurs if the proof is successful since the action would be completely barred thereby, we feel that the application of comparative-negligence principles to strict liability and implied warranty achieves a fair and equitable result in the apportionment of damages.

. . .

QUESTIONS AND NOTES

1. In recent years comparative-fault or comparative-negligence rules have been adopted in the majority of states. In the negligence area they replace contributory-negligence rules under which a plaintiff whose own negligence was to any degree a cause of the injury was barred from recovery. The move to comparative fault was, therefore, a liberalizing rule that allowed previously barred plaintiffs to recover.

This stands in sharp contrast to the effect of applying those rules to implied-warranty actions. Before adoption of the comparative-negligence statutes, most courts had taken the position of the Restatement (Second) of Torts § 402A, comment n that in implied-warranty and strict-tort actions, only assumption of the risk—not ordinary negligence—is a defense to a strict-tort (or warranty) action. Therefore, as to strict-tort or warranty actions, use of comparative-fault principles *reduces* plaintiffs' recoveries below what they would have been under prior law.

2. *Correia* and *Fiske* show that courts (and legislatures) have disagreed as to whether comparative fault ought to be applied in strict tort or warranty actions. What do you think? Does comparative fault undercut the policy behind strict tort and warranty liability? Is it possible to compare plaintiff's negligent conduct with defendant's non-negligent-based strict tort or warranty liability?

If comparative fault is to apply in strict tort or warranty actions, to what plaintiff's conduct should it apply? *Fiske* suggests that assumption of the risk should still be a complete defense. Do you agree? At the other extreme, should comparative fault apply only to assumption of the risk, with other negligent conduct of the plaintiff being no defense at all?

How is comparative fault to be measured in a strict tort or warranty action? Should the comparison be of relative degrees of blameworthiness? Or should the comparison be of relative degrees of causation? or of both? or of neither? Observe that relative degrees of causation might be said to be also dealt with as a part of proximate cause. For a good discussion of the questions just asked, see the opinion of Justice Linde in Sandford v. Chevrolet Division of General Motors, 292 Or. 590, 642 P.2d 624 (1982).

D.   FEDERAL AND STATE STATUTES APPLYING SPECIAL RULES TO CONSUMER TRANSACTIONS

1.   THE MAGNUSON-MOSS CONSUMER WARRANTY ACT

a.   INTRODUCTION

Dissatisfaction with the operation of certain UCC rules in consumer transactions led Congress in 1975 to enact the Magnuson–Moss Consumer Warranty Act. Primary among the points of dissatisfaction was the deception implicit in the ubiquitous practice of giving something with one hand (viz., an express warranty) while simultaneously taking away much more with the other (viz., disclaimer of implied warranties and exclusion of liability for damages for breach of the express warranty). To address the deception and perceived unfairness in this practice, the Act has three principal components: (1) disclosure; (2) a ban on disclaimers; and (3) enhanced remedies.

To understand the Act, careful attention to the definitions is essential. Please read the definition of "written warranty" (§ 101(6), 15 U.S.C.A. § 2301(6)). How does it differ from the definition of "express warranty" in Article 2? Please read the definitions of "supplier," "consumer," and "consumer product."

The Act does not require a supplier to give a written warranty. That remains entirely within the discretion of the supplier. If, however, the supplier does give a written warranty, the requirements of the Magnuson–Moss Act apply.

(1) Section 103 (15 U.S.C.A. § 2303) requires suppliers of consumer goods who give written warranties to label those warranties either "full" or "limited." To be a full warranty, the warranty must meet the standards specified in section 104 (15 U.S.C.A. § 2304). If a written warranty does not meet those standards, it may not properly be labeled "full warranty." If the supplier nevertheless labels it "full warranty," then it is deemed to incorporate all the standards specified for full warranties (§ 104(e), 15 U.S.C.A. § 2304(e)). In addition, the Act requires "full and conspicuous" disclosure of the terms of the warranty (§ 102(a), 15 U.S.C.A. § 2302(a)). The Federal Trade Commission is authorized to promulgate implementing regulations, and it has done so. FTC, Disclosure of Written Consumer Product Warranty Terms and Conditions, 16 C.F.R. §§ 701.1–701.4.

(2) Section 108 (15 U.S.C.A. § 2308) sweeps away disclaimers of implied warranties. If a supplier gives a written warranty, the supplier may not disclaim implied warranties. This is true even if the written warranty is a "limited warranty." The supplier may, however, be able to limit the duration of the implied warranties.

(3) Finally, if the warrantor breaches a written warranty or an Article 2 implied warranty, the consumer has a federal cause of action and, if successful, may recover attorney's fees. (§ 110(d), 15 U.S.C.A. § 2310(d)). Article 2 contains no provision making attorney's fees available to a successful litigant, so the Magnuson–Moss Act provides a huge benefit to those who can assert its provisions.

Although the Act is entitled, "Consumer Warranty Act," its reach extends beyond consumer transactions. This is a function of the definitions of "consumer product" and "consumer." A "consumer product" is any goods that are normally used for personal, family, or household purposes. This means that an automobile or a television, for example, is within the definition even if the purchaser is a commercial entity. "Consumer" includes a buyer who purchases for use rather than resale. So when section 108 bans disclaimers on consumer products that are sold to consumers, it bans disclaimers on televisions sold to sports bars. And when section 110(d) gives a right of action to consumers, it confers a right of action on a corporation that purchases a car for its sales rep.

b. INVALIDATION OF DISCLAIMERS

The Act invalidates disclaimers of implied warranties, but only if the supplier makes a written warranty. "Supplier" includes the manufacturer of a consumer product, intermediate distributors, and the retailer. In any sale to a consumer, some of the suppliers may make written warranties and some may not. It is important to determine whether a particular supplier has made a written warranty. If it has, then the consumer may recover for any breach of an implied warranty by that supplier. Please read the definition of "implied warranty."

In Ventura v. Ford Motor Corp., 180 N.J.Super. 45, 433 A.2d 801 (App.Div.1981), plaintiffs purchased a new car that turned out to be defective. When repairs proved ineffective, plaintiffs sued the dealer (Marino Auto Sales) and the manufacturer, seeking to revoke their acceptance of the car and recover the price. The manufacturer warranted that the dealer would "repair or replace free any parts found ... to be defective ... within the earlier of 12 months or 12,000 miles." The contract between plaintiffs and the dealer contained a disclaimer of "all warranties" and a provision that "[t]he selling dealer ... agrees to promptly perform and fulfill all terms and conditions of the [manufacturer's warranty]." The court granted rescission:

> We will first consider the application of this act to the dealer, Marino Auto. As quoted above, paragraph 7 of the purchase order contract provides that there are no warranties, express or implied, made by the selling dealer or manufacturer except, in the case of a new motor vehicle, "the warranty expressly given to the purchaser upon delivery of such motor vehicle. . . ." This section also provides: "The selling dealer also agrees to promptly perform and fulfill all terms and conditions of the owner service policy." ... The provision in paragraph 7 in these circumstances is a "written warranty" within the meaning

of § 101(6)(B) since it constitutes an undertaking in connection with the sale to take "remedial action with respect to such product in the event that such product fails to meet the specifications set forth in the undertaking. . . ." In our view the specifications of the undertaking include, at the least, the provisions of the limited warranty furnished by Ford. . . .

... Accordingly, having furnished a written warranty to the consumer, the dealer as a supplier may not "disclaim or modify [except to limit in duration] any implied warranty to a consumer. . . ." The result of this analysis is to invalidate the attempted disclaimer by the dealer of the implied warranties of merchantability and fitness. Being bound by those implied warranties arising under state law, N.J.S.A. 12A:2–314 and –315, Marino Auto was liable to plaintiff for the breach thereof as found by the trial judge, and plaintiff could timely revoke his acceptance of the automobile and claim a refund of his purchase price. N.J.S.A. 12A:2–608 and N.J.S.A. 12A:2–711. . . .

Plaintiff also could have recovered damages against Ford for Ford's breach of its written limited warranty. Marino Auto was Ford's representative for the purpose of making repairs to plaintiff's vehicle under the warranty. . . .

One question posed by this case is whether recovery of the purchase price from the manufacturer was available to plaintiff for breach of the manufacturer's warranty. If the warranty were a full warranty plaintiff would have been entitled to a refund of the purchase price under the Magnuson–Moss Warranty Act. Since Ford's warranty was a limited warranty we must look to state law to determine plaintiff's right to damages or other legal and equitable relief § 110(d)(1). Once privity is removed as an obstacle to relief we see no reason why a purchaser cannot also elect the equitable remedy of returning the goods to the manufacturer who is a warrantor and claiming a refund of the purchase price less an allowance for use of the product. . . .

c. IMPACT ON THE REQUIREMENT OF PRIVITY

In the last paragraph of the *Ventura* excerpt, the court states that a consumer may sue under the Act for a remote seller's breach of the implied warranty of merchantability. You will recall that as a matter of state law, the states are split on this question (pages 307–20 supra). Hence, *Ventura* suggests that section 110(d) eliminates any requirement of privity of contract for implied warranty. The Supreme Court of Illinois agreed:

> The Act broadly defines "consumer" in section 101(3) as "a buyer (other than for purposes of resale) of any consumer product, any person to whom such product is transferred during the duration of an implied or written warranty * * * and any other person who is entitled by the terms of such warranty * * * or under applicable State law to enforce against the warrantor * * * the obligations of the warranty." It has been suggested that this broad definition of "consumer" and the provisions of section 110(d)(1), which section authorizes a "consumer"

to maintain a civil action for damages for failure of a "supplier" or "warrantor" to comply with any obligation of a written or implied warranty, effectively abolish vertical privity. We do not think we can focus on any one section of Magnuson–Moss but should read the sections referred to together to accomplish the purpose of Magnuson–Moss of furnishing broad protection to the consumer.

. . . In cases where no Magnuson–Moss written warranty has been given, Magnuson–Moss has no effect upon State-law privity requirements because, by virtue of section 101(7), which defines implied warranty, implied warranty arises only if it does so under State law. However, if a Magnuson–Moss written warranty (either "full" or "limited") is given, by reason of the policy against disclaimers of implied warranty expressed in Magnuson–Moss and the provisions authorizing a consumer to sue a warrantor, the nonprivity "consumer" should be permitted to maintain an action on an implied warranty against the "warrantor." . . . [A] warrantor, by extending a written warranty to the consumer, establishes privity between the warrantor and the consumer which, though limited in nature, is sufficient to support an implied warranty under sections 2–314 and 2–315 of the UCC. The implied warranty thus recognized, by virtue of the definition in section 101(7) of Magnuson–Moss, must be one arising under the law of this State.

Szajna v. General Motors Corp., 115 Ill.2d 294, 104 Ill.Dec. 898, 503 N.E.2d 760, 768–69 (1986). Not all courts agree. In Walsh v. Ford Motor Co., 588 F.Supp. 1513, 1524–26 (D.D.C.1984), the court took a decidedly different approach:

Ford argues that State privity laws are preserved under the Act and must be considered by the Court before a plaintiff may assert an implied warranty claim under Magnuson–Moss. Ford bases its privity argument on the express provisions of the Act. It notes that although the Act provides for a Federal cause of action for breach of implied warranty, the Act defines implied warranty as "an implied warranty arising under State law (as modified by sections 108 and 104(a) of this act) in connection with the sale by a supplier of a consumer product." Section 101(7), 15 U.S.C. § 2301(7). . . .

In response plaintiffs have argued that State law privity doctrines do not apply under Magnuson–Moss because the Act creates a new Federal private cause of action for breach of implied warranty. Therefore, plaintiffs assert, the requirement that vertical privity exist between the purchaser and Ford is eliminated under the Act and cannot serve as a barrier for pursuing implied warranty claims. Specifically, plaintiffs cite to the Act's definition of "consumer," "supplier," and "warrantor" as a basis for arguing that state privity law has been superseded. When reading those definitions into section 110(d)(1), plaintiffs argue, the Court must conclude that any person to whom the vehicle is transferred during the life of the implied warranty is entitled to enforce that warranty by bringing suit.

Certainly, it is axiomatic that where the meaning of the statute is plain on its face, this Court need not take further inquiry into its purpose. Here, Congress has specifically provided that implied warranties "arise" under State law. Section 101(7), 15 U.S.C. 2301(7). If, in this action, there are to be any implied warranty claims at all under Magnuson–Moss, they must "originate" from or "come into being" from state law.[4] Therefore, if a State does not provide for a cause of action for breach of implied warranty where vertical privity is lacking, there cannot be a Federal cause of action for such a breach.

The statutory history in this matter is also clear. In a Senate report from the Committee on Commerce, the committee stated that:

It is not the intent of the Committee to alter *in any way* the manner in which implied warranties are created under the Uniform Commercial Code. For instance, an implied warranty of fitness for a particular purpose which might be created by an installing supplier is not, in many instances, enforceable by the consumer against the manufacturing supplier. *The Committee does not intend to alter currently existing state law on these subjects.*

Senate Comm. on Commerce, S.Rep. No. 151, 93d Cong., 1st Sess. 21 (1973) (emphasis added). . . .

Plaintiffs, however, argue that the definitions "consumer," "supplier," and "warrantor" in section 101 abolish any state law privity requirements. They assert that by transposing these definitions into the subsection that provides for civil actions by consumers for breach of warranty, the Court is compelled to conclude that State privity requirements are abolished. When transposing these definitions of section 101, section 110(d)(1) provides:

. . . a consumer [including "a buyer (other than for purposes of resale) of any consumer product, any person to whom such product is transferred"] who is damaged by the failure of a supplier ["any person engaged in the business of making a consumer product directly or indirectly available to consumers"] [or] warrantor ["any supplier or other person who . . . is or may be obligated under an implied warranty"] ["arising under State law"] . . . to comply with . . . an implied warranty ["arising under State law"] . . . may bring suit. . . .

In adding these definitions to section 110(d)(1), it is still evident to this Court that an action under Magnuson–Moss may be brought by a "consumer who is damaged by the failure of a supplier to comply with any obligation under [the act] . . . includ[ing] implied warranties arising under State law." H.R.Rep. No. 93–1107, 93d Cong., 2d Sess., reprinted in 1974 U.S.Code Cong. & Ad.News 7702, 7723. The definitions do not alter the requirement that an implied warranty, if it is to arise at all, must arise under State law and "[i]f state law requires

---

4. The Random House Dictionary of the English Language (Random House, N.Y. 1969) defines arise as "1. to come into being, action, or notice; originate; appear; spring up."

vertical privity to enforce an implied warranty and there is none, then, like the yeastless souffle, the warranty does not 'arise.' " Feinstein v. Firestone Tire & Rubber Co., 535 F.Supp. at 605 n. 13.

Which view is correct? Does the Magnuson–Moss Act override state law in those states that require vertical privity for implied-warranty liability?

In *Szajna* the Illinois Supreme Court believed that it is a question of state law whether the state's requirement of privity survives enactment of Magnuson–Moss. The federal courts disagree. For example, in Larry J. Soldinger Associates, Ltd. v. Aston Martin Lagonda of North America, Inc., 1999 WL 756174 (N.D.Ill.1999), the United States District Court for the Northern District of Illinois stated:

> ... In Illinois, a plaintiff may pursue a UCC breach of implied warranty claim for economic damages only if he is in privity of contract with the seller. Rothe v. Maloney Cadillac, Inc., 119 Ill.2d 288, 292, 518 N.E.2d 1028, 1029–30 (1988) (noting that "with respect to purely economic loss, the UCC article II implied warranties give a buyer of goods a potential cause of action only against his immediate seller")). . . .

> Count II ... alleges breach of implied warranty of merchantability [and] relies on the Magnuson–Moss Act. See 15 U.S .C. § 2310(d). . . . Defendant's argument, in a nutshell, is as follows. Section 2310(d) of the Act allows for suits based on breach of implied warranties; section 2301(7) defines implied warranties as "an implied warranty arising under State law (as modified by section 2308 and 2304(a) of this title)." 15 U.S.C. § 2301(7). Under Illinois law, as discussed above, contractual privity is a prerequisite for UCC breach of implied warranty claims. Plaintiff had no privity of contract with Aston Martin. Because Magnuson–Moss defines breach of implied warranty claims by reference to Illinois law, Defendant contends, Plaintiff's claims must fail. Defendant urges the court to follow several federal decisions that support this conclusion, including Walsh v. Ford Motor Co., 807 F.2d 1000, 1014 (D.C.Cir.1986), Abraham v. Volkswagen of Am., 795 F.2d 238, 247–48 (2d Cir.1986), Walsh v. Ford Motor Co., 106 F.R.D. 378, 395–96 (D.D.C.1985), *rev'd on other grounds,* 807 F.2d 1000 (D.C.Cir.1986), and Skelton v. General Motors Corp., No. 79 C 1243, 1985 WL 1860, at *2–3 (N.D.Ill. June 21, 1985).

> Plaintiff, on the other hand, contends that Defendant here ignores controlling law: in both *Rothe* and *Szajna,* the Illinois Supreme Court has ruled that contractual privity is not required to maintain a breach of implied warranty claim under the Act. These cases held that, although "the UCC article II implied warranties give a buyer of goods a potential cause of action only against his immediate seller," Magnuson–Moss "broadens the reach of the UCC ... affording consumers substantially greater protection," so implied warranty claims under the federal statute do not require contractual privity. *Rothe,* 119 Ill.2d at 293–95, 518 N.E.2d at 1030–31 (citing *Szajna*). In light of the "crystal clear pronouncements of the Illinois Supreme Court on what Illinois

law requires," Plaintiff argues that an absence of privity of contract does not preclude his Magnuson–Moss breach of implied warranty claims. . . .

. . . After carefully considering the arguments of both sides, the court finds the *Abraham* line of authority more persuasive.

Szajna, on which Plaintiff relies, was the Illinois Supreme Court's seminal case . . . . Because the plaintiff was not in privity of contract with GM, and claimed only economic losses, the court decided that he could not proceed with his claim under the UCC.

Moving on to the Magnuson–Moss claim, the court perused the text of the statute, beginning with Section 2301(7), which defines implied warranties as those "arising under state law (as modified by section 2308 and 2304(a) of this title)." . . .

. . . The court's rationale was that by extending a written warranty, the manufacturer establishes a privity-like relationship with the consumer sufficient to support an implied warranty. This result, the court believed, was consistent with the broad policy goals of the statute: "Magnuson–Moss broadens the reach of the UCC article II implied warranties, affording consumers substantially greater protection against defective goods." *Rothe,* 119 Ill.2d at 295, 518 N.E.2d at 1031 (characterizing the reasoning of *Szajna*).

Several federal courts—*Abraham,* the court of appeals in *Walsh, Skelton*—have taken a view contrary to that of the Illinois Supreme Court. The Second Circuit's analysis in *Abraham* is the most comprehensive. . . . The court of appeals observed that the " 'arising under' phrase [in Section 2301(7) of the Act] strongly suggests that the obligations of the warranty are solely the creation of state law, an inference further strengthened by the explicit reference [in Section 2301(7)] to 'modifications' of such state law elsewhere in the Act, none of which deal with privity." [*Abraham,* 795 F.2d] at 247. Still, the court acknowledged that a liberal reading of the statutory text arguably "provide[s] for an action by a consumer without privity against a supplier on an implied warranty arising under the law of a state that does not allow transferees without privity to sue." *Id.* The court therefore considered the extent to which Magnuson–Moss added a new layer of federal law to existing state warranty doctrines.

Parsing the statute's legislative history, *Abraham* found "that with regard to written warranties . . . privity is not required," and that Congress clearly intended to limit the ability of sellers to disclaim implied warranties. *Id.* at 248. The *Abraham* court determined that Congress nevertheless intended that state law would govern the applicability of implied warranties, except where Sections 2308 and 2304(a) explicitly modified state law. . . .

The court concurs with the conclusion of *Abraham* for several reasons. First, although this court technically is not bound by a Second Circuit decision, *Abraham* holds greater sway than *Szajna,* since the Seventh

Circuit asks that district courts give "substantial weight" to the "direct authority of a sister circuit." Richards v. Local 134, Int'l Bhd. of Electrical Workers, 790 F.2d 633, 636 (7th Cir.1986). Additionally, *Szajna's* decision to review and interpret not only Section 2308 but also Sections 2301(3) and 2310, while neglecting to consider 2304(a), is inconsistent with plain language of the touchstone Section 2301(7), which defines "implied warranty" by reference to state law and Sections 2308 and 2304(a) only.

. . .

Moreover, the decisions of these federal courts are consistent with the plain language of Section 2301(7), which refers to state law and Sections 2308 and 2304(a) to define the parameters of implied warranties. Sections 2308 and 2304(a) deal primarily with limitations on disclaimers, however; they do not discuss privity at all. What remains to guide the interpretation of the Act on the question of privity, then, is state law, which in Illinois is as follows: under the Illinois UCC, contractual privity is a prerequisite for recovery under a theory of breach of implied warranty. In sum, because Plaintiff was not in contractual privity with Aston Martin, summary judgment is appropriate . . . .

The Seventh Circuit has since endorsed this conclusion. Voelker v. Porsche Cars North America, Inc., 353 F.3d 516 (7th Cir. 2003).

d. LEASES

The definition of "consumer" begins, "The term 'consumer' means a buyer . . . ." Similarly, the Act defines "written warranty" as an affirmation "made in connection with the sale of a consumer product . . . ." If a consumer acquires goods by means of a lease, does the consumer have the benefit of Magnuson–Moss? The issue was before the court in *Voelker*, and it stated:

The Magnuson–Moss Act defines three categories of "consumer[s]"[1]: a category one consumer is "a buyer (other than for the purposes of resale) of any consumer product"; a category two consumer is "any person to whom such product is transferred during the duration of an implied or written warranty (or service contract) applicable to the product"; and, a category three consumer is "any other person who is entitled by the terms of such warranty (or service contract) or under applicable State law to enforce against the warrantor (or service contractor) the obligations of the warranty (or service contract)." 15 U.S.C. § 2301(3). Voelker claims to be a consumer under all three categories.

The first category of consumer would require Voelker to be a "buyer," which presupposes a sale. The "sale" that Voelker identifies

---

1. For ease of reference, we refer to the three types of consumers as category one, two or three consumers, although the statute itself does not use this terminology.

in his brief is the lease, which he argues is functionally equivalent to a sale. No binding authority governs the question of whether a lease can constitute a sale under the Magnuson–Moss Act. Persuasive authorities, for their part, are divided. See Szubski v. Mercedes–Benz, U.S.A., LLC, 796 N.E.2d 81 (Ohio Com. Pleas 2003) (collecting cases on both sides of the issue).

As the Court of Appeals of New York has pointed out, the Act does not define "sale." DiCintio v. DaimlerChrysler Corp., 97 N.Y.2d 463, 768 N.E.2d 1121, 1124, 742 N.Y.S.2d 182 (N.Y. 2002). Under the Uniform Commercial Code, however, it is well established that a sale occurs only where there is a passing of title to a buyer. In common speech, similarly, a sale is typically understood to require the transfer of title. See Webster's Ninth New Collegiate Dictionary 1037 (1987) (defining "sale," in relevant part, as "the transfer of ownership of and title to property from one person to another for a price.") Against this backdrop, we conclude that no reasonable person reading the Magnuson–Moss Act would conclude that there is a sale to Voelker under the Act where title does not pass to him. Here, it is undisputed that title never passed to Voelker under the lease agreement, and so the lease cannot constitute a sale for purposes of making Voelker a category one consumer.

When Voelker signed his lease, however, title had already passed from the car's manufacturer, Porsche, to the lessor, Copans. . . . Voelker argues that the sale needed to qualify him as a category one consumer occurred when the manufacturer sold the vehicle to Copans, who in turn became Voelker's lessor. We disagree because, for a sale to qualify a plaintiff as a category one consumer, it must be made to a buyer *"other than for purposes of resale."* 15 U.S.C. § 2301(3) (emphasis added). In other words, it is a final sale to a user, not a sale to an intended reseller. But whenever a lessor takes title to a car, at least one of its purposes is, presumably, the actual resale of the vehicle. DiCintio, 768 N.E.2d at 1127. In this particular case, Voelker's lease, a copy of which is attached to the complaint, establishes that Copans took title of the vehicle with intent ultimately to resell it: Paragraph 17 gives Voelker first option to buy the car at the end of the lease term or even before the end of the lease term . . . .

In short, for Voelker to qualify as a category one consumer under the Magnuson–Moss Act, there must have been a sale of the automobile "other than for the purposes of resale," and that sale must have included the transfer of title. Here, the only sale alleged in relation to the car was between the manufacturer, Porsche, and the lessor, Copans, and that sale occurred for the purposes of resale. Accordingly, accepting all facts alleged in the complaint as true, the transfer of the possession of the car to Voelker was not a sale and thus he is not entitled to proceed under the Magnuson–Moss Act as a category one consumer.

The next question is whether Voelker has stated a claim as a category two consumer. In other words, has Voelker alleged facts that would show that he is "any person to whom such product is *transferred during the duration* of an implied or written warranty (or service contract) applicable to the product"? 15 U.S.C. § 2301(3) (emphasis added). The "written warranty ... applicable to the product" that Voelker identifies is the New Car Limited Warranty, which Voelker has attached to his complaint. That warranty, however, did not begin until after possession of the car was transferred to Voelker, and not "during [the warranty's] duration." By its own terms, the warranty did not take effect until one of four antecedents occurred: "the date the car [was] first delivered to the first retail purchaser, or the date it was first used as a demonstrator, lease, or company car, whichever came first." The only triggering event that Voelker identifies is the date that the car was first used—by himself—as a lease car. Because the warranty did not begin until the date the car was "first used as a ... lease" car, the warranty did not begin until after he took possession. Thus, Voelker has failed to allege that the car was "transferred [to him] during the duration" of the New Car Limited Warranty, and, accepting all of the allegations in his complaint as true, he does not qualify as a category two consumer.

Finally, we consider whether Voelker has stated a claim as a category three consumer. That is, we ask whether he is "any other person who is entitled by the terms of such warranty (or service contract) or under applicable State law to enforce against the warrantor (or service contractor) the obligations of the warranty (or service contract)." 15 U.S.C. § 2301(3) (emphasis added). Copans, as the defendants assert, assigned to Voelker "all its rights under the Porsche Limited Warranty." Under the state law of Illinois, as an assignee of that warranty, a lessee like Voelker was entitled to enforce the rights arising from the warranty. Dekelaita v. Nissan Motor Corp., 343 Ill.App.3d 801, 799 N.E.2d 367 (Ill.App.2003). Therefore, Voelker qualifies as a category three consumer.

2. State Statutes Modifying Article 2 for Consumer Transactions

The Magnuson–Moss Act significantly limits a seller's right to disclaim warranties in consumer goods transactions *if* the seller gives a written warranty as defined in the Act: if the seller does not give a written warranty, the Magnuson–Moss limitations on disclaimers do not apply. However, many states have enacted legislation that limits or forbids warranty disclaimers whether or not the seller has given a written warranty. Most states that limit or forbid disclaimers have amended or eliminated UCC 2–316 and 2–719,[1] but others have adopted totally separate consumer

---

1. Alabama, Ala.Code 1975 §§ 7—2–316(5), 7–2–719(4); Connecticut, Conn.Gen. Stat.Ann. § 42a–2–316(5); District of Columbia, D.C.Code § 28:2–316.01; Maine, Me.Rev.

protection acts.[2] In addition, one state has recently adopted a consumer protection statute, but has incorporated it directly into the Article 2.[3]

Five eastern states (Connecticut, Maine, Maryland, Massachusetts, and Vermont), as well as the District of Columbia, have amended 2–316 to provide that 2–316 does not apply to sales of consumer goods or services.[4] The statutes provide that any language, oral or written, that attempts to exclude or modify implied warranties as to consumer goods cannot be enforced. These sections also affect 2–719 (which generally permits modification or limitation of remedy) by providing that an exclusion or modification of consumer's remedies for breach of an implied warranty cannot be enforced.

New Hampshire follows a more lenient approach than that of many of its neighbors. New Hampshire's 2–316(4) provides that disclaimers of implied warranties in sales of goods for personal, family, or household use are effective to limit the liability of merchant sellers, but only if the disclaimer strictly complies with specified statutory requirements. To limit liability for breach of an implied warranty, the seller must provide the buyer with a conspicuous writing, either before or at the time of sale, which clearly informs the buyer in simple and concise language that (1) the goods are being sold on an "as is" or "with all faults" basis, (2) the entire risk as to quality and performance of the goods is with the buyer, and (3) the buyer will assume the entire cost of necessary servicing or repair. These disclaimer requirements are identical to those contained in California's and Rhode Island's consumer protection statutes discussed below. In addition, the New Hampshire statute provides that the writing must be signed by the buyer.

Massachusetts, Maryland, and the District of Columbia also extend consumer protection by qualifying manufacturers' attempts to limit or modify remedies available to consumers for breach of *express* warranties. Any language that attempts to limit or modify a consumer's remedies for

---

Stat.Ann. tit. 11, § 2–316(5); Maryland, Md. Code Com.Law § 2–316.1; Massachusetts, Mass. Ann.Laws ch. 106, § 2–316A; Mississippi, Miss.Code, §§ 75–2–314(1), (3), 75–2–315, 75–2–719(4); New Hampshire, N.H.Rev. Stat.Ann. § 382–A:2–316(4); South Carolina, S.C.Code tit. 36, § 2–316(5) (2002); Washington, Wash.Rev.Code § 62A.2–316(4), 62A.2–719(3).

2. California,   Cal.Civ.Code   Ann. §§ 1790–1795.7;   Kansas,   Kan.Stat.Ann. §§ 50–639, 50–644; Minnesota, Minn.Stat. Ann. §§ 325G.17–325G.20; West Virginia, W.Va.Code §§ 46A–1–107, 46A–8–102.

3. Rhode Island, R.I.Gen.Laws § 6A–2–329.

4. Consumer goods and services are those which are used or bought primarily for

personal, family, or household purposes (see UCC 9–109). The Connecticut and Vermont statutes provide that disclaimers of implied warranties are unenforceable only as to new or unused consumer goods. As to used goods, the provisions of 2–316(2), (3), and (4) still operate to permit disclaimers of the implied warranties. In addition, the California and Rhode Island consumer protection statutes discussed below apparently apply only to sales of new consumer goods. The implied warranties of merchantability and fitness do not arise in sales of used consumer goods under those statutes. The Maryland statute provides that disclaimers of implied warranties are effective as to certain used automobiles if the disclaimers meet specified requirements.

breach of the manufacturer's express warranties is unenforceable unless the manufacturer provides reasonable and expeditious means of performing the warranty obligations.[5]

Other states modify Article 2's disclaimer provisions, but most do not provide consumers with the kind of protection found in the statutes of the states discussed in the preceding paragraphs. The Alabama law, for example, permits enforceable disclaimers, but includes a new subsection (5) to 2–316, which provides that a seller cannot limit or exclude his liability for damages for personal injury in the case of consumer goods.

Washington has also modified 2–316 and 2–719. The Washington statute provides that in any case where goods are purchased primarily for personal, family, or household use, disclaimers by merchant sellers of the warranty of merchantability or fitness for particular purpose are not effective except insofar as the disclaimer sets forth with particularity the qualities and characteristics that are not being warranted. This means that a seller may not simply say, "All implied warranties are disclaimed," but instead must state specifically the characteristics of the product which are not warranted.

Several other states, notably California, Kansas, Minnesota, Rhode Island, and West Virginia, have adopted consumer-protection statutes that affect sellers' warranties. Under the California Song–Beverly Consumer Warranty Act a manufacturer, distributor, or retailer who makes express warranties may not limit, modify, or disclaim the implied warranties of merchantability and fitness that arise in every sale of consumer goods. These implied warranties may not be disclaimed except on an "as is" or "with all faults" basis and then only if the seller strictly complies with the statute's provisions. To disclaim, the manufacturer must attach to the goods a conspicuous writing that clearly informs the buyer prior to the sale in simple and concise language that (1) the goods are being sold on an "as is" or "with all faults" basis, (2) the entire risk as to the quality and performance of the goods is with the buyer, and (3) the buyer will assume the entire cost of all necessary servicing or repair.

Rhode Island has adopted a consumer protection statute very similar to the Song–Beverly Act, but has incorporated it directly into its version of the Uniform Commercial Code as 2–329. The Rhode Island statute provides that implied warranties can only be disclaimed on an "as is" or "with all faults" basis, and then only if the disclaimer complies with the statute's requirements, which are identical to those in the California Act. Rhode Island's 2–329 also provides that no express warranty may disclaim implied warranties.

As with the Song–Beverly Act, the Minnesota statute permits "as is" sales of new goods so long as the seller makes proper disclosure that the sale is on an "as is" or "with all faults" basis and that the entire risk as to

---

5. Massachusetts law provides that the manufacturer must maintain facilities within the Commonwealth, but the District of Co-lumbia and Maryland laws are silent as to what constitutes "reasonable and expeditious means."

quality and performance is with the buyer. The Minnesota Act, like Rhode Island's 2–329, provides that no express warranty may disclaim implied warranties.

The West Virginia Consumer Credit and Protection Act prohibits any exclusion, modification, or limitation of express and implied warranties and of remedies for breach of warranty. In the event that a manufacturer violates the Act, an aggrieved consumer may recover actual damages or $200, whichever is greater.

Kansas also has a statute that prohibits disclaimers. In the case of a consumer transaction, no supplier may exclude, modify, or limit the implied warranties or any remedy for breach. Such disclaimers or limitations are void, and if a consumer prevails in an action based upon breach of warranty and the supplier has violated the statute, the court may award reasonable attorney's fees, a civil penalty of $2,000, *and* actual damages.

Breach of warranty gives rise to a cause of action under the UCC. It also may give rise to a cause of action under other law. For example, the Texas Deceptive Trade Practices Act, which enumerates various kinds of conduct that amount to deceptive practices, provides that a consumer may recover under that Act for breach of express or implied warranty. Tex. Bus. & Com. Code § 17.50(a)(2). Many states have statutes, modeled after the Federal Trade Commission Act, which broadly prohibit "unfair or deceptive acts or practices" in consumer transactions. These statutes may apply in warranty-related situations. The manufacturer of a temperature controller told a buyer that the product had been used only at a trade show. It actually had been sold and returned as defective. When the manufacturer resold it without any repair or reconditioning, a Massachusetts court held that the seller violated the little-FTC act, Mass.Gen.L. ch. 93A, § 2. Polycarbon Industries, Inc. v. Advantage Engineering, Inc., 260 F.Supp.2d 296 (D.Mass.2003). Note that both the Texas and Massachusetts statutes apply these consumer-protection statutes in such a way as to encompass certain commercial buyers.

Finally, between 1983 and 1986 virtually every state enacted a warranty law pertaining solely to new motor vehicles. These statutes respond to a shortcoming in Article 2's remedial scheme. Known as "lemon laws," they offer additional protection to buyers of new cars when the dealer and manufacturer fail to make good on their promises to repair defects. We will return to these laws in Chapter 6 in connection with the buyer's remedies for breach of warranty.

CHAPTER 6

BUYER'S REMEDIES FOR BREACH BY THE SELLER

A. INTRODUCTION

Section 2–301 states the basic obligations of the parties as, respectively, "to transfer and deliver" and "to accept and pay," both "in accordance with the contract." Sections 2–507 and 2–511 elaborate: the seller must tender delivery of the goods, and until the seller does so, the buyer does not have to accept the goods or pay for them (2–507(1)). The buyer must tender payment, and until the buyer does so, the seller does not have to tender or complete delivery of the goods (2–511(1)). Putting these together, we see that Article 2 embraces the common-law rule that ordinarily the parties must perform simultaneously. This chapter considers the rights of the parties when the seller allegedly fails to perform in accordance with the contract and the UCC.

A seller may breach by repudiating the contract, by failing to deliver the goods, or by making a tender of delivery that does not conform to the contract. The nonconformity may be either a defect in the goods or a defect in tender (e.g., late delivery). Article 2 gives the buyer several remedies for each of these kinds of breach, but not all of the remedies are available all the time.

If a seller makes a nonconforming tender the buyer often is entitled to reject the goods or revoke acceptance of them. Sometimes, however, the buyer must accept the goods even though they do not conform to the contract. If the buyer rightfully rejects nonconforming goods or revokes acceptance of them, the buyer may cancel the contract and recover damages (2–711(1)). If the buyer accepts the nonconforming goods and keeps them, the buyer cannot cancel the contract but may have a damages remedy. This chapter considers each of these alternatives, starting with the right to reject or revoke acceptance of nonconforming goods.

B. REJECTION, CURE, AND REVOCATION OF ACCEPTANCE

1. SINGLE-DELIVERY CONTRACTS

Under the common law, unless the parties have agreed otherwise, the performance of each party is a condition of the other party's obligation to perform. This leads to the common-sense conclusion that if one party refuses to perform, the other need not perform either. But what if the party does not refuse to perform, but just does not perform exactly as required? In the eighteenth and nineteenth centuries, the courts developed the substantial-performance doctrine, under which substantial performance—albeit not complete or perfect—triggers the obligation of the other. The second party may refuse to perform only if the performance of the first falls short of substantial performance. This rule applies today in may kinds of contracts, e.g., contracts for construction. At one time it applied to contracts for the sale of goods, too. But that changed in 1877, with the English case of Bowes v. Shand, L.R. 2 App.Cas. 455 (H.L.1877). *Bowes* involved a contract for the sale of 600 tons of rice, to be shipped in March or April of 1874. The seller tendered to the buyer 600 tons of merchantable rice, but almost all of the rice had been put on board the carrier ship in February, and only a small part of the rice was put on board in March. The term "shipped" as used in the contract was construed to mean "put on board," and under this construction the House of Lords held that the seller had breached by tendering rice that had been shipped in February and not in March or April as required by the contract. It held that this breach by the seller justified the buyer's rejection of all of the rice upon its arrival.

Seven years after *Bowes,* the United States Supreme Court followed its reasoning in two companion cases, Norrington v. Wright, 115 U.S. 188, 6 S.Ct. 12, 29 L.Ed. 366 (1885), and Filley v. Pope, 115 U.S. 213, 6 S.Ct. 19, 29 L.Ed. 372 (1885). *Norrington* involved a contract for the sale of 5,000 tons of iron rails, to be shipped at the rate of about 1,000 tons per month, beginning in February of 1880, the whole of the contract goods to be shipped before August 1, 1880. The Supreme Court construed the contract to mean that the seller was obligated to ship as close to 1,000 tons as possible in the months of February–June and any deficiencies were to be made up by shipments in July. The seller shipped 400 tons in February and 885 tons in March. The Court held that the seller's actions constituted breach justifying rescission by the buyer, even though shipment at the rate of 1,000 tons thereafter would have achieved shipment of the whole of the 5,000 tons before August 1. In *Filley,* the seller agreed to ship Scotch iron from Glasgow as soon as possible. He was unable to obtain a vessel out of Glasgow, so he shipped the iron from Leith. The market price of iron declined, and the buyer rejected the goods when they arrived. The Supreme Court held the rejection rightful, stating that a court could not inquire into the reasons the parties had for stipulating shipment from Glasgow, or whether the place of shipment was of any moment to the parties. The fact that the tender was not in strict compliance with the terms of the contract was enough to justify rejection.

The rule of *Bowes, Norrington*, and *Filley* is known as the perfect-tender rule. The Uniform Sales Act adopted the perfect-tender rule, but courts in states that adopted the Act sometimes failed to follow its provisions. For example, in National Import & Trading Co. v. E.A. Bear & Co., 324 Ill. 346, 155 N.E. 343 (1927), the buyer, relied on Bowes v. Shand to claim that the seller breached by loading eggs on March 31st when the contract called for the first shipment in April. It appeared that the market price for the eggs had declined sharply. Even though Illinois had adopted the Uniform Sales Act more than a decade earlier, the court did not refer to the Act and applied the substantial-performance rule.

For the position of the UCC on this question, see 2–601, which continues the perfect-tender rule in single-delivery contracts, and 2–612, which adopts a version of the substantial-performance rule in installment contracts (2–612), except as to defects in documents, where it adheres to the perfect-tender rule. The comments to 2–601 and 2–612 do not state any reason for the difference in treatment of single-delivery and installment-delivery contracts. Can you think of any justification for the different treatment?

D.P. Technology Corp. v. Sherwood Tool, Inc.

United States District Court, District of Connecticut, 1990.
751 F.Supp. 1038.

■ NEVAS, DISTRICT JUDGE. . . . On January 24, 1989, the defendant entered into a written contract to purchase a computer system, including hardware, software, installation and training, from the plaintiff. The complaint alleges that the computer system was "specifically" designed for the defendant and is not readily marketable. The contract, executed on January 24, 1989, incorporates the delivery term set forth in the seller's amended letter of January 17, 1989, stating that the computer system would be delivered within ten to twelve weeks. The delivery period specified in the contract ended on April 18, 1989. The software was delivered on April 12, 1989, and the hardware was delivered on May 4, 1989. On May 9, 1989, the defendant returned the merchandise to the plaintiff, and has since refused payment for both the software and the hardware. Thus, the plaintiff alleges that the defendant breached the contract by refusing to accept delivery of the goods covered by the contract while the defendant argues that it was rather the plaintiff who breached the contract by failing to make a timely delivery. [Defendant moved to dismiss plaintiff's complaint for failure to state a claim.]

. . .

Because the contract between the parties was a contract for the sale of goods, the law governing this transaction is to be found in Article 2 of the Uniform Commercial Code ("UCC"); Conn Gen.Stat. §§ 42a–2–101 et seq. In its motion to dismiss, the defendant argues that the plaintiff fails to state a claim upon which relief can be granted because the plaintiff breached the contract which provided for a delivery period of ten to twelve weeks from the date of the order, January 24, 1989. Since the delivery period ended on April 18, 1989, the May 4 hardware delivery was 16 days late. The defendant contends that because the plaintiff delivered the hardware after the contractual deadline, the late delivery entitled the defendant to reject delivery, since a seller is required to tender goods in conformance with the terms set forth in a contract. U.C.C. § 2–301; Conn.Gen.Stat. § 42a–2–301.

. . .

. . . [P]laintiff argues that the defendant relies on the perfect tender rule, allowing buyers to reject for any nonconformity with the contract. Plaintiff points out that the defendant has not cited one case in which a buyer rejected goods solely because of a late delivery, and that the doctrine of "perfect tender" has been roundly criticized. While it is true that the perfect tender rule has been criticized by scholars principally because it allowed a dishonest buyer to avoid an unfavorable contract on the basis of an insubstantial defect in the seller's tender, . . . the basic tender provision of the Uniform Commercial Code continued the perfect tender policy developed by the common law and embodied in the Uniform Sales Act. Section 2–601 states that with certain exceptions,[5] the buyer has the right to reject "if the goods or the tender of delivery fail *in any respect* to conform to the contract." (emphasis supplied). Conn.Gen.Stat. § 42a–2–601. The courts that have considered the issue have agreed that the perfect tender rule has survived the enactment of the Code. . . . Similarly, courts interpreting § 2–601 have strictly interpreted it to mean any nonconformity, thus excluding the doctrine of substantial performance.[6] Printing Center of Texas, Inc. v. Supermind Pub. Co., Inc., 669 S.W.2d 779, 783 (Tex.App. 1984) (the term "conform" within § 2–601 authorizing the buyer to reject the whole if the goods or tender of delivery fail in any respect to conform to the contract does not mean substantial performance but complete performance); Astor v. Boulos Co., Inc., 451 A.2d 903, 906 (Me.1982) (the generally disfavored "perfect tender rule" survives enactment of the UCC as respects a contract for sale of goods but does not control in the area of service contracts which are governed by the standard of substantial performance); Moulton Cavity & Mold, Inc. v. Lyn–Flex Indus., Inc., 396 A.2d 1024, 1027– 28 (1979) (holding that the doctrine of substantial performance "has no application to a contract for the sale of goods"); Jakowski v. Carole Chevrolet, Inc., 180 N.J.Super. 122, 125, 433 A.2d 841, 843 (1981) (degree of nonconformity of goods is irrelevant in assessing buyer's concomitant right to reject them). These courts have thus found that the tender must be

5. See, e.g., §§ 2–508 (seller's limited right to cure defects in tender), 2–608 (buyer's limited right to revoke acceptance) and 2–612 (buyer's limited right to reject nonconforming tender under installment contract). See also Calamari and Perillo, Contracts, (2d ed.1972) at 413 n. 81 ("It has been suggested that these exceptions in fact represent a new rule, supplanting the traditional perfect tender rule in that despite § 2–601, the intent of the Code is to apply the doctrine of substantial performance to sales contracts.").

6. This interpretation allowing a buyer to cancel a contract for any nonconformity dates back to the common law interpretation of the perfect tender rule in the law of sales which differed from the law of contracts, which allows rescission only for material breaches. Ramirez v. Autosport, 88 N.J. 277, 284, 440 A.2d 1345, 1349 (1982). Thus, Judge Learned Hand stated in Mitsubishi Goshi Kaisha v. J. Aron & Co., Inc., 16 F.2d 185, 186 (2d Cir.1926), that "[t]here is no room in commercial contracts for the doctrine of substantial performance." While Judge Hand wrote in a pre–UCC context, modern courts have reiterated the view that perfect tender does not require substantial performance but complete performance.

perfect in the context of the perfect tender rule in the sense that the proffered goods must conform to the contract in every respect. Connecticut, however, appears in this regard to be the exception. Indeed, in the one Connecticut case interpreting § 2–601, Franklin Quilting Co., Inc. v. Orfaly, 1 Conn.App. 249, 251, 470 A.2d 1228, 1229 (1984), in a footnote, the appellate court stated that "the 'perfect tender rule' requires a *substantial nonconformity* to the contract before a buyer may rightfully reject the goods." Id. at 1229 n.3, citing White & Summers, Uniform Commercial Code, (2d ed.), § 8–3 (emphasis supplied). Thus, the Connecticut Appellate Court has adopted "the White and Summers construction of § 2–601 as in substance a rule that does not allow rejection for insubstantial breach such as a short delay causing no damage." Id., (3rd ed.). § 8–3. See also National Fleet Supply, Inc. v. Fairchild, 450 N.E.2d 1015, 1019 n. 4 (Ind.App.1983) (despite UCC's apparent insistence on perfect tender, it is generally understood that rejection is not available in circumstances where the goods or delivery fail in some small respect to conform to the terms of the sales contract (citing White and Summers)); McKenzie v. Alla–Ohio Coals, Inc., 29 U.C.C.Rep.Serv. (Callaghan) 852, 856–57 (D.D.C.1979) (there is substantial authority that where a buyer has suffered no damage, he should not be allowed to reject goods because of an insubstantial nonconformity).

As noted above, a federal court sitting in diversity must apply the law of the highest court of the state whose law applies. Since this court has determined that Connecticut law governs, the next task is to estimate whether the Connecticut Supreme Court would affirm the doctrine of substantial nonconformity, as stated in *Orfaly*, an opinion of the Connecticut Appellate Court. When the highest state court has not spoken on an issue, the federal court must look to the inferior courts of the state and to decisions of sister courts as well as federal courts. As noted, the weight of authority is that the doctrine of substantial performance does not apply to the sale of goods. However, as noted by White and Summers, in none of the cases approving of perfect rather than substantial tender was the nonconformity insubstantial, such as a short delay of time where no damage is caused to the buyer. White and Summers, Uniform Commercial Code (3rd ed.), § 8–3 n.8. In the instant case, there is no claim that the goods failed to conform to the contract. Nor is there a claim that the buyer was injured by the 16–day delay. There is, however, a claim that the goods were specially made, which might affect the seller's ability to resell. Thus Connecticut's interpretation of § 2–601 so as to mitigate the harshness of the perfect tender rule reflects the consensus of scholars that the rule is harsh and needs to be mitigated. Indeed, Summers and White state that the rule has been so "eroded" by the exceptions in the Code that "relatively little is left of it; the law would be little changed if § 2–601 gave the right to reject only upon 'substantial' nonconformity," especially since the Code requires a buyer or seller to act in good faith. R. Summers and J. White, Uniform Commercial Code (3rd ed.1988), § 8–3, at 357. See also Alden Press Inc. v. Block & Co., Inc., 123 Ill.Dec. 26, 173 Ill.App.3d 251, 527 N.E.2d 489, 493 (1988) (notwithstanding the perfect tender rule, the reasonableness of buyer's rejection of goods and whether such rejection of goods is in good faith are ultimately matters for the trier of fact); Printing Center of Texas v. Supermind Pub. Co., Inc., 669 S.W.2d 779, 784 (Tex.App.1984) (if the evidence establishes any nonconformity, the buyer is entitled to reject the goods as long as it is in good faith); Neumiller Farms, Inc. v. Cornett, 368 So.2d 272, 275 (Ala.1979) (claim of dissatisfaction with delivery of goods so as to warrant their rejection must be made in good faith, rather than in an effort to escape a bad bargain). A rejection of goods that have been specially manufactured for an insubstantial delay where no damage is caused is arguably not in good faith.

Although the Connecticut Supreme Court has not yet addressed the issue of substantial nonconformity, it has stated, in a precode case, Bradford Novelty Co. v. Technomatic, 142 Conn. 166, 170, 112 A.2d 214, 216 (1955), that although "[t]he time fixed by the parties for performance is, at law, deemed of the essence of the contract," where, as here, goods have been specially manufactured, "the time specified for delivery is less likely to be considered of the essence ... [since] in such a situation there is a probability of delay, and the loss to the manufacturer is likely to be great if the buyer refuses to accept and pay because of noncompliance with strict performance." Id. But see Marlowe v. Argentine Naval Com'n, 808 F.2d 120, 124 (D.C.Cir.1986) (buyer within its rights to cancel a contract for 6-day delay in delivery since "time is of the essence in contracts for the sale of goods") citing Norrington v. Wright, 115 U.S. 188, 203 n.6 (1885) ("In the contracts of merchants, time is of the essence.")

After reviewing the case law in Connecticut, this court finds that in cases where the nonconformity involves a delay in the delivery of specially manufactured goods, the law in Connecticut requires substantial nonconformity for a buyer's rejection under § 2–601, and precludes a dismissal for failure to state a claim on the grounds that the perfect tender rule, codified at § 2–601, demands complete performance. Rather, Connecticut law requires a determination at trial as to whether a 16–day delay under these facts constituted a substantial nonconformity. [Defendant's motion to dismiss is denied.]

QUESTIONS AND NOTES

1. The perfect-tender rule can be defended on the grounds that (1) in the usual case the seller can resell the goods to someone else and therefore is not substantially harmed by the rejection, and (2) the rule avoids difficult fact determinations as to whether any particular breach is material. However, in cases like *D.P. Technology*, when the goods are specially manufactured for the buyer, it seems unfair to the seller to permit the buyer to reject for inconsequential breaches. The court in *D.P. Technology* applies a Connecticut rule requiring "substantial nonconformity" for the right to reject goods under the perfect-tender rule to override the apparent rigidity of 2–601. What would the court have done if the computer or the software contained some minor defect, which the seller could not fix?

2.   Problem. Buyer contracts to buy 100,000 lbs. of sugar at a price of 20 cents per lb., delivery to be May 15. Seller tenders the sugar on May 14th, at which time the price of sugar is 12 cents per lb. Buyer refuses to accept the sugar, even though she has storage space and would incur no additional expense by accepting it. Is the rejection rightful?

3.   Good-faith limitation on the buyer's right to reject. Section 1–203 provides, "Every contract or duty within this Act imposes an obligation of good faith in its performance or enforcement." Does this limit the buyer's right to reject goods under 2–601? Is rejection within the universe of "performance or enforcement"? Consider the following excerpt from Honnold, Buyer's Right of Rejection, 97 U.Pa.L.Rev. 457, 475–476 (1949):

> The precise scope intended for [1–203] is not apparent. But its language is sufficiently vague to invite the argument that a rejection in a falling market was engendered by an ulterior motive to avoid the price decline and therefore was not made in "good faith."
>
> This new legal tool may be used to good effect to bar untoward rejection. But it gives little aid in determining whether in any specific case rejection is an appropriate remedy. In its customary setting in problems of *bona fide* purchase, a concept such as "good faith" is necessary, and reasonably workable. In dealing with the propriety of rejection, however, a legal test framed in terms of the buyer's state of mind is much more elusive. Presumably a rejection of goods which were seriously defective would not be held improper on evidence that the buyer was aware of a market decline and was delighted to have an avenue of escape from the purchase. In this field, less subjective tests are needed.

What is the content of this obligation to act in good faith?

4.   Exactly what does it mean to say that a buyer may reject goods if the goods or the tender fail in any respect to conform to the contract? How does the Code define "conform"? If a contract calls for the sale of 100,000 bushels of wheat, does the buyer have a right to reject if the seller delivers 100,001 bushels? 99,999 bushels?

While the case from which the following excerpt is taken did not involve an attempted rejection, the idea expressed may be relevant.

> Fargo's complaint alleges that the H–100 is "defective in material and workmanship" and "has required numerous and repetitive repairs, including some thirty-seven separate repair jobs." Certainly, however, every mechanical failure in a new and complex machine does not constitute a breach of warranty. N.C.R. v. Adell, 57 Mich.App. 413, 225 N.W.2d 785 (1975). At the outset then, it is necessary to distinguish and segregate those defects which merely required that [repairs] be performed and those legally significant defects which either remained uncured after reasonable opportunity to correct them or which are otherwise related to plaintiff's damage claims. Fargo does not contend that it was entitled to a perfect machine, nor that the installation and break-in period should have been completely service free.

Fargo Machine & Tool Co. v. Kearney & Trecker Corp., 428 F.Supp. 364, 370 (E.D.Mich.1977).

5.   Cure. Section 1–203 is not the only section that imposes some limits on a buyer's right to reject nonconforming goods or a nonconforming tender. Consider 2–508, which permits a seller, after a buyer has rejected goods, to cure the nonconformity for which the buyer rejected. In Problem 2, then, even if Buyer's rejection is proper, Seller may re-tender the goods on May 15. Hence 2–508 mitigates the harshness of the perfect-tender rule. It does not eliminate the harshness, however, because (1) re-tender will cause at least some additional expense, and (2) it may not be possible for the seller to acquire the necessary information and take the necessary steps to make an appropriate re-tender, as, for example, when tender is being made by a third party.

6.   Problem. Buyer orders 5,000 electric knives from Seller. When the knives arrive, Buyer discovers that there are only 4,500 in the shipment. The 4,500 all seem to conform to the contract. May Buyer reject the shipment? What if Buyer wants to reject 2,500 and keep 2,000: may it do so? Please consult 2–307, 2–601, 2–612, 2–105(6), 2–106(2). Is 1–203 relevant, too?

If the shipment is the first of two 5,000–unit shipments under a single contract, may Buyer reject all or part of the shipment? What additional facts are relevant?

7.   Problem. One morning as you are having your first mug of coffee, a long-time client, the owner of a chain of independent grocery stores, phones you. She tells you that she has a contract with a beer bottler for 1,000 cases of premium microbrew. The price is $25 per case FOB Seller's loading dock, and the delivery date is today. A truck driver has just arrived at her dock, but he has only 600 cases. He said the other 400 were stolen while he was in a truck stop having lunch. And, she reports, the seller permitted the trucking company to issue a bill of lading for the beer that limits the trucking company's liability to $20 per case. She asks, "What should I do? Should I reject the beer? Should I take the 600 cases and deduct $10,000? $2,000?" How do you respond?

8.   Problem. Buyer, the plumbing subcontractor on a construction job requiring Crane brand plumbing fixtures, contracts with Seller for delivery on March 1st of 100 Crane fixtures. The fixtures arrive in shipping cartons marked Crane, but the individual boxes containing the fixtures are marked American Standard. The fixtures themselves contain no identifying marks. May the buyer rightfully reject the fixtures? Does it make a difference whether or not the fixtures actually are Crane? That the seller, at time of delivery, notifies the buyer that the fixtures are Crane?

What if Buyer operates a plumbing supply store and purchases the fixtures for resale?

9.   CISG. The Convention on Contracts for the International Sale of Goods rejects the perfect tender rule. See Articles 25, 49(1)(a), 46(2), 47, 51. But see Article 52 as to early delivery. The CISG does not use the term rejection, but the apparent assumption is that the buyer can properly reject the goods only if it is "avoiding" the contract, and a contract can be avoided only for "fundamental breach," which is defined in Article 25.

In international sales, sellers could be substantially inconvenienced if a buyer in the country of destination could reject for minor defects, leaving the seller to arrange for their disposition. This may be true of sellers in some domestic transactions, too. Would you be in favor of abandoning the perfect-tender rule in domestic sales?

2.   INSTALLMENT CONTRACTS

As noted above, although Article 2 nominally adopts the perfect-tender rule for single-delivery contracts, it adopts essentially the substantial-performance rule for installment contracts. Section 2–612(2) provides that the buyer may reject an installment only if the installment has a nonconformity, the nonconformity substantially impairs the value of the installment, and the nonconformity cannot be cured. If the nonconformity substantially impairs the value of the whole contract—as opposed to just the value of the installment—the buyer may cancel the contract and recover damages for total breach 2–612(3), 2–711(1)).

In Graulich Caterer, Inc. v. Hans Holterbosch, Inc., 101 N.J.Super. 61, 243 A.2d 253 (App.Div.1968), Holterbosch contracted with Graulich for a large quantity of frozen meals to be heated in microwave ovens and sold at the Lowenbrau Pavilion at the 1964 New York World's Fair. The first delivery was made on April 23, 1964. Holterbosch's personnel were "stunned" by the product initially delivered and complained immediately that the units did not match previously furnished samples. The first delivery was rejected as "bland, unpresentable, tasteless," and generally unsaleable. The second delivery was no better than the first. Holterbosch cancelled the contract and installed conventional ovens to prepare food. Graulich sued for lost profits, claiming unjustifiable termination of the contract. The trial court held for Holterbosch. The appellate court affirmed:

> Since warranties of sample and description are characterized as "express warranties," the "whole of the goods shall conform to the sample or model." N.J.S. 12A:2–313(1)(c). The "goods" to "conform" to the sample or model must be "in accordance with the obligations under the contract," N.J.S. 12A:2–106(2); here, to comply with the standards established by the March 17 taste-test of the samples. . . . Additionally, the implied warranty of fitness for purpose attaches to contracts of this type, where, as here, they are not specifically excluded. A breach of these warranties triggers a buyer's rights following seller's breach as catalogued in N.J.S. 12A:2–711. These remedies include, but are not limited to, cancellation, N.J.S. 12A:2–711(1), 2–106(4), "if the breach goes to the whole of the contract." N.J.S. 12A:2–612(3).
>
> . . .
>
> Here, Holterbosch had the right to reject any installment that was nonconforming, provided that the nonconformity substantially im-

paired the value of that installment and could not be cured. N.J.S. 12A:2–612(2). "Cure," novel to New Jersey's jurisprudence, permits the seller to cure a defective tender through repair, replacement or price allowance if he reasonably notifies the buyer of his curative intention and, in effecting the cure, makes a timely conforming delivery. N.J.S. 12A:2–508(1).

. . . We find that Holterbosch was justified in rejecting Graulich's tender of the April 23 initial installment since the nonconformity of the tendered goods with the accepted sample was incurable, and thus substantially impaired the value of that installment.

Replacing considerations of anticipatory repudiation and the material injury with the test of substantial impairment, N.J.S. 12A:2–612 adopts a more restrictive seller-oriented approach favoring "the continuance of the contract in the absence of an overt cancellation." See Comment [6]. To allow an aggrieved party to cancel an installment contract, N.J.S. 12A:2–612(3) requires (1) the breach be of the whole contract which occurs when the nonconformity of "one or more installments substantially impairs the value of the whole contract"; and (2) that seasonable notification of cancellation has been given if the buyer has accepted a nonconforming installment.

What amounts to substantial impairment presents a question of fact . . . . Comment [4] states that "substantial impairment of the value of an installment can turn not only on the quality of the goods but also on such factors as time, quantity, assortment and the like. It must be judged in terms of the normal or specifically known purposes of the contract."

At the Lowenbrau Pavilion on April 23, 1964 plaintiff Graulich, timely noticed of the nonconforming initial tender, gave assurance that future tenders would be cured to match the original samples. Unequivocally committed to the microwave kitchen method, defendant lent plaintiff three members from its staff in aid of this adjustment. Since plaintiff was given the opportunity to cure, there is no need to touch upon the substantiality of the initial nonconforming installment.

The second installment tender was as unsatisfactory as the first. The meat was dry, the gravy "gooey" and the complaints abundant. After the nonconforming second delivery it became apparent that eleventh-hour efforts attempting to rework and adjust the platters failed. Translating this into legal parlance, there was a nonconforming tender of the initial installment on a contract for the sale of goods; upon tender the buyer Holterbosch notified the seller Graulich of the nonconformity and unacceptable nature of the platters tendered; the failure of the cure assured by plaintiff, seller, was evidenced by a subsequently defective nonconforming delivery. The second unacceptable delivery and the failure of plaintiff's additional curative efforts left defendant in a position for one week without food. Time was critical. Plaintiff knew that platters of maximum quality were required on a daily installment basis. Because of defendant's immediate need for quality food and plaintiff's failure to cure, we find that the nonconformity of the second delivery, projected upon the circumstances of this case, "substantially impair[ed] the value of the whole contract [and resulted in] a breach of the whole." N.J.S. 12A:2–612(3). If the breach goes to the whole contract the buyer may cancel the whole contract. N.J.S. 12A:2–711(1). Accordingly, we find that Holterbosch was justified in canceling the installment agreement signed on April 1, 1964.

Midwest Mobile Diagnostic Imaging, L.L.C. v. Dynamics Corporation of America

United States District Court, Western District of Michigan, 1997.
965 F.Supp. 1003.

■ ENSLEN, CHIEF JUDGE. [After extensive negotiations, in August 1995 plaintiff (MMDI) contracted to purchase four trailers from Ellis & Watts (E & W), doing business as Dynamics Corp. The seller was to outfit each of the trailers to accommodate an MRI unit to be supplied by Phillips, which was to certify that the completed trailers were satisfactory. MMDI paid $63,000 of the price at the signing of the contract. The delivery dates initially were left open, but the parties subsequently fixed December 1 as the date for delivering the first fully-equipped trailer. MMDI thereupon scheduled patients for visits starting on December 4.

[In mid-November E & W completed assembly, including installation of the MRI units supplied by Phillips, and sent a bill to MMDI, which paid another $321,500. Upon inspection on November 28, Phillips concluded that the trailer did not meet the contract specifications because the walls were not sufficiently stable. E & W accepted this conclusion and attempted to cure the nonconformities. Its cure, tendered on December 13, however, consisted of a system of large steel beams that were aesthetically unpleasing and impeded the servicing of the machine. After an exchange of correspondence, MMDI cancelled the contract on December 18 and sued for damages caused by E & W's breach.]

ANALYSIS

A. *Breach of contract*

The primary issue for resolution by the Court is whether MMDI rightfully rejected E & W's tender of the first trailer and then subsequently canceled the contract, or if its actions in mid-December constituted anticipatory repudiation of the contract. . . .

1. Installment Contract

Before turning to the specific questions of rejection and cancellation, the Court must first resolve a threshold issue. Under the UCC, the parties' rights to reject, cure, and cancel under an installment contract differ substantially from those defined under a single delivery contract. Consequently, resolution of whether the contract is an installment contract is of primary concern. Section 2–612(1) defines an "installment contract" as "one which requires or authorizes the delivery of goods in separate lots to be separately accepted . . . ." The commentary following this section emphasizes that the "definition of an installment contract is phrased more broadly in this Article [than in its previous incarnation as the Uniform Sales Act] so as to cover installment deliveries tacitly authorized by the circumstances or by the option of either party." § 2–612, cmt. 1.

Plaintiff argues that the contract between itself and E & W does not constitute an installment contract because it authorizes delivery in commercial units, and not lots, as required by subsection (1). However, upon review of the Code section defining those terms, it becomes clear that those terms are not mutually exclusive. Section 2–105 defines a "lot" as a "parcel or single article which is the subject matter of a separate sale or delivery, whether or not it is sufficient to perform the contract." The same section defines a commercial unit as "such a unit of goods as by commercial usage is a single whole for purposes of sale and division of which materially impairs its character or value on the market or in use. A commercial unit may be a single article (as a machine) or a set of articles (as a suite of furniture or an assortment of sizes) or a quantity (as a bale, gross, or carload) or any other unit treated in use or in the relevant market as a single whole." Thus, a lot, which is the measure of goods that the contract states will be delivered together in one installment, can be a single commercial unit. Consequently, § 2–612 applies wherever a contract for multiple items authorizes the delivery of the items in separate groups at different times, whether or not the installment constitutes a commercial unit.

. . . [N]either party disputes that they agreed to have the trailers delivered at four separate times. Therefore, the Court finds that the contract in dispute is an installment contract.

2.   Right of Rejection

Section 2–612, therefore, is the starting point for the Court's analysis of MMDI's actions on December 13, 1995. Under § 2–612, the buyer's right to reject is far more limited than the corresponding right to reject under a single delivery contract defined under § 2–601. Under § 2–601, a buyer has the right to reject, "if the goods or tender of delivery fail in any respect to conform to the contract. . . ." Known as the "perfect tender" rule, this standard requires a very high level of conformity. Under this rule, the buyer may reject a seller's tender for any trivial defect, whether it be in the quality of the goods, the timing of performance, or the manner of delivery. To avoid injustice, the Code limits the buyer's correlative right to cancel the contract upon such rejection by providing a right to cure under § 2–508. § 2–508, cmt. 2. Under § 2–508, the seller has a right to cure if s/he seasonably notifies the buyer of the intent to do so, *and* either 1) the time for performance has not yet passed, or 2) the seller had reason to believe that the goods were in conformity with the contract. Thus, § 2–508's right to cure serves to temper the buyer's expansive right to reject under a single delivery contract.

Section 2–612 creates an exception to the perfect tender rule. Under subsection (2), a buyer may not reject nonconforming tender unless the defect substantially impairs the value of the installment. In addition, "if the nonconformity is curable and the seller gives adequate assurances of cure," the buyer must accept the installment. § 2–612, cmt. 5. But even if rejection is proper under subsection 2, cancellation of the contract is not appropriate unless the defect substantially impairs the value of the whole contract. § 2–612(3), cmt. 6. Because this section significantly restricts the buyer's right to cancel under an installment contract, there is no corresponding necessity for reference to § 2–508; the seller's right to cure is implicitly defined by § 2–612.[6]

a. *Delivery Date*

Before proceeding with the analysis of MMDI's December 13 rejection, the Court initially notes that E & W's tender on December 13 constituted a cure attempt for the wall-flexing defect which delayed the delivery of the first trailer beyond the agreed upon delivery date. Although under § 2–612 the delivery date does not cut off the seller's right to cure, it does have an effect on the rights of the parties. *See* Graulich Caterer, Inc. v. Hans Holterbosch, Inc., [101 N.J.Super. 61, 243 A.2d 253, 261 (1968)].

In the instant case, the original, written contract included no definite delivery date. Instead, the contract left the delivery term to be agreed upon at a later date. At the time of execution, the parties both expected delivery of the first trailer to take place in October. During the months after the execution of the contract, however, the parties modified the deadline for the first installment of the contract on several occasions. As noted above, upon review of the testimony and documentary evidence, the Court finds that, whatever delivery date the parties had agreed upon prior to November 1995, by early November they had renegotiated their agreement to establish a December 1, 1995 delivery date. *See* § 2–209 (sales contract may be modified by oral or written agreement without consideration, so long as agreement does not state otherwise).

Defendant argues, however, that, even if the parties had at one point agreed upon a December 1, 1995 deadline, when the first trailer failed the Philips road test on November 28, 1995, the parties renegotiated the delivery term to allow E & W a reasonable time to cure the defect. While E

---

6. Courts of other jurisdictions have reached differing conclusions with regard to the interaction between §§ 2–612 and 2–508. *See, e.g. Arkla Energy Resources v. Roye Realty & Dev., Inc.,* 9 F.3d 855 (10th Cir.1993). This Court does not find the arguments of these other courts persuasive, however, and notes that their decisions are not binding on this Court. Nevertheless, the Court also notes that, since the time for delivery of the first installment had already passed on December 1, 1995 … and defendant could not have reasonably believed and, in fact, did not believe that the trailer was in conformity with the contract on that date, defendant had no right to cure under § 2–508.

& W is correct that, as of December 1, it had a reasonable time in which to cure the wall-flexing problem, the Court disagrees that MMDI's willingness to wait for a cure constitutes an agreement to extend the delivery deadline. Because the parties believed that the defect was curable and E & W, without solicitation, unequivocally promised to cure it, under § 2–612, MMDI had no choice but to accept an offer of cure. To reject the installment on November 28 would have constituted a violation of § 2–612. The Court, therefore, finds that any negotiations the parties engaged in regarding delivery after discovery of the wall-flexing problem, did not constitute a modification of the delivery date for the first installment, but rather involved negotiation regarding cure. Since no specific date for delivery of a cure was agreed upon during those negotiations, under section 2–309(1), E & W had a reasonable time to effectuate a cure. Although there is some question as to whether further delay would have been reasonable, the Court finds that, as of December 13, 1995, a reasonable time had not yet passed. Therefore, defendant's tender of a cure was timely.

b. Substantial Impairment of the Installment

The Court's conclusion that E & W's December 13 tender was an attempt to cure the November 28 breach raises another question: which standard of conformity applies to cure under an installment contract, perfect tender or substantial impairment? Looking to the rationale behind § 2–612, the Court notes that the very purpose of allowing the seller time to cure under this section is to permit it additional time to meet the obligations of the contract. The assumption is that, because the parties have an ongoing relationship, the seller should be given an opportunity to make up the deficiency. This section was not designed to allow the seller to have a never-ending series of chances to bring the item into conformity with the contract. Nor was it enacted to force the buyer to accept a nonconforming product as satisfaction of the contract. Consequently, it is logical that a tender of cure should be required to meet the higher "perfect tender" standard. On its face, however, § 2–612, which generally defines a buyer's right to reject goods under an installment contract, requires . . . substantial impairment in this context as well. Thus, there is some question as to which is the appropriate standard. The answer is not crucial however, since the trailer in this case fails under *both* standards. Because a decision on this point will not affect the ultimate outcome in this case, the Court declines to address the issue. Instead, the Court proceeds with the substantial impairment analysis provided by § 2–612.

To establish substantial impairment of the value of an installment, the buyer " 'must present objective evidence that with respect to its own needs, the value of the goods was substantially impaired.' " *Arkla Energy Resources v. Roye Realty & Dev., Inc.,* 9 F.3d 855, 862 (10th Cir.1993) (quoting *Bodine Sewer, Inc. v. Eastern Illinois Precast, Inc.,* 143 Ill.App.3d 920, 97 Ill.Dec. 898, 906, 493 N.E.2d 705, 713 (1986)). *See also* § 2–612, cmt. 4. The existence of such nonconformity depends on the facts and circumstances of each case, and "can turn not only on the quality of the goods but also on such factors as time . . ., and the like." § 2–612, cmt. 4.

See eg., Colonial Dodge, Inc. v. Miller, 420 Mich. 452, 457–58, 362 N.W.2d 704 (1984) (holding missing spare tire in new car had special devaluing effect for the buyer and thus could constitute substantial impairment). Finally, whether nonconformity rises to the level of substantial impairment may be judged by reference to the concept of material breach under traditional contract law. *See Durfee v. Rod Baxter Imports, Inc.,* 262 N.W.2d 349 (Minn.1977).

In the instant case, plaintiff alleges several aspects in which defendant's December 13 tender failed to conform to contract obligations. Plaintiff contends that the trailer tendered on December 13 with the bracing structure did not conform to the parties' agreement because: 1) it was not and could not be certified by Philips without conditions for use with the 1.5T scanner and 2) its interior design did not conform with the parties' agreements. Because of these defects, MMDI argues that the value of trailer was reduced substantially. Defendant, on the other hand, contends that the contract required only that the trailer meet the technical specifications provided by Philips, and that, therefore, the December 13 trailer was in complete compliance with its terms.

The written contract signed by the parties in this case is relatively skeletal and thus, requires interpretation. The Court's fundamental purpose in interpreting the terms of the contract is to give effect to the intent of the parties as it existed at the time the agreement was made. . . .

As instructed by the commentary to § 2–612, the Court begins the substantial impairment analysis by looking to the "normal and specifically known purposes of the contract." § 2–612, cmt. 4. Reviewing the evidence presented, the Court finds that the primary purpose of the contract was to provide the plaintiff with four trailers for use with the Philips 1.5T scanner. With that in mind, the parties agreed that the trailers would be constructed in accordance with the specifications provided by Philips and that the trailer would be not be ready for delivery until Philips certification had been received. Philips did not, however, ever certify the trailer for unconditional use with the bracing structure. Because the bracing structure prevented normal service of the scanner magnet, it was only approved as a temporary fix.

. . . The bracing structure's shape and orientation prevented removal of the outer panels from the scanner magnet and made some repairs to the magnet more difficult and more dangerous. Furthermore, in order to perform certain repairs, the steel brace would have to be unbolted and removed. Once removed, the scanner magnet would have to be recalibrated and retested. Consequently, Philips' decision to refuse certification was entirely justified. Having found no evidence of bad faith or dishonesty on the part of Philips, the Court finds that defendant's failure to meet this condition constituted a breach of the parties' agreement. . . . The Court, therefore, finds that this failure to conform to the parties' agreement, in and of itself, constituted a material breach.

In addition to violating the requirement that the trailer receive certification from Philips, plaintiff correctly asserts that defendant breached yet another term of the contract. The Court notes that the bracing structure also violated the parties' implied agreement regarding the design of the interior of the trailer. . . .

. . . [W]hen the contract was executed, the parties both understood that the trailer's interior was meant to be aesthetically pleasing. It is the very nature of a mobile MRI trailer to function as an extension of the hospital it services. Since E & W was in the business of constructing trailers for mobile medical uses, it no doubt understood that the appearance of the trailer's interior could impact the comfort of MMDI's patients. Indeed, it is apparent that E & W realized such aesthetics were important to the value of the trailer, since, in its initial negotiations with MMDI, E & W included a cut-away drawing of the interior of a mobile unit which read: "Spacious, efficient layout with clean, *aesthetically pleasing* interior." The Court, therefore, finds that the agreement between the parties required that the interior of the trailer be aesthetically pleasing.

Such a condition of satisfaction by one of the parties to the contract will only be excused if approval is withheld unreasonably. *See American Oil Company v. Carey*, 246 F.Supp. 773 (E.D.Mich.1965); Restatement (Second) of Contracts, § 228. In the instant case, upon review of photographs of the bracing structure and testimony of those experienced in this industry, and in light of the fact that the interior of the trailer should match that of a hospital and not a construction site, the Court finds that plaintiff's refusal to approve the aesthetics of the design was commercially reasonable. Given that an integral aspect of the trailer's function is to serve as a clinic for patients undergoing medical procedures, and given MMDI's clients' expectations after having viewed the trailer at [a preview before the unit was formally delivered in late November], such a defect in the trailer's interior also reduced the value of the trailer substantially.

Upon review of the evidence, the Court finds that the bracing structure substantially impaired the value of the first trailer. Although the trailer met the express technical Philips' specifications for wall-flexing, it was never certified by the manufacturer. The failure of this condition does not relieve defendant of liability because it was defendant's failure to properly construct the trailer that prevented certification. In light of the specific facts and circumstances of this case, the Court finds that this deficiency substantially impaired the value of the installment. When coupled with the trailer's failure to conform with the aesthetic requirements of the contract and the delay caused by the cure attempt, the Court holds that the cure attempt clearly constitutes a substantial breach within the meaning of § 2–612(2).

Substantial impairment, however, does not in itself justify rejection of the installment. As noted above, the buyer must still accept tender if the defect can be cured and the seller gives adequate assurances. . . . Defendant has failed in this regard. The Court notes that neither E & W's statements during the December 13 conference call nor the letter sent the following day constituted adequate assurances. On the contrary, during the December 13 conference call, Andrew Pike, the President of E & W denied the existence of a defect, disclaimed any continuing obligation to cure under the contract, and stated that he did not believe a better design could be made which would remedy the wall-flexing problem. Furthermore, on December 14, Mr. Pike again ignored the servicing problems that the bracing structure had caused, ignored the fact that the bracing structure had not been approved for permanent use by Philips, and reiterated his doubt that the design could be constructed in a more aesthetically pleasing manner. Under these circumstances, the Court finds that MMDI's rejection of E & W's cure on December 13 constituted a rightful rejection under § 2–612(2).

3. Cancellation

a. *Substantial Impairment of Contract as a Whole*

The fact that rejection of one installment is proper does not necessarily justify cancellation of the entire contract. Under § 2–612(3) the right to cancel does not arise unless the nonconforming goods substantially impair the value of the *entire* contract. Indeed, as noted above, the very purpose of the substantial impairment requirement of § 2–612(3) is to preclude parties from canceling an installment contract for trivial defects.

Whether a breach constitutes "substantial impairment" of the entire contract is a question of fact. To make such a determination, the Court should consider "the cumulative effect of [the breaching party's] performance under the contract, based on the totality of the circumstances. . . ." *Neufer v. Video Greetings, Inc.*, 931 F.2d 56, 1991 WL 65439 (6th Cir.1991) (unpublished). Ultimately, "[w]hether the nonconformity in any given installment justifies cancellation as to the future depends, not on whether such nonconformity indicates an intent or likelihood that future deliveries will also be defective, but whether the nonconformity substantially impairs the value of the whole contract." § 2–612, cmt. 6. Thus, the question is one of present breach which focuses on the importance of the nonconforming installment relative to the contract as a whole. If the nonconformity only impairs the aggrieved party's security with regard to future installments, s/he "has the right to demand adequate assurances but [ ] not an immediate right to cancel the entire contract." § 2–612, cmt. 6. The right to cancel will be triggered only if "material inconvenience or injustice will result if the aggrieved party is forced to wait and receive an ultimate tender minus the part or aspect repudiated." § 2–610, cmt. 3 (noting the test for anticipatory repudiation under § 2–610 is the same as the test for cancellation under § 2–612(3)).

In the instant case, there is substantial evidence that one of the primary purposes of this contract was to provide MMDI with a fourth mobile MRI trailer so that it could meet the growing demand for its services. Thus, impairment of one of the four installments would have a substantial negative impact on MMDI. Moreover, an early delivery time was of primary importance to MMDI, as E & W was well aware. By failing to cure the November 28 breach on the first installment, E & W substantially delayed completion of the remainder of the contract which delayed

MMDI's ability to begin use of the 1.5T MRI trailer it had promised to its customers at the [preview event] on November 3. Having found that substantial injustice would be done to plaintiff if it were required to accept the remaining three trailers after substantial delay as satisfaction of the contract, the Court finds that plaintiff rightfully canceled the contract on December 18, 1995.

4.   Damages

Having found that plaintiff rightfully rejected defendant's tender of cure on December 13, 1995, and subsequently properly canceled the contract, the Court finds that plaintiff is entitled to damages. Plaintiff has requested reimbursement of the amount it already paid for the nonconforming installment in the amount of $384,500 as well as damages in the amount of $185,250 incurred for the lease of a rental mobile MRI trailer between December 19, 1995 and April 20, 1996, to replace the trailer E & W failed to produce. Under § 2–711, a buyer who has rightfully canceled a contract may recover, among other things: 1) the amount that has already been paid, 2) damages for "cover" as defined in § 2–712, and 3) any damages of nondelivery, including consequential and incidental damages, as defined by § 2–715. Under § 2–715, incidental damages include "any reasonable expense incident to the delay or other breach." Thus, plaintiff is clearly entitled to return of the amount already paid for the item it never received. Plaintiff is also entitled to recover the amount paid for a replacement rental unit. Though this amount does not constitute cover it is allowable as incidental to the delay produced by E & W's breach. Had E & W made conforming tender on December 13, 1995, plaintiff would not have been forced to contract with another company for the trailers and to wait until spring for the first one. The Court, therefore, finds plaintiff is entitled to both expectation and consequential damages under the Code and awards plaintiff a sum total of $569,250 for the breach of contract.

QUESTIONS AND NOTES

1.   In *Graulich* (page 359 supra) the contract called for daily delivery. When the first delivery was nonconforming, the buyer rejected it. This was permissible only if the nonconformity substantially impaired the value of the installment—which it did—and the nonconformity could not be cured. Was the nonconformity non-curable?

2.   In *Graulich* the buyer rejected the first installment. The next day it properly rejected the next installment, and it also cancelled the contract. Granted that the quality of the food was wholly unacceptable, why does unsatisfactory performance on two of 180 installments justify cancellation of the entire contract?

3.   Problem. Seller contracts to deliver six generators (one per month), each of which is to be capable of producing 1000 Kw/hour, plus or minus

2%. In due course, Seller tenders delivery of a generator that produces 900 Kw/hour. Must Buyer accept it?

Assume that when Buyer complains, Seller agrees to correct the problem. A week after picking up the generator, Seller returns it to Buyer. If the generator produces 960 Kw/hour, and Seller tells Buyer, "That's the best I can do," may Buyer reject it?

4. In Holiday Mfg. Co. v. B.A.S.F. Systems, Inc., 380 F.Supp. 1096 (D.Neb.1974), the parties entered into a contract for the manufacture and sale of 6 million tape player cassettes. The cassettes were to be delivered at the rate of 500,000 per month. A year later, however, only 1.5 million cassettes had been delivered. In addition, the seller had a number of difficulties in producing those cassettes: there were depressions in the cassette surface, cracks, oversize cassettes, and tape leader misalignment. Each time a problem appeared, the buyer called it to the attention of the seller, and the seller was able to change the manufacturing process to correct it. Then, nearly a year after first deliveries under the contract were due, the seller delivered cassettes with a new defect, improper guide-hole spacing. At that point the buyer cancelled the contract claiming that, under § 2–612(3), the seller's delays and the numerous defects had substantially impaired the value of the whole contract.

The court held that the buyer improperly terminated. It stated that the buyer had not treated the delays as being serious but rather seemed willing to allow whatever time was needed to correct the various defects. As to the defects, the court said that all were corrected except the last and that under the circumstances there was no substantial impairment. Does this mean that as long as a seller is willing and able to remedy defects in its performance, the buyer must continue accepting that performance?

Compare the result in Rester v. Morrow, 491 So.2d 204 (Miss.1986), involving an attempt by the purchaser of an automobile to revoke acceptance of the goods in a single-delivery contract, pursuant to 2–608. that section employs the same test for revocation of acceptance that 2–612(3) uses for the buyer's right to cancel an installment contract, viz., substantial impairment to the buyer of the value of the whole contract. Over the course of an entire year, the dealer had repaired a number of defects, but finally as to three defects that were themselves fairly trivial, the dealer did not make the repairs as promised. The court held that whether the value of the car to be buyer was substantially impaired was a jury question. The court said: "[On the day of revocation] Rester pointed out a soiled carpet, an unrepaired fuse panel, and an unreplaced piece of chrome. Unquestionably these are minor defects. . . . But our law does not allow a seller to postpone revocation in perpetuity by fixing everything that goes wrong with the automobile. There comes a time when enough is enough—when an automobile purchaser, after having to take his car to the shop for repairs an inordinate number of times and experiencing all of the attendant inconvenience, is entitled to say, 'That's all,' and revoke, notwithstanding the seller's repeated good faith efforts to fix the car."

Which of these decisions is more faithful to Article 2?

5.   Revised Article 2. The revision changes 2–612(2), by dropping the requirement of "cannot be cured" from the first sentence. Under the revised section, "The buyer may reject any installment which is nonconforming if the nonconformity substantially impairs the value of that installment to the buyer or if the nonconformity is a defect in documents." The second sentence states, "However, if the nonconformity does not fall within subsection (3) and the seller gives adequate assurance of its cure the buyer must accept that installment." What does this change mean? If the nonconformity substantially impairs the value of the installment to the buyer and cannot be cured, may the buyer reject? If it *can* be cured, may the buyer reject?

6.   Leases. Article 2A follows the approach of Article 2 to installment contracts. See 2A–510.

3.   PROCEDURE FOR EFFECTIVE REJECTION AND DUTIES AFTER REJECTION

If the goods and the tender conform to the contract, the buyer must accept them. If either the goods or the tender of them does not conform to the contract, in a single-delivery contract the buyer may reject them. Sections 2–513 and 2–602 govern rejection; the former provides that the buyer has a right to inspect the goods before accepting them, and the latter provides that rejection must occur within a reasonable time after tender and is ineffective unless the buyer gives timely notice to the seller. Section 2–606 governs acceptance of the goods and provides the ways in which acceptance may occur. Please read these sections, and note that under 2–606 acceptance does not depend on the buyer's intent to accept.

As a general rule, a person who brings a lawsuit must establish by a preponderance of the evidence every fact essential to the claim being asserted. This is true of actions under the UCC, and one of the elements of a seller's claim is that the goods conform to the contract. Hence, the burden of proving that fact is on the seller. If, however, the buyer has accepted the goods and refuses to pay for them because they allegedly fail to conform to the contract, 2–607(4) places the burden of proving the fact of nonconformity on the *buyer*, even if the seller is asserting a claim to recover the price of the goods. Sometimes it is not easy to determine whether the goods conform. In those instances, and some others as well, it is essential to know whether the buyer has accepted or rejected the goods.

———

Miron v. Yonkers Raceway, Inc.

United States Court of Appeals, Second Circuit, 1968.
400 F.2d 112.

■ J. JOSEPH SMITH, CIRCUIT JUDGE: Yonkers Raceway, Inc. and Saul Finkelstein appeal from a judgment of the District Court for the Southern District of New York, Richard H. Levet, Judge, entered after a trial without a jury, rendering them liable to plaintiffs for the purchase price of a horse and dismissing their counterclaims on the merits. . . .

I.

In September 1965, plaintiffs entered the horse "Red Carpet" in an auction called the "Old Glory Horse Sale," sponsored by Raceway. The contract by which Red Carpet was consigned to Raceway for sale provided that Raceway would act as plaintiffs' exclusive agent for the sale of the horse and would receive a commission of 10% on the accepted bid, and incorporated by reference the "Terms and Conditions of Sale." The Terms and Conditions of Sale provided, *inter alia:* that the horses were offered for sale according to the laws of New York, that title and "all risk and responsibility for the horse" pass to the buyer at the fall of the auctioneer's hammer, that "No delivery will be made until final settlement," and that "unless otherwise expressly announced at time of sale, there is no guarantee of any kind as to the soundness or condition or other quality of any horse sold in this Sale except that horses which are unsound in eyes or wind, or are 'cribbers,' must be announced at time of sale * * * Any horse whose condition is as aforesaid and is not so announced at time of sale, or where sex is incorrectly represented at time of sale, will be subject to return to Consignor * * * [provided that the buyer gives notice in writing] within seven days of sale. Any other representation, warranty or guarantee of the Consignor which is announced or otherwise given shall not extend beyond 24 hours after the fall of the Auctioneer's hammer or until final payment has been made, whichever is sooner."

Plaintiffs delivered Red Carpet to Raceway on October 17, 1965; the auction of the horse took place early in the afternoon of October 19. At $17,000 there was a lull in the bidding, whereupon Murray Brown, plaintiffs' employee, took the microphone and said:

> This horse has won 2 of his last 3 starts. On September 24, he raced on a muddy track, big stake race in Montreal * * * beating Mr. Sea Song. Now, you know what Mr. Sea Song has done this year * * * he's a top free-for-all horse and this horse beat him racing a good trip, and this is just recently. He's as sound—as, as gutty a horse as you want to find anywhere. He'll race a good mile for you every time. He's got loads of heart and you're way off on the price of this horse.[2]

The bidding then resumed, and defendant Finkelstein submitted the highest bid, which was $32,000.

By about 3:00 p.m. that day, Raceway delivered possession of Red Carpet to Finkelstein without obtaining any part of the purchase price, and Finkelstein immediately had the horse transported to his barn at Roosevelt Raceway, Westbury, Long Island. The next morning, Cruise, the trainer for

---

2. This statement was recorded on tape. Plaintiffs have conceded that it consti-   tuted a warranty that the horse was sound.

Finkelstein's horses, took Red Carpet out of his stall and hitched him to a jog cart. He observed some swelling of the horse's left hind leg at that time, and when the horse was caused to walk and trot, it limped and favored its left hind leg. Cruise returned Red Carpet to the stall, and summoned Dr. Bernard F. Brennan, a veterinarian, who found that Red Carpet's left hind leg was swollen, warm and sensitive.

Finkelstein notified Raceway, at about 11:30 a.m. that day, October 20, that Red Carpet was lame and not sound, and that afternoon an official of Raceway notified Brown, at plaintiffs' stables, of Finkelstein's complaint. Finkelstein subsequently demanded, as we have said, that plaintiffs take back the horse because it was not sound, as warranted, but they have continued to refuse to accept its return. Neither Raceway nor Finkelstein has paid plaintiffs any part of the purchase price for Red Carpet.

The basic factual issue tried below was whether Red Carpet was sound, as warranted, at the time when the auctioneer's hammer fell and all risks passed to Finkelstein as the buyer. The defendants' evidence on this issue consisted of X-rays of the horse's left hind leg.

Dr. Brennan testified that he took X-rays of Red Carpet's leg on the afternoon of October 20, and prints were introduced as the defendants' Exhibits B, C, D1 and E1. The X-rays revealed a broken splint bone, which, it was agreed by witnesses for all of the parties, is enough to render a racehorse unsound. Both of the defendants' expert witnesses ... testified that Exhibits B and D1 revealed calcification around the site of the fracture indicating that the fracture was two or three weeks old. The plaintiffs' experts testified, however, that Exhibit D1, unlike Exhibit B, did not show calcification, and concluded that the X-rays must have been taken on different days. The defendants countered by offering testimony that a difference in intensity between the exhibits explained the fact that callus growth was less visible on D1 than on B, but the court found that Exhibit D1 showed no calcification and that it therefore was not taken on the same day as Exhibit B. The court also found that Exhibits D1 and E1 were undated, that Exhibits B and C were admittedly incorrectly dated, and that no business records sufficient to prove the date on which the X-rays were taken had been produced, and concluded that the exhibits lacked sufficient probative force to establish the date on which the fracture occurred. We see no reason why this conclusion should not stand.

The expert witnesses were in substantial agreement that the symptoms of a broken splint bone are swelling, heat which is perceptible to the touch, and sensitivity and lameness, and that these symptoms become apparent immediately or very soon after the occurrence of the fracture. Thus if Red Carpet's splint bone was broken at the time of sale, an examination of the horse after the sale would have disclosed that fact. Finkelstein testified that he was not an experienced horse buyer, and ordinarily has a trainer or veterinarian examine the legs of horses he buys, but he went to the auction on October 19, 1965 intending to buy two brood mares, and for that reason did not have his trainer or a veterinarian with him. Although he observed the horse when it was led into the ring at the auction, he did not examine it or look at its legs at the time of the sale. The court found that neither Finkelstein nor his agents inspected or examined the horse prior to the time when Cruise observed a swelling of its left hind leg on the day after the sale.

The plaintiffs offered, on the basic issue of the time of the fracture, testimony of persons who had observed and examined Red Carpet on the day of the sale. Roger White, a competitor of the Mirons, testified that he inspected the horse with the intention of buying it if the price was right, and that he couldn't see anything wrong with it. Dr. Rene Rosaire Gauthier, who accompanied White to the auction and examined Red Carpet for him, testified that when he examined Red Carpet's legs he observed no heat or swelling, and that he saw the horse trotting and walking without limping or manifesting any lameness. The court found, on the basis of this and other testimony, that "On October 19, 1965, prior to sale, the horse's left hind leg was neither swollen, hot, nor lame."[5]

The District Court's finding on the basic factual issue was expressed in terms of failure to carry the burden of proof. Concluding that under New York law Finkelstein had accepted Red Carpet and therefore had the burden of proving a breach of warranty, the court found: "Defendant Finkelstein has failed to prove by a fair preponderance of the credible evidence that the horse was not 'sound' at the time of its sale to him on October 19, 1965."

We will first consider the questions relevant to whether there was a breach of warranty, and then turn to the issues raised by the counterclaims.

II.

We affirm the judgment below on the breach of warranty issue, because we agree with the District Court that under New York law Finkelstein had the burden of proving a breach of warranty and we find ample support in the record for the finding that Finkelstein did not carry that burden successfully. The plaintiffs have argued forcefully that we need not consider who had the burden of proof on the issue, but we must disagree.

. . .

The District Court based its determination that Finkelstein had the burden on New York Uniform Commercial Code ("U.C.C.") § 2-607(4), which provides: "The burden is on the buyer to establish any breach with respect to the goods accepted." The question thus is whether Finkelstein

5. The horse's groom, who cared for it from September 24, 1965 to October 19, exercising it and rubbing its legs daily, did not see any swelling on the left hind leg, and did not see the horse limping. An X-ray of the horse's left hind leg taken on September 30, 1965 showed that on that date Red Carpet did not have a broken splint bone. Red Carpet raced on September 24, 1965, finishing first; on October 2, 1965, finishing first; and on October 16, 1965, finishing sixth.

accepted the horse, and we turn for guidance to U.C.C. § 2–606(1), which states:

> Acceptance of goods occurs when the buyer
>
> (a) after a reasonable opportunity to inspect the goods signifies to the seller that the goods are conforming or that he will take or retain them in spite of their nonconformity; or
>
> (b) fails to make an effective rejection (subsection (1) of Section 2–602), but such acceptance does not occur until the buyer has had a reasonable opportunity to inspect them; or
>
> (c) does any act inconsistent with the seller's ownership; but if such act is wrongful as against the seller it is an acceptance only if ratified by him.

It has not been argued that Finkelstein accepted the horse under subsection (a). We doubt he could be said to have done any act inconsistent with the plaintiffs' ownership of the horse, within the meaning of subsection (c), but we need not decide the applicability of that subsection, for we think the trial judge was right in finding that Finkelstein failed to make an effective rejection of the horse under U.C.C. § 2–602(1), thereby accepting it under subsection (b). U.C.C. § 2–602(1) provides: "Rejection of goods must be within a reasonable time after their delivery or tender. It is ineffective unless the buyer seasonably notifies the seller."

Finkelstein accepted the horse, then, if having had a reasonable opportunity to inspect it, he did not reject it within a reasonable time.[14] What is reasonable depends upon an evaluation of all of the circumstances, and we would therefore be reluctant to overturn the findings and conclusions of the trial judge on these issues. He has a feel for the circumstances of the case which we could not possibly have.[15] Moreover, the finding that Finkelstein did not reject the horse within a reasonable time seems to us to be clearly correct.

As the trial judge rightly pointed out, "The fact that the subject matter of the sale in this case was a live animal * * * bears on what is a reasonable time to inspect and reject." Finkelstein's own testimony showed that it is customary, when buying a racehorse, to have a veterinarian or trainer examine the horse's legs, and we agree that the existence of this custom is very important in determining whether there was a reasonable

---

14. A "reasonable opportunity to inspect," U.C.C. § 2–606(1)(b), may of course encompass more than merely a reasonable time to inspect; here, there is no question that Finkelstein had the facilities for inspection available, and the only question on appeal was whether he waited too long.

A reasonable period for rejection overlaps a reasonable opportunity to inspect under U.C.C. § 2–606(1)(b). Thus if inspection discloses a defect, there remains the obligation to reject within a reasonable time. But in many cases where the buyer passes up a reasonable opportunity to inspect, he thus fails to reject within a reasonable time, and we think that this is one of those cases, for reasons stated in the text.

15. Cf. the cases in which it has been said that what is a reasonable time for inspection is a question of fact for the jury; e.g., C.W. Anderson Hosiery Co. v. Dixie Knitting Mills, Inc., 204 F.2d 503, 505 (4 Cir.1953); see Annot., 52 A.L.R.2d 900 (1957).

opportunity to inspect the horse. See Official Comment to U.C.C. § 1–204, para. 2. We gather from the record that the reason it is customary to examine a racehorse's legs at the time of sale is that a splint bone is rather easily fractured (there was testimony that a fracture could result from the horse kicking itself), and although the judge made no specific findings as to this, we assume that is generally what he had in mind when he pointed out that "a live animal is more prone to rapid change in condition and to injury than is an inanimate object." As we have said, Finkelstein did not have the horse examined either at the place of sale or at his barn later the day of the sale. He thus passed up a reasonable opportunity to inspect Red Carpet.

Finkelstein having had a reasonable opportunity to inspect Red Carpet on the day of the sale, we have no problem with the finding that the attempted rejection on the next day did not come within a reasonable time. In addition to our reluctance to question the trial judge's finding as to what is a reasonable time, we take into account that what is a reasonable time for rejection depends on the purpose of rejection. See U.C.C. § 1–204(2). Where goods are effectively rejected for breach of warranty, the burden of proving that they conform presumably remains on the seller,[17] whereas upon acceptance the buyer has the burden to establish any breach. U.C.C. § 2–607(4). In this case, the subject of the sale is a racehorse warranted to be sound, and the record clearly shows that an injury such as occurred here, rendering a horse unsound, may be a matter of chance, proof of the exact time of injury being very difficult to make. In these circumstances, the burden of proof on the issue of soundness at the time of sale cannot fairly rest on the seller where the buyer has taken possession of the horse, transported it to his barn, and kept it overnight before discovering the injury and informing the seller of it. We conclude that rejection did not take place within a reasonable time after delivery, and Finkelstein thus accepted the horse. In short, since one of the consequences of acceptance is that the buyer bears the burden of proving any breach, the fairness of allocating the burden one way or the other is relevant in determining whether acceptance has occurred—here, whether rejection took place within a reasonable time.

The defendants have argued strenuously that inspection and rejection on the day after the sale is certainly soon enough, and the argument would gain substantial strength if another sort of defect were involved and we took into account that the customary type of inspection at the time of sale might not disclose aspects of a horse's soundness other than the condition of its legs, and that these aspects, unlike the condition of the legs, would be

---

17. The official comment to U.C.C. § 2–602, para. 3, states that the section applies only to rightful rejection by the buyer. Yet acceptance may depend upon whether there has been a rejection under that section, and the allocation of the burden of proving whether there was a defect, and thus whether or not there was "rightful rejection," depends upon whether there has been accep-tance. See U.C.C. §§ 2–606(1)(b) and 2–607(4). The only sensible construction of these sections would seem to be that non-acceptance, consisting of attempted rejection within a reasonable time after delivery or tender, amounts to rightful rejection if the seller fails to prove that the goods conform, but is a breach if the seller proves conformity.

very unlikely to change overnight. There is nothing in the record as to how much the customary inspection at the time of sale would show; Finkelstein testified only that he has a trainer or veterinarian examine the legs of horses he buys. In any case, if there are defects which are not discoverable by the inspection which the District Court found Finkelstein had a reasonable opportunity to make, the problem is taken care of by U.C.C. § 2–608(1), which provides in relevant part:

> The buyer may revoke his acceptance of a lot or commercial unit whose nonconformity substantially impairs its value to him if he has accepted it.

> * * *

> (b) without discovery of such nonconformity if his acceptance was reasonably induced either by the difficulty of discovery before acceptance or by the seller's assurances.

The answer to the argument is that inspection is not necessarily final; where there are defects discoverable by a customary inspection at the time of sale, a buyer in Finkelstein's position will not be excused from making that inspection and rejecting the goods within a reasonable time, if a defect is disclosed, on the ground that there are possible critical defects which only a more thorough inspection would disclose. There are no conceptual problems involved in this approach, for there is nothing ultimate about any of the conceptions we are using. Since a finding of acceptance depends upon a finding that there was a reasonable opportunity to inspect, the question whether acceptance may be revoked as reasonably induced by the difficulty of discovery before acceptance, within the meaning of U.C.C. § 2–608(1), must be answered by reference to the scope of the inspection which there was a reasonable opportunity to make. Thus if Finkelstein had carried out the customary inspection and accepted the horse, and the defect allegedly rendering Red Carpet unsound at the time of sale were a defect not discoverable by inspection on the day of sale, rather than a broken splint bone, we may presume the District Court would not have placed the burden of proof on Finkelstein, and would have said that he had "revoked his acceptance."

The defendants argue that the provision in the Terms and Conditions of Sale that any warranty of the consignor "shall not extend beyond 24 hours after the fall of the Auctioneer's hammer or until final payment has been made, whichever is sooner," fixes by agreement, a reasonable time for rejection, U.C.C. § 1–204(1), and that since Finkelstein rejected within 24 hours of the fall of the hammer, he did not accept Red Carpet under U.C.C. § 2–606(1)(b). There was considerable confusion over the meaning of this provision at the trial; Finkelstein submitted a memorandum in which it was argued that under the provision any defect violating the warranty appearing within 24 hours is presumed to be a defect existing at the time of sale, so that the seller must show that "some external, intervening cause occurred after the horse passed from its possession." The trial judge interpreted this as an argument that the provision converted any warranty into a 24–hour insurance policy, and, not surprisingly, rejected that notion. He concluded that "At most, the clause means that if any futuristic warranty is stated, it could extend no longer than the period mentioned."

We think this provision must be construed simply as setting a time within which defects must be reported in order for the warranty to be valid. The setting of such a deadline does not necessarily mean that any unreasonable delay in inspection or rejection is acceptable so long as it does not extend past the deadline. Had Red Carpet been obviously lame, hobbling badly at the time he was delivered to Finkelstein, and had Finkelstein nonetheless taken the horse away to his barn without comment, it would be unreasonable to say that Finkelstein nonetheless had twenty-four hours to report the defect, because of this provision. On our view of the case, whether rejection was within a reasonable time must be answered with reference to what inspection for defects is customary, and it appears that Finkelstein had no more excuse for taking the horse away without giving its legs the customary inspection than he would have had for taking it away without comment if it had been hobbling. We will not construe a provision which by its terms sets a maximum time for reporting defects to set a minimum time as well, for some defects may be more readily discoverable than others.

We conclude, then, that Finkelstein accepted the horse by failing to reject it within a reasonable time, and thus had the burden of proving any breach of warranty. As we have already said, we find ample support for the finding that he failed to prove a breach by a fair preponderance of the credible evidence. The only evidence submitted by the defendants to establish the time of the fracture was the X-rays discussed above, and we have explained why the trial judge found that these lacked sufficient probative force to establish the date of the fracture.[18]

. . .

Affirmed.

QUESTIONS AND NOTES

1. Assume that a consumer finds a car for sale on an Internet website that brings buyers and sellers together. After agreeing to a transaction, the buyer learns that the seller lives only a short distance away, and they agree that instead of handling payment and delivery of the car through the website's mechanism, the buyer will pick it up at the seller's home and pay for it with a cashier's check. When the buyer arrives at the seller's house, he asks to take the car for a little drive. The seller refuses to hand over the keys until the buyer hands over the check, and the buyer refuses to pay

---

18. If Finkelstein, having accepted the horse, had met his burden of proof, he would have been entitled to damages for nonconformity; see U.C.C. § 2–714.

until he has a chance to drive the car. The seller sues, and the buyer counterclaims. Who wins?

2. Section 2–602(1), as explained by 1–204(2)-(3), requires that (a) rejection be within a reasonable time after delivery, and (b) notice of rejection occur within a reasonable time. Which of these is in issue in *Miron*?

The concepts of reasonable time for rejection and for notification of rejection are elastic. The resolution of the issue is normally one for the jury. It has been held that three hours after delivery was an unreasonably long time to defer rejection (Max Bauer Meat Packer, Inc. v. United States, 198 Ct.Cl. 97, 458 F.2d 88 (1972) (perishable goods)), and that 12 months was not unreasonably long. (Trailmobile Div. of Pullman, Inc. v. Jones, 118 Ga.App. 472, 164 S.E.2d 346 (1968) (motor vehicle)). What is a reasonable time in which to reject is closely related to what is a reasonable time in which to exercise the right to inspect before acceptance (see § 2–513(1)). This will vary with the nature of the goods, the kind of inspection that is required, and the ability of the buyer to make the necessary inspection. The reasonable time for inspection shrinks when the goods are perishable (Appeal of Mazur Bros. & Jaffee Fish Co., Inc., 3 UCC Rep.Serv. 419 (Veterans Administration Contract Appeals Board, VACAB–512, June 25, 1965)) or when the inspection consists of a simple measurement of the size of the goods delivered (Michael M. Berlin & Co., Inc. v. T. Whiting Mfg., Inc., 5 UCC Rep.Serv. 357 (N.Y.Tr.Ct.1968)). Also, when goods are seasonal, there may be an obligation to inspect and reject in time for the seller to dispose of the goods before they become obsolete (Societé Nouvelle Vaskene v. Lehman Saunders, Ltd., 14 UCC Rep.Serv. 692 (N.Y.Sup.Ct.1974) (dresses)).

When a seller delivers nonconforming goods and responds to the buyer's complaint with a promise to bring the goods up to contract specifications, courts discount the time during which the seller attempts to remedy the defect in the goods in computing a reasonable time for rejection. See Trailmobile Div. of Pullman, Inc. v. Jones, 118 Ga.App. 472, 164 S.E.2d 346 (1968); Fablok Mills, Inc. v. Cocker Machine & Foundry Co., 125 N.J.Super. 251, 310 A.2d 491 (1973); Continental Concrete Pipe Corp. v. Century Road Builders, Inc., 195 Ill.App.3d 1, 142 Ill.Dec. 291, 552 N.E.2d 1032 (1990).

The contract may specify the period within which rejection must take place and that provision will be effective unless it is "manifestly unreasonable" (1–204). If the time limitation is so short that the contract time for rejection would expire before the buyer has a reasonable chance to discover the defect, the time set is manifestly unreasonable. Neville Chemical Co. v. Union Carbide Corp., 422 F.2d 1205 (3d Cir.1970); Koch Supplies, Inc. v. Farm Fresh Meats, Inc., 630 F.2d 282 (5th Cir.1980).

3. Problem. Buyer, a retail carpet dealer, purchased a roll of carpet. It was delivered on June 1, and placed in Buyer's warehouse. Nine months later, when Buyer first had a customer who wished to buy that particular type of carpet, it was unrolled and was found to be defective. May Buyer reject?

Would it matter if the contract had provided that notification of rejection must occur within 30 days after delivery. See 1–204.

4. It is not enough for the buyer to record its decision to reject. The rejection is ineffective unless the buyer communicates it to the seller. The reasons are obvious: upon rejection, the seller may have a right to cure the nonconformity but cannot do so unless informed of the problem. Even if the seller has no right to cure, the policy of the Code is to promote negotiation with respect to troublesome transactions. See, e.g., 2–607(3), which requires the buyer to give the seller notice of a breach even if the buyer already has accepted the goods and intends to keep them.

In the typical case notification of rejection is virtually contemporaneous with rejection. If the rejection is within a reasonable time, then the notification will be held to have been seasonably made.

In DeJesus v. Cat Auto Tech Corp., 161 Misc.2d 723, 615 N.Y.S.2d 236 (N.Y.City Civil Ct.1994), defendant took delivery of 10,000 printed certificates and paid for them by check. He then examined the certificates, concluded that they were defective, and stopped payment on the check. He did not notify the seller of this action nor of his rejection of the certificates. The seller did not learn of the problem until her bank returned the buyer's check to her. The court held that the stop order on the check was not an effective rejection because it did not give the seller a reasonable time and opportunity to cure. As authorized by 2–709(1)(a), the court gave the seller judgment for the balance due.

In *Miron* if the x-rays had proven that Red Carpet was lame at the time of the sale, would defendant's rejection have been effective?

5. Courts have sometimes confused rejection or revocation of acceptance with "rescission." (E.g., Sarnecki v. Al Johns Pontiac, 3 UCC Rep.Serv. 1121 (Pa.Com.Pl.1966); Menard & Holmberg Rambler, Inc. v. Shea, 44 Mass.App.Dec. 204 (1970)). However, rejection is merely a refusal to take the tendered goods: it need not be accompanied by a decision not to sue on the contract for breach. Rescission of the contract, on the other hand, is a choice among several available remedies for breach. A person who rescinds is seeking to escape from the contract and return to its pre-contract status, as opposed to enforcing the contract by seeking expectancy damages for the loss cause by the other person's breach.

Courts also have sometimes failed to distinguish between rejection and revocation of acceptance. Revocation of acceptance (authorized by 2–608) is an "undoing" of acceptance and is available in only limited circumstances. Rejection is a refusal to accept and is much more readily available. While the carelessness of courts in this regard is understandable, since rejection and revocation of acceptance both force the goods back on the seller, you should not be similarly careless. The two concepts are different and apply in different situations.

Rejection or revocation of acceptance is in no way an election of remedy and, after either rejection or revocation of acceptance, the buyer might either ask for rescission or for damages for breach. Incidentally, asking for return of any of the purchase price paid would not necessarily be a request for rescission, since on breach-of-contract principles, a seller is not entitled to retain the price of goods not accepted. See 2–711 and Official Comment 1 to 2–608. (By the way, in the last sentence of the middle paragraph on page 376, the court's assertion with respect to the burden of proof if defendant had revoked acceptance, is wrong. Do you see why?) Revocation of acceptance is covered in more detail later in this chapter.

6. Acceptance by conduct inconsistent with the seller's ownership. The foregoing materials concern acceptance of goods under 2–606(1)(b), as a result of the buyer's failure to make an effective rejection. Acceptance of the goods also may occur even if the buyer purports to reject but then engages in conduct inconsistent with the seller's ownership (2–606(1)(c)).

Problem. Buyer purchases a dining room suite from Seller, a furniture dealer. When the furniture arrives, it is the wrong color. Buyer immediately notifies Seller that she does not want the furniture and that Seller should come pick it up. Several days later, before Seller has picked up the furniture, one of the pieces, a buffet, is substantially damaged by workers installing a new floor in Buyer's apartment. Buyer accepts a check for the full purchase price of the buffet from the insurance company for the flooring company and allows the insurance company to take it. When Seller's truck arrives to pick up the furniture, the driver sees that the buffet is missing. He phones Seller to report this, and Seller directs him to leave all the furniture where it is and to return to the store. Relying on 2–607(1) and 2–709(1)(a), Seller sues for the price of all the furniture. What result? (In addition to the sections already discussed, please consult 2–603 and 2–604.)

Suppose that, in the above problem, Seller is located in Los Angeles, Buyer lives in Bakersfield (110 miles away), and that after rejection Seller requests Buyer to make arrangements to return the suite of furniture to Los Angeles. Is Buyer obligated to do so?

7. Acceptance by using the goods after rejection. In Bowen v. Young, 507 S.W.2d 600 (Tex.Civ.App.1974), Young purchased a mobile home from Bowen in El Paso, Texas. It was taken to Columbia, South Carolina, where Young had taken a job. When it was set up, Young discovered numerous defects and, 17 days after delivery, sent a notice of rejection. At the time of rejection, Young was paying rent on a space for the trailer, storage charges on his furniture, and rent on the place where he was living. When the seller failed to return his deposit, Young moved into the trailer to minimize his expenses. He spent $581.00 to make the heating system conform to the contract, lived in the trailer for a year, and then spent $1,880 to have it taken back to El Paso. The trial court held that Young had properly rejected. Reversing, the appellate court stated:

> Section 2.602 requires that the rejection be within a reasonable time after delivery, with notice to the seller. Then in § 2.711 there is the following provision:

"(c) On rightful rejection or justifiable revocation of acceptance a buyer has a security interest in goods in his possession or control for any payments made on their price and any expenses reasonably incurred in their inspection, receipt, transportation, care and custody and may hold such goods and resell them in like manner as an aggrieved seller."

In this case, Appellee received the mobile home in South Carolina on January 4, 1971. On January 21st, he rejected the unit and advised the seller. Where goods fail "in any respect" to conform to the contract the buyer may . . . reject the entire unit. Certainly the telegram dated January 21, 1971, was evidence to support the trial Court's finding that the Appellee rightfully rejected the mobile home. It did not conform in every respect to the one ordered, particularly with regard to the size of the air conditioner. The rejection within a few days after the unit had been connected up and all equipment tested, but before Appellee moved into it, was under the circumstances a rejection within a reasonable time and notice was given to the seller by telegram to comply with § 2.602.

Although § 2.711(c) gives a buyer a security interest in goods in his possession, and even a right to resell them, it does not give a right to continued use of the goods until the security interest is satisfied. The Appellee testified that after discovering the defects in the mobile home, he telephoned both the seller and manufacturer to obtain some satisfaction toward the repairs and change of the defects. When he sent his telegram on January 21st to the seller, he said therein "Unable to secure commitment from factory." A week earlier he had wired the seller and General Electric Credit Corporation, who was to originally finance the mobile home, that the unit was damaged and that he would not pay until it was completely repaired.

Failing to get satisfactory assurance from either the seller or manufacturer concerning the damaged and nonconforming mobile home, Appellee did not seek to foreclose his security interest for the down-payment, transportation and storage expense. Nor did he act in accordance with § 2.604, which provides: " * * * if the seller gives no instructions within a reasonable time after notification of rejection the buyer may store the rejected goods for the seller's account or reship them to him or resell them for the seller's account with reimbursement as provided in the preceding section. Such action is not acceptance or conversion." Instead, he decided sometime in February to move into the mobile home and spent nearly $600.00 to repair the heating unit and change from an electric to a gas heater. By doing so he accepted the goods under § 2.606, and under § 2.607 became obligated to pay at the contract price for the goods accepted, retaining such rights, if any, as existed for damages under § 2.714 and § 2.715.

Keeping in mind that the goods in question were a mobile home, exactly what should Young have done? Why was his occupancy of it not an appropriate response? We will return to this problem in connection with revocation of acceptance.

8.   Revised Article 2. Revised 2–608 makes no substantive change in current 2–608, but it adds a new subsection (4):

(4) If a buyer uses the goods after a rightful rejection … , the following rules apply:

> (a) Any use by the buyer which is unreasonable under the circumstances is wrongful as against the seller and is an acceptance only if ratified by the seller.

> (b) Any use of the goods which is reasonable under the circumstances is not wrongful as against the seller and is not an acceptance, but in an appropriate case the buyer is obligated to the seller for the value of the use to the buyer.

Under the rule of revised 2–608, do you think that the use by Young in Bowen v. Young was reasonable under the circumstances?

If the use was not reasonable and Bowen chose not to ratify the use as an acceptance, what is the legal situation between Bowen and Young? between Bowen and Young's creditors? If Bowen does ratify the use as acceptance, what is the answer to these two questions?

9.   Problem. Buyer, a retail dress shop, contracts to purchase 15 "wet-look" vinyl skirts. The skirts delivered are not "wet-look," and Buyer immediately telephones Seller and rejects them. Seller tells Buyer to try to sell the skirts. Instead of following that instruction, Buyer puts the skirts back in the packing boxes in which they were shipped and places them in a storage room. Seller sues for the price (2–607(1) and 2–709(1)(a)), alleging that Buyer accepted the skirts. What result? Did Buyer act properly after rejection?

10.   CISG and the burden of proving nonconformity. In disputes under Article 2, allocation of the burden of proving whether goods conform to the contract can be critical. The same is true of the Convention on Contracts for the International Sale of Goods. For example, under Article 67(1), the risk of loss passes to the buyer when the goods are delivered to the carrier. Under Article 36(1) the seller is liable for any nonconformity that exists at the time the risk passes to the buyer. In the case of perishable goods that, upon arrival, the buyer discovers to be spoiled, it is critical to know whether the goods already were spoiled when the seller delivered them to the carrier. Who has the burden of proving that the goods did or did not conform to the contract? This was an issue in Chicago Prime Packers, Inc. v. Northam Food Trading Co., 408 F.3d 894 (7th Cir.2005), in which a U.S. seller sued a Canadian buyer for the purchase price of pork ribs that arrived in a spoiled condition. The court held that the burden of proof rested on the buyer:

> [The buyer] asserts that [the seller] should bear the burden of proving that the ribs were not spoiled at the time of transfer because the quality of the goods is an essential element of [the seller's] breach

of contract claim. [The seller] counters that nonconformity is an affirmative defense for which [the buyer] has the burden of proof. Proper assignment of the burden of proof is a question of law that we review de novo.

The CISG does not state expressly whether the seller or buyer bears the burden of proof as to the product's conformity with the contract. Because there is little case law under the CISG, we interpret its provisions by looking to its language and to "the general principles" upon which it is based. See CISG Art. 7(2); see also Delchi Carrier SpA v. Rotorex Corp., 71 F.3d 1024, 1027–28 (2d Cir.1995). The CISG is the international analogue to Article 2 of the Uniform Commercial Code. Many provisions of the UCC and the CISG are the same or similar, and "caselaw interpreting analogous provisions of Article 2 of the [UCC], may ... inform a court where the language of the relevant CISG provision tracks that of the UCC." Delchi Carrier SpA, 71 F.3d at 1028. "However, UCC caselaw 'is not per se applicable.'" Id.

A comparison with the UCC reveals that the buyer bears the burden of proving nonconformity under the CISG. Under the UCC, the buyer may plead breach of the implied warranty of fitness for ordinary purpose as an affirmative defense to a contract action by the seller for the purchase price. In such an action it is the defendant-buyer's burden to prove the breach of the warranty.

Section 2–314 of the UCC provides that a warranty that goods are "fit for the ordinary purpose for which such goods are used" is implied unless the contract states otherwise. Mirroring the structure and content of this section, Article 35(2) of the CISG provides that unless the contract states otherwise, "goods do not conform with the contract unless they ... are fit for the purposes for which goods of the same description would ordinarily be used." Accordingly, just as a buyer-defendant bears the burden of proving breach of the implied warranty of fitness for ordinary purpose under the UCC, under the CISG, the buyer-defendant bears the burden of proving nonconformity at the time of transfer. See Larry A. DiMatteo et al., The Interpretive Turn in International Sales Law: An Analysis of Fifteen Years of CISG Juris-prudence, 24 Nw.J.Int'l L. & Bus. 299, 400 (2004) (Under the CISG, "the buyer is allocated the burden of proving that the goods were defective prior to the expiration of the seller's obligation point."); see also R. Folsom, 1 International Business Transactions § 1.15, at 41 (2d ed.2002). The district court was correct to conclude that [the buyer] bears the burden of proving that the ribs were spoiled at the time of transfer.

What is wrong with the court's reasoning?

4. Cure

We have seen that under 2–612(2) a buyer in an installment contract may not reject nonconforming goods if the nonconformity can be cured. In a single-delivery contract, the matter is governed by 2–508. That section contemplates that the buyer may reject goods that fail in any respect to conform to the contract (2–601), but in some instances gives the seller a right to cure. Under 2–508, then, the buyer's rejection of the goods is a prerequisite to the seller's right to cure. If the buyer accepts nonconforming goods and asserts a claim because of the nonconformity, the seller has no right to cure (unless the contract provides otherwise). Please read 2–508. Note that subsection (1) governs the seller's right to cure when the buyer rejects the goods before the time for the seller's performance has expired. Subsection (2) applies when the time for the seller's performance has expired.

Zabriskie Chevrolet, Inc. v. Smith

New Jersey Superior Court, Law Division, 1968.
99 N.J.Super. 441, 240 A.2d 195.

■ DOAN, J.D.C. (temporarily assigned). This action arises out of the sale by plaintiff to defendant of a new 1966 Chevrolet automobile. Within a short distance after leaving the showroom the vehicle became almost completely inoperable by reason of mechanical failure. Defendant the same day notified plaintiff that he cancelled the sale and simultaneously stopped payment on the check he had tendered in payment of the balance of the purchase price. Plaintiff sues on the check and the purchase order for the balance of the purchase price plus incidental damages and defendant counterclaims for the return of his deposit and incidental damages.

The facts are not complex nor do they present any serious dispute.

On February 2, 1967 defendant signed a form purchase order for a new 1966 Chevrolet Biscayne Sedan which was represented to him to be a brand-new car that would operate perfectly. On that occasion he paid plaintiff $124 by way of deposit. On February 9, 1967 defendant tendered plaintiff his check for $2069.50 representing the balance of the purchase price ($2064) and $5.50 for license and transfer fees. Delivery was made to defendant's wife during the early evening hours of Friday, February 10, 1967, at which time she was handed the keys and the factory package of printed material, including the manual and the manufacturer-dealer's warranty, none of which she or her husband ever read before or after the sale was made, nor were the details thereof specifically explained to or agreed to by defendant. While en route to her home, about 2-1/2 miles away, and after having gone about 7/10 of a mile from the showroom, the car stalled at a traffic light, stalled again within another 15 feet and again thereafter each time the vehicle was required to stop. When about halfway home the car could not be driven in "drive" gear at all, and defendant's wife was obliged to then propel the vehicle in "low-low" gear at a rate of about five to ten miles per hour, its then maximum speed. In great distress, defendant's wife was fearful of completing the journey to her home and called her husband, who thereupon drove the car in "low-low" gear about seven blocks to his home. Defendant, considerably upset by this turn of events, thereupon immediately called his bank (which was open this Friday evening), stopped payment on the check and called plaintiff to notify them that they had sold him a "lemon," that he had stopped payment on the check and that the sale was cancelled. The next day plaintiff sent a wrecker to defendant's home, brought the vehicle to its repair shop and after inspection determined that the transmission was defective.

Plaintiff's expert testified that the car would not move, that there was no power in the transmission and in that condition the car could not move. Plaintiff replaced the transmission with another one removed from a vehicle then on plaintiff's showroom floor, notifying defendant thereafter of what had been done. Defendant refused to take delivery of the vehicle as repaired and reasserted his cancellation of the sale. Plaintiff has since kept the vehicle in storage at his place of business. Within a short period following these occurrences plaintiff and defendant began negotiations for a new 1967 Chevrolet, but these fell through when plaintiff insisted that a new deal could only be made by giving defendant credit for the previously ordered 1966 Chevrolet. This defendant refused to do because he considered the prior transaction as cancelled.

The issues in this case present problems for disposition under the Uniform Commercial Code (Code). The Code . . . provides that the act shall be liberally construed and applied to promote its underlying purposes and policies. N.J.S. 12A:1–102[;] . . . that unless displaced by the particular provisions of the Code, the principles of law and equity or other validating or invalidating cause shall supplement its provisions, N.J.S. 12A:1–103; and . . . that the remedies provided by the Code shall be liberally administered to the end that the aggrieved party may be put in as good a position as if the other party had fully performed. N.J.S. 12A:1–106.

. . .

Plaintiff urges that defendant accepted the vehicle and therefore under the Code (N.J.S. 12A:2–607(1) is bound to complete payment for it. Defendant asserts that he never accepted the vehicle and therefore under the Code properly rejected it; further, that even if there had been acceptance he was justified under the Code in revoking the same. Defendant supports this claim by urging that what was delivered to him was not what he bargained for, i.e., a new car with factory new parts, which would operate perfectly as represented and, therefore, the Code remedies of rejection and revocation of acceptance were available to him. These remedies have their basis in breach of contract and failure of consideration although they are also viewed as arising out of breach of warranty. The essential ingredient which determines which of these two remedies is brought into play is a determination, *in limine,* whether there had been an "acceptance" of the goods by the buyer. Thus, the primary inquiry is whether the defendant had "accepted" the automobile prior to the return thereof to the plaintiff.

. . .

The New Jersey Study Comment to 12A:2–606 states:

> "2. Subsection 2–606(1)(a) is similar to the first clause of section 48 of the U.S.A. (N.J.S.A. 46:30–54). See also, Paul Gerli & Co. v. Mistletoe Silk Mills, 80 N.J.L. 128, 76 A. 335 (1910)."

The *Gerli* case states:

> *"The question arises whether the defendant accepted it.* The defendant had a right to inspect and examine (Sales Act, § 47), and, if necessary, to test the goods even though the test involved destruction of a part. Williston on Sales, § 475. If, however, the defendant intimated to the plaintiff that it had accepted the goods, or if the defendant did any act inconsistent with the ownership of the plaintiff, or if, after the lapse of a reasonable time, it retained the goods without intimating to the plaintiff a rejection, then the defendant must be deemed to have accepted the goods and the right of rescission is gone. Sales Act, § 48." (at p. 129, at p. 336 of 76 A.)

> . . .

It is clear that a buyer does not accept goods until he has had a "reasonable opportunity to inspect." Defendant sought to purchase a new car. He assumed what every new car buyer has a right to assume and, indeed, has been led to assume by the high powered advertising techniques of the auto industry—that his new car, with the exception of very minor adjustments, would be mechanically new and factory-furnished, operate perfectly, and be free of substantial defects. The vehicle delivered to defendant did not measure up to these representations. Plaintiff contends that defendant had "reasonable opportunity to inspect" by the privilege to take the car for a typical "spin around the block" before signing the purchase order. If by this contention plaintiff equates a spin around the block with "reasonable opportunity to inspect," the contention is illusory and unrealistic. To the layman, the complicated mechanisms of today's automobiles are a complete mystery. To have the automobile inspected by someone with sufficient expertise to disassemble the vehicle in order to discover latent defects before the contract is signed, is assuredly impossible and highly impractical. Consequently, the first few miles of driving become even more significant to the excited new car buyer. This is the buyer's first reasonable opportunity to enjoy his new vehicle to see if it conforms to what it was represented to be and whether he is getting what he bargained for. How long the buyer may drive the new car under the guise of inspection of new goods is not an issue in the present case. It is clear that defendant discovered the nonconformity within 7/10 of a mile and minutes after leaving plaintiff's showroom. Certainly this was well within the ambit of "reasonable opportunity to inspect." That the vehicle was grievously defective when it left plaintiff's possession is a compelling conclusion, as is the conclusion that in a legal sense defendant never accepted the vehicle.

> . . .

Nor did plaintiff have reasonable grounds to believe that a new automobile which could not even be driven a bare few miles to the buyer's residence would be acceptable. The dealer is in an entirely different position from the layman. The dealer with his staff of expert mechanics and modern equipment knows or should know of substantial defects in the new automobile which it sells. There was offered into evidence the dealer's inspection and adjustment schedule containing over 70 alleged items that plaintiff caused to be inspected, including the transmission. According to that schedule the automobile in question had been checked by the seller for the satisfaction of the buyer, and such inspection included a road test. The fact that the automobile underwent a tortured operation for about 2–1/2 miles from the showroom to defendant's residence demonstrates the inherent serious deficiencies in this vehicle which were present when the so-called inspection was made by plaintiff, and hence plaintiff was aware (or should have been) that the vehicle did not conform to the bargain the parties had made, and plaintiff had no reasonable right to expect that the vehicle in that condition would be accepted.

There having been no acceptance, the next issue presented is whether defendant properly rejected under the Code. That he cancelled the sale and rejected the vehicle almost concomitantly with the discovery of the failure of his bargain is clear from the evidence. [Section 2–601] delineates the buyer's rights following nonconforming delivery and reads as follows: . . .

Section 12A:2–602 indicates that one can reject after taking possession. Possession, therefore, does not mean acceptance and the corresponding loss of the right of rejection; nor does the fact that buyer has a security interest along with possession eliminate the right to reject. . . .

N.J.S. 12A:2–106 defines conforming goods as follows:

"(2) Goods or conduct including any part of a performance are 'conforming' or conform to the contract when they are in accordance with the obligations under the contract."

The Uniform Commercial Code Comment to that section states:

"2. Subsection (2): It is in general intended to continue the policy of requiring *exact performance* by the seller of his obligations as a condition to his right to require acceptance. However, the seller is in part safeguarded against surprise as a result of sudden technicality on the buyer's part by the provisions of Section 2–508 on seller's cure of improper tender or delivery. Moreover usage of trade frequently permits commercial leeways in performance and the language of the agreement itself must be read in the light of such custom or usage and also, prior course of dealing, and in a long term contract, the course of performance."

There was no evidence at the trial concerning any "custom or usage," although plaintiff in its brief argued that it is the usage of the automobile trade that a buyer accept a new automobile, although containing defects of manufacture, if such defects can be and are seasonably cured by the seller. Perhaps this represents prevailing views in the automobile industry which have, over the years, served to blanket injustices and inequities committed upon buyers who demurred in the light of the unequal positions of strength between the parties. The spirit of the [opinion in Henningsen v. Bloomfield Motors, Inc., 32 N.J. 358, 161 A.2d 69 (1960)], supra, contemplated these conditions which cried out for correction. In the present case we are not dealing with a situation such as was present in Adams v. Tramontin Motor Sales, 42 N.J.Super. 313, 126 A.2d 358 (App.Div.1956). In that case, brought for breach of implied warranty of merchantability, the court held that minor defects, such as adjustment of the motor, tightening of loose elements, fixing of locks and dome light, and a correction of rumbling noise, were not remarkable defects, and therefore there was no breach. Here the breach was substantial. The new car was practically inoperable and endowed with a defective transmission. This was a "remarkable defect" and justified rejection by the buyer.

Lastly, plaintiff urges that under the Code, N.J.S. 12A:2–508, it had a right to cure the nonconforming delivery. . . .

The New Jersey Study Comment to 12A:2–508 reads:

"3. Subsection 2–508(2) has been applauded as a rule aimed at ending 'forced breaches.' See, Hawkland, Sales and Bulk Sales Under the Uniform Commercial Code, 120–122 (1958). * * *

"Section 2–508 prevents the buyer from forcing the seller to breach by making a surprise rejection of the goods because of some minor nonconformity at a time at which the seller cannot cure the deficiency within the time for performance."

The Uniform Commercial Code Comment to 12A:2–508 reads:

"2. Subsection (2) seeks to avoid injustice to the seller by reason of a surprise rejection by the buyer. However, the seller is not protected unless he had 'reasonable grounds to believe' that the tender would be acceptable."

It is clear that in the instant case there was no "forced breach" on the part of the buyer, for he almost immediately began to negotiate for another automobile. The inquiry is as to what is intended by "cure," as used in the Code. This statute makes no attempt to define or specify what a "cure" shall consist of. It would appear, then, that each case must be controlled by its own facts. The "cure" intended under the cited section of the Code does not, in the court's opinion, contemplate the tender of a new vehicle with a substituted transmission, not from the factory and of unknown lineage from another vehicle in plaintiff's possession. It was not the intention of the Legislature that the right to "cure" is a limitless one to be controlled only by the will of the seller. A "cure" which endeavors by substitution to tender a chattel not within the agreement or contemplation of the parties is invalid.

For a majority of people the purchase of a new car is a major investment, rationalized by the peace of mind that flows from its dependability and safety. Once their faith is shaken, the vehicle loses not only its real value in their eyes, but becomes an instrument whose integrity is substantially impaired and whose operation is fraught with apprehension. The attempted cure in the present case was ineffective.

Accordingly, and pursuant to N.J.S. 12A:2–711, judgment is rendered on the main case in favor of defendant. On the counterclaim judgment is rendered in favor of defendant and against plaintiff in the sum of $124, being the amount of the deposit, there being no further proof of damages.

Defendant shall, as part of this judgment, execute for plaintiff, on demand, such documents as are necessary to again vest title to the vehicle in plaintiff.

QUESTIONS

1.   Which subsection of 2–508 governs *Zabriskie*?

2.   The seller attempted to cure the nonconformity by replacing the defective transmission with one from another car. The court held that this was not sufficient. Can you think of any other way the seller might have cured the nonconformity?

3.   Shaken-faith doctrine. The court creates what has come to be known as the "shaken-faith doctrine." Some other courts have embraced it, too. But not all. For example, in Sinco, Inc. v. Metro–North Commuter Railroad Co., 133 F.Supp.2d 308 (S.D.N.Y.2001), Metro–North was undertaking a renovation of Grand Central Terminal in New York City. It invited proposals for a fall-restraint system to protect its workers when they were working high off the floor in the terminal. Ultimately, it contracted with Sinco for a system in which workers would wear a harness that would be connected to a cable system by metal clips. If a worker fell, the harness and cable system would prevent any serious injury or death. When Sinco came to the work site to show the system to the workers, one of the metal clips fell apart in a worker's hand. The worker's union asserted that its members would under no circumstances work with the Sinco system. The contract provided that on material breach, Sinco would have seven days to cure the breach. Sinco proposed a cure by reworking some clips and supplying others that did not have the flaw. Metro–North refused to accept this cure. When Sinco sued, Metro–North counterclaimed to recover the excess cost it paid another supplier for a fall-restraint system. Each party filed a motion for summary judgment. The court's response:

> Metro–North alleges that Sinco's delivery of the defective Sayf-links was so material a breach that Metro–North was entitled to terminate the contract without even providing an opportunity for cure. This argument conflicts with both the language of the contract and the substantive law of New York. Article 7.01 of the contract provides that a "material breach" by Sinco may be considered an "Event of Default." "The remedy of termination—or, more accurately, the 'right' to terminate—is available only where one party has materially breached the contract. . . . Where a breach is material, the party is justified in refusing to go on, and thus the law provides that party with the right to terminate." ESPN, Inc. v. Office of the Comm'r of Baseball, 76

F.Supp.2d 383, 392 (S.D.N.Y.1999). It is well-settled under New York law that in order to justify termination, "a breach must be . . . so substantial and fundamental as to strongly tend to defeat the object of the parties in making the contract." Babylon Assocs. v. County of Suffolk, 101 A.D.2d 207, 475 N.Y.S.2d 869, 874 (App. Div.2d Dep't 1984). Termination is an "extraordinary remedy" to be permitted only when the breach goes to "the root of the agreement." Septembertide Publishing, B.V. v. Stein & Day, Inc., 884 F.2d 675, 678 (2d Cir.1989).

An injured party's right of termination, however, is limited by the doctrine of cure.

. . .

. . . Metro–North argues that the delivery of defective Sayflinks was so severe a breach that it irremediably undermined Metro–North's confidence in the fall-protection system, rendering futile any attempt at cure. Following the discovery of the defect, Metro–North's unions reported that their members would not use the system, and the unions repeatedly expressed a complete lack of confidence in Sinco and its products. Metro–North contends that nothing Sinco did—no curative performance of any sort—could restore this lost confidence. In other words, the breach could not be cured.

In support of this "shaken faith" or "loss of confidence" theory, Metro–North cites case law from states other than New York. I find these authorities not entirely applicable to the case before me.

Zabriskie Chevrolet, Inc. v. Smith, 99 N.J.Super. 441, 240 A.2d 195 (N.J.Sup.Ct.1968) involved a car dealer's efforts to cure its delivery of new car with a faulty transmission by replacing the transmission with one removed from a showroom model. The court found that the substitution of a transmission "not from the factory and of unknown lineage" was "not within the agreement or contemplation of the parties." *Id.* at 458, 240 A.2d 195. In short, the cure did not conform to the terms of the contract. The court's discussion of "shaken faith" is not essential to its conclusion; it appears from the text of the opinion that the attempted cure was objectively unreasonable.

Hemmert Agricultural Aviation, Inc. v. Mid–Continent Aircraft Corp., 663 F.Supp. 1546 (D.Kan.1987), decided under Kansas state law, better illustrates Metro–North's theory. The flaws in a "crop-duster" airplane purchased by the plaintiff created "fear and apprehension" in the pilot. The court held that, "[w]here the buyer's confidence in the dependability of the machine is shaken because of the defects and possibly because of seller's ineffective attempts to cure, revocation appears justified." *Id.* at 1552.

There appear to be no New York cases treating the "shaken faith" theory articulated in *Hemmert* under Kansas law. I am not prepared to hold that Sinco's breach rendered futile any potential cure. A materially breaching party generally is entitled, subject to the relevant terms and conditions of the contract and the Uniform Commercial Code, to cure its breach within a reasonable period of time. Cure, in this case, required not only the timely delivery of conforming replacement parts, but a convincing showing of the reliability of the equipment. Such a showing would have required a description of Sinco's manufacturing methods and a precise explanation of the reasons why the demonstration parts failed in relation to such methods. If Sinco had timely tendered such a cure, Metro–North would have been able to assess the reasons for the failure and the reliability of the cure. If, objectively, the cure was shown to be reliably safe, Metro–North would have been obligated to accept the cure, despite, perhaps, any lingering subjective misgivings of its employees. Ultimately, however, Sinco failed to cure and Metro–North justifiably terminated the contract.

. . .

It is undisputed that Sinco's attempted performance under the contract—its delivery of a fall-protection system that included the defective Sayflinks—did not satisfy its contractual obligations. Pursuant to the Code and the contract, Sinco had the opportunity following this breach to cure.

Sinco, as the party attempting to effect a cure, had the burden to show that its proffered cure did, in fact, conform to the terms of the contract. Those terms included stringent conditions regarding quality control and reliability. It is uncontested that the welded Sayflinks, manufactured and delivered within two days after the equipment failure, were not subjected to Sinco's internal quality controls. The contractual conditions regarding reliability also applied to the replacement Sayflinks that came from the regular assembly line that did not include the additional welding. Sinco had to show exactly what had caused the defect in the demonstration parts, that the underlying problem had been remedied, and that the defect would not recur. Furthermore, in order to conform to the contract, any replacement system had to be demonstrably reliable. In a situation such as this, involving the failure of vital safety equipment in front of the very individuals the equipment was designed to protect, the injured party did not have to accept at face value the word of the breaching party regarding the reliability of replacement equipment. Metro–North was entitled to objective evidence of such reliability.

Sinco did not satisfy that obligation by delivering to Metro–North a videotape of a welded and staked Sayflink surviving a single "pull test" of over 6200 pounds of stress. The replacement parts sent by Sinco included four Sayflinks that had been staked, and four that had been both welded and staked. The videotaped test was performed only on a Sayflink with the supplemental welding, not on a "standard" Sayflink that lacked the welding. Moreover, the test involved the application of stress in a different direction than the direction in which the failure occurred, and did not show reliability over time and frequent use. Finally, the videotape was produced by Sinco itself, not by a disinterested and objective third party. The videotaped stress test did not demonstrate the reliability of Sinco's attempted cure.

. . .

When Metro–North did not accept Sinco's first attempted cure, Sinco proposed several ideas for other possible cures during discussions with Metro–North. However, these mere offers of potentially curative performance did not adequately cure Sinco's breach.

Pursuant to Section 2–508(2) of the New York Uniform Commercial Code, Sinco had to notify Metro–North of its intention to cure and had to make a "conforming tender." "This clearly entails *more than a mere offer,* but less than actual physical delivery." Allied Semi–Conductors Int'l, Ltd. v. Pulsar Components Int'l, Inc., 907 F.Supp. 618, 624 (E.D.N.Y.1995) (emphasis added).

. . .

Sinco's bare offers of potentially curative performance were not enough. The contract called for reliable equipment to protect Metro–North's employees from grave injury or death, and Sinco's equipment had been shown to be unreliable. In order to effectuate a cure, Sinco was obliged to make a conforming tender—that is, to put a fall protection system and proof of its reliability at Metro–North's disposition, leaving it to Metro–North to accept the tender. In essence, Sinco had to take the initiative; it could not shift any part of its burden to Metro–North. It was not enough for Sinco merely to suggest possible solutions. Because Sinco failed to cure its breach, I deny its motion for summary judgment and grant Metro–North's motion for summary judgment on the issue of liability.

4. The court in *Sinco* suggests that when the first attempt at cure failed, Sinco had the right to try again. What language in 2–508 supports this position? How many attempts does the seller get?

5. Would appropriate "cure" in *Sinco* require the seller to convince the buyer's employees to use the seller's system?

6. The court in *Sinco* applies subsection (2) of 2–508, which applies when the seller has reasonable grounds to believe that the nonconforming tender would be acceptable. What basis is there for saying that Sinco had reasonable grounds to believe that the clips would be acceptable?

7. Cure by repair vs. cure by substitution of new goods. In Wilson v. Scampoli, 228 A.2d 848 (D.C.App. 1967), the buyer purchased a color TV in 1965 for $675. When delivered and set up, the picture had a red tinge. Two days later a service representative was unable to fix the problem and said he needed to take the chassis to the seller's shop. The buyer refused to permit this and demanded another brand new TV set. The seller refused to replace the TV unless it proved incapable of repair. The buyer demanded return of the purchase price and, when the seller refused, sued. The trial court granted the relief plaintiff requested, but the appellate court reversed. Citing 2–508, it stated:

A retail dealer would certainly expect and have reasonable grounds to believe that merchandise like color television sets, new and delivered as crated at the factory, would be acceptable as delivered and that, if defective in some way, he would have the right to substitute a conforming tender. The question then resolves itself to whether the dealer may conform his tender by adjustment or minor repair or whether he must conform by substituting brand new merchandise. The problem seems to be one of first impression in other jurisdictions adopting the Uniform Commercial Code as well as in the District of Columbia.

Although the Official Code Comments do not reach this precise issue, there are cases and comments under other provisions of the Code which indicate that under certain circumstances repairs and adjustments are contemplated as remedies under implied warranties. In L & N Sales Co. v. Little Brown Jug, Inc., 12 Pa.Dist. & Co.R.2d 469 (Phila.County Ct.1957), where the language of a disclaimer was found insufficient to defeat warranties under §§ 2–314 and 2–315, the court noted that the buyer had notified the seller of defects in the merchandise, and as the seller was unable to remedy them and later refused to accept return of the articles, it was held to be a breach of warranty. In Hall v. Everett Motors, Inc., 340 Mass. 430, 165 N.E.2d 107 (1960), decided shortly before the effective date of the Code in Massachusetts, the court reluctantly found that a disclaimer of warranties was sufficient to insulate the seller. Several references were made in the ruling to the seller's unsuccessful attempts at repairs, the court indicating the result would have been different under the Code.

While these cases provide no mandate to require the buyer to accept patchwork goods or substantially repaired articles in lieu of flawless merchandise, they do indicate that minor repairs or reasonable adjustments are frequently the means by which an imperfect tender may be cured. In discussing the analogous question of defective title, it has been stated that:

> The seller, then, should be able to cure [the defect] under subsection 2–508(2) in those cases in which he can do so without subjecting the buyer to any great inconvenience, risk or loss. Hawkland, Curing an Improper Tender of Title to Chattels: Past, Present and Commercial Code, 46 Minn.L.Rev. 697, 724 (1962).

Removal of a television chassis for a short period of time in order to determine the cause of color malfunction and ascertain the extent of adjustment or correction needed to effect full operational efficiency presents no great inconvenience to the buyer. In the instant case, appellant's expert witness testified that this was not infrequently necessary with new televisions. Should the set be defective in workmanship or parts, the loss would be upon the manufacturer who warranted it free from mechanical defect. Here the adamant refusal of [the buyer] to allow inspection essential to the determination of the cause of the excessive red tinge to the picture defeated any effort by the seller to provide timely repair or even replacement of the set if the difficulty could not be corrected. The cause of the defect might have been minor and easily adjusted or it may have been substantial and required replacement by another new set—but the seller was never given an adequate opportunity to make a determination.

... We therefore reverse the judgment of the trial court granting rescission and directing the return of the purchase price of the set.

8.   Under 2–508(1) seller's right to cure within "time for performance" or "contract time" is absolute. After the "contract time," however, cure is available only if the seller had reasonable grounds to believe that the original, nonconforming tender would be acceptable. If the seller does not have reasonable grounds to believe that, it is critical to the seller's right to cure that the time for performance not have expired when the buyer rejects the goods.

When does the time for performance expire? Ordinarily, we would expect it to be the last date on which the seller could deliver the goods. But what if the seller also promises to provide some form of support for a specified period of time after delivery: does this mean that the "contract time" extends to the end of that period, so that if the goods do not conform, the seller may cure the nonconformity long after the deadline for delivery? One court has held just that. Peter Pan Seafoods, Inc. v. Olympic Foundry Co., 17 Wash.App. 761, 565 P.2d 819 (1977), but other courts have not adopted this position. See the Official Comments to 2–508.

The *Zabriskie* court discusses cure and seems to assume that any available cure would be under 2–508(2). This assumption rests on the conclusion that "time for performance" in 2–508(1) refers to the time when, under the contract, the goods must be delivered. Of course, it might be that February 9th, the day on which the automobile was delivered to Smith, was not the last day on which delivery could be made without a breach of the time provisions of the contract. If so, then if a delivery on, say, February 15th would have been within the contract time requirements, the seller might have had a right to cure under subsection (1) until at least the 15th. Assuming that the contract time for delivery had expired in *Zabriskie* before seller tendered the repaired automobile, did the seller have a right to cure?

9.   The court in *Zabriskie*, in the first partial paragraph on page 387, seems to say that since the dealer claimed to have inspected the car prior to delivery, he knew "or should have known" that the car was defective. The next step in that line of reasoning, although the court does not overtly make it, is that since the dealer ought to have known he was selling a defective machine, he could not reasonably expect that it would be acceptable with or without money allowance, and thus had no right to cure. The reverse of that argument is that if the dealer neither knew nor had reason to know of the defect, he had a right to cure no matter how serious the defect is. On page 388, however, the court seems to take a somewhat different view of cure, suggesting that it is available after the time for performance has passed only if the rejection is an attempt to force a breach. Presumably, that idea is that cure is available only if the defect is so minor that ordinarily a buyer would go ahead and take the goods anyway "with or without money allowance." See Official Comment 2 to 2–508. In the view of most commentators, this "surprise rejection" situation is the only one contemplated by 2–508(2). R.Nordstrom, Law of Sales § 105, 317–322 (1970); R.Dusenberg & L.King, Sales and Bulk Transfers § 14.02 (1974); W.Hawkland, A Transactional Guide to the UCC § 1.37, at 198–200 (1964); Peters, Remedies For Breach of Contract Relating to the Sale of Goods Under the Uniform Commercial Code; A Roadmap For Article Two, 73 Yale L.J. 199, 209–216 (1963).

10.   Presumably, it will be a rare case in which a seller who was aware of substantial defects in tendered goods will be able to establish a reasonable belief that they would be acceptable so as to support a right to cure under 2–508(2). In Wilson v. Scampoli, however, the seller did not know of the defect in the television set and the court held that he therefore was reasonable in believing that the set would be acceptable and had the right to cure whether or not the defect was substantial.

Under that view, the right to cure applies not only to trivial defects, but also to substantial ones if the seller is (reasonably?) unaware of the defects. See, in favor of the result in *Scampoli*, J.White & R.Summers, Uniform Commercial Code § 8–5 (4th ed.1995). For a commentary critical of the result, see R.Nordstrom, Sales 320–321 (1970). In Johannsen v. Minnesota Valley Ford Tractor Co., Inc., 304 N.W.2d 654 (Minn.1981), the court held that the right to cure is limited to cases in which the defects are minor and that the seller has no right to cure defects that substantially impair the value of the goods.

11.   Occasionally, commentators on the Code have professed to believe that it is not clear whether the phrase "with or without money allowance" in 2–508(2) modifies the language preceding it or the language following it. That is, they are not sure whether, if a comma were added to the section, it should be placed after the word "acceptable" or after the word "allowance." What do you think? If the section should be read as if there were a comma after "acceptable," what does the phrase after the comma mean? See Peters, Remedies for Breach of Contracts Relating to the Sale of Goods Under the Uniform Commercial Code: A Roadmap for Article Two, 73 Yale L.J. 199, 211 (1963).

12.   Problem. Your client, the owner of a small chain of discount houses, sells a number of different brands of television sets. They have not previously carried Westminster sets, which are made by a Japanese manufacturer. Westminster's U.S. distributor, however, persuaded your client to purchase 200 nine-inch portable TVs, to be delivered in four equal monthly installments, starting in October. The first shipment arrived on October 3rd and when store employees on October 4th opened the first box to put out the sets, they discovered that the sets had six-inch screens. Your client immediately phones you and asks whether she can refuse the sets and terminate the contract. What do you advise?

Does the concept of cure have any relevance?

Do you need any additional facts to determine whether the defect "substantially impairs the value of that installment?"

13. In Jakowski v. Carole Chevrolet, page 201 supra, the seller delivered a car without the undercoating required by the contract. The buyer brought the car back in for the seller to apply the undercoating, and while the car was on the dealer's lot, it was stolen. The court looked to 2–510 to determine the risk of loss because the car as delivered failed to conform to the contract. In view of 2–508, however, was the court right: should risk of loss have been governed by 2–509?

14. Revised Article 2. Revised 2–508(2) abandons the "reasonable grounds to believe" element and changes the period for cure from "a further reasonable time" to "if the cure is appropriate and timely under the circumstances." See Official Comments 3–4 to revised 2–508.

5. REVOCATION OF ACCEPTANCE

Once the buyer has accepted the goods, it is too late to reject them, even if they are grossly nonconforming. The buyer may, however, be able to revoke acceptance of them. Like rejection, revocation of acceptance has the effect of putting the goods back into the hands of the seller. To that extent, it may seem that it does not matter whether the buyer rejects or revokes acceptance. But it matters a lot: as noted earlier, the burden of proving whether the goods are nonconforming depends entirely on whether the buyer wants to reject or revoke acceptance (2–607(4)). Furthermore, although rejection is permitted if the goods or the tender fail in any respect to conform to the contract, revocation of acceptance is permitted only under the circumstances specified in 2–608. Please read that section.

Jorgensen v. Pressnall

Oregon Supreme Court, 1976.
274 Or. 285, 545 P.2d 1382.

■ O'CONNELL, CHIEF JUSTICE. This is a suit for the rescission of a mobile home purchase contract and for the recovery of plaintiffs' down payment and damages. Defendants are Pressnall, the seller of the mobile home, and Commercial Credit Company, the company financing the transaction. Commercial Credit counterclaims for losses incurred in repossession of the mobile home and, in the event rescission is granted, seeks recovery of damages from Pressnall for breach of a warranty. The trial court found for plaintiffs against Pressnall and for Commercial Credit on its cross-complaint against Pressnall. Pressnall appeals.

Plaintiffs purchased a new mobile home from Pressnall, using their old mobile home as a down payment and financing the balance. Pressnall assigned the financing contract to Commercial Credit, warranting the enforceability of the assigned contract.

Pressnall represented the mobile home to plaintiffs as being of "good, sound construction," and of "medium quality." He also represented to plaintiffs that the mobile home was strong enough to stand up to frequent moves. Plaintiffs were assured that any defects present in the mobile home delivered to them from the factory would be repaired promptly.

The mobile home was delivered to plaintiffs' lot on November 1, 1972. Soon after they moved in plaintiffs discovered water and air leaks, gaps in the "tip out,"[1] as well as defective doors, cabinets, vents and walls. Plaintiffs promptly gave Pressnall a list of these defects and were assured by Pressnall that the problems would be corrected. Thereafter, a series of repair requests yielded no action except the appearance of workmen who were not prepared to make repairs. Finally, plaintiffs, having decided that it was futile to attempt to have the unit properly repaired through Pressnall's efforts, turned the matter over to their attorney and rejected Pressnall's further efforts to make repairs. Thereafter, negotiations were held with a representative of the mobile home manufacturer and as a result three repairmen worked approximately ten hours each repairing defects. However, plaintiffs were not satisfied with the quality of repairs and when a release was tendered to them they refused to sign it. Although some of the defects were cured, the serious problems such as leakage continued and new problems were created.

Concluding that further requests to repair the unit would be futile, plaintiffs instructed their attorney on December 27th, 1972, to send letters to both defendants notifying them of plaintiffs' decision to rescind the purchase contract. Plaintiffs tendered back the new mobile home, subject to their security interest, and demanded return of the down payment as well as consequential damages. On advice of counsel plaintiffs continued to occupy the mobile home until November 15, 1973, approximately three weeks before the trial. The mobile home was repossessed by Commercial Credit in January of 1974 and resold at a loss.

Pressnall contends that plaintiffs did not prove facts sufficient to justify rescission, asserting (1) that there is no evidence of a material misrepresentation inducing plaintiffs' purchase; (2) that there is no evidence that the uncorrected defects were material or that they rendered the trailer unfit for use as a dwelling; (3) that rescission is not a proper remedy because plaintiffs refused to allow reasonable efforts to repair, and (4) that plaintiffs' continued possession and use of the mobile home constituted an assertion and exercise of the right of ownership inconsistent with their attempted revocation of acceptance.

The contract in question is governed by the Uniform Commercial Code. Specifically, the buyer's right to revoke acceptance is defined in ORS 72.6080 . . . .

---

1. The "tip out" is a hinged section that is transported inside the mobile home and then tipped out to widen the living room when the mobile home is set up. This method of construction is necessitated by width limitations for transportation over highways.

Plaintiffs' rescission letter constituted a revocation of acceptance within the meaning of the code. When cast in language of the Uniform Commercial Code, Pressnall's contentions are that there is no proof of nonconformities substantially impairing the value of the goods and that there has been no failure to seasonably cure the nonconformities.

Whether plaintiffs proved nonconformities sufficiently serious to justify revocation of acceptance is a two-step inquiry under the code. Since ORS 72.6080(1) provides that the buyer may revoke acceptance of goods "whose nonconformity substantially impairs its value *to him*," the value of conforming goods *to the plaintiff* must first be determined. This is a subjective question in the sense that it calls for a consideration of the needs and circumstances of the plaintiff who seeks to revoke; not the needs and circumstances of an average buyer.[3] The second inquiry is whether the nonconformity in fact substantially impairs the value of the goods to the buyer, having in mind his particular needs. This is an objective question in the sense that it calls for evidence of something more than plaintiff's assertion that the nonconformity impaired the value to him; it requires evidence from which it can be inferred that plaintiff's needs were not met because of the nonconformity. In short, the nonconformity must *substantially* impair the value of the goods to the plaintiff buyer. The existence of substantial impairment depends upon the facts and circumstances in each case.

In the present case plaintiffs purchased the mobile home for the purpose of using it as their residence. Because of the defects described above and defendant's failure to cure them, the value of the mobile home to plaintiffs as a residence was substantially impaired. Defendant argues that since plaintiffs did not produce any evidence showing that the cost of repairs was substantial in relation to the purchase price, there was no proof of substantial impairment of value. This argument would have some force if the test for a substantial impairment of value were an objective one. However, since, as we have shown, the test is a subjective one, permitting revocation of acceptance if it is shown that the value *to the purchaser* is impaired, the relatively small amount of money needed to repair the defect is not necessarily relevant because the impairment of the value to the purchaser may be substantial even though the cost of curing the defect may be relatively small. Thus, in the present case, although the defects in the mobile home probably could have been repaired at a relatively small cost, plaintiffs were deprived of the benefits of a comfortable home for a substantial period of time as a result of defendant's failure to make timely repairs.

---

3. See, Uniform Commercial Code § 2-608, comment 2: "The test is not what the seller had reason to know at the time of contracting; the question is whether the nonconformity is such as will in fact cause a substantial impairment of value to the buyer though the seller had no advance knowledge as to the buyer's particular circumstances." See also, Tiger Motor Co. v. McMurtry, 284 Ala. 283, 292, 224 So.2d 638 (1969): "We are aware that what may cause one person great inconvenience or financial loss, may not another."

Defendant also seems to argue that impairment of value is not shown unless the goods are useless for the purchaser's purposes. This is not true; revocation of acceptance is permissible not only where there is complete impairment, but also where the impairment is substantial but not complete.

Pressnall contends that any failure to cure the nonconformities was excused because plaintiffs unreasonably refused to allow further attempts to repair the unit. The record indicates, however, that Pressnall had ample opportunity to cure the defects before the revocation of acceptance occurred, but that he did not act seasonably. A seller does not have an unlimited amount of time to cure the nonconformity.

Pressnall's final argument is that plaintiffs' use of the mobile home after the notice of rescission constituted a use of the goods inconsistent with the seller's ownership and that therefore a new acceptance of the goods occurred. The answer to this contention is that plaintiffs retained a security interest in the mobile home after the revocation of acceptance. This entitled them to continue in possession to preserve their collateral. Continued occupancy was the most feasible method of protecting the mobile home from water damage. The alternative was to find covered storage, which would have been expensive. Defendant suffered no loss as a result of plaintiffs' occupancy since the trial court awarded an offset to defendant for the rental value of the mobile home during plaintiffs' occupancy.

Plaintiffs having successfully revoked their acceptance of the mobile home, Pressnall thereby breached the warranty given on assignment of the financing contract to Commercial Credit. Damages were, therefore, properly awarded to Commercial Credit.

The decree of the trial court is affirmed.

QUESTIONS AND NOTES

1.   Is *Jorgensen* a subsection (1)(a) case or a subsection (1)(b) case?

2.   Subsection (2) permits revocation of acceptance only if the buyer acts within a reasonable time after discovering the grounds for it. Did the Jorgensens revoke within a reasonable time?

In Tiger Motor Co. v. McMurtry, 284 Ala. 283, 224 So.2d 638 (1969) (cited in footnote 3 of the *Jorgensen* opinion), the buyer was allowed to revoke his acceptance of a new automobile even though he had kept it for 344 days and driven it more than 14,000 miles. The buyer recovered all payments he had made, the court refusing to allow the seller any rental value as a set-off. The buyer testified that he had taken the automobile back to the dealer at least 30 times for repair and that it had been in the seller's shop for a total of 40 to 50 days.

On the other hand, in Green Chevrolet Co. v. Kemp, 241 Ark. 62, 406 S.W.2d 142 (1966), the court held that the buyer could not revoke his acceptance after keeping an automobile for six months and driving it 3,000 miles.

3. Subsection (2) also requires that revocation occur "before any substantial change in condition of the goods which is not caused by their own defects." Was there no substantial change in the condition of the Jorgensens' mobile home as a result of their living in it for more than a year?

4. Continued use after revocation of acceptance. In Bowen v. Young (Question 7, page 380 supra) the purchaser of a mobile home rejected it, but then moved into and occupied it for a year. The court held that after first rejecting the home, the buyer's occupation of it amounted to acceptance under 2–606(1)(c). A similar issue arises with respect to revocation of acceptance. The court in *Jorgensen* concluded that the buyers' continued occupancy did not amount to acceptance. Why not?

In Fablok Mills, Inc. v. Cocker Machine & Foundry Co., 125 N.J.Super. 251, 310 A.2d 491 (1973), the plaintiff purchased 10 knitting machines that were delivered over a nine-month period. Before all were delivered, the plaintiff experienced problems with some of the machines and complained. The seller undertook to correct the defects and continued to make those efforts until two years after the last machines were delivered, at which point plaintiff notified defendant that it was revoking its acceptance of the machines. After this notification, the plaintiff stopped using some of the machines and put them in storage. It continued to use others (the court's opinion does not indicate the period of use). The trial court held that, as a matter of law, the revocation did not come within reasonable time and that use after the revocation was inconsistent with revocation. The appellate court reversed. The attempts of the seller to repair may have induced the buyer reasonably to believe that the defects would be cured. What is a reasonable time within which to revoke is a matter for the jury. Further, whether use after revocation is inconsistent with revocation is also a matter for the jury. The court stated that the overriding requirement of reasonableness which permeates the Code counsels against any absolute rule against continued use after revocation of acceptance. Use may be the most appropriate means of mitigating damages. Here the seller was the only domestic maker of knitting machines: plaintiff's choice was to either close down its business or continue using some of the machines. The defendant did not show that it objected to the continued use, that the delay in stopping use prejudiced it, or that the buyer had any reasonable alternative. Accord, Toshiba Machine Co. v. SPM Flow Control, Inc., 180 S.W.3d 761, 772–75 (Tex.App.2005). On the other hand, in another case a consumer revoked acceptance of a car but continued using it because she did not have access to public transportation and could not afford to buy another one. The court held that it was not reasonable for her to have continued using the car indefinitely (driving it some 37,000 miles between the date of revocation and the date of the decision). Barrett v. Brian Bemis Auto World, 408 F.Supp.2d 539 (N.D.Ill.2005).

5. Revocation of acceptance and privity of contract. In Durfee v. Rod Baxter Imports, Inc., 262 N.W.2d 349 (Minn.1977), plaintiff purchased a Saab that proved to be seriously nonconforming. He sent the dealer and the manufacturer's U.S. distributor notice of revocation of acceptance and sued to recover the purchase price, as permitted by 2–711(1). The court permitted recovery:

> Defendant Saab–Scania suggests that it cannot be liable because, as the distributor of the Saab, it had no direct contractual relationship with plaintiff. If this is the case, plaintiff may well be left without relief, for Saab–Scania was unable to assure us at oral argument of the continued existence of Rod Baxter. Although the relevant sections of Article 2 of the Uniform Commercial Code seem to require a buyer-seller relationship, Saab–Scania does not escape liability on this ground in these circumstances.

> The existence and comprehensiveness of a warranty undoubtedly are significant factors in a consumer's decision to purchase a particular automobile. Saab–Scania evidently warrants its automobiles to increase retail sales and indirectly its own sales of Saab automobiles. When the ... defects are substantial enough to justify revocation of acceptance, we think the buyer is entitled to look to the warrantor for relief. If plaintiff had sued Saab–Scania for breach of either express warranty or implied warranty, the absence of privity would not bar the suit despite the language of the pertinent Code sections. We see no reason why the result should differ merely because plaintiff has chosen to revoke his acceptance instead of suing for breach of warranty. The remedies of the Code are to be liberally administered. Minn.St. 336.1–106(1). We think liberal administration does not envision forcing a consumer to keep a car which is sufficiently defective so as to justify his returning it and then requiring him to sue the distributor for damages merely because the dealer is insolvent or no longer in business. The distributor of the automobile, who profits indirectly from retail sales, must take responsibility for the solvency of its dealers when its warranty is breached. A consumer cannot be expected to foresee the demise of local dealerships; instead he is entitled to rely on the distributor who induced him to buy the automobile. The lack of privity between the parties does not relieve Saab–Scania of liability.

Compare Gasque v. Mooers Motor Car Co., Inc., 227 Va. 154, 313 S.E.2d 384 (1984):

> The remedy of revocation of acceptance ... lies only against a seller of goods, not against a remote manufacturer. This is so because the remedy, where successful, cancels a contract of sale, restores both title to and possession of the goods to the seller, restores the purchase price to the buyer, and as fairly as possible, returns the contracting parties to the status quo ante. The remote manufacturer, having no part in the sale transaction, has no role to play in such a restoration of former positions.

The buyers argue that this limitation on revocation revivifies the "archaic doctrine of privity." We disagree. A remote manufacturer is liable to a buyer for damages arising from negligence or from breach of warranty, and the defense of lack of privity has been abolished as to such cases. Code § 8.2–318. But the remedy of revocation of acceptance under Code § 8.2–608 is conceptually inapplicable to any persons other than the parties to the contract of sale sought to be rescinded.

Under the language of 2–608, which court is right?

Gappelberg v. Landrum

Texas Court of Appeals, 1983.
654 S.W.2d 549, rev'd, 666 S.W.2d 88 (Tex.1984).

■ STOREY, JUSTICE.

This is a sale of goods case under the Uniform Commercial Code presenting the novel question of the duration of the right to cure after acceptance of goods without knowledge of any defects. The seller, Landrum, contends that the right to cure by replacement outlasts the buyer's right to revoke acceptance of the original, defective goods. We conclude that there is a right to cure by replacement apart from the right to repair the original product and that this right survives the substantial impairment of the value of the original good as long as the right is asserted within a reasonable time after notification of revocation by the buyer. Accordingly, we affirm.

The case was tried before the court on extensive stipulated facts. In exchange for Gappelberg's used Advent-brand big-screen television and $2,231.25, Landrum sold him a new Advent Model V–125 big-screen television. Landrum represented that the Advent Model V–125 was the best television set he had. The same day of the purchase Gappelberg informed Landrum that the screen was damaged. Within the next two days, several other defects surfaced: an unclear picture due to a faulty color convergence board, a red spot on the screen, a chipped mirror, a slight tilt in the screen, and minor damage and scratches on surfaces. Landrum or his service representatives repaired some of these defects over the next two weeks. Three weeks after the sale, the television stopped functioning altogether; Gappelberg notified Landrum of the problem. The service representative told Gappelberg that the television would need to be taken to the repair shop. However, despite a number of calls to Landrum, the television was not removed for the repairs, although Landrum offered assurances that he would repair the set or replace it. On that day or the following day, Gappelberg requested the return of consideration and asked the service representative to pick up the set but not to repair it because he would not accept it or a replacement. A day or two later, Landrum offered to replace the set with another new one of the same make and model. At the time of the stipulated revocation of acceptance, Landrum had not repaired the color convergence problem, the red spot on the screen, or the slight tilt of the screen. The trial court denied Gappelberg's relief by holding that while the power failure and convergence problem substantially impaired the value of the set, Gappelberg prevented Landrum from curing the nonconforming good by his refusal to accept a replacement set.

While both parties agree that Gappelberg's revocation of acceptance was proper under Tex.Bus. & Com.Code Ann. § 2.608, Gappelberg contends that Landrum was not entitled to cure by replacing the television set because the right to cure under § 2.508 is limited to cases of rejection and is not available after revocation of acceptance under § 2.608. Consequently, Gappelberg concludes that he was not obligated to permit Landrum to replace the defective television with a new one after he had already justifiably revoked acceptance of the original set he agreed to buy.

Citing authority from other jurisdictions, Landrum replies that the seller should always have an opportunity to cure nonconforming goods within a reasonable time of notification concerning a defect. More specifically, Landrum contends that the seller has a right to cure after revocation of acceptance because the right to cure is incorporated into § 2.608(c) because "[a] buyer who so revokes has the same rights and *duties* with regard to the goods * * * as if he had rejected them" and one of these *duties* obligates the buyer to allow the seller to cure.

In the absence of guidance from Texas authorities, we have examined the authorities from other states and found that the greater weight of authority provides support for the conclusion that the right to cure *by repair* ends when the buyer justifiably exercises his right to revoke acceptance of goods due to a substantial impairment in their value.

. . .

The test that the courts have applied to rule on the propriety of revocation requires a substantial impairment in the value of the goods. This substantial impairment, in turn, has depended upon such factors as the ease of correcting the defect and the seller's diligence in attempting these repairs. See, e.g., Don's Marine, Inc. v. Haldeman, 557 S.W.2d 826, 829–30 (Tex.Civ.App.-Corpus Christi 1977, writ ref'd n.r.e.). Because these factors relate only to the repair of defects, revocation for ineffective repairs should not preclude an attempt to cure by replacement. Therefore, the seller's right to replace should survive a buyer's revocation following ineffective repairs.

. . .

The courts that discuss the relationship between the seller's right to cure and the buyer's right to revoke were not presented with such a generous offer as Landrum's offer to replace. It is easier to understand the motivation of a buyer who demands replacement in the face of ineffective repairs than the whim of the buyer who wants his used trade-in product returned to him when he could have a brand new product. Section 2.508 is aimed at avoiding this sort of "surprise rejection" which effectuates a "forced breach." See Tex.Bus. & Com.Code Ann. § 2.508 official comment

(Vernon 1968). "If a merchant sells defective goods, the reasonable expectation of the parties is that the buyer will return those goods and that the seller will repair or replace them." Ramirez v. Autosport, 88 N.J. 277, 440 A.2d 1345, 1351 (1982).

Gappelberg relies heavily upon Johannsen v. Minnesota Valley Ford Tractor Co., 304 N.W.2d 654 (Minn.1981) (en banc), in which the Minnesota Supreme Court held that despite the language in § 2–608(3) regarding the buyer's post-revocation duties, the seller has no right to repair defects that substantially impair the value of the goods to the buyer because the right to cure is limited to minor defects. The reasoning of *Johannsen* is not applicable to an offer to replace the defective product. The severity of the defect in the original product should have little if any influence upon the value of the replacement product, unless the confidence of the buyer in a brand or line of products is justifiably undermined by the nature of the defect.

A survey of the cases reveals three lines of cases: (1) the seller's right to cure [by repair] ends where the buyer's right to revoke begins, see, e.g., Johannsen, 304 N.W.2d at 657; (2) the seller has no right to cure [by repair] in a case of revocation of acceptance unless § 2.608(a)(1) applies (that is, when the buyer accepts with knowledge of the defect and the seller agrees to repair); see, e.g., Werner v. Montana, 117 N.H. 721, 378 A.2d 1130, 1136 (1977); and (3) the seller's right to cure by repair is cut off by the subverted confidence of the buyer in the reliability of a major purchase, such as a car or a mobile home, see, e.g., Zabriskie Chevrolet, Inc. v. Smith, 99 N.J.Super. 441, 240 A.2d 195, 205 (1968). Landrum's offer to replace does not fall into any of these three categories, and, therefore, in the spirit of the Code, we conclude that following three weeks of diligent attempted repairs, Landrum was entitled to replace the television when faced with the unexpected demand of Gappelberg for the return of consideration when the television stopped operating completely.

In view of our conclusion that Landrum had a right to cure by replacement, Gappelberg is not entitled to the damages he claims under Tex.Bus. & Com.Code Ann. § 2.711 (Vernon 1968). . . .

The judgment is affirmed.

———

Gappelberg v. Landrum

Texas Supreme Court, 1984.
666 S.W.2d 88.

■ KILGARLIN, J. This case presents an issue previously undecided in Texas, or for that matter, any other American jurisdiction. Under the Uniform Commercial Code, does the seller have the right to cure a substantial defect by making a replacement of the product after the buyer has revoked acceptance?

. . .

The concept of revocation of acceptance is relatively new. During early years of the Code, "the courts did not take to it." J.White & R.Summers, Handbook of the Law Under the Uniform Commercial Code 302 (2d ed.1979). Early court decisions interpreting the Code confused the terms "revocation" with "rescission" and "rejection." Gradually, however, the concept of revocation of acceptance has taken hold. Its principle is simple. The right of a buyer to revoke exists only when the buyer has initially accepted the goods in question. Rejection, however, is an initial act of the buyer, meaning there was never an acceptance.

The right of the seller to cure by repair or replacement clearly exists in instances of rejection. UCC § 2.508. This, of course, is not a rejection case. It is a case in which, under the fact findings, the buyer was clearly entitled to revoke his acceptance. . . .

. . . The only reference to cure in § 2.608 is in situations when the buyer knew of the defects at the time of acceptance of the goods. There is no reference to cure for our situation where Gappelberg accepted the television set without knowing of the defects. The court of appeals, in its opinion, has listed the numerous cases from other jurisdictions which hold that once a buyer properly revokes acceptance, the seller no longer has the right to cure by repair. This is likewise the conclusion of White and Summers, Handbook of the Law Under the Uniform Commercial Code, supra, at 293, who state that revocation of acceptance is not limited by the right to cure. We do not consider paragraph (c) in UCC § 2.608 as having any reference to UCC § 2.508. It is more logically related to UCC §§ 2.603 and 2.604, as UCC § 2.608(c) makes absolutely no mention of seller's rights.

. . .

The court of appeals in this case notes that in none of the cases in which a seller's right to cure has been denied once revocation of acceptance occurs was the buyer presented with such a generous offer as Landrum's offer to replace. The court of appeals concluded that "in the spirit of the Code," cure by replacement even in revocation situations should be authorized.

Although a rejection case, in Zabriskie Chevrolet, Inc. v. Smith, 99 N.J.Super. 441, 240 A.2d 195 (1968), the court observed that "for a majority of people, the purchase of a new car is a major investment, rationalized by the peace of mind that flows from its dependability and safety. Once their faith is shaken, the vehicle loses not only its real value in their eyes, but becomes an instrument whose integrity is substantially impaired and whose operation was fraught with apprehension." In *Zabriskie*, a new 1966 Chevrolet ceased to operate within one mile of being removed from the showroom, because of a faulty transmission. The buyer was not forced to take the Chevrolet with a different transmission in it, his faith in the whole automobile having been shaken. By the same token, Gappelberg had seen one Advent television perform, or fail to perform as the case may be, and there certainly is justification for his not wanting to go through experiences with another Advent.

Professor Wallach states, "the seller is ordinarily in a better position to maximize the return on the resale of the goods, and his disposition of the goods eliminates the storage and other incidental expenses that may be involved in the unsatisfactory transaction." G.Wallach, The Law of Sales Under the Uniform Commercial Code 9–30 (1981). This is probably the best policy reason of all for denying replacement after revocation * * * the relative position of the parties. It is true that a new machine provided by Landrum could have proved perfectly free of defects. It is equally possible that such a new machine would have defects, perhaps similar to those of the old Advent or entirely different ones. No one contends that the seller's right to cure is limitless. Even Landrum, in argument, admits that a day of reckoning must come, although he earnestly contends that the three weeks in the situation at bar was not adequate time to allow cure.

We are cited no good policy reason why different rules should attain as to cure by replacement instead of cure by repair. Indeed, we cannot envision any basis for a distinction. Thus, we state that once a buyer has properly revoked acceptance of a product, the seller has neither the right to cure by repair nor by replacement.

. . .

Therefore, the judgments of the courts below are reversed and judgment is here rendered that Gappelberg recover of Landrum $3,731.25 with both pre-judgment and post-judgment interest. . . .

QUESTIONS

1. If cure is available after revocation of acceptance, as the Court of Appeals held, then presumably the requirements of 2–508 must be satisfied. The Court of Appeals does not discuss the requirement in 2–508(2) that the seller have reason to believe that the tender would be acceptable. Did the seller have reasonable grounds to believe the TV would be acceptable? If so, then on the Court of Appeals' view of things the seller had a right to cure, which it exercised by trying to repair the TV. When those attempts failed, by what authority might the Court of Appeals think that the seller was entitled to tender a new TV? Should 2–508(2) be read as saying that there is a right to cure if the seller had reason to believe that *cure* would be acceptable, at least where that cure is by a tender of replacement goods? If that is not a permissible reading of 2–508(2), on the facts did the seller have reason to believe that the original tender would be acceptable?

2. The case was tried to the court "on extensive stipulated facts." One of those facts was that the buyer had revoked acceptance of the TV. What is the legal effect of that stipulation? Was it malpractice for the seller's lawyer to make that concession?

3. The Court of Appeals echoes the idea seen in Wilson v. Scampoli (Question 7, page 392 supra) that cure by repair is not permissible in the case of a defect that substantially impairs the value of the goods. Is that sound policy? Is that position consistent with 2–608 and 2–508?

4. Now the important question: Do you agree with the Court of Appeals or with the Supreme Court? If there had been an acceptance, a revocation of acceptance, and a tender of a replacement TV all before the time for delivery had expired, could the buyer properly refuse the new TV? If you conclude that the buyer could, what statutory language are you relying on? If you conclude that the buyer could not, what statutory language are you relying on?

5. Revised Article 2. Under revised 2–508(2) the seller may cure only if cure is "appropriate and timely under the circumstances." Presumably, a court could say that a cure by repair is not "appropriate." Could a court also say that cure by replacement is not appropriate?

Revised 2–508 extends the right to cure to certain transactions in which a commercial buyer revokes acceptance, but a consumer buyer need not accept a tender of cure after a revocation of acceptance. On the other hand, if a consumer has *rejected* the goods, the consumer must accept the cure. That is an odd result since the more obvious the defect, the more likely that the consumer will discover it before acceptance and will reject the goods. Therefore, a consumer who does not want to accept a seller's cure will argue that he or she had accepted the goods and now is revoking acceptance. Under current 2–508 and 2–608, of course, it is in the buyer's interest to argue rejection rather than revocation of acceptance. This anomaly results from the exclusion of consumer buyers from the newly created right of cure for sellers whose buyers have revoked acceptance.

Question 3 revisited. What position does revised 2–508 take with respect to the view of *Scampoli* and the Court of Appeals in *Gappelburg* that cure by repair is not permissible in the case of a defect that substantially impairs the value of the goods? Subsection (2) permits cure after the time for performance only if it is "appropriate and timely under the circumstances." At least in a consumer contract, perhaps a court might be persuaded that a tender of repaired goods for goods that were substantially defective is not "appropriate" under revised 2–508(2). However, there is no similar requirement that the cure be "appropriate" under 2–508(1).

In the hypothetical in Question 4, what is the result under revised 2–508?

6. CISG. Article 48 of the Convention on Contracts for the International Sale of Goods provides that even after the date of delivery the seller may "remedy at his own expense any failure to perform his obligations, if he can do so without unreasonable delay and without causing the buyer unreasonable inconvenience." But this right is "subject to article 49," which provides that the buyer may declare the contract avoided if the seller's failure to perform amounts to a "fundamental breach of contract." Article 25 defines "fundamental breach." Please read Articles 25, 48, and 49.

Problem. In a transaction governed by the CISG, Seller contracts to sell a road grader to Buyer. The grader is delivered and placed in operation. In the second week of operation, the engine seizes up because of a failure of the oil pump. Cure would require replacement of the engine. Buyer notifies Seller of the problem, and informs Seller that Buyer is avoiding the sale because of fundamental breach by Seller. Seller, in turn, asserts that Buyer cannot avoid the sale and states that he will be able to replace the engine within two weeks. Buyer refuses to allow Seller to repair. Has Buyer breached?

What additional facts are needed, if any? Is the CISG approach to cure preferable to that of Article 2?

C.   REMEDIES WHEN THE BUYER DOES NOT HAVE THE GOODS

1.   THE RIGHT TO GET THE GOODS

According to 2–711(2), "Where the seller fails to deliver or repudiates the buyer may . . .

(a) if the goods have been identified recover them as provided in this Article (Section 2–502); or

(b) in a proper case obtain specific performance or replevy the goods as provided in this Article (Section 2–716)."

Section 2–502 addresses some of the situations in which a buyer forms a contract with a seller who encounters financial difficulty before delivering the goods. The problem is especially acute if the buyer has paid all or part of the price. The section permits the buyer to recover the goods from the seller, but only if (a) the buyer tenders any balance of the price of the goods, and (b) the seller's insolvency arose within ten days after the buyer's first payment. This ten-day limitation deprives the section of much of its utility. (Revised 2–502 drops the insolvency-of-the-seller limitation altogether for consumer transactions.) Under the current version of 2–502, if the seller is insolvent (defined in 1–102(23)) at the time the contract is formed, the buyer gains no rights under the section, even if the buyer has no reason to suspect the insolvency. Further, even if 2–502 gives the buyer rights to the goods as against the seller, the seller's creditors also may have rights to them. These conflicts are resolved elsewhere in the Code and are the subject of Chapter 10.

Section 2–716(1) states that the seller is entitled to specific performance "where the goods are unique or in other proper circumstances." Other than heirlooms, art objects, and certain collectibles, when are goods unique? In what other circumstances is specific performance appropriate? See Official Comment 2.

Sedmak v. Charlie's Chevrolet, Inc.

Missouri Court of Appeals, 1981.
622 S.W.2d 694.

In their petition, plaintiffs, Dr. and Mrs. Sedmak (Sedmaks), alleged they entered into a contract with defendant, Charlie's Chevrolet, Inc. (Charlie's), to purchase a Corvette automobile for approximately $15,000.00. The Corvette was one of a limited number manufactured to commemorate the selection of the Corvette as the Pace Car for the Indianapolis 500. Charlie's breached the contract, the Sedmaks alleged, when, after the automobile was delivered, an agent for Charlie's told the Sedmaks they could not purchase the automobile for $15,000.00 but would have to bid on it.

The trial court found the parties entered into an oral contract and also found the contract was excepted from the Statute of Frauds. The court then ordered Charlie's to make the automobile "available for delivery" to the Sedmaks.

Charlie's raises three points on appeal: (1) the existence of an oral contract is not supported by the credible evidence; (2) if an oral contract exists, it is unenforceable because of the Statute of Frauds; and (3) specific performance is an improper remedy because the Sedmaks did not show their legal remedies were inadequate.

. . .

. . . [T]he record reflects the Sedmaks to be automobile enthusiasts, who, at the time of trial, owned six Corvettes. In July, 1977, "Vette Vues," a Corvette fancier's magazine to which Dr. Sedmak subscribed, published an article announcing Chevrolet's tentative plans to manufacture a limited edition of the Corvette. The limited edition of approximately 6,000 automobiles was to commemorate the selection of the Corvette as the Indianapolis 500 Pace Car. The Sedmaks were interested in acquiring one of these Pace Cars to add to their Corvette collection. In November, 1977, the Sedmaks asked Tom Kells, sales manager at Charlie's Chevrolet, about the availability of the Pace Car. Mr. Kells said he did not have any information on the car but would find out about it. Kells also said if Charlie's were to receive a Pace Car, the Sedmaks could purchase it.

On January 9, 1978, Dr. Sedmak telephoned Kells to ask him if a Pace Car could be ordered. Kells indicated that he would require a deposit on the car, so Mrs. Sedmak went to Charlie's and gave Kells a check for $500. She was given a receipt for that amount bearing the names of Kells and Charlie's Chevrolet, Inc. At that time, Kells had a pre-order form listing both standard equipment and options available on the Pace Car. Prior to tendering the deposit, Mrs. Sedmak asked Kells if she and Dr. Sedmak were "definitely going to be the owners." Kells replied, "yes." After the deposit had been paid, Mrs. Sedmak stated if the car was going to be theirs, her husband wanted some changes made to the stock model. She asked Kells to order the car equipped with an L82 engine, four speed standard transmission and AM/FM radio with tape deck. Kells said that he would try to arrange with the manufacturer for these changes. Kells was able to make the changes, and, when the car arrived, it was equipped as the Sedmaks had requested.

Kells informed Mrs. Sedmak that the price of the Pace Car would be the manufacturer's retail price, approximately $15,000. The dollar figure could not be quoted more precisely because Kells was not sure what the ordered changes would cost, nor was he sure what the "appearance package"—decals, a special paint job—would cost. Kells also told Mrs. Sedmak that, after the changes had been made, a "contract"—a retail dealer's order form—would be mailed to them. However, no form or written contract was mailed to the Sedmaks by Charlie's.

On January 25, 1978, the Sedmaks visited Charlie's to take delivery on another Corvette. At that time, the Sedmaks asked Kells whether he knew anything further about the arrival date of the Pace Car. Kells replied he had no further information but he would let the Sedmaks know when the car arrived. Kells also requested that Charlie's be allowed to keep the car in their showroom for promotional purposes until after the Indianapolis 500 Race. The Sedmaks agreed to this arrangement.

On April 3, 1978, the Sedmaks were notified by Kells that the Pace Car had arrived. Kells told the Sedmaks they could not purchase the car for the manufacturer's retail price because demand for the car had inflated its value beyond the suggested price. Kells also told the Sedmaks they could bid on the car. The Sedmaks did not submit a bid. They filed this suit for specific performance.

Mr. Kells' testimony about his conversations with the Sedmaks regarding the Pace Car differed markedly from the Sedmaks' testimony. Kells stated that he had no definite price information on the Pace Car until a day or two prior to its arrival at Charlie's. He denied ever discussing the purchase price of the car with the Sedmaks. He admitted, however, that after talking with the Sedmaks on January 9, 1978, he telephoned the zone manager and requested changes be made to the Pace Car. He denied the changes were made pursuant to Dr. Sedmak's order. He claimed the changes were made because they were "more favorable to the automobile" and were changes Dr. Sedmak "preferred." In ordering the changes, Kells said he was merely taking Dr. Sedmak's advice because he was a "very knowledgeable man on the Corvette." There is no dispute, however, that when the Pace Car arrived, it was equipped with the options requested by Dr. Sedmak.

Mr. Kells also denied the receipt for $500 given him by Mrs. Sedmak on January 9, 1978, was a receipt for a deposit on the Pace Car. On direct examination, he said he "accepted a five hundred dollar ($500) deposit from the Sedmaks to assure them the first opportunity of purchasing the car." On cross-examination, he said: "We were accepting bids and with the five hundred dollar ($500) deposit it was to give them the first opportunity to bid on the car." Then after acknowledging that other bidders had not paid for the opportunity to bid, he explained the deposit gave the Sedmaks the "last opportunity" to make the final bid. Based on this evidence, the trial court found the parties entered into an oral contract for the purchase and sale of the Pace Car at the manufacturer's suggested retail price.

. . .

[The court's discussion of statute of frauds issues is omitted. It found that the $500 payment took the contract out of the statute.]

Finally, Charlie's contends the Sedmaks failed to show they were entitled to specific performance of the contract. We disagree. Although it has been stated that the determination whether to order specific performance lies within the discretion of the trial court, Landau v. St. Louis Public Service Co., 273 S.W.2d 255, 259 (Mo.1954), this discretion is, in fact, quite narrow. When the relevant equitable principles have been met and the contract is fair and plain, " 'specific performance goes as a matter of right.' " Miller v. Coffeen, 280 S.W.2d 100, 102 (Mo.1955). Here, the trial court ordered specific performance because it concluded the Sedmaks "have no adequate remedy at law for the reason that they cannot go upon the open market and purchase an automobile of this kind with the same mileage, condition, ownership and appearance as the automobile involved in this case, except, if at all, with considerable expense, trouble, loss, great delay and inconvenience." Contrary to defendant's complaint, this is a correct expression of the relevant law and it is supported by the evidence.

Under the Code, the court may decree specific performance as a buyer's remedy for breach of contract to sell goods "where the goods are unique or in other proper circumstances." § 400.2–716(1) RSMo 1978. The general term "in other proper circumstances" expresses the drafters' intent to "further a more liberal attitude than some courts have shown in connection with the specific performance of contracts of sale." § 400.2–716, UCC, Comment 1. This Comment was not directed to the courts of this state, for long before the Code, we, in Missouri, took a practical approach in determining whether specific performance would lie for the breach of contract for the sale of goods and did not limit this relief only to the sale of "unique" goods. Boeving v. Vandover, 218 S.W.2d 175 (Mo.App.1949). In *Boeving*, plaintiff contracted to buy a car from defendant. When the car arrived, defendant refused to sell. The car was not unique in the traditional sense but, at that time, all cars were difficult to obtain because of war-time shortages. The court held specific performance was the proper remedy for plaintiff because a new car "could not be obtained elsewhere except at considerable expense, trouble or loss, which cannot be estimated in advance and under such circumstances [plaintiff] did not have an adequate remedy at law." Id. at 177–178. Thus, *Boeving* presaged the broad and liberalized language of § 400.2–716(1) and exemplifies one of the "other proper circumstances" contemplated by this subsection for ordering specific performance. § 400.2–716, Missouri Code Comment 1. The present facts track those in *Boeving*.

The Pace Car, like the car in *Boeving*, was not unique in the traditional legal sense. It was not an heirloom or, arguably, not one of a kind. However, its "mileage, condition, ownership and appearance" did make it difficult, if not impossible, to obtain its replication without considerable expense, delay and inconvenience. Admittedly, 6,000 Pace Cars were produced by Chevrolet. However, as the record reflects, this is limited production. In addition, only one of these cars was available to each dealer, and only a limited number of these were equipped with the specific options ordered by plaintiffs. Charlie's had not received a car like the Pace Car in the previous two years. The sticker price for the car was $14,284.21. Yet Charlie's received offers from individuals in Hawaii and Florida to buy the Pace Car for $24,000 and $28,000 respectively. As sensibly inferred by the trial court, the location and size of these offers demonstrated this limited edition was in short supply and great demand. We agree, with the trial court. This case was a "proper circumstance" for ordering specific performance.

Judgment affirmed.

Hilmor Sales Co. v. Helen Neushaefer Div. of Supronics Corp.

New York Supreme Court, Queens County, 1969.
N.Y.L.J., April 21, 1969, Part I, p. 22, 6 U.C.C. Rep.Serv. 325.

■ CRISONA, J. Plaintiff moves by order to show cause for an order (1) enjoining the defendant from disposing of goods which the defendant has allegedly contracted to sell to plaintiff, and (2) directing that the defendant specifically perform its contract.

The subject matter of the contract in dispute here is a substantial quantity of lipsticks and containers of nail polish. The only claim made by plaintiff with respect to these chattels being unique is that they were purchased at close-out prices and cannot be replaced at the contract price.

Section 2–716(1) of the Uniform Commercial Code provides with respect to a buyer's right to specific performance that it may be decreed "where the goods are unique or in other proper circumstances." Plaintiff has failed to establish that there is anything unique about these chattels. It appears to the court that plaintiff can be adequately compensated for any breach of the contract herein by an award of money damages. In such a situation, "there should be no specific performance" (Glick v. Beer, 263 App.Div. 599, 600–601). Finally, plaintiff has failed to demonstrate that it will be irreparably damaged if the injunction which it seeks is not granted (cf. Camp v. Brengel, 286 App.Div. 1031).

For the foregoing reasons, the motion is denied. Settle order.

QUESTIONS AND NOTES

1. Are the two preceding cases inconsistent with each other? What is the best ground you can think of for distinguishing them? If you think they are inconsistent, which reaches the better result?

2. A glimpse at the history of specific performance in contracts for the sale of goods. Early case law limited specific performance of contracts for the sale of chattels to unique or one-of-a-kind goods (heirlooms, etc.), but there are a fair number of pre-Code cases giving specific performance of sales contracts in other situations. A sampling includes The Equitable Gas Light Co. of Baltimore City v. Baltimore Coal Tar & Manufacturing Co., 63 Md. 285, 3 A. 108 (1885) (specific performance granted on allegations that the goods were indispensable to plaintiff's business, were not available in Baltimore except from defendant, and if defendant did not perform plaintiff would have to procure the goods from distant cities); Eastern Rolling Mill Co. v. Michlovitz, 157 Md. 51, 145 A. 378 (1929) (specific performance granted in a 5–year output contract because the goods were not otherwise obtainable in the locale and the uncertainty concerning quantity makes damages so uncertain that an action for damages would be an inadequate remedy); Paullus v. Yarbrough, 219 Or. 611, 347 P.2d 620 (1959) (contract for the sale of standing timber enforced because of the increasing difficulty that small operators like plaintiff were having in finding timber tracts that they can purchase); and Strause v. Berger, 220 Pa. 367, 69 A. 818 (1908) (specific enforcement granted to the buyer of timber, because the quality of the timber and the difficulty of procuring timber of that quality in the locality in which his business was conducted gave it special value to the buyer).

3. Replevin. Section 2–716 also provides that buyer has a right of replevin for goods identified to the contract if he is unable to procure substitute goods ("effect cover") or if the "goods have been shipped under reservation and satisfaction of the security interest in them has been made or tendered." As amended in 1999 in connection with the comprehensive revision of Article 9, subsection (3) also gives a *consumer* buyer the right to replevy goods that have been identified to the contract for sale under 2–501 "even if the seller has not repudiated or failed to deliver." Therefore, there is no requirement that the goods be otherwise unique or that the consumer buyer be unable to cover. This new provision has some importance in cases in which a creditor of the seller claims an interest in goods that have not yet been delivered to the buyer. In revised Article 2, 2–716 drops this special rule for consumer buyers.

In most states the plaintiff in a replevin (or claim and delivery) action gets possession of the goods pending suit by posting a bond and having the sheriff seize them. In nearly all states, however, the defendant can retake the property pending final determination of rights by posting a bond. The effect is to convert the replevin action into an action for either damages or the property, whichever the defendant chooses. But recovery of damages is exactly what the plaintiff does not want in a 2–716 replevin action: the plaintiff wants the goods. It is not clear whether the courts will conclude that 2–716 modifies the replevin statute in accordance with the purpose of 2–716.

4. Revised Article 2 and contracted-for specific performance. Historically the courts have refused to enforce provisions in a contract stipulating that one of the parties is entitled to an award of specific performance if the other party breaches. They have reasoned that an award of specific performance, as with all equitable remedies, rests within the sound discretion of the court, and the parties by their agreement cannot bind the court. Revised 2–716 seeks to change this. It provides that in contracts other than consumer contracts, specific performance may be decreed if the parties have agreed to that remedy. If the parties have agreed to specific performance as a remedy, it is not necessary that the court find that there is any other reason such as inability to cover, as a condition to the granting of specific performance. The section also says that, even if the parties have agreed to specific performance, specific performance "may not" be granted if the breaching party's sole remaining contractual obligation is the payment of money. Specific performance of an obligation to pay money would smack of debtor's prisons and similar personal compulsion. Except as to the obligation to pay money, if specific performance is the stipulated remedy for breach, must the court grant specific performance? The statute provides that the court "may" grant specific performance. Does that suggest that the court may ignore the contract provision if the court thinks that enforcing the provision would be "inequitable"? Notice that if the only obligation to be enforced is the payment of money the court "may not" grant specific performance. In that sentence "may not" is mandatory. Is "may" in the preceding sentence in the section also mandatory, or is it permissive?

5. CISG. In many civil law countries, the law generally provides that the buyer is entitled to specific performance by the seller. The Convention on Contracts for the International Sale of Goods follows that tradition by providing in Article 46(1), "The buyer may require performance by the seller of his obligations unless the buyer has resorted to a remedy which is inconsistent with this requirement." In recognition of the variant common law position, however, and the strength of attachment of common law lawyers to their tradition, Article 28 provides: "If, in accordance with the provisions of this Convention, one party is entitled to require performance of any obligation by the other party, a court is not bound to enter a judgment for specific performance unless the court would do so under its own law in respect of similar contracts of sale not governed by this Convention."

The buyer's right to specific performance generated strong feelings on both sides of the issue during the drafting of Convention. After noting that specific performance will almost never be sought in either international or domestic sales situations if replacement goods are available, Professor Honnold commented:

> It is not easy to understand the intractability of the opposing views on the scope of specific performance. In preparing the Convention issues of practical importance have usually yielded to reconciliation or compromise. But on this issue one bred in the common law remains puzzled at the civil lawyer's insistence on a remedy that rarely is

useful, while a scion of the civil law must be dismayed by an attitude that seems to subvert the sanctity of obligations.

J. Honnold, Uniform Law for International Sales Under the 1980 United Nations Convention 286 (2d ed.1991).

In accordance with the Convention's preference for specific performance, if the lack of conformity of the original goods constitutes a fundamental breach of contract, Article 46(2) authorizes the buyer to compel delivery of substitute goods. Article 46(3) authorizes the buyer to "require the seller to remedy the lack of conformity by repair, unless this is unreasonable having regard to all the circumstances." But note that if the nonconformity does not constitute a fundamental breach, the buyer is not entitled to reject them, but, as noted, can ask for "repair."

2. The Right to Damages

Section 2–711 sets out a roadmap for damages when a seller breaches a sales contract. It addresses the various remedies available to the buyer who does not have the goods, either because the seller did not tender them or because the buyer has properly rejected or revoked acceptance of the goods. It is not a complete roadmap, however, because it does not address the remedies of a buyer who accepts and keeps nonconforming goods. Please read 2–711 now.

1. Problem. Buyer, in New York, contracts to buy 1,000 cases of grade A, large eggs from Seller, who is located in Atlanta. The contract price is $15.00 per case, FOB Atlanta. The eggs are to be loaded on June 1 and shipped by rail to New York. On June 7th the eggs arrive in New York, and Buyer inspects them, determines that they are not grade A, and properly rejects them. The market price of grade A, large eggs in Atlanta on the 7th is $15.00 per case. In New York, the market price is $16.25. The cost of transportation from Atlanta to New York is $1.00 per case by rail and $1.25 per case by truck. What are Buyer's damages under 2–713?

If Seller had repudiated the contract and therefore had not shipped the eggs, to what damages would Buyer be entitled?

2. Problem. Farmer contracts to sell 10,000 bushels of corn to Elevator at a price of $1.50 per bushel, delivery on September 30. Elevator's business consists of purchasing from farmers and selling to processors. Farmer fails to deliver. On September 30 Elevator is buying at $2.35 per bushel and selling at $2.50 per bushel. Elevator claims damages under 2–713, of $1.00 per bushel. Is Elevator entitled to $1.00 per bushel?

3. Problem. In December 2006 Seller contracts to sell Buyer a new midnight blue 2006 Porsche 911 Carrera for $72,000, delivery in two days. When Buyer returns to pick it up, Seller informs her that he sold the car to someone else. Buyer attempts to find another midnight blue Carrera, but the 2007 models are out, and she cannot find a blue 2006 model. She is, however, able to find a forest green 2006 Carrera, which she purchases for $76,000. She sues Seller to recover $4,000. Is she entitled to it?

What if she cannot find any 2006 Carrera (even colors other than midnight blue), so she purchases a 2006 Ferrari F430 for $195,000. Can she recover the excess of that over the price of the Porsche?

What if she cannot find any 2006 Carrera, so she purchases a new 2007 midnight blue Carrera, for $76,000, plus $400 to ship it to her location. What damages can she recover?

Valley Die Cast Corp. v. A.C.W. Inc.

Michigan Court of Appeals, 1970.
25 Mich.App. 321, 181 N.W.2d 303.

■ HOLBROOK, JUDGE.

. . .

In 1965, Paul Stafford became interested in the car wash business as an investment. In January 1966, after learning that plaintiff was the manufacturer of [the "Thrift–I–Matic pressure] car wash system, Stafford arranged to talk with William Alkire, sales manager of plaintiff corporation. He was shown a working model of a car wash system which was allegedly different from and inferior to the newer stationary model he subsequently purchased. The sales brochure which he was given explained the operation of the new system, emphasized its dependability and profitability as an investment, and represented that it would wash cars "sparkling clean."

During preliminary sales conversations, Stafford [told] Alkire that he knew nothing about the car wash business. Stafford, his father, and his uncle invested in the purchase from plaintiff of its car wash system and, together with their wives, organized the defendant corporation. A purchase agreement was executed by Stafford, president of the corporation, on January 18, 1966, as a part of which a deposit of $1,000 was made to plaintiff by certified check. The purchase agreement included a stationary car wash system for $16,950, a rinse unit for $1,950, and a blower-dryer for $4,800, with a total price of $24,448. Because plaintiff was unable to deliver a blower-dryer as ordered, defendant secured one from another source. The price of plaintiff's blower-dryer was deducted from the total price of the sale. A building was constructed to accommodate plaintiff's system, built pursuant to plans prepared by plaintiff, costing defendant $26,000.

On July 13, 1966, defendant executed a note for $15,802.80, the balance of the purchase price, and a security agreement, providing for payment on September 1, 1966, and every month thereafter, of $263.38 until the full sum was paid. At the time suit was commenced, defendant had made 5 payments pursuant to the note, through January 1967 and was not in default.

The equipment was delivered to defendant's completed building on July 15, 1966. Several of plaintiff's employees assisted the building contractor in installing its system, together with the blower-dryer and an additional wax tower, purchased elsewhere. Defendant gave a certified check for $6,500, representing the balance of the down payment.

Installation of the equipment was completed on July 30, 1966. Plaintiff's employees checked and tested the equipment, following which defendant opened for business in early September 1966.

Stafford and his father testified that the equipment never ran right, and that by October 1966 it became necessary to wash cars by hand, forcing defendant to employ extra help. . . .

On November 30 and December 30, 1966, defendant, per Paul Stafford, forwarded to plaintiff the December 1966 and January 1967 payments, respectively, on its note, with accompanying letters advising that the equipment did not work properly and that payment was not intended as a waiver of defendant's legal rights.

On January 10, 1967, defendant notified plaintiff by letter of its rejection of the auto wash equipment, claiming breach of warranties, demanding that plaintiff remove its equipment and pay to defendant $11,943.90 ($8,816.90 in payments under the contract, and $3,127 installation cost) in discharge of defendant's security interest in the equipment, and giving notice of defendant's intention to resell the equipment should plaintiff fail to remove the same and discharge defendant's security interest therein by 5:00 p.m. January 20, 1967.

Stafford continued to use plaintiff's system until brush equipment, ordered from another source, was delivered on May 16, 1967, and also continued to request and receive necessary service from plaintiff on its equipment. On May 12, 1967, defendant wrote plaintiff that it was in the process of acquiring new auto wash equipment and removing and storing that of plaintiff's with the exception of a boiler, pump and sign which defendant was able to retain and use.

[Plaintiff sued for the balance of the price, and defendants counterclaimed for breach of warranty and fraud. The trial court entered judgment on a jury verdict for defendants for $9,000. Both parties appealed.]

I.

Plaintiff contends that defendant did not rescind but, rather, accepted plaintiff's system as a matter of law, and, in this regard, refers to certain acts of defendant which it claims were inconsistent with plaintiff's ownership of the equipment, viz: defendant's continued use of all of the equipment after January 10, 1967, until May 12, 1967; its use thereafter of a part of a "commercial unit" up to the trial of the case and its request for service after January 10, 1967; and defendant's act of taking depreciation on the equipment through August 31, 1967. In support of its position, plaintiff cites section 2606 of the uniform commercial code, M.C.L.A. § 440.2606 . . . .

It is defendant's position that utilization of plaintiff's equipment before replacement machinery was secured, and utilization of the useable units of the system after replacement, was necessary to mitigate damages, and was limited to "commercial units." . . .

Defendant's assertion that that portion of plaintiff's system which it utilized prior to acquisition of, and in conjunction with, the replacement brush system, could be found by a jury to be a "commercial unit," refers to M.C.L.A. § 440.2601, which allows a buyer to "accept any commercial unit or units and reject the rest." A "commercial unit" is defined in M.C.L.A. § 440.2105 as "a unit of goods as by commercial usage is a single whole for purposes of sale and division of which materially impairs its character or value on the market or in use. A commercial unit may be a single article (as a machine) or a set of articles * * * or a quantity * * * or any other unit treated in use or in the relevant market as a single whole." Testimony revealed that in addition to retaining plaintiff's sign, of a value of $400, which was available from plaintiff as optional equipment, the other items retained by defendant were collectively known as a "power pack" unit, suitable for use with both a brush and pressure system, and which was also available separately as optional equipment.

We conclude that defendant is correct, that the existence of acts tending to show an acceptance or rejection of goods as well as the ultimate fact of acceptance or rejection are, under the facts in this case, for the jury to determine.

Plaintiff claims that the taking of depreciation by defendant upon the value of plaintiff's equipment for the years ending August 31, 1966 and 1967, for tax purposes, considered in conjunction with other actions by defendant in regard to the equipment, amounted to an acceptance by defendant of the equipment as a matter of law. We rule that this contention is [a question for the jury], in view of the uncontradicted testimony by defendant's accountant that the use of depreciation was a proper accounting practice.

. . .

III.

Plaintiff, citing section 2715 of the uniform commercial code, dealing with incidental and consequential damages resulting from a seller's breach, M.C.L.A. § 440.2715, contends that the costs allegedly incurred by defendant in renovating its building to accommodate the substitute brush system, including $1,300.00 as the cost of electrical work to install the brush unit in its building, and $6,519.62 as the amount paid to Center Line Construction Incorporated for renovation of the building, are not recoverable. Plaintiff claims that, there being no special circumstances known to the seller when it entered into the contract which would distinguish the contract here involved from other contracts of the same kind, and no proof of actual damages, recovery of damages includes only such as would result from the natural and usual course of things.

The testimony revealed that the building, as originally built to accommodate plaintiff's equipment, was constructed by Center Line Construction

Incorporated for $26,000. Peter Cedroni, president of Center Line Construction Company testified that if he had originally constructed defendant's building to house the brush equipment, he would have done the same work with the exception of replacing the concrete floor. Defendant's proofs included an itemized statement of renovation costs, showing a total cost of $6,519.62.

Defendant asserts that renovation costs were within the contemplation of the parties, inasmuch as plaintiff should have known that if its system failed to perform properly defendant would have to install a system which would wash cars clean, requiring a modification of the building to house a substitute system; that, in any event, the costs of renovation proximately resulted from the failure of performance of the equipment, which plaintiff had reason to know had been purchased for a particular purpose, i.e., that of washing cars clean, citing section 2715 of the uniform commercial code, M.C.L.A., § 440.2715, and American Vitrified Products Company v. Wyer (C.A.6, 1955), 221 F.2d 447. We are convinced that the record contained sufficient proofs to enable the jury to determine whether renovation costs should be included in the award of damages to defendant as a proximate result of the failure of plaintiff's equipment to function properly. There was no substantial error committed by the court in submitting this question of fact to the jury.

IV.

Plaintiff contends that defendant cannot properly claim damages for loss of profits based upon plaintiff's sales brochure, which pointed out that the car wash equipment as sold would wash a car per minute and that by washing the number of cars listed per day and month, the operator could expect to show a profit. Plaintiff relies upon Allis v. McLean (1882), 48 Mich. 428, 12 N.W. 640 and Stevenson v. Brotherhoods Mutual Benefit (1945), 312 Mich. 81, 19 N.W.2d 494, in support of its position that the elements that go to make up a successful car wash business are beyond the control of the manufacturer and are too speculative to allow loss of profits as an element of defendant's damages.

Defendant asserts that the question of profits is one of fact for the jury, and that the law of this State is to the effect that loss of profits is a proper element of damages in contract cases, Atkinson v. Morse (1886), 63 Mich. 276, 29 N.W. 711, and in tort cases, Allison v. Chandler (1863), 11 Mich. 542. Defendant further contends that the proofs in the instant case established loss with reasonable certainty and, although defendant was not required to establish the amount of loss with absolute certainty, Callender v. Myers Regulator Co. (1930), 250 Mich. 298, 230 N.W. 154, there was mathematical certainty in much of defendant's evidence.

In the case of Allis v. McLean, supra, it was stated in 48 Mich. at pp. 431, 432, 12 N.W. at p. 642:

> " * * * But the difficulty in measuring damages by profits is that they are commonly uncertain and speculative, and depend upon so many contingencies that their loss cannot be traced with reasonable certainty

to the breach of contract. When that is the case they are said to be too remote; and the damages must be estimated on a consideration of such elements of injury as are more directly and certainly the result of the failure in performance. *But in some cases profits are the best possible measure of damage, for the very reason that the loss is indisputable, and the amount can be estimated with almost absolute certainty.* * * * " (Emphasis supplied).

The *Atkinson* and *Allison* cases, supra, cited by defendant, approve the recovery of damages for loss of profits where, based upon the factual circumstances of a given case, such profits are not subject to mere speculation. In this regard, the *Atkinson* case states as follows in 63 Mich. at p. 281, 29 N.W. at p. 713:

> "Damages for * * * loss of profits are more frequently allowed to be recovered in cases of tort than contract; but when loss of profits arising from a breach of contract can be proved with a reasonable degree of certainty, and [such loss is] directly traceable to the breach of the contract, there is no reason why [such damages] may not be recovered. * * * "

We note that the trial court did instruct the jury against speculation as to damages. Although recovery of damages for loss of profits is a close question, resolution of this question was confined to that measure of damages controlled by the evidence which was reasonably certain and not speculative.

V.

Defendant claims that the trial court's ruling that defendant had not "covered," pursuant to sections 2711 and 2712 of the uniform commercial code, M.C.L.A. §§ 440.2711, 440.2712 by installing a brush wash system in place of plaintiff's pressure system was erroneous and resulted in an insufficient verdict; that the jury should have been allowed to consider evidence of the cost of "cover" which, pursuant to section 2712, consists of the difference between the cost of the defective pressure equipment and the cost of the replacement brush equipment; and that it was for the jury to determine whether, under the circumstances, defendant acted reasonably. Defendant further argues that the uniform commercial code does not limit "cover" to identical goods, but requires only good faith, reasonably prompt action and a reasonable purchase. Defendant concedes that the price of the substituted brush system was $3,328.56 more than that of the pressure system sold by plaintiff, and that the pressure system washed cars while in a stationary position, using high pressure jets of water, while the brush system, using rotating brushes which touched the cars, creating friction, carried cars through the brushes by a conveyor. Defendant states that the important difference was that the brush system washed cars clean, while the pressure system did not.

The trial court, in ruling that defendant had not covered by installing a more expensive brush system, which operated upon a principle entirely different from the pressure system purchased from plaintiff, stated:

"* * * you put an entirely different system in. If you had gone out and gotten the same system there wouldn't be any question about it."

We rule that the question of admissibility of defendant's offer of evidence of "cover" was one for the court, and that its rejection was not an abuse of discretion but was proper under the facts.

. . .

Affirmed. No costs, neither party having prevailed on its appeal.

QUESTIONS AND NOTES

1. After removing the equipment supplied by plaintiff, defendants replaced it with other equipment that cost $3,300 more than the equipment supplied by plaintiff. In the last section of the opinion, the court upholds the trial court's denial of the $3,300 excess. In reaching that conclusion, what factors does the court consider? Was the court correct? Please read the Official Comments.

What if the evidence showed that the maintenance costs of the jet spray system supplied by plaintiff averaged $5,000 per year, while the maintenance costs of the brush system that defendants later acquired were $3,000 per year. Would those facts be relevant? If so, to what issue?

What if the evidence also showed that the expected life of a spray system is 10 years and the expected life of a brush system is 12 years. To what issue is that relevant? Alternatively, what if the expected life of the brush system is only 8 years. To what issue is that relevant?

2. Problem. Seller agreed to supply Buyer with its requirements of ethanol for three years for $2.00 per gallon. After one year the market price rose dramatically, and Seller refused to continue performing unless Buyer agreed to pay $3.00 per gallon. Buyer paid the higher price, reserving its rights under the original contract. Buyer, who had been charging its customers $2.30 per gallon, increased its price to $3.40 per gallon. At the expiration of the three-year period, Buyer sued. You may assume that Seller's refusal to deliver except at the higher price is a breach. Is Buyer entitled to recover under 2–712?

Seller claims that Buyer's damages should be reduced by the $1.10 per gallon that he raised his own prices to his customers. Is Seller correct?

3. The court holds (Part III of the opinion) that it was a question for the jury whether the defendants could recover the $6,500 cost of renovating the building and the $1,300 electrical work to accommodate the brush system. What section authorizes recovery of those amounts?

4. In holding that there was sufficient evidence to permit the jury to consider awarding lost profits (Part IV), the court does not cite any section of the Code. Does Article 2 permit a buyer to recover lost profits?

5.   Leases. Problem. Lessor contracts to acquire and lease a Model 5025 John Deere farm tractor to Lessee for a two-year period beginning April 1. Rent is $650 per month and Lessee has the obligation to insure and maintain the tractor and to return it to Lessor at the end of the lease term in good condition "reasonable wear and tear excepted."

On April 1 Lessor fails to deliver the tractor and notifies Lessee that it will not deliver in the future. On April 15, Lessee leases the same model tractor from another person for a one-year period beginning immediately, at a monthly rental of $700. The other lease terms are the same as those of the original lease. Can Lessee can recover as damages the $50 per month excess cost of the replacement lease? See 2A–518, 2A–519(1).

Suppose the new lease had been for three years? Is there any reason to treat the one-year lease and the three-year lease differently?

6.   Problem. Buyer contracts to purchase 3,000 tons of fertilizer from Seller at a price of $21.00 per ton. Seller fails to deliver. The market price at the place for tender at the time buyer learns of Seller's breach is $23.00 per ton. Fifteen days later he purchases replacement goods at $22.00 per ton. May buyer recover as damages the excess of the market price over the contract price, or is he limited to his excess cost of cover?

Suppose that, within the 30–day period following Seller's breach, Buyer purchases 10,000 tons from others at prices ranging from $22.00 to $23.50 per ton. Can Buyer claim that the purchases at $23.50 are "cover" purchases?

If, when Seller breaches, Buyer could purchase fertilizer for $22.00 per ton but does not do so, can Buyer recover damages measured by market price less contract price? See 2–715(2).

Allied Canners & Packers, Inc. v. Victor Packing Co.

California Court of Appeal, 1984.
162 Cal.App.3d 905, 209 Cal.Rptr. 60.

■ ROUSE, J.

[Victor contracted to deliver a large quantity of raisins to Allied in October 1976, at a price of 29.75 cents per pound minus a discount of 4 percent. Allied had in turn contracted to sell the raisins to a Japanese buyer for 29.75 cents per pound. Therefore, the profit that Allied was to receive on the transaction was only the 4 percent discount from the price of 29.75 cents per pound.

The raisin market is subject to the control of the federal government, which divides raisins into various categories, some of which may only be sold to specified buyers and only for resale to exporters. When Victor contracted to sell to Allied, the market price—which Victor would have to pay in order to acquire raisins for delivery to Allied—was 22 cents per pound. After Victor contracted with Allied, but before Victor actually contracted to acquire the raisins from its supplier, a heavy rain damaged the raisin crop, and the government prevented the sale of raisins for export. Victor was unable to acquire raisins and, therefore, failed to deliver to Allied. When Allied sued, Victor conceded that its failure to deliver was a breach of the contract with Allied.]

. . .

Allied did not cover by purchasing raisins on the open market. The earliest that either party could have bought raisins was October 1976, when the price of raisins was in the vicinity of 80 to 87 cents per pound. . . . [Allied's] buyer, Shoei Foods Industrial Co., Ltd. (Shoei), demanded delivery . . . . Allied's contract with Shoei, however, contained a provision holding it harmless from liability caused by strikes, fires, accidents and other developments beyond its control. At trial, Allied conceded that it had not been sued by Shoei for any damages resulting from its failure to deliver raisins to Shoei, but suggested that Shoei would hold off suing it until this action against Victor was concluded. Judgment was entered in this case in July 1981, nearly five years after the transaction occurred. Although the statute of limitations for a breach of contract action had expired (Code Civ.Proc. § 337, subd. 1), Shoei had never brought suit against Allied, and there is no indication that Allied voluntarily paid damages to Shoei.

. . .

Allied contends that pursuant to § 2713, subdivision (1), it is entitled to damages in the amount of $150,281.25, representing the difference between the contract price of 29.75 cents per pound and a market price of 87 cents per pound for 262,500 pounds . . . [of] raisins. The trial court, however, refused to apply § 2713 because it determined, purportedly as a matter of fact, that Allied was a broker, not a buyer, and therefore not subject to the provisions of the Commercial Code governing a buyer's remedies for breach of contract by a seller. The court concluded that Allied was damaged only to the extent of its lost "commission" as a broker in the sum of $4,462.50. Judgment for that amount was entered in Allied's favor.

While we perceive that the trial court was attempting to limit Allied's damages to those actually suffered, and felt that application of the formula set forth in § 2713, subdivision (1), would result in a windfall to Allied, it could not properly do so on the basis that Allied was not a "buyer" within the meaning of the Commercial Code. . . .

. . .

We conclude that Allied was a buyer in its contract with Victor and that it had a "forward contract" to sell the raisins to Shoei. As such, the remedies provided to a buyer by the Commercial Code are applicable to it. Thus, we turn to a consideration of the correct application of such remedies in this case.

. . .

Sections 2–712 and 2–713 of the Uniform Code are sometimes referred to as "cover" and "hypothetical cover," since the former involves an actual entry into the market by the buyer while the latter does not. (See Childres, Buyer's Remedies: The Danger of Section 2–713 (1978) 72 Nw.U.L.Rev. 837, 841 [applying those terms] (hereafter cited as Buyer's Remedies); Peters, Remedies for Breach of Contracts Relating to the Sale of Goods Under the Uniform Commercial Code: A Roadmap For Article Two (1963) 73 Yale L.J. 199, 259 [market under § 2–713 is "purely theoretical"] (hereafter cited as Remedies for Breach of Contracts).) It has been recognized that the use of the market price-contract price formula under § 2–713 does not, absent pure accident, result in a damage award reflecting the buyer's actual loss. (Buyer's Remedies, supra, at pp. 841–842; Remedies for Breach of Contracts, supra, at p. 259; [Simon & Novack, Limiting the Buyer's Market Damages to Lost Profits: A Challenge to the Enforceability of Market Contracts (1979)], 92 Harv.L.Rev. 1395 [hereafter cited as Market Damages]; White & Summers, Uniform Commercial Code 224 [2d ed. 1980].)

For example, in this case it is agreed that Allied's actual lost profit on the transaction was $4,462.50, while application of the market-contract price formula would yield damages of approximately $150,000. In Market Damages, supra, Simon and Novack describe the courts as divided on the issue of whether market damages, even though in excess of the plaintiff's loss, are appropriate for a supplier's breach of his delivery obligations and observe: "Strangely enough, each view has generally tended to disregard the arguments, and even the existence, of the opposing view. These two rival bodies of law, imposing in appearance, have passed each other like silent ships in the night." (92 Harv.L.Rev. 1395, 1397.) In Buyer's Remedies, supra, Professor Childres similarly points out that the courts have generally not undertaken any real analysis of the competing considerations involved in determining the correct measure of damages in such circumstances. (72 Nw.U.L.Rev. 837, 844 et seq.) We will undertake such an analysis.

Professors White and Summers, after noting their belief that "the Code drafters did not by [§ 2–713] intend to put the buyer in the same position as performance would have" (White & Summers, Uniform Commercial Code, supra, at p. 224), advance two possible explanations for the section. First, they suggest that it is simply a historical anomaly:

"Since cover was not a recognized remedy under pre-Code law, it made sense under that law to say that the contract-market formula put buyer in the same position as performance would have *on the assumption that the buyer would purchase substitute goods*. If things worked right, the market price would approximate the cost of the substitute goods and buyer would be put 'in the same position . . . .' But under the Code, 2–712 does this job with greater precision, and 2–713 reigns over only those cases in which the buyer does not purchase a substitute. Perhaps the drafters retained 2–713 not out of a belief in its appropriateness, but out of fear that they would be dismissed as iconoclasts had they proposed that the court in noncover cases simply award the buyer any economic loss proximately caused by seller's breach." (Ibid.)

They conclude, however, that probably the best explanation for § 2–713 "is that it is a statutory liquidated damage clause, a breach inhibitor the payout of which need bear no close relation to plaintiff's actual loss." (White & Summers, Uniform Commercial Code, supra, at p. 225.) They then observe that this explanation conflicts with the policy set forth in § 1–106, which provides in subdivision (1): "The remedies provided by this code shall be liberally administered *to the end that the aggrieved party may be put in as good a position as if the other party had fully performed* but neither consequential or special nor penal damages may be had except as specifically provided in this code or by other rule of law." (Emphasis added.) They find § 2–713 consistent, however, with a belief that plaintiffs recover too little and too infrequently for the law of contracts to be effective, and offer no suggestion for resolution of the conflict. (Ibid.)

In her article Remedies for Breach of Contracts, supra, then-Professor Peters states:

"Perhaps it is misleading to think of the market-contract formula as a device for the measurement of damages. . . . An alternative way of looking at market-contract is to view this differential as a statutory liquidated damages clause, rather than as an effort to calculate actual losses. If it is useful in every case to hold the party in breach to some baseline liability, in order to encourage faithful adherence to contractual obligations, perhaps market fluctuations furnish as good a standard as any." (73 Yale L.J. 199, 259.)

She does not discuss the conflict between the market-contract formula and the "only as good a position as performance" policy embodied in § 1–106.

Simon and Novack state:

"While it is generally recognized that the automatic invocation of market damages may sometimes overcompensate the plaintiff, a variety of arguments have been employed by commentators and courts to justify this result: the desirability of maintaining a uniform rule and of facilitating settlements; the public interest in encouraging contract performance and the proper functioning of the market; the prevention of defendant's unjust enrichment; the restoration of the very 'value' promised to plaintiff; and the inherent difficulty and complexity of proving actual economic losses not encompassed within the contract terms." (Fns. omitted; Market Damages supra, 92 Harv.L.Rev. 1395, 1403.)

That a defendant not be unjustly enriched by a bad faith breach is a concern widely shared by commentators and courts. (Id., at p. 1406, fn. 51, and cases there cited.)

Viewing § 2–713 as, in effect, a statutory provision for liquidated damages, it is necessary for us to determine whether a damage award to a buyer who has not covered is ever appropriately limited to the buyer's actual economic loss which is below the damages produced by the market-contract formula, and, if so, whether the present case presents a situation in which the damages should be so limited.

One view is that § 2–713 of the Uniform Code, or a substantively similar statutory provision, establishes the principle that a buyer's resale contract and damage claims made thereunder are irrelevant to an award of damages, and that damages therefore cannot be limited to a plaintiff's actual economic loss. . . . Simon and Novack, while favoring that view, concede that it can be argued that the provision of § 1–106 that an aggrieved party be put " 'in as good a position as if the other party had fully performed' " calls for an opposite conclusion. (Market Damages, supra, 92 Harv.L.Rev. 1395, 1412–1413, fn. 71.)

Although we find no cases discussing the interaction of § 1–106 and § 2–713, we note that some pre-Uniform Code cases held that a limitation to actual losses should be placed upon the market price-contract price measure of damages under general contract principles. (See, e.g., Foss v. Heineman, (1910) 144 Wis. 146 [128 N.W. 881]; Isaacson v. Crean (1917) 165 N.Y.S. 218; Texas Co. v. Pensacola Maritime Corporation (5th Cir. 1922) 279 F. 19.) One author on the subject has apparently concluded that such a limitation is appropriate under the Uniform Code when the plaintiff-buyer has a resale contract and the existence of the resale contract is known to the defendant-seller:

> "It may be supposed . . . that the buyer was bound by a contract made before the breach to deliver to a third person the very goods which the buyer expected to obtain from the seller, and the price under the resale contract may be less than the market price at the time of the breach. If the reason generally given for the rule permitting the recovery of additional damage because of an advantageous resale contract existing and known to the defendant when he contracted be applied, namely, that such consequential damages are allowed because the parties supposedly contract for them, it would follow that in every case the damage that the defendant might normally expect to follow from breach of his contract should be recovered even though the plaintiff actually suffered less damage than the difference between the contract price and the market price." (4 Anderson, Uniform Commercial Code (3d ed.1983) § 2–711:15, pp. 430–431.)

. . .

We conclude that in the circumstances of this case—in which the seller knew that the buyer had a resale contract, the buyer has not been able to show that it will be liable in damages to the buyer on its forward contract, and there has been no finding of bad faith on the part of the seller—the policy of § 1106, subdivision (1), that the aggrieved party be put in as good a position as if the other party had performed requires that the award of damages to the buyer be limited to its actual loss, the amount it expected to make on the transaction.[7] . . .

We need not determine in this case what degree of bad faith on the part of a breaching seller might warrant the award of market-contract price damages without limitation, in circumstances otherwise similar to those involved here, in order to prevent unjust enrichment to a seller who deliberately breaches in order to take advantage of a rising market. Although Allied implies that Victor was guilty of bad faith here because after its breach it [sold] raisins to which [Allied] was entitled at 36.25 cents per pound, rather than acquiring the raisins and delivering them to Allied, the record is simply not clear on Victor's situation following the rains. It does appear clear, however, that, as the trial court found, the rains caused a severe problem, and Victor made substantial efforts to persuade [the government] to release . . . raisins to it . . . . We do not deem this record one to support an inference that windfall damages must be awarded the buyer to prevent unjust enrichment to a deliberately breaching seller. (Compare Sun–Maid Raisin Growers v. Victor Packing Co., supra, 146 Cal.App.3d 787 [where, in a case coincidentally involving Victor, Victor was expressly found by the trial court to have engaged in bad faith by gambling on the market price of raisins in deciding whether to perform its contracts to sell raisins to Sun–Maid].)

The judgment is affirmed. Each party is to bear its own costs on appeal.

TexPar Energy Inc. v. Murphy Oil USA, Inc.

United States Court of Appeals, Seventh Circuit, 1995.
45 F.3d 1111.

■ Reavley, Circuit Judge.

. . .

On May 29, 1992, TexPar contracted to purchase 15,000 tons of asphalt from Murphy at an average price of $53 per ton. On the same day, TexPar contracted to sell the 15,000 tons to Starry Construction Company at an average price of $56 per ton. Hence, TexPar stood to profit by $45,000 if both contracts were performed.

During the first half of 1992, the price of asphalt varied widely. Evidence was presented of prices ranging from $40 to $100 per ton. The

---

7. Allied suggested at trial that it had suffered additional consequential damages through the loss of its entire account with Shoei. Although it might have been able to establish such damages under § 2715, subdivision (2)(a), little evidence on that issue was presented and Allied has made no contention on appeal that it was entitled to such damages. The view that the true damages it had suffered were $4,462.50 was expressed by its own president when the trial court asked him whether in the event that damages of $150,281 were awarded, he would consider that to be his company's own money. He replied that he would not.

wide range of prices reflected volatile market forces. From the supply standpoint, asphalt is one of the end products of petroleum refining, and must be sold or stockpiled to accommodate the production of more valuable petroleum products. Demand depends in large measure on the availability of government funding for highway construction. Weather also affects asphalt supply and demand. The price rose rapidly in June of 1992, and consequently, the sale price of $53 per ton lost its attractiveness to Murphy.

In May and early June TexPar took delivery of 690 tons of asphalt; but, on June 5, Murphy stopped its deliveries and notified TexPar that its sales manager lacked authority to make the contract. By then, the price of asphalt had risen to $80 per ton. Starry insisted that TexPar deliver the full 15,000 tons at $56 per ton as TexPar and Starry had agreed. Ultimately, with TexPar's approval, Starry and Murphy negotiated directly and agreed on a price of $68.50 per ton. This arrangement was reached several weeks after the repudiation by Murphy. By this time the market price had dropped, according to TexPar. TexPar agreed to pay Starry the $12.50 difference between the new price of $68.50 per ton and the original $56 per ton price. TexPar therefore paid Starry approximately $191,000 to cover the price difference.

The jury found that the difference between the market price ($80) and the contract price ($53) of the undelivered asphalt (14,310 tons) on the date of repudiation (June 5), amounted to $386,370. The court entered judgment for this amount.

DISCUSSION

The parties agree that Wisconsin law, and particularly Wisconsin's version of the Uniform Commercial Code, applies to this dispute.

A.   *Damages Under UCC § 2–713*

The district court applied UCC § 2–713 . . . .

Murphy does not dispute that if this provision is applied, the damages awarded are proper, since Murphy does not dispute the quantity of goods, the market price or the date of notice of repudiation used by the jury to calculate damages. Instead, Murphy argues that the general measure of damages in a breach of contract case is the amount needed to place the plaintiff in as good a position as he would have been if the contract had been performed. Murphy argues that since TexPar's award—$386,370—far exceeds its out-of-pocket expenses ($191,000) and lost profits ($45,000) occasioned by the repudiation, the court erred in instructing the jury merely to find the difference in market price and entering judgment in that amount.

We cannot quarrel with Murphy that the general measure of damages in contract cases is the expectancy or "benefit of the bargain" measure. The UCC itself embraces such a measure in § 1–106, providing that the UCC remedies "shall be liberally administered to the end that the aggrieved party may be put in as good a position as if the other party had fully performed . . . ." Wis.Stat.Ann. § 401.106 (West 1994).

Nevertheless, we do not believe that the district court erred in awarding damages based on a straightforward application of § 402.713. That provision is found in the article on the sale of goods, and specifies a remedy for the circumstances presented here—the seller's nondelivery of goods for which there is a market price at the time of repudiation.

We can see no sound reason for looking to an alternative measure of damages. Murphy argues that TexPar shouldn't be awarded a "windfall" amount in excess of its out-of-pocket damages. Since it depends on the market price on a date after the making of the contract, the remedy under § 402.713 necessarily does not correspond to the buyer's actual losses, barring a coincidence. Our problem with Murphy's suggested measure of damages is that limiting the buyer's damages in cases such as this one to the buyer's out-of-pocket losses could, depending on the market, create a windfall for the seller. If the price of asphalt had fallen back to $56 per ton by the time Starry and Murphy had arranged for replacement asphalt, TexPar's damages would have been zero by this measure,[2] and Murphy could have reaped a windfall by selling at the market price of $80 in early June instead of the $53 price negotiated with TexPar.

Murphy argues that it did not in fact realize a windfall, since its cost of production was $70 per ton and it eventually agreed to sell to Starry for $68.50. We find this argument unpersuasive. Applying the market value measure of damages under UCC § 2–713, as the district court did, is expressly allowed under the Code. Since § 2–713 addresses the circumstances of a seller's nondelivery of goods with a market price, we see no error in applying this specific provision over the more general remedies provision found at § 1–106. See Tongish v. Thomas, 251 Kan. 728, 840 P.2d 471, 474 (1992) ("[B]ecause it appears impractical to make [§ 1–106] and [§ 2–713] harmonize in this factual situation, [§ 2–713] should prevail as the more specific statute according to statutory rules of construction."). The UCC § 2–713 remedy serves the purpose of discouraging sellers from repudiating their contracts as the market rises, if the buyer should resell as did TexPar, or gambling that the buyer's damages will be small should the market drop. It also has the advantage of promoting uniformity and predictability in commercial transactions, by fixing damages on the date of the breach, rather than allowing the vicissitudes of the market in the future to determine damages. *Id.* 840 P.2d at 476 ("Damages computed under [§ 2–713] encourage the honoring of contracts and market stability.")

. . .

AFFIRMED.

---

2. TexPar would not even have received its lost profits, because Murphy had persuaded the district court that its acknowledgment form effectively precluded the recovery of lost profits. The district court so ruled in granting a partial summary judgment.

QUESTIONS AND NOTES

1. Is it relevant in cases like *Allied Canners* and *TexPar* whether the seller knows that the buyer is purchasing for resale? that the buyer already has a resale contract when it contracts with the seller?

2. With which court do you agree? Or are the cases distinguishable, so that you agree with both?

3. Is it relevant to the question whether to use 2–713 or 1–106 that the seller opportunistically used an increase in the market price to make more money by selling to someone else?

4. For a case agreeing with *Allied Canners*, see H–W–H Cattle Co. v. Schroeder, 767 F.2d 437 (8th Cir.1985), in which the buyer also had already contracted to resell the goods (cattle). The court did not discuss the question whether the seller knew that the buyer had already made a resale contract. Most courts, however, agree with the result in *TexPar*. E.g., Tongish v. Thomas, 16 Kan.App.2d 809, 829 P.2d 916, aff'd 251 Kan. 728, 840 P.2d 471 (1992), in which the court stated:

> We are not persuaded that the lost profits view under *Allied* should be embraced. It is a minority rule that has received only nominal support. We believe the majority rule or the market damages remedy as contained in [2–713] is more reasoned and should be followed as the preferred measure of damages. While application of the rule may not reflect the actual loss to a buyer, it encourages a more efficient market and discourages the breach of contracts.
>
> The majority rule further permits the parties to measure the expectancy of what might happen if the seller does not perform the contract. The buyer has an option at the beginning of the contract to take actions to protect against an uncertain future. The parties both know that the option is an election that can be exercised by the buyer to protect against future losses. This generates stability in the market by discouraging the seller from breaching the contract when the market fluctuates to his advantage. The rule is further in accord with the rule of statutory construction that a specific statute shall prevail over a conflicting general statute dealing with the same subject matter unless the legislature intended to make the general statute control.

5. Problem 3, page 415 revisited. Assume that when Seller breaches, Buyer purchases another 2006 midnight blue Porsche 911 Carrera for $72,500. If Buyer proves that the market price for 2006 Carreras in December 2006 was $76,000, can she recover the $4,000 difference?

6. CISG. The Convention on Contracts for the International Sale of Goods provides for damages in Articles 74–77. Note the similarity of Articles 75 and 76 to 2–712 and 2–713. If *Allied Canners* were decided under the Convention, what would the result be?

D. REMEDIES WHEN THE BUYER GETS AND KEEPS THE GOODS

The buyer who accepts and keeps goods is obligated to pay for them, and 2–607(1) requires the buyer to pay the price even if the goods do not conform to the contract. The catalog of remedies in 2–711 does not include any remedy for the situation in which the buyer accepts and keeps goods even though the goods or the tender fail to conform and the buyer could have rejected them or revoked acceptance of them. The buyer does, of course, have a remedy in this situation. It appears in 2–714. Please read that section and consider the following excerpt from Chatlos Systems, Inc. v. National Cash Register Corp., 670 F.2d 1304 (3d Cir.1982), which deals with the application of subsection (2). In a transaction that occurred before the enactment of Article 2A, plaintiff leased a computer system from defendant. Applying the Article 2 rules to the transaction, the trial court held that plaintiff's damages for breach of warranty were $201,826.50, the value the system would have had if it had been as warranted less its actual value, which the court estimated at $6,000. Defendant claimed that trial court should have used the contract price of the computer ($46,020) as the value the computer would have had if it had been as warranted, so that plaintiff's damages were only $40,020. The court responded:

> Waiving the opportunity to submit additional evidence as to value on the remand which we directed, appellant chose to rely on the record of the original trial and submitted no expert testimony on the market value of a computer which would have performed the functions NCR had warranted. Notwithstanding our previous holding that contract price was not necessarily the same as market value, 635 F.2d at 1088, appellant faults the district judge for rejecting its contention that the contract price for the NCR 399/656 was the only competent record evidence of the value of the system as warranted. The district court relied instead on the testimony of plaintiff-appellee's expert, Dick Brandon, who, without estimating the value of an NCR model 399/656, presented his estimate of the value of a computer system that would perform all of the functions that the NCR 399/656 had been warranted to perform. Brandon did not limit his estimate to equipment of any one manufacturer; he testified regarding manufacturers who could have made systems that would perform the functions that appellant had warranted the NCR 399/656 could perform. He acknowledged that the systems about which he testified were not in the same price range as the NCR 399/656. Appellant likens this testimony to substituting a Rolls Royce for a Ford, and concludes that the district court's recomputed damage award was therefore clearly contrary to the evidence of fair market value—which in NCR's view is the contract price itself.

> Appellee did not order, nor was it promised, merely a specific NCR computer model, but an NCR computer system with specified capabili-

ties. The correct measure of damages, under N.J.Stat.Ann. § 12A:2–714(2), is the difference between the fair market value of the goods accepted and the value they would have had if they had been as warranted. Award of that sum is not confined to instances where there has been an increase in value between date of ordering and date of delivery. It may also include the benefit of a contract price which, for whatever reason quoted, was particularly favorable for the customer. Evidence of the contract price may be relevant to the issue of fair market value, but it is not controlling. [Defendant] limited its fair market value analysis to the contract price of the computer model it actually delivered. [Plaintiff] developed evidence of the worth of a computer with the capabilities promised by NCR, and the trial court properly credited the evidence.

[Plaintiff] was aided, moreover, by the testimony of Frank Hicks, NCR's programmer, who said that he told his company's officials that the "current software was not sufficient in order to deliver the program that the customer (Chatlos) required. They would have to be rewritten or a different system would have to be given to the customer." Hicks recommended that Chatlos be given an NCR 8200 but was told, "that will not be done." . . . [A]nother NCR witness admitted that the 8200 series was two levels above the 399 in sophistication and price. This testimony supported [the testimony of a third witness] that the price of the hardware needed to perform Chatlos' requirements would be in the $100,000 to $150,000 range.

Essentially, then, the trial judge was confronted with the conflicting value estimates submitted by the parties. Chatlos' expert's estimates were corroborated to some extent by NCR's supporters. NCR, on the other hand, chose to rely on contract price. Credibility determinations had to be made by the district judge. Although we might have come to a different conclusion on the value of the equipment as warranted had we been sitting as trial judges, we are not free to make our own credibility and factual findings. . . .

The judgment of the district court will be affirmed.

A dissenting judge thought that plaintiff should have produced evidence of the value the particular system delivered would have had if it had performed as warranted, rather than evidence of what another system that performed all the warranted functions would have cost.

What do you think? Do you think the plaintiff got a larger recovery than it was entitled to? Why do you answer the way you do?

———

Section 2–607(3)(a) provides that a buyer who wants to keep the goods but assert a claim for damages "must within a reasonable time after he discovers or should have discovered the breach notify the seller of the breach or be barred from any remedy." Lockheed Electronics Co. v.

Keronix, Inc., 114 Cal.App.3d 304, 170 Cal.Rptr. 591 (1981), a contract for the sale of computer cores, is illustrative of the rationale for this requirement. After some of the cores had been delivered, the buyer notified the seller to "put a hold on the order." Four months later the buyer cancelled the rest of the order, justifying the cancellation by claiming that the cores were defective. The seller defended by arguing that the buyer had not given timely notice of defects. The court held that the buyer was precluded from relying on any defects in the goods to establish the seller's breach, because if the seller had been notified, it could have cured the defects by making delivery of replacement cores.

This makes sense and is reinforced by 2–605(1), which applies when the buyer rejects the goods. Does it also make sense if the seller breaches not by delivering defective goods, but rather by delivering conforming goods after the date on which delivery was to be made?

————

Jay V. Zimmerman Co. v. General Mills, Inc.

United States District Court, Eastern District of Missouri, 1971.
327 F.Supp. 1198.

■ Regan, District Judge.

[Plaintiff contracted to sell defendant 3.6 million toy "dune buggies," at a price of 2.63 cents each, to be used as an inpack premium in defendant's cereal "Clackers." Defendant also was to pay $16,400 for a mold to be used in manufacturing the dune buggies. Plaintiff was late in making deliveries, but defendant accepted and paid for them. Defendant refused, however, to pay the price of the mold, and plaintiff sued. Defendant counterclaimed for damages.]

. . .

Plaintiff also urges that defendant waived the requirement of prompt delivery. We find against plaintiff on this issue. The rule followed by the Missouri courts is that a purchaser who accepts late delivery does not thereby, as a matter of law, waive his right to recover damages which have resulted from the delay. . . .

We find as a fact that by accepting late delivery of the dune buggies defendant did not intend to and did not waive its right to damages. Under the facts of this case, all that defendant waived by accepting the dune buggies was its right to rescind the contract by reason of plaintiff's breach.

This brings us to the question of whether the Uniform Commercial Code of Missouri, and in particular Section 400.2–607(3), bars defendant from recovering damages as plaintiff insists. This statute provides in substance that where a tender has been accepted, the buyer must, within "a reasonable time" after the breach has been discovered or should have been discovered, notify the seller of the breach "or be barred from any remedy."

The statute refers to a breach which is discovered or discoverable only *after* acceptance of tender of the goods. The Missouri courts have not yet construed this section. However, in construing statutes generally, the Missouri courts act on the presumption that the Legislature never intends to enact an absurd law or to intend to require the performance of a needless and useless act.

In the present, as in any case involving late delivery, both the seller and the buyer are necessarily fully aware *prior* to tender that the seller's contract obligation to timely deliver has not been complied with. It would be an unreasonable, if not absurd, construction of the statute to require a renewed notice of breach *after* acceptance of the goods under the facts here involved. A party has notice of a fact when he has actual knowledge of it. Section 400.1–201(25) of the Uniform Commercial Code. The purpose of a notice in the context of this section (Cf. the definition of "notice" in Section 400.1–201(26)) is to *inform* the seller of matters which would not normally come to the buyer's attention until *after* the goods came into his possession. The legislative intent was to make provision with respect to the effect of acceptance of allegedly defective or inferior goods or those allegedly not meeting warranted standards of quality. In that situation it is reasonable to require the buyer to inform the seller of the existence of a possible factual dispute relating to matters of which the buyer presumably was not aware prior to his acceptance of a tender of the goods.

If perchance the statute should be construed to require a useless notice of a breach which is known to both parties prior to tender, we find under the facts that notice of breach sufficient to comply with the statute was given by defendant within a "reasonable time" after acceptance of the tender as well as prior thereto. In his letter of November 13, 1969, Nelles explicitly stated that plaintiff had failed to achieve its obligation to meet defendant's tight timing schedule "by wide margin." This language clearly "informs" plaintiff of the fact of its breach as to time of delivery, and by giving such information defendant has met the only burden the statute places on a buyer who has accepted a tender. He is not required to give notice of breach in any particular manner or form nor is he required to assert an intention to make a claim for damages or to pursue any other available remedy. In view of the actual knowledge of the seller concerning its untimely deliveries, the notice of breach in defendant's November 13, 1969 letter was given within a "reasonable time" after acceptance of the dune buggies. We are confirmed in this view by the further fact that numerous telephone discussions, beginning at least as early as mid-August and continuing through November, 1969, were had relating to plaintiff's inability to meet defendant's "tight timing schedule," and that in the course of these discussions plaintiff was "informed" of its breach of contract. A verbal notice of breach is sufficient to meet the requirements of Section 400.2–607(3). When the Legislature intended that a notice be given in writing, it carefully and explicitly so provided. Cf. Section 400.2–607(5)(a) and (b).

Having found a breach of contract for which plaintiff is liable, the remaining issue is that of damages. Plaintiff was aware that defendant intended to use the dune buggies as an inpack premium in promoting the sale of its Clackers cereal and that the "tight timing schedule" was for the purpose of assuring that the promotion would be made at the particular period of the year which in the judgment of the defendant was best suited to overcome consumer sales resistance. Relying on plaintiff's agreement to conform to the "tight timing schedule," defendant purchased cereal cartons on which were imprinted dune buggy advertisements and in addition contracted and paid for the preparation of TV commercials. When it became obvious that the "tight timing schedule" could not and would not be met, defendant was forced to change its plans for the use of the dune buggies.

In order to avoid a vacuum during the period in which the dune buggies were to be used as premiums, defendant hurriedly arranged for another premium which was far from satisfactory as a substitute for the dune buggies. Because of the shortness of time, defendant was required to ship the substitute premium by air-freight at a cost of $2,831.98 and was also required to pay the seller the cost of overtime labor to produce the substitute premium, at an additional cost to defendant of $320. These two expenses totaling $3,151.98 would not have been incurred but for plaintiff's breach of contract, and we find that they constitute "incidental damages" in connection with effecting cover, incident to the breach, within the meaning of Section 400.2–715 of the Uniform Commercial Code of Missouri. These damages would have been sustained even if the dune buggies had been rejected.

As for the other damages sought, the evidence shows that in April, 1970, defendant destroyed the dune buggy Clackers cartons at a net loss to defendant of $31,498.04. Defendant seeks to impose liability upon plaintiff for the amount of this loss, its theory being that the specially imprinted Clackers cartons were time coded so that they became worthless for later use.

We hold that defendant is not entitled to recover this item of damages. We find that the cartons were not actually time coded and that they could have been used for a Clackers dune buggy promotion at any time after the dune buggies were accepted had defendant desired to do so. That defendant was impressed with the value of the dune buggies as an inpack premium and for that reason accepted the late deliveries admits of no doubt. We are convinced, however, that defendant's decision not to use the dune buggies to advertise its Clackers cereal was due to its reasonable belief that these premiums could more profitably be used to promote another of its cereals in view of the rapidly declining sales of Clackers commencing long prior to the agreed dates of delivery.

The Clackers cartons became obsolescent and were ultimately destroyed solely because of defendant's change in promotion plans and not because of plaintiff's default in making timely deliveries. For the same reason we find that the defendant is not entitled to recover the cost of the

Clackers' dune buggy commercials, advertising which it could have used had it not decided to abandon the use of dune buggies in promoting Clackers. Defendant presented no substantial evidence to support an award for loss of profits and has now waived any such claim.

It follows from the foregoing that defendant is entitled to recover only the sum of $3,151.98 on its counterclaim.

. . .

Eastern Air Lines, Inc. v. McDonnell Douglas Corp.

United States Court of Appeals, Fifth Circuit, 1976.
532 F.2d 957.

■ AINSWORTH, C.J.

[Plaintiff contracted to buy 99 jet passenger aircraft from the defendant to be delivered over a period of years. There were substantial delays in delivery of the planes and plaintiff sued to recover the resulting damages. The District Court gave judgment for plaintiff on a jury verdict of just under 25 million dollars. Defendant appealed.]

. . .

During the trial and in final instructions to the jury, the District Court held that Eastern need not prove, as a predicate for recovery in this suit, that it had given McDonnell Douglas reasonable and timely notice of the delivery delays. McDonnell strongly contests the trial judge's rulings for Eastern on this issue and argues either that the airline should, as a matter of law, be barred from any recovery or, alternatively, that the issue of timely notice should have been submitted to the jury.

. . .

McDonnell contends that the trial judge denied it the benefits of [section 2–607(3)(a)], both by ruling that section 2–607 does not apply to late deliveries and by holding in the alternative that Eastern gave adequate notice. Because we are unable to agree with the District Court's ruling on either ground, we hold that the question of timely notice under section 2–607 should have been submitted to the jury.

A. *Applicability of U.C.C. § 2–607(3)(a)*

Even though section 2–607, by its very terms, governs "any breach," the trial court found the notice requirement to be inapplicable to delivery delays because a seller necessarily has knowledge of this sort of contract violation. Relying on the case of Jay V. Zimmerman Company v. General Mills, Inc., E.D.Mo., 1971, 327 F.Supp. 1198, 1204, the District Judge concluded that notice is useless where a breach is apparent to both parties. The trial court apparently was of the view that the sole function of section 2–607 is to inform the seller of hidden defects in his performance. Under this approach, the only purpose of notice is to provide the seller with an opportunity to remedy an otherwise unknown nonconforming tender.

Section 2–607's origins, however, reveal that it has a much broader function. The Code's notice requirement was derived from decisional law in California and several other states which sought to ameliorate the harsh common law rule that acceptance of goods by the buyer waived any and all of his remedies. This approach was codified under section 49 of the Uniform Sales Act which was adopted in California as Civ.Code § 1769.

As Professor Williston, the author of the Sales Act, has noted, section 49 continued the common law rule treating a seller's tender of goods as an offer of them in full satisfaction. 3 S.Williston, Contracts § 714 (rev.ed. 1961). The buyer, though, was permitted to accept the offer without waiving any claims if he gave the seller prompt notice to this effect. This approach reconciled the desire to give finality to transactions in which goods were accepted with the need to accommodate a buyer who, for business reasons, had to accept the tendered goods despite unsatisfactory performance by the seller. Pre–U.C.C. decisions in California and else-where, therefore, recognized that the primary purpose of notice is to inform the seller that, even though his tender has been accepted by the buyer, his performance is nonetheless considered a breach of contract.

Under section 49 it was irrelevant whether a seller had actual knowl-edge of a nonconforming tender. Instead, the critical question was whether the seller had been informed that the buyer considered him to be in breach. Consequently, in Professor Williston's words, "the section is applicable not only to defects in quality but to breach of any promise or warranty, as, for instance, *delay in time*." 5 S.Williston, Contracts § 714 at 409 (3d ed.1961) (emphasis supplied). Pre–U.C.C. decisions, therefore, applied the notice requirement in delivery delay cases. Judge Learned Hand, for example, applied section 49 in a case in which performance had been delayed, noting:

> The plaintiff replies that the buyer is not required to give notice of what the seller already knows, but this confuses two quite different things. The notice "of the breach" required is not of the facts, which the seller presumably knows quite as well as, if not better than, the buyer, but of buyer's claim that they constitute a breach. The purpose of the notice is to advise the seller that he must meet a claim for damages, as to which, rightly or wrongly, the law requires that he shall have early warning.

American Mfg. Co. v. United States Shipping Board E.F. Corp., 2 Cir., 1925, 7 F.2d 565, 566.

As the drafters of Article 2 acknowledge, section 2–607 continues the basic policies underlying section 49 of the Uniform Sales Act. Indeed, the notice requirement developed in pre-U.C.C. cases is entirely consistent with the Article 2 goals of encouraging compromise and promoting good faith in commercial relations. As Comment 4 to section 2–607 indicates, the pur-pose of notice is not merely to inform the seller that his tender is nonconforming, but to open the way for settlement through negotiation between the parties. In the words of the California Supreme Court, "the sound commercial rule" codified in section 2–607 also requires that a seller be reasonably protected against stale claims arising out of transactions which a buyer has led him to believe were closed. Pollard v. Saxe & Yolles Development Company, 1974, 12 Cal.3d 374, 115 Cal.Rptr. 648, 525 P.2d 88. Early warning permits the seller to investigate the claim while the facts are fresh, avoid the defect in the future, minimize his damages, or perhaps assert a timely claim of his own against third parties.

Given these undeniable purposes, it is not enough under section 2–607 that a seller has knowledge of the facts constituting a nonconforming tender; he must also be informed that the buyer considers him to be in breach of the contract. The Code's notice requirement, then, is applicable to delivery delays as well as other breaches. Accordingly, we decline to follow the reasoning of the *Zimmerman* decision, and we find that the trial court erred in not applying section 2–607 to the delivery delays at issue in this case.

. . .

QUESTIONS AND NOTES

1. With which court do you agree?

2. Revised Article 2. Revised 2–607 takes another step in the evolution of the rule requiring notice of breach: under revised 2–607(3)(a) "failure to give timely notice bars the buyer from a remedy only to the extent that the seller is prejudiced by the failure." Is this a desirable step? Was McDonnell Douglas prejudiced by Eastern's failure to give notice?

3. In *Zimmerman* the court awards the defendant $2,800 for air freight and $320 for overtime labor in connection with obtaining substitute goods. To justify this award, the court cites 2–715. But if you read that section carefully, you will see that it does not provide that a buyer is entitled to damages. So what authority is there for the court's conclusion?

E.   CONTRACTUAL LIMITATIONS OF REMEDIES

It may surprise you to realize that almost all of the provisions in Part 7 of Article 2 are merely gap-fillers, for 2–718 and 2–719 specifically authorize the parties to displace those provisions by agreement. Section 2–718 specifically authorizes the parties to stipulate the damages that will be available in the event of breach. Section 2–719 authorizes them to modify or exclude the remedies that would be available in the absence of their agreement on remedies. The latter section is related to 2–316, which authorizes warranty disclaimers, but it is conceptually very different, and that difference is extremely important to understand. If a seller disclaims warranties, that means there are no warranties and the seller is not in breach just because the goods are defective. If, on the other hand, a seller excludes damages, a defect in the goods may amount to a breach of the contract but the buyer has no claim to damages for loss caused by that breach. See 2–316(4). Please read 2–719(1) now.

1. Subsection (1) refers to two possible remedies that the parties might place in their contract: refund of the price and repair or replacement of nonconforming goods or parts. No doubt you have encountered each of these in your own purchases. Can you think of other remedies the parties might place in their contract?

2.   Problem. Buyer purchases a non-stick fry pan. Accompanying the pan is a statement:

> GlideFree Cookware is warranted to free from defects in material and workmanship under normal household use for a period of 10 years. This pan will continue to release food for a full 10 years when our care and use instructions are followed. We will repair or replace (at our option) any defective part or item during the guarantee period. Should you have a problem with your pan, please return it to us at 136 Woodlawn Rd., Waterloo, IA.
>
> This warranty does not cover damage caused by overheating, accident, misuse, or abuse. Incidental or consequential damages are expressly excluded by this warranty.

After three years food no longer glides out of the pan without sticking. May Buyer recover damages for this breach of warranty?

3. Many contracts—both consumer and commercial, even highly negotiated ones—provide that the buyer's *exclusive* remedy is repair or replacement. What reasons might a seller have for wanting this provision? What reasons might a buyer have? Please write down at least two reasons for each.

The adequacy of the remedy to achieve these purposes depends on two things: the parties' willingness to attempt repairs (or replacement) and the seller's ability to accomplish it successfully and expeditiously. Occasionally, when a buyer complains about a nonconformity, the seller refuses to take any action, perhaps because the seller does not agree that there is a nonconformity or because the seller thinks that the buyer's misuse of the product caused the problem. If the seller is wrong and in fact the goods do not conform, the seller's refusal leaves the buyer without any remedy. In other instances the seller may attempt to repair the goods—even repeatedly—but simply be unable to make the goods conform. (Obvious examples are those motor vehicles that properly are described as lemons, but the phenomenon occurs with respect to commercial equipment, too.) Here, also, the buyer is left without any remedy. In recognition of these scenarios, subsection (2) provides a remedy. Please read subsection (2) now.

If an exclusive repair-or-replace remedy fails of its essential purpose, the Article 2 remedies are available. Assuming that the seller is willing to attempt repairs, the remedy fails of its essential purpose if the seller's attempts are unsuccessful. This may occur in at least two ways: the defect repeatedly manifests itself, as when the seller simply cannot, despite repeated repairs, solve the problem with a car's transmission. It also may occur, however, if notwithstanding the successful repair of a defect, another defect becomes evident. At some point, a succession of defects, even if each (except perhaps the last one) is repaired, justifies a conclusion that the remedy has failed of its essential purpose. As one court stated in connection with a series of attempts to repair a motor home:

> It is the position of the defendants that KOA successfully repaired every defect complained of by the Murrays . . . .

> Although the Murrays agreed that KOA had never refused to attempt a requested repair, this testimony does not affect their right to revoke acceptance. The limited remedy of repair or replacement of defective parts fails of its essential purpose whenever, despite reasonable opportunity for repair, the goods are not restored to a nondefective condition within a reasonable time, whether or not the failure to do so is willful.

Murray v. Holiday Rambler, Inc., 83 Wis.2d 406, 265 N.W.2d 513 (1978).

> Another court stated:

> To be effective the repair remedy must be provided within a reasonable time after discovery of the defect. It is not necessary to show negligence or bad faith on the part of the seller, S.M. Wilson & Co. v. Smith International, Inc., 587 F.2d 1363, 1374–75 (9th Cir.1978). The detriment to the buyer is the same whether the seller diligently but unsuccessfully attempts to honor his promise or acts negligently or in bad faith.

Chatlos Systems, Inc. v. National Cash Register Corp., 635 F.2d 1081 (3d Cir.1980).

4. Besides a seller's refusal or inability to effect repairs, when might an exclusive repair-or-replace remedy fail of its essential purpose?

(a) Problem. Buyer purchases an SUV, pursuant to a contract that contains an express warranty of no defects and an exclusive repair-or-replace remedy. Six months after purchase, a defective $10 part in the steering mechanism causes Buyer to lose control and crash. The vehicle sustains $2,000 of damage, and the new HDTV that she is bringing home from the store is destroyed. Has the exclusive remedy failed of its essential purpose?

(b) Problem. Seller, an oil refiner, delivers petroleum to Buyer, a chemical company that produces resins, which it sells to manufacturers of floor tile, shoe soles, paint, and other products. The contract states that the seller's liability is limited to return of the purchase price and requires the buyer to inform the seller of any nonconformity within ten days after delivery. The petroleum is contaminated with a substance that causes the floor tile and other end products to emit a foul odor, rendering them unsaleable. Has the exclusive remedy failed of its essential purpose?

5. Sections 2–712, 2–713, and 2–714 each provides that the buyer may recover consequential damages. But 2–719(3) provides that, whether or not the parties agree on any remedies not found in Article 2, they are free to agree that in the event of the seller's breach, the seller is not liable for consequential damages. Please read subsection (3) now.

Problem. Seller delivers a diesel truck tractor to Buyer, who is a long-distance trucker. The contract provides:

> There are no warranties, expressed or implied, made by either the Dealer or the Manufacturer on new GMC motor vehicles, chassis or parts furnished under this Order except the Manufacturer's Warranty against defects in material and workmanship set out below:

> GMC, as Manufacturer, warrants each new motor vehicle, including all equipment and accessories (except tires and tubes), to be free from defects in material and workmanship under normal use and service; GMC's obligation under this warranty being limited to repairing or replacing at its option any part or parts thereof that shall, within twenty-four (24) months after delivery of the vehicle to the original retail purchaser, be returned to an authorized GMC Truck Dealer. The repair or replacement of defective parts under this warranty will be made by such Dealer without charge for parts and labor.

The vehicle has defect that Seller cannot repair within a reasonable time and number of attempts. Is Buyer entitled to resort to the remedies in Article 2? (What remedies might those be?)

Buyer claims that he was out of business numerous days while Seller attempted to repair the vehicle and that he lost $16,000 in net profits. Can Buyer recover the $16,000?

———

Smith v. Navistar International Transportation Corporation

United States Court of Appeals, Seventh Circuit, 1992.
957 F.2d 1439.

■ Coffey, Circuit Judge. . . . In 1984, Smith, an independent owner-operator of long distance trucks, decided to purchase a new truck, and Smith requested a list of sixteen options and/or components on the truck. After discussing the proposed purchase with several dealers, Smith decided to buy the Navistar semi-tractor truck Model 9370 as specified, from Jones (a Navistar authorized dealership), on November 7, 1984. . . .

Upon delivery of the truck Smith received an Owner's Limited Warranty booklet which in pertinent part read:

"[Navistar] will repair or replace any part of this vehicle which proves defective in material and/or workmanship in normal use and service, with new or ReNewed parts, for the first twelve months from new vehicle delivery date or for 50,000 miles (90,000 Km), whichever occurs first, except as specified under 'What is Not Covered.' "

On the second page of the Owner's Limited Warranty booklet are additional warranty disclaimers:

"NOTE: DISCLAIMER!

THERE ARE NO WARRANTIES WHICH EXTEND BEYOND THE DESCRIPTION ON THE FACE HEREOF. THIS WARRANTY IS IN LIEU OF ALL OTHER WARRANTIES, EXPRESSED OR IMPLIED. THE COMPANY SPECIFICALLY DISCLAIMS WARRANTIES OF *MERCHANTABILITY AND FITNESS FOR A PARTICULAR PURPOSE*, ALL OTHER REPRESENTATIONS TO THE FIRST USER/PURCHASER, AND ALL OTHER OBLIGATIONS OR LIABILITIES. THE COMPANY FURTHER EXCLUDES LIABILITY FOR INCIDENTAL AND CONSEQUENTIAL DAMAGES, ON THE PART OF THE COMPANY OR THE SELLER. No person is authorized to give any other warranties or to assume any liabilities on the Company's behalf unless made or assumed in writing by the seller." (emphasis in original). . . .

Some nine days after Smith's purchase of the truck, he experienced problems with the truck's braking system. On no fewer than ten separate occasions between November 7, 1984 and April 1985, Smith brought the truck to authorized Navistar dealers for repairs. Thus, the truck was out of service for a period of forty-five days.[3] Smith alleges that throughout the period of repair, the defendants were aware that he had a contract with one firm that he relied upon for his business and that if he was unable to operate his truck he would lose the contract. Notwithstanding Smith's dissatisfaction with the number and frequency of the alleged defects, Smith continued to use the truck during the problem time period and eventually ran up some 48,488 miles on it. On June 6, 1985, Smith sent a letter to the three named defendants expressing his intention to revoke his contract based upon his dissatisfaction with the final repair effort. At this same time Smith ceased making installment payments on the truck.

[Two years later Smith sued the seller, the manufacturer, and the lender that financed the purchase.] After extensive discovery, the defendants moved for summary judgment, and on January 27, 1989, the district court denied defendants' motion for summary judgment on the issue of liability, but granted defendants' motion as to damages . . . . The practical effect of this order was to limit the amount of damages a jury could award to $19,527.70, the amount Smith had paid for the truck prior to the revocation of his acceptance. [Ultimately, the court entered judgment for Smith for this amount.] Smith appeals.

. . .

---

3. Neither Navistar nor any of its dealers ever refused to work on Smith's truck, and Smith was never charged for any of the repairs undertaken.

Illinois law applies in this diversity action, and the transaction is governed under Article 2 of the Uniform Commercial Code. The plaintiff Smith argues that, because this is a diversity action, the district court was required to determine the applicable law of the State of Illinois when determining whether the plaintiff was entitled to consequential damages. The plaintiff contends that because, "the Illinois Supreme Court has not addressed the issue in question, the district court was required to use the predictive approach and in applying this approach, the district court disregarded the sole Illinois appellate decision on point and chose a resolution having no basis in Illinois law."

Our review of the district court's grant of partial summary judgment in favor of the defendants is de novo: "We must decide whether the record shows that there is no genuine issue of material fact and that the moving party is entitled to judgment as a matter of law." Dribeck Importers v. G. Heileman Brewing Co., 883 F.2d 569, 573 (7th Cir.1989) (citations omitted). In its denial of partial summary judgment, the district court cited two conflicting cases which dealt with the issue of whether consequential damages could be awarded when a limited warranty failed to provide the protection the buyer expected. The first of these cases was a decision of an intermediate appellate court, Adams v. J.I. Case Co., 125 Ill. App. 2d 388, 261 N.E.2d 1 (4th Dist.1970). The second was a decision of this court, AES Technology Systems, Inc. v. Coherent Radiation, 583 F.2d 933 (7th Cir. 1978). Smith in essence argues that the district court erred in granting partial summary judgment because it chose to follow *AES* rather than *Adams*. However, federal courts are not bound by the decision of a lower state court unless the state's highest court in the jurisdiction whose law governs the diversity action has ruled on the matter.

Smith's signature on the Retail Order would ordinarily constitute an effective waiver of any right to recover incidental and consequential damages arising from the loss of his single employment contract.[6] However, the U.C.C. provides that "where circumstances cause an exclusive or limited remedy to fail of its essential purpose, remedy may be had as provided in this Act." Ill. Rev. Stat. ch. 26, § 2-719(2). In *Adams*, the Illinois Appellate Court adopted a categorical approach and held that the seller's breach of a limited warranty to repair or replace defective tractor parts automatically exposes the seller to liability for the buyer's consequential damages despite an otherwise enforceable disclaimer:

> "The limitations of remedy and of liability are not separable from the obligations of the warranty. Repudiation of the obligations of the warranty destroyed its benefits. . . . It should be obvious that they cannot at once repudiate their obligation under the warranty and assert its provisions beneficial to them."

Adams, 261 N.E.2d at 7-8.

---

6. . . . [T]he Retail Order, as well as the owner's manual that Smith received, disclaimed any warranties of merchantability and fitness for a particular purpose and any liability for incidental and consequential damages.

However, in *AES*, this court rejected the categorical approach enunciated in Adams, and refused to automatically sever a consequential damage disclaimer from a contract merely on the failure of a limited warranty to provide the benefits that the parties bargained for:

"Some courts have awarded consequential damages, when a remedy failed of its essential purpose, in the face of prohibitions in the contract against consequential damages. However, we reject the contention that failure of the essential purpose of the limited remedy automatically means that a damage award will include consequential damages. An analysis to determine whether consequential damages are warranted must carefully examine the individual factual situation including the type of goods involved, the parties and the precise nature and purpose of the contract. The purpose of the courts in contractual disputes is not to re-write contracts by ignoring parties; intent; rather, it is to interpret the existing contract as fairly as possible when all events did not occur as planned."

AES, 583 F.2d at 941 (footnote omitted) (emphasis added).

Other courts have similarly adopted this case-by-case approach. In Chatlos Systems v. National Cash Register Corp., 635 F.2d 1081 (3d Cir.1980), the court held that the failure of the essential purpose of a limited remedy does not automatically mean that a damage award will include consequential damages:

"New Jersey has not taken a position on this question, so in this diversity case we must predict which view the New Jersey Supreme Court would adopt if the question were presented to it.

It appears to us that the better reasoned approach is to treat the consequential damage disclaimer as an independent provision, valid unless unconscionable. This poses no logical difficulties. A contract may well contain no limitation on breach of warranty damages but specifically exclude consequential damages. Conversely, it is quite conceivable that some limitation might be placed on a breach of warranty award, but consequential damages would expressly be permitted.

The limited remedy of repair and a consequential damages exclusion are two discrete ways of attempting to limit recovery for breach of warranty. The Code, moreover, tests each by a different standard. The former survives unless it fails of its essential purpose, while the latter is valid unless it is unconscionable. We therefore see no reason to hold, as a general proposition, that the failure of the limited remedy provided in the contract, without more, invalidates a wholly distinct term in the agreement excluding consequential damages. The two are not mutually exclusive."

Id. at 1086 (footnotes and citations omitted).

Similarly, in S.M. Wilson & Co. v. Smith International, Inc., 587 F.2d 1363 (9th Cir.1978) (California law), the court determined that consequential damages were not warranted even though the limited repair warranty failed to achieve its essential purpose:

> "The issue remains whether the failure of the limited repair remedy to serve its purpose requires permitting the recovery of consequential damages . . . . We hold it does not. In reaching this conclusion we are influenced heavily by the characteristics of the contract between [seller] and [buyer] . . . . Parties of relatively equal bargaining power negotiated an allocation of their risks of loss. Consequential damages were assigned to the buyer, Wilson. The machine was a complex piece of equipment designed for the buyer's purposes. The seller Smith did not ignore his obligation to repair; he simply was unable to perform it. This is not enough to require that the seller absorb losses the buyer plainly agreed to bear. Risk shifting is socially expensive and should not be undertaken in the absence of a good reason. An even better reason is required when to so shift is contrary to a contract freely negotiated. The default of the seller is not so total and fundamental as to require that its consequential damages limitation be expunged from the contract."

Id. at 1375.

We believe the district court's reliance on *AES* rather than *Adams* was correct. The case-by-case approach adopted by *AES* and the other decisions allows some measure of certainty in that parties of relatively equal bargaining power can allocate all of the risks that may accompany a breach of warranty, and prevents the court from upsetting that allocation upon a breach of contractual duties. Moreover, in those situations where the limited warranty fails to provide the benefits that the buyer expected (i.e., to repair or replace defective parts) and the parties are clearly on unequal terms with respect to relative bargaining power, the case-by-case approach enunciated in *AES* enables the courts to examine "the intent of the parties, as gleaned from the express provisions of the contract and the factual background" to determine whether consequential damages are warranted, rather than automatically exposing the seller to liability for consequential damages despite an otherwise valid disclaimer. *AES*, 583 F.2d at 941. Thus, we agree with the district court that the rationale underlying *AES* and the other decisions adopting the case-by-case approach is more compelling than the categorical approach enunciated in Adams.

Smith also argues that "even if the district court was correct in the approach that it chose, the case-by-case approach, it misapplied that approach." Smith contends that the district court failed to analyze "all of the attendant objective facts and circumstances, including the language of the agreement, the relative bargaining power of the parties and the commercial context of the transaction" in order to determine which party should bear the risk of consequential damages. In our opinion, this argument is without merit as the district court noted that Smith failed to present any evidence in opposition to the damages awarded in the summary judgment motion. Moreover, our review of the record reveals that at the time Smith purchased the truck he was an experienced operator of long-distance trucks and had visited at least six different truck dealers in Indiana and Illinois, and had drawn up a list of sixteen specifications for the truck that he felt met his specific need. Having refused to accept any truck that did not meet his list of sixteen requirements, Smith presented the necessary components and options to defendant Jones, who offered the plaintiff-appellant the Navistar truck that met his specifications. At the time of purchase, Smith signed a Retail Order specifically excluding liability on the part of the seller for incidental and consequential damages:

> "THIS WARRANTY IS IN LIEU OF ALL OTHER WARRANTIES, EXPRESSED OR IMPLIED, INCLUDING WITHOUT LIMITATION, WARRANTIES OF MERCHANTABILITY AND FITNESS FOR PARTICULAR PURPOSE, ALL OTHER REPRESENTATIONS TO THE FIRST USER PURCHASER, AND ALL OTHER OBLIGATIONS OR LIABILITIES, INCLUDING LIABILITY FOR INCIDENTAL AND CONSEQUENTIAL DAMAGES ON THE PART OF THE COMPANY OR THE SELLER."

Moreover, Smith accepted a warranty which also clearly excluded seller liability for incidental and consequential damages in a section set off with the words, "NOTE: DISCLAIMER!" Smith read the terms and conditions of the warranty and failed to ask any questions regarding the terms of the Retail Order or warranty before signing the same. We have failed to discover evidence in the record that the parties intended that the defendants bear the risk of consequential damages or that the parties' relative bargaining power was so unequal that the disclaimer was unconscionable and we refuse to re-write the contract including the Retail Order's clear exclusion of consequential damages.

. . .

The decision of the district court is AFFIRMED.

QUESTIONS AND NOTES

1. What warranty did defendants allegedly breach?

2. The court rejects the conclusion that if the exclusive remedy fails of its essential purpose, the buyer necessarily can recover consequential damages, when the contract contains a separate term specifically excluding liability for consequential damages. Rather, the recoverability of consequential damages must be determined on a case-by-case approach. By what standard is the court to determine whether the buyer may recover consequential damages in the particular case before it?

3. In Milgard Tempering, Inc. v. Selas Corp., 902 F.2d 703 (9th Cir.1990), the buyer paid $1.45 million for a furnace for tempering glass. The design of the furnace was complex, and the parties contemplated it would take several months after delivery to get it to work properly. The contract limited the buyer's remedy to repair or replacement and specifically excluded liability for consequential damages. Three years after the scheduled delivery date, the furnace still did not operate as warranted. In the buyer's suit for lost profits, the court held that the exclusive remedy had failed of its essential purpose. As to the buyer's ability to recover lost profits notwithstanding the exclusion of them in the contract, the court stated:

> The task before the district court was to examine the remedy provisions and determine whether Selas' default caused a loss which was not part of the bargained-for allocation of risk. . . . We agree with the district court's decision to lift the cap on consequential damages. Milgard did not agree to pay $1.45 million in order to participate in a science experiment. It agreed to purchase what Selas represented as a cutting-edge glass furnace that would accommodate its needs after two months of debugging. Selas' inability to effect repair despite 2.5 years of intense . . . effort caused Milgard losses not part of the bargained-for allocation of risk. Therefore, the cap on consequential damages is unenforceable.

4. In the commercial setting, the most commonly occurring example of consequential damages is lost profits. In the consumer context, of course, the buyer cannot incur that kind of loss. Besides personal injuries, what kinds of loss might be within the definition of consequential damages in 2–715(2)?

5. Problem. Buyer purchases a lathe for its factory. The contract provides:

> Seller warrants this product against defects in manufacture. This is the only warranty made by Seller, and Seller expressly disclaims all implied warranties. Seller will repair or replace any parts that prove defective within 24 months after the product is first placed in service. Repair or replacement of defective parts is Buyer's exclusive remedy under this warranty.

The lathe breaks down, and Buyer wants to return it. Seller insists on repair. Buyer consults you to determine if she can force Seller to take it back or can get damages, or must she allow Seller to attempt repair. What do you advise?

6. Please look at 2–714. Subsection (2) states the measure of damages for breach of warranty. Subsection (3) states that the buyer may recover incidental and consequential damages "in a proper case." What is "a proper case"? Compare 2–712(2) and 2–713(1).

In Beal v. General Motors Corp., 354 F.Supp. 423 (D.Del.1973), the court addressed this issue:

> Few courts have spoken to the question what is a "proper case" for the award of consequential damages within the contemplation of § 2–714(3). The Pennsylvania Supreme Court in the case of Keystone Diesel Engine Company v. Irwin, 411 Pa. 222, 191 A.2d 376 (1963) relied on pre-Code common law principles in holding that:

"Special circumstances" entitling the buyer to damages in excess of the difference between the value as warranted and the value as accepted exist where the buyer has communicated to the seller at the time of entering into the contract sufficient facts to make it apparent that the damages subsequently claimed were within the reasonable contemplation of the parties. Wolstenholme, Inc. v. Jos. Randall & Bro., 295 Pa. 131, 144 A. 909 (1929). * * *

In the *Birdsboro* case this test was construed as requiring a tacit agreement that consequential damage would be recoverable:

> * * * Under Pennsylvania interpretation of the general Code provisions dealing with damages, therefore, the plaintiff, in order to collect damages in excess of the difference between the value of the goods as warranted and as accepted, must prove that the seller was on notice of the fact that the plaintiff would hold it responsible for any loss of profit or loss due to "down time" arising from the inability to use the machinery and equipment in question. Jones & McKnight Corp. v. Birdsboro Corporation, 320 F.Supp. 39, 45 (N.D.Ill.1970).

The "tacit agreement" concept has elsewhere been rejected, however. In the Illinois case of Adams v. J.I. Case Co., 125 Ill.App.2d 388, 261 N.E.2d 1 (1970), the court, relying on the statutory language of § 2–715(2) opted for a different test:

> * * * In their Official Comment upon UCC 2–715(2) its framers make it clear that the "tacit agreement" test for the recovery of consequential damages is rejected. The language of that section should not be so narrowly construed as to require a prior understanding or agreement that the seller would be bound for consequential damages in the event of his breach. If that is the holding * * * of Keystone * * * it must be rejected. The Official Comment further states that the older Common Law rule which made the seller liable for all consequential damages of which he had "reason to know" in advance is followed, modified to require reasonable prevention of loss by cover or otherwise. The Code provision and the Official Comment makes it clear that strictures are not to be applied to the plain meaning of the Code by adherence to what the parties may have agreed or contemplated at the time of sale. * * *

> ... [This court adopts] the test of the *Adams* case. Under that test, the question then is whether the loss for which recovery is sought is one that results from general or particular requirements or needs of which the seller at the time of contracting had reason to know. If it is, then consequential damages are proper provided that those damages could not have been reasonably prevented by action of the buyer.

What is the flaw in this reasoning? What is the proper analysis?

7. Lemon laws. Every state has enacted a so-called lemon law to provide relief to purchasers of defective motor vehicles. The impetus to these laws was a shortcoming of 2–719. Granted, subsection (2) provides that if an exclusive remedy fails of its essential purpose, the buyer may pursue all Article 2 remedies. But it does not provide any standard for when an exclusive remedy fails of its essential purpose. The historic attitude of the automobile manufacturers was to offer repeated repairs, no matter how many prior attempts they had made and no matter how long a vehicle may have been out of service for repairs.

One great innovation of the lemon laws is to establish a bright-line test, typically an alternative test of either four attempts to repair a single defect or the vehicle's being out of service for more than 30 days during the first year after its purchase. There is considerable variation among the states concerning the precise details of this standard. For example, some have specified the number of repair attempts as three or five; some have extended the one-year period to 18 or 24 months.

The other great innovation of the lemon laws is to eliminate the bar of privity and enable the buyer in effect to revoke acceptance as against the remote manufacturer.

9. Revised Article 2. To repeat Question 1 on page 446 above, what warranty did the seller breach? Whether or not it is possible to identify a warranty, the seller undoubtedly made a promise to repair or replace. That promise traditionally has been viewed as a part of the warranty obligation of the seller. Therefore, some courts have applied the warranty statute of limitations to enforcement of repair-or-replacement promises. Under the general rule of 2–725, the statute of limitations starts running when tender of delivery is made. This means that the four-year statute of limitations might have run before the seller failed to perform its repair or replacement promise. Other courts have measured the limitations period from the time the seller breaches the promise to repair or replace.

Revised Article 2 addresses that problem by creating a new statutory concept, a "remedial promise." Remedial promise is defined in revised 2–103(n) as "a promise by the seller to repair or replace the goods or to refund all or part of the price of goods upon the happening of a specified event." Revised 2–725(c) provides that "For breach of a remedial promise, a right of action accrues when the remedial promise is not performed when performance is due."

You may have noticed that revised 2–313, 2–313A, 2–313B, and 2–318 also refer to remedial promises. Those references assure that remedial promises run to remote parties to the same extent as the "obligations" under 2–313A and 2–313B, and to the same extent as the warranties or obligations under 2–318.

CHAPTER 7

Seller's Remedies for Breach by the Buyer

A. Introduction

A buyer may breach, among other ways, by not making a payment when it is due, by repudiating the contract, or by wrongfully rejecting the goods or revoking acceptance of them. Section 2–703 is a catalog of the seller's remedies if one of these events occurs. Subsection (e) specifies the principal damages remedies of the seller: the contract-market differential (analogous to the buyer's remedy under 2–713) and the action for the price. Please read 2–703 and 2–709.

B. Remedies on Wrongful Rejection or Repudiation

1. Action for the Price

Industrial Molded Plastic Products, Inc. v. J. Gross & Son, Inc.

Pennsylvania Superior Court, 1979.
263 Pa.Super. 515, 398 A.2d 695.

■ HOFFMAN, JUDGE. This is a breach of contract action brought by Industrial Molded Plastic Products, Inc. (Industrial) against J. Gross & Son, Inc. (Gross). In a non-jury trial below, the court awarded Industrial $2,494.52 damages representing lost profits. Industrial now contends that the proper measure of damages was the contract price of the goods. Gross has cross-appealed on the issue of liability, contending that the salesman who signed the contract lacked the authority to bind the corporate entity.

Industrial is in the business of manufacturing custom injection molded plastics by specification for various manufacturers. Industrial also manufactures various "fill-in" items during slack periods, such as electronic parts, industrial components, mirror clips, and plastic clothing clips. Industrial manufactured plastic clothing clips only for its house accounts of H. Daroff & Sons and Joseph H. Cohen & Sons. Gross is a wholesaler to the retail clothing industry, selling mostly sewing thread, but also other items such as zippers, snaps, and clips. Gross sold only a small amount of plastic clothing clips, never having more than $100–$200 worth of clips in inventory at any one time.

Sometime in the fall of 1970, Mr. Stanley Waxman (Gross' President and sole stockholder) and his son Peter (a 22 year old salesman for Gross) appeared at the offices of Industrial's President, Mr. Judson T. Ulansey. They suggested to him that they might be able to market Industrial's plastic clothing clips in the retail clothing industry, in which they had an established sales force. At this initial meeting, there was no discussion of Peter Waxman's authority or lack thereof in the company. After this meeting, Stanley authorized Peter to purchase a "trial" amount of clips (not further specified) to test the market, but neither this authorization nor its limitation was communicated to Ulansey. All subsequent negotiations were between Ulansey and Peter Waxman only. Deceiving both his father and Ulansey, Peter held himself out as Vice–President of Gross, and on December 10, 1970, signed an agreement obligating Gross to purchase from Industrial five million plastic clothing clips during the calendar year of 1971, at a price of $7.50 per thousand units, delivery at Industrial's plant in Blooming Glen, Pennsylvania. Gross was granted an exclusive distributorship in the clips for the same time, excepting Industrial's two house accounts mentioned above. Before the execution of this agreement, Ulansey telephoned Stanley Waxman, who told Ulansey that Peter could act on behalf of Gross. There was no discussion of the specific terms of the agreement, such as the quantity purchased.

Industrial immediately began production of the five million clips during "fill-in" time. As they were manufactured, they were warehoused in Industrial's plant as per the contract. In February, 1971, Peter Waxman picked up and paid for 772,000 clips. Stanley Waxman, who had to sign Gross' check for payment, thought that this was the "trial amount" he had authorized Peter to buy. These were the only clips which Gross ever took into its possession. On numerous occasions during the year Ulansey urged Peter to pick up more of the clips, which were taking up more and more storage space at Industrial's plant as they were being manufactured. Peter told Ulansey that he was having difficulty selling the clips and that Gross had no warehousing capacity for the inventory that was being accumulated. At no time, however, did Peter repudiate the contract or request Industrial to halt production. By the end of 1971, production was completed and Industrial was warehousing 4,228,000 clips at its plant.

On January 19, 1972, Industrial sent Gross an invoice for the remaining clips of $31,710, less credit of $203.55, for a balance due of $31,506.45. However, Gross did not honor the invoice or pick up any more of the clips. Ulansey wrote to Stanley Waxman on February 7, 1972, requesting him to pick up the clips. Receiving no response, Ulansey wrote to Stanley Waxman again on February 23, 1972, threatening legal action if shipping instructions were not received by March 1, 1972. Finally, on March 30, 1972, Peter Waxman responded with a letter to Ulansey, which stated that Gross' failure to move the clips was due to a substantial decline in the clothing industry in 1971 and competition with new lower-cost methods of hanging and shipping clothes. The letter asked for Industrial's patience and predicted that it would take at least the rest of the year to market the clips successfully. At this point, Industrial initiated legal action. Stanley Waxman learned of the five million clip contract for the first time when informed by his lawyer of the impending lawsuit. Industrial filed its complaint in August of 1972, and at the same time Peter began an extended (four years) leave of absence from Gross.

Ulansey testified that Industrial was unable to resell any of the 4.2 million clips because of a lack of market generally. Additionally, Industrial lost its two house accounts for plastic clothing clips because Daroff went bankrupt and Cohen refused to do further business with Industrial, citing a close personal relationship with Stanley Waxman. Industrial, being a manufacturer, had no sales force to find new customers. However, Industrial did receive a small quantity of new orders from 1972 to 1976, for which new clips were manufactured.

. . .

Industrial contends that the court below erred in entering judgment based upon its lost profits, on the grounds that the proper measure of damages was the unpaid balance of the contract price. The court below limited damages to lost profits because it found in fact that Industrial "did not make a good faith or reasonable effort to resell the goods * * * nor did he demonstrate the futility of any resale attempt."

It is true that in order to maintain an action for the contract price of goods which are merely *identified,* the seller must mitigate damages or show that such effort would be unavailing. Uniform Commercial Code, 12A PS § 2–709(1)(b). However, a seller of goods is also entitled to recover the contract price due for goods *accepted* by the buyer. 12A PS § 2–709(1)(a). Under the Code, a buyer's acceptance of goods occurs, inter alia, when, after a reasonable opportunity to inspect the goods, the buyer fails to make an effective rejection of them. 12A PS § 2–606(1)(b). To preserve his rights, the seller is only obligated to tender the goods in accordance with the terms of the contract. 12A PS § 2–507(1). The seller is under no obligation to resell accepted goods in order to maintain his action for price. 12A PS § 2–709(1)(a). See generally Unlaub Co., Inc. v. Sexton, 568 F.2d 72, 76–77 (8th Cir.1977).

Here, Industrial wholly performed its obligations under the contract, manufacturing five million clips and delivering them to its plant in Blooming Glen, Pennsylvania. For over a year, Industrial entreated Gross to take possession of the growing pile of clips. Thus, Gross had ample opportunity to inspect, but never rejected the goods. In fact, even as late as March 30, 1972, Gross still indicated that it intended to market the clips, but would need more time to do so. As such, Gross accepted the clips and breached its contract by failure to pay for them. Since the goods were accepted, Industrial is entitled to the full unpaid balance of the contract price, notwithstanding its failure to attempt to resell the clips.

The order below is reversed and the court below is directed to enter judgment in favor of Industrial against Gross for $31,506.45, plus interest from January 19, 1972.

QUESTIONS AND NOTES

1.   By failing to reject the clips for more than ten months, the buyer accepted them and was liable for the price. A similar result may occur even if the delay in the buyer's action is much less than that. Consider N. Bloom & Son (Antiques) Limited v. Skelly, 673 F.Supp. 1260 (S.D.N.Y.1987). In August 1985 Skelly purchased two candelabras and a centerpiece from Bloom in London, England, for $45,000, delivery at Skelly's home in Newport, R.I. Bloom's carrier, Artworld, made several attempts to deliver the goods in September but Skelly was not at home, did not authorize anyone to receive the goods on her behalf, and did not respond to Artworld's written notices of its attempts to deliver. On October 1st Skelly instructed Artworld to return the goods to Bloom. Two weeks later she informed Bloom that she was rejecting the items because an appraiser had looked at photographs of them and had informed her that they were not worth the price she had agreed to pay. Bloom sued Skelly for the price. Upholding the seller's claim, the court stated:

> Skelly contends that she never accepted the candelabras and centerpiece, and that instead she rejected them. This distinction affects the measure of damages. The measure of damages in a case of non-acceptance is the difference between the contract price and the market price at the time and place of tender, or lost profits. N.Y.U.C.C. § 2–708. In a case in which goods are accepted but not paid for, the seller may bring an action for the full contract price. N.Y.U.C.C. § 2–709(1)(a).

> N.Y.U.C.C. § 2–507(1) provides:

> > Tender of delivery is a condition to the buyer's duty to accept the goods and, unless otherwise agreed, to his duty to pay for them. *Tender entitles the seller to acceptance of the goods and to payment according to the contract.* [emphasis added]

> The requirements for an effective tender are set forth in § 2–503(1):

> > Tender of delivery requires that the seller put and hold conforming goods at the buyer's disposition and give the buyer any notification reasonably necessary to enable him to take delivery. The manner, time and place for tender are determined by the agreement and this Article, and in particular

> > (a) tender must be at a reasonable hour, and if it is of goods they must be kept available for the period reasonably necessary to enable the buyer to take possession . . . .

> Bloom, through Artworld, attempted on several occasions to deliver the candelabras and centerpiece to Skelly's home in Newport, as the parties had agreed. Although Skelly herself was not present when tender was made, she could have authorized someone else to accept delivery on her behalf. She could also have responded to the notices left by Artworld, in order to arrange a time for delivery when she would be

present. She did neither because she had decided not to accept delivery. Since Bloom made proper tender of the goods pursuant to § 2–503(1), it is entitled to acceptance pursuant to § 2–507(1).

Acceptance is also governed by § 2–606(1), which provides:

Acceptance of goods occurs when the buyer . . .

(b) fails to make an effective rejection (subsection (1) of Section 2–602), but such acceptance does not occur until the buyer has had a reasonable opportunity to inspect them . . . .

Section 2–602(1) mandates that "[r]ejection of goods must be within a reasonable time after their . . . tender." The determination of what constitutes a reasonable time period depends on the particular circumstances of each case and is generally a question of fact. In this case, Skelly, after being informed of Artworld's attempts to deliver the candelabras and centerpiece throughout September 1985, did not take any active steps to reject them until October 1. Under the circumstances, this was not within a "reasonable time" after tender under § 2–602(1). During the month of September 1985, Skelly did have a "reasonable opportunity to inspect" the goods under § 2–606(1). Skelly proffered no good reason for her repeated failure to take delivery of the goods. Had she done so, an inspection could have been accomplished in a matter of minutes.

Skelly's argument that she cannot be held to have accepted the goods because she did not inspect them, as she has a right to do under N.Y.U.C.C. § 2–513, is untenable. Section 2–513(1), like the N.Y.U.C.C. provisions discussed above, provides a right of inspection "at any reasonable place and time and in any reasonable manner." This provision does not mean that if a buyer chooses not to inspect the goods, she thereby acquires a defense of non-inspection. By refusing to respond to Artworld's repeated attempts at delivery, Skelly gave up her right of inspection, and thus accepted the goods. Under N.Y.U.C.C. § 2–709(1)(a), the amount Bloom may recover is therefore the full contract price of $45,000.

2. If the buyer has received conforming goods and refuses or fails to pay for them, it makes sense for 2–709 to give the seller an action for the price. But in neither *Industrial Molded Plastic Products* nor *N. Bloom & Son* did the buyer have the goods or want the goods. Granted, the buyers breached, and the sellers are entitled to damages to place them in their expectancy positions. But they still have the goods and presumably can resell them to other buyers. What, then, is the sense in saying that they can recover the price?

3. What could the buyers in these cases have done to avoid being held liable for the price?

4. Problem. Radcliff Manufacturing Co., of Denver, Colorado, contracted to sell 5,000 electric knives to Rearson, Inc., a large retailer located in Phoenix, at a price of $50,000. A half hour after delivery at Rearson's warehouse in Phoenix, Rearson sent Radcliff an e-mail stating that the knives were being rejected because the handles were not the proper color. In fact, the knives conformed to the contract in every respect. May Radcliff recover the price of the knives from Rearson? Are 2–401(2) and (4) relevant?

5.   Problem. Buyer contracts with a furrier for a natural, alabaster-colored mink coat to be specially made for her in an extra large size and with an unusually large flare, for $7,500. After the coat is made, she announces that she no longer desires it. Seller makes no effort to resell the coat, but sues for the price. Is he entitled to it?

[handwritten margin note: 2–709 (1) (b) / good identified / → circumstances indicate / that effort to resell / will be unavailing]

6.   Problem. Assume in Problem 4 above that Rearson's trademark had been molded into the handles of the knives. Would 2–709(1)(b) enable Radcliff to recover the price?

(In connection with this question, consider McCoy v. Mitsuboshi Cutlery, Inc., 67 F.3d 917 (Fed.Cir.1995). The holder of a patent on a shrimp knife contracted for a manufacturer to fabricate and deliver 150,000 of the knives. When the buyer refused to accept delivery of the knives or pay for them, the seller resold them to another. In rejecting the buyer's claim that the seller had violated its patent, the court held that the seller had an implied license to sell and was not liable for violating the buyer's patent. How does this case affect Radcliff's right to recover the price?)

Now assume that the knives did not have the Rearson trademark and Rearson held them for two weeks before notifying Radcliff that it was returning the knives? Is Radcliff entitled to the price?

Would it help Rearson to point to 2–608? See 2–709(3).

7.   Leases. Problem. Lessor leases to Lessee a road-grading machine for 24 months at a rental of $2,000 per month. The contract provides that if Lessee fails to make any monthly payment within 30 days of the date it is due, Lessor has the option to treat the transaction as a sale of the machine to Lessee for $84,000, which is the price that Lessor had paid to acquire the machine. After nine months, Lessee defaults. If Lessor does not assert any rights under the treat-as-a-sale provision, what is Lessor's remedy? See 2A–529.

If Lessor does assert rights under that provision, what is the remedy? Is the contract provision enforceable? See 2A–503, 2A–504, 2A–523, 2A–528, 2A–529.

Suppose Lessor argues that the provision is enforceable, that Lessee cannot rightfully reject the goods after nine months, and that, therefore, Lessor is entitled to the price. What is Lessor's remedy? See 2A–529.

Suppose Lessor argues that the provision is enforceable but agrees that it will take back the machine and sue for its damages as seller. Is the clause enforceable? See 2A–503, 2A–504, 2A–523.

8.   CISG. Article 62 of Convention on Contracts for the International Sale of Goods provides "The seller may require the buyer to pay the price, take delivery or perform his other obligations, unless the seller has resorted to a remedy which is inconsistent with this requirement." Therefore, the basic rule of CISG is the direct opposite of the Article 2 rule. (See Official Comment 6 to 2–709.) As noted earlier, however, CISG Article 28 provides that a state does not have to grant specific performance of the contract if it would not do so under similar circumstances under its own law. See also Articles 85 and 88. It may be doubted whether in practice there are any significant number of cases in which international sellers would try to force goods on buyers if the buyer repudiates before the goods have been shipped. If the goods have been shipped, the widespread use of letters of credit moots the issue. A letter of credit represents an irrevocable commitment of a third party to pay the seller upon presentation of documents showing shipment of goods. Hence, buyers in international transactions cannot avoid paying the price by rejecting the goods. Chapter 11 provides an introduction to letters of credit.

2.   Action for Damages

As the problems in the preceding section indicate, the seller has only a very limited right to recover the price from a reluctant buyer who does not have the goods. Notice, by the way, that passage of title has nothing to do with the seller's right to recover the price, as 2–401 provides, "Each provision of this Article with regard to the rights, obligations and remedies of the seller, the buyer, purchasers or other third parties applies irrespective of title to the goods except where the provision refers to such title." Therefore, even if title already has passed to the buyer, the seller can recover the price and force the goods on the buyer only in the situations described in 2–709.

The seller's basic remedy, then, for a buyer's unjustified rejection of goods is recovery of damages (as distinguished from recovery of the price), and in recovering damages, the seller typically has the choice of two measures:

(1) the contract price less the market price at the time and place for tender, under 2–708(1), or

(2) upon resale of the goods to another buyer, the contract price less the resale price, under 2–706.

Alternatively, in some circumstances the seller is entitled to recover the lost profit on the transaction, under 2–708(2). What are those circumstances? Please read 2–708.

QUESTIONS

1.   Problem. On February 1st of the current year, Buyer contracts to purchase 120,000 pounds of yarn from Seller, a manufacturer of yarn, for $4.00 per pound. Buyer is a manufacturer of clothing and needs yarn to produce sweaters. Seller is to deliver 20,000 pounds every six months, on June 1st and December 1st of this year and the next two years. Buyer is to pay for each installment no later than 30 days after delivery. On June 1st of the current year, Seller delivers and Buyer pays for 20,000 pounds. On December 1st of the current year, Seller delivers another 20,000 pounds, which Buyer accepts. Two weeks later, on December 15th, Buyer informs Seller that it has decided to cease manufacturing sweaters and will not take any more yarn. On February 1st of the next year, Seller sues.

    a. The market price of yarn varies over time. On the following dates in the current year, it is:

February 1: $3.95 per pound

June 1: $3.90

December 1: $3.85

December 15: $3.65

On February 1st of the next year, when Seller sues: $3.75.

How should Seller's damages be measured?

    b. When Buyer repudiates the contract, Seller ceases manufacturing the yarn. Assume that Buyer can prove that if Seller had completed manufacturing the yarn for Buyer, its costs of production would have been $3.80 per pound. Should Seller recover $.35 per pound or $.20 per pound for the yarn that was never delivered? Is 1–106 (revised 1–305) relevant?

    c. In 2–713(1) how does the phrase, "less expenses saved in consequence of the buyer's breach," affect the answer to Problem a?

2. Problem. Seller has a contract to purchase its requirements of gasoline additive for $400 per ton. Seller contracts to sell Buyer 1,000 tons of the gasoline additive for $450 per ton. Before Seller delivers any of the additive to Buyer, the market price drops to $350 per ton and Buyer repudiates the contract. When Seller sues, how should its damages be measured?

3. Problem. On January 20, 2007, Buyer contracts to purchase a 2006 Chrysler 300 from Dealer for $36,000, delivery on February 1st, the day after she is to receive her annual bonus. On January 26th Buyer decides she would rather have a Toyota Avalon and therefore fails to return to Dealer's lot on February 1st. When Dealer phones her, she explains that she no longer wants the car. Dealer insists that she complete the purchase, but Buyer is adamant. Dealer informs her, "I'm holding you responsible for the car, and if you don't pick it up and pay me by February 7th, I'll sell it to someone else and hold you responsible for my damages." On March 20th Dealer sells the car at an auction attended by dealers from a four-state region. The successful bidder pays $28,000, of which the auction company retains $300 for its services in selling the car. How should Dealer's recovery be measured?

4. Problem. Buyer, the owner of a tavern, contracts to purchase a large-screen TV from Seller for $2,600, to be delivered to Buyer's tavern. When Seller's delivery truck arrives with the TV, Buyer states that he has found a better TV at a lower price, and he refuses to accept the TV. The truck driver returns the TV to Seller. Without further communicating with

Buyer, Seller sells the TV during her semiannual clearance sale, for $2,000. How should Seller's damages be measured?

5. Proof of the market price at the relevant time may be difficult. For long-term contracts 2–723 helps to ease the difficulties of proof. Alternatively, the seller may avoid the problem by reselling the goods under 2–706 and recovering damages based on the resale price rather than the market price. Notice the specific requirements for that resale, especially the requirement that the seller notify the breaching buyer of the anticipated sale.

Tesoro Petroleum Corp. v. Holborn Oil Co., Ltd.

New York Supreme Court, New York County, 1989.
145 Misc.2d 715, 547 N.Y.S.2d 1012.

■ LEHNER, J. [Defendant contracted to purchase 10 million gallons of gasoline at $1.30 per gallon from plaintiff, who had acquired it a few days earlier for $1.26 per gallon. Plaintiff notified defendant of the name of the vessel that would deliver the gasoline in New York, but defendant, evidently reacting to a sudden sharp decline in the market price, repudiated the contract. Plaintiff thereupon sold the gasoline on the specified ship to another purchaser, Esso Sapa, in Argentina for $1.10 per gallon. Plaintiff sued to recover the excess of the contract price ($1.30 per gallon) over the market price at the time for tender ($.80 per gallon). Defendant claimed that plaintiff was not entitled to more than the excess of the contract price ($1.30 per gallon) over the resale price ($1.10 per gallon). Thus, plaintiff's recovery would be either $5 million or $2 million. Both parties moved for partial summary judgment.]

Plaintiff justifies this recovery by asserting that it, rather than the defaulting buyer, is entitled to the benefit of its ability to resell the gasoline at above market price. Although the price for which one actually sells merchandise is evidence as to its market value, and there is no explanation as to why Esso Sapa was willing to pay a premium of about 40% above market to obtain this cargo, the question as to the actual market value is not raised for determination on this motion.

Plaintiff maintains that since gasoline is fungible, it, as a dealer in that commodity, could have made a profit not only on the sale to defendant, but also could have purchased gasoline on the open market and made a second profit on the resale to Esso Sapa. Hence it asserts (putting aside incidental damages) that by recovering damages of $.50 per gallon (assuming a market price of $.80 per gallon at the time) from defendant, it will be in the same position as if defendant had complied with its alleged contract and accepted the gasoline and paid $1.30 per gallon. . . . To support its position, plaintiff relies on U.C.C. § 2–703 as giving it the option to proceed against a defaulting buyer under either § 2–706 or § 2–708.

Defendant, on the other hand, asserts that if plaintiff establishes a breach, its damages should be limited to its actual loss resulting therefrom, which would be $.20 per gallon plus incidental damages. In this regard defendant points to U.C.C. § 1–106, which it asserts sets forth the policy of the Code to place an aggrieved party in as good a position as if the other party had fully performed, and contends that granting plaintiff the profit it seeks would result in a windfall which would be inconsistent with such policy. Further, defendant maintains that permitting plaintiff to choose its remedy to maximize its damages would be inconsistent with the requirement that a party mitigate damages.

. . .

Although the Official Comment to § 2–703 states that the "Article rejects any doctrine of election of remedy as a fundamental policy and thus the remedies are essentially cumulative in nature," it concludes that "(w)hether the pursuit of one remedy bars another depends entirely on the facts of the individual case."

In White & Summers, 1 Uniform Commercial Code 354 (3rd ed.1988), the distinguished authors indicate that the Code and Comments in this area are "equivocal," and that "(w)hether the drafters intended a seller who has resold to recover more in damages under § 2–708 * * * is not clear." (*Op. cit.*, at 352.)

On this question, White and Summers conclude:

" . . . a seller who resells goods reasonably identified to the broken contract for a price above the § 2–708(1) market price should be limited to the difference between the contract price and his actual resale price. We believe that this is an exact measure of his expectation and that he should not recover more than that. As indicated above, the buyer bears the burden of showing that the seller was not a lost volume seller, and that the goods which in fact were resold were those that would have been delivered to him, the breaching buyer." (*Op. cit.*, at 356)

In so concluding the authors expressed the following caveat:

"All of the foregoing discussion assumes that the buyer who wishes to limit the seller to the difference between the contract and the resale price can show that the goods resold were in fact the goods contracted for. If the seller could have fulfilled the buyer's contract by buying on the market or by a choice among a variety of fungible goods, the buyer will be unable to limit the seller to § 2–706 damages. The buyer will not be able to prove that the resale is 'reasonably identified as referring to the broken contract.' Put another way, the difference between the contract and a specific resale price is not the proper measure of the seller's expectation damages unless that resale is a substitute for the one actually conducted." (*Op. cit.*, at 355.)

The foregoing position has generally been that enunciated by the courts that have considered the issue. In Nobs Chemical, U.S.A., Inc. v. Koppers Co., Inc., 616 F.2d 212 (5th Cir.1980), the court (after observing the lack of "any law directly on point") limited damages on a breach of contract for the sale of chemicals to that provided in § 2–706. It heavily relied on the policy provision set forth in § 1–106 that "the remedies provided by this Act shall be liberally administered to the end that the aggrieved party may be put in as good a position as if the other party had fully performed," concluding:

> "No one insists, and we do not think they could, that the difference between the fallen market price and the contract price is necessary to compensate the plaintiffs for the breach. Had the transaction been completed, their 'benefit of the bargain' would not have been affected by the fall in market price, and they would not have experienced the windfall they otherwise would receive if the market price-contract price rule contained in [§ 2–708(1)] is followed."

Supra, at 215. Accord: ... Union Carbide Corp. v. Consumers Power Co., 636 F.Supp. 1498, 1501 (E.D.Mich.1986), where it was stated that § 2–708 did "not authorize awards of damages which put the seller in a better position than performance would have put them."

The *Union Carbide* case properly distinguished Trans World Metals, Inc. v. Southwire Co., 769 F.2d 902 (2d Cir.1985), relied upon by plaintiff, as there it was found that the parties to the contract assumed the risks of price variations, and to deny plaintiff a gain from a drop in prices would unjustly deny it the benefit of its bargain.

Here the alleged contract would not in any way be affected by the sharp drop in prices that occurred, as the contract was for a fixed price of goods already purchased. Hence, the result reached by the Second Circuit in *Trans World* is not pertinent to the case at bar.

Plaintiff asserts that the foregoing cases are inapposite because New York legislative history calls for a different result. This argument is based on the 1956 New York Law Revision Commission recommendation to delete language in the draft of § 2–703(e) that would have limited § 2–708 to situations where the "goods have not been sold." This recommendation was apparently accepted by the Commissioners on Uniform State Laws, and hence the Code in New York, and elsewhere, does not contain such language. This is hardly reason to call for an interpretation of the Code in New York different from that in other states.

In explaining this deletion, White and Summers state:

> "It is possible that the New York Law Revision Commission had in mind the seller who would not receive a windfall by suing under 2–708(1) and simply wanted to make it clear that a seller who makes a good faith attempt to comply with 2–706 but fails may then resort to 2–708(1). Nothing in their report suggests that they considered the case in which 2–706 recovery would be small because the seller sold at a price very near to the contract price yet the contract-market differential under 2–708 would be large." (*Op. cit.*, at 354.)

In B & R Textile Corp. v. Paul Rothman Industries, Ltd., 101 Misc.2d 98 (Civ.Ct.N.Y.Co., 1979), § 2–708 was used in the type of situation contemplated by the authors. There damages were measured by that section because a § 2–706 recovery was not permissible due to the seller's failure to give the required notice of intention to resell. In that case, however, damages were the same under either measure as the market price was found to be the same as the resale price.

Further, Official Comment 2 under § 2–706 states that "(f)ailure to act properly under this section deprives the seller of the measure of damages here provided and *relegates* him to that provided under section 2–708" (emphasis supplied), thus implying that it was contemplated that § 2–708 recoveries would be less than the contract-resale price differential authorized in § 2–706.

Moreover, if § 2–708 could not be employed if the goods had been sold, a merchant who sells from inventory would lose his profit if required to reduce damages recoverable from a defaulting buyer by the amount of the sale price of the item when sold to another customer. Thus, in Neri v. Retail Marine Corporation, 30 N.Y.2d 393, 400 (1972), the Court of Appeals, in allowing a § 2–708(2) recovery of lost profits by a retailer of boats, quoted the following from an illustration contained in Hawkland, Sales and Bulk Sales (1958 ed):

> "Thus, if an automobile dealer agrees to sell a car to a buyer at the standard price of $2,000, a breach by the buyer injures the dealer, even though he is able to sell the automobile to another for $2,000. If the dealer had an inexhaustible supply of cars, the resale to replace the breaching buyer costs the dealer a sale, because, had the breaching buyer performed, the dealer would have made two sales instead of one. The buyer's breach, in such a case, depletes the dealer's sales to the extent of one, and the measure of damages should be the dealer's profit on one sale."

Thus, it is clear that the deletion of the proposed condition for the use of § 2–708 does not mean that the drafters of the Code contemplated the type of recovery sought by plaintiff herein.

Plaintiff, in essence, wishes to be accorded the same treatment as the car dealer in Professor Hawkland's illustration. However, there are significant differences that warrant the court declining such application. Here plaintiff was selling to Esso Sapa a specific cargo aboard a specific vessel, and thus the gasoline aboard that ship may be considered as goods identified [see § 2–501(1)(a)] to a broken contract.

On page 2 of plaintiff's initial memorandum of law it is stated:

> "After unsuccessfully attempting to convince (defendant) to honor its contract, (plaintiff) scrambled to find a new buyer and, on July 17, after feverish, lengthy and deliberate negotiations, concluded a sale to Esso Sapa."

On page 348 of the deposition of plaintiff's witness he testified that, in seeking to sell the gasoline to a representative of Esso Sapa, "I asked him to buy the cargo."

These statements are illustrative of the fact that although gasoline of the type involved in the action is fungible, and thus may be purchased in the marketplace by anyone (including traders such as plaintiff) in a position to finance the transaction, the sale here to Esso Sapa was clearly a substitute for the one plaintiff claims it actually contracted for with defendant.

If plaintiff's damages are measured in accordance with § 2–706, it would be receiving the benefit reasonably to be expected when it entered into the alleged contract with defendant. Granting it the approximately $3,000,000 additional recovery that it seeks would result in a windfall which cannot be said to have been in the contemplation of the parties at the time of their negotiations, and would be inconsistent with the policy of the Code as expressed in § 1–106.

Accordingly, the court concludes that the proper interrelationship of §§ 2–706 and 2–708 is that summarized by White and Summers above and followed in the cases cited. Thus, in the event plaintiff prevails and establishes a breach of contract at trial, its damages will be measured in accordance with § 2–706.

The situation would be different if plaintiff's sale were from its inventory (in which case it would be treated as the car dealer mentioned above), or if it had already contracted to sell the product to Esso Sapa, or perhaps even if it was then actually engaged in negotiations for trades in this type of gasoline. However, no such claim is made. The statement in plaintiff's reply memorandum of law that "in all likelihood, (plaintiff) would have negotiated such a sale (to Esso Sapa) even in the absence of (defendant's) breach" is not supported by any facts in the record, as there are no allegations that plaintiff had any negotiations then pending for the sale of this type of gasoline with Esso Sapa or any other party. This is simply a case where plaintiff, in an effort to mitigate its damages, went out and made a sale of a specific identified cargo of gasoline aboard a vessel then proceeding to New York.

. . .

The motions for partial summary judgment are decided in accordance with the foregoing.

QUESTIONS AND NOTES

1. The court cites *Nobs Chemical* (page 459). That case is the basis of Problem 2, page 457 supra. How do the facts of *Tesoro* differ from the facts of that problem?

2. To be entitled to contract price less resale price under 2–706, the resale must be "identified as referring to the broken contract," though it is not necessary that the goods have been identified to the broken contract before the breach occurred. Was the resale in *Tesoro* identified to the broken contract?

Of course, if a court is using the measure in 2–706 because the *buyer* wants it used, it is not relevant that the requirements of 2–706 have not been met. (Do you see why?)

3. The seller in *Tesoro* argued that if the buyer had not breached, it (the seller) could have purchased more gasoline in the open market and sold that gasoline to Esso Sapa, so that the sale to Esso Sapa is irrelevant to the amount it should recover from the defendant. The court rejects this argument. Should it have done so?

4. In *Tesoro* the contract with the defendant called for a fixed price of $1.30 per gallon regardless of the market price at the time of delivery. In a fixed-price contract, the risk of a rising market price is on the seller, and the risk of a falling market price is on the buyer. If there is a decline in the market price, the benefit of that decline belongs to the seller, and the cost of the decline goes to the buyer. But the court in *Tesoro* cut off that cost at the price at which the seller sold to Esso Sapa. Was this appropriate?

5. Compare Trans World Metals, Inc. v. Southwire Co., 769 F.2d 902 (2d Cir.1985), a contract for the sale of aluminum, with monthly deliveries that would not be completed until 20 months after the contract was formed. The price was $.77 per pound, and with more than 10 installments remaining, the market price declined steeply. The buyer breached, and the seller sued, seeking damages measured by the contract price less the market price on each of the delivery dates. Rejecting the buyer's argument that 2–708(2) should apply when 2–708(1) overcompensates the seller, the court held that the seller was entitled to damages measured by the excess of the contract price over the market price at the several times of tender:

> [We are not] convinced that Trans World has been overcompensated. No measure other than the contract/market price differential will award Trans World the "benefit of its bargain," that is, the "amount necessary to put [it] in as good a position as [it] would have been if the defendant had abided by the contract." The contract at issue in this case is an aluminum supply contract entered into eight months prior to the initial deliveries called for by its terms. The last of the anticipated deliveries of aluminum would not have been completed until a full twenty months after the negotiations took place. It simply could not have escaped these parties that they were betting on which way aluminum prices would move. Trans World took the risk that the price would rise; Southwire took the risk that the price would fall. Under these circumstances, Trans World should not be denied the benefit of its bargain, as reflected by the contract/market price differential.
>
> The decision primarily relied upon by Southwire is distinguishable from this case. *Nobs Chemical* involved a seller acting as a middleman. The seller in *Nobs* had entered into a second fixed-price contract with its own supplier for purchase of the goods to be sold under the contract sued upon; its "market price" thus had been fixed in advance by contract. Because the seller had contractually protected itself against market price fluctuation, the Fifth Circuit concluded that it would have been unfair to permit the seller to reap a riskless benefit. As that

Court noted, "the difference between a fallen market price and the contract price is [not] necessary to compensate the plaintiffs for the breach. Had the transaction been completed, their 'benefit of the bargain' would not have been affected by the fall in the market price. * * * " Whether or not we would have reached the same result in *Nobs*, here the benefit of the bargain under a completed contract would have been affected by the fall in aluminum prices. Because Trans World accepted the risk that prices would rise, it is entitled to benefit from their fall.

In contrast, the court in Union Carbide Corporation v. Consumers Power Co., 636 F.Supp. 1498 (E.D.Mich.1986), stated that 2–708(2), which authorizes the award of lost profits when the remedy in 2–708(1) is "inadequate to put the seller in as good a position as performance would have done," must be understood to authorize the award of lost profits when 2–708(1) is "incapable or inadequate to accomplish the stated UCC remedies of compensating the aggrieved person but not overcompensating that person or specifically punishing the other person." Is this an appropriate reading of subsection (1)?

6. Revised Article 2. Revised 2–706 and 2–708 do not change the answers to the issues discussed above.

7. Leases. Section 2A–528, the analog of 2–708, contains the same ambiguity as to the relationship between a recovery based on resale and a recovery of lost profits. Official Comment 4 to 2A–501, however, tilts Article 2A toward the result in *Tesoro*. Subsection (4), on which that Comment is based, provides: "Except as otherwise provided in Section 1–106(1) or this Article or the lease agreement, the rights and remedies referred to in subsections (2) and (3) are cumulative." Section 1–106 provides that the remedies provided by Code are to be "liberally administered to the end that the aggrieved party may be put in as good a position as if the other party had fully performed . . . ." The Comment interprets the reference to 1–106 as denying a party the right to cumulation of, or selection among, remedies if the result would be to place the aggrieved party in a better position than it would have been in had there been full performance. Of course, it could be argued that 1–106 says only that an aggrieved party should never recover less than the amount that is necessary to put that aggrieved party in as good a position as if the other party had performed, and does not address the issue whether the aggrieved party might ever recover more than the amount necessary to attain expectancy. The revisions to Article 2A leave Official Comment 4 intact, and the revisions to Article 2 do not add any comparable comment to 2–703.

8. CISG. Article 75 of the Convention on Contracts for the International Sale of Goods provides a much simpler substitute-transaction based remedy. It merely provides that if, "in a reasonable manner and within a reasonable time . . . the buyer has bought goods in replacement or the seller has resold the goods, the party claiming damages may recover the difference between the contract price and the price in the substitute transaction as well as any further damages recoverable under Article 74."

If there has not been a substitute transaction, Article 76 provides that the aggrieved party may measure damages by the difference between the contract price and the "current" price. In either case, the aggrieved party may also recover other damages, such as lost profit, limited by rules dealing with foreseeability (Article 74) and mitigation of damages (Article 77).

9. Problem 5, page 455 revisited. What if Buyer repudiates the contract for the mink coat before Seller has completed making it. Indeed, assume that the repudiation occurs after Seller has taken all the appropriate measurements and made a pattern for the coat, but before he has acquired the materials needed to make it. Is Seller entitled to the price under 2–709? Why or why not? If not, what is Seller's remedy?

10. Problem. Assume in the above problem that the repudiation occurs after Seller has received and cut the pelts according to the pattern for the coat. Can Seller complete the coat and recover the price?

———

lost profit   2579
expenses   C74
*   32,53*

Neri v. Retail Marine Corp.

New York Court of Appeals, 1972.
30 N.Y.2d 393, 334 N.Y.S.2d 165, 285 N.E.2d 311.

Seller

■ GIBSON, JUDGE. . . . *→ buyer*

The plaintiffs contracted to purchase from defendant a new boat of a specified model for the price of $12,587.40, against which they made a deposit of $40. They shortly increased the deposit to $4,250 in consideration of the defendant dealer's agreement to arrange with the manufacturer for immediate delivery on the basis of "a firm sale," instead of the delivery within approximately four to six weeks originally specified. Some six days after the date of the contract plaintiffs' lawyer sent to defendant a letter rescinding the sales contract for the reason that plaintiff Neri was about to undergo hospitalization and surgery, in consequence of which, according to the letter, it would be "impossible for Mr. Neri to make any payments." The boat had already been ordered from the manufacturer and was delivered to defendant at or before the time the attorney's letter was received. Defendant declined to refund plaintiffs' deposit and this action to recover it was commenced. Defendant counterclaimed, alleging plaintiffs' breach of the contract and defendant's resultant damage in the amount of $4,250, for which sum defendant demanded judgment. Upon motion, defendant had summary judgment on the issue of liability tendered by its counterclaim; and Special Term directed an assessment of damages, upon which it would be determined whether plaintiffs were entitled to the return of any portion of their down payment.

Upon the trial so directed, it was shown that the boat ordered and received by defendant in accordance with plaintiffs' contract of purchase was sold some four months later to another buyer for the same price as that negotiated with plaintiffs. From this proof the plaintiffs argue that defendant's loss on its contract was recouped, while defendant argues that

contract - resale = 0
contract - market = 0

but for plaintiffs' default, it would have sold two boats and have earned two profits instead of one. Defendant proved, without contradiction, that its profit on the sale under the contract in suit would have been $2,579 and that during the period the boat remained unsold incidental expenses aggregating $674 for storage, upkeep, finance charges and insurance were incurred. Additionally, defendant proved and sought to recover attorneys' fees of $1,250.

The trial court found "untenable" defendant's claim for loss of profit, inasmuch as the boat was later sold for the same price that plaintiffs had contracted to pay; found, too, that defendant had failed to prove any incidental damages; further found "that the terms of section 2–718, subsection 2(b), of the Uniform Commercial Code are applicable and same make adequate and fair provision to place the sellers in as good a position as performance would have done" and, in accordance with paragraph (b) of subsection (2) thus relied upon, awarded defendant $500 upon its counterclaim and directed that plaintiffs recover the balance of their deposit, amounting to $3,750. The ensuing judgment was affirmed, without opinion, at the Appellate Division, and defendant's appeal to this court was taken by our leave.

The issue is governed in the first instance by section 2–718 of the Uniform Commercial Code which provides, among other things, that the buyer, despite his breach, may have restitution of the amount by which his payment exceeds: (a) reasonable liquidated damages stipulated by the contract or (b) absent such stipulation, 20% of the value of the buyer's total performance or $500, whichever is smaller (§ 2–718, subsection [2], pars. [a], [b]). As above noted, the trial court awarded defendant an offset in the amount of $500 under paragraph (b) and directed restitution to plaintiffs of the balance. Section 2–718, however, establishes, in paragraph (a) of subsection (3), an alternative right of offset in favor of the seller, as follows: "(3) The buyer's right to restitution under subsection (2) is subject to offset to the extent that the seller establishes (a) a right to recover damages under the provisions of this Article other than subsection (1)."

Among "the provisions of this Article other than subsection (1)" are those to be found in section 2–708, which the courts below did not apply. . . . [Subsection (2) of that section provides,] "If the measure of damages provided in subsection (1) is inadequate to put the seller in as good a position as performance would have done then the measure of damages is the profit (including reasonable overhead) which the seller would have made from full performance by the buyer, together with any incidental damages provided in this Article (Section 2–710), due allowance for costs reasonably incurred and due credit for payments of proceeds of resale."

. . .

Prior to the code, the New York cases "applied the 'profit' test, contract price less cost of manufacture, only in cases where the seller [was] a manufacturer or an agent for a manufacturer" (1955 Report of N.Y.Law Rev.Comm., vol. 1, p. 693). Its extension to retail sales was "designed to eliminate the unfair and economically wasteful results arising under the older law when fixed price articles were involved. This section permits the recovery of lost profits in all appropriate cases, which would include all standard priced goods." (Official Comment 2, McKinney's Cons.Laws of N.Y., Book 62–1/2, Part 1, p. 605, under Uniform Commercial Code, § 2–708.) Additionally, and "[i]n all cases the seller may recover incidental damages" (id., Comment 3). The buyer's right to restitution was established at Special Term upon the motion for summary judgment, as was the seller's right to proper offsets, in each case pursuant to section 2–718; and, as the parties concede, the only question before us, following the assessment of damages at Special Term, is that as to the proper measure of damage to be applied. The conclusion is clear from the record—indeed with mathematical certainty—that "the measure of damages provided in subsection (1) is inadequate to put the seller in as good a position as performance would have done" (Uniform Commercial Code, § 2–708, subsection [2]) and hence—again under subsection (2)—that the seller is entitled to its "profit (including reasonable overhead) * * * together with any incidental damages * * *, due allowance for costs reasonably incurred and due credit for payments or proceeds of resale."

It is evident, first, that this retail seller is entitled to its profit and, second, that the last sentence of subsection (2), as hereinbefore quoted, referring to "due credit for payments or proceeds of resale" is inapplicable to this retail sales contract.[2] Closely parallel to the factual situation now before us is that hypothesized by Dean Hawkland as illustrative of the operation of the rules: "Thus, if a private party agrees to sell his automobile to a buyer for $2,000, a breach by the buyer would cause the seller no loss (except incidental damages, i.e., expense of a new sale) if the seller was able to sell the automobile to another buyer for $2000. But the situation is different with dealers having an unlimited supply of standard-priced goods. Thus, if an automobile dealer agrees to sell a car to a buyer at the standard price of $2000, a breach by the buyer injures the dealer, even though he is able to sell the automobile to another for $2000. If the dealer has an inexhaustible supply of cars, the resale to replace the breaching buyer costs the dealer a sale, because, had the breaching buyer performed, the dealer would have made two sales instead of one. The buyer's breach, in such a case, depletes the dealer's sales to the extent of one, and the measure of damages should be the dealer's profit on one sale. Section 2–708 recognizes this, and it rejects the rule developed under the Uniform Sales Act by many

---

2. The concluding clause, "due credit for payments or proceeds of resale," is intended to refer to "the privilege of the seller to realize junk value when it is manifestly useless to complete the operation of manufacture" (Supp. No. 1 to the 1952 Official Draft of Text and Comments of the Uniform Commercial Code, as Amended by the Action of the American Law Institute of the National Conference of Commissioners on Uniform Laws [1954], p. 14). The commentators who have considered the language have uniformly concluded that "the reference is to a resale as scrap under * * * Section 2–704." Another writer, reaching the same conclusion, after detailing the history of the clause, says that " 'proceeds of resale' previously meant the resale value of the goods in finished form; now it means the resale value of the components on hand at the time plaintiff learns of breach" (Harris, Seller's Damages, 18 Stanf. L.Rev. 66, 104).

courts that the profit cannot be recovered in this case." (Hawkland, Sales and Bulk Sales [1958 ed.], pp. 153–154.)

The record which in this case establishes defendant's entitlement to damages in the amount of its prospective profit, at the same time confirms defendant's cognate right to "any incidental damages provided in this Article (Section 2–710)" (Uniform Commercial Code, § 2–708, subsection [2]). From the language employed it is too clear to require discussion that the seller's right to recover loss of profits is not exclusive and that he may recoup his "incidental" expenses as well. Although the trial court's denial of incidental damages in the uncontroverted amount of $674 was made in the context of its erroneous conclusion that paragraph (b) of subsection (2) of section 2–718 was applicable and was "adequate * * * to place the sellers in as good a position as performance would have done," the denial seems not to have rested entirely on the court's mistaken application of the law, as there was an explicit finding "that defendant completely failed to show that it suffered any incidental damages." We find no basis for the court's conclusion with respect to a deficiency of proof inasmuch as the proper items of the $674 expenses (being for storage, upkeep, finance charges and insurance for the period between the date performance was due and the time of the resale) were proven without objection and were in no way controverted, impeached or otherwise challenged, at the trial or on appeal. Thus the court's finding of a failure of proof cannot be supported upon the record and, therefore, and contrary to plaintiffs' contention, the affirmance at the Appellate Division was ineffective to save it.

The trial court correctly denied defendant's claim for recovery of attorney's fees incurred by it in this action. Attorney's fees incurred in an action such as this are not in the nature of the protective expenses contemplated by the statute (Uniform Commercial Code, § 1–106, subd. [1]; § 2–710; § 2–708, subsection [2] . . .).

It follows that plaintiffs are entitled to restitution of the sum of $4,250 paid by them on account of the contract price less an offset to defendant in the amount of $3,253 on account of its lost profit of $2,579 and its incidental damages of $674.

The order of the Appellate Division should be modified, with costs in all courts, in accordance with this opinion, and, as so modified, affirmed.

QUESTIONS AND NOTES

1. In view of *Neri*, was the judgment of the court in *Tesoro* correct?

2. In *Neri*, what section authorizes the seller's recovery of incidental damages?

3. Did the court correctly conclude that the $674 in charges for storage and upkeep, insurance premiums, and interest payments were recoverable as incidental damages?

Was the sale of the boat facilitated by the fact that it was available for viewing at the seller's place of business? Why is this question relevant to the recoverability of the $674?

4. Assume that in *Neri* Retail Marine's contract with the manufacturer of the boat in question provided that if Retail Marine sold a specified number of those boats in that calendar year, the manufacturer would pay Retail Marine a bonus of $5,000. If the Neris' breach caused Retail Marine to fall one sale short of that number, would they be liable for the $5,000?

5. In R.E. Davis Chemical Corp. v. Diasonics, Inc., 826 F.2d 678 (7th Cir.1987), Davis contracted to buy medical diagnostic equipment from Diasonics, making a $300,000 down payment. When Davis refused to take delivery, Diasonics sold the same equipment to another buyer for the same price that Davis had agreed to pay. Davis sued for return of its down payment, and Diasonics claimed that it was entitled to deduct its lost profit before returning any of the $300,000. The trial court held that when a seller has resold, it is limited to recovery of the excess of the contract price over the resale price under 2–706. The Court of Appeals reversed. After stating that lost-volume sellers are entitled to recover lost profits, it continued:

> However, we disagree with the definition of "lost volume seller" adopted by other courts. Courts awarding lost profits to a lost volume seller have focused on whether the seller had the capacity to supply the breached units in addition to what it actually sold. In reality, however, the relevant questions include, not only whether the seller could have produced the breached units in addition to its actual volume, but also whether it would have been profitable for the seller to produce both units. Goetz & Scott, Measuring Sellers' Damages: The Lost–Profits Puzzle, 31 Stan.L.Rev. 323, 332–33, 346–47 (1979). As one commentator has noted, under
>
>> "the economic law of diminishing returns or increasing marginal costs[,] ... as a seller's volume increases, then a point will inevitably be reached where the cost of selling each additional item diminishes the incremental return to the seller and eventually makes it entirely unprofitable to conclude the next sale."
>
> Shanker, [The Case for a Literal Reading of UCC Section 2–708(2), 24 Case W.Res.L.Rev. 697, 705 (1973)]. Thus, under some conditions, awarding a lost volume seller its presumed lost profit will result in overcompensating the seller, and § 2–708(2) would not take effect because the damage formula provided in § 2–708(1) does place the seller in as good a position as if the buyer had performed. Therefore, on remand, Diasonics must establish, not only that it had the capacity to produce the breached unit in addition to the unit resold, but also that it would have been profitable for it to have produced and sold both. Diasonics carries the burden of establishing these facts because the burden of proof is generally on the party claiming injury to establish the amount of its damages; especially in a case such as this, the plaintiff has easiest access to the relevant data.

. . .

We therefore reverse the grant of summary judgment in favor of Davis and remand with instructions that the district court calculate Diasonics' damages under § 2–708(2) if Diasonics can establish, not only that it had the capacity to make the sale to Davis as well as the sale to the resale buyer, but also that it would have been profitable for it to make both sales. Of course, Diasonics, in addition, must show that it probably would have made the second sale absent the breach.

On remand, the trial court awarded Diasonics lost profit of $453,050. On appeal (924 F.2d 709 (7th Cir.1991)), that award was affirmed. The court held that it was clearly established on remand that Diasonics had the capacity to manufacture one more machine and that it was searching for all possible buyers. Therefore, it was a lost-volume seller. The buyer argued on appeal that Diasonics had not proven its profit on the lost sale because it had used average costs rather than actual costs. Presumably that argument is that Diasonics should have had to show the actual marginal cost of producing an additional unit. In any event, the court approved the use of average cost data, saying that Diasonics only had to prove its damages with reasonable certainty, not with mathematical precision.

Davis also argued that the seller had to identify the particular buyer of the rejected machine and show that the buyer would have bought another machine if it had not been able to receive the machine originally intended for Davis. The court also rejected that argument. It stated that the Diasonic units were interchangeable and that it was not necessary for Diasonics to "trace the exact resale buyer for that unit."

6. "Including reasonable overhead." The parenthetical in 2–708(2), "including reasonable overhead," means that the seller is entitled to be repaid for the overhead allocable to the breached contract. Compensation for the out-of-pocket expenses that the seller has incurred before the breach is provided by the phrase at the end of the subsection, "due allowance for costs incurred." The allowance for reasonable overhead, therefore, refers to the portion of the seller's fixed overhead that is allocable to the breached contract. These are the costs the seller incurs regardless of whether it ever formed the contract with the buyer. They include rent, salaries, insurance, and all the other expenses that are to be paid regardless of the existence of the contract in question. To see why this is so, consider the following example.

Bulldozers, Inc., has succeeded in securing contracts this year for the sale of 10 bulldozers at a price of $30,000 each. Therefore gross income for the year will be $300,000 if all 10 contracts are performed,

Suppose costs for the year are:	
10 Bulldozers @ $20,000	$200,000
Rent	10,000
Secretary	10,000
Utilities and office expense	10,000
Insurance	5,000
Sales rep's commission ($1000 per bulldozer)	10,000
Total Cost	$245,000
Net Profit:	$55,000
(per unit	$5,500)

Now suppose one of the buyers repudiates an agreement to buy one bulldozer. What are the damages? The above numbers change. Gross income (prior to any award for damages for the breach) will be $270,000 (rather than $300,000 as it would have been but for the breach).

Costs will be

9 Bulldozers @ $20,000	$180,000
Rent	10,000
Secretary	10,000
Utilities and office expenses	10,000
Insurance	5,000
Sales rep's commission ($1000 per bulldozer)	9,000
Total Cost	$224,000
Net Profit:	$46,000

If we allow only the per-unit $5,500 as damages for the lost sale, the seller's net profit for the year will be $46,000 plus $5,500, or $51,500, not the $55,000 it would have had the buyer not repudiated.

On the other hand, if we compute lost profit by deducting only the expenses that were saved as a result of the breach (the $20,000 cost of the bulldozer and the $1000 commission) from the breaching buyer's purchase price of $30,000, seller's damages will be $9,000. If we add $9,000 to the $46,000 profit made on the other nine sales occurring the year, we get total profit for the year of $55,000. Therefore, the $9,000 recovery puts the seller in the position it would have been had the contract been performed. The expenses saved sometimes are referred to as variable costs, as contrasted with the fixed costs of running the business. The lost profit is determined by starting with the contract price and deducting the variable costs that the seller has not incurred. The remainder, the lost profit, therefore includes a portion of the fixed costs. This is the "reasonable overhead" to which 2–708(2) refers.

7.   "Due credit for payments and proceeds of resale." The primary application of 2–708(2) is to the "lost-volume seller." This is the seller who has sufficient supply to handle the entire demand for its goods. When a buyer breaches, there is no way for the seller to recoup the loss by making a second sale. Another buyer may take the goods, but as this second buyer would presumably have bought from the seller anyway, the seller has irretrievably lost the volume of the breached contract. The only way to make the seller whole, then, is to allow lost profit on the breached contract.

What, then, is the effect of the last phrase of 2–708(2), "due credit for ... proceeds of resale"? Since the seller in the typical lost-volume case resells the goods for approximately the same price the breaching buyer had promised, allowing credit for proceeds of resale in the lost-volume case normally will result in little or no recovery under 2–708(2). The Code could not mean to give with one hand and take with the other, say the commentators. But backing up that view with Code analysis has proved a rather difficult thing to do.

One approach is to view "proceeds of resale" as applying only to unfinished goods sold for salvage. This gives lost profits to the components assembler and the lost-volume seller. It is the view of the court in *Neri* and is the approach taken by several leading commentators, including J.White & R.Summers, *Uniform Commercial Code* §§ 7–8, 7–13 (4th ed.1995); Harris, A Radical Restatement of the Law of Seller's Damages: Sales Act and Commercial Code Results Compared, 18 Stan.Law Rev. 66, 105–106 (1965); and R.Nordstrom Handbook of the Law of Sales § 177, at 541 (1970).

A different approach has been offered by Schlosser, Construing Section 2–708(2) to Apply to the Lost–Volume Seller, 24 Case W.Res.L.Rev. 686 (1973). *Schlosser* reads the words, "profit ... which the seller would have made from full performance by the buyer," as including not only the profit the seller would have made on the breached contract, but also the profit on the resale to buyer #2. The profit on the sale to buyer #2 is "lost" since buyer #2 did not buy the goods she otherwise would have bought, as the seller sold her the breaching buyer's goods instead. Allowing credit for proceeds of resale then cancels out one profit, but since, if buyer #1 had not breached, the seller would have had two profits, the seller still recovers lost profit.

Though these two approaches seem to produce the same result, they will not always do so. To discover the difference, consider the following problem, derived from a hypothetical posed by *White & Summers*: Boeing has contracts to produce 100 747's in a given year. American Airlines has contracted to buy the third one off the line, and Delta, the fourth. American breaches, so Boeing sells the third one off the line to Delta and manufactures only 99. The analysis of *White & Summers*, *Harris*, and *Nordstrom* is as follows. Assume the cost of making a 747, including reasonable overhead, is $17 million, and that Boeing was selling them for $20 million. The "profit" is $3 million, "costs reasonably incurred" are all allocated to Delta and thus saved, and "proceeds of resale" is ignored. Boeing thus recovers $3 million.

Schlosser, on the other hand, analyzes the situation in terms of two unit profits for Boeing, which may or may not be equal, depending on economic factors in Boeing's operation. Suppose that although it cost $17 million to produce the plane earmarked for American and sold to Delta, it would have cost only $16 million to produce the 100th plane. Suppose further that Delta paid only $19.5 million instead of $20 million for the plane it bought. Then under *Schlosser's* analysis the profit Boeing lost from American is $3 million ($20 million minus $17 million) and the profit it lost from Delta as a result of American's breach is $3.5 million ($19.5 million minus $16 million). The total lost profit is $6.5 million. Add "costs reasonably incurred" ($17 million) and subtract "proceeds of resale" ($19.5 million), and Boeing's recovery is $4 million. This, *Schlosser* argues, is obviously the correct result, as "full performance" by American would have resulted in profit of $6.5 million, and $4 million, added to Boeing's actual profit of $2.5 million, will place Boeing in its expectancy position. Thus, *Schlosser* argues that its test is really a different test, as it is a more accurate measure of what "full performance" by the breaching buyer would have meant to the seller.

All of the foregoing analysis has assumed the result, and then tried to find a rational way of reading 2–708(2) to get that result from it. The difficulty that the commentators have had in trying to find a believable reading that produces the desired result could indicate that the result they assume is not the correct result at all. Shanker, The Case for a Literal Reading of UCC Section 2–708(2), 24 Case W.Res.L.Rev. 697 (1973), argues that 2–708(2) is to be read literally, and that reducing seller's recovery by the amount of "proceeds of resale" is not only the intended result, but the better rule.

One of *Shanker's* arguments is that to give to 2–708(2) the construction urged by the commentators would discourage aggrieved sellers from relying on 2–706, and as that section was intended by the drafters to be the reselling seller's primary remedy, this cannot be the correct result. More fundamentally, the article attacks the concept of the lost-volume seller, arguing that this creature seldom if ever exists in the real world. It asserts that production problems, personnel problems, unavailability of supplies, and the whole gamut of a business' headaches will eventually produce a situation in most businesses where the goods not bought by the breaching buyer will sooner or later make possible a sale that the seller would have had to turn down due to lack of supply had the buyer not breached. (The truth of this assertion is, it would seem, a factual inquiry, and as such, might be more appropriate as a defense to a 2–708(2) action than as an aid in construing the section.) *Shanker* also argues that the typical merchant is happy to have "gotten his money out of" the goods as to which the buyer breached and does not expect to recover a second profit on goods that already have been sold for a fair profit. In essence *Shanker* argues that since the seller *feels* whole, there is no point using other analytical constructs to determine whether or not the seller *is* whole.

Similarly, Goetz & Scott, in Measuring Seller's Damages: The Lost Profits Puzzle, 31 Stan.L.Rev. 323 (1979), using detailed economic analysis, argues that sellers' actual losses are almost never the lost profit allowed in such cases as *Neri*. In *Neri*, for example, they suggest that the second sale, which they say was probably a spot sale, rather than a contractually obligated future sale, was made possible, or at least made possible at less expense, by the Neris' breach. Therefore, a showing by a seller that it could acquire or produce all the contracted-for items that it could reasonably expect to sell should not be enough to establish its right to a recovery larger than contract price less market price.

The economic arguments in *Goetz & Scott* may be sound, but the better policy choice may be to allow sellers to recover lost profits once they show ability to supply all reasonably expectable buyers, with the burden on the breaching buyer to show, if it can, that the seller's loss was less than the claimed lost profits. In a case like *Neri*, for example, it is hard, if not impossible, to know whether the second sale would have been made even if the Neris had not breached. Also, it is difficult to know whether the second sale, if it would have been made anyway, would have been at a higher cost to Retail Marine (or at a lower price) if the Neris had not breached. On the other hand, it is practically certain that Retail Marine could have acquired a second boat from the manufacturer at about the same price it paid for the one that the Neris had contracted to buy.

8. Revised Article 2. Revised 2–708(2) deletes the reference to "due allowance for costs reasonably incurred and due credit for payment or proceeds of resale." Presumably, however, it would continue to be appropriate to reduce a seller's recovery by any sums the seller receives when it sells for salvage the uncompleted goods or any materials that would have been used in manufacturing the goods.

9. Problem. Seller contracted with Buyer, a furniture retailer, to manufacture and deliver 4,000 wooden end tables of a specified design, for $100,000. Six weeks later Buyer repudiated. At that time, Seller had acquired all the materials it needed and had cut the tops and legs for the tables. The cost of the materials was $20,000, and the cost of the labor to cut the wood was $10,000. The salvage value of the materials is about $3,000. Seller estimates that the total additional cost of finishing the 4,000 tables would be $50,000 and that they would sell for a total of between $70,000 and $90,000 on the market. Should Seller complete the tables? If it does, what is its recovery? If it does not complete the tables, what is its recovery?

10. In Lee Oldsmobile, Inc. v. Kaiden, 32 Md.App. 556, 363 A.2d 270 (1976), the buyer contracted to purchase a Rolls–Royce for $29,500. When the buyer repudiated, the seller resold the automobile for $26,500. It claimed as damages the following:

Contract price of $29,500 less resale price of $26,500	$3,000
Commission to salesman on second sale	600
Commission to broker on second sale	1,000
Floor plan interest on cost of car, 52 days	335
Transportation expenses	140
Total	$5,075

The court held that since the seller had not given notice of intention to resell, it was not entitled, under 2–706, to the excess of the contract price over the resale price of the automobile. The court, however, did allow recovery of the other claimed items of damage.

(a) Can you think of any basis for awarding the $3,000?

(b) Is it appropriate to give as damages the expenses of a sale not meeting the requirements of 2–706? If so, under what section?

(c) Was the seller's attorney guilty of malpractice in bringing a suit claiming 2–706 damages, rather than seeking to recover lost profits under 2–708(2)?

3. CONTRACTED-FOR DAMAGES

Kvassay v. Murray

Kansas Court of Appeals, 1991.
15 Kan.App.2d 426, 808 P.2d 896.

■ WALKER, D.J.

Plaintiff Michael Kvassay, d/b/a Kvassay Exotic Food, appeals the trial court's finding that a liquidated damages clause was unenforceable and from the court's finding that damages for lost profits were not recoverable. Kvassay contends these damages occurred when Great American Foods, Inc., (Great American) breached a contract for the purchase of baklava. . . .

On February 22, 1984, Kvassay, who had been an independent insurance adjuster, contracted to sell 24,000 cases of baklava to Great American at $19.00 per case. Under the contract, the sales were to occur over a one-year period and Great American was to be Kvassay's only customer. The contract included a clause which provided: "If Buyer refuses to accept or repudiates delivery of the goods sold to him, under this Agreement, Seller shall be entitled to damages, at the rate of $5.00 per case, for each case remaining to be delivered under this Contract."

. . . After producing approximately 3,000 cases, Kvassay stopped producing the baklava because [Great American] refused to purchase any more of the product.

. . .

In April 1985, Kvassay filed suit for damages arising from the collapse of his baklava baking business. . . . The trial court ruled that liquidated damages could not be recovered and . . . "as a matter of law" that Kvassay would not be able to recover damages for lost profits in the action because they were too "speculative and conjectural." . . .

Kvassay first attacks the trial court's ruling that the amount of liquidated damages sought by him was unreasonable and therefore the liquidated damages clause was unenforceable.

Kvassay claimed $105,000 in losses under the liquidated damages clause of the contract, representing $5 per case for the approximately 21,000 cases of baklava which he was not able to deliver. The trial court determined that Kvassay's use of expected profits to formulate liquidated damages was improper because the business enterprise lacked duration, permanency, and recognition. The court then compared Kvassay's previous yearly income (about $20,000) with the claim for liquidated damages ($105,000) and found "the disparity becomes so great as to make the clause unenforceable."

Since the contract involved the sale of goods between merchants, the Uniform Commercial Code governs. See K.S.A. 84–2–102. "The Code does not change the pre-Code rule that the question of the propriety of liquidated damages is a question of law for the court." 4 Anderson, Uniform Commercial Code § 2–718:6, p. 572 (3d ed. 1983). Thus, this court's scope of review of the trial court's ruling is unlimited.

Liquidated damages clauses in sales contracts are governed by K.S.A. 84–2–718 . . . .

[Under the common law] a "stipulation for damages upon a future breach of contract is valid as a liquidated damages clause if the set amount is determined to be reasonable and the amount of damages is difficult to ascertain." This is clearly a two-step test: damages must be reasonable and they must be difficult to ascertain. Under the UCC, however, reasonableness is the only test. K.S.A. 84–2–718 provides three criteria by which to measure reasonableness of liquidated damages clauses: (1) anticipated or actual harm caused by breach; (2) difficulty of proving loss; and (3) difficulty of obtaining an adequate remedy.

In its ruling, the trial court found the liquidated damages clause was unreasonable in light of Kvassay's income before he entered into the manufacturing contract with Great American. There is no basis in 84–2–718 for contrasting income under a previous unrelated employment arrangement with liquidated damages sought under a manufacturing contract. Indeed, the traditional goal of the law in cases where a buyer breaches a manufacturing contract is to place the seller "in the same position he would have occupied if the vendee had performed his contract." Outcault Adv. Co. v. Citizens Nat'l Bank, 118 Kan. 328, 330–31, 234 Pac. 988 (1925). Thus, liquidated damages under the contract in this case must be measured against the anticipated or actual loss under the baklava contract as required by 84–2–718. The trial court erred in using Kvassay's previous income as a yardstick.

. . .

Kvassay produced evidence of anticipated damages at the bench trial showing that, before the contract was signed between Kvassay and Great American, Kvassay's accountant had calculated the baklava production costs. The resulting figure showed that, if each case sold for $19, Kvassay would earn a net profit of $3.55 per case after paying himself for time and labor. If he did not pay himself, the projected profit was $4.29 per case. Nevertheless, the parties set the liquidated damages figure at $5 per case. In comparing the anticipated damages of $3.55 per case in lost net profit with the liquidated damages of $5 per case, it is evident that Kvassay would collect $1.45 per case or about 41 percent over projected profits if Great American breached the contract. If the $4.29 profit figure is used, a $5 liquidated damages award would allow Kvassay to collect 71 cents per case or about 16–1/2 percent over projected profits if Great American breached the contract.

An examination of these pre-contract comparisons alone might well lead to the conclusion that the $5 liquidated damages clause is unreasonable because enforcing it would result in a windfall for Kvassay and serve as a penalty for Great American. A term fixing unreasonably large liqui-dated damages is void as a penalty under 84–2–718.

A better measure of the validity of the liquidated damages clause in this case would be obtained if the actual lost profits caused by the breach were compared to the $5 per case amount set by the clause. . . . Given the trial court's ruling that lost profits were not recoverable and could not be presented to the jury, it is questionable whether the court would have permitted evidence concerning lost profits at the bench trial.

The trial court utilized an impermissible factor to issue its ruling on the liquidated damages clause and the correct statutory factors were not directly addressed. We reverse the trial court on this issue and remand for further consideration of the reasonableness of the liquidated damages clause in light of the three criteria set out in 84–2–718 . . . .

. . .

Given the quantity of evidence offered to prove the profitability of Kvassay's business, it is clear the trial court was premature in ruling, as a matter of law, that lost profits could not be proved. Kvassay should have been permitted to offer his evidence and meet his burden of proof on damages . . . .

QUESTIONS AND NOTES

1. Section 2–718 validates the use of a liquidated damages clause, but only if it stipulates damages "at an amount which is reasonable in light of the anticipated or actual harm caused by the breach, the difficulties of proof of loss, and the inconvenience or nonfeasibility of otherwise obtaining an adequate remedy." Does the damages clause in *Kvassay* meet this stan-dard?

2. During the initial proceedings, Kvassay attempted to introduce proof of his actual lost profits. The trial court erred in excluding this evidence and on remand must consider it. If Kvassay proves what his profits were on the 3,000 cases he produced, one could project the profits lost on the 21,000 cases not produced. What rationale would justify awarding him the liqui-dated damages of $105,000 rather than the amount so projected?

———

Superfos Investments Limited v. FirstMiss Fertilizer, Inc.

United States District Court, Southern District of Mississippi, 1993.
821 F.Supp. 432.

■ Lee, J.

Superfos Investments Limited, t/a Superfos Trading, Inc., brought this action seeking damages from defendant FirstMiss Fertilizer, Inc. (First-

Miss) for defendant's alleged breach of its obligations under a contract for the sale and purchase of anhydrous ammonia, a liquid fertilizer. The contract, executed between FirstMiss as buyer and Superfos as seller, was for a term commencing April 1, 1988 and ending December 31, 1990, and required FirstMiss to purchase a minimum of 80,000 tons of anhydrous ammonia in each year of the contract. The contract further provided that should FirstMiss fail to purchase the specified minimum annual volume, it was nevertheless obligated to make payment, upon being invoiced for such deficiency by Superfos, as though the required minimum annual volume of product had been delivered.

In its complaint, Superfos alleges that FirstMiss failed to take delivery of the requisite minimum amounts of anhydrous ammonia dictated by the parties' contract in contract years 1989 and 1990, having taken only 62,856 tons of the product in 1989 and 78,588 tons in 1990. Superfos demands payment of $1,478,670 for the 1989 shortfall and $163,438 for the 1990 shortfall, contending that under the terms of the agreement, it is entitled to recover the full contract purchase price for product not taken by FirstMiss in accordance with the minimum annual purchase obligations.

FirstMiss has now moved the court for partial summary judgment asking that the court resolve the following issue: Whether that provision in its contract with Superfos which provides that FirstMiss must pay the full amount of the purchase price of product for deficiencies or shortfalls in its annual "takes" is enforceable, or whether the provision amounts to a damages penalty for FirstMiss' alleged failure to perform. . . . [T]he court concludes that FirstMiss' motion is well taken and should be granted.

Superfos argues that the subject contract is a typical "take-or-pay" contract, which is reasonable, just and enforceable according to its terms. According to Superfos, the provision in the contract which requires First-Miss to pay for product that it does not take in compliance with the annual minimum requirements imposed by the contract is not a penalty provision, but rather is an alternative means by which FirstMiss may perform its obligations under the contract. In other words, according to Superfos, the contract is, like any other take-or-pay contract, an alternative performance contract, in which the alternatives of taking and paying for the requisite annual volume, on the one hand, and on the other hand of paying for product not taken, are merely the buyer's alternative methods of perform-ing its bargain. FirstMiss maintains that while the contract may superfi-cially resemble a take-or-pay contract, this resemblance is betrayed by its substance and the "pay" option purported to be provided is a penalty in disguise. Thus, the question presented for resolution on the present motion is whether the contract at issue is a true "alternative performance" contract (giving the buyer the option of taking and paying for product or of paying for product not taken), or whether the contract is, in fact, one which provides for a primary obligation (taking and paying for product) with provision for the payment of liquidated damages or a penalty (paying for product not taken) as a means of encouraging or ensuring the buyer's performance of the primary obligation. If the contract falls in the former category, it is enforceable according to its terms. If not, then it devolves upon the court to determine whether the "pay" provision can be construed as an enforceable liquidated damages stipulation or whether it is, in fact, a penalty which cannot be enforced under any circumstances.

Regarding alternative performance contracts, Professor Williston has explained:

> A contract may give an option to one or both parties either to perform a specified act or to make a payment; and though this form of contract cannot be used as a cover for the enforcement of a penalty, yet if on a true interpretation it appears that it was intended to give a real option, that is, that it was conceived possible that at the time fixed for performance, either alternative might prove the more desirable, the contract will be enforced according to its terms. The fact that a promise is expressed in the alternative, however, may easily be given too much weight. As the question of liquidated damages or penalty is based on equitable principles, it cannot depend on the form of the transaction, but rather on its substance. It follows that a contract expressed in the alternative, when examined in the light of the existing facts may prove to be:
>
> (1) A contract contemplating a single definite performance with a penalty stated as an alternative;
>
> (2) a contract contemplating a single definite performance with a sum named as liquidated damages as an alternative; or
>
> (3) a contract by which either alternative may prove the more advantageous and is as open to the promisor as the other.

5 S.Williston, A Treatise on the Law of Contracts § 781, at 706–07 (W.H.E. Jaeger, ed. 3d ed.1961). See also Restatement (Second) of Contracts § 356, Comment c ("although parties may in good faith contract for alternative performances . . . a court will look to the substance of the agreement to determine whether this is the case or whether the parties have attempted to disguise a provision for a penalty that is unenforceable. . . ."). A number of factors lead the court to conclude that the contract at issue in the case sub judice is not a true alternative performance contract.

Courts have recognized, almost without exception, that "take-or-pay" contracts are alternative performance contracts such that the "pay" option in a "take-or-pay" contract is not a penalty provision, and in fact is not a damages provision at all, but rather is one of the buyer's performance alternatives. [The court cites 12 cases, all involving the sale of natural gas.] The contract at issue in the case at bar, however, is not a typical take-or-pay contract.

Take-or-pay contracts, which are common in the natural gas industry, are viewed as risk-allocation contracts:

> The purpose of the take-or-pay clause is to apportion the risks of natural gas production and sales between the buyer and seller. The seller bears the risk of production. To compensate the seller for that risk, buyer agrees to take, or pay for if not taken, a minimum quantity of gas. The buyer bears the risk of market demand. The take-or-pay clause insures that if the demand for gas goes down, seller will still receive the price for the Contract Quantity delivered each year.

[Universal Resources Corp. v. Panhandle Eastern Pipe Line Co., 813 F.2d 77, 80 (5th Cir.1987)]. And they are enforced primarily on the basis that what the buyer is actually paying for is not so much a "product"—gas—as the process by which the gas is made available. The payment is intended to compensate the producer for the costs associated with production and to ensure a steady source of income so that he may continue production.

Superfos argues that the very reason for its entering into this contract with FirstMiss was to ensure a source of payment with which Superfos could meet its own "take-or-pay" obligations under a separate contract into which Superfos had entered with Farmland Industries, Inc., a producer of anhydrous ammonia. In terms nearly identical to the Superfos/FirstMiss contract (with the exception of the minimum tonnage requirements), the Farmland/Superfos contract required Superfos to take and pay for a minimum annual amount of product or to pay for product not taken in accordance with the required minimum annual quantities. Superfos contends that just as with any other take-or-pay contract, under the terms of their agreement, FirstMiss acquired a contractually assured supply of anhydrous ammonia, while Superfos was assured of a source of payment for Farmland's product so that Farmland could continue to produce, even in the event of a change in the marketplace. FirstMiss accepted the risk of changing market conditions, while Superfos accepted the supply risks associated with Farmland's production since, according to Superfos, it guaranteed FirstMiss a constant supply of anhydrous ammonia even if Farmland failed to meet its "obligations to Superfos." Were that the case, then perhaps the question here would be close. However, while a seller's assumption of the risks associated with production is a fundamental feature of take-or-pay contracts, the parties' agreement in this case belies Superfos' contention that it assumed a production risk. In the following terms, the agreement explicitly relieved Superfos of the risk of Farmland's failure to supply the product:

> Neither party will be liable for failure to perform or for delay in performing this Agreement where such failure or delay is occasioned by . . . "Events of Force Majeure." The parties hereto contemplate that Seller will receive the Product which it needs in order to fulfill its obligations hereunder from Farmland, pursuant to the agreement between Seller and Farmland . . . . Therefore, failure of Farmland to deliver a supply of product to Seller pursuant to said agreement, to the extent not excused by acts or omissions of Seller, shall be an Event of Force Majeure that can be exercised by Seller.

Superfos did not, therefore, bear the risk of production; the contract itself eliminated that risk from Superfos' perspective.

Another factor which confirms usual take-or-pay contracts as alternative performance contracts is a buyer's contractual right to "make-up" for gas paid for but not taken. See [Day v. Tenneco, Inc., 696 F.Supp. 233, 234 (S.D.Miss.1988)] (take-or-pay clauses generally grant pipelines a period of five years to take gas paid for under the clause).

. . .

. . . Thus, a determinative factor in the analysis of provisions of a contract to ascertain whether those provisions truly do provide "alternative obligations" is whether the buyer is given a "real choice" of alternatives. . . . [T]he inclusion of a make-up provision in a take-or-pay contract does just that; it gives the buyer that choice. Conversely, . . . the absence of such a provision would provide the buyer no real choice.

. . .

The principal question which has arisen in this case is whether the contract provided FirstMiss a "real choice" of performance alternatives—that is, whether the "pay" alternative was or could be construed under any circumstances to be equally as advantageous as the take-and-pay option, for absent a "real choice," the contract cannot legitimately be treated and enforced as a valid alternative performance agreement. Determining the answer to this question involves construction of the contract; FirstMiss relies heavily on the absence of a make-up provision for its position that this was not a true alternative performance contract, whereas Superfos insists that the contract did, in fact, give FirstMiss a right to make up for "takes" below the minimum annual quantities. While the contract at issue does provide that FirstMiss may make up deficiencies in its quarterly takes, contrary to Superfos' position, nothing in the parties' contract grants FirstMiss the right to make up any annual shortfalls. . . .

The court is, of course, cognizant that a contract which provides for the payment of a liquidated sum of money as one of the alternative methods of performance can be a valid alternative performance contract. But where it cannot reasonably be concluded that at the time the contract was entered, paying for a product not taken might prove as desirable as taking the product and paying for it, then it cannot be reasonably concluded that the "pay" alternative is a true alternative. In the court's opinion, the "pay" option in this contract was not a "real option."

. . .

The court, having concluded that the contract is not a true alternative performance contract despite its superficial appearance as such, must now determine whether the "pay" alternative may be construed as a valid liquidated damages provision, or whether it is, instead, a penalty which may not be enforced against FirstMiss. The question whether the contract establishes a penalty is one of law to be resolved by the court. Virginia law[, which governs this dispute,] recognizes that the parties to a contract may liquidate damages if they do so in an "amount which is reasonable in light of the anticipated or actual harm caused by the breach, the difficulties of proof of loss, and the inconvenience or nonfeasibility of otherwise obtaining an adequate remedy." Va. Code. § 8.2–718. However, "[a] term fixing unreasonably large liquidated damages is void as a penalty." Id. Professor Williston has said:

> Though difficulties frequently arise in the application of the principle distinguishing [a provision for liquidated damages from a provision for a penalty], the fundamental basis of the distinction at least is evident: A penalty is a sum named, which is disproportionate to the damage which could have been anticipated from breach of the contract, and which is agreed upon to enforce performance of the main purpose of the contract by the compulsion of this very disproportion. It is held in terrorem over the promisor to deter him from breaking his promise. Liquidated damage, on the other hand, is a sum fixed as an estimate made by the parties at the time when the contract is entered into, of the extent of the injury which a breach of the contract will cause.

Williston § 776. In the case at bar, FirstMiss maintains that at the time the parties entered into the contract, they should have anticipated that upon breach by FirstMiss, at worst, Superfos would have been required to resell the product at a reduced price, if Farmland would not release Superfos from its own purchase obligations, and that Superfos' anticipated losses would have been no greater than the difference between the contract price and the market price at the time of resale, plus costs incident to the resale less any amounts saved as a result of not having to deliver the product to FirstMiss. According to FirstMiss, requiring it to pay the full contract price for any shortfall in tonnage is grossly disproportionate to the losses which could have been anticipated or which were actually suffered by Superfos. Superfos counters that at the time of contracting, the parties should have anticipated that Superfos might find itself in a situation where it was obligated to pay Farmland for product not taken by FirstMiss and, since Superfos could not store the product and neither party knew what the market conditions would be or whether Superfos would be able to sell the product on the spot market, the only damages which were reasonably ascertainable at the time of contracting were based on Superfos' obligation to Farmland and that provided a reasonable basis for estimating potential damages in the event of breach. The court cannot accept Superfos' position. It simply does not follow from the fact that predicting market conditions is difficult or impossible that it is reasonable to assume that there will be no market for the product. For the parties here to have anticipated that Superfos would be damaged to the extent of the full contract price for any shortfall, they would have had to have anticipated that the market for anhydrous ammonia would disappear entirely. The court hardly considers that this could have been a reasonable assumption of the parties' contract. And in the court's view, to require FirstMiss to pay the full price for any shortfall in tonnage would, indeed, be grossly disproportionate to any actual or anticipated losses. As such, the provision must be viewed as an unenforceable penalty.[8]

Based on the foregoing, it is ordered that the motion of FirstMiss for partial summary judgment is granted.

QUESTIONS AND NOTES

1. Exemplary of enforcement of a take-or-pay clause in a contract for the purchase of natural gas is Sabine Corp. v. ONG Western, Inc., 725 F.Supp. 1157 (W.D.Okla.1989). Defendant failed to take the specified minimum amount and plaintiff sued to recover the price due under the take-or-pay clause. Defendant asserted that the take-or-pay provision was not an enforceable liquidated damages clause. The court responded:

VI. Penalty or Liquidated Damages

The essence of defendant ONG's fourth affirmative defense, on which plaintiff seeks summary judgment, is that because ONG will not, due to market conditions, be able by later takes to make up payment for gas previously not taken, Sabine will remain free to resell such gas paid for but not taken by ONG, resulting in a windfall to Sabine and demonstrating that Sabine "has not suffered damage to the full extent of the contract price for the gas not taken by the buyer." Therefore, ONG alleges, the take-or-pay provisions operate as a penalty or liquidated damages provision and are unenforceable pursuant to Okla.Stat. title 12A, § 2–718(1) and Okla.Stat. title 15, § 214 because the amount of the deficiency sought by plaintiff bears no reasonable relationship to plaintiff's actual damages and the amount of actual damages is not impracticable or extremely difficult to determine.

Sabine asserts that the payment obligation under a take-or-pay contract is a promise or obligation, not a punishment for breach, and that payment pursuant to such contract provision constitutes performance thereof, not payment for breach of the contract of an amount stipulated as damages. Thus, plaintiff asserts that the payment obligation is neither a penalty or a liquidated damages provision, citing Resources Investment Corp. v. Enron Corp., 669 F.Supp. 1038 (D.Colo. 1987) and Universal Resources Corp. v. Panhandle Eastern Pipe Line Co., No. CA3–85–0723–R, slip op. (N.D.Tex. April 1, 1986), aff'd 813 F.2d 77 (5th Cir.1987).

ONG ... makes a minimal response, asserting on the basis of the Hughes Affidavit that material issues of fact exist as to whether ONG will be able to recoup take-or-pay payments made to Sabine and as to whether the amount of take-or-pay payments demanded by Sabine

---

8. Of course, this does not mean that Superfos is precluded from recovering damages for any breach; it merely means that Superfos' damages would be calculated based on the ordinary rules of contract law.

bears any reasonable relationship to any actual and potential damages of Sabine due to ONG's alleged breach. . . .

Whether or not ONG will be able to recoup take-or-pay payments is not material. An assumption that ONG cannot recoup such payments does not render the take-or-pay provisions or the payment obligation under the contract a penalty or a liquidated damages provision. The court agrees with plaintiff and with the United States District Court for the Northern District of Texas that "[t]he take-or-pay provision . . . specifies a contractual obligation rather than dictates damages upon breach." Accordingly, the take-or-pay provision, or more particularly the payment provision, cannot constitute a penalty for failure to perform or a liquidated damages provision specifying damages for breach of the "take" obligation. . . . See also International Minerals & Chemical Corp. v. Llano, Inc., 770 F.2d 879, 885 (10th Cir.1985), cert. denied, 475 U.S. 1015 (1986) (take-or-pay contracts impose alternative obligations); Comment b, Restatement (Second) of Contracts § 361 (1981) (distinguishing provision for alternative performance from liquidated damages provision).

2. Does the take-or-pay clause in *Sabine* meet the standards of 2–718 for enforceability of a damages clause?

3. How is the clause in *Sabine* different from the clause in *Superfos*?

––––––––

Martin v. Sheffer

North Carolina Court of Appeals, 1991.
102 N.C.App. 802, 403 S.E.2d 555.

■ LEWIS, JUDGE.

In December of 1987 Daniel Martin and John Duke contracted with J & S Distributors, Inc. to purchase a KIS Magnum Speed printer for $17,000. The parties agreed that Martin and Duke would send one half of the money as a deposit and would pay the balance upon delivery. On 28 December 1987 the KIS machine arrived in Georgia but Duke and Martin refused to accept it, stating that the delivery was five days late and they had purchased a substitute machine elsewhere. The plaintiffs requested return of their deposit and were refused.

... Duke and Martin sued Jeff Sheffer and J & S Distributors for breach of contract, fraud, breach of good faith and unfair and deceptive trade practices. Defendants answered and counterclaimed for full performance of the contract pursuant to a clause in the contract which provides:

7. In the event of non-payment of the balance of the purchase price reflected herein on due date and in the manner recorded or on such extended date which may be caused by late delivery on the part of DIS, the Customer shall be liable for

7.1   immediate payment of the full balance recorded herein; and

7.2 payment of interest at the rate of 12% per annum calculated on the balance due, when due, together with any attorney's fees, collection charges and other necessary expenses incurred by DIS.

. . . [D]efendants moved for summary judgment on their counterclaim. The trial court granted this motion and ordered specific performance of the contract, costs and attorney's fees.

Appellants argue that the trial court erred in ordering them to accept delivery of the KIS machine and pay the entire balance of the contract. They contend that the determination of seller's damages is controlled by U.C.C. § 2–708 and is limited to lost profits. N.C.G.S. § 25–2–708. Appellants fail to take note of N.C.G.S. § 25–1–102(3) and (4) which provide:

> (3) The effect of provisions of this chapter may be varied by agreement except as otherwise provided in this chapter and except that the obligations of good faith, diligence, reasonableness and care prescribed by this chapter may not be disclaimed by agreement . . .

> (4) The presence in certain provisions of this chapter of the words "unless otherwise agreed" or words of similar import does not imply that the effect of other provisions may not be varied by agreement under subsection (3).

The official comment to Subsection 25–1–102(4) expressly states the general rule that all provisions of the UCC may be varied by contract. Finally, N.C.G.S. § 25–2–719(1)(a) provides that a contract for sale of goods "may provide for remedies in addition to or in substitution for those provided in this article and may limit or alter the measure of damages recoverable under this article, . . . " *Id.* The official comment to this subsection states that "parties are free to shape their remedies to their particular requirements and reasonable agreements limiting or modifying remedies are given effect." Official Comment to N.C.G.S. § 25–2–719.

A contractual provision expanding seller's damages upon breach of the buyer will therefore be upheld where the contractual provision is reasonable and in good faith. N.C.G.S. § 25–1–102. Appellants have signed a contract agreeing to a specific performance clause upon breach. Appellants do not argue in their brief that they were fraudulently induced into signing the contract, that the clause authorizing specific enforcement is ambiguous or a mistake, or that the seller breached the contract by failing to deliver at the time promised.

The appellants argue that the clause should be struck as an "unconscionable and oppressive" liquidated damages clause pursuant to N.C.G.S. § 25–2–718. A contractual clause authorizing specific performance is different in kind from a liquidated damages clause. Even were this not the case, enforcement of the price the appellant freely agreed to pay for the KIS machine cannot be considered unreasonable or a penalty.

Neither do we find this contractual clause to be otherwise unreasonable or contrary to public policy. N.C.G.S. § 25–1–102(3). To find unconscionability there must be an absence of meaningful choice on part of one of the parties together with contract terms which are unreasonably favorable to the other. Appellant does not argue that he lacked meaningful choice in negotiating the terms of the contract. As a merchant, appellant is presumed to be familiar with the terms and practices of contracts for the purchase of the tools of his trade; as such "it is rare that a limitation of remedy will be held unconscionable in a commercial setting since the relationship between business parties is usually not so one-sided as to force an unconscionable limitation on a party." Byrd Motor Lines v. Dunlop Tire and Rubber Corp., 63 N.C.App. 292, 296, 304 S.E.2d 773, 776 (1983). The contractual clause authorizing specific performance does not undermine the essential purpose of the contract.

While this is a case of first impression in this jurisdiction, cases from other jurisdictions serve as guidance and explanation as to the purpose of the Uniform Commercial Code, which is "to make uniform the law among the various jurisdictions." Accordingly, in Frank LeRoux v. Burns, 4 Wash.App. 165, 480 P.2d 213 (1971), the Washington Court of Appeals upheld a similar clause which gave the seller the option of demanding the balance of payments on the contract in the case of any delinquent payment for the goods. The Court held that the parties were free to shape their remedies according to their particular needs, and that an expansion of the seller's remedies beyond those specified in the Uniform Commercial Code to include specific performance is neither unreasonable nor unconscionable. *Id.* The same rationale applies to the case before us.

. . .

Affirmed.

QUESTIONS AND NOTES

1. How is *Sheffer* different from a dispute in which the buyer breaches a contract in which the seller promises to deliver a printer to the buyer and the buyer promises to pay the seller $17,000?

2. How is the litigation in *Sheffer* different from a seller's action for the price? Under 2–709, is the seller entitled to the price? Is Official Comment 6 relevant to the dispute in *Sheffer*?

3. The court's reasoning emphasizes 1–102 and 2–719, both empowering the parties to stipulate the remedies in the event of breach. Please consider the accuracy of this proposition: an agreement that specific performance is the remedy for breach is not within the contemplation of those sections.

4. Revised Article 2 and liquidated damages. Revised 2–718 makes two important changes in an attempt to liberalize the ability of the parties to stipulate damages in the event of breach. It deletes the reference to difficulty of proof of loss and difficulty of obtaining an adequate remedy, except in consumer contracts. It also deletes the second sentence of 2–718(1), stating that a term fixing unreasonably large liquidated damages is void as a penalty. Revised Official Comment 2 states that this latter provision is redundant and misleading, because it could be read to say that even though the damages provision meets the test of the first sentence of 2–718(1), the provision might nevertheless be struck as unreasonably large.

Revised 2–718 also deletes the provision in 2–718(2) which permits a seller to retain the lesser of $500 or 20 percent of any payments made by the buyer without having to prove that it has suffered any loss or conferred any benefit on the buyer.

5. Revised Article 2 and specific performance as an agreed remedy. As noted earlier (pages 413–14 supra), revised 2–716 expressly allows the court to grant specific performance if the parties have contracted for it, except that specific performance may not be granted if the only remaining performance is the payment of money. In *Sheffer*, since the buyers also had to accept the goods, was their remaining obligation more than the payment of money? If so, does this mean that under revised 2–716 sellers can always get specific performance?

6. Interest charges as liquidated damages. It is common for contracts to provide that if the buyer fails to pay when payment is due, the seller is entitled to a finance charge or default charge of a specified amount or rate. Are these provisions enforceable? In N. Bloom & Son (Antiques) Ltd. v. Skelly, 673 F.Supp. 1260 (S.D.N.Y.1987), the buyer contracted to purchase two candelabras and a centerpiece for $45,000. The contract called for an interest charge of 24 percent per year on contract balances not paid according to the contract terms. The prevailing interest rate when the contract was made was 13 percent, and the court held that the 11 percent premium above the base rate was not reasonably related to the actual damages (viz., collection costs) that the seller would suffer from delayed payment. It held the provision to be an unenforceable penalty under 2–718.

7. Leases. It is very common for leases of goods to stipulate a formula for calculating the lessor's damages in the event of breach by the lessee. These formulas can be quite intimidating. For example, in Northwest Acceptance Corp. v. Hesco Construction, Inc., 26 Wash.App. 823, 614 P.2d 1302 (1980), a construction company defaulted on a four-year lease of a backhoe. The lessor repossessed and sued to enforce a clause of the lease contract that provided:

Lessor and lessee agree, for the purpose of this lease, that:

(A) The cost to the lessor of the equipment hereby leased was $55,544.50.

(B) The fair market value of the equipment hereby leased, at the end of the term of this lease shall be $8,331.67.

(C) At any time during the period of this lease, the present value of rent contracted to be paid in the future (said present value to be computed on the basis of a 5 per cent per annum yield) shall be computed as if the monthly rental was a monthly annuity for the number of future months the rent is promised to be paid.

(D) The total depreciation of the leased equipment during the term of the lease shall be the cost of the equipment to the lessor (Item 'A' above) less its residual value at the end of the lease (Item 'B' above).

(E) For the purpose of this section, the depreciated value of the leased equipment at any particular time during the term of this lease shall be the cost of the leased equipment to the lessor, as above set forth, less the depreciation thereon to such time computed on an accelerating depreciation basis, said computation to be made by dividing the term of the lease into semi-annual periods and spreading the total depreciation over such periods under the sum of the digits method. The sum of the digits computation shall be accomplished by numbering the last semi-annual period with the digit '1'; the next prior to the last period with the digit '2', and so on back, until the first semi-annual period is numbered, and then forming a fraction with a denominator equal to the sum of all the digits used and a numerator equal to the digit of the semi-annual period containing the day to which depreciation is being computed, plus the digits for all prior semi-annual periods. The fraction thus formed shall be used to multiply the total depreciation of the leased equipment during the term of the lease established in paragraph (D) above, and the result shall be the depreciation of the leased equipment to the day selected.

(F) In the event the lessee during the term of the lease elects to reject the lease or defaults in performance thereof and surrenders the leased equipment to the lessor or such equipment otherwise comes into the possession of the lessor, the damage to the lessor because of the lessee's default or breach of the lease exclusive of costs enumerated herein above shall be established as follows: The amount of all rent due and unpaid at the time of the computation of such damage shall be added to the present value of all rent contracted to be paid in the future (item C above) and the sum shall be Item 1 of this computation. If the equipment has been surrendered to the lessor or the lessor has otherwise come into the possession of it, there shall be subtracted from the depreciated value of the equipment at the time it came into the possession of the lessor (established pursuant to paragraph 'E' above), the residual value of the chattel at the end of the term of the lease (item 'B' above) and the difference which is Item 2 shall be subtracted from Item 1. The result, when added to the costs herein provided for, plus 5 per cent interest thereon from the date of computation to date of payment, or if judgment is entered for such damages, to date of judgment, shall be the amount of the damages suffered and costs expended by the lessor because of the lessee's breach of the lease. Interest after judgment shall be at the highest lawful rate permitted by law.

In the event the lessee during the term of the lease elects to reject it or defaults in performance thereof, but the leased equipment does not come into the possession of the lessor, the amount of damages suffered and costs expended by the lessor shall be Item 1 above plus the residual value of the chattels at the end of the term of the lease, which is item B above, plus interest at the rate of 5 per cent per annum from the date of computation to the date of payment, or if judgment is entered for such damages, to the date of judgment, plus the costs expended.

The court applied this formula as follows:

1. The aggregate of rental payments in arrears ($6,640.00) is added to the present value of all future rentals contracted to be paid over the unexpired term of the lease ($34,090.64), which is discounted at the agreed rate of 5 percent, to $32,754.75, for a total of $39,394.75.

2. That total is reduced by the difference between (a) the current depreciated value of the equipment at the time of repossession by the lessor ($21,169.59), and (b) the agreed fair market or residual value of the equipment upon its return at the end of the lease ($8,331.67), or $12,837.92. The total damages under this formula are $39,394.75 minus $12,837.92, or $26,556.83.

It agreed with the trial court that "The liquidated damages are reasonably related to anticipation of possible problems with the leased equipment, the condition it would be in upon its return to the plaintiff and the value of the lease agreement to the plaintiff if the defendants had fully performed said lease." The appellate court stated:

> The hydraulic backhoe is a specialized piece of construction equipment, the marketability of which is dependent upon many factors including a fluctuating economy, the state of the construction industry, and the demand for used equipment. Because this was a lease agreement, Hesco is not entitled to a credit for the resale price of the equipment following repossession. But, two features of this formula make it a fair liquidated damages provision—(1) the lessor's expectation for future rentals under the lease were reduced to the present value; and (2) the lessee was given a credit for depreciation savings because the equipment was returned to the lessor before the end of the lease.

> There is no basis for a finding of unconscionability. We have here two contracting parties, both with extensive experience in construction equipment. Contrary to assertions by Hesco, the damage formula is not impossible to understand. Mr. Schimmels complains that Northwest did not volunteer an explanation of the formula, but he also admitted that he never bothered to read the contract, and did not ask for an explanation. His son, who was serving as Hesco's secretary-treasurer at the time, is a certified public accountant. Given these circumstances, the trial court properly refused to find the lease unconscionable.

> There is no reason why persons, competent and free to contract, may not agree upon this subject (liquidated damages) as fully as upon any other, or why their agreement when fairly and under-

standingly entered into with a view to just compensation for the anticipated loss, should not be enforced.

Underwood v. Sterner, 63 Wash.2d 360, 366, 387 P.2d 366 (1963)

8. Liquidated damages clauses of the type used in *Hesco Construction* are common. If the calculation of damages is tied to the time of occurrence of the breach, the clause is likely to be sustained. Several elements of the formula might, however, be attacked, depending upon the facts of a particular case.

(1) The present discounted value of future rents varies inversely with the discount rate: the lower the discount rate, the higher the value of future rents. The five-percent discount rate used in Northwest was below the market rate of interest in the late 1970s by a substantial amount. The market rate was probably around ten percent. It might be possible to attack the discount rate as being unreasonably low and therefore overcompensating the lessor.

(2) The sum-of-the-digits depreciation method might assume unrealistically high loss of value in the leased goods during the early part of the lease and, again, overcompensate the lessor. For example, in a four-year lease, the sum-of-the-digits depreciation method leads to about 50% depreciation in the first year. (The sum of the digits 1 through 48 is 1168. The sum of the digits 37 through 48 is 547, so the first year depreciation is 547/1168, or 46.83%, of the total depreciation over the four years.)

(3) The value of the leased property at the end of the lease (the "residual value") might be set lower than the lessor actually or reasonably expects it to be at the end of the lease.

Section 2A–103(u) of the UCC, which defines present value, states that in determining present value the contracted-for discount rate will be used if it was not manifestly unreasonable at the time the transaction was entered into; "otherwise," the discount is determined by a commercially reasonable rate that takes into account the facts and circumstances of each case at the time the transaction was entered into. See 2A–503 and 2A–504 as to contracted-for remedies and liquidated-damages clauses in lease contracts.

CHAPTER 8

REPUDIATION AND THE PROSPECT OF BREACH

A. THE PROSPECT OF BREACH

A party to a sales contract may breach that contract in any number of different ways. Perhaps the most extreme and dramatic of them is by renouncing the obligations of the contract. The law refers to this as a repudiation, and if the renunciation occurs in advance of the time for performance, it is known as an anticipatory repudiation. Under 2–610(b), a repudiation operates as a material breach. Under 2–703 a repudiation by the buyer triggers the seller's right to all of the remedies specified there. Similarly, under 2–711(1) a repudiation by the seller triggers the buyer's right to all the remedies specified there and in 2–711(2).

Repudiation, then, is a very serious matter. But what exactly is a repudiation? Official Comment 1 to 2–610 states, "anticipatory repudiation centers upon an overt communication of intention or an action which renders performance impossible or demonstrates a clear determination not to continue with performance." If any of these occurs, there is a repudiation, and the other party may invoke the appropriate remedies of Article 2. But the party who invokes one of those remedies may be taking a large risk, because a judge or jury reviewing the situation after the fact may conclude that the other party's conduct or statements do not amount to a repudiation. If this happens, then the party who resorted to the Article 2 remedies is the party in breach. This, then, poses a dilemma for a party who has significant doubt about whether the other party will perform as promised: "should I continue to perform even though I may not get what I bargained for, or should I refuse to perform and be liable for breach if I'm wrong?"

Fortunately, Article 2 provides a way out this dilemma, a mechanism by which an insecure party may suspend performance until the insecurity is resolved. The first sentence of subsection (1) of 2–609 states the important proposition that a "contract for sale imposes an obligation on each party that the other's reasonable expectation of receiving due performance will not be impaired." The second sentence states the prerequisites for suspending performance. Please read all of 2–609.

————

Clem Perrin Marine Towing, Inc. v. Panama Canal Co.

United States Court of Appeals, Fifth Circuit, 1984.
730 F.2d 186.

■ PATRICK E. HIGGINBOTHAM, CIRCUIT JUDGE. Defendant Panama Canal Company [hereinafter PCC] appeals from an adverse judgment for breach of a lease-purchase of a tugboat. . . .

I

Effective March 15, 1974, PCC and [Clem Perrin Marine Towing, Inc., (hereinafter CPMT)] agreed to a "Bareboat Charter Party," providing for a three-year bareboat charter of a tug at a cost of $344,880.* The agreement called for payments in seven installments, the last five of which were to be paid in advance [of each of the last five] six-month periods. Article XIX of the agreement gave PCC an "option" to purchase the tug during the final ninety days of the three-year period for $26,400, well below CPMT's claimed market value of $190,000. CPMT agreed to provide merchantable title upon exercise of the option. . . .

During August 1976, PCC received information that CPMT was not making its payments on the tug's first mortgage. It also claims it learned for the first time during August that CPMT had encumbered the tug with a third mortgage in addition to the two mortgages outstanding against the tug when the contract was signed. The final installment of $49,480 was due on September 15, 1976, to cover the six-month period from that date until March 15, 1977. On August 27, 1976, PCC wrote to CPMT that "[i]t has come to our attention that one of the outstanding mortgages on this boat has fallen into default and the Panama Canal Company therefore considers that reasonable grounds exist for requiring assurance that clear title to the boat will be perfected on or before December 15, 1976," the date the option to purchase became exercisable. Further, PCC stated that it would not forward the payment due September 15 until it received assurance.

CPMT's only response was to file this suit [on September 17,] two days after PCC withheld payment. On December 20, after the purchase option matured, PCC tendered the final charter-hire installment along with the option payment. Delivery was made subject to the condition that CPMT furnish merchantable title. CPMT did not reply.

On April 13, 1977, the companies holding the first and second mortgages on the tug gave notice to PCC that they planned to foreclose and seize the vessel. On June 2, 1977, PCC bought those mortgages for $111,897. In its countersuit ..., PCC contends that CPMT breached its agreement to provide merchantable title and seeks damages plus interest, in addition to its request for title to the tug.

After discovery and after the denial of several motions for summary judgment filed by both parties, trial in the case was set for May 8, 1978. On

---

* Under a bareboat charter, the charterer (here, PCC) takes control of the vessel for the period of the charter as though it owns the vessel, with the obligation of returning it to the owner (here, CPMT) at the end of that period.—Ed.

March 28, 1978, however, Clem and Marie Perrin filed Chapter XI bankruptcy petitions, and this case was stayed. On January 9, 1979, CPMT was declared bankrupt. The trustee in bankruptcy obtained an order allowing further prosecution of this suit on October 17, 1979, and PCC says it became aware the stay had been lifted when the trustee commenced new discovery proceedings on March 16, 1981.

. . .

IV

UCC § 2–609 provides that when reasonable grounds for insecurity arise, a party may in writing demand assurance and, if commercially reasonable, suspend performance for which he has not already received the agreed return. A ground for insecurity need not arise from or be directly related to the contract under which a party suspends performance. UCC § 2–609, Comment 3. Here PCC had not already received the return for the performance it suspended; the payment was to be made at the beginning of the last six-month lease-period and title to the vessel had not yet been transferred. Under this standard, PCC need only prove it had reasonable doubt that CPMT would provide merchantable title, and need not prove, for example, that CPMT was insolvent, so long as the doubt is otherwise reasonable. See UCC § 2–609, Comment 4. If PCC further can carry its related burden of proving that it was commercially reasonable to suspend performance in light of that doubt, then its case will be made under the UCC standard. . . .

. . .

VI

CPMT claims it was not reasonable for PCC to ask for assurance because CPMT was actually in good financial shape at the time PCC suspended performance and could have provided merchantable title, and further that PCC did not adequately investigate CPMT's financial situation before asking for assurance. The district court made no distinct finding on the reasonableness of PCC's suspension of performance, but did hold that PCC had failed to use "due diligence" in investigating CPMT's financial situation. Whether a buyer has reasonable grounds for insecurity is a question of fact. To the extent CPMT is correct in saying this finding of a lack of "due diligence" may be interpreted to be a finding that PCC was not reasonable in its suspension of performance and request for assurance, we hold that the finding was clearly erroneous.

What prompted PCC's concern was a phone call from Mr. H.J. Lopez of the George Engine Company to the PCC informing PCC that CPMT was not making its mortgage payments on the vessel and that George Engine Company was making them instead. CPMT argues that PCC should have inquired more deeply to determine the extent of any financial difficulty, because in reality CPMT was in no danger of defaulting on its mortgages. CPMT further argues it was unreasonable to suspend performance because PCC was aware that CPMT was relying on the payment to pay off the mortgages. CPMT's argument about the extent of PCC's inquiry misses the point, however. If CPMT was in the fine financial shape it argues it was in, all CPMT had to do in response to PCC's request for assurance was to explain the situation. It was certainly not unreasonable for PCC to become alarmed at Lopez' call, enough so for the call in itself to constitute a reasonable ground for insecurity. Lopez had played a major role in brokering the deal between PCC and CPMT and could reasonably have been considered to have good information about CPMT's financial status. Cf. UCC § 2–609, Comment 3 ("[A] report from an apparently trustworthy source that the seller had shipped defective goods * * * would normally give the buyer reasonable grounds for insecurity.") The standard is one of reasonable insecurity, not absolute certainty. See UCC § 2–609, Comment 4, citing Corn Products Refining Co. v. Fasola, 94 NJL 181, 109 A. 505 (1920). Here PCC's suspicion was reasonable, as was their action in asking for assurance. Further, in the face of CPMT's silence after the demand for assurance, it was obviously reasonable for PCC to protect itself by withholding payment, notwithstanding that it was aware that doing so would probably hurt CPMT. That suspending performance might hurt CPMT was not reasonably PCC's concern.

VII

We therefore reverse the district court's finding that PCC breached the contract. Instead, we hold that CPMT breached its agreement to provide merchantable title and is liable for the damages PCC incurred in buying the mortgages on the vessel. Of course, CPMT is still owed the last payment of charter hire and the option payment. We therefore remand the case to the district court for the purpose of offsetting the amounts owed and then awarding PCC the remaining amount. The district court is further directed to award PCC prejudgment interest, see Com. Standard Ins. Co. v. Bryce St. Apts., Ltd., 703 F.2d 904 (5th Cir. 1983), and to enter an order for specific performance compelling CPMT to deliver clear title to the vessel to PCC. Finally, since the parties did not brief the issue on appeal of whether the third-party defendants may be reached by piercing the corporate veil, we remand that issue to the district court for its consideration.

Reversed and remanded.

QUESTIONS AND NOTES

1. An omitted portion of the opinion reveals that the contract contained a provision that allowed CPMT to cancel the contract if PCC defaulted in payment. In view of the existence of this provision, did the court err in holding for PCC?

2. Problem. Seller contracts to deliver over a 12–month period 100 gasoline pumps at Buyer's chain of convenience stores. The contract calls for Seller to install them, get them operating properly, and service them for

90 days after delivery. Payment is due 30 days after installation. Of the first 20 pumps that are delivered and installed, 12 do not operate as they are supposed to.

a. Can Buyer properly send Seller a letter refusing to permit Seller to install any more pumps until it provides satisfactory proof that they will operate as warranted?

b. Can Buyer withhold payment for the 12 nonconforming pumps? for the other eight?

c. Can Buyer demand an extension of the 30–day warranty of repairs provided in the contract?

3. Problem. Tophat Company contracted to sell Warren Construction Company a large construction crane for $250,000, delivery on June 1st. The contract called for payment of 50% of the price on delivery and the balance in two annual payments, with Tophat taking a security interest in the crane to secure those two payments. On May 10th, Teri Toroian, president of Tophat Company, was having coffee with Laurie Liu, an attorney friend. Liu remarked that she had heard that Warren was losing a lot of money on a large apartment building it was building. When Toroian got back to the office she phoned Warren and asked whether Warren's financial position was impaired by losses on the apartment building. Warren's treasurer said, "It's not true that we have lost money. In fact, we are fine, and we don't appreciate your asking." With that the conversation ended.

Toroian, however, then sent a letter to Warren Construction relating the statements she had heard and asking whether there was any truth to the assertion. Warren again responded, this time in writing, "we are not losing money, we are fine"; "keep your nose out of our business"; and "why are you so worried, you're fully secured for the amount we owe you after the crane is delivered."

On May 29th Toroian asks you whether she can safely withhold delivery because, she says, she is afraid that Warren Construction is overextended and may get into trouble. She also asks how, if she may indeed withhold delivery, she should proceed, both before and after June 1st. How do you respond?

Would your answer to the above problem change if Toroian told you that she also had heard the same rumors from persons other than Liu before she had made the contract with Warren?

4. Note that 2–609(1) speaks of a *written* demand for adequate assurance. Does an oral demand suffice to trigger the other party's obligation to respond? Several cases have held that, on the facts of the case, an oral demand for assurances was effective under 2–609. E.g., Diskmakers, Inc. v. DeWitt Equipment Corp., 555 F.2d 1177 (3d Cir.1977); ARB, Inc. v. E–Systems, Inc., 663 F.2d 189 (D.C.Cir.1980).

5. As perhaps suggested by Problem 3, the financial condition of a business may change significantly over a relatively short period of time. A change in the financial condition of the seller may affect the seller's ability to deliver the goods, and the buyer may invoke 2–609 to demand assurances that the seller will perform as agreed. A change in the financial condition of the buyer may affect the buyer's ability to pay for the goods, and the seller may demand adequate assurance. For this particular cause of insecurity, however, Article 2 has two other provisions to alleviate the seller's insecurity. Under the conditions specified in 2–702, the seller may convert a credit transaction into a cash transaction. Under the conditions specified in 2–705, the seller may withhold delivery of the goods. Please read those sections.

6.   Problem. Noflat Tire Company contracted to ship a carload of tires to TBA Stores, Inc. The shipment was to be F.O.B. Noflat's plant and was on open account on 90–day payment terms. While the carload was in transit, Noflat's credit department received a report that TBA was running four months or more behind in paying bills. Noflat calls you and asks whether there is anything it can do to protect itself against the possibility that TBA will pay very late or not at all. The shipment was under a straight bill of lading naming TBA as consignee. (Under a straight bill, the carrier will deliver to the named consignee without requiring payment or the surrender of any document or other evidence of ownership.)

    a.   What do you advise? *Get assurances, stop performance*

    b.   May Noflat direct the carrier to stop the train? *2–705*

    c.   If Noflat decides to stop the shipment, does it have to notify TBA of that action and the reasons for it? *no*

7.   Problem. Global Controls contracted to deliver certain instruments to MissileCo for use in a missile system that MissileCo was installing. The contract called for payment to be made monthly for deliveries made the previous month. Final inspection and acceptance of the goods were to take place at the various missile sites (which were not the place of delivery). About six weeks before making the first delivery, Global began to receive unfavorable credit reports on MissileCo. About three weeks before the first delivery Global secured a Dun & Bradstreet credit report that showed a reduction in MissileCo's credit rating from A1 to A1–1/2 and delays in payment to its suppliers. Global then contacted some individual suppliers, who reported substantial delays in payment. Instead of shipping the goods under a straight bill of lading, Global sent the first order under a sight-draft-with-order bill of lading. (Under that document the carrier will not deliver the goods to the buyer until the price is paid. It permits the buyer to inspect the goods in the hands of the carrier, but requires payment of the price before the buyer is entitled to possession of the goods.) MissleCo refused to pay against the sight draft and the goods were returned to Global Controls. When Global Controls sued, MissleCo filed a counterclaim. Which party has breached? See 2–702, 2–310, 2–505, 2–513.

8. If the seller learns of the buyer's insolvency before the seller has shipped the goods, may the seller cancel the contract without offering the goods for cash?

9.   Subsection (1) of 2–702 provides that if the seller discovers the buyer to be insolvent, the seller may (a) refuse to deliver except for cash, and (b) stop delivery under 2–705. If a seller learns of a buyer's insolvency after the seller has shipped the goods, may the seller exercise the second alternative in 2–702 independently of the first: may a seller stop delivery of the goods without offering to deliver them for cash? Should the seller who already has shipped the goods be treated differently than the seller who has not shipped?

B.   Repudiation

1.   Definition

The preceding section explores the rights of one party to a sales contract when the words or conduct of the other party have created insecurity about whether that other party will perform in accordance with the contract. If that other party's words or conduct amount to a repudiation of the contract, the aggrieved party need not go through the procedures of 2–609 but instead may treat the repudiation as a breach. See 2–610(b). Alternatively, the aggrieved party may refuse to treat the repudiation as a breach and may continue to await performance by the repudiating party. See 2–610(a). Conversely, 2–611 recognizes that the repudiating party may have a change of heart and want to retract the repudiation.

1.   Problem. Assume that there are only five remaining operable U.S. Army amphibious vehicles of World War Two vintage (Ducks) in the entire world. Two of these are owned by Fraley Motors in Houston, Texas; two are owned by Motion Picture Props, Inc., of Long Beach, California; and one is owned by Eduardo Robles of Atlanta, Georgia. Robles contracts with Motion Picture Props to sell his Duck at a price of $25,000, delivery in Atlanta on June 2nd.

a.   On May 15th Motion Picture Props learns that Eduardo Robles has just leased his Duck to Fraley Motors for 18 months. Props also understands that Fraley is willing to sell one of its Ducks for $35,000. Props is afraid that Fraley may sell the Duck momentarily and asks whether they can buy it immediately and charge Robles with the increased cost. What do you advise?

b.   Since delivery of the Duck is to be made in Atlanta, Props has arranged for one of its large tractor-trailers to leave Long Beach for Atlanta on May 25th. On May 23rd, Props receives an e-mail from Robles saying that he has decided to lease the Duck (to Fraley) instead of selling it (to Props), so he would not be delivering it to Props. Props e-mails back, "We expect you to perform," and sends the truck on its way. The truck arrives in Atlanta on June 2nd, and the driver tenders the purchase price and demands delivery. Robles refuses. May Props recover as an element of damages the expense of sending the truck to Atlanta? What arguments would you make on behalf of Motion Picture Props? on behalf of Eduardo Robles?

2. Problem. In a series of six separate contracts, Seller contracts to deliver 100 barrels of kosher dill pickles to Buyer, who operates a chain of specialty grocery stores. The contracts call for delivery on the first day of each month, April through September. The price of each delivery is $10,000, and payment is due 10 days after delivery. Seller delivers on the first of April, May, June, and July. Buyer pays for the April delivery on April 12th, for the May delivery on May 20th, and has not paid for the deliveries in June and July. On July 25th, Seller informs Buyer that it will not deliver the pickles on the August and September contracts unless it has received payment on the two earlier contracts on which it has not been paid. Buyer immediately purchases pickles elsewhere for $11,500 per month and sues Seller. Is Seller liable?

3. Consider the following excerpt from Ewanchuk v. Mitchell, 154 S.W.3d 476 (Mo.App.2005):

> Ewanchuk and Mitchell are both in the business of breeding and raising registered Boston terriers. Ewanchuk has been licensed in this business for twelve years and resides in Alberta, Canada. Mitchell has been licensed in this business for three years and operates a kennel in Cabool, Missouri. Mitchell sold only puppies, and she mainly marketed her animals to brokers that purchased animals for resale to pet stores.

> On January 20, 2003, one of Mitchell's breeding females whelped two male Boston terrier puppies ("the puppies.") Rather than being the black and white color normally found in Boston terriers, the puppies were red and white in color. This made them very unique and desirable animals.

> On February 20, 2003, Mitchell offered to sell the puppies by placing an ad on the internet. That same day, Ewanchuk responded to the ad by leaving a message on Mitchell's answering machine. In the message, Ewanchuk expressed her interest in purchasing the puppies. She asked Mitchell to return the call, which Mitchell did. Ewanchuk and Mitchell had several more telephone conversations about the puppies, and Mitchell sent photographs of them to Ewanchuk. During these conversations, Ewanchuk did not commit to purchasing the puppies because they were still too young.

> On March 21, 2003, Mitchell called Ewanchuk to inform her that the puppies were eight weeks old and were going to be sold to a broker the following Monday unless Ewanchuk agreed to buy them. The timing of the sale was very important to Mitchell because pet stores would not purchase puppies older than nine weeks of age, so she had to get them to a broker immediately if Ewanchuk did not buy them. Otherwise, the value of the puppies would decline because Mitchell would no longer be able to sell them to a broker or a pet store.

> Mitchell initially priced the puppies at $350 each, but she agreed to sell the puppies for a total of $600 because Ewanchuk wanted to buy both of them. Ewanchuk provided Mitchell with a credit card number which was used to charge the $600 payment.

Although Ewanchuk and Mitchell were able to agree on the puppies' price, they were unable to agree on when and how the puppies would be delivered to Ewanchuk. . . . Mitchell, however, insisted that Ewanchuk accept delivery by April 15, 2003.

. . .

. . . On [April 15] Ewanchuk telephoned Mitchell to discuss shipping arrangements. In this telephone call, Ewanchuk insisted Mitchell ship the puppies together in one crate. Ewanchuk testified that "I wanted the two puppies shipped together in one kennel, and they [Mitchell and her husband] refused to do that." Mitchell would not ship the three-month-old puppies together because she believed they "would fight and that it was not safe for the puppies to be in the same crate at that age." Mitchell was willing to send one puppy in one crate, but Ewanchuk wanted both delivered together. Ewanchuk testified that Mitchell "repudiated" the contract during that call and said she would refund Ewanchuk's money.

After April 15, 2003, Ewanchuk made no further arrangements to have the puppies delivered to her and had no further direct contact with Mitchell. Ewanchuk later hired an attorney, who filed suit on her behalf on May 16, 2003, seeking specific performance of the oral agreement and injunctive relief to prevent Mitchell from selling the puppies to someone else. . . .

. . . [T]he trial court entered judgment for Mitchell . . . . The trial court found for Mitchell, in pertinent part, for the following reason:

> There was no meeting of the minds as to one of the essential terms of the contract, namely when the puppies would be shipped to the Plaintiff in Canada, and how the shipment would be arranged . . . . Further, a dispute arose as to whether the puppies should be shipped in one crate or two crates. Therefore, the Court finds that all of the essential terms of the contract were not agreed upon and that the Agreement lacked a definiteness necessary for its enforcement.

Ewanchuk appealed.

. . . The oral agreement between Ewanchuk and Mitchell was a contract for the sale of goods within the meaning of Missouri's version of the Uniform Commercial Code ("UCC.") See § 400.2–105(1). Therefore, this transaction in goods is governed by the law of sales found in Article 2 of the UCC, which is codified in § 400.2–101 through § 400.2–725.

. . .

The trial court misapplied the law by concluding that the parties' agreement "lacked a definiteness necessary for its enforcement." On appeal, however, we are "primarily concerned with the correctness of the trial court's result, not the route taken by the trial court to reach that result." Business Men's Assur. Co. of America v. Graham, 984

S.W.2d 501, 506 (Mo. banc 1999). "The judgment will be affirmed if cognizable under any theory, regardless of whether the reasons advanced by the trial court are wrong or not sufficient." Id.

The second prong of Ewanchuk's argument is that Mitchell breached the contract by refusing to deliver the puppies. We reject this aspect of Ewanchuk's argument. The trial court entered judgment for Mitchell after concluding the contract was unenforceable. This conclusion is correct, but for a different reason than the one upon which the trial court relied.

. . . Ewanchuk insisted the puppies be shipped to her in one crate, and Mitchell refused. Mitchell offered to ship one dog in one crate, but Ewanchuk was adamant that she wanted the puppies shipped together. At that point, Mitchell cancelled the contract and said she would refund Ewanchuk's money. Thereafter, Ewanchuk made no further arrangements to have the puppies delivered to her, and she never contacted Mitchell directly again.

As noted above, the parties failed to reach an agreement upon the manner and place of delivery during their negotiation. Therefore, the UCC supplied that term of the agreement by requiring Ewanchuk to pick up the puppies at Mitchell's place of business in Cabool. Ewanchuk did not pick up the puppies by April 15, 2003. Instead, on the date delivery was due to occur, Ewanchuk insisted that Mitchell ship both puppies by air in one crate to Alberta, Canada. It was this demand which caused Mitchell's refusal to deliver the puppies and consequent cancellation of the contract. Absent Mitchell's agreement, the UCC did not give Ewanchuk the right to receive delivery of the puppies in this fashion.

Both by decisional law and statute, Missouri recognizes the doctrine of anticipatory repudiation. Missouri Public Service Co. v. Peabody Coal Co., 583 S.W.2d 721, 724 (Mo.App.1979); § 400.2–610. A party repudiates a contract by manifesting a positive intention not to perform by words or conduct. Gateway Aviation, Inc. v. Cessna Aircraft Co., 577 S.W.2d 860, 862 (Mo.App.1978). Section 400.2–610 states in pertinent part that, "when either party repudiates the contract with respect to a performance not yet due the loss of which will substantially impair the value of the contract to the other, the aggrieved party may . . . (b) resort to any remedy for breach (section 400.2–703 or section 400.2–711) . . . ." Upon a buyer's repudiation of the contract, in whole or in part, one of the seller's available remedies is cancellation of the contract. § 400.2–703(f).

Here, Ewanchuk's own testimony demonstrated that she insisted upon a mode of delivery (both puppies in one crate) and a place of delivery (Alberta, Canada, via air transportation) to which Mitchell had not agreed and to which Ewanchuk was not entitled under the UCC. After making this impermissible demand, Ewanchuk also testified that she never contacted Mitchell directly again and made no further arrangements to have the puppies delivered to her.

Thus, Ewanchuk's trial testimony, by which she was bound, proved that she repudiated the contract on April 15, 2003. Since the puppies were then 12 weeks old, Ewanchuk's repudiation impaired the value of the contract to Mitchell because she could no longer sell the puppies to a broker or pet store. Based on this repudiation, Mitchell was authorized to cancel the contract, which she did.

In conclusion, the trial court properly denied Ewanchuk's request for specific performance and other relief because the contract was unenforceable. The reason the contract was unenforceable, however, was because it had been cancelled by Mitchell after repudiation by Ewanchuk. Although the trial court did not rely on the doctrine of repudiation as the basis for its decision, we may do so to uphold the judgment based on the record before us. The judgment of the trial court is affirmed.

4. Problem. Scott Kim contracted to sell Meredith Hendon three holographic-image-making machines for a total price of $50,000, delivery on February 1. On January 15 Kim called Hendon and notified her that he would be unable to supply the machines except at a price of $75,000. Hendon replied, "What! Our contract clearly calls for a price of $50,000. You can't get away with this. I'll see you in court!" Taken aback by her vehemence, Kim retreated, "All right, never mind. I'll perform on the original terms." Hendon said, "No, I'm through with you."

Kim tendered the machines on February 1, and Hendon refused to accept them. Who breached?

5. Problem. Smith, a farmer, contracted to sell soybeans to LDC. Because of bad weather, Smith had substantially fewer beans to deliver than he had contracted to sell. On December 8th, immediately after a telephone conversation with Smith, LDC covered and ultimately sued Smith for $21,655, the excess of the cover price over the contract price. If LDC had delayed cover until December 12th, the damages would have been about $10,000 less. Smith claimed that he had not repudiated in the telephone conversation on the 8th and that cover was inappropriate. On cross-examination, he testified as follows (Transcript pp. 104–106):

Q. And let me talk with you very briefly about that phone conversation on the 8th.

A. Go ahead.

Q. That was you, wasn't it, that called Mr. Cox?

A. Yes, sir.

Q. And that was early in the morning?

A. Yes, sir.

Q. At 7:45 A.M. In fact it was before the prices on the Chicago Board of Trade opened for the day?

A. Yes, sir.

Q. And you told him you'd finished cutting beans, is that correct?

A.   Yes, sir.

Q.   What else did you tell him?

A.   We had a—we talked about the beans that were over at Gulf Grain and everything.

Q.   Did you know how much was over at Gulf Grain then to be cleaned?

A.   There were three loads.

Q.   Three truckloads?

A.   Yes, sir.

Q.   So a couple of thousand bushels at most?

A.   Yes, sir.

Q.   Twenty-five hundred bushels at most?

A.   Yes, sir.

Q.   Did you discuss anything else?

A.   No, sir.

Q.   Do you recall stating in that phone conversation to Mr. Cox you wanted to pay up?

A.   I didn't say that.

Q.   You never said that?

A.   No, sir.

Q.   When you called did you intend to convey the message to him that you wanted to pay him?

A.   I said that we would get together and settle up when they got everything in.

Q.   Now you knew you were short on your deliveries?

A.   Yes, sir.

Q.   Very short?

A.   Yes, sir.

Q.   But it's your testimony now that you never said you wanted to pay up?

A.   No, sir, I never did say that.

Q.   Never said that? You're absolutely certain about that?

A.   Yes, sir.

[Continuing the cross examination, plaintiff's counsel questions Smith about his deposition (Transcript p. 106).]

Q.   Do you remember my asking you back then about that phone conversation?

A.   Yes, sir.

Q. What was your answer at that time?

A. I reckon it was the same thing I said now.

[Referring now to the deposition:] The witness is Michael Smith, on direct examination. (Deposition Transcript pp. 82–84).

Q. Tell us then on December 8th what happened in relationship to your conversation with Mr. Cox and how you produced on your contract.

A. Well, I called him and told him that we'd finished cutting our beans and wanted to set up a date, you know, that we could go down and get with him and, you know, settle up our contract, at which time he told me that all of our beans hadn't come in from Gulf Grain. And at that time he said he didn't know and he would get back in touch with me when they did come in and we could get down. And he just never did. As soon as he hung up the phone he was burning it, I reckon.

Q. Pardon?

A. I said as soon as he hung up the phone he was burning it trying to sell them, I reckon.

Q. Did he ever call you and tell you that?

A. No, sir.

Q. Did he tell you on December 8th that he was going to purchase beans for [LDC] to fulfill your contract?

A. No, sir, he didn't.

Q. When is the first time that you knew that he had done that?

A. On the 12th of December.

Q. All right, sir. Did you authorize him to sell or purchase beans to supply your contract on December 8th?

A. No, sir.

Q. Have you at any time authorized him to purchase beans to fulfill your contract at any time?

A. No, sir.

Q. You didn't say then you wanted to pay up, is that correct?

A. I believe I said "settle up."

The deposition is handed to Smith. [Plaintiff's counsel asks some preliminary questions. Then the questioning continues (Transcript p. 107).]

Q. All right. The next question I asked was: "What was your purpose in calling him?" Now this was back on the 2nd day of December, 1981, this was down in my office, and your answer at that time was the following: "I called him and was going to see if we could settle our contract. We was, you know, going to pay up. He told me he didn't have all the beans in and stuff and wait three or four days and he'd call me back." Now is it your testimony today you didn't tell him you were going to pay up?

A.   Well, I must have did if that's what I said.

[On redirect (Transcript p. 141), Smith testified:]

Q.   You were asked on cross examination, particularly from Pages 20 and 21 of the deposition, about having told Mr. Cox that you would come down or either that you would come down and pay up. Tell the Jury what you meant when you said that to Mr. Cox.

A.   What I meant when I said it?

Q.   Yes, sir.

A.   Well, he was going to call me back when all of our stuff got in from Gulf Grains, all of our beans and everything was in, and we were going to get together and either pay him or him pay us what the difference was on our contracts that we were short on.

The jury found for Smith, but the trial judge entered judgment n.o.v. for LDC. What result on appeal?

---

2. DAMAGES

Once the court concludes that one party has repudiated the contract, the problem of assessing damages remains. If a buyer repudiates, 2–703 permits the seller to recover under 2–706 (contract price less resale price) or under 2–708 (either contract price less market price or lost profits).

1. Problem. On March 1 Seller, a grain elevator, contracts to sell 30,000 bushels of corn to Buyer, a cereal manufacturer. The price is $75,000, and delivery is to be October 31. On August 1 Buyer repudiates. The market price of this quantity of corn fluctuates as follows:

August 1:	$72,000
September 1:	$72,500
October 1:	$72,250
October 31:	$72,600

To what damages is Seller entitled?

2. Problem. When Buyer in Problem 1 repudiates, Seller sells the corn on August 21 for $73,000 to a manufacturer of corn meal. To what damages is he entitled?

If a seller repudiates, 2–711 permits the buyer to recover under 2–712 (cover price less contract price) or under 2–713 (market price less contract price). Unlike the apparent ease of determining the seller's damages in the case of repudiation by the buyer, however, it is considerably more difficult to determine the buyer's damages when the seller repudiates.

Oloffson v. Coomer

Illinois Appellate Court, 1973.
11 Ill.App.3d 918, 296 N.E.2d 871.

■ ALLOY, PRESIDING JUSTICE. Richard Oloffson, d/b/a Rich's Ag Service appeals from a judgment of the circuit court of Bureau County in favor of appellant against Clarence Coomer in the amount of $1,500 plus costs. The case was tried by the court without a jury.

Oloffson was a grain dealer. Coomer was a farmer. Oloffson was in the business of merchandising grain. Consequently, he was a "merchant" within the meaning of section 2–104 of the Uniform Commercial Code. Coomer, however, was simply in the business of growing rather than merchandising grain. He, therefore, was not a "merchant" with respect to the merchandising of grain.

On April 16, 1970, Coomer agreed to sell to Oloffson, for delivery in October and December of 1970, 40,000 bushels of corn. Oloffson testified at the trial that the entire agreement was embodied in two separate contracts, each covering 20,000 bushels and that the first 20,000 bushels were to be delivered on or before October 30 at a price of $1.12–3/4 per bushel and the second 20,000 bushels were to be delivered on or before December 15, at a price of $1.12–1/4 per bushel. Coomer, in his testimony, agreed that the 40,000 bushels were to be delivered but stated that he was to deliver all he could by October 30 and the balance by December 15.

On June 3, 1970, Coomer informed Oloffson that he was not going to plant corn because the season had been too wet. He told Oloffson to arrange elsewhere to obtain the corn if Oloffson had obligated himself to deliver to any third party. The price for a bushel of corn on June 3, 1970, for future delivery, was $1.16. In September of 1970, Oloffson asked Coomer about delivery of the corn and Coomer repeated that he would not be able to deliver. Oloffson, however, persisted. He mailed Coomer confirmations of the April 16 agreement. Coomer ignored these. Oloffson's attorney then requested that Coomer perform. Coomer ignored this request likewise. The scheduled delivery dates referred to passed with no corn delivered. Oloffson then covered his obligation to his own vendee by purchasing 20,000 bushels at $1.35 per bushel and 20,000 bushels at $1.49 per bushel. The judgment from which Oloffson appeals awarded Oloffson as damages, the difference between the contract and the market prices on June 3, 1970, the day upon which Coomer first advised Oloffson he would not deliver.

Oloffson argues on this appeal that the proper measure of his damages was the difference between the contract price and the market price on the dates the corn should have been delivered in accordance with the April 16 agreement. Plaintiff does not seek any other damages. The trial court prior to entry of judgment, in an opinion finding the facts and reviewing the law, found that plaintiff was entitled to recover judgment only for the sum of $1,500 plus costs as we have indicated which is equal to the amount of the difference between the minimum contract price and the price on June 3, 1970, of $1.16 per bushel (taking the greatest differential from $1.12–1/4 per bushel multiplied by 40,000 bushels). We believe the findings and the judgment of the trial court were proper and should be affirmed.

It is clear that on June 3, 1970, Coomer repudiated the contract "with respect to performance not yet due." Under the terms of the Uniform Commercial Code the loss would impair the value of the contract to the remaining party in the amount as indicated. (Ill.Rev.Stat.1969, ch. 26, § 2–610.) As a consequence, on June 3, 1970, Oloffson, as the "aggrieved party," could then:

> "(a) for a commercially reasonable time await performance by the repudiating party; or

> "(b) resort to any remedy for breach (Section 2–703 or Section 2–711), even though he has notified the repudiating party that he would await the latter's performance and has urged retraction; * * * "

If Oloffson chose to proceed under subparagraph (a) referred to, he could have awaited Coomer's performance for a "commercially reasonable time." As we indicate in the course of this opinion, that "commercially reasonable time" expired on June 3, 1970. The Uniform Commercial Code made a change in existing Illinois law in this respect, in that, prior to the adoption of the Code, a buyer in a position as Oloffson was privileged to await a seller's performance until the date that, according to the agreement, such performance was scheduled. To the extent that a "commercially reasonable time" is less than such date of performance, the Code now conditions the buyer's right to await performance. (See Ill.Rev.Stat.Ann. 1969, ch. 26, § 2–610, Illinois Code Comment, Paragraph (a)).

If, alternatively, Oloffson had proceeded under subparagraph (b) by treating the repudiation as a breach, the remedies to which he would have been entitled were set forth in section 2–711, which is the only applicable section to which section 2–610(b) refers, according to the relevant portion of 2–711:

> "(1) Where the seller fails to make delivery or repudiates or the buyer rightfully rejects or justifiably revokes acceptance then with respect to any goods involved, and with respect to the whole if the breach goes to the whole contract (Section 2–612), the buyer may cancel and whether or not he has done so may in addition to recovering so much of the price as has been paid

> (a) 'cover' and have damages under the next section as to all the goods affected whether or not they have been identified to the contract; or

> (b) recover damages for non-delivery as provided in this Article (Section 2–713). * * *"

Plaintiff, therefore, was privileged under Section 2–610 of the Uniform Commercial Code to proceed either under subparagraph (a) or under subparagraph (b). At the expiration of the "commercially reasonable time" specified in subparagraph (a), he in effect would have a duty to proceed under subparagraph (b) since subparagraph (b) directs reference to remedies generally available to a buyer upon a seller's breach.

Oloffson's right to await Coomer's performance under section 2–610(a) was conditioned upon his:

(i) waiting no longer than a "commercially reasonable time"; and

(ii) dealing with Coomer in good faith.

Since Coomer's statement to Oloffson on June 3, 1970, was unequivocal and since "cover" easily and immediately was available to Oloffson in the well-organized and easily accessible market for purchases of grain to be delivered in the future, it would be unreasonable for Oloffson on June 3, 1970, to have awaited Coomer's performance rather than to have proceeded under Section 2–610(b) and, thereunder, to elect then to treat the repudiation as a breach. Therefore, if Oloffson were relying on his right to effect cover under section 2–711(1)(a), June 3, 1970, might for the foregoing reason alone have been the day on which he acquired cover.

Additionally, however, the record and the finding of the trial court indicates that Oloffson adhered to a usage of trade that permitted his customers to cancel the contract for a future delivery of grain by making known to him a desire to cancel and paying to him the difference between the contract and market price on the day of cancellation. There is no indication whatever that Coomer was aware of this usage of trade. The trial court specifically found, as a fact, that, in the context in which Oloffson's failure to disclose this information occurred, Oloffson failed to act in good faith. According to Oloffson, he didn't ask for this information:

"I'm no information sender. If he had asked I would have told him exactly what to do. * * * I didn't feel my responsibility. I thought it his to ask, in which case I would tell him exactly what to do."

We feel that the words "for a commercially reasonable time" as set forth in Section 2–610(a) must be read relatively to the obligation of good faith that is defined in Section 2–103(1)(b) and imposed expressly in Section 1–203.

The Uniform Commercial Code imposes upon the parties the obligation to deal with each other in good faith regardless of whether they are merchants. The Sales Article of the Code specifically defines good faith, "in the case of a merchant * * * [as] honesty in fact and the observance of reasonable commercial standards of fair dealing in the trade." For the foregoing reasons and likewise because Oloffson's failure to disclose in good faith might itself have been responsible for Coomer's failure to comply with the usage of trade which we must assume was known only to Oloffson, we conclude that a commercially reasonable time under the facts before us expired on June 3, 1970.

Imputing to Oloffson the consequences of Coomer's having acted upon the information that Oloffson in good faith should have transmitted to him, Oloffson knew or should have known on June 3, 1970, the limit of damages he probably could recover. If he were obligated to deliver grain to a third party, he knew or should have known that unless he covered on June 3, 1970, his own capital would be at risk with respect to his obligation to his own vendee. Therefore, on June 3, 1970, Oloffson, in effect, had a duty to proceed under subparagraph (b) of Section 2–610 and under subparagraphs (a) and (b) of subparagraph 1 of Section 2–711. If Oloffson had so proceeded under subparagraph (a) of Section 2–711, he should have effected cover and would have been entitled to recover damages all as provided in section 2–712, which requires that he would have had to cover in good faith without unreasonable delay. Since he would have had to effect cover on June 3, 1970, according to section 2–712(2), he would have been entitled to exactly the damages which the trial court awarded him in this cause.

Assuming that Oloffson had proceeded under subparagraph (b) of Section 2–711, he would have been entitled to recover from Coomer under Section 2–713 and Section 2–723 of the Commercial Code, the difference between the contract price and the market price on June 3, 1970, which is the date upon which he learned of the breach. This would produce precisely the same amount of damages which the trial court awarded him.

Since the trial court properly awarded the damages to which plaintiff was entitled in this cause, the judgment of the circuit court of Bureau County is, therefore, affirmed.

Affirmed.

QUESTIONS AND NOTES

1. In a well known pre-Code case, Reliance Cooperage Corp. v. Treat, 195 F.2d 977 (8th Cir.1952), a seller contracted to deliver barrel staves on December 31, at $450 per thousand. In late August, when the price was around $525 per thousand, he repudiated. On December 31 the price was $750 per thousand. The buyer sued, seeking recovery of damages based on the market price on December 31. The trial judge charged the jury that buyer could not recover damages based on the price on the date of delivery if he could have avoided loss by purchasing the staves earlier. The jury returned a verdict for the buyer for $500. The Eighth Circuit reversed, holding that damages should have been measured by looking to the market price on the date of delivery.

Among other stated reasons for the decision, the court commented that requiring the innocent party to make an immediate purchase upon notice of the repudiation would encourage repudiation as the market rose. Moreover, an immediate purchase might not actually mitigate the loss, since the market might fall prior to the delivery date. The result in *Reliance Cooperage* was generally assumed to be correct and was approved by both

Corbin and Williston. 5 A.Corbin, Contracts § 1053 (1964); 3 S.Williston, The Law Governing Sales of Goods § 588 (1948).

In addition to the reasons given in *Reliance Cooperage*, Williston argued that "the plaintiff is entitled to use such money or credit as he has for making all the forward contracts he is able to make for his own benefit."

Corbin, in the section cited above, comments as follows:

> "In cases like these under discussion, it should be observed that the repudiator has the same opportunity to avoid consequences of his repudiation as has the injured party. If it appears probable that the making of a new speculative future contract will result in advantage that can be set off against the loss caused by breach of the first contract, the repudiator can himself make such a contract. If this is true, there is no sufficient reason for requiring the injured party to make this speculative contract for the benefit of the repudiator. If the injured party makes such a contract and it results in profit, let him keep that profit himself. Let the repudiator use his own prophetic judgment, take the risks that are involved therein, and get the profit or suffer the loss that may be the result."

What do you think? Is *Oloffson* wrong as a matter of policy? Do you think it conceivable that the court misconstrued Article 2? What inference do you draw from 2–723? J.White & R.Summers, Uniform Commercial Code, 4th ed. (1995) § 6–7, suggests that the Code drafters did not intend to change the result of cases like *Reliance Cooperage*.

2. In First National Bank of Chicago v. Jefferson Mortgage Co., 576 F.2d 479 (3d Cir.1978), Kislak Mortgage Company, purporting to act as agent of the defendant, contracted to sell $5,000,000 worth of GNMA mortgage-backed securities to the plaintiff. The delivery date was March 31, 1974. Defendant repudiated the contract on October 1, 1973. The trial court held that Kislak had no authority to contract for defendant and, therefore, was liable to plaintiff for breach. It awarded damages measured by the market-contract differential, based on the market price as of March 31, 1974. On appeal, the court applied by analogy the repudiation and damages rules of Article 2. It reversed, holding that the market-contract damages should have been measured as of the date of the repudiation, October 1, 1973:

> The district court found that Jefferson unequivocally repudiated the contract on October 1, 1973, long before the date set for perform-ance. UCC Section 2–610 provides that upon anticipatory repudiation, an aggrieved party may "(a) for a commercially reasonable time await performance by the repudiating party; or (b) resort to any remedy for breach (12A:2–703 or 12A:2–711) * * * (c) in either case suspend his own performance * * *" According to 2–711, when a seller repudiates, a buyer may "cover" under 2–712 or may recover damages under 2–713. The district court held that the Bank did not "cover," and therefore 2–713 measures the damages the Bank may recover.

Section 2–713 (NJSA 12A:713) provides: * * *.

The most obvious interpretation of the phrase "learned of the breach" appears to be "learned of the repudiation." This much White and Summers, Uniform Commercial Code (1972), §§ 6–7 at 198 concedes. However, the district court interpreted the phrase "at the time when the buyer learned of the breach" to mean at the time of performance, in reliance upon the contrary conclusions of the same treatise §§ 6–7, pp. 196–206. See also, Cargill v. Stafford, 553 F.2d 1222 (10th Cir.1977). We find the New Jersey Study Comment to be a more persuasive authority on the meaning of Section 2–713 as enacted by the New Jersey legislature. The Comment adopts the view that the date of anticipatory repudiation is the "time when the buyer learned of the breach":

> * * * the buyer may elect to recover damages for non-delivery, including repudiation, based on the difference between the price current at the time the buyer learned of the breach and the contract price together with consequential damages, but less any expense saved as a result of the seller's breach. This is the meaning of Section 2–713. This changes the rule of the Uniform Sales Act that the buyer's damages for non-delivery are the difference between the contract price and the market or current price of the goods at the time or times when they ought to have been delivered.

> Because an aggrieved buyer is permitted to cover at any time after the breach and recover as damages from the seller the difference between the cost of cover and the contract price, it would be inconsistent to make a non-covering buyer compute his damages by reference to the time of performance instead of the time of breach. Such a rule would force a buyer to speculate on the wisdom of covering, and such speculation should not be encouraged by positive law.

We note that the New Jersey Study Comment supports the plain meaning of Section 2–713. The New Jersey Study Comments were distributed throughout the State of New Jersey prior to the enactment of the Code and were before the New Jersey legislature at the time the Code was adopted. See Abrams, Introduction and New Jersey History of the Uniform Commercial Code, 17 Rutgers L.Rev. 1–4 (1962). The New Jersey courts have in fact relied on the New Jersey Study Comments and the Official Comments in interpreting the Code.

Kislak argues that the word "breach" should not be interpreted to include a "repudiation" that technically a breach does not occur until the time for performance has arrived, and further, that if the drafters had intended to include repudiation the word would have been expressly used. However, it is clear from a careful reading of Section 2–711, that the word "breach" as used in the Code is not a narrow term pertaining to only one time period, but rather is a general one that can apply to a number of situations. Section 2–711 reads in part:

"(1) Where the seller fails to make delivery or *repudiates* or the buyer rightfully rejects or justifiably revokes acceptance then with respect to any goods involved, and with respect to the whole if the *breach* goes to the whole contract * * * the buyer may cancel * * *." (Emphasis added.)

It is apparent that the word "breach" in Section 2–711 refers to any of four contingencies, one of which is repudiation.

Our interpretation of Section 2–713 is further supported by the policy expressed in Section 2–610. Under the latter section an aggrieved party is not entitled to await performance by the repudiating party indefinitely or until the performance date, but may await performance "for a commercially reasonable time only." The Official Comment to this section elaborates: "[If an aggrieved party] awaits performance beyond a commercially reasonable time he cannot recover resulting damages which he should have avoided." It would be illogical to allow an aggrieved party to await performance for only a commercially reasonable time and to limit damages as of that point under Section 2–610, and then allow a recovery of damages computed as of the performance date under Section 2–713.

These two sections of the Code should be interpreted in a consistent manner. Since under Section 2–610, an aggrieved party may for a commercially reasonable time await performance, Section 2–713 should be interpreted to measure damages within a commercially reasonable time after learning of the repudiation.

We are mindful that the views of the experienced trial judge on the subject of uncertain local law in the district within which he sits are entitled to special respect. Were it not for our firm conviction that an error has been made as to the measure of damages we would feel bound to accept them. Entertaining such a firm opinion for the reasons indicated, however, we find it necessary to reverse as to the interpretation of Section 2–713 and to hold that within the contemplation of the New Jersey statute in question the expression "at the time the buyer learned of the breach" means "at the time the buyer learned of the repudiation."

Jefferson unequivocally repudiated on October 1. The Bank claims that a commercially reasonable time after Jefferson's repudiation ended on October 5, when Wertz, the Bank employee who dealt in GNMA securities, returned to his office after completing various prearranged business meetings in New Jersey and New York. We are not persuaded that "a commercially reasonable time" should be determined on the basis of the availability of any particular Bank employee. On the contrary, the very failure of the Bank otherwise to define and support by proof any commercially reasonable time beyond October 1 lends weight to the appropriateness of the latter date as a cut-off.

Ordinarily the circumstances of the particular market involved should determine the duration of a "commercially reasonable time."

The district court found that GNMA securities in the fall of 1973 were treated like stock. Several Wall Street firms had established themselves as dealers in GNMA securities and were actively trading them. Thus, comparable GNMA securities likely were available for immediate purchase. * * *

3.   Problems, page 504 revisited. On March 1 Seller and Buyer formed a contract for the sale of 30,000 bushels of corn for $75,000, delivery on October 31. On September 1 Seller (rather than Buyer) repudiated the contract. The market price of that quantity of corn fluctuated as follows:

May 1:	$78,000
June 1:	$76,000
July 1:	$77,000
August 1:	$77,500
September 1:	$77,000
October 1:	$78,000
October 31:	$79,000

a. If Buyer purchased 30,000 bushels of corn on October 15 for $78,600, to what damages is it entitled?

b. If Buyer did not replace the corn, to what damages is it entitled?

4. If you agree with the result in Oloffson v. Coomer that the buyer's damages should be measured at the expiration of a commercially reasonable time after the buyer learned of the seller's repudiation, do you need to reconsider your answer to Problem 1 on page 504?

5.   Revised Article 2. The revision moves the quasi-definition of "repudiation" that now appears in Official Comment 1 into subsection (2) of revised 2–610. Revised 2–708(1)(b) and revised 2–713(1)(b) adopt the position of the court in Oloffson v. Coomer that the measure of damages for repudiation "is the difference between the contract price and the market price ... at the expiration of a commercially reasonable time after the [aggrieved party] learned of the repudiation . . . . "

6.   CISG. The Convention on Contracts for the International Sale of Goods takes a different approach than Article 2 to the issues of insecurity and suspension of performance. Article 71 provides that a party may suspend performance if it becomes apparent that the other party will not perform a substantial part of his obligations as a result of a serious deficiency in his ability to perform, his creditworthiness, or his conduct in preparing to perform or performing the contract. The party suspending performance, however, must immediately give notice of suspension and continue with performance if the other party provides adequate assurance of his performance.

Article 72 provides that if it is "clear that one of the parties will commit a fundamental breach of contract, the other party may declare the contract avoided, but, unless the other party has declared that he will not perform, the party declaring the contract avoided must, 'if time allows,'" give reasonable notice to the other party so that he may provide adequate assurance of his performance.

The difference between the events that trigger rights under Article 71 and the events that trigger the greater rights under Article 72 seems very slight and possibly non-existent. Presumably, however, the ambiguity in the sections will encourage an insecure party to be cautious about declaring the contract at an end. Is that good or bad?

Note that the Convention provides no right to demand assurances unless there is a right to suspend performance, and the right to suspend does not arise unless "it becomes apparent that the other party will not perform a substantial part of his obligations. . . ." Therefore, the right to demand assurances is more limited than the right under UCC 2–609.

As for the measurement of damages when a party repudiates, Article 76 provides that a party who has not entered into a substitute transaction can recover the difference between the contract price and the "current" price at the time of avoidance. To what date does "current" refer? Article 72 permits a party to declare the contract avoided if it is clear that the other party will commit a fundamental breach, but it does not say that the contract is avoided, or that there is a present breach by repudiation. It merely states that the aggrieved party may avoid the contract. Does this mean that the aggrieved party is in control of the time for measuring contract-market damages in the repudiation case by deciding whether and when to declare the contract avoided?

In connection with that question, Articles 49 and 64, which relate to fundamental breach by seller and buyer respectively, state that the aggrieved party "may declare the contract avoided." It seems very unlikely that CISG would be interpreted to allow the aggrieved party to choose the time for measuring damages by delaying a declaration that the contract is avoided in the case, for example, where the seller fails to deliver the goods, or the buyer wrongfully rejects the goods. But, in the case of repudiation, since there is a strong argument for allowing the injured party to measure damages at the time set for performance of the other party, courts might, indeed, give the aggrieved party the power to choose the time to determine contract-market damages by choosing the time to announce avoidance.

CHAPTER 9

DISCHARGE BY IMPOSSIBILITY OR FRUSTRATION OF PURPOSE

Occasionally unanticipated events occur that either impair the ability of the parties to perform or destroy the utility of the performance for which they have contracted. To deal with these situations, the courts of England developed the doctrines of impossibility of performance and frustration of purpose. Taylor v. Caldwell, 3 Best & S. 826 (K.B.1863); Krell v. Henry, 2 K.B. 740 (Ct.App.1903). American courts have embraced these doctrines, excusing the parties from their contractual obligations when an unforeseen, supervening event makes the performance of one of them impossible or frustrates the purpose for which they formed the contract. In 2–613 through 2–616, Article 2 adopts these doctrines for sales contracts.

———

United States v. Wegematic Corp.

United States Court of Appeals, Second Circuit, 1966.
360 F.2d 674.

■ FRIENDLY, CIRCUIT JUDGE. The facts developed at trial in the District Court for the Southern District of New York, fully set forth in a memorandum by Judge Graven, can be briefly summarized: In June 1956 the Federal Reserve Board invited five electronics manufacturers to submit proposals for an intermediate-type, general-purpose electronic digital computing system or systems; the invitation stressed the importance of early delivery as a consideration in determining the Board's choice. Defendant, a relative newcomer in the field, which had enjoyed considerable success with a smaller computer known as the ALWAC III–E, submitted a detailed proposal for the sale or lease of a new computer designated as the ALWAC 800. It characterized the machine as "a truly revolutionary system utilizing all of the latest technical advances," and featured that "maintenance problems are minimized by the use of highly reliable magnetic cores for not only the high speed memory but also logical elements and registers." Delivery was offered nine months from the date the contract or purchase order was received. In September the Board acted favorably on the defendant's proposal, ordering components of the ALWAC 800 with an aggregate cost of $231,800. Delivery was to be made on June 30, 1957, with liquidated damages of $100 per day for delay. The order also provided that in the event the defendant failed to comply "with any provision" of the agreement, "the Board may procure the services described in the contract from other sources and hold the Contractor responsible for any excess cost occasioned thereby." Defendant accepted the order with enthusiasm.

The first storm warning was a suggestion by the defendant in March 1957 that the delivery date be postponed. In April it informed the Board by letter that delivery would be made on or before October 30 rather than as agreed, the delay being due to the necessity of "a redesign which we feel has greatly improved this equipment"; waiver of the stipulated damages for delay was requested. The Board took the request under advisement. On August 30 defendant wrote that delivery would be delayed "possibly into 1959"; it suggested use of ALWAC III–E equipment in the interim and waiver of the $100 per day "penalty." The Board also took this request under advisement but made clear it was waiving no rights. In mid-October defendant announced that "due to engineering difficulties it has become impracticable to deliver the ALWAC 800 Computing System at this time"; it requested cancellation of the contract without damages. The Board set about procuring comparable equipment from another manufacturer; on October 6, 1958, International Business Machines Corporation delivered an IBM 650 computer, serving substantially the same purpose as the ALWAC 800, at a rental of $102,000 a year with an option to purchase for $410,450.

In July 1958 the Board advised defendant of its intention to press its claim for damages; this suit followed. The court awarded the United States $46,300 for delay under the liquidated damages clause, $179,450 for the excess cost of the IBM equipment, and $10,056 for preparatory expenses useless in operating the IBM system—a total of $235,806, with 6% interest from October 6, 1958.

The principal point of the defense, which is the sole ground of this appeal, is that delivery was made impossible by "basic engineering difficulties" whose correction would have taken between one and two years and would have cost a million to a million and a half dollars, with success likely but not certain. Although the record does not give an entirely clear notion what the difficulties were, two experts suggested that they may have stemmed from the magnetic cores, used instead of transistors to achieve a solid state machine, which did not have sufficient uniformity at this stage of their development. Defendant contends that under federal law, which both parties concede to govern, the "practical impossibility" of completing the contract excused its defaults in performance.

. . .

We find persuasive the defendant's suggestion of looking to the Uniform Commercial Code as a source for the "federal" law of sales. The Code has been adopted by Congress for the District of Columbia, 77 Stat. 630 (1963), has been enacted in over forty states, and is thus well on its way to becoming a truly national law of commerce . . . . When the states have gone so far in achieving the desirable goal of a uniform law governing commercial transactions, it would be a distinct disservice to insist on a different one for the segment of commerce, important but still small in relation to the total, consisting of transactions with the United States.

Section 2–615 of the UCC, entitled "Excuse by failure of presupposed conditions," provides that:

> "Except so far as a seller may have assumed a greater obligation * * * delay in delivery or non-delivery * * * is not a breach of his duty under a contract for sale if performance as agreed has been made impracticable by the occurrence of a contingency the non-occurrence of which was a basic assumption on which the contract was made. * * *"

The latter part of the test seems a somewhat complicated way of putting Professor Corbin's question of how much risk the promisor assumed. Recent Developments in the Law of Contracts, 50 Harv.L.Rev. 449, 465–66 (1937); 2 Corbin, Contracts § 1333, at 371. We see no basis for thinking that when an electronics system is promoted by its manufacturer as a revolutionary breakthrough, the risk of the revolution's occurrence falls on the purchaser; the reasonable supposition is that it has already occurred or, at least, that the manufacturer is assuring the purchaser that it will be found to have when the machine is assembled. As Judge Graven said: "The Board in its invitation for bids did not request invitations to conduct a development program for it. The Board requested invitations from manufacturers for the furnishing of a computer machine." Acceptance of defendant's argument would mean that though a purchaser makes his choice because of the attractiveness of a manufacturer's representation and will be bound by it, the manufacturer is free to express what are only aspirations and gamble on mere probabilities of fulfillment without any risk of liability. In fields of developing technology, the manufacturer would thus enjoy a wide degree of latitude with respect to performance while holding an option to compel the buyer to pay if the gamble should pan out. We do not think this the common understanding—above all as to a contract where the manufacturer expressly agreed to liquidated damages for delay and authorized the purchaser to resort to other sources in the event of non-delivery. If a manufacturer wishes to be relieved of the risk that what looks good on paper may not prove so good in hardware, the appropriate exculpatory language is well known and often used.

Beyond this the evidence of true impracticability was far from compelling. The large sums predicted by defendant's witnesses must be appraised in relation not to the single computer ordered by the Federal Reserve Board, evidently for a bargain price, but to the entire ALWAC 800 program as originally contemplated. Although the record gives no idea what this was, even twenty-five machines would gross $10,000,000 if priced at the level of the comparable IBM equipment. While the unanticipated need for expending $1,000,000 or $1,500,000 on redesign might have made such a venture unattractive, as defendant's management evidently decided, the sums are thus not so clearly prohibitive as it would have them appear. What seemingly did become impossible was on-time performance; the issue whether if defendant had offered prompt rectification of the design, the Government could have refused to give it a chance and still recover not merely damages for delay but also the higher cost of replacement equipment, is not before us.

Affirmed.

QUESTIONS AND NOTES

1. In *Wegematic,* Judge Friendly says: "If a manufacturer wishes to be relieved of the risk that what looks good on paper may not prove so good in hardware, the appropriate exculpatory language is well known and often used." It is not clear whether he had in mind a special clause for contracts for the sale of new technology machines or the more usual "force majeure" clause. In any event, sales contracts frequently contain a clause reading something like the following (from 5A–2 Bender's Forms and Procedures Under the UCC ¶ 24.22(1)):

> *Force majeure.* Neither party shall be held responsible if fulfillment of any terms or provisions of this contract are delayed or prevented by revolutions or other disorders, wars, acts of enemies, strikes, fires, floods, acts of God, by any other cause not within the control of the party whose performance is interfered with, and which by the exercise of reasonable diligence, the party is unable to prevent, whether of the class of causes above enumerated or not.

These clauses typically excuse one or both parties from performing in situations in which 2–615 would not provide an excuse. Absent such defenses as duress or unconscionability, are these clauses enforceable? Note that 2–615 opens with the language: "Except so far as a seller may have assumed a greater obligation . . . ." Does this mean that 2–615 renders unenforceable a contract clause under which a seller assumes a *lesser* obligation in relation to performing notwithstanding the occurrence of uncertain events?

The drafting history of 2–615 reveals that the introductory language was intended to make it clear that a seller might assume greater liability by implication as well as by express agreement. That language apparently was used without any thought that it might restrict a seller's ability to contract for discharge in the event of occurrences that would not operate as a discharge under 2–615. See Hawkland, The Energy Crisis and Section 2–615 of the Uniform Commercial Code, 79 Comm.L.J. 75 (1974).

2. Problem. In April Farmer contracts to deliver 20,000 bushels of soybeans to Elevator between October 1 and October 31, for $2.15 per bushel. As a result of drought, Farmer's land yields only 12,000 bushels, which she delivers to Elevator. Perhaps because of the draught, perhaps not, the market price at that time is $3.50 per bushel. Elevator purchases 8,000 bushels at that price from someone else and sues Farmer for $10,800, the excess of the cover price over the contract price. Is she liable?

Would it matter if the soybeans already were planted when the parties formed the contract?

3. Problem. During a visit to Seller's showroom, Buyer contracts to purchase a new Volvo S60 for $30,000. As part of the contract, Seller agrees to upgrade the sound system, and Buyer is to return the next day to take delivery. That night the car is stolen, and it is never recovered. It is the end of the model year, and Seller has no more S60's. Though Seller might be able to find one at another dealership, Seller does not offer to do so. Instead, it attempts to sell Buyer the next year's model. Unable to afford that, she declines and sues to recover the excess of the market value, which she can establish to be $33,000, over the contract price, or $3,000. Is Seller liable?

———

Chase Precast Corporation v. John J. Paonessa Company, Inc.

Massachusetts Supreme Judicial Court, 1991.
409 Mass. 371, 566 N.E.2d 603.

■ LYNCH, JUSTICE.

This appeal raises the question whether the doctrine of frustration of purpose may be a defense in a breach of contract action in Massachusetts, and, if so, whether it excuses the defendant John J. Paonessa Company, Inc. (Paonessa), from performance.

. . .

The pertinent facts are as follows. In 1982, the Commonwealth, through the Department of Public Works (department), entered into two contracts with Paonessa for resurfacing and improvements to two stretches of Route 128.* Part of each contract called for replacing a grass median strip between the north and southbound lanes with concrete surfacing and precast concrete median barriers. Paonessa entered into two contracts with Chase under which Chase was to supply, in the aggregate, 25,800 linear feet of concrete median barriers according to the specifications of the department for highway construction. The quantity and type of barriers to be supplied were specified in two purchase orders prepared by Chase.

The highway reconstruction began in the spring of 1983. By late May, the department was receiving protests from angry residents who objected to use of the concrete median barriers and removal of the grass median strip. Paonessa and Chase became aware of the protest around June 1. On June 6, a group of about 100 citizens filed an action in the Superior Court to stop installation of the concrete median barriers and other aspects of the work. On June 7, anticipating modification by the department, Paonessa notified Chase by letter to stop producing concrete barriers for the projects. Chase did so upon receipt of the letter the following day. On June 17, the department and the citizens' group entered into a settlement which provided, in part, that no additional concrete median barriers would be installed.

* A road that rings Boston.—Ed.

On June 23, the department deleted the permanent concrete median barriers item from its contracts with Paonessa.

Before stopping production on June 8, Chase had produced approximately one-half of the concrete median barriers called for by its contracts with Paonessa, and had delivered most of them to the construction sites. Paonessa paid Chase for all that it had produced, at the contract price. Chase suffered no out-of-pocket expense as a result of cancellation of the remaining portion of barriers. [But Chase lost the profit it would have generated from producing the remaining portion of the barriers. Chase sued to recover this profit, but the trial court held that Paonessa was excused from its obligations on the basis of impossibility of performance. An intermediate appellate court affirmed, but rested its decision on the excuse of frustration of purpose. Chase appealed.]

This court has long recognized and applied the doctrine of impossibility as a defense to an action for breach of contract. See, e.g., Butterfield v. Byron, 153 Mass. 517, 27 N.E. 667 (1891). Under that doctrine, "where from the nature of the contract it appears that the parties must from the beginning have contemplated the continued existence of some particular specified thing as the foundation of what was to be done, then, in the absence of any warranty that the thing shall exist ... the parties shall be excused ... [when] performance becomes impossible from the accidental perishing of the thing without the fault of either party." Boston Plate & Window Glass Co. v. John Bowen Co., 335 Mass. 697, at 700, 141 N.E.2d 715 (1957).

On the other hand, although we have referred to the doctrine of frustration of purpose in a few decisions, we have never clearly defined it.

Other jurisdictions have explained the doctrine as follows: when an event neither anticipated nor caused by either party, the risk of which was not allocated by the contract, destroys the object or purpose of the contract, thus destroying the value of performance, the parties are excused from further performance.

In Mishara Construction Co. v. Transit–Mixed Concrete Corp., 365 Mass. 122, at 129, 310 N.E.2d 363 (1974), we called frustration of purpose a "companion rule" to the doctrine of impossibility. Both doctrines concern the effect of supervening circumstances upon the rights and duties of the parties. The difference lies in the effect of the supervening event. Under frustration, "[p]erformance remains possible but the expected value of performance to the party seeking to be excused has been destroyed by [the] fortuitous event. . . ."[3] Lloyd v. Murphy, 25 Cal.2d 48, at 53, 153 P.2d 47 (1944). The principal question in both kinds of cases remains "whether an unanticipated circumstance, the risk of which should not fairly be thrown

---

3. Clearly frustration of purpose is a more accurate label for the defense argued in this case than impossibility of performance, since, as the Appeals Court pointed out, "[p]erformance was not literally impossible. Nothing prevented Paonessa from honoring its contract to purchase the remaining sections of median barrier, whether or not the [department] would approve their use in the road construction." 28 Mass.App.Ct. 639, 644 n.5, 554 N.E.2d 868 (1990).

on the promisor, has made performance vitally different from what was reasonably to be expected." See *Lloyd, supra,* at 54, 153 P.2d 47 (frustration); *Mishara Constr. Co., supra,* 365 Mass. at 129, 310 N.E.2d 363 (impossibility).

Since the two doctrines differ only in the effect of the fortuitous supervening event, it is appropriate to look to our cases dealing with impossibility for guidance in treating the issues that are the same in a frustration of purpose case.[4] The trial judge's findings with regard to those issues are no less pertinent to application of the frustration defense because they were considered relevant to the defense of impossibility.

Another definition of frustration of purpose is found in the Restatement (Second) of Contracts § 265 (1981):

"Where, after a contract is made, a party's principal purpose is substantially frustrated without his fault by the occurrence of an event the non-occurrence of which was a basic assumption on which the contract was made, his remaining duties to render performance are discharged, unless the language or the circumstances indicate the contrary."

This definition is nearly identical to the defense of "commercial impracticability," found in the Uniform Commercial Code, G.L. c. 106, § 2–615 (1988 ed.), which this court, in *Mishara Constr. Co., supra* at 127–128, 310 N.E.2d 363, held to be consistent with the common law of contracts regarding impossibility of performance. It follows, therefore, that the Restatement's formulation of the doctrine is consistent with this court's previous treatment of impossibility of performance and frustration of purpose.

Paonessa bore no responsibility for the department's elimination of the median barriers from the projects. Therefore, whether it can rely on the defense of frustration turns on whether elimination of the barriers was a risk allocated by the contracts to Paonessa. *Mishara Constr. Co.* articulates the relevant test:

"The question is, given the commercial circumstances in which the parties dealt: Was the contingency which developed one which the parties could reasonably be thought to have foreseen as a real possibility which could affect performance? Was it one of that variety of risks which the parties were tacitly assigning to the promisor by their failure to provide for it explicitly? If it was, performance will be required. If it could not be so considered, performance is excused." This is a question for the trier of fact.

Paonessa's contracts with the department contained a standard provision allowing the department to eliminate items or portions of work found unnecessary.[6] The purchase order agreements between Chase and Paonessa

---

4. Those issues include the foreseeability of the supervening event, allocation of the risk of occurrence of the event, and the degree of hardship to the promisor.

6. The contracts contained the following provision:

"4.06 Increased or Decreased Contract Quantities.

do not contain a similar provision. This difference in the contracts does not mandate the conclusion that Paonessa assumed the risk of reduction in the quantity of the barriers. It is implicit in the judge's findings that Chase knew the barriers were for department projects. The record supports the conclusion that Chase was aware of the department's power to decrease quantities of contract items. The judge found that Chase had been a supplier of median barriers to the department in the past. The provision giving the department the power to eliminate items or portions thereof was standard in its contracts. See Standard Specifications for Highways and Bridges, Commonwealth of Massachusetts Department of Public Works § 4.06 (1973). The judge found that Chase had furnished materials under and was familiar with the so-called "Unit Price Philosophy" in the construction industry, whereby contract items are paid for at the contract unit price for the quantity of work actually accepted. Finally, the judge's finding that "[a]ll parties were well aware that lost profits were not an element of damage in either of the public works projects in issue" further supports the conclusion that Chase was aware of the department's power to decrease quantities, since the term prohibiting claims for anticipated profit is part of the same sentence in the standard provision as that allowing the engineer to eliminate items or portions of work.

In *Mishara Constr. Co.* we held that, although labor disputes in general cannot be considered extraordinary, whether the parties in a particular case intended performance to be carried out, even in the face of a labor difficulty, depends on the facts known to the parties at the time of contracting with respect to the history of and prospects for labor difficulties. In this case, even if the parties were aware generally of the department's power to eliminate contract items, the judge could reasonably have concluded that they did not contemplate the cancellation for a major portion of the project of such a widely used item as concrete median barriers, and did not allocate the risk of such cancellation.[7]

Our opinion in Chicopee Concrete Serv., Inc. v. Hart Eng'g Co., 398 Mass. 476, 498 N.E.2d 121 (1986), does not lead to a different conclusion. Although we held there that a provision of a prime contract requiring city approval of subcontractors was not incorporated by reference into the subcontract, we nevertheless stated that, if the record had supported the

"When the accepted quantities of work vary from the quantities in the bid schedule, the Contractor shall accept as payment in full, so far as contract items are concerned, payment at the original contract unit prices for the accepted quantities of work done.

"The Engineer may order omitted from the work any items or portions of work found unnecessary to the improvement and such omission shall not operate as a waiver of any condition of the Contract nor invalidate any of the provisions thereof, nor shall the Contractor have any claim for anticipated profit.

"No allowance will be made for any increased expenses, loss of expected reimbursement therefor or from any other cause."

7. The judge did not explicitly find that cancellation of the barriers was not contemplated and that the risk of their elimination was not allocated by the contracts. However, the judge's decision imports every finding essential to sustain it if there is evidence to support it. Mailer v. Mailer, 390 Mass. 371, 373, 455 N.E.2d 1211 (1983).

conclusion that the subcontractor knew, or at least had notice of, the approval clause, the result might have been different. *Id.* at 478–479, 498 N.E.2d 121.[8]

. . .

Judgment affirmed.

QUESTIONS

1. The court states the issue as whether the doctrine of frustration of purpose may be a defense, but 2–615 does not mention frustration of purpose. Was it proper for the court to analyze the case in terms of frustration of purpose?

2. The court barely mentions 2–615 and does not seem to apply it to determine whether the parties were excused from their obligations to perform. Was this proper?

Waldinger Corp. v. CRS Group Engineers, Inc.

United States Court of Appeals, Seventh Circuit, 1985.
775 F.2d 781.

■ WOOD, CIRCUIT JUDGE.

In 1977, the Urbana and Champaign Sanitary District was engaged in planning two waste water treatment facilities. CRS Group Engineers, Inc., Clark Dietz Division ("Dietz,") as engineer for the Sanitary District, prepared the specifications for these facilities. Among the equipment necessary for the facilities were belt filter presses.[1] The specifications for these

---

8. This court held in John Soley & Sons v. Jones, 208 Mass. 561, 566–567, 95 N.E. 94 (1911), that, where by its terms the prime contract could be cancelled if the defendant was not making sufficient progress on the work, and the plaintiff knew of the article of cancellation, nevertheless, even if it was mutually understood that the defendant did not intend to perform unless the prime contract remained in force, the defendant was not relieved from performance on the ground of impossibility where it failed to provide for the risk of cancellation in its contract with the plaintiff. To the extent that holding is contrary to our decision in this case, we decline to follow it, and refer to our adoption in *Mishara Constr. Co., supra*, 365 Mass. at 130, 310 N.E.2d 363, of the following statement:

"Rather than mechanically apply any fixed rule of law, where the parties themselves have not allocated responsibility, justice is better served by appraising all of the circumstances, the part the various parties played, and thereon determining liability." See West Los Angeles Inst. for Cancer Research v. Mayer, 366 F.2d 220, 225 (9th Cir.1966), cert. denied, 385 U.S. 1010, 87 S.Ct. 718, 17 L.Ed.2d 548 (1967) ("foreseeability of the frustrating event is not alone enough to bar rescission if it appears that the parties did not intend the promisor to assume the risk of its occurrence").

1. The function of a belt filter press is to remove waste solids from the waste water. The district court explained the manner in which it accomplishes this goal:

presses detailed two types of requirements—performance capabilities and mechanical components. The Waldinger Corporation ("Waldinger,") a mechanical contractor, preparing to bid on the mechanical portions of the projects, received quotations for sludge dewatering equipment from four belt press manufacturers, including Ashbrook–Simon–Hartley, Inc. ("Ashbrook.") Waldinger successfully bid on the projects and became the mechanical subcontractor; Ashbrook was successful in its bid to be the supplier of the sludge dewatering equipment. Ashbrook, however, was unable to supply the equipment described in the specifications set forth in its contract with Waldinger, and Waldinger obtained the equipment from The Ralph B. Carter Company ("Carter.")

Waldinger then sued Ashbrook for breach of contract. Ashbrook, in defense, claimed impracticability of performance due to Dietz's intentional or negligent drafting of restrictive specifications. Waldinger also sued Dietz, claiming that Dietz intentionally interfered with the contract between Ashbrook and Waldinger and, alternatively, that Dietz negligently failed to draft proper specifications for the sludge dewatering equipment.

Following a bench trial, the district court found that Dietz intentionally prepared exclusionary specifications, and insisted without justification that Ashbrook comply literally with those specifications. The court also found that Ashbrook did not bid with the realization that it could not comply with the specifications. The court concluded as a matter of law that Dietz intentionally interfered with the contract between Ashbrook and Waldinger and that Ashbrook was excused from performing its contract with Waldinger because performance was impracticable. Waldinger v. Ashbrook–Simon–Hartley, Inc., 564 F.Supp. 970 (C.D.Ill.1983).

I.

The district court made the following factual findings, none of which is clearly erroneous. In the summer of 1977, Dietz decided to use equipment manufactured by Carter as the model for the sludge dewatering equipment to be used on the projects, though Dietz had never seen the Carter 15–31 machine perform.[2] Carter supplied the data and performance descriptions which were incorporated in the specifications drawn by Dietz. Dietz took the Carter performance claims at face value, making no independent study of them. Dietz knew that no manufacturer but Carter recycled the belt wash water used in the machine but nevertheless specified that subsystem.[3]

"Sewage enters the belt filter press as a slurry of solids and water. The slurry is mixed with polymers, organic compounds which cause the solids in the slurry to floculate. The floculated sludge is deposited in a section of the machine where gravity dewatering takes place and excess water drains off from the floculated sludge. The floculated sludge is then fed into a shear press section of the machine where more water is extracted by shear pressure and the sludge emerges from the filter press as a friable, cake solid."

Waldinger v. Ashbrook–Simon–Hartley, Inc., 564 F.Supp. 970, 973 (C.D.Ill.1983).

2. At the time the specifications were drafted, Carter had no 15–31 machine in operation.

3. Carter has since returned to its pre–1975 flat belt press design and no longer manufactures a machine that recycles belt wash water.

Dietz had no data proving that such recycling would increase solid removal or reduce polymer consumption in the sludge dewatering process. Indeed, the evidence adduced at trial showed that recycling had no positive effect on a filter press' production capacities, but likely had a negative effect. Dietz had no scientific basis for including in the specifications other features of the Carter machine, specifically, the 540 square foot dewatering area and the stainless steel clad rollers. The structure designed to house the filter presses was sized to fit the Carter 15–31 machine.

In November and December of 1977, Ashbrook contacted Dietz concerning the sludge dewatering equipment to be used in the facilities. Ashbrook subsequently asked Dietz to approve its size 1–V Winkelpress for use on the projects. The evidence established that as early as January, 1978, Dietz had decided to reject the Ashbrook machine. Ashbrook, believing it could meet the performance requirements of the specifications and relying on its experience that specific mechanical subsystems were ordinarily waived by an owner's engineer if a supplier could show that its equipment met performance specifications, bid to supply the sludge dewatering equipment in March, 1978. A March 10, 1978, evaluation prepared by a member of the Dietz design team concluded that Ashbrook's equipment did indeed meet the performance specifications.

Subsequently, on April 5, 1978, Dietz retreated from that conclusion, stating that the size 1–V Winkelpress did not have the performance capacity required by the specifications because the machine did not recycle belt wash water. Dietz also questioned the limitation on maintenance space created by the use of an Ashbrook machine in a building designed to house a Carter machine. Dietz stated that it would not approve the machine for use on the projects based upon the information then in its possession. Ashbrook replied that it would provide actual operation data to confirm the machine's capacity and that it would supply equipment that would comply with the specifications.

On May 1, 1978, Waldinger issued, and on May 22, 1978, Ashbrook executed, purchase orders under which Ashbrook agreed to furnish the sludge dewatering equipment "in complete accordance with plans and specifications § 11140—sludge dewatering system . . . ." The purchase orders further provided that the equipment furnished by Ashbrook would require the approval of Dietz. Ashbrook, in executing the purchase orders, agreed to furnish the required submittal data for approval by Dietz. General Condition No. 10 of the purchase orders provided as follows:

> "All material and equipment furnished under this Purchase Order shall be subject to the approval of the Owner, architect [or] engineer . . . , and Seller shall furnish the required submittal data . . . for said approval. In the event such approval is not obtained, this Purchase Order shall be deemed to be cancelled, with no liability on the part of either Purchaser or Seller, *unless* this Purchase Order is placed with the requirement that the material [or] equipment . . . is to be

supplied of the type and in such a manner as to meet requirements of plans and specifications. In the latter case the material [or] equipment . . . furnished hereunder shall be in strict accordance with plans [and] specifications . . . , and Seller shall be bound thereby. In the event the material [or] equipment . . . does not meet the foregoing requirements, Seller shall, upon receipt of notice, immediately replace same, or remedy any deficiency, without expense to the Purchaser, and further, Seller shall pay to Purchaser all loss or damage resulting therefrom.''

At the beginning of the relationship between Ashbrook and Dietz, Dietz requested only performance data on the 1–V machine. Ashbrook set about meeting the production test requirements laid down by Dietz. In August of 1978, Dietz concluded that the 1–V machine met the performance requirements of the specifications. Dietz then demanded performance data on the machine's dewatering capacity with alum sludge. Throughout the testing period, Dietz rejected Ashbrook's performance data as insufficient even though it had no data from Carter. Dietz ultimately rejected the 1–V machine because it did not have proven dewatering capacity with alum sludge; the Carter machine, to the knowledge of Dietz, had never been tested on alum sludge.[4] On November 16, 1978, Dietz discussed with Ashbrook for the first time the mechanical aspects of the Winkelpress, stating that Ashbrook must strictly comply with the mechanical specifications. When Ashbrook notified Dietz that it could not guarantee the machine's performance if built according to Dietz's mechanical specifications, Dietz told Ashbrook not to submit the size 1–V machine again.

. . . Ashbrook notified Waldinger that it was unable to supply the equipment described in the specifications. Waldinger then terminated the purchase orders and obtained the equipment from Carter.[5]

The district court found that no manufacturer but Carter could have literally complied with the specifications for the sludge dewatering equipment; that Dietz intended to use Carter equipment on the projects to the exclusion of other manufacturers; that Dietz's decision to use Carter equipment was conscious and in deliberate disregard of the EPA regulation requiring free and open competition, 40 C.F.R. § 35.936–3 (1976); and that there was no scientific or empirical basis for Dietz's insistence on strict compliance with the specifications. The district court further found that Ashbrook did not bid the project with the realization that it could not meet the specifications; rather, relying upon the EPA requirements that specifications foster competition and that specifications not be exclusionary or discriminatory and upon its experience that specific mechanical subsystems

---

4. In the interim between the letting of the bids and the rejection of the Ashbrook machine, Dietz was reassuring Carter that Dietz would insist on rigid adherence to the specifications. Carter expressed the hope that the "successful manufacturer" would be required to meet all process requirements.

5. Carter ceased manufacturing the 15–31 machine in February, 1978 and began manufacturing instead the 15–32 model. This machine, which Waldinger was required to install, was too large for the structure designed to house the 15–31 machine. The building had to be redesigned to accommodate the 15–32 machine.

are ordinarily waived if a supplier can demonstrate that its equipment meets performance specifications, Ashbrook bid the project believing it could perform. Ashbrook, the district court found, could not have known that Dietz would interpret its specifications in such a way as to require Ashbrook to manufacture a Carter machine.

II.

Waldinger challenges the district court's conclusion that Ashbrook was excused from performing its contract with Waldinger on the ground of commercial impracticability. Ill.Rev.Stat. ch. 26, § 2–615. Assuming the seller has not assumed the greater obligation under the agreement, three conditions must be satisfied before performance is excused: (1) a contingency has occurred; (2) the contingency has made performance impracticable; and (3) the nonoccurrence of that contingency was a basic assumption upon which the contract was made. . . . The rationale for the defense of commercial impracticability is that the circumstance causing the breach has rendered performance "so vitally different from what was anticipated that the contract cannot be reasonably thought to govern." Eastern Air Lines, Inc. v. McDonnell Douglas Corp., 532 F.2d 957, 991 (5th Cir.1976). Because the purpose of a contract is to place the reasonable risk of performance upon the promisor, however, it is presumed to have agreed to bear any loss occasioned by an event that was foreseeable at the time of contracting.

The applicability of the defense of commercial impracticability, then, turns largely on foreseeability. The relevant inquiry is whether the risk of the occurrence of the contingency was so unusual or unforeseen and the consequences of the occurrence of the contingency so severe that to require performance is to grant the buyer an advantage he did not bargain for in the contract. If the risk of the occurrence of the contingency was unforeseeable, the seller cannot be said to have assumed that risk. If the risk of the occurrence of the contingency was foreseeable, that risk is tacitly assigned to the seller. The seller's failure to provide a contractual excuse against the occurrence of a foreseeable contingency may be deemed to be an assumption of an unconditional obligation to perform. Phrased somewhat differently, if a contingency is foreseeable, the § 2–615 defense is unavailable because the party disadvantaged by the fruition of the contingency might have contractually protected itself.

This analysis assumes, of course, that the parties have not restricted the excusing contingencies or eliminated the protection of § 2–615 by imposing upon the seller an absolute contractual duty to deliver. If a particular contingency is contemplated and the risk of its occurrence specifically assigned to the seller, foreseeability is not an issue. The parties will be held to their bargain.

The district court found that a basic assumption of the contract between Waldinger and Ashbrook was that Ashbrook equipment was competitive and would comply with the specifications drafted by Dietz. That assumption was based upon the belief that Dietz would interpret its specifications in a competitive and nonrestrictive manner. Because Dietz did not do so, performance by Ashbrook was rendered impracticable.

Waldinger contends that Ashbrook assumed a greater obligation to it under their agreement, an issue not specifically addressed by the district court; specifically, Waldinger argues that Ashbrook unconditionally obligated itself to supply whatever equipment was necessary to meet the specification requirements to the satisfaction of Dietz. In support, Waldinger cites the purchase order in which Ashbrook agreed to furnish equipment "in strict accordance with plans, specifications and general conditions applicable to the contract of Purchaser with the Owner or other contractor." Waldinger further points out that Ashbrook failed to indicate, in the space provided on the purchase order, any specific exceptions to the terms and conditions of the purchase order. Thus, although Ashbrook could have attempted to contractually protect itself by making its obligation to supply the equipment contingent upon Dietz's approval, it did not, and now, according to Waldinger, must be held accountable for its breach.

Ashbrook contends that Waldinger views too broadly the scope of the obligation it assumed. Ashbrook argues that it cannot be deemed to have assumed the obligation to meet all mechanical specifications—that is, to build a Carter machine—because Dietz was required, under EPA regulations incorporated in all sub-agreements on EPA projects, 40 C.F.R. §§ 35.9361(b); 35.937–9(a); 35.938–4(c)(5) (1976), to draft and interpret its specifications in a non-proprietary, non-restrictive manner. There is, Ashbrook contends, an "irreconcilable conflict" between the language of General Condition No. 10 which required it to provide equipment in "strict accordance" with the specifications and the EPA regulations prohibiting specifications drawn to only one manufacturer. Ashbrook apparently argues that it obligated itself to supply equipment that would meet the specifications only insofar as Dietz, in accordance with EPA regulations, drafted and interpreted those specifications in a non-proprietary, non-restrictive manner.

Pursuant to the terms of General Condition No. 10 of the purchase orders, the risk of non-approval by Dietz was specifically allocated to Ashbrook. Under those terms, Ashbrook assumed the obligation of providing equipment that strictly complied with the specifications. Although the § 2–615 defense would be unavailable to Ashbrook if this contractual provision stood alone, we are presented with EPA regulations that Ashbrook contends narrow the scope of its otherwise broad contractual obligation to Waldinger. We believe, in light of the express contractual terms prohibiting exclusionary specifications, that Ashbrook obligated itself to provide equipment that would satisfy the specifications when interpreted in a competitive, non-restrictive manner. Ashbrook assumed the risk that it could not supply a machine that satisfied specifications so interpreted, but it did not assume the risk that it could not manufacture a Carter machine. To hold otherwise is to read out of the contract the EPA regulations in which the federal public policy of free and open competition is incorporated. 40 C.F.R. § 35.936–3 (1976). We decline to do so.

The district court found that it was not foreseeable at the time of contracting that Dietz would require strict compliance with all specifications. A district court's factual findings may not be overturned unless they are clearly erroneous. Fed.R.Civ.P. 52. . . . Waldinger has not persuaded us that this finding is clearly erroneous. True, Ashbrook knew that Dietz's approval was required and that at the time it signed the purchase orders Dietz had not expressly approved its 1–V machine. The refusal of an engineer to waive certain mechanical specifications is foreseeable, and a supplier normally assumes the risk of non-approval. But these general principles cannot be deemed to apply where an engineer's insistence on literal compliance with exclusionary specifications has no scientific or rational basis. Given industry practice on waiver of mechanical specifications and the EPA regulations prohibiting exclusionary specifications upon which Ashbrook could rightly rely, Ashbrook could not have foreseen the possibility that Dietz would require it to build a Carter machine even if its machine met the performance specifications. The § 2–615 defense is therefore available to Ashbrook if performance was rendered commercially impracticable by Dietz's insistence upon compliance with the exclusionary specifications.

Ashbrook based its claim that performance was commercially impracticable on the evidence that it could not have supplied a filter press that met both the mechanical and performance specifications. Waldinger argues that performance was not commercially impracticable because Ashbrook could have built and supplied a filter press that met Dietz's mechanical specifications. According to Waldinger, Ashbrook's evaluation that the machine would not meet performance standards did not render performance of the contract impracticable because an owner impliedly warrants that the mechanical specifications it furnishes will, if strictly adhered to, permit the contractor to achieve the desired result; the owner, not the contractor, assumes this risk. Bates & Rogers Construction Corp. v. North Shore Sanitary District, 92 Ill.App.3d 90, 94, 414 N.E.2d 1274, 1278 (2d Dist. 1980).

Initially, we note that if the record contains evidence that Ashbrook could have supplied a machine that met both the mechanical and the performance specifications, Waldinger has not pointed to it. Ashbrook produced evidence that it could not have supplied such a machine. Because Carter had no 15–31 machine in operation and because Dietz made no independent study of Carter's performance claims, Dietz apparently could offer no concrete evidence that the mechanical filter press it demanded would satisfy the performance standards.

Secondly, an owner's implied warranty that its specifications are not defective, the effect of which is to shield the contractor from liability when the machine it builds according to the specifications does not serve the intended purpose, yields to a contrary express contractual provision. Specification 11140 provided that the supplier of the sludge dewatering system was responsible for meeting certain performance standards; if it did not, the owner had the options of reducing the contract price, requiring the supplier to replace the equipment, or waiving the penalty.

Under the contract documents, then, Ashbrook was required to guarantee performance. This, the evidence shows, it could not do if required to build its filter press according to Dietz's mechanical specifications. We conclude that Ashbrook's inability to supply a filter press that would both satisfy Dietz's mechanical specifications and perform as required is sufficient to establish that performance of its contract with Waldinger was commercially impracticable.

. . .

In conclusion, we affirm the district court's determination that Ashbrook was excused from performing its contract with Waldinger on the ground of commercial impracticability. . . .

■ PELL, SENIOR CIRCUIT JUDGE, concurring in part and dissenting in part.

. . . I respectfully dissent from that portion of the opinion [affirming the district court's determination that Ashbrook was excused from contractual performance on the ground of commercial impracticability].

In final analysis this is simply a case where a subcontractor apparently anxious to secure a contract, although knowing that he could not meet all of the requirements of that contract, nevertheless was willing to take a chance that it could vary the terms. In this case the effort was not successful and Ashbrook should also be responsible for damages to Waldinger.

The majority opinion accepts the district court's findings of fact as being not clearly erroneous. I cannot agree. Thus a finding that Ashbrook did not bid the project with the realization it could not meet the specifications simply is not supported by the record. Further, it is not clear to me whether there was any evidence in the trial that Ashbrook relied upon the EPA's requirements that specifications foster competition or whether this is merely a post hoc argument advanced by Ashbrook after it found itself in a trial. Ashbrook may have relied upon its experience that specific mechanical subsystems are ordinarily waived if a supplier can demonstrate that its equipment can meet performance specifications but here Ashbrook had no basis for calling that experience into play. There was nothing in the specifications authorizing an "equal" substitute. I am at a loss to find support for the district court's finding that Ashbrook could not have known that Dietz would interpret its specification in such a way as to require Ashbrook to manufacture a Carter machine.

On the reverse side of the purchase orders, at the top of the page in capital letters, Ashbrook was admonished that "SELLER MUST INDICATE IN WRITING THE SPECIFIC EXCEPTIONS, IF ANY, TO THE TERMS AND CONDITIONS OF THIS PURCHASE ORDER." Ashbrook executed the purchase order as written. No exceptions to the purchase order were taken by Ashbrook. I fail to comprehend why Ashbrook did not here assume a "greater obligation." The plain situation was that there was an unconditional obligation to Waldinger, under the circumstances and the contract documents, to provide the materials necessary to satisfy the specification requirements to the approval of the engineer. Ashbrook knew at the time it signed the Purchase Orders that the engineer had expressly not approved acceptability of its 1–V machine to satisfy the performance specifications and knew its subsystem parts were sufficiently different that a waiver of the specifications by the engineer on six separate items would be required. Ashbrook admittedly made the business decision to bid the project under those circumstances, without exculpatory language in the contract. Its decision to do so under those known contingencies was not in accord with custom in the industry, which according to the evidence would be to submit a bid identifying your equipment as an "or equal."

While I regard § 2–615 as not being applicable, even in the event it were, a person seeking its shelter must establish that performance was "impracticable." In Neal–Cooper Grain Co. v. Texas Gulf Sulphur Co., 508 F.2d 283 (7th Cir.1974), this court stated in denying a defense of commercial impracticability:

> "The fact that performance has become economically burdensome or unattractive is not sufficient for performance to be excused." Id. at 293.

> "We will not allow a party to a contract to escape a bad bargain merely because it is burdensome. After one party has entered a contract for supply, he ceases to look for other sources and does not enter other contracts." Id. at 294.

Further, Ashbrook has completely failed to prove that its loss if it had complied with the specification would have been excessive or unreasonable. The district court properly did not find this to be the case. In applying § 2–615 to the circumstances of a case, the courts have uniformly held that the specific contingency which occurred need not have been contemplated but only that the occurrence be in some degree foreseeable.

In the present case, refusal of the engineer to agree to waive all or part of the mechanical specifications in interpreting compliance with the project specifications, could have been foreseen as a distinct possibility that would affect performance.

Ashbrook contends it is excused from performance because it did not obtain the expected performance from the engineer. Ashbrook, however, was aware of the fact that its desired performance of the contract would be possible only to the extent that it was able to obtain the consent or cooperation of the engineer.

An agreement which cannot be performed without the consent or cooperation of a third party is not excused by reason of the inability of the promisor to obtain such consent or cooperation.

Waldinger bargained with Ashbrook to receive sludge dewatering equipment which would meet the specifications and receive the Engineer's approval, without restriction or limitation as to source of supply. Whether the necessary equipment was manufactured by Ashbrook in whole or in part or by other suppliers was of no consequence to Waldinger. It offered that contract in the form of two purchase orders to Ashbrook. Ashbrook accepted the contract on those terms without reservation or exception.

Ashbrook contends performance was impossible because the equipment required by the engineer in satisfaction of the specifications could not (in Ashbrook's opinion) have performed and, therefore, Ashbrook would have become subject to those provisions of the contract which required Ashbrook to repair or replace equipment which did not satisfy the performance specifications. The law of Illinois is clearly to the contrary. If Ashbrook had supplied the equipment under its approved drawings, and that equipment did not satisfy the performance specifications by reason of the fact that the approved and specified equipment being supplied could not meet the performance specifications, as contended by Ashbrook, then Ashbrook would be excused from operation of the penalty provisions. Bates & Rogers Const. Corp. v. North Shore Sanitary Dist., 92 Ill.App.3d 90, 94, 414 N.E.2d 1274, 1278 (1980). . . .

Regardless of the ultimate allocation of responsibility between Ashbrook and Dietz, Ashbrook, in my opinion, should be held accountable to Waldinger under the terms of its contract with Waldinger.

QUESTIONS AND NOTES

1. Why do you suppose Waldinger used a subcontractor for the belt filter presses?

2. As between Waldinger and Ashbrook, which of them was likely to have greater knowledge of the risk that Dietz would reject Ashbrook's equipment? Is this question relevant?

3. As between Waldinger and Ashbrook, which of them should bear the extra expense resulting from Dietz's insistence upon Carter equipment?

4. How relevant is it that Ashbrook did not anticipate that Dietz would insist not only on compliance with performance specifications but also with exact design specifications? It is common in construction bidding to specify the use of specific equipment, identified by manufacturer and model number. But the specifications usually add, "or equal," to give bidders the chance to base their bid on competing equipment if it can be shown to be equivalent to the specified item. What is the significance, if any, of the absence of this language in the specifications here?

5. A number of commentators have pointed out that the frequently stated requirement that the discharging event be "unforeseeable" or "unforeseen" (repeated in Official Comment 1 to 2–615) is not workable or accurate. A good, short statement is the following from Joskow, Commercial Impossibility, The Uranium Market and the Westinghouse Case, 6 J. Legal Stud. 119, 157 (1977):

> The foreseeability doctrine appears to raise a number of difficulties. To some extent every occurrence is foreseeable. There is always

some probability that a fire will destroy the anticipated source of supply, that a key person will die, that various acts of God—like floods—will occur, that there will be an embargo or war, etc. In an objective sense, virtually nothing is truly unforeseeable to the extent that theoretically every possible state of the world could be enumerated and some probability assigned to its occurrence.

The foreseeability requirement may only make sense if we introduce the concept of "bounded rationality." . . . [T]he concept of bounded rationality recognizes that human beings cannot evaluate all possible states of the world or all available information that might affect a particular situation. One way of thinking about the foreseeability doctrine is as delineating the boundary between those contingencies that are reasonably part of the decisionmaking process and those that are not. This recognizes that most contracts are not complete contingent claims contracts, commonly including only some subset of all possible occurrences as a reasonable basis for decisionmaking and appropriately included either explicitly or implicitly in the terms of the contract.

For an argument that, in applying impossibility and frustration rules, courts should, and largely do, put the risk of the unexpected contingency on the party able at least cost to assess and bear the risk, see Posner & Rosenfield, Impossibility and Related Doctrines in Contract Law: An Economic Analysis, 6 J. Legal Stud. 83 (1977).

6. Problem. PlayTime contracts to manufacture, deliver, and install 50 swing sets at School District's elementary schools. The contract, which does not contain a force majeure clause, calls for delivery and installation during the third week of April. As it completes the swing sets, PlayTime must store them in its warehouse until all 50 are completed. During the second week of April, when PlayTime has 80 of these completed swing sets in its warehouse, a fire destroys 40 of them.

a. Is PlayTime excused from performing?

b. Assume that PlayTime also has a contract with DayCareCo for 15 swing sets. If PlayTime delivers 15 to DayCareCo, must School District accept delivery of the other 25?

c. If School District accepts delivery of the 25, can it insist on later delivery of the other 25 swing sets for which it contracted? If so, is it entitled to compensation for the delay?

7. Problem. Buyer contracts to purchase a coat custom-made of an exotic fur by Seller, for $6,500. He pays $2,500 down and agrees to return in six months to be measured for the coat and to approve the pelts. Before he returns, Congress passes legislation to protect that species of animal by prohibiting the use of its fur for any purpose. Under 2–615(a) Seller's failure to deliver is not a breach. But is Buyer entitled to the return of his $2,500 down payment? See 2–616. Subsection (1)(b) provides that in the event of impracticability under 2–615, the buyer may terminate the contract. But it does not specifically address whether the buyer may recover back a down payment. Is Seller liable for the $2,500?

Now assume that the government has not banned the use of the fur specified for Buyer's coat, but that Buyer becomes concerned about preservation of that species and informs Seller that he does not want the coat after all and will not take it or pay for it. If this communication occurs before Seller has incurred any expenses, is Buyer entitled to the return of his down payment?

8. Leases. Article 2A contains rules similar to the rules of Article 2. See 2A–221, 2A–405, 2A–406.

9. CISG. Article 79 of the Convention on Contracts for the International Sale of Goods relieves a party from liability for failure to perform if "he proves that the failure was due to an impediment beyond his control and that he could not reasonably be expected to have taken the impediment into account at the time of the conclusion of the contract or to have avoided or overcome it or its consequences." The "impediment" language of Article 79 seems to describe impossibility rather than frustration of purpose. In contrast, it is at least arguable that frustration of purpose may be a defense under UCC 2–615. See Official Comment 3 to 2–615. Note that Article 79 applies both to sellers and to buyers, while 2–615 by its terms applies only to sellers. In a proper case, however, it is likely that courts applying Article 2 would apply similar rules to buyers. See Northern Indiana Public Service Co. v. Carbon County Coal Co., 799 F.2d 265 (7th Cir.1986).

Article 79, like UCC 2–615, avoids using "unforeseen" to describe the kind of event that will discharge the parties. Compare the CISG language, "could not reasonably be expected to have taken into account," with the somewhat circuitous language of 2–615, "the occurrence of a contingency the non-occurrence of which was a basic assumption on which the contract was made."

Note also that Article 79(2) requires that if the claimed impediment is the inability of a third party to perform, both the third party and the person claiming discharge must meet the "impediment" test stated above. If Article 79(2) governed the dispute in *Chase Precast* (page 518 supra), what result?

CHAPTER 10

RIGHTS AND LIABILITIES OF THIRD PARTIES

A. TITLE

For purposes of Article 2, title is irrelevant to the determination of the rights of the buyer and the seller against each other. Article 2 allocates risk of loss according to the rules of 2–509 and 2–510 rather than according to who has title. The right of a buyer to get contracted-for goods from a seller who refuses to deliver is determined by 2–716 and 2–502, and it does not suffice under those sections that the buyer has title. (If the buyer has title but is unable to obtain possession of the goods under 2–716 or 2–502, title revests in the seller. Compare 2–401(4).)

Section 2–401 states that the buyer acquires, by identification of goods to the contract, a "special property." This "special property" is, however, no more than the right to exercise rights under 2–716 and 2–502, the right to insure (2–501), and the right to sue third parties for injury to the goods (2–722).

While rights between buyer and seller do not turn on title, 2–401 does state rules from which one may determine when title passes to the buyer. Official Comment 1 indicates that these rules are necessary in connection with implementing "public regulation" that depends on title. This public regulation includes such things as ad valorem taxes that are assessed against the person who has title to goods on a particular date. Title also may be important in determining which of the parties, buyer or seller, has tort liability to third parties.

Home Indemnity Co. v. Twin City Fire Insurance Co.

United States Court of Appeals, Seventh Circuit, 1973.
474 F.2d 1081.

■ HASTINGS, SENIOR CIRCUIT JUDGE. [Parker G.M.C. Truck Sales, Inc., contracted to sell a new G.M.C. semi-tractor to Bodge Lines, Inc., a trucking business. As part of the price, Bodge was to trade in a used Mack semi-tractor. The certificate of title to the trade-in vehicle was held by a lender, and Parker Truck promised Bodge that it would to pay the lender the balance due on the trade-in. The parties also agreed that Bodge could remove some new tires on the trade-in and replace them with used tires.

Sometime after Bodge took possession of the new tractor, two of Parker Truck's employees went to Bodge's premises to pick up the trade-in. Bodge's mechanic, Rex Imlay, informed them that he had not yet swapped out the tires and would himself drive the trade-in to Parker Truck's premises after he completed the exchange of the tires.

Later that afternoon, while driving the trade-in to Parker Truck's premises, Imlay was involved in an accident, injuring two persons as well as the trade-in vehicle. The vehicle was towed to the premises of Parker Truck, which repaired it, paid off the lender, and sold it. In a separate proceeding, the two persons injured in the accident sued. In this proceeding, Bodge's insurer, Home Indemnity Co., filed a declaratory judgment action against Parker Truck's insurer, Twin City Fire Insurance Co., to determine which of them is liable.] This question, in turn, is answered by determining who owned the Mack truck at the time of the accident.

. . .

The instant cause was submitted to the trial court upon a joint stipulation . . . . The stipulation further provided:

" * * * the sole issue for determination is whether said plaintiff or said defendant insures one Rex Imlay for his liability, if any, arising out of an accident which occurred on March 24, 1968 and out of which said accident claims have been presented . . . .

" * * * there is a single issue of fact which will be determinative of this question, to wit: Was the vehicle driven by said Rex Imlay, at the time of the accident in question, 'owned' by Bodge Lines, Inc. (insured by The Home Indemnity Company), or by Parker GMC Truck Sales, Inc. (insured by Twin City Fire Insurance Company)?"

. . .

The trial court, upon consideration of the record as stipulated and briefs by the parties in lieu of oral argument, found the facts as above set out favorable to Home. The court further found that the trade-in Mack tractor was owned at the time of the collision by Parker Truck and that ownership was acquired at the time of the execution of the contract the morning of March 24, 1969, as a partial payment by Bodge for the new G.M.C. truck. The court further found that the arrangement [for Imlay to deliver] the Mack tractor was made at a time when the vehicle was owned by Parker Truck and was not authorized by Bodge. The court finally concluded that Imlay was not insured by Home but rather was insured by Twin City, and it rendered judgment favorable to Home and adverse to Twin City.

Twin City and Parker Truck alone have appealed. We affirm.

The burden of appellants' appeal is their contention that the trial court erred as a matter of law in finding that the title to the trade-in vehicle had passed from Bodge to Parker Truck before the vehicle left the premises of Bodge. They rely upon certain sections of the Uniform Commercial Code as authority for their claim.

Whether this challenged action of the trial court was a conclusion of law, a finding of fact or a mixed question of law and fact is not determinative of this appeal, and we shall not fashion a label for it. . . .

It is undisputed that the purchase and sale of a motor vehicle is a transaction involving goods governed by Article 2 of the Uniform Commercial Code, Ind.Code § 26–1–2–101, et seq. (1971). We are concerned here with the sale of the new G.M.C. truck by Parker Truck to Bodge and the trade-in of the Mack tractor by Bodge to Parker Truck. Each party to the transaction is the "seller" of the goods it is to deliver. U.C.C. § 2–304(1) provides: "The price can be made payable in money or otherwise. If it is payable in whole or in part in goods each party is a seller of the goods which he is to transfer." Hence, both parties agree that Bodge is the "seller" of the trade-in vehicle.

Again, the parties agree that the place for delivery of the trade-in vehicle is governed by U.C.C. § 2–308, which provides, in relevant part: "Unless otherwise agreed * * * the place for delivery of goods is the seller's place of business or if he has none his residence * * *." Hence, "unless otherwise agreed," the place for delivery of the trade-in vehicle was Bodge's place of business.

Concerning the passage of title, U.C.C. § 2–401(2) provides: "Unless otherwise explicitly agreed title passes to the buyer [Parker Truck] at the time and place [Bodge's place of business] at which the seller [Bodge] completes his performance with reference to the physical delivery of the goods, despite any reservation of a security interest and even though a document of title is to be delivered at a different time or place * * *."

Relevant to the tender of delivery of the trade-in vehicle, appellants cite U.C.C. § 2–503(1), which states, in relevant part: "Tender of delivery requires that the seller put and hold conforming goods at the buyer's disposition and give the buyer any notification reasonably necessary to enable him to take delivery."

Based upon the foregoing sections of the Uniform Commercial Code, appellants advance the following line of reasoning. When Parker Truck sought delivery of the trade-in vehicle at Bodge's place of business, the trade-in unit was not prepared for tender of delivery because the substitution of the used tires for the new tires had not been accomplished. At that time the parties orally agreed through their respective employees ... to change the place of delivery from Bodge's place of business to Parker Truck's. Since Bodge was unwilling to tender the trade-in vehicle at that time the "otherwise" agreement of § 2–308 was made. Finally, appellants argue, since Bodge had not completed the physical delivery of the vehicle at the time of the accident, and since the accident occurred while the tractor was being operated by an employee of Bodge en route to Parker Truck's premises, in performance of the changed agreement as to delivery, title had not passed to the buyer but remained in the seller. Hence, appellants conclude, Home was obligated to defendant and pay on behalf of Imlay any liability found against him. We disagree.

The trial court found as a fact that when [Parker Truck] called at Bodge's for the trade-in vehicle to take delivery and transport it to the premises of Parker Truck, they were told by Imlay that he had not completed the tire exchange; that [Parker Truck's representative] said he could not return that day; that Imlay then *volunteered* to drive it for them when it was ready; and that [Parker Truck's representative] said that would be all right. We cannot fault this finding of fact. Imlay was driving as a volunteer to accommodate [Parker Truck], rather than as a Bodge employee under a new agreement as to place of delivery which would have affected ownership of the vehicle. Further, our reading of [the deposition of Bodge's president] indicates that he never authorized Imlay or any other employee to make delivery of a truck at any place other than Bodge's premises.

As earlier set out, the trial court found as undisputed facts that, after the accident in question, the damaged trade-in vehicle was removed to the premises of Parker Truck; it was repaired by Parker Truck at its own expense; Parker Truck paid the balance owing on it to the lien holder and later resold the repaired tractor; and no adjustment was made to the contract between the parties because of the damage sustained by that vehicle. . . .

It seems clear to us, as it was to the trial court, that Parker Truck by its own course of conduct placed its mark of approval on the meaning of the agreement of the parties by completing its performance in a manner consistent with the transfer of ownership to it prior to the accident in question.

We have examined the authorities cited by appellants concerning passage of title and ownership upon or after physical delivery of goods sold. We are not persuaded that they are inconsistent with the result reached here. This case is limited to and controlled by the factual situation present here.

We hold that the factual findings of the trial court are not clearly erroneous and that the conclusions reached below are proper and correct. In short, we have determined that the correct result was reached, and the judgment appealed from is affirmed.

Affirmed.

QUESTIONS

If Parker Truck had not repaired and sold the damaged trade-in, would the result change? Why or why not? If Parker Truck had sought to reduce the trade-in allowance (or recover for the reduced value of the damaged trade-in), would the result change? Why or why not?

B. SITUATIONS IN WHICH THE BUYER GETS BETTER TITLE THAN THE SELLER HAD

1. RIGHTS OF THE BUYER AGAINST A SECURED CREDITOR OF THE SELLER

A seller of goods often grants a security interest in those goods to secure a debt owed to some lender or supplier. That security interest gives the lender or supplier (the creditor) the right to seize and sell the goods to satisfy the debt if the seller does not pay the debt. If the seller sells goods that are subject to a security interest, the question arises whether the buyer takes free of the security interest. That issue is dealt with in substantial detail in Article 9 of the Uniform Commercial Code and in the law school course that covers secured transactions. This note and the next two cases provide a brief introduction.

To protect its security interest in a seller's goods against the claims of third parties, a creditor (known as a "secured party") must "perfect" its interest, usually by filing a document (a "financing statement") in the relevant state's secretary of state's office showing the existence of the security interest. (A security interest in a motor vehicle, other than one given by a debtor who is a dealer in motor vehicles, must be perfected by notation on the vehicle's certificate of title. A security interest given by a dealer in motor vehicles is perfected by filing a financing statement, rather than by notation on the certificate of title.)

When a dealer in goods borrows money to finance its business and grants a security interest in the goods it holds for sale, its lender expects it to sell those goods. This, of course, enables the seller to pay the debt owed to the lender. Persons who purchase goods from a dealer do not expect that they must search in the secretary of state's office to determine whether the dealer has granted a security interest in the goods being bought. (For example, did it ever occur to you to ask whether the electronics dealer from whom you purchased your last computer had granted its creditor a security interest in it?) Under Article 9 the ordinary buyer from a dealer in goods of the kind being purchased takes free of a perfected security interest created by the seller even if the buyer knows that the goods are subject to a security interest. That buyer is called a "buyer in ordinary course of business." The requirements necessary to achieve the status of "buyer in ordinary course" are set out in 1–201(9) [revised 1–201(a)(9)]. Please read that definition, and see also 9–320(a).

If the grantor of a security interest is not a merchant who deals in goods of the kind, perfection of the security interest gives the secured party rights superior to the person in possession of the goods, including subsequent good faith buyers. If the debtor defaults, the secured party can repossess the goods, even from a good faith purchaser. If the security interest is not perfected, the secured party may enforce it as against buyers who know of the interest or act in bad faith when they take possession of the goods.

The following cases and problems explore some of the rules briefly summarized above. Article 9 was revised in 1999, and all states have now adopted the 1999 version. Both the following cases cite sections in the pre–1999 version, but nothing in the current version would affect the outcome of these cases.

Snap–On Tools Corporation v. Rice

Arizona Court of Appeals, 1989.
162 Ariz. 99, 781 P.2d 76.

■ Roll, Presiding Judge.

. . .

FACTS

Snap–On sold tools to Larry Neal, who operated a tire business in Benson, Arizona. The goods included an air compressor and wheel balancer and were sold pursuant to purchase money security agreements. Snap–On did not perfect its interest in these tools because it is a Snap–On policy not to record financing statements for contracts involving less than $7,500.

In March 1987, Rice entered into a contract with Neal to purchase the tire business, including some tools which constituted collateral covered by the security agreements. Rice had worked for Neal for approximately one and one-half years prior to the purchase.

In July 1987, Rice applied for credit from Snap–On with the intent of taking over Neal's outstanding tool account. The credit application was denied. Snap–On told Rice that it "would not be able to do business with [Rice] and in his name." Based on Snap–On's refusal to extend Rice credit to take over the tool account, Rice and Neal modified the purchase contract. The price was reduced to $4,000 and Neal kept most of the tools that had been part of the original contract for the sale of the business. Neal did purport to sell the air compressor and wheel balancer to Rice. Neal then moved to Kansas and shortly thereafter filed bankruptcy. After the purchase of the business, Rice made no payments to Snap–On. Thereafter, Snap–On attempted to recover the air compressor and wheel balancer from Rice.

PROCEDURAL BACKGROUND

Snap–On filed a complaint and application for provisional remedy of replevin without notice. An order was issued directing the sheriff to replevy the collateral. Rice was served with the summons, complaint, and an application for provisional remedy. Rice filed a request for hearing pursuant to A.R.S. § 12–2402. After the hearing, the court quashed the provisional remedy, ordered the return of the collateral, and awarded Rice his costs and attorneys' fees. Snap–On appeals from this order.

ISSUES

. . .

Snap–On's Right to Replevin

Snap–On argues that its unperfected purchase money security interest in the air compressor and wheel balancer is superior to Rice's interest. A.R.S. § 47–9301(A) provides in part:

A. Except as otherwise provided in subsection B of this section, an unperfected security interest is subordinate to the rights of:

* * *

3. In the case of goods . . . a person who is not a secured party and who is a . . . buyer not in ordinary course of business, to the extent that he gives value and receives delivery of the collateral *without knowledge of the security interest*. . . . [Emphasis added]

Snap–On does not deny that goods are involved, that Rice was a buyer not in the ordinary course of business, or that Rice received delivery of the collateral. Snap–On does contend that Rice had knowledge of Snap–On's security interest and that Rice did not give value for the air compressor and wheel balancer. These are questions of fact which the trial court resolved in favor of Rice. Our standard of review is limited to a determination as to whether substantial evidence exists to support the decision of the trial court.

a. *Knowledge*

For purposes of the Uniform Commercial Code, the definition of knowledge is set forth in A.R.S. § 47–1201(25)(c), which states: "[A] person 'knows' or has 'knowledge' of a fact when he has actual knowledge of it." A.R.S. § 47–9301 does not mandate good faith; it only requires that delivery be taken without actual knowledge of Snap–On's security interest. *Southland Corp. v. Emerald Oil Co.*, 789 F.2d 1441, 1446 (9th Cir.1986) (interpreting UCC § 9–301 under California law). Actual knowledge does not include a reason to know of the security interest. The purchaser must have actual knowledge that the security interest exists at the time the collateral is purchased.

The code does not require an inquiry into whether a security interest exists. In *Clark Oil and Refining Co. v. Liddicoat*, 65 Wis.2d 612, 622–23, 223 N.W.2d 530, 536 (1974), the court stated:

By this definition [of knowledge], it is apparent that the framers of the Code required proof of actual knowledge on the part of the lien creditor if he is to be subordinated to the holder of an unfiled security interest. Whether the judgment creditor had reason to know, or might have been alerted to, circumstances that should reasonably have impelled him to check beyond the filed record is irrelevant under the Code.

Snap–On argues that Rice had actual knowledge of the security interest of Snap–On in the wheel balancer and air compressor because Rice worked at the store for a year and a half prior to that purchase, Rice made payments to Snap–On on behalf of Neal, Rice made a credit application to assume the obligation of the tool account, Rice was told of Snap–On's interest in the collateral, and Snap–On demanded that Rice turn over the collateral to Snap–On. Snap–On contends that Scott Garvin's testimony proved that Rice was told of Snap–On's interest in the collateral. Garvin, who was Snap–On's credit manager, testified: "I told Mr. Rice we would not be able to do business with him and we needed to pick up the tools."

Rice testified that when he entered into the contract to purchase the business from Mr. Neal in March 1987, he had no knowledge that Snap–On claimed a lien or held an unfiled purchase money security interest in the air compressor and wheel balancer. Rice did admit that although Neal had indicated that the wheel balancer was not "free and clear," Rice believed Neal was to pay off the balancer.

The judge found that "there may be knowledge on the part of the defendant that a contract exists between the person from whom he purchased his business and your client" and that "he may have some knowledge of the existence of an agreement." However, the judge did not find that Rice had actual knowledge of a security interest. We agree that the fact that Rice knew that Neal owed money to Snap–On does not prove that Rice knew of Snap–On's security interest in the air compressor and wheel balancer. Substantial evidence exists to support the trial court's decision that Rice did not acquire the compressor and balancer with actual knowledge of Snap–On's interest.

b.   *Value*

Snap–On also maintains that Rice did not give value for the air compressor and wheel balancer as required by A.R.S. § 47–9301(A)(3) because Rice did not pay the full value of the items. Value is defined in A.R.S. § 47–1201(44).

[A]   person gives "value" for rights if he acquires them:

* * *

(d) Generally, in return for any consideration sufficient to support a simple contract.

The only testimony presented regarding the value of the two items came from Rice, who stated that the air compressor and wheel balancer had a combined value of $2,500. The $4,000 Rice paid for the business was for good will, some used tires, the compressor, and the balancer. Ample evidence existed to support the trial court's conclusion that Rice gave value for the two items in question. That Snap–On's lien on the compressor and the balancer exceeded $4,000 does not prove that these two items had a value equal to the lien. Once again, substantial evidence exists to support the trial court's conclusion that Rice gave value for the compressor and balancer.

There was substantial evidence to support the trial court's quashing of the provisional remedy. Rice will be awarded attorneys' fees on appeal upon compliance with Rule 21(c), Ariz.R.Civ.App.P., 17B A.R.S. We affirm the trial court's granting of Rice's motion to quash provisional remedy and remand this matter for further proceedings.

QUESTIONS AND NOTES

1. The rule applied in *Snap–On Tools* now appears in 9–317(b). Please read that section. Observe that to prevail against a secured party with an unperfected secured interest, the buyer must both give value and receive delivery of the goods without knowledge of the security interest. Therefore, if the buyer pays the price, but before receiving delivery, acquires knowledge of the unperfected security interest, the buyer will lose. The buyer also loses if the secured party perfects its security interest (generally by filing) before the buyer gets possession, even if the buyer has given value before the secured party perfects. On the other hand, the giving of value doesn't mean that the price actually must be paid. Since 1–201(44) [revised 1–204(4)] defines "value" as "any consideration sufficient to support a simple contract," a contractually binding promise is value. Therefore, if a buyer takes possession of goods pursuant to a contract that calls for deferred payment, the buyer will not lose to the holder of an unperfected security interest of which the buyer learns before actually paying for the goods or which the secured party perfects before the buyer pays for the goods.

2. Was the fair market value of the goods bought by Rice relevant to whether Rice took free of *Snap–On Tools'* unperfected security interest?

3. The court states (third paragraph on page 540) that 9–301 (current 9–317) "does not mandate good faith." In light of 1–203 (revised 1–304), is the court correct?

4. Rice was not a buyer in ordinary course because Neal, from whom he bought, was not a dealer in air compressors or wheel balancers. Neal may have been a dealer in tires and other goods, but Rice could have been a buyer in ordinary course only if Neal was in the business of selling the particular items that Rice bought. Nevertheless, even though Rice was not a buyer in ordinary course, he took free of Snap–On Tool's security interest. If, however, Snap–On Tools had filed a proper financing statement, its interest would have been superior to Rice's interest.

5. Former Article 9 called a person like Rice, who did not buy from a person in the business of selling goods of the kind, a "buyer not in ordinary course" just to make it clear that there was a different rule for "buyers in ordinary course." Current 9–317(b) drops the "buyer not in ordinary course" language but does not change the rule. The next case in the materials involves a "buyer in ordinary course of business."

General Electric Credit Corporation v. Humble

United States District Court, Middle District of Alabama, 1982.
532 F.Supp. 703.

MEMORANDUM OPINION

■ HOBBS, DISTRICT JUDGE.

Plaintiff General Electric Credit Corporation (GECC), a New York corporation with its principal place of business in Connecticut, brought this diversity action against H. C. Humble, individually and d/b/a H & H Mobile Homes Sales, a citizen of Alabama. In its complaint, GECC seeks possession of three mobile homes which were sold to Humble by Sanderson Mobile Homes, Inc., or, in the alternative, plaintiff seeks the value of the three mobile homes, alleged to total $23,800.00, plus damages for defendant's wrongful detention of the mobile homes.[1]

The facts in this case have been submitted to the Court on a stipulation of the parties and are not disputed. On January 2, 1980, Sanderson Mobile Homes, Inc. entered into an agreement with GECC in which Sanderson granted to GECC a security interest in all of its inventory, including but not limited to mobile homes, both new and used, presently owned and thereafter acquired, together with all proceeds of the sale or the disposition thereof. GECC subsequently perfected its security interest under Alabama law by filing the appropriate financing statements.

On September 25, 1981, Sanderson transferred one used, repossessed 1976 model mobile home to Humble; and on October 7, 1981, Sanderson transferred two used, repossessed 1976 and 1977 mobile homes to Humble. All of these transfers were made pursuant to bills of sale. Although the price paid for each mobile home was less than the NADA wholesale book value, no claim has been made that the sum paid for these used, repossessed mobile homes was less than fair market value for such sales, and plaintiff presented no evidence that the sales reflected less than fair market value for the particular mobile homes. The Court has no evidence before it on the condition of these repossessed mobile homes at the time of their sale by Sanderson to Humble.

By a letter dated November 11, 1981, GECC notified Humble that Sanderson had defaulted in its obligations to GECC and that GECC had a perfected security interest in the mobile homes transferred to Humble. GECC demanded that Humble release the mobile homes to GECC or pay the value of the mobile homes. Humble acknowledged receipt of the letter, but has refused to deliver possession of the mobile homes to GECC or pay GECC the value of the mobile homes.

---

1.   GECC initially sought an interlocutory order for the issuance of a writ of detinue to acquire possession of the mobile homes in question pending the outcome of the instant suit, see Fed.R.Civ.P. 64; Ala. Code § 6–6–250 (1975), but at the hearing on GECC's request for an interlocutory order both parties agreed that Humble could maintain possession of the mobile homes upon the condition that the proceeds from any sales would be held in trust pending this Court's ruling. The parties further agreed to submit this case for decision on the stipulations and briefs now before the Court.

As the basis of its claim, GECC relies on Section 7–9–306(2)* of the Alabama Code, which provides: "Except where this article otherwise provides, a security interest continues in collateral notwithstanding sale, exchange or other disposition thereof by the debtor unless his action was authorized by the secured party in the security agreement or otherwise. . . ." Humble, on the other hand, relies on an exception to the protection afforded creditors by Section 7–9–306(2). This exception arises under Section 7–9–307(1)** of the Alabama Code when a buyer in the ordinary course of business purchases the collateral from the debtor and such purchase is valid even though the buyer knows of the existence of the security interest created by the debtor. According to these provisions of the Alabama version of the Uniform Commercial Code, the determinative factor in deciding if Humble takes the mobile homes free of GECC's security interest is whether Humble qualifies as a buyer in the ordinary course of business.

A buyer in the ordinary course of business is defined in Section 7–1–201(9)*** as "a person who in good faith and without knowledge that the sale to him is in violation of the ownership rights or security interest of a third party in the goods buys in ordinary course from a person in the business of selling goods of that kind." Good faith is defined in Section 7–1–201(19) of the Alabama Code to be "honesty in fact in the conduct or transaction concerned." This definition creates a subjective standard of good faith. Good faith is also defined in Section 7–2–103(1)(b), which is expressly applicable to merchants, as "honesty in fact and the observance of reasonable commercial standards of fair dealing in the trade." This definition creates an objective standard of good faith. GECC contends that the objective standard of Section 7–2–103(1)(b) is applicable in this case since Humble is a merchant in the business of buying and selling mobile homes. Specifically, GECC contends that Humble was not observing reasonable commercial standards of fair dealing and, consequently, was not acting in good faith so as to qualify as a buyer in the ordinary course of business when Humble purchased the three mobile homes from Sanderson without making a record inquiry to determine if the mobile homes were subject to a security interest.

GECC argues that a sale between dealers is not in the ordinary course of business unless the merchant buyer makes a record inquiry to determine if the mobile homes are subject to a security interest. GECC further contends that upon discovery of a security interest, the merchant buyer must also investigate to see if the sale violates the terms of the security agreement. In support of its argument, GECC relies on the case of Swift v. J. I. Case Co., 266 So.2d 379 (Fla.Dist.Ct.App.1972).

If this Court agreed with the sweeping holding of the Florida court, it would follow that GECC would be entitled to the relief it seeks. This Court does not agree, however. Section 7–9–307(1) of the Alabama Code provides

---

* Now 9–315.—Ed.

** Now 9–320(a).—Ed.

*** Now 1–201(a)(9) and slightly modified.—Ed.

that even actual knowledge that a perfected security interest exists would not defeat a buyer in the ordinary course of business. To prevent a buyer in the ordinary course of business from taking free of the security interest, the secured party must also show that the buyer had knowledge that the sale by the debtor was unauthorized under some term of the security agreement.[2]

In their commentary on the UCC, Willier and Hart question the holding of the Florida court in the *Swift* case as follows:

> It is doubtful that a security agreement between a manufacturer and a dealer would prevent resale. The decision of the court produces the strange result that the buyer fails to take free of the security interest merely because he did not inquire as to the existence of a security agreement covering the goods, when had he so done, he would have discovered nothing to impair his right to take a clear title to the goods. This decision, in effect, at least for a merchant buyer, changes the requirement of 9–307 that the buyer not have actual knowledge that the sale violates a security agreement, to a requirement that buyer have taken measures to acquire positive knowledge that the sale is not in violation of a security agreement.[3]

In the instant case, GECC has failed to present any evidence that there was anything unusual in the sale of used mobile homes from dealer Sanderson to dealer Humble. In fact, the parties have stipulated that such sales were made on other occasions by the debtor Sanderson. Under modern business practices, it would seem surprising if most automobiles and mobile homes in the hands of dealers were not financed with security agreements, and Section 7–9–307 expressly provides that a buyer in the ordinary course of business takes free of a valid security interest "even though the buyer knows of its existence." In order for such a security instrument to defeat a sale between merchant dealers, the buyer must have knowledge of facts that would put him on notice that the sale is in violation of some term of the security agreement. GECC not only failed to show the existence of such facts; it failed to offer evidence of any facts that would even suggest that any inquiry be made.

GECC argues that Humble was particularly at fault for failing to make a record inquiry in this case because the purchases of the mobile homes were pursuant to bills of sale[4] rather than the assignment of certificates of

---

2. "Reading the two provisions (Sections 7–9–307 and 7–1–201(9)) together, it results that the buyer takes free if he merely knows that there is a security interest which covers the goods but takes subject if he knows, in addition, that the sale is in violation of some term in the security agreement not waived by the words or conduct of the secured party." Ala.Code § 7–9–307, Official Comment 2 (1975); see Cessna Fin. Corp. v. Skyways Enterprises, Inc., 580 S.W.2d 491 (Ky.1979).

3. Willier and Hart, U.C.C. Reporter–Digest § 9–307 A50 (Matthew Bender & Co. 1981). See also Taft v. Kaplan (In re Dexter Buick–GMC Truck Co.), 2 B.R. 253 (D.R.I. 1980).

4. Mobile homes may be transferred by bills of sale in Alabama because mobile homes are exempted under the provisions of the Alabama Uniform Certificate of Title and Antitheft Act. See Ala.Code § 32–8–31(9) (1975).

origin, which GECC contends is the customary method of transferring title to a mobile home. Argument is not a substitute for evidence. Plaintiff has offered no evidence that the sale of mobile homes between dealers in Alabama or elsewhere is customarily accompanied by an assignment of a certificate of origin. Consequently, there is no evidentiary basis for the proposition that the failure to make the transfer with a certificate of origin would alert an Alabama mobile home dealer to any probable flaw in the sale.

In *Swift* the Florida court apparently relied on the objective standard of good faith in reaching its decision. A number of courts, however, have applied the subjective standard of good faith in determining whether a purchaser of collateral qualifies as a buyer in the ordinary course of business. Although it appears that the subjective standard found in Section 7–1–201(19) is operative in this case since the objective standard expressed in Section 7–2–103(1)(b) is only applicable to Article 2 transactions under the Alabama Code, this Court is of the opinion that GECC is not entitled to prevail under either the objective or subjective standard.

If GECC hoped to prevail under either standard, it would have to show more than that Humble failed to inquire about a security interest. In the opinion of this Court, GECC must show that the merchant buyer either had knowledge that the sale violated a security agreement or at least that it had knowledge of facts that would make a reasonable prudent buyer undertake some inquiry. GECC must offer some proof that would take these sales out of the ordinary course of business.

If GECC had shown by the evidence that the failure to accompany the transfer of these used mobile homes with certificates of origin was so unusual as to put a prudent merchant dealer on notice of a possible flaw in the transaction, or if it had presented evidence of such inadequate payment for the mobile homes that would have created a reasonable doubt as to the good faith of the seller, this Court would be required to examine carefully the good faith of the merchant buyer under either standard. But no evidence was offered, and GECC's sole reliance that Humble's purchase was not in the ordinary course of business is based on its contention, rejected by this Court, that a merchant buyer with respect to all purchases must make record inquiry of any security interests before claiming the protection afforded by Section 7–9–307(1).

GECC also maintains that, by virtue of Sanderson's default on its properly perfected security agreements with GECC prior to the transfer of the mobile homes from Sanderson to Humble, GECC had title to and a right to the immediate possession of the mobile homes prior to their transfer to Humble. GECC contends that under Section 7–9–306(2) its right to possession is consequently superior to any right of Humble. As previously mentioned, Section 7–9–306(2) does afford a creditor a degree of protection by providing that a security interest continues in collateral notwithstanding sale by the debtor. Nevertheless, an exception to the creditor's continuing security interest arises under Section 7–9–307(1) when a buyer in the ordinary course of business purchases the collateral from the debtor. Since the Court finds that Humble was a buyer in the ordinary course of business under Section 7–9–307(1) for the reasons previously discussed, Humble took title to the mobile homes regardless of GECC's perfected security interest. GECC clearly had the right to take possession of the collateral from Sanderson upon default; but, having failed to do so, GECC may not now recover against Humble.

An order will be entered this date finding all issues in favor of defendant Humble.

QUESTIONS AND NOTES

1. *Snap-On Tools* and *GECC* are similar in that in both cases the major fact issue is the buyer's knowledge with respect to the prior security interest. The rules applicable to the two cases, however, are different. For example, 9–317(b) does not specifically state that the buyer must be in good faith to take free of the prior unperfected interest. On the other hand, a buyer in ordinary course under 9–320 must "buy in good faith." The court in *GECC* suggests that the good faith requirement of 1–201(9) might in some situations impose a duty on a buyer to inquire about the existence of a security interest. It also suggests that paying a price substantially below the market value of the goods might show lack of good faith. What do you think of that suggestion?

2. Under 9–317, for a buyer not in ordinary course to prevail over the secured party, the buyer must get possession of the goods without knowledge of the security interest and before it is perfected. In 9–320(a), which covers purchasers from a dealer, there is no statement that the buyer must get possession of the goods in order to prevail over the secured party. Prior to the 1999 revision of Article 9, neither Article 9 nor Article 1 addressed the issue of the precise point in the progression of the sales contract at which a person becomes a buyer in ordinary course.

Once a purchaser takes possession of the goods under a sales contract, the purchaser surely is a "buyer" and can be a buyer in ordinary course. But what if the secured party repossesses the goods from the seller after the sales contract is formed, but before the goods have been delivered to the buyer: can the buyer be a buyer in ordinary course and get the goods from the possession of the secured party free of the security interest? If it cannot be determined which goods were to be delivered under the sales contract, it seems difficult for the buyer to ask the finder of fact to designate goods to which it is entitled as a buyer in ordinary course. If the goods have been identified to the contract by the seller, however, it may be reasonable to allow the buyer to be a buyer in ordinary course and get the goods from the secured party. Before the 1999 revision, some courts held that a purchaser could not be a "buyer" and therefore a buyer in ordinary course until it obtained possession of the goods, while other courts held that a purchaser becomes a buyer when the seller identifies particular goods to the contract. (See 2–501 on identification.) One case even held that a buyer was a buyer in ordinary course when the seller had sold the buyer a farm drill and the seller had a number of such drills in its inventory but had not yet identified any particular drill to the contract. Wilson v. M & W Gear, 110 Ill.App.3d 538, 66 Ill.Dec. 244, 442 N.E.2d 670 (1982). A good case discussing the above issues prior to the 1999 revisions is Big Knob Volunteer Fire Co. v. Lowe & Moyer Garage, Inc., 338 Pa.Super. 257, 487 A.2d 953 (1985).

The revision of Article 9 also revised 1–201(9), 2–501, 2–502, and 2–716, to create greater certainty as to the time at which the purchaser becomes a "buyer" entitled to assert rights as a buyer in ordinary course. Please read those sections now, and consider the following problems.

3.   Problem. Buyer entered into a contract for the purchase of a new car, for use as the family vehicle, and made a deposit of $100 toward the total purchase price of $25,000. The contract provided that Buyer could pay the balance of the purchase price in equal monthly payments over five years at an interest rate of 8% per year. Seller wrote the vehicle identification number (VIN) on the contract. Before the automobile was delivered to Buyer, Dealer's lender, which had a security interest in dealer's inventory, seized the automobile. Can Buyer get the automobile from the lender free of the lender's security interest? That question seems easy, right? But what about the payment: must Buyer pay the entire unpaid balance of the price to the lender immediately, or must the lender comply with the credit terms of the sales contract?

4.   Problem. In which of the following variations of Problem 3 does Buyer have the same rights as above?

a.   Dealer did not write the VIN on the contract but directed its service employees to begin to prepare a particular car for delivery to Buyer, and the employees had done so.

b.   The employees had not yet begun to prepare the car when it was seized by the lender.

c.   Dealer had only one car that would satisfy the contract, and Dealer intended to deliver that car, but had not so indicated by either notation of specific VIN number or by directing its employees to begin preparing it for delivery.

d.   Dealer had two identical cars on hand, either of which would satisfy the contract, but had taken no steps to indicate which car would be delivered.

5.   A buyer for personal, family, or household use may recover the goods from the seller's secured creditor under either 2–502 or 2–716. The latter section reads:

"(3) The buyer has a right of replevin for goods identified to the contract if after reasonable effort he is unable to effect cover for such goods or the circumstances reasonably indicate that such cover will be unavailing or if the goods have been shipped under reservation and satisfaction of the security interest in them has been made or tendered. *In the case of goods bought for personal, family or household purposes, the buyer's right of replevin vests upon acquisition of a special property, even if the seller had not then repudiated or failed to deliver."* [emphasis added]

Does 2–716(3) state for the consumer buyer essentially the same rule as 2–502 but without the requirement that the buyer have paid part of the price?

A buyer acquires a special property in goods when they are identified to the contract. Therefore, the second sentence of 2–716(3) really says the same thing as the first sentence with respect to the time when a consumer buyer's right to replevy the goods arises. What the second sentence does not repeat is the requirement that the buyer be unable to cover (or, if the goods have been shipped under reservation, pay the price). Is the intention of the second sentence, therefore, to permit a consumer buyer to replevy goods even if the buyer could purchase identical goods from another source? If so, the rule is like that of 2–502, except that the buyer need not have paid any part of the price. See Official Comment 3 to 2–716, which notes the distinction between non-consumer buyers and consumer buyers under 2–716(3).

6. A buyer who has made a down payment of only $100, as in Problems 3 and 4, is not likely to go through the hassle of trying to get an automobile away from the secured party unless the price is an exceptionally good price. It will often be better just to forget the $100 or try to get the money back from the dealer. If, however, the buyer has paid a substantial part, or all, of the price, the ability to get the automobile free of the lender's security interest can be important. If the buyer does not recover the goods, the buyer becomes a general unsecured creditor of the dealer.

Notice how limited the commercial buyer's right is under 2–502. Even if the full price of the goods has been paid, the buyer can get the goods from the secured party only if the seller becomes insolvent within 10 days after the receipt of the *first* installment on their price. It is very unlikely that the buyer can prove that the seller became insolvent within that period. A commercial buyer who is otherwise a buyer in ordinary course might seek specific performance or replevin under 2–716 as a means of taking property free of the security interest of a repossessing secured party.

7. Revised Article 2. Recall (from Chapters 6 and 7) that revised 2–716 permits the parties in a contract other than a consumer contract to contract for specific performance as a remedy for breach. If a buyer has contracted for specific performance and is otherwise a buyer in ordinary course who would take free of a security interest created by its seller, would the contracted-for remedy of specific performance be available against the secured party who had repossessed the goods? See again 1–201(9) [revised 1–201(a)(9)].

The revision deletes the second sentence of 2–716(3). This means that a consumer buyer, like any other buyer, would be able to seek specific performance or replevin, even from a secured party, only if the requirements set out in subsections (1) or (3), respectively, are satisfied. The revision adds a new subsection, which reads: "(4) The buyer's right under subsection (3) vests upon acquisition of a special property, even if the seller had not then repudiated or failed to deliver." The new subsection therefore avoids any implication that a consumer buyer could get replevin without meeting the requirements of subsection (3). Giving the buyer a right of replevin even though the seller has not repudiated or failed to deliver makes it clear that replevin can be used against the seller's secured party as well as against the seller itself. See Official Comment 5.

2. RIGHTS OF THE BUYER WHEN THE SELLER DOES NOT OWN THE GOODS: ENTRUSTMENT

Owners of goods often place those goods in the possession of others. Common examples include delivery to a consignment shop for the purpose of selling the goods and delivery to a dealer for the purpose of repairing the goods. If the owner of a TV takes it to a dealer for repairs, what happens if the dealer wrongfully sells the TV to a third person? Please read 2–403 and consider the following problems.

1. Problem. Bill Lawton took his stereo radio receiver to Radio Hospital, Inc., for repairs. Radio Hospital is also a dealer in new and used radios, and it sold Lawton's radio to Tami Konuk, who purchased in good faith and without knowledge of Lawton's rights. May Lawton recover the radio from Konuk?

2. Problem. If Radio Hospital had given a security interest in Lawton's radio to First Bank to secure a loan, would First Bank's security interest have been superior to the rights of Lawton?

———

Atlas Auto Rental Corp. v. Weisberg

New York City Civil Court, 1967.
54 Misc.2d 168, 281 N.Y.S.2d 400.

■ EDWARD J. GREENFIELD, JUDGE. Plaintiff is an automobile rental concern which from time to time would sell off its used automobiles as they were replenished with new ones. On August 23, 1965 plaintiff was offering for sale a two year old Chevrolet station wagon for $1250. One Herbert Schwartzman, who had previously attempted to lease a car, offered to purchase the station wagon, and tendered his check, but it was not certified, and plaintiff's manager testified he rejected it. Nevertheless, he permitted Schwartzman to take a test run. Schwartzman got into the station wagon, drove off, and was never seen again. Plaintiff's manager then had Schwartzman's check, which he says he found on his desk, deposited, but alas, it was returned marked "No funds."

A week later, the car was traced to the premises of defendant Weisberg, a licensed auto wrecker and junk dealer in the Bronx. Weisberg was also licensed as a used car dealer in Yonkers. Weisberg claimed he had purchased this car from Schwartzman for $900. He actually paid Schwartzman only $300 down, the balance to be paid at a later time. Schwartzman has never been heard from again. Weisberg received from him neither a bill of sale nor a registration certificate for the motor vehicle, but he immediately resold it the same day to a dealer for $1200.

Plaintiff now sues for conversion, seeking to recover from Weisberg and his firm the value of its station wagon. Defendant resists, insisting that he had acquired good title to the motor vehicle. He invokes the provisions of the Uniform Commercial Code to substantiate his argument that he could acquire good title from a merchant, or even from a thief. There appear to be no reported cases on these provisions of the Code.

At common law, one could convey only such title as he himself possessed. Thus no one could obtain good title from a thief, no matter how innocent the circumstances of his acquisition.

The harshness of this rule with respect to innocent purchasers who had paid their money in perfect good faith without any indication of anything amiss in the transaction led to statutory modifications of the common law rule, so that where the title owner had conveyed a voidable title he would not be permitted to revoke it as against a bona fide purchaser for value. Personal Property Law § 105. Innocence would thus transmute the imperfect title into a state of perfection and impregnability. Impeccable virtue would receive its just reward, and title would pass from a swindler, if not from a thief. Stanton Motor Corp. v. Rosetti, 11 A.D.2d 296, 203 N.Y.S.2d 273.

The protection of the innocent was further developed to cover situations where the title owner had not conveyed even a voidable title, but had so clothed the transferor with apparent vestiges of authority and indicia of title that equitable principles of estoppel were invoked to preclude the title owner from asserting his title. This would cover such circumstances as the delivery of goods to a retail merchant on consignment, or other situations in which the transferor was permitted to retain and sell inventory, with title retained purely as a security device. Personal Property Law, § 104. Zendman v. Harry Winston, Inc., 305 N.Y. 180, 111 N.E.2d 871. Possession alone by the transferor was not enough; he must have been authorized to sell the goods. Barnard v. Campbell, 55 N.Y. 456. Thus where the goods had been obtained by false representations the true owner was not estopped. Hentz v. Miller, 94 N.Y. 64.

The Uniform Commercial Code has expanded the rights of a third person who has purchased the property in all innocence, even from a thief, or from a person who has been entrusted with possession, even if not authorized to sell. UCC § 2–403. Under the Code, title ordinarily passes when goods are delivered, unless otherwise explicitly agreed. UCC § 2–401(2). If passage of title is dependent upon the performance of some condition subsequent, this is a voidable title which can be transferred to a bona fide purchaser for value even if the transferor was deceived as to the identity of the purchaser, the delivery was in exchange for a check later dishonored, or procured through a fraud punishable as larcenous under the criminal law. Thus what was formerly ambiguous has been made explicit. UCC § 2–403(1).

Subdivision (2) provides that the entrusting of goods to a person in the business of selling goods of that kind can validate a transfer to a buyer in the ordinary course of business. This is so even if procurement of the entrusting was larcenous. (Subd. 3.)

Under these provisions, the first question posed is whether plaintiff conferred a voidable title upon Schwartzman, which could be perfected in the hands of a bona fide purchaser for value. Plaintiff put the vehicle in Schwartzman's hands, according to its testimony, solely for the purpose of permitting a test run, and not with any idea of conferring title upon him. The fact that this was done *after* Schwartzman's offer of purchase ostensibly had been rejected, and that after he took the car, plaintiff's manager "found" his check and immediately deposited it raises troublesome questions as to whether or not plaintiff had in fact intended to convey a voidable title dependent on whether the check cleared.

Defendant argues further that irrespective of questions of title, plaintiff did entrust possession of the car to Schwartzman, who was a dealer in wholesale automobiles, and he therefore comes within the protective ambit of UCC § 2–403(2). Do the facts here spell out an "entrusting" of the car to Schwartzman? Even if they do, there is no competent evidence to establish that Schwartzman was "a merchant who deals in goods of that kind." Defendant offered in evidence an invoice he had received from Schwartzman in a prior transaction headed "Herb Schwartzman, Wholesale Automobiles," but this would not suffice to establish the fact, and certainly would not have indicated to plaintiff that Schwartzman was in fact a merchant. Since the "entrusting" provisions of UCC § 2–403 are an extension of the principle of estoppel, it would appear to be essential that the actual vocational status of the merchant be established, but also that the original owner and the ultimate purchaser must be shown to have been aware of that status. An owner entrusting his goods to another cannot be said to have conferred the indicia of ownership and apparent authority to deal with the goods unless he knows he has transferred possession to a dealer. Similarly, the ultimate purchaser can demonstrate reliance and invoke the statutory provision only if he believed he was buying from a dealer. The proof here is wholly lacking in both respects.

Beyond that, defendant's claim to good title must founder on considerations of his own status. If he acquired the property from one who had a voidable title, he must show that he was a "good faith purchaser for value." UCC § 2–403(1). That term is defined in UCC §§ 1–201 and 2–103(1)(b). The requirement of good faith for a merchant like defendant is simply "honesty in fact and the observance of reasonable commercial standards of fair dealing." UCC § 2–103(1)(b). If he acquired the property from a merchant who was entrusted with possession, he must demonstrate that he was a "buyer in ordinary course of business." UCC § 2–403(2). This term is likewise defined in § 1–201, subd. 9, and in requiring the purchase from one in the business of selling goods of that kind, is more restrictive than the term "good faith purchaser for value." See Commentary to UCC § 2–403, McKinney's Consol.Laws of N.Y. Annotated, Book 62½, Part 1, p. 397.

The facts of this case indicate that defendant does not fit in either category. He was not registered or licensed to buy or sell used cars in New York City, but could legally deal only in "junk." He paid Schwartzman $300 in cash for a car he was able to resell immediately for $1200. He was shown no bill of sale or owner's registration, and he resold the car without transferring any owner's registration. Simple prudence would have put anyone in an honest transaction on guard. Certainly the standards of honesty in fact and reasonable commercial standards of fair dealing have not been met. He took the risks involved, and was out of pocket $300 for a two year old station wagon. His claim that he is still holding the "balance" for the vanished Schwartzman against the day of eventual return is far from convincing. It was he who had prior dealings with Schwartzman. Certainly if he was not working with him, he had every reason to be skeptical of Schwartzman's claim of ownership. The Uniform Commercial Code protects the innocent purchaser, but it is not a shield for the sly conniver, the blindly naive, or the hopelessly gullible.

Plaintiff is therefore entitled to judgment in the amount of $1200, with interest from the 30th day of August, 1965.

QUESTIONS AND NOTES

1.   The court suggests that, for an entruster to lose title under 2–403(2), both the entruster and the buyer must know that the seller is a merchant. What language in 2–403 supports this construction? If the statutory language is not clear, what factors are relevant in deciding the issue? Suppose the entruster knows that he is giving the possession to a merchant but the buyer does not know that she is buying from a merchant. What result? If the entruster doesn't know of merchant status, but the buyer does, what result?

2.   If Schwartzman had sold the automobile to Christa Harrow, a consumer who purchased in good faith, would Harrow have won as against plaintiff? Did Schwartzman have "voidable title"?

3.   Subsection (1) provides that a person with voidable title has power to transfer good title to a good faith purchaser for value. Subsection (2) provides that a merchant who deals in goods of the kind has the power to transfer good title to a buyer in the ordinary course of business. What are the policy justifications for protecting a broader range of purchasers under subsection (1) (voidable title cases) than under subsection (2) (entrusting-to-merchant cases)?

4. Suppose a buyer contracts to buy goods without knowledge of the true owner's interest, but learns of that interest before paying any part of the price: is the buyer a good faith purchaser for value under 2–403(1)?

See 1–201(9), (44) [revised 1–201(a)(9), 1–204]. Compare 9–320(a), 9–317(b), and 3–303.

5. At the time of the events described in *Atlas*, New York did not have a certificate-of-title law. In a state with a certificate-of-title law, can a person in possession of the motor vehicle but not in possession of the certificate of title transfer good title under either 2–403(1) or (2)? In Mattek v. Malofsky, 42 Wis.2d 16, 165 N.W.2d 406 (1969), the court held that a dealer who purchased without seeing the certificate of title could not be in good faith. The court stated that the dealer, being chargeable with notice that a certificate of title was outstanding and that the seller was required by law to give him the certificate, was unreasonable, as a matter of law, in not procuring the certificate. In Medico Leasing Co. v. Smith, 457 P.2d 548 (Okl.1969), however, a dealer who purchased from another dealer without securing the certificate of title was held to be a buyer in ordinary course under 2–403(2) because the purchaser had been told that the original certificate of title had been lost. (That the purchaser was able to procure another title certificate, in its own name, does not encourage confidence in certificate-of-title procedures.)

The courts of some states have held that, under their certificate-of-title laws, title does not pass until the certificate of title is delivered to the purchaser. See Gicinto v. Credithrift of America, No. 3, Inc., 219 Kan. 766, 549 P.2d 870 (1976).

6. Problem. Murphy leased a road grader from Ross Implements, Inc. for a period of six months at a rental of $500 per month. Four months into the lease Murphy sold the grader to Jacobi, who paid value and took in good faith. Does Jacobi take free of Ross Implements' rights? Was Murphy a purchaser? Could he transfer greater rights than Ross intended to give to him? See 2A–305(1)-(2).

7. Problem. Owner delivered two front-end loaders to Trico, a dealer in front-end loaders, for repair. Without authority, an employee of Trico transferred the two machines to a corporation she had set up, and that corporation sold the machines to Bayer, a buyer in ordinary course. Does Bayer take free of Owner's interest?

8. Problem. Owner, not a dealer in front-end loaders, sold a front-end loader to Pecci, who paid in full for the loader and was to pick it up in two days. Owner then sold the loader to Kang, who paid in full and took possession. Owner is insolvent. As between Pecci and Kang, who is entitled to the loader? See 2–401(2)-(3).

C. Situations in Which the Buyer Gets Worse Title Than the Seller Had

1. Fraudulent Conveyances

No debtor should be free to conceal or dispose of his property with a view to preventing his creditors from satisfying their legal claims. He must be just to his creditors before he can rightfully be generous with his property for the benefit of others. These basic principles are, in Anglo-American law, associated with the Statute of 13 Elizabeth, c. 5, which declared conveyances with intent to delay, hinder or defraud creditors utterly void, frustrate and of no effect against the persons so hindered, delayed or defrauded.

J.MacLachlan, Bankruptcy 253 (1956).

The clearest example of a fraudulent conveyance is a gift of assets to a family member for the purpose of putting the assets beyond the reach of the donor's creditors. The law of fraudulent conveyances, however, extends far beyond this archetype. The original Statute of 13 Elizabeth invalidated conveyances made with the actual intent to hinder creditors, and over time the courts identified indicia of that intent. Known as "badges of fraud," these indicia created a presumption of fraudulent conveyance when one of them was present. Something of these badges of fraud remain, and the current law of fraudulent conveyances is found in the Uniform Fraudulent Transfer Act (or its predecessor the Uniform Fraudulent Conveyances Act), the Bankruptcy Code, the UCC, and the common law.

Fraudulent conveyance law employs an extraordinary notion—that a transfer of title, valid between the parties, is invalid as to creditors of the transferor. Since creditors protected by the rule do not have to be secured, a fraudulent conveyance of unencumbered goods may be set aside. This means, in effect, that the transferee gets less than a complete interest in fraudulently conveyed goods, even if the transferor had a perfect, unencumbered title. The law is designed to protect creditors, within limits, by enabling them to rely on the property of their debtors. The protection is given at the expense, at least initially, of the transferee.

While a debtor should not be able to frustrate his creditors by fraudulently conveying goods, the interest of the innocent transferee must be considered. Normally, therefore, fraudulent conveyance law is limited by the principle that a transfer will not be upset unless some guilt or fault can be assigned to the transferee.

a. SELLER'S RETENTION OF POSSESSION AFTER THE SALE

Three main classes of cases constitute the great bulk of fraudulent conveyances. The first is "fraudulent retention," in which the seller continues in possession of goods after selling them. Creditors of the seller may be misled by the seller's ostensible ownership. The buyer's failure to take possession causes the ambiguous situation, but the buyer's "guilt" is not necessarily sufficient to justify the ability of a creditor to disregard the conveyance and seize the property conveyed. After all, the buyer may have a good reason for not taking possession. Should that matter?

Lefever v. Mires

Illinois Supreme Court, 1876.
81 Ill. 456.

■ MR. JUSTICE SCHOLFIELD. The contest here is between appellant, as purchaser, and appellee, as judgment creditor, in regard to which has the prior right to certain hay and corn, and a cow.

The property originally belonged to one Brewer, against whom appellee's judgment was obtained, who was tenant of a farm of appellant for the year 1874.

Appellant claims that Brewer sold the property to him on the 21st of October, 1874, which was before the levy of appellee's execution. The corn and hay were raised on the farm of appellant, of which Brewer was tenant, and the hay was in stack and the corn cut up and in shocks on the land where grown, at the time of the alleged sale, and the cow was also then on the same farm.

The evidence fails to show other than a contract of sale. The property remained where it was before the sale—Brewer still being in possession of the farm—until the levy of the execution; and there is no proof of even a symbolical delivery to appellant.

It is argued that the court erred in instructing the jury that, to make the sale valid as against appellee, it was essential the proof should show that there was an actual delivery of possession to the appellant.

The rule undoubtedly is, as contended by appellant, where the goods are ponderous or bulky, or can not be conveniently delivered manually, there may be a symbolical delivery; but we are unable to see why there could not have been an actual delivery of, at least, the cow, here, even if it shall be conceded the shocks of corn and hay were too ponderous for manual delivery. But what act tending to show symbolical delivery can be claimed to have been proven? We have been unable to find evidence of any. It does not appear that the property was present when the contract for sale was made, or that anything else was done between the parties than merely to make the agreement to sell. The property remained in the possession, and, so far as the entire world could see, was still owned by Brewer, after as well as before the sale. This, as against creditors, in our opinion, was insufficient to pass the title.

. . .

The judgment is affirmed.

QUESTIONS

1. The rationale for viewing a seller's retention of possession as fraud against the seller's creditors is that the seller's apparent ownership of the goods may mislead the creditors. How was the creditor misled in *Lefever*?

2. The court suggests that if Brewer had handed the purchaser a handful of hay, a stalk of corn, and the bell that hung around the neck of the cow, the result would be different. Presumably, of course, the creditor's perception of Brewer's continued ownership would not have been any different than it was in the case. Why would a different result be justified?

————

Blumenstein v. Phillips Insurance Center, Inc.

Alaska Supreme Court, 1971.
490 P.2d 1213.

■ Connor, Justice. . . .

The background of this case is connected with a recurrence of gold fever which for a short time struck the community of Nome, Alaska. In the mid–1960's a venture was launched to recover gold from submerged deposits in the ocean offshore from the town. Lucrative dreams of a bygone era were revived briefly by the prospect of recovering this wealth through new dredging technology. But in 1967 the vision faded into the chill reality of economic failure. On the beach at Nome a converted landing craft, the Mermaid I, stands vigil as a tangible but lonely witness to the vanished hopes of a modern day gold stampede. However, it is only with the fate of the Mermaid I as a means of satisfying indebtedness that this appeal is concerned.

On May 14, 1966, appellant, Bernard Blumenstein, conveyed the landing craft Mermaid I to Martin Dredging, Inc. The transaction entered into between Blumenstein and Martin Dredging was labeled a "Conditional Sale Agreement." Although it was apparently intended to leave Blumenstein with a security interest in the Mermaid I, the agreement was never recorded.

The conditional sale agreement called for an initial down payment by Martin Dredging to Blumenstein of 4,000 shares of its stock. At that time the stock was selling for about a dollar a share. A balance of $11,000 was to be paid in installments. Two installments of $1,250 each were due in the summer of 1966. Further payment was then to be deferred until July 15 of the following year, at which time installments were to resume at a monthly rate of $2,500 until the balance had been paid. The terms of the sale also provided for alteration of the boat by Martin Dredging to suit its purposes. Martin Dredging was at the time embarking on the project to mine underwater gold deposits in the offshore area near Nome, and wanted the Mermaid I for test dredging to prove the theory that gold could profitably be retrieved from the underwater deposits. The vessel was converted as planned and was used during the summer of 1966 for mining operations, which initially proved to be successful. With the onset of winter, the Mermaid I was beached near Nome; the boat has not been used since that time, and it remains, to this date, at the location where it was left in the fall of 1966.

In the spring of 1967 Martin Dredging drastically increased the scope of its undertaking by purchasing and outfitting a surplus minesweeper, subsequently named the Mermaid II. Appellee [Phillips Insurance Center, Inc.] was called upon to provide insurance for the Mermaid II. After summoning an underwriter to examine Martin Dredging's operation, Phillips contracted to provide insurance to the company.

The operation of the Mermaid II during the summer months of 1967 proved to be the undoing of Martin Dredging. Through a combination of unfortunate circumstances, the mining operation met with little success, while Martin Dredging incurred inordinately heavy expenses. By late summer it was generally known that the Mermaid II had proved to be a colossal failure. By that time Martin Dredging had been rendered insolvent, with no substantial assets besides the Mermaids I and II, and no funds with which it could pay outstanding obligations.

The financial collapse of Martin Dredging and the failure of the Mermaid II precipitated the events which culminated in this appeal. On July 15, 1967, the day upon which Martin Dredging was to resume monthly installments for the Mermaid I, Blumenstein failed to receive payment; he contacted the company and was assured that the money would be forthcoming within 30 days. However, by August 15, the date set for the second monthly payment of 1967, it became apparent that he would receive neither the delinquent July payment nor the August payment.

Blumenstein made several formal requests for payment at this time and contacted individual members of Martin Dredging's board of directors persistently. Finally, through the efforts of his attorney, Blumenstein persuaded the members of the board to call a special meeting concerning payment of the amounts due on the Mermaid I. In the course of this meeting, which was held on September 7, 1967, Blumenstein apparently proposed that Martin Dredging quitclaim its interest in the Mermaid I to him, in return for which Blumenstein would relinquish any claim for payment which he might have against the company. The members of the board ultimately acquiesced to this arrangement, and the Mermaid I was thus quit-claimed back to Blumenstein.

Testimony adduced below shows that shortly after this reconveyance of the Mermaid I, Blumenstein boarded the vessel and removed several items. A few days later he returned with a workman and spent several hours removing some more equipment and preparing the boat for the onset of winter. Some welding equipment which belonged to the boat was also retrieved from the Martin Dredging shop. Blumenstein took no further measures in reasserting his possession of the Mermaid I.

During this same period of time, Phillips ran into trouble collecting premiums on the insurance which it had procured for the operations of the Mermaid II. On August 19, 1967, Phillips sent Martin Dredging a notice of cancellation, giving the Mermaid II 30 days to repair to a safe port. Nome was not considered a safe port, and at some time around the end of August the Mermaid II was taken to Seward, where she was later sold to satisfy a judgment for unpaid seamen's wages. In the first week of September 1967 Phillips filed suit against Martin Dredging to recover $7,931.25 in unpaid premiums. On September 15, about a week after Martin Dredging had quitclaimed the Mermaid I to Blumenstein, Phillips attached the boat.

At first Blumenstein did nothing about the attachment papers affixed to the Mermaid I. Not until it became evident that Phillips might actually sell the boat did he act. Accordingly, on September 3, 1968, almost a full year after issuance of the quitclaim deed by Martin Dredging, Blumenstein first filed a complaint in intervention against Phillips, alleging that the Mermaid I was his by virtue of the quitclaim deed. Phillips answered, denying the validity of the quitclaim transaction and affirmatively asserting that the conveyance to Blumenstein amounted to an attempt to defraud creditors.

On December 22, 1969, Blumenstein's claim came on for trial in the superior court at Anchorage, and on January 15, 1970, the court entered findings of fact and conclusions of law in favor of Phillips. Specifically, the court found that Blumenstein either knew or should have known of Martin Dredging's insolvency at the time he procured the quitclaim deed, "and that the transfer amounted to a preference of the creditor Blumenstein over the Plaintiff creditor of Martin Dredging Incorporated." The court further held that Blumenstein's conduct was not sufficient to reassert possession of the Mermaid I in a manner which would give public notice of his interest in the boat, and that the quitclaim transaction consequently fell within the presumption of fraud created by AS 09.25.060.[2] It was the court's conclusion that Blumenstein had failed to overcome the statutory presumption.

On appeal, Blumenstein asserts that the trial court erred in deciding that he had failed to properly retake possession of the Mermaid I. It is thus argued that the statutory presumption of fraud should not have been held applicable in the circumstances of this case, and that the quitclaim deed from Martin Dredging to Blumenstein constituted a valid conveyance of the vessel. Phillips rebuts Blumenstein's arguments on appeal, maintaining that the trial court correctly invalidated as fraudulent the conveyance in question. Phillips points out that the essential concern in determining whether possession over an object has been established should be whether the conduct of the party claiming possession would have sufficiently given

---

2. AS 09.25.060 provides in relevant part:

"Every sale or assignment of personal property unless accompanied by the immediate delivery and the actual and con-

tinued change of possession of the thing sold or assigned is presumed prima facie to be a fraud against the creditors of the vendor or assignor * * *."

notice to the general public of the party's interest in the property possessed. It is urged that Blumenstein's actions in the present case were insufficient under this criterion. Phillips additionally points to various badges of fraud in the transaction between Blumenstein and Martin Dredging, which, it is claimed, support the conclusion that this conveyance was made with intent to defraud creditors.

Although the primary focus of the controversy on appeal has been upon the adequacy of the possession which Blumenstein established over the Mermaid I, we have concluded that the trial court's decision would require reversal regardless of the proper disposition of this issue. Thus, in our consideration of this matter, we may assume that the trial court was correct in finding that Blumenstein's conduct was insufficient as a retaking of possession of the Mermaid I. We will further assume that the trial court properly held that Blumenstein was aware of Martin Dredging's impending insolvency.

Given these assumptions, it is apparent that Blumenstein, under the conditional sale agreement, did not perfect a security interest in the Mermaid I which would give him priority over Phillips' attachment lien.

. . .

Though Blumenstein could not prevail on the basis of his intended security interest, he also has a claim as a grantee for valuable consideration. We turn next to the question whether the quitclaim deed delivered to Blumenstein by Martin Dredging should properly have been invalidated under Alaska's law governing fraudulent conveyances.[6] AS 34.40.010 provides that a conveyance of goods made with intent to hinder, delay or defraud creditors is invalid. This statute provides Alaska's basic prohibition against transactions in fraud of creditors. AS 34.40.090 complements the basic prohibition by providing that the existence of fraudulent intent is a question of fact. Thus, under normal circumstances, fraud will not be presumed.

However, AS 09.25.060 qualifies the provisions of AS 34.40.010 and AS 34.40.090, by erecting a prima facie presumption of fraud in cases where a sale of personal property is not "accompanied by the immediate delivery and the actual and continued change of possession" by the vendee. Since we have accepted as valid the finding that Blumenstein did not sufficiently retake possession of the Mermaid I after receiving the quitclaim deed from Martin Dredging, the conclusion seems inescapable that the statutory presumption of fraud created by AS 09.25.060 was correctly held to apply to the circumstances of the present case by the trial court. Yet by no means does it follow that the result reached by the lower court was correct.

---

6. Given our conclusion that no security interest in the Mermaid I was perfected by Blumenstein, and assuming that Blumenstein did not adequately retake possession of the Mermaid I following reconveyance to him by Martin Dredging, it is evident that the provisions of the Uniform Commercial Code do not govern this transaction. Except in cases involving retention by a merchant seller in the course of trade, the code specifically leaves the validity of sales where the seller retains possession of goods sold to determination under existing state laws. See AS 45.05.128(b). [2–402(2).—Ed.]

We must emphasize initially that AS 09.25.060 establishes only a prima facie presumption. This presumption is rebuttable. It serves merely to shift to the vendee the burden of proving that a conveyance was made without fraudulent intent. Under AS 09.25.060, if a vendee has failed to establish immediate and continued possession over personalty which he has purchased, and if he makes no effort to show that the transaction was entered into in good faith, then a finding of fraud will be compelled. Where, on the other hand, the grantee introduces evidence tending to show that the conveyance in question was transacted in good faith, then the presumption will be dispelled, and it will be incumbent upon the finder of fact to determine whether there was actually an intent to defraud creditors.

In ruling upon the circumstances of the present case, the trial court stopped short of reaching the issue of actual intent to defraud. Instead, its decision was confined to the finding that Blumenstein had failed to overcome the presumption erected by AS 09.25.060. In our view, the court's exclusive reliance on the AS 09.25.060 presumption was unwarranted. Ample and convincing evidence was introduced by Blumenstein to show that the conveyance of the Mermaid I by Martin Dredging was undertaken in good faith.

It is significant that Blumenstein furnished a plausible, and, indeed, entirely believable explanation for his failure to take more positive steps in establishing possession of the Mermaid I after receiving the quitclaim deed from Martin Dredging. At the time of the conveyance, the Mermaid I had been beached for approximately one year. The boat was beached at the same location where it had usually been kept by Blumenstein prior to its conveyance to Martin Dredging. With winter impending, refloating of the boat would have been difficult and impracticable. It should further be noted that many indicia of ownership—such as the ship's Coast Guard number and its radio license—which might normally be expected to change with transfer of a boat, had remained unaltered since Blumenstein's original possession. Moreover, it must be considered that, while Blumenstein might not have actively and openly asserted his repossession of the boat, neither can it be said that the Mermaid I was, in any practical sense, retained by Martin Dredging. All of these factors, taken together, tend to explain Blumenstein's failure to retake possession of the Mermaid I, and thereby substantially weaken any inference of fraud which might be drawn.[7]

Even more significant than the facts surrounding Blumenstein's failure to take possession of the Mermaid I is the showing that the quitclaim deed to the Mermaid I was given in consideration for the discharge of a

---

7. It is relevant to note that even in jurisdictions where legislation provides that failure of a vendee to take possession of purchased goods must conclusively be presumed to be fraudulent, the nature of the purchased goods and the circumstances surrounding the failure to take immediate possession may warrant exceptions to the rule. For example, in California it has been held that "[w]here a movable is bulky and not readily transferable by manual delivery the rule of that section [section conclusively presuming fraud] is relaxed by reason of the impracticability of actual delivery by ordinary means and methods." Shepherd v. Gamble, 95 Cal.App.2d 890, 214 P.2d 403, 405 (1950).

valid debt owed by Martin Dredging to Blumenstein.[8] The validity of Martin Dredging's obligation to Blumenstein under the terms of the original conditional sale agreement is not contested, and, in fact, seems to be assumed in the findings of the trial court. Similarly uncontested is the fact that Blumenstein discharged the debt owed to him by Martin Dredging in return for the quitclaim deed to the Mermaid I. It has previously been held that such a showing tends strongly, if not conclusively, to overcome the type of presumption created by AS 09.25.060. For example, in Scruggs v. Blackshear Manufacturing Company, 45 Ga.App. 855, 166 S.E. 249, 251 (1932), under circumstances not unlike those of the present case, the court reversed a finding of fraud by the lower court, holding that while retention of possession by a vendor gives rise to a prima facie presumption of fraud, "[p]roof of payment of valuable consideration for the property rebuts the presumption * * *."[9]

Because Blumenstein offered a satisfactory explanation for his failure to take more overt steps in attempting to reestablish possession of the Mermaid I, and because he further showed that the quitclaim deed delivered by Martin Dredging was issued in exchange for valuable consideration, we think that the trial court was unjustified in relying on the statutory presumption to invalidate as fraudulent the conveyance in question. Under these circumstances, the trial court should have considered the validity of the transaction as a question of fact pursuant to AS 34.40.010 and AS

---

8. Phillips has argued that the consideration paid by Blumenstein for the quitclaim of the boat was inadequate. At the time of the conveyance, a balance of approximately $8,500 remained to be paid on the original conditional sale agreement; Phillips contends that this amount was insufficient consideration for a vessel which had originally been sold for $15,000, and subsequently re-equipped with costly machinery. However, it must be remembered that Martin Dredging, at the time of the quitclaim transaction, was insolvent and had no funds available to meet its current obligations. The company was already two installments in arrears, and apparently Blumenstein was making persistent demands for payment. Moreover, under the terms of the conditional sale agreement, if Martin Dredging had insisted on removing, prior to returning the boat to Blumenstein, the equipment which it had installed, then it would have been obligated to restore the vessel to the condition in which it had been at the time of the purchase in 1966.

The adequacy of consideration in any given instance cannot be viewed apart from the particular circumstances in which the parties find themselves. Any sale conducted under the pressure of economic necessity is bound to produce less than an optimal consideration; however, this fact will not affect the adequacy of consideration. Thus, for the purpose of determining whether fraud is indicated in a transaction, adequacy of consideration is usually judged by broad standards. As the court held in White v. Nollmeyer, 151 Mont. 387, 443 P.2d 873, 883 (1968), in order to determine whether a fair consideration had been paid,

"the test to be applied is whether the disparity between the true value * * * and the price paid is so great as to shock the conscience and strike the understanding at once with the conviction that such transfer never could have been made in good faith."

Applying this standard, we are unable to conclude in the present situation that the consideration paid by Blumenstein for the return of the Mermaid I was inadequate.

9. See also Andrews v. Lorraine Dance Studios, Inc., 189 A.2d 802, 804–805 (R.I. 1963), where the court states that "a showing that there was adequate consideration for the sale of property retained by a vendor tends to rebut the presumption of fraud that arises from its retention."

34.40.090. Accordingly, the court should have ruled on the issue whether, in the conveyance of the Mermaid I to Blumenstein, there was an actual, as opposed to a presumed intent to hinder, delay or defraud creditors.

Under normal circumstances a remand to the superior court might be appropriate in order to allow the lower court the opportunity to rule upon the question of actual fraudulent intent. However, in the present case we feel that the necessity for a remand is obviated, since, in our view, the findings of fact rendered below preclude a conclusion of fraud.

In its fourth finding of fact, the trial court ruled that Blumenstein

"reasonably knew or should have known the corporation [Martin Dredging] was insolvent and that the transfer amounted to a preference of the creditor Blumenstein over the Plaintiff creditor of Martin Dredging Incorporated."

Both the tenor of the court's language and the context within which it is placed leave an indelible impression that the court believed that a preferential payment to one of several creditors by an insolvent debtor is in itself an unlawful or fraudulent act. Indeed, this appears to be a notion shared by the parties on appeal.

Yet the rule is settled that in the absence of bankruptcy laws or express statutory prohibition, an insolvent debtor may convey property to one creditor, even if it means that the debtor's assets will thereby be depleted, and that the claims of other creditors will be defeated. . . .

As Corbin states in his treatise on contracts:

"At common law it was not illegal for a debtor to pay one of his creditors in full even though he did not have enough left to pay his other creditors in full or even in part. Such a payment was not, and is not now, a fraudulent conveyance. The payment is merely the performance of an existing legal duty. Nor is it illegal for the debtor to transfer property as security for an existing debt; the value of the property in excess of the debt remains available to other creditors. The conveyance of property to a creditor in satisfaction of an existing debt is a fraudulent conveyance only in case its value is in excess of the debt and the purpose of the debtor is to keep that excess out of the hands of his other creditors."[10]

The rational underpinning of the rule which allows preferential transfers is not difficult to perceive, and has been aptly stated by the court in Irving Trust Company v. Kaminsky, 19 F.Supp. 816, 818 (S.D.N.Y.1937):

"[T]he rule against fraudulent conveyances may be availed of by a single creditor. To allow such a creditor, acting in his own interest alone, to set aside a preferential transfer as one in fraud of creditors

---

10. 6A A.Corbin, Contracts § 1467, at 566 (1962) (Footnote omitted). 1 G.Glenn, Fraudulent Conveyances and Preferences §§ 289 & 289a (rev.ed.1940), is in accord with Corbin:

"If there is in our law one point which is more ungrudgingly accepted than others, it is that the preferential transfer does not constitute a fraudulent conveyance." Id. § 289, at 488.

would amount to substituting that creditor as the person preferred in place of the creditor chosen by the debtor."

Thus, numerous courts hold that a bona fide preference of one creditor over others will be upheld even where the debtor is or will be rendered insolvent, or where other creditors are threatening suit, or where the preferred creditor is aware of the debtor's insolvency. Some courts have held that even if the debtor's intent is fraudulent, and even if the preferred creditor is aware of that intent, a preferential transaction will not be set aside so long as the preferred creditor, by accepting the conveyance from the debtor, is only protecting his own interests as a creditor. Accordingly, it is the rule that a bona fide preference by an insolvent debtor does not, in itself, constitute evidence of fraud.

. . . Here, both Blumenstein and Phillips were found to be creditors of Martin Dredging at the time of the challenged conveyance. In quitclaiming the Mermaid I to Blumenstein, Martin Dredging chose to prefer his claim over that of Phillips. To invalidate this transfer now would accomplish nothing more than the substitution of Phillips for Blumenstein as the preferred creditor of Martin Dredging. This we refuse to do.

. . .

The judgment of the superior court is reversed and this matter is remanded for entry of judgment in favor of the appellant.

QUESTIONS AND NOTES

1. If a debtor sells one of its assets for the fair value of that asset, the asset is replaced by the price the debtor receives. Creditors of the debtor thus have no complaint. This is not necessarily true if the debtor transfers an asset in exchange for cancellation of debt. Though the debtor's balance sheet shows the same degree of (in)solvency, there are fewer assets for the creditors to reach. Nevertheless, as *Blumenstein* reveals, transfer of goods for extinguishment of an equivalent amount of debt is not a fraudulent conveyance. Whether Martin Dredging received fair value for the vessel is, of course, another matter altogether.

2. Presumption of fraud: conclusive or rebuttable. Article 2 preserves the various statutory and decisional rules on whether a seller's retention of sold goods is fraudulent as against the seller's creditors, but it limits those rules by stating that "retention of possession in good faith and current course of trade by a merchant-seller for a commercially reasonable time after a sale or identification is not fraudulent" (2–402).

As *Lefever* indicates, in some states retention of possession by the seller after sale is "conclusive fraud." That is just another way of saying that seller's creditors can reach the goods if they are not delivered to the buyer with some promptness. *Blumenstein* illustrates that in other states, retention of goods after sale creates a presumption of fraud, but this presumption may be rebutted by showing that the transaction was bona fide.

There are several somewhat different underlying reasons for the retention-of-possession rules. Most important, perhaps, is the fact that a debtor in financial difficulty may try to put his goods beyond the reach of creditors by entering into a sham sale, and a claimed sale without change of possession is some indication that the transfer is a sham. That is, the purported sale may actually be a fraudulent transfer, one intended to "delay, hinder, or defraud creditors."

Second, creditors may rely on the fact that the debtor apparently owns goods in making the decision to extend credit. It is clear that the likelihood of creditor reliance on appearances was a substantial factor in the early common-law development. See Twyne's Case, 3 Co.Rep. 806, 76 Eng.Rep. 809 (1601). (Today, however, unsecured creditors ordinarily rely not on a debtor's apparent ownership of particular tangible goods, but rather on the debtor's anticipated future income stream, which is estimated from financial reports and other sources.)

Third, creditors who have a judgment against the debtor will rely on debtor's apparent ownership of particular goods by levying on them and foregoing a search for, or levy on, other goods.

These different justifications for the fraudulent-retention-of-possession rules suggest the reasons for the fact that some states treat retention as conclusively fraudulent while others treat it as only presumptively fraudulent. They also explain the rather curious fact that, in a number of states, once the buyer has taken possession of the goods, the goods no longer can be reached by seller's levying creditors, no matter how long possession was left with seller after sale. If retention is prima facie evidence of actual fraud, and is not rebutted, then, as in any actual fraud case, the levying creditor should be able to reach the goods even after their ultimate delivery to the buyer. Similarly, the same result should obtain if the rationale for the fraudulent-retention rules is that creditors will extend credit relying on the seller's ownership of the goods in question. If the rule is based upon the levying creditor's change of position in levying on particular goods, however, the rule that once the goods are delivered to the buyer they are no longer subject to claims of seller's creditors, makes perfectly good sense. As you might surmise, in states in which retention is said to be conclusively fraudulent, there is a strong chance that, once the goods are delivered to the buyer, the seller's creditors can no longer reach them. (Even if such a state bases its rule also on the creditor's reliance in extending credit, the courts may suggest that, since the levying creditor would have lost to another creditor who levied first, it is appropriate to conclude that the levying creditor also loses to a buyer who took possession before the levy.) On the other hand, in a state where retention is only presumptively fraudulent and the presumption is not rebutted, the levying creditor is likely to be able to reach the goods in the buyer's hands.

See generally, G.Glenn, Fraudulent Conveyances §§ 344–363 (1940); S.Williston, Sales ch. 15 (Rev.Ed.1948) (state-by-state summary of the applicable rules). And see P.Alces, The Law of Fraudulent Transactions § 308 (1989).

3. Problem. On January 3rd Bill Lawton purchased a new sound system from Hi–Tech Electronics for $1,000 during a special sale. Since he was going to be moving into a new apartment on March 15th, he asked Hi–Tech if he might leave the unit in the store until then. Hi–Tech agreed.

a. If Hi–Tech sells the system to Tami Konuk, who buys without knowledge of Lawton's interest, does she take free of his interest?

b. Does Lawton take free of a security interest in the system created by Hi–Tech (i) on January 2nd; (ii) on January 4th? See 9–320(a).

c. On January 4th a creditor with a judgment against Hi–Tech Electronics levies on the sound system. Is the creditor's interest superior to Lawton's interest? Or does the stereo belong to Lawton, so that it cannot be reached by Hi–Tech's creditors?

———

b. SALES MADE WITH ACTUAL INTENT TO DEFRAUD CREDITORS

There are two main types of fraudulent transfers other than those involving seller's retention of possession. One is a transfer that is in fact fraudulent—transfers made with actual intent to hinder, delay, or defraud creditors. The other is a transfer at less than fair value which leaves the transferor insolvent or with insufficient assets to reasonably continue a business. Fraudulent transfers of these two types are dealt with in the Uniform Fraudulent Conveyance Act, drafted in 1918 and adopted by 25 jurisdictions, and the Uniform Fraudulent Transfer Act (UFTA), drafted in 1984 to replace the earlier Act. The UFTA has been adopted in more than 40 states (and the District of Columbia).

The transferor's actual intent to hinder, delay, or defraud creditors is not necessarily enough to defeat a transfer made to implement that intent. The transfer cannot be set aside as against a transferee who took in good faith and for reasonably equivalent value.[1] The Act does not define "good faith" and it is, therefore, unclear exactly what the term means. Section 548 of the Bankruptcy Code also permits the avoidance of fraudulent conveyances. It, too, insulates a transfer—even if made with actual intent to hinder creditors—to the extent that the transferee took in good faith and for value.[2] Like the UFTA, the Bankruptcy Code does not contain a definition of "good faith," and courts in the bankruptcy context have resisted a single definition, saying that the content of the requirement depends on the circumstances of the particular case.[3] If the transferee was in good faith but gave less than equivalent value, the transfer can be set

---

1. U.F.T.A. § 8(a).

2. 11 U.S.C.A. § 548(c).

3. E.g., In re Hannover Corp., 310 F.3d 796 (5th Cir.2002); In re Financial Federated Title & Trust, 309 F.3d 1325 (11th Cir.2002).

aside, but the transferee is entitled to the return of the value actually given.[4]

The actual-intent rules are relatively unimportant for sales law purposes, because transfers made in exchange for consideration are usually purchases in good faith. Occasionally, it is possible to prove that the buyer dealt with the seller for the express purpose of hindering, delaying or defrauding the latter's creditors. In these cases, there is a fraudulent conveyance even though the transferee has paid fair consideration. Many of these cases involve family transactions, such as sales to a spouse.[5]

c. SALES FOR LESS THAN FAIR VALUE BY SELLERS WHO ARE INSOLVENT OR WHO ARE LEFT WITH INSUFFICIENT CAPITAL

The third type of fraudulent transfer—transfers made for less than fair consideration by a transferor who is either insolvent, thereby rendered insolvent, or left with unreasonably small assets for the business in which the transferor is engaged—does have importance for sales law. The applicable rules are in sections 4 and 5 of UFTA. If the transfer is for less than "reasonably equivalent value," the transfer is assailable irrespective of the good faith of the transferee, although, a good faith transferee is entitled to a return of the consideration paid. Since the statutory test is fair or reasonably equivalent value, it would seem to follow that a buyer who innocently gets a very good bargain from an insolvent seller runs the risk of participating in a fraudulent conveyance. This has not necessarily been the case. In the application of the "fair equivalence" rule of the 1918 Act in the seller-buyer situation, the courts usually have not resolved the matter solely by determining the value of the thing sold and comparing it to the price paid. Rather they have taken into account all the surrounding circumstances attending the sale, and declare the conveyance fraudulent only when the consideration paid by the buyer is so short of the real value of the property conveyed "as to startle a correct mind."[6] The same rule may be applied under the UFTA, but a Seventh Circuit case has rejected that test, holding instead that under the "fair equivalent value" test in section 8(a) of the Act, if the net effect of the transfer is to diminish the transferor's estate, any difference in value between the property transferred and the price paid for it could be recovered by the creditors of the transferor.[7]

If a conveyance is found to be fraudulent, protected creditors may set it aside to the extent necessary to satisfy their claims, or disregard it and attach and levy execution on the property conveyed. See section 7, which makes it clear that a fraudulent conveyance is not "utterly void, frustrate

---

4. Bankruptcy Code § 548(c), 11 U.S.C.A. § 548(c); UFTA § 8(a), (d).

5. E.g., Winter v. Welker, 174 F.Supp. 836 (E.D.Pa.1959); see also, Farrell v. Paulus, 309 Mich. 441, 15 N.W.2d 700 (1944).

6. Neal v. Clark, 75 Ariz. 91, 251 P.2d 903 (1952).

7. Scholes v. Lehmann, 56 F.3d 750 (7th Cir.1995). The case involved a Ponzi scheme, and the excess value received by the transferee was clear. It is unclear whether the court would have imposed such a burden on a good faith buyer in a different context.

and of no effect," to quote the Statute of 13 Elizabeth c. 5, but is merely voidable. It follows from this that a bona fide purchaser from a fraudulent grantee is protected against the rights of the creditors of the fraudulent transferor.[8]

2.   BULK SALES

The rules regarding fraudulent conveyances protect creditors of a seller by allowing them to subject the transferred goods to their claims if the transferee has participated in a scheme to hinder or defraud them, has taken with notice of such a scheme, or has taken as a donee or for less than fair consideration. These fraudulent-conveyance rules do not protect creditors of transferors who, at one stroke, sell their entire assets for fair value to a person who has no intention of defrauding anyone. Yet such bulk sales enable fraudulent debtors to convert their inventories into cash and to disappear with the proceeds before their creditors learn of the transaction.

Around 1890 it became common in America for unethical debtors to defeat their creditors in this way. In response, the National Association of Credit Men drafted the first bulk-sales statute, and by 1950 all states had some form of bulk-transfer legislation. There were marked differences in the laws of the various states, however, and creditors involved in interstate transactions sometimes were injured by their ignorance of the scope and operation of the bulk-sales laws in other states.

When the UCC was being drafted in the 1940s and 1950s, the drafters decided to include a bulk sales law as Article 6 of the Code. That law requires the buyer of a major part of a seller's inventory in certain situations to notify creditors of the seller of the impending sale. In some states the buyer also is obligated to make payment directly to certain creditors of the seller. If the buyer fails in its obligations under the bulk sales law, the transfer of goods to the buyer is ineffective as to the seller's creditors. Therefore, a buyer who has in good faith paid full value to the seller may lose the goods to a creditor (or have to pay a second time to be able to retain the goods). To avoid this, the buyer must get a list of creditors from the seller and notify those creditors of the impending sale. Compliance with this requirement can be a major burden, particularly in transactions involving the acquisition of a major business with hundreds or thousands of creditors. When it applies, the bulk sales law, in effect, makes the buyer an uncompensated policeman for the seller's creditors.

From the beginning Article 6 was controversial. Some thought it bad policy to require good faith buyers to incur the expense and delay necessary to assure that creditors of a seller were paid or had an opportunity to protect their right to be paid. Contrarily, others thought that Article 6 should be expanded and strengthened to provide even greater protection for creditors of the seller when the seller engaged in a bulk sale.

---

8.   Section 8(a) expressly protects a subsequent bona fide purchaser.

In the 1970s, therefore, the American Bar Association appointed a committee to study Article 6 and make recommendations. The members of that committee were split between those who believed that bulk-sales legislation should be repealed altogether and those who thought it should be strengthened. After due deliberation, the committee recommended revision of Article 6, largely to make it less onerous for buyers, but also to provide some additional protection to the seller's creditors.

Based on the recommendations of the ABA committee, the National Conference of Commissioners on Uniform State Laws appointed a drafting committee to redraft Article 6. The drafting committee ultimately presented alternative recommendations: the first alternative was repeal of Article 6; the second, adoption of a revised version of Article 6 (which the committee had prepared). In 1987 NCCUSL and ALI (co-sponsor of the UCC) chose the first alternative but straddled the fence: they recommended that the states repeal Article 6 but also approved a revised Article 6 as an alternative for states that might choose not to repeal it.

Most states have opted for repeal: 44 (as well as Puerto Rico and the U.S. Virgin Islands) have repealed Article 6, four jurisdictions (California, the District of Columbia, Indiana, and Virginia) have adopted revised Article 6; and three states (Georgia, Maryland, and Wisconsin) still have original Article 6.

a. TRANSACTIONS COVERED

Article 6 applies to a sale not in the ordinary course of the seller's business of "more than half in value" of a seller's inventory (6–102). It applies only to sales by sellers whose principal business is the sale of inventory from stock (6–103(1)(a)). Official Comment 2 to 6–102 of original Article 6 states that the provisions of Article 6 are aimed primarily at businesses to whom unsecured credit normally is advanced on the faith of their stock in trade:

> The businesses covered are defined in subsection (3). Notice that they do not include farming nor contracting nor professional services, nor such things as cleaning shops, barber shops, pool halls, hotels, restaurants, and the like whose principal business is the sale not of merchandise but of services. While some bulk sales risk exists in the excluded businesses, they have in common the fact that unsecured credit is not commonly extended on the faith of a stock of merchandise.

The comments to current Article 6 do not repeat this language, but the intent is unchanged in this respect. See 2–603, Official Comment 1.

b. TRANSFERS EXCEPTED

Before enactment of the UCC, transfers in the ordinary course of business were not regarded as falling within the proscription of bulk transfer statutes. Article 6 preserves this point of view by exempting from the scope of Article 6 all bulk transfers in the ordinary course of business (6–102(1)). This exemption excludes routine transfers from the operation of the statute. In addition, 6–103(3) excludes from coverage the creation of security interests, sales under judicial process or in foreclosure of security interests, and sales by a general assignee for the benefit of creditors. It also excludes (a) sales in which the transferee assumes all the debts of the seller and is not insolvent after the transfer; and (b) sales in which the buyer gets from the seller a list of all known creditors and agrees to pay those creditors. Finally, it excludes from coverage very small transactions and very large ones: sales of assets having a net value of less than $10,000 or more than $25,000,000. Official Comment 7 states that the potential loss to creditors in small transactions does not justify the costs of compliance and the publicity that usually attends large transactions obviates the creditors' need for notification from the buyer to alert them to protect their interests.

c. COMPLIANCE WITH THE ACT

(1) Compliance Procedures

The buyer must obtain from the seller a verified list of "claimants" (defined in 6–102(1)(e)), prepare a schedule of distribution of the price being paid, and give all claimants notice of the sale and the planned distribution of the price. If there are more than 200 claimants, however, instead of sending notice to individual claimants, the buyer can file a notice of the bulk sale in the office of the secretary of state. The notice must be sent (or the filing made) at least 45 days before the buyer pays more than 10% of the price or takes delivery of the goods, whichever occurs first. The requirement of a schedule of distribution does not mean that the buyer must make a distribution to creditors. The plan of distribution could merely state that the entire price will be paid to the seller. If, however, the schedule of distribution lists amounts to be paid to creditors, the buyer is liable to creditors who do not receive the amounts on that schedule (6–106(3), 6–107(1)).

(2) Effect of Failure to Comply

A failure by the buyer to comply with the provisions of Article 6 does not make the transfer ineffective. Rather, the buyer is liable for damages caused individual creditors (6–107). Those damages are measured by the amount the seller owes the creditor minus the amount that the creditor would not have realized had the buyer complied with the statute. The buyer has the burden of proving the amount that the creditor would not have realized.

Defenses to the buyer's liability include (a) the buyer's good faith and commercially reasonable belief that the sale was not subject to Article 6; and (b) the buyer's good faith and commercially reasonable effort to comply with the statute. Unless the buyer has concealed the fact of sale, any action by a creditor against a buyer must be brought within one year of the sale.

This overview of the Article 6 is an extreme oversimplification. The statute contains substantial detail and must be read carefully by a lawyer handling a bulk sales transaction.

D. Right of the Seller, As Against Creditors of the Buyer, to Recover Goods from a Buyer Who Is Insolvent

1. Rights Against Lien Creditors and the Trustee in Bankruptcy

In re Mel Golde Shoes, Inc.

United States Court of Appeals, Sixth Circuit, 1968.
403 F.2d 658.

■ O'Sullivan, Circuit Judge. We consider the appeal of Johnston & Murphy Shoes, Inc., from a judgment of the District Court for the Western District of Kentucky holding that such company's right to reclaim a shipment of shoes from an insolvent purchaser—Mel Golde Shoes, Inc.—under the Uniform Commercial Code of Kentucky, K.R.S. § 355.2–702(2), was subordinate to attachments levied thereon by creditors of such debtor-purchaser. The judgment of the District Court vacated a contrary holding by the Bankruptcy Referee.

On January 23, 1967, Johnston & Murphy Shoes, Inc., delivered a shipment of shoes to Mel Golde Shoes, Inc., at Louisville, Kentucky. The following day appellees, Meinhard Commercial Corporation and William Iselin & Company, levied attachments against the entire inventory of Golde. On February 2, Golde filed a petition in the United States District Court seeking relief under Chapter XI of the Bankruptcy Act. The petition's averment that Golde was "unable to pay its unsecured debts as they mature" disclosed Golde's insolvency within the meaning of Kentucky's Uniform Commercial Code and the Referee* so found. On February 1, 1967, the day before the Chapter XI petition was filed,** Johnston & Murphy, exercising the right given by above K.R.S. § 355.2–702(2), made timely demand for the return of the shoes. This was followed by a reclamation petition in the bankruptcy court. The Referee held that Johnston & Murphy's right of reclamation was superior to any lien rights of the attaching creditors. He was of the view, however, that the Chapter XI proceeding would be unworkable if the shoes were returned and granted appellant the status of a secured creditor in lieu of return of the shoes. The propriety of this procedure is not challenged if Johnston & Murphy's reclamation right is superior to any rights of the attaching creditors. In the District Court, the Referee's order was overruled in an Opinion and Order which concluded as follows:

---

* Now known as Bankruptcy Judge.—Ed.

** Chapter XI provided a mechanism for reorganizing and rehabilitating businesses in financial difficulty. It has been superseded by Chapter 11 of the Bankruptcy Code of 1978.—Ed.

"It is Therefore Ordered that the Referee's order dated April 7, 1967, is hereby overruled and that Johnston & Murphy Shoes, Inc., having failed to establish its statutory right to reclamation before certain other creditors became lien creditors, is to be treated as a creditor with an unperfected security interest."

We reverse.

Under K.R.S. § 355.2–702(2), supra, Johnston & Murphy had the right to reclaim the shoes shipped to the insolvent Mel Golde unless such right is taken away by subparagraph (3) of § 355.2–702, which reads:

"(3) The seller's right to reclaim under subsection (2) is subject to the *rights* of a buyer in ordinary course or other good faith purchaser *or lien creditor under this article* (KRS 355.2–403). * * *." (Emphasis supplied.)

It is, and was, the contention of the appellee creditors that they became "lien creditors" by virtue of their attachments, pursuant to K.R.S. § 355.9–301(3). We must, accordingly, look to K.R.S. § 355.2–403 for delineation of the "rights" of lien creditors. The caption of K.R.S. § 355.2–403 advises that it deals with "Power to transfer; good faith purchase of goods; 'entrusting' " and provides no help to a solution of the problem here, but concludes in its final subsection (4) that,

"(4) the rights of other purchasers of goods and of lien creditors are governed by the Articles on Secured Transactions (Article 9), Bulk Transfers (Article 6) and Documents of Title (Article 7)."

Inasmuch as Bulk Transfers and Documents of Title have no relevance here, we move on to Article 9, which in its first section, K.R.S. § 355.9–101, states, "This article shall be known and may be cited as Uniform Commercial Code—*Secured Transactions.*" (Emphasis supplied.) The District Judge and the appellee creditors assume that the section of Article 9 that has relevance here is in its Part 3 which bears the catchline "Rights of Third Parties; Perfected and Unperfected Security Interest; Rules of Priority." They rely specifically on K.R.S. § 355.9–301 entitled, "Persons who take priority over *unperfected security interests;* 'lien creditor' " and providing, in relevant part:

"(1) Except as otherwise provided in subsection (2), an unperfected security interest is subordinate to the rights of * * *

"(b) a person who becomes a lien creditor without knowledge of the security interest and before it is perfected;"

Basically, appellees' position, upheld by the District Judge, is that Johnston & Murphy's status is "to be treated as a creditor with an *unperfected* security interest." We do not read the quoted section of the statute as defining or throwing any light upon the "rights" of a "lien creditor" vis-a-vis the right of reclamation of a defrauded seller under § 355.2–702(2). This latter right is not a "security interest" in the goods sold and Johnston & Murphy are not attempting to assert a "security interest" to support their position. Thus, at the end of this circuitous statutory journey, we arrive at the conclusion that Kentucky's Commercial Code does not contain any provision defining the relative priorities of a creditor as against a reclaiming seller. Such being the situation, we must turn to relevant common law of Kentucky for the needed answer. The Commercial Code in K.R.S. § 355.1–103 provides:

"355.1–103 *Supplementary general principles of law applicable.* Unless displaced by the particular provisions of this chapter, the principles of law and equity * * * shall supplement its provisions."

We consider that the early decision of Lane & Bartlett v. Robinson, 57 Ky.Rep. 496 (1857) announced Kentucky's agreement with the general rule that a defrauded seller's right to reclaim his goods is superior to any right of attaching creditors. The Court said:

"And no reason exists why, as between attaching creditors and vendors asserting an enforceable equity growing out of the contract of sale, the latter should not be preferred. It would certainly be unjust to subject to the payment of the debts of their fraudulent vendee, goods he had improperly obtained from them, and which, in equity, they were entitled to reclaim. This would virtually secure to such vendee the fruits of his fraud by the payment of his debts to the extent of the value of the goods, and defeat the equity of the vendor and the object of the statute." 57 Ky.Rep. at 502–503.

We consider that the rights of the unpaid seller—given by § 355.2–702(2)—were tantamount to those available to a defrauded seller. In the Official Comment to the Code, its draftsmen say:

"2. Subsection (2) takes as its base line the proposition that any receipt of goods on credit by an insolvent buyer amounts to *a tacit business misrepresentation of solvency and therefore is fraudulent as against* the particular seller." Uniform Commercial Code, 1962 Official Text with Comments, p. 190. (Emphasis supplied.)

In In re Monson, 127 F.Supp. 625, 626 (W.D.Ky.1955), Chief Judge Roy Shelbourne recognized and enforced Kentucky law which gives priority to a defrauded seller's right of reclamation over the liens of a trustee in bankruptcy. This view received support in Volume 79 of the Harvard Law Review at p. 610:

"The lack of substantive direction in the Code as to the power of a lien creditor suggests that prior state law may still be followed. * * * Where, as in the majority of jurisdictions, pre-Code law allows the defrauded seller to defeat the claim of a levying creditor, * * * the seller will prevail."

The case of In re Kravitz, 278 F.2d 820 (3rd Cir.1960), has been cited by both the appellant and the appellees in support of their respective positions, but we consider that if it has any relevance here it supports the position we take. The question there involved was whether a seller's right of reclamation granted by § 2–702 of the Uniform Commercial Code could be enforced against the lien of a trustee in bankruptcy. The Third Circuit held that it could not because *under Pennsylvania law* the rights of a trustee in bankruptcy as a "lien creditor" were superior to a defrauded seller. The Court there recognized that the Code Sections did not contain the needed rule. It said,

> "It is perfectly clear that, while Section 70, sub. c of the Bankruptcy Act makes the trustee an ideal lien creditor, what such a lien creditor gets is determined by the law of the state involved, here Pennsylvania." 278 F.2d at 822.

Conversely, looking to Kentucky law, we hold that the appellant Johnston & Murphy's right to reclaim the goods sold to the debtor took priority over appellees' attachment liens.

The judgment of the District Court is reversed with direction that further proceedings be had in conformity with the order of the Referee.

NOTES

1. As revealed in *Mel Golde Shoes*, the original version of 2–702(3) provides that a seller's right to reclaim is "subject to the rights of a buyer in ordinary course or other good faith purchaser *or lien creditor* under this Article (Section 2–403)." A number of states deleted the reference to lien creditor in their initial adoption of the Code, and in 1966 the Permanent Editorial Board approved an amendment to the Code deleting "or lien creditor." Therefore, the present official version of the Code does not contain the lien creditor language. In approximately half the states, however, 2–702(3) still contains the reference to "lien creditor," so the issue raised in *Mel Golde Shoes* remains.

2. Perhaps the most celebrated case interpreting 2–702(3) is *In re Federal's, Inc.*, which moved from the Bankruptcy Court (12 UCC Rep.Serv. 1142 (Bkrtcy.E.D.Mich.1973)) to the District Court (402 F.Supp. 1357 (E.D.Mich. 1975)) to the Sixth Circuit (553 F.2d 509 (6th Cir.1977)). Matsushita Electric Corporation of America (distributor of Panasonic products) had delivered merchandise to Federal's Inc., which filed a bankruptcy petition six days after the delivery. Panasonic sought to reclaim the goods from the trustee in bankruptcy. The Bankruptcy Court stated:

> Panasonic contends that the rights of a reclaiming seller as against a lien creditor are governed not by the Code but by the common law of Michigan and that pursuant to such law the right of reclamation may be exercised as against the trustee in bankruptcy. This conclusion apparently is reached as follows: Section 2.702(3) provides that the seller's right to reclaim is subject to the rights of "lien creditors under this Article (Section 2.403)." Section 2.403 does not spell out any rights of lien creditors but merely states in paragraph 4 that the rights of lien creditors "are governed by the articles on secured transactions (Article 9), bulk transfers (Article 6) and documents of title (Article 7)." While Article 9 defines a lien creditor, this section deals only with the right of a lien creditor as against an unperfected security interest. Since the

rights of a lien creditor vis à vis an alleged defrauded seller are not dealt with in Article 9, the right of a lien creditor and therefore a trustee in bankruptcy as against a reclaiming seller is not to be found in the Code and therefore it is to the common law of Michigan that we must look for a determination of this question. The difficulty with this argument is that:

> "It does have the effect of ignoring the express statutory language which includes not only the cross reference but also includes the very specific wording in Section 2.702(3) which states that the rights of the reclaiming seller are subject to the rights of 'lien creditors.' " Dusenberg and King, Sales and Bulk Transfers Under the UCC (Volume 3 of Benders UCC Service § 13.03(4) (1966)).

A study of the drafting history of § 2.702(3) suggests an alternative interpretation that is more reasonable and plausible and accounts for the presence of the ambiguous references. Between 1945 and 1952 a number of drafts and redrafts of the Code were prepared. The first complete draft was completed in 1951. During the next year a limited number of further amendments were made and in October of 1952 an official edition of the Code with explanatory comments was published as the 1952 Official Text and Comments Edition. The early drafts of § 2.702(3) did not contain any reference to "lien creditor." The inclusion of the term "lien creditor" first appears in the 1952 draft of that section. Prior to the inclusion of the term lien creditor in § 2.702(3) the reference to § 2.403 was appropriate and applicable since buyers in the ordinary course of business and good faith purchasers (the only parties mentioned in the 1951 approved draft) are dealt with in § 2.403. It is readily understandable how in concentrating upon the preparation of the amended version of the Code for submission to the States the drafters could overlook the need for a clarifying correction of the references appearing in the 1951 version of § 2.702(3). In adding the term "lien creditor" the drafters had to be aware that the Code in § 9.301 defined the term lien creditor—viz.

> "A 'lien creditor' means a creditor who has acquired a lien on the property involved by attachment, levy or the like and includes * * * a trustee in bankruptcy from the date of the filing of the petition. * * *"

The drafters also had to be aware of the fact that an avowed purpose of the Code was to make uniform the laws governing commercial transactions among all the States that would enact the Code. In addition, the drafters must have been aware that Article 2 was intended to be a complete revision and modernization of the Uniform Sales Act. It would seem that if the drafters had intended that the rights of a lien creditor be defined otherwise than that defined in § 9.301 and had intended to exclude from its coverage the determination of controversies between sellers of personal property as against lien creditor, and had intended to depart from the principle of uniformity to make sources of non-Code law applicable to such controversies, this intent would have been simply and explicitly expressed. If such had been the intent of the drafters there would have been no need to adopt an approach that ends in futility after a circuitous exploration of the Code.

In light of this background the most plausible assumption is that the drafters intended the rights of a reclaiming seller as against a lien creditor to be determined solely by reference to the Code.[11] As Professor Shanker of the Western Reserve University Law School observes:

> "It is the definition of a 'lien creditor' and not his rights which is found elsewhere in Article 2, particularly in Section 2.403. Then, the cross-reference by Section 2.403 to Article 9 becomes less confusing since Article 9 clearly defines a lien creditor.

> "The actual right of the lien creditor to defeat the seller's reclamation right, however, is given by the language of Section 2.702(3), itself. It is merely the definition of a lien creditor which is found elsewhere.

> "Such a view seems completely consistent with the language of Section 2.702(3). Further, it obviates the serious problems which arise when one looks for lien creditor's rights in sources beyond the Code."[12]

In a similar vein, Professor Vern Countryman of Harvard Law School comments:

> "As to lien creditor, the provision would then simply say that the seller's right to reclamation is 'subject to the rights of * * * a lien creditor,' which would without strain be read to mean is 'subject to the lien of a lien creditor.' This interpretation would still leave it to the court to determine whether 'lien creditor' means the sort of levying creditor whose hypothetical status the bankruptcy trustee acquired under § 70c, and here the definition provided for Article 9 provides a persuasive analogy. But if the court resolved that question in favor of the trustee, no resort to pre-code law would be necessary to conclude that the goods should remain in the bankruptcy estate."[13]

The Code aside, most states did not permit reclamation absent the seller establishing that the buyer had an intent to defraud. The Code now takes the position that "any receipt of goods on credit by an

---

11. Even commentators who conclude that the ultimate determination of the respective rights of a lien creditor and a reclaiming seller is to be made by reference to non-Code sources concede that "the language used by the draftsmen of the Code renders entirely plausible the assumption that the right to reclaim is completely cut off by a creditors levy or by bankruptcy." Kennedy, The Trustee in Bankruptcy Under the Uniform Commercial Code: Some Problems Suggested by Articles 2 and 9, 14 Rutgers Law Review 518, 551 (1960).

12. A Reply to the Proposed Amendment of UCC Section 2.702(3): Another View of Lien Creditors' Rights Against Rights of a Seller to an Insolvent, 14 Western Reserve Law Review 93, 98 (1962).

13. Buyers and Sellers of Goods in Bankruptcy, 1 New Mex.Law Rev. 435, 457 (1971).

insolvent buyer amounts to a tacit misrepresentation of solvency and is therefore fraud as against the seller." Official Comment to § 2.702. If state law were to be applied but with the rule of proof as modified by the Code, clearly the protection given to the sellers of goods would be enhanced. In fact, the official comment to the Code explicitly states that § 2.702 intended to extend "the protection given to a seller who has sold goods to the buyer immediately preceding his insolvency." Therefore, it has been suggested that to hold that the respective rights of a reclaiming seller and a lien creditor are to be determined solely by reference to the Code would defeat this intent. However, this intent was expressed prior to the inclusion of the term "lien creditor" in § 2.702(3). Legislation is rarely enacted in the form introduced. Substance and policy are modified by negotiation and compromise. Whatever the drafters of the Code had originally intended should not and cannot influence the construction of a statute as finally written and adopted.

In light of this analysis, if I were free to do so, I would hold that rights of a reclaiming seller as against a lien creditor are to be determined solely by reference to the Uniform Commercial Code and the Bankruptcy Act and I would further hold that since by reference to the Code a defrauded seller's right to reclaim is divested by a lien creditor, the trustee, since he is given the right of a lien creditor by Section 70c of the Bankruptcy Act must prevail. However, since the Sixth Circuit Court of Appeals in In re Mel Golde Shoes, Inc., 403 F.2d 658 (1968), held to the contrary, I am permitted no such freedom.

* * * Panasonic has conceded that Federal's did intend to pay for the goods purchased. Under Michigan law prior to the Code, the failure to establish intent not to pay would have defeated Panasonic's right to reclaim. However, under the Code it is not necessary to establish an intent not to pay. The Code now imports an irrebuttable presumption of fraud from the mere receipt of purchased goods while insolvent. The Official Comment to § 2.702 states:

> "Subsection (2) takes as its base line the proposition that any receipt of goods on credit by an insolvent buyer amounts to a tacit business misrepresentation of solvency and therefore is fraudulent as against the particular seller."

Should Panasonic, therefore, establish that Federal's was insolvent within the meaning of § 1.201(23) on the date it received the merchandise, ... the court would be compelled to grant the reclamation petition.

On appeal, the District Court held that Michigan non-Code law applies and under that law Panasonic loses to a lien creditor who extended credit after delivery of the merchandise and that the trustee in bankruptcy was to be treated as such a creditor. On further appeal, the Sixth Circuit, adhering to its decision in *Mel Golde Shoes*, applied non-Code Michigan law and concluded that Michigan courts would hold that Panasonic could reclaim as against lien creditors.

3. Another issue much discussed before the comprehensive revision of the Bankruptcy Act in 1978 was whether, under the Bankruptcy Act itself, the seller's right under 2–702 to reclaim goods could be exercised as against the trustee in bankruptcy. Complex analysis led most courts to conclude that the seller prevailed. The Bankruptcy Code now clearly resolves the issue:

§ 545.   Statutory Liens

The trustee may avoid the fixing of a statutory lien on property of the debtor to the extent that such lien

(1) first becomes effective against the debtor

(A) when a case under this title concerning the debtor is commenced;

(B) when an insolvency proceeding other than under this title concerning the debtor is commenced;

(C) when a custodian is appointed or takes possession;

(D) when the debtor becomes insolvent;

(E) when the debtor's financial condition fails to meet a specified standard; or

(F) at the time of an execution against property of the debtor levied at the instance of an entity other than the holder of such statutory lien;

(2) is not perfected or enforceable on the date of the filing of the petition against a bona fide purchaser that purchases such property on the date of the filing of the petition, whether or not such a purchaser exists;

(3) is for rent; or

(4) is a lien of distress for rent.

§ 546.   Limitations on Avoiding Powers

. . .

(c) Except as provided in subsection (d) of this section, the rights and powers of a trustee under sections 544(a), 545, 547, and 549 of this title are subject to any statutory right or common law right of a seller of goods that has sold goods to the debtor, in the ordinary course of such seller's business, to reclaim such goods if the debtor has received such goods while insolvent, but

(1) such a seller may not reclaim any such goods unless such seller demands in writing reclamation of such goods

(A) before ten days after receipt of such goods by the debtor; or

(B) if such 10–day period expires after the commencement of the case, before 20 days after the receipt of such goods by the debtor, and

(2) the court may deny reclamation to a seller with such a right of reclamation that has made such a demand only if the court

(A) grants the claim of such a seller priority as a claim of a kind specified in section 503(b) of this title, or

(B) secures such claim by a lien.

Subsection (d) of 546 contains some special rules for grain producers and fishermen who deliver their goods to, respectively, a grain storage facility or a fish processing facility.

4. Under 2–702 the seller does not have to make demand within 10 days if the buyer has made a written misrepresentation of solvency within three months prior to delivery of the goods. Under the Bankruptcy Code (§ 546), however, the seller's rights as against the trustee in bankruptcy depend on the seller's making a demand within the 10– or 20–day period provided therein, even though the buyer made a written misrepresentation of solvency.

Section 546(c), in addition to referring to § 545, also refers to rights of the bankruptcy trustee under §§ 544(a), 547, and 549. Section 544(a) gives the trustee the rights of lien creditors as of the date of bankruptcy; § 547 gives the trustee power to avoid certain preferential transfers by the bankrupt within specified time periods before bankruptcy; and § 549 allows the trustee to avoid certain post-petition transfers by the bankrupt.

5. Revised Article 2. Revised 2–702 deletes the 10–day requirement of current 2–702 and also deletes the reference to misrepresentation of solvency. In all cases, the demand must be made within a reasonable time after buyer's receipt of the goods. Of course, that change does not affect the demand requirements applicable if the buyer is in bankruptcy.

————

2. Rights Against Secured Creditors

A seller asserting a right to reclaim under 2–702 must be concerned about two classes of competing parties other than lien creditors and the trustee in bankruptcy: subsequent buyers and secured parties. The rights of subsequent buyers are dealt with in 2–403(1) and (2), and there seems little doubt that good faith buyers for value under 2–403(1) and buyers in the ordinary course of business under 2–403(2) take priority over the seller's reclamation rights. In those cases, of course, the goods are in the hands of the buyer who purchased from the seller, and the subsequent buyer presumably relies on that possession in making the purchase.

A secured creditor who takes a security interest in the goods after they are delivered also relies on the fact that the buyer has possession of the goods. Often, however, creditors take security interests not only in property then in the possession of the debtor, but also in property to be acquired in the future (known as after-acquired property). A secured party whose security interest arises under a general after-acquired-property clause in a security agreement that was taken prior to the sale in question typically does not extend credit in reliance upon having a security interest in the particular goods that the seller seeks to reclaim. Therefore, it has been suggested that a seller's reclamation right ought to take priority over an interest of a secured party which arises under an after-acquired-property clause. The following case addresses that issue.

In re Emery Corp.

United States Bankruptcy Court, Eastern District of Pennsylvania, 1984.
38 B.R. 489.

■ EMIL F. GOLDHABER, BANKRUPTCY JUDGE. The basis of the dispute at bench is whether a seller's right of reclamation under § 2702 of the Uniform Commercial Code ("the UCC") of Pennsylvania is precluded by the existence of a creditor holding a security interest in the debtor's after-acquired property. For the reasons stated herein we find that the seller may reclaim the goods.

. . . [The debtor] executed security agreements with several creditors, which agreements were duly perfected prior to February 24, 1983. At all times pertinent to this action, these secured creditors were owed in excess of $10,490.24. Lavonia delivered on credit $10,490.24 worth of yarn to the debtor on March 1, 1983. Two days later the debtor filed a petition for reorganization under chapter 11 of the Bankruptcy Code. The debtor received a letter from Lavonia which demanded the return of the yarn.

We will commence our discussion in the abstract with an historical review of the common-law antecedents of the issues underlying the dispute at bench. At common law a seller of goods who failed to receive payment at or after delivery of the goods to the purchaser had a right of reclamation under certain circumstances. A distinction was drawn between credit sales and cash sales based on the theory that one selling on credit had voluntarily subjected himself to greater risk in dealing with the purchaser than an individual selling for cash. The consequences of this theoretical distinction became manifest in the application of the "void-voidable" transaction doctrine. A buyer who obtained goods in a cash sale without payment of the purchase price, usually through the use of a check subsequently dishonored, obtained no title to the goods. His title was void rather than voidable.* The seller could reclaim the goods merely upon the failure of payment. The seller who delivered goods on credit had a more restricted right of reclamation. Generally, a purchaser's failure to comply with the credit terms of the arrangement gave the seller nothing more than the rights of a general unsecured creditor with no right of reclamation. But if the buyer purchased goods on credit while insolvent, knowing that he would be unable to pay for them, he committed a fraud on the seller. The

---

* Section 2–402 changes this, so that the cash buyer's title is merely voidable if the buyer's payment fails.—Ed.

purchaser's title to the goods was voidable and the seller could reclaim the goods upon establishing the existence of the fraud.

The UCC preserves in modified form a creditor's right of reclamation although the drafters of the statute dispensed with the requirement of proving fraud for the sake of simplicity and uniformity. In re PFA Farmers Market Assoc., 583 F.2d 992, 994 n.2 (8th Cir.1978). As to credit sellers, this change expanded the right of reclamation. Hereafter we shall deal exclusively with sales on credit under § 2702. . . .

Under the former bankruptcy statute—the Bankruptcy Act of 1898—the applicability of the right of reclamation against a debtor in possession or a trustee in bankruptcy was uncertain. With the passage of the Code in 1978, the trustee's ability to restrict a seller's right of reclamation was circumscribed through § 546 of that statute . . . . The legislative history of § 546 indicates that, as "under nonbankruptcy law, the right [of reclamation] is subject to any superior rights of secured creditors. The purpose of the provision is to recognize, in part, the validity of section 2–702 of the Uniform Commercial Code, which has generated much litigation, confusion, and divergent decisions in different circuits." S.Rep. No. 95–989, 95th Cong., 2d Sess. 86–87 (1978), reprinted in 1978 U.S.Code Cong. & Ad.News 5787, 5872–73. . . .

. . .

The parties in the case at bench do not dispute that the seller has a prima facie right of reclamation under § 2702(b) since the goods were delivered to the debtor when it was insolvent and since the debtor received the notice of reclamation within the requisite ten day period. The first issue stems from the meaning of the limitation provisions of § 2702(c) as to whether a creditor with a security interest in the debtor's after-acquired property is a "good faith purchaser" who, by that status, cuts off the seller's right to reclaim his goods. The debtor contends that under § 2702(c) the holder of a security interest is a "purchaser" within the meaning of § 1201 of the UCC which states in part as follows:

"§ 1201. General definitions

"Subject to additional definitions contained in the subsequent provisions of this title which are applicable to specific provisions of this title, the following words and phrases when used in this title shall have, unless the context clearly indicates otherwise, the meanings given to them in this section:

* * *

" 'Purchase.' Includes taking by sale, discount, negotiation, mortgage, pledge, lien, issue or reissue, gift or any other voluntary transaction creating an interest in property.

" 'Purchaser.' A person who takes by purchase."

The debtor then relies on § 2403(d) which states that the "rights of other purchasers of goods and of lien creditors are governed by * * * Division 9 (relating to secured transactions)." The debtor concludes that the reclamation creditor's rights are subordinate to the rights of the secured creditor under § 9312(e)(2), which states that, "[s]o long as conflicting security interests are unperfected, the first to attach has priority."

Although the debtor's theory is supported by notable authority we find it flawed on two bases, the first of which is the debtor's conclusion that the term "purchaser" in § 2702 includes a secured creditor who obtained his security interest *prior* to the seller's delivery of the goods. The pertinent question is, when must the interest of the buyer, purchaser or lien creditor first arise for these interests to defeat the rights of a reclaiming [seller].

. . . In light of the spirit and purpose of § 2702(c) as well as the express language of that section, we find that the term "purchaser" in § 2702(c) includes a secured creditor only to the extent that such creditor gives value to the debtor and receives a security interest thereon after the delivery of the goods and prior to the demand for reclamation.

Since § 2702 is largely a codification of the common law, such common law is persuasive in establishing the meaning of § 2702(c). In credit sales the common law of reclamation, which below is denominated as rescission, has been described as follows:

> "In cases of this character the contract is voidable at the election of the vendor, upon discovery of the fraud. He must rescind promptly upon the discovery, or a conclusive presumption of ratification will arise, but he is not put to his election until he knows, or ought to have known, of the fraud. The right of rescission will not avail when the goods have passed into the hands of an innocent purchaser for value, without notice of the fraud, nor against the execution of a creditor whose debt was contracted, by the fraudulent purchaser, subsequently to his possession under this title. * * * As against a creditor whose debt was in existence at the time the debtor fraudulently obtained possession of the property, the vendor may, if not estopped upon other grounds, assert his right to rescind after the goods have been levied upon."

Mann v. Salsberg, 17 Pa.Super. 280, 284–85 (1901). As stated in *Mann*, a creditor who holds a preexisting debt at the time the goods are sold, has no ability to terminate a seller's right of reclamation although it can be precluded if the debt is incurred and the security interest granted after the goods are delivered to the debtor. In light of *Mann*, our interpretation of the term "purchaser" in § 2702(c) comports well with its common law antecedent.

Although the debtor's request for denial of the reclamation claim is without merit on the first issue under the above stated holding, we continue with the debtor's argument in order to enunciate alternate holdings. As stated above, the debtor relies on § 2403, to which § 2702 refers, which states that the "rights of other purchasers of goods and of lien creditors are governed by * * * Division 9 (relating to secured transactions)." § 2403(d). The debtor claims that the rights of a reclamation creditor are subordinate to the rights of a secured creditor under § 9312(e), which states that "so long as conflicting security interests are unperfected, the first to attach has priority." By its language § 9312(e) is applicable only in a contest between competing security interests. We are aware of no provision of the UCC which states that a creditor's right to reclaim goods is, or should be deemed, a security interest. In essence, § 2702(b) is but one manifestation of the equitable right of rescission. On the creditor's reclamation of the goods, the parties are returned to the same relative positions they occupied before the transaction occurred. More particularly, a reclamation creditor has no Article 9 security interest in the goods unless there was an intent to create a security interest and that intent was committed to a signed agreement. § 9203(a)(1) and § 9102(a). In the case at issue, there is no proof of either of these elements and thus there is no Article 9 security interest. . . .

. . .

In summary, we find that the debtor's analysis is flawed for two reasons. First, we hold that a creditor who advances credit and obtains a security interest prior to the seller's delivery of goods is not a purchaser within the meaning of § 2702. Second, we hold that § 2702 has displaced state law, which holds that a claimant who obtains a security interest prior to the seller's delivery of goods does not have priority under the UCC against the reclaiming creditor. Had we not found that § 2702 displaced non-UCC state law, then our result would not have changed since state common law grants the reclaiming seller the same rights over a secured creditor as § 2702.

———

The debtor appealed Judge Goldhaber's decision. The District Court's opinion follows.

Lavonia Manufacturing Co. v. Emery Corp.

United States District Court, Eastern District of Pennsylvania, 1985.
52 B.R. 944.

■ CAHN, DISTRICT JUDGE. Appellant, Emery Corporation ("Emery,") appeals under Bankruptcy Rule 8001(a), 11 USC § 8001(a) (1984), from a decision of the United States Bankruptcy Court for the Eastern District of Pennsylvania allowing the seller, Lavonia Manufacturing Company ("Lavonia,") to reclaim property delivered to Emery shortly before it filed for bankruptcy. The Bankruptcy Court concluded that the seller's right of reclamation under 13 Pa.C.S.A. § 2702 (1984), the Uniform Commercial Code of Pennsylvania ("UCC,") was superior to the secured creditors' perfected security interests in Emery's after-acquired property. For the reasons stated below, I will reverse the decision of the bankruptcy court.

I.

. . .

[T]he bankruptcy court granted Lavonia's request to reclaim the property delivered to Emery. The court held that although a seller's right of reclamation is subordinate to the rights of a "good faith purchaser," the term "purchaser" in § 2702 of the UCC includes a secured creditor only to the extent that the creditor gives value to the debtor and receives a security interest in the goods after delivery of the goods and prior to the demand for reclamation. The issue presented on appeal is whether, under § 2–702, Emery's perfected secured creditors are considered to be good faith purchasers to whom the seller's right of reclamation is subordinate.

II.

Section 2–702 of the UCC governs the reclamation rights of credit sellers. To reclaim goods under § 2–702, the seller must establish that the debtor was insolvent and that the seller made a timely demand for return of the delivered goods. The parties here do not dispute that Lavonia has met these requirements; Emery was insolvent when the goods were received and acknowledges receipt of the reclamation demand within the required ten day period. Subsection (c) of § 2–702, however, specifically subordinates a seller's reclamation right to the rights of a "good faith purchaser."

The bankruptcy court found that Emery's creditors were not "good faith purchasers" capable of subordinating Lavonia's right to reclamation. The court declined to apply the UCC's broad definitions of "purchase" and "purchaser" for purposes of § 2–702. Instead, the court held that "the term 'purchaser' in § 2–702(c) includes a secured creditor only to the extent that such creditor gives value to the debtor and receives a security interest thereon after the delivery of the goods and prior to the demand for reclamation." In reaching this conclusion, the court first interpreted § 2–403 of the UCC to mean that, because a debtor has voidable title in goods received from a seller, the seller can divest the debtor of the voidable title after delivery by giving notice under § 2–702(b). Therefore, a good faith purchaser must take some action to prevent the seller of delivered goods from divesting the debtor of his § 2–403 right to transfer good title to the good faith purchaser. The court concluded that "[t]he only reasonable triggering event which could occur after delivery . . . is the issuance of credit and the receipt of a security interest."

III.

Section 2–403 grants a person with voidable title and possession of goods the "power to transfer good title to a good faith purchaser for value." 13 Pa.C.S.A. § 2403(a). See Independent News Co. v. Williams, 293 F.2d 510, 512 (3d Cir.1961) ("any entrusting of possession of goods to a merchant who deals in goods of that kind gives him power to transfer all rights of the entrustor"); In re Holiday Meat Packing, Inc., 30 B.R. 737, 740 (Bkrtcy.W.D.Pa.1983) ("a purchaser of goods from a dealer therein takes good title thereto under 13 Pa.C.S.A. § 2403.") I am unaware, however, of any authority supporting the view that § 2–403 gives a seller the right to divest the debtor of title and reclaim goods unless the creditor gives new value, thereby defeating a prior secured creditor's interest in after-acquired property. To the contrary, numerous courts have held that a perfected secured creditor with an interest in after-acquired property is a good faith purchaser within the meaning of § 2–403. A review of the applicable Code sections leads me to concur in this view.

First, the statutory definitions of the UCC are persuasive on the point. Section 1–201 of the Code defines purchaser as "a person who takes by purchase." Purchase, also defined in § 1–201, includes "taking by sale, discount, negotiation, mortgage, pledge, lien, issue or reissue, gift or any voluntary transaction creating an interest in property." A security interest in after-acquired property certainly falls within the broad boundaries set by the above definition. Moreover, the inclusiveness of the definition, particularly of the final phase, suggests that the Code's drafters intended "purchaser" to encompass holders of valid security interests of all types, including interests in after-acquired property. Second, Emery's creditors clearly gave "value" under § 1–201 of the Code, which provides that a "person gives 'value' for rights if he acquires them . . . as security for or in total or partial satisfaction of a preexisting debt." At the time of Lavonia's delivery, Emery owed the three creditors in excess of $10,490.24. The secured creditors gave value when they took an after-acquired interest in the yarn in exchange for this preexisting debt. The Code imposes no demand that a secured creditor give "new" value to maintain a perfected interest in after-acquired property. I find that Emery's three perfected creditors were good faith purchasers under § 2–702, whose rights are superior to Lavonia's rights to reclaim.

. . .

Any seeming unfairness to Lavonia in this result is dispelled by recognition of the fact that the seller could have protected its interest by complying with the UCC's purchase money provisions. As the United States Court of Appeals for the Fifth Circuit noted in Stowers v. Mahon ("Samuels & Co."), 526 F.2d 1238 (5th Cir.) (en banc), cert. denied, 429 U.S. 834 (1976), the Code seeks to encourage specific types of commercial behavior, most importantly, the notice filing of security interests. Specifically, the UCC "limits the seller's ability to reserve title once he has voluntarily surrendered possession to the buyer," Id. at 1246, by requiring that the seller perfect a security interest in the delivered goods to become superior to any prior perfected security interests. Under § 9–107, a seller may take a purchase money security interest ("PMSI") in goods delivered to a debtor. A PMSI in inventory offers a seller unusually good priority. In fact, a PMSI grants a seller of goods the power to defeat a prior perfected secured creditor with an interest in after-acquired inventory. See § 9–312(c).* This favored status is the Code's way of mitigating the potential inequity of security interests in after-acquired property.

---

* This provision now appears in 9–324(b).—Ed.

The various sections and Articles of the UCC work together as an integrated whole. As part of the Code's overall scheme favoring notice filing of nonpossessory security interests in goods, a perfected security interest unquestionably holds a superior position to an unperfected interest. Excusing Lavonia's failure to perfect would frustrate the Code's purpose. Lavonia neglected to take advantage of the Code-provided means for gaining priority over the creditors here, and cannot now contest the loss of its interest.

For the reasons stated above, I will reverse the decision of the Bankruptcy Court. An appropriate order will issue.

QUESTIONS AND NOTES

1. The result reached by the District Court is in accord with essentially all cases to deal with the issue. Is that result good policy? Under which rule, that of the Bankruptcy Judge or the District Judge, are sellers more likely to get paid for their goods?

2. An early case concluding that a secured party's interest in after-acquired property was superior to that of a reclaiming seller was Matter of Samuels & Co., 526 F.2d 1238 (5th Cir.1976). In that case the seller sold cattle to a meat processor and received payments by check. Before the checks were paid, the packer went into bankruptcy. The packer had given a security interest in its inventory to C.I.T. The court held that C.I.T.'s interest in the cattle as after-acquired property took priority over the unpaid cash seller's right to reclaim under 2–507(2). The seller argued that under a federal statute, the Packers and Stockyards Act, 7 U.S.C.A. §§ 181–229, a trust for the benefit of the seller was created in the sold cattle until payment and that, under that trust, it was entitled to recover the cattle (or their proceeds) as against C.I.T. The U.S. Supreme Court rejected that argument (Mahon v. Stowers, 416 U.S. 100, 94 S.Ct. 1626, 40 L.Ed.2d 79 (1974)). In 1976, however, Congress amended the Packer's and Stockyards Act to give the seller a trust in goods sold and in their proceeds. 7 U.S.C.A. § 196. Therefore, in transactions governed by that Act the rights of a reclaiming seller now take priority over the rights of an Article 9 secured party.

3. On the facts of *Atlas Auto Rental Corp.*, page 550 supra, if Schwartzman had received voidable title, would Atlas have lost its right to reclaim as against a secured party's rights under an after-acquired property clause? (Section 9–204 establishes the validity of after-acquired-property clauses in security agreements.)

CHAPTER 11

DOCUMENTARY TRANSACTIONS

A. INTRODUCTION

The issues dealt with in this chapter generally arise when the seller and the buyer are separated by substantial distances. In these transactions the parties typically use common carriers to transport the goods to the buyer, and the seller extends credit to the buyer for 30, 60, or 90 days after the goods arrive. Credit sales offer substantial advantages to both parties: for the seller, they cut down costs because the seller does not have to engage in the special techniques that are necessary to assure that the buyer does not receive the goods before paying for them. For the buyer, credit sales permit the processing of payments on an orderly, routine basis rather than having to take the special steps necessary to pay before receipt of the goods. In credit sales, of course, the buyer also has the use of additional capital and has the ability to withhold payment if the buyer believes that the seller has breached the contract. The seller's pricing, however, presumably takes account of the fact that the seller loses the use of capital, bears the risk of the buyer's failure to pay, and is in an unfavorable position as to disputes during the credit period.

Credit selling is widespread in this country because there are reliable credit reporting agencies that provide accurate information about the financial position of businesses and because most businesses have sufficient financial strength that the risks involved in selling to them on credit are negligible. Also, the legal systems in the various states are similar and familiar so that, if the buyer does not pay, collection efforts can be made in a relatively efficient manner. In spite of the fact that credit selling is the norm rather than the exception, 2–310 says that "unless otherwise agreed, payment is due at the time and place at which the buyer is to receive the goods . . . ." Therefore, if the contract (including implied terms incorporated by virtue of trade usage or course of dealing) does not provide credit terms, the buyer must pay when the goods arrive.

Sometimes, however, either because insufficient information is available or because the available information shows a weak financial position, sellers refuse to extend credit. In these cases there are standardized mechanisms by which a seller can use the services of the shipping and banking industries to assure that a distant buyer pays the price on or before receipt of the goods.

Sales on credit are less common in foreign transactions than in domestic transactions. In addition to the problem of acquiring reliable information as to the credit standing of foreign buyers, there are problems of the use of unfamiliar legal systems, possible governmental impediments to removal of currency from the buyer's country, and so on, which make credit selling riskier than it is in domestic sales. Indeed, the risks in foreign sales are such that sellers very commonly refuse to sell unless they have the guarantee (in the form of a letter of credit) of a bank in the seller's country that it will pay the price of the goods upon submission to the bank of documents indicating that the goods have been shipped.

The reasons for use of the letter of credit are compelling. Even if a seller has shipped goods to a foreign buyer in such a way that the buyer cannot get possession of the goods before paying for them, the seller may be in a very unsatisfactory position if the buyer does not pay. To be sure, the seller still has control of the goods, but they are in another country, which may be far away. There may be a limited market for the goods in question in that country, and the seller may have little knowledge about the market and may have few business contacts there. Thus even though the seller still has control of the goods, it may be difficult and expensive to sell or re-ship them. Sellers may avoid these risks by requiring bank payment against documents showing shipment of the goods. Similarly, while a bank is perhaps more likely than a buyer to honor its commitments, the possible expense and loss if a foreign bank does fail to honor its commitments leads sellers to want a promise from a bank in their own country.

This chapter explores the obligations of carriers as to the goods they carry, the various mechanisms used by sellers to assure payment when they do not extend credit, and some particular problems of letters of credit.

B. OBLIGATIONS OF CARRIERS

Carriers in practically all cases issue bills of lading* covering goods accepted for shipment. Bills of lading have three functions: (1) receipt for the goods, (2) statement of the terms of the shipment agreement, and (3) evidence of ownership of the goods. (As we shall see, "evidence" may be too weak a word in the case of negotiable bills of lading.) "Bill of lading" is defined in 1–201(6) [revised 1–201(a)(6)]. As evidence of ownership, a bill of lading is a document of title, as is a "warehouse receipt" (1–201(45) [revised 1–201(a)(42)]). Bills of lading and warehouse receipts are the two most common documents of title.

A bill of lading is either negotiable (sometimes called an "order" bill of lading) or non-negotiable (also called a "straight" bill of lading). A straight bill states that the goods are consigned to a named person, and the carrier will deliver the goods to the named consignee without requiring surrender of any copy of the bill. A negotiable bill, on the other hand, states that the goods are consigned *to the order of* a named person, and the carrier will deliver the goods only upon the surrender of the bill of lading. Therefore, in

---

* "Lade" appears to have been the Middle English word preferred for what we would now call "load"—hence bill of lading rather than bill of loading—"the bills of lading do declare what goods are laden. . . ." Malyn, Lex Mercatoria 97 (1636).

the case of a negotiable bill, the seller can control the delivery of the goods by controlling the bill of lading. Negotiable bills are transferable by proper indorsement and have many of the characteristics of negotiable money instruments, such as checks and promissory notes. Examples of a negotiable and a non-negotiable bill of lading follow.

The "Consigned to Order of" language makes this bill negotiable. Notice also the sentence in the paragraph at the top of the page which requires surrender of the bill properly indorsed before delivery of the property.

The provisions set out on the next page are on the back of the bill. The same provisions would also apply to a staright bill.

CONTRACT TERMS AND CONDITIONS

Sec. 1. (a) The carrier or party in possession of any of the property herein described shall be liable as at common law for any loss thereof or damage thereto, except as hereinafter provided.

(b) No carrier or party in possession of all or any of the property herein described shall be liable for any loss thereof or damage thereto or delay caused by the act of God, the public enemy, the authority of law, or the act or default of the shipper or owner, or for natural shrinkage. The carrier's liability shall be that of warehouseman, only, for loss, damage, or delay caused by fire occurring after the expiration of the free time allowed by tariffs lawfully on file (such free time to be computed as therein provided) after notice of the arrival of the property at destination or at the port of export (if intended for export) has been duly sent or given, and after placement of the property for delivery at destination, or tender of delivery of the property to the party entitled to receive it, has been made. Except in case of negligence of the carrier or party in possession (and the burden to prove freedom from such negligence shall be on the carrier or party in possession), the carrier or party in possession shall not be liable for loss, damage, or delay occurring while the property is stopped and held in transit upon the request of the shipper, owner, or party entitled to make such request, or resulting from a defect or vice in the property, or for country damage to cotton, or from riots or strikes.

(c) In case of quarantine the property may be discharged at risk and expense of owners into quarantine depot or elsewhere, as required by quarantine regulations or authorities, or for the carrier's dispatch at nearest available point in carrier's judgment, and in any such case carrier's responsibility shall cease when property is so discharged, or property may be returned by carrier at owner's expense to shipping point, earning freight both ways. Quarantine expenses of whatever nature or kind upon or in respect to property shall be borne by the owners of the property or be a lien thereon. The carrier shall not be liable for loss or damage occasioned by fumigation or disinfection or other acts required or done by quarantine regulations or authorities even though the same may have been done by carrier's officers, agents, or employees, nor for detention, loss, or damage of any kind occasioned by quarantine or the enforcement thereof. No carrier shall be liable, except in case of negligence, for any mistake or inaccuracy in any information furnished by the carrier, its agents, or officers, as to quarantine laws or regulations. The shipper shall hold the carriers harmless from any expense they may incur, or damages they may be required to pay, by reason of the introduction of the property covered by this contract into any place against the quarantine laws or regulations in effect at such place.

Sec. 2. (a) No carrier is bound to transport said property by any particular train or vessel, or in time for any particular market or otherwise than with reasonable dispatch. Every carrier shall have the right in case of physical necessity to forward said property by any carrier or route between the point of shipment and the point of destination. In all cases not prohibited by law, where a lower value than actual value has been represented in writing by the shipper or has been agreed upon in writing as the released value of the property as determined by the classification or tariffs upon which the rate is based, such lower value plus freight charges if paid shall be the maximum amount to be recovered, whether or not such loss or damage occurs from negligence.

(b) As a condition precedent to recovery, claims must be filed in writing with the receiving or delivering carrier, or carrier issuing this bill of lading, or carrier on whose line the loss, damage, injury or delay occurred, within nine months after delivery of the property (or, in case of export traffic, within nine months after delivery at port of export) or, in case of failure to make delivery, then within nine months after a reasonable time for delivery has elapsed; and suits shall be instituted against any carrier only within two years and one day from the day when notice in writing is given by the carrier to the claimant that the carrier has disallowed the claim or any part or parts thereof specified in the notice. Where claims are not filed or suits are not instituted thereon in accordance with the foregoing provisions, no carrier hereunder shall be liable, and such claims will not be paid.

(c) Any carrier or party liable on account of loss of or damage to any of said property shall have the full benefit of any insurance that may have been effected upon or on account of said property, so far as this shall not avoid the policies or contracts of insurance; Provided, That the carrier reimburse the claimant for the premium paid thereon.

Sec. 3. Except where such service is required as the result of carrier's negligence, all property shall be subject to necessary cooperage and baling at owner's cost. Each carrier over whose route cotton or cotton linters is to be transported hereunder shall have the

privilege, at its own cost and risk, of compressing the same for greater convenience in handling or forwarding, and shall not be held responsible for deviation or unavoidable delay in procuring such compression. Grain in bulk consigned to a point where there is a railroad, public or licensed elevator, may (unless otherwise expressly noted herein, and then if it is not promptly unloaded) be there delivered and placed with other grain of the same kind and grade without respect to ownership (and prompt notice thereof shall be given to the consignor), and if so delivered shall be subject to a lien for elevator charges in addition to all other charges hereunder.

Sec. 4. (a) Property not removed by the party entitled to receive it within the free time allowed by tariffs lawfully on file (such free time to be computed as therein provided) after notice of the arrival of the property at destination or at the port of export (if intended for export) has been duly sent or given, and after placement of the property for delivery at destination has been made, may be kept in vessel, car, depot, warehouse or place of delivery of the carrier, subject to the tariff charge for storage and to carrier's responsibility as warehouseman, only, or at the option of the carrier, may be removed to and stored in a public or licensed warehouse at the place of delivery or other available place, at the cost of the owner, and there held without liability on the part of the carrier, and subject to a lien for all freight and other lawful charges, including a reasonable charge for storage.

(b) Where nonperishable property which has been transported to destination hereunder is refused by consignee or the party entitled to receive it, or said consignee or party entitled to receive it fails to receive it within 15 days after notice of arrival shall have been duly sent or given, the carrier may sell the same at public auction to the highest bidder, at such place as may be designated by the carrier: Provided, That the carrier shall have first mailed, sent, or given to the consignor notice that the property has been refused or remains unclaimed, as the case may be, and that it will be subject to sale under the terms of the bill of lading if disposition be not arranged for, and shall have published notice containing a description of the property, the name of the party to whom consigned, or, if shipped order notify, the name of the party to be notified, and the time and place of sale, once a week for two successive weeks, in a newspaper of general circulation at the place of sale or nearest place where such newspaper is published; Provided, That 30 days shall have elapsed before publication of notice of sale after said notice that the property was refused or remains unclaimed was mailed, sent, or given.

(c) Where perishable property which has been transported hereunder to destination is refused by consignee or party entitled to receive it, or said consignee or party entitled to receive it shall fail to receive it promptly, the carrier may, in its discretion, to prevent deterioration or further deterioration, sell the same to the best advantage at private or public sale: Provided, That if time serves for notification to the consignor or owner of the refusal of the property or the failure to receive it and request for disposition of the property, such notification shall be given, in such manner as the exercise of due diligence requires, before the property is sold.

(d) Where the procedure provided for in the two paragraphs last preceding is not possible, it is agreed that nothing contained in said paragraphs shall be construed to abridge the right of the carrier at its option to sell the property under such circumstances and in such manner as may be authorized by law.

(e) The proceeds of any sale made under this section shall be applied by the carrier to the payment of freight, demurrage, storage, and any other lawful charges and the expense of notice, advertisement, sale, and other necessary expense and of caring for and maintaining the property, if proper care of the same requires special expense, and should there be a balance it shall be paid to the owner of the property sold hereunder.

(f) Property destined to or taken from a station, wharf, or landing at which there is no regularly appointed freight agent shall be entirely at risk of owner after unloaded from cars or vessels or until loaded into cars or vessels, and, except in case of carrier's negligence, when received from or delivered to such stations, wharves, or landings shall be at owner's risk until the cars are attached to and after they are detached from locomotive or train or until loaded into and after unloaded from vessels.

Sec. 5. No carrier hereunder will carry or be liable in any way for any documents, specie, or for any articles of extraordinary value not specifically rated in the published classifications or tariffs unless a special agreement to do so and a stipulated value of the articles are indorsed hereon.

Sec. 6. Every party, whether principal or agent, shipping explosives or dangerous goods, without previous full written disclosure to the carrier of their nature, shall be liable for and indemnify the carrier against all loss or damage caused by such goods, and such goods may be warehoused at owner's risk and expense or destroyed without compensation.

Sec. 7. The owner or consignee shall pay the freight and average, if any, and all other lawful charges accruing on said property; but, except in those instances where it may lawfully be authorized to do so, no carrier by railroad shall deliver or relinquish possession at destination of the property covered by this bill of lading until all tariff rates and charges thereon have been paid. The consignee shall be liable for the freight and all other lawful charges, except that if the consignor stipulates, by signature, in the space provided for that purpose on the face of this bill of lading that the carrier shall not make delivery without requiring payment of such charges and the carrier, contrary to such stipulation, shall make delivery without requiring such payment, the consignor (except as hereinafter provided) shall not be liable for such charges. Provided, that, where the carrier has been instructed by the shipper or consignor to deliver said property to a consignee other than the shipper or consignor, such consignee shall not be legally liable for transportation charges in respect of the transportation of said property (beyond those billed against him at the time of delivery for which he is otherwise liable) which may be found to be due after the property has been delivered to him, if the consignee (a) is an agent only and has no beneficial title in said property, and (b) prior to delivery of said property has notified the delivering carrier in writing of the fact of such agency and absence of beneficial title, and, in the case of a shipment reconsigned or diverted to a point other than that specified in the original bill of lading, has also notified the delivering carrier in writing of the name and address of the beneficial owner of said property; and, in such cases the shipper or consignor, or, in the case of a shipment so reconsigned or diverted, the beneficial owner, shall be liable for such additional charges. If the consignee has given to the carrier erroneous information as to who the beneficial owner is, such consignee shall himself be liable for such additional charges. On shipments reconsigned or diverted by an agent who has furnished the carrier in the reconsignment or diversion order with a notice of agency and the proper name and address of the beneficial owner, and where such shipments are refused or abandoned at ultimate destination, the said beneficial owner shall be liable for all legally applicable charges in connection therewith. If the reconsignor or diverter has given to the carrier erroneous information as to who the beneficial owner is, such reconsignor or diverter shall himself be liable for all such charges.

If a shipper or consignor of a shipment of property (other than a prepaid shipment) is also the consignee named in the bill of lading and, prior to the time of delivery, notifies, in writing, a delivering carrier by railroad (a) that such party is the beneficial owner of such property, and (b) the name and address of the beneficial owner of such property, and (c) that delivery is to be made to such party only upon payment of all transportation charges in respect of the transportation of such property, and delivery is made by the carrier to such party without such payment, such shipper or consignor shall not be liable (as shipper, consignor, consignee, or otherwise) for such transportation charges but the party to whom delivery is so made shall in any event be liable for any additional charges billed against the property at the time of such delivery, and also for any additional charges which may be found to be due after delivery of the property, except that if such party prior to such delivery has notified in writing the delivering carrier the name and address of the beneficial owner of the property, and has given in writing to such delivering carrier the name and address of such beneficial owner, such party shall not be liable for any additional charges which may be found to be due after delivery of the property; but if the party to whom delivery is made has given to the delivering carrier erroneous information as to who the beneficial owner is, such party shall nevertheless be liable for such additional charges. If the shipper or consignor has given to the delivering carrier erroneous information as to who the beneficial owner is, such shipper or consignor shall himself be liable for such transportation charges, notwithstanding the foregoing provisions of this paragraph and irrespective of any provisions to the contrary in the bill of lading or in the contract of transportation under which the shipment was made. The term "delivering carrier" means the line-haul carrier making ultimate delivery.

Nothing herein shall limit the right of the carrier to require at time of shipment the prepayment or guarantee of the charges. If upon inspection it is ascertained that the articles shipped are not those described in this bill of lading, the freight charges must be paid upon the articles actually shipped.

Where delivery is made by a common carrier by water the foregoing provisions of this section shall apply, except as may be inconsistent with Part III of the Interstate Commerce Act.

Sec. 8. If this bill of lading is issued on the order of the shipper, or his agent, in exchange or in substitution for another bill of lading, the shipper's signature to the prior bill of lading as to the statement of value or otherwise, or election of common law or bill of lading liability, in or in connection with such prior bill of lading, shall be considered a part of this bill of lading as fully as if the same were written or made in or in connection with this bill of lading.

Sec. 9. (a) If all or any part of said property is carried by water over any part of said route, and loss, damage or injury to said property occurs while the same is in the custody of a carrier by water the liability of such carrier shall be determined by the bill of lading of the carrier by water (this bill of lading being such bill of lading if the property is transported by such water carrier thereunder) and by and under the laws and regulations applicable to transportation by water. Such water carriage shall be performed subject to all the terms and provisions of, and all the exemptions from liability contained in, the Act of the Congress of the United States, approved on February 13, 1893, and entitled "An act relating to the navigation of vessels, etc.", and of other statutes of the United States according carriers by water the protection of limited liability, as well as the following subdivisions of this section; and to the conditions contained in this bill of lading not inconsistent with this section, when this bill of lading becomes the bill of lading of the carrier by water.

(b) No such carrier by water shall be liable for any loss or damage resulting from any fire happening to or on board the vessel, or from explosion, bursting of boilers or breakage of shafts, unless caused by the design or neglect of such carrier.

(c) If the owner shall have exercised due diligence in making the vessel in all respects seaworthy and properly manned, equipped, and supplied, no such carrier shall be liable for any loss or damage resulting from the perils of the lakes, seas, or other waters, or from latent defects in hull, machinery, or appurtenances whether existing prior to, at the time of, or after sailing, or from collision, stranding, or other accidents of navigation, or from prolongation of the voyage. And, when for any reason it is necessary, any vessel carrying any or all of the property herein described shall be at liberty to call at any port or ports, in or out of the customary route, to tow and be towed, to transfer, tranship, or lighter, to load and discharge goods at any time, to assist vessels in distress, to deviate for the purpose of saving life or property, and for docking and repairs. Except in case of negligence such carrier shall not be responsible for any loss or damage to property if it be necessary or is usual to carry the same upon deck.

(d) General Average shall be payable according to the York-Antwerp Rules of 1924, Sections 1 to 15, inclusive, and Sections 17 to 22, inclusive, and as to matters not covered thereby according to the laws and usages of the Port of New York. If the owners shall have exercised due diligence to make the vessel in all respects seaworthy and properly manned, equipped and supplied, it is hereby agreed that in case of danger, damage or disaster resulting from faults or errors in navigation, or in the management of the vessel, or from any latent or other defects in the vessel, her machinery or appurtenances, or from unseaworthiness, whether existing at the time of shipment or at the beginning of the voyage (provided the latent or other defects or the unseaworthiness was not discoverable by the exercise of due diligence), the shippers, consignees and/or owners of the cargo shall nevertheless pay salvage and any special charges incurred in respect of the cargo, and shall contribute with the shipowner in general average to the payment of any sacrifices, losses or expenses of a general average nature that may be made or incurred for the common benefit or to relieve the adventure from any common peril.

(e) If the property is being carried under a tariff which provides that any carrier or carriers party thereto shall be liable for loss from perils of the sea, then as to such carrier or carriers the provisions of this section shall be modified in accordance with the tariff provisions, which shall be regarded as incorporated into the conditions of this bill of lading.

(f) The term "water carriage" in this section shall not be construed as including lighterage in or across rivers, harbors, or lakes, when performed by or on behalf of rail carriers.

Sec. 10. Any alteration, addition, or erasure in this bill of lading which shall be made without the special notation hereon of the agent of the carrier issuing this bill of lading, shall be without effect, and this bill of lading shall be enforceable according to its original tenor.

724 — SOUTHERN RAILWAY SYSTEM — **724**

FORM 407 C-6 (REV. 12-77)

277 19 012

STRAIGHT BILL OF LADING—SHORT FORM   ORIGINAL—NOT NEGOTIABLE

RECEIVED, subject to the classifications and tariffs in effect on the date of the issue of this Bill of Lading.

FINAL DESTINATION AND ADDITIONAL ROUTING

SPECIAL INSTRUCTIONS

ALLOWANCE NET

INVOICE NO.

If charges are to be prepaid, write or stamp here, "TO BE PREPAID".

NOTE – Where the rate is dependent on value, shippers are required to state specifically in writing the agreed or declared value of the property. This agreed or declared value of the property is hereby specifically stated by the shipper not to exceed

Subject to Section 7 of Conditions:

SIGNATURE OF CONSIGNOR

PER

NO. PKGS. | DESC. OF ARTICLES, SPEC. MARKS AND EXCEPTIONS | COMMODITY CODE NUMBER

DATE REV W/B PREP | FOR THE CARRIER

WEIGHT | RATE | FREIGHT | ADVANCES | PREPAID

DESTN. AGENT'S F/B NO

FIRST JUNCTION | SECOND JUNCTION | THIRD JUNCTION | FOURTH JUNCTION

Outbound Junction Stamps Here. Yard Stamps on Back.

DESTINATION AGENT STAMP

724 — SOUTHERN RAILWAY SYSTEM — 724

[This short form straight bill does not reprint the Contract Terms and Conditions on the back. Rather the very small print in the upper right hand corner states that the goods are received on the terms and conditions of the Uniform Domestic Straight Bill of Lading in effect on the date of the bill. The small print also states that the shipper certifies that he is familiar with the terms of the Uniform Straight Bill including the terms on the back thereof. This form can be filled out by a computer printer.

[A more recent computer form used by some railroads does not contain the small print on the top right but is otherwise identical with this form. In the most recent form, the bill is negotiable or not depending on whether the words "Order Of" appear before the name of the consignee in the block for consignee and address. The form makes no reference at all to any contract terms. Presumably, the Uniform Bill of Lading terms nevertheless apply.—ed.]

There are several sources of law governing bills of lading. For inter-state carriers, the basic law is the Federal Bills of Lading Act (Pomerene

Act), 49 U.S.C.A. §§ 80101–80166. For intrastate shipments, UCC Article 7 controls. Overseas shipments may be subject to the Carriage of Goods by Sea Act (46 U.S.C.A. § 1300ff), or to the provisions of various treaties, or, of course, to the law of other nations. The Federal Bills of Lading Act, adopted in 1916 and recodified without substantive change in 1994, is practically identical with the Uniform Bills of Lading Act, which was promulgated in 1909 and ultimately adopted in most states. That Act was replaced by UCC Article 7, which deals with both bills of lading and warehouse receipts. Under the Supremacy Clause of the United States Constitution, of course, the Federal Bills of Lading Act displaces Article 7.

In the typical sale on credit, the seller obtains a straight bill and sends it to the buyer. Upon arrival at the buyer's location, the carrier delivers the goods. But what if the goods do not conform to the contract?

Fine Foliage of Florida, Inc. v. Bowman Transportation, Inc.

United States Court of Appeals, Eleventh Circuit, 1990.
901 F.2d 1034.

■ KRAVITCH, CIRCUIT JUDGE:

This case involves an appeal by a common carrier, Bowman Transportation, Inc. ("Bowman.") from the district court's order finding it liable to Fine Foliage of Florida, Inc. ("Fine Foliage,") for the value of ferns damaged due to an incorrect temperature setting on a refrigerated container unit. Bowman contends that the lower court erred in finding that Fine Foliage established a prima facie case under the Carmack Amendment, 49 U.S.C. § 11707.[a] ... Because we find that the district court ruled correctly ... , we affirm.

I.   Background

Fine Foliage, a Florida corporation located in DeLeon Springs, Florida, is a grower and international shipper of decorative ferns used in floral arrangements. Bowman is an interstate trucking company that was employed for the inland transportation of the ferns from DeLeon Springs, Florida to Savannah, Georgia.

In April of 1987, Fine Foliage, through its freight forwarder, Wilk Forwarding Company ("Wilk.") arranged for the shipment of 939 cartons of leatherleaf fern from DeLeon Springs, Florida to Tokyo, Japan. Wilk arranged to have Bowman undertake the inland transportation from DeLeon Springs to Jacksonville, Florida and then arranged for sea passage with Mitsui Lines ("Mitsui.") Mitsui arranged through its agent, Strachan

---

a. Now recodified as 49 U.S.C.A. 11706 for rail carriers and as 49 U.S.C.A. 14706 for   motor carriers.—Ed.

Shipping, to have the ferns transported by Bowman from a terminal in Jacksonville to its port in Savannah.

The bill of lading covering the DeLeon Springs to Jacksonville portion of the trip specified that the ferns were to be transported by Bowman at a temperature of 39 Fahrenheit. The bill also had printed on it the words "PERISHABLE Keep From Heat or Frost." Leonard Davis, Bowman's driver, testified that he signed the bill of lading without reading it. Testimony at trial established, however, that it is common knowledge among fern growers and truck drivers who transport ferns that the plant must be shipped at temperatures between 38 and 40 Fahrenheit. Davis testified that he knew that ferns should be shipped between 38 and 40.

. . .

[The refrigeration control in the transportation trailer was set for 0 F. When the truck arrived in Savannah, Georgia, the zero temperature in the trailer was discovered by a Savannah marine surveyor who noted that ice appeared on some of the containers holding the ferns. A visual examination of the ferns at that time did not show damage from freezing. They were loaded on a ship for Japan, but the bill of lading issued by the ocean carrier noted "EXCEPTION: CONTAINER RECEIVED BY CARRIER SET AT ZERO DEGREES FAHRENHEIT CARRIER NOT RESPONSIBLE FOR POSSIBLE DAMAGE TO CARGO DUE TO INCORRECT TEMP." When the ferns arrived in Toyko, they were found to be a "total loss."]

II.   The Carmack Amendment

. . .

The Carmack Amendment provides that a common carrier is liable for the actual loss or injury to goods in an interstate commerce shipment. It states in part that:

> A common carrier providing transportation or service subject to the jurisdiction of the Interstate Commerce Commission . . . and a freight forwarder shall issue a receipt or bill of lading for property it receives for transportation under this subtitle. That carrier or freight forwarder and any other common carrier that delivers the property and is providing transportation or service subject to the jurisdiction of the Commission . . . are liable to the person entitled to recover under the receipt or bill of lading. . . . Failure to issue a receipt or bill of lading does not affect the liability of a carrier or freight forwarder.

The purpose of the Carmack Amendment is to protect shippers against the negligence of interstate carriers and "to relieve shippers of the burden of searching out a particular negligent carrier from among the often numerous carriers handling an interstate shipment of goods." Reider v. Thompson, 339 U.S. 113, 119, 70 S.Ct. 499, 502, 94 L.Ed. 698 (1950). Once liability is established, the defendant carrier may then seek to recover damages from the connecting carrier which had possession of the goods when loss was sustained.

A. *Fine Foliage's Prima Facie Case*

A shipper establishes a prima facie case of the carrier's negligence and liability under the Carmack Amendment by evincing proof by a preponderance of the evidence that the goods "1) were delivered to the carrier in good condition, 2) arrived in damaged condition, and 3) resulted in the specified amount of damage." Offshore Aviation v. Transcon Lines, Inc., 831 F.2d 1013, 1014 (11th Cir.1987) (per curiam).

At trial Fine Foliage put forth evidence in support of each of these elements, and the district court found that Fine Foliage succeeded in establishing a prima facie case. First, it found that "the subject fern was in good condition when loaded by the plaintiff's employees into the reefer for transportation by the defendant on the morning of April 29, 1987." Second, the district court found that "the subject fern was ruined upon arrival in Savannah, although the total loss of the shipment was not declared until arrival and inspection in Tokyo." Finally, it found that the "plaintiff had substantiated its damages attributed to the loss of the subject fern at $21,035.60."

Bowman claims that Fine Foliage's testimony at trial was insufficient to establish a prima facie case against the carrier and that the district court erred in failing to grant Bowman's motion for involuntary dismissal under Fed.R.Civ.P. 41(b). As the trial judge's ruling on Fine Foliage's prima facie case was based on his findings of fact, we review his conclusions under the clearly erroneous standard.

Bowman argues that the court erred in finding that the ferns were initially in good condition, when the only evidence as to the condition of the ferns when they left Fine Foliage was a Department of Agriculture certificate which showed lack of insect infestation. It argues that prior decisions of this and other courts have required that the condition of the contents of a container be established by eyewitness or other direct reliable testimony. In support of that assertion, Bowman points to Highlands Insurance Company v. Strachan Shipping Company, 772 F.2d 1520 (11th Cir.1985); Pillsbury Co. v. Illinois Central Gulf Railroad, 687 F.2d 241 (8th Cir.1982); and D.P. Apparel Corp. v. Roadway Express, Inc., 736 F.2d 1 (1st Cir.1984).

We find that Bowman's reliance on these cases is misplaced. *Highlands* involved a situation in which there was no proof, other than a bill of lading, that TV sets, reported stolen, had actually been placed in a sealed seagoing container. It stands only for the proposition that evidence "such as the testimony of an eyewitness to the loading of the container is necessary to confirm the contents." *Highlands*, 772 F.2d at 1521. Here, there is no dispute that the ferns were loaded into the container. In *Pillsbury*, the court held that where goods are shipped under seal, a bill of lading does not establish a prima facie case for the shipper that the goods were in good order. Instead, the shipper must "present[ ] additional evidence sufficient to establish by preponderance of all the evidence the condition of the goods upon delivery." 687 F.2d at 244. The *Pillsbury* court relied on circumstantial evidence to find that the plaintiff had demonstrated that the cars, when loaded, were free of insect infestation. In *D.P. Apparel,* the court found that the plaintiff failed to establish a prima facie case by relying primarily on the bill of lading for the proposition that the goods were delivered to the carrier in good condition. 736 F.2d at 4.

In the instant case, neither the plaintiff nor the trial judge relied on the bill of lading to establish delivery of the goods to Bowman in good condition. Instead, the trial court based its finding regarding the original condition of the ferns on "the approval of the fern by the Department of Agriculture; the testimony as to the care and temperature control of the fern after its harvest; and the fact that other fern, packaged in the identical manner and stored in the same cooler as the subject fern, arrived at overseas destinations in acceptable condition." We find no support for Bowman's assertion that a judge may not rely on circumstantial evidence to establish the original condition of goods when that evidence is substantial and reliable.[3] In light of the evidence in the instant case, we find that the judge did not err in holding that Fine Foliage had established the first prong of its prima facie case.

Bowman further contends that the court erred in finding that the ferns arrived at their destination in a damaged condition. The court based this finding "upon the 0 Fahrenheit temperature setting in the container as evidenced by the temperature chart and the credible testimony regarding the consequent detriment to fern caused by freezing temperatures." Bowman argues that Fine Foliage did not establish the accuracy of the particular Ryan recorder used to record the temperature in the container. We note, however, that there was substantial evidence introduced at trial that the temperature setting on the container was at 0: the Mitsui equipment interchange receipt lists a temperature setting of 0, and the marine surveyor in Savannah found both that the temperature had been set at zero and that there was a layer of ice on the ferns. Fine Foliage also presented sufficient testimony to establish that ferns that are subjected to such temperatures for a period of hours cannot possibly remain unharmed. In sum, our review of the record indicates that there was ample evidence presented at trial from which the trial judge could conclude that the ferns were destroyed while in Bowman's possession and we cannot say that the judge erred in finding that Bowman established this prong of the prima facie case.

. . . Because Fine Foliage established each prong of its prima facie case, the district judge did not abuse his discretion in failing to dismiss the case.

B.   *Defenses to a Prima Facie Case under the Carmack Amendment*

Once a plaintiff has established a prima facie case under the Carmack Amendment, the burden of proof shifts to the carrier to show that it was free from negligence and the damage was caused solely by "(a) the act of

---

3. Indeed, the evidence relied on in *Pillsbury* was similar to that presented in the instant case. Pillsbury produced evidence of its preloading inspection and cleaning procedures and also showed that a test car switched through the defendant carrier's yard became infested while one switched to another carrier's yard did not. *Pillsbury,* 687 F.2d at 245.

God; (b) the public enemy; (c) the act of the shipper himself; (d) public authority; (e) or the inherent vice or nature of the goods." Missouri Pacific R. Co. v. Elmore & Stahl, 377 U.S. 134, 137, 84 S.Ct. 1142, 1144, 12 L.Ed.2d 194 (1964); Frosty Land Foods v. Refrigerated Transport, 613 F.2d 1344, 1346–47 (5th Cir.1980).

The district court found that Bowman was negligent in failing to notice and correct the temperature setting on the reefer containing the ferns. It found that there was no reason that Davis should not have noted the incorrect temperature setting of the container prior to loading the ferns, particularly in light of Davis's knowledge of the correct temperature. In finding that Bowman failed to rebut Fine Foliage's prima facie case, the court relied on the fact that the 39 temperature was noted on the bill of lading signed by Davis. It also took note of Bowman's course of dealing with Fine Foliage, Bowman's knowledge of the proper temperature, and Davis' knowledge that the cooling system had malfunctioned. The court stressed that it would have been logical and reasonable for Davis, who had some knowledge of the time required for cooling a container, to check the temperature setting of the container prior to or during the loading of the ferns in order to determine whether the reefer had adequately pre-cooled. The court found that even if Davis was not able to adjust the temperature setting, he could have called the improper setting to the attention of one of the Fine Foliage employees. There is ample support in the testimony introduced at trial for the district court's finding of negligence. We also find no error in the district court's finding that even if Bowman was not negligent, it had not established any of the accepted defenses to Fine Foliage's prima facie case.

. . .

For the foregoing reasons, the opinion of the district court is affirmed. . . .

NOTES

1. The Carmack Amendment is a codification of the common law rule on the liability of common carriers. The Amendment applies to interstate transportation by railroads, highway common carriers, and some freight forwarders. The Amendment does not apply to contract carriers or to intrastate shipments. Common carriers are carriers that hold themselves out as available to the general public for the carriage of goods. Contract carriers, in contrast, are carriers who contract with one or more individual shippers for carriage but who do not hold themselves out as being available to carry for everyone.

While rail and truck carriers are almost strictly liable, the damages allowed a shipper are limited by the classification and tariffs in effect on the day the carrier issues a bill of lading. For intrastate shipments not governed by the federal law, 7–309(2) recognizes limited-liability tariffs.

The carrier-liability rules, the rate charges, and the limitations on the dollar amount of the carrier's liability may bind the carrier and shipper even if no bill of lading is issued. Consequently, it seems correct to say that the rights and duties of the parties do not flow from contract but rather from positive law.

The liability of contract carriers and of common carriers as to intrastate shipments is determined by the law of each state. To determine the law of any particular state it is necessary to examine (1) state statutes for any possible statutory change of the common law rules or any statutory limitation upon the ability of carriers to contract out of those rules, (2) the regulations of any state agency regulating intrastate carriers and (3) the state decisional law to determine the extent to which local decisions have modified the traditional common law rules or permit carriers to contract out of their common law liability. Section 7–309(1) provides that a carrier that issues a bill of lading "shall exercise the degree of care in relation to the goods which a reasonably careful man would exercise under like circumstances," but then states that the section "does not affect any statute, regulation, or rule of law that imposes liability on a common carrier for damages not caused by its negligence." The Code itself, therefore, does not affect existing liability rules.

2. Ocean carriers. The liability of ocean carriers is prescribed by the Carriage of Goods by Sea Act, enacted in 1936. 46 U.S.C.A. §§ 1300–1315. The Act is based on the Brussels Convention of 1924, which was signed by many leading commercial countries. Under the Act and the Convention, the liability of ocean carriers is considerably lighter than that imposed on rail, truck, and air carriers. For example, section 4(2) of the Act (U.S.C.A. § 1304(2)) provides that "Neither the carrier nor the ship shall be responsible for loss or damage arising or resulting from—(a) act, neglect, or default of the master, mariner, pilot, or the servants of the carrier in the navigation or in the management of the ship; (b) Fire, unless caused by the actual fault or privity of the carrier; (c) Perils, dangers, and accidents of the sea or other navigable waters ..." (etc., specifying seventeen specific types of exemptions). Section 4(3) adds: "The shipper shall not be responsible for loss or damage sustained by the carrier or the ship arising or resulting from any cause without the act, fault, or neglect of the shipper, his agents, or his servants." And section 4(5) limits the amount of the carrier's liability for loss to $500 per package or in the case of goods not shipped in packages, $500 per customary freight unit, unless the nature and value of such goods have been declared by the shipper before shipment and inserted in the bill of lading.

3. Air carriers. Liability of domestic carriers is controlled by tariffs published by the airline. Those tariffs generally exclude liability except for loss caused by the carrier's negligence and also contain provisions limiting the dollar amount of liability unless the shipper states a higher value and pays a higher charge.

The liability of international air carriers is governed by a treaty, the Warsaw Convention, since 1934 adhered to by over 90 countries, including the United States. One authority summarizes liability under the treaty as follows:

> The international air carrier is not liable if it proves that all necessary measures were taken to avoid the damage or that it was impossible for the carrier or its agents to take such measures, or if the carrier proves that the damage was occasioned by an error in piloting, in the handling of the aircraft, or in navigation and that, in all other respects, the carrier and his agents have taken all necessary measures to avoid the damage.

S.Sorkin, How to Recover for Loss or Damage to Goods in Transit 5–43 (1977).

4.   Risk of the seller or buyer vs. risk of the carrier. It sometimes happens that goods are totally destroyed while in the possession of a carrier en route from the seller to the buyer under a contract in which the delivery term is "f.o.b. Seller's plant." Under that delivery term the buyer usually has the risk of loss (2–509(1)(a)), but if the goods do not conform to the contract, 2–510(1) provides that the risk remains on the seller. If the goods have been damaged but not destroyed, it may be easy to prove whether or not they conformed to the contract. If they are destroyed, however, proof of this matter is difficult, and the outcome of the case may turn on which party has the burden of proof.

At common law and under the Uniform Sales Act, the burden of proving that the goods conformed to the contract was on the seller, but evidence that the seller delivered goods to the carrier which he claimed conformed to the contract made out a prima facie case. The burden of going forward with the evidence was then on the buyer, but "if the goods had been destroyed while in the carrier's hands this proof would of course be difficult to make and it is probable that the seller's prima facie proof would remain unrebutted." J.Waite, Sales 54 (1921); see Levy v. Radkay, 233 Mass. 29, 123 N.E. 97 (1919); Skinner v. James Griffiths & Sons, 80 Wash. 291, 141 P. 693 (1914). Nothing in Article 2 changes this.

In *Fine Foliage* the court states that under the Carmack Amendment, to shift the risk of loss to the carrier, the shipper (i.e. the seller) must prove that the goods were in good condition at the time of delivery to the carrier. If the seller proves that the goods conformed to the sales contract, then the risk of loss, as between the seller and the buyer, is on the buyer. Depending on the nonconformity, of course, the goods may be in good condition for purposes of the Carmack Amendment but nonconforming for purposes of 2–509 and 2–510 (e.g., a latent breach of warranty).

G.A.C. Commercial Corp. v. Wilson

United States District Court, Southern District of New York, 1967.
271 F.Supp. 242.

■ FREDERICK VAN PELT BRYAN, DISTRICT JUDGE. Plaintiff G.A.C. Commercial Corporation (G.A.C.), a Delaware corporation, brings this action sounding in ... negligence against a New York corporation, Norwood & St. Lawrence Railroad Co. (Norwood), a rail carrier in interstate commerce. Defendant Norwood now moves ... for summary judgment under Rule 56, F.R.Civ.P.

... [O]n October 17, 1963, plaintiff G.A.C. entered into an accounts receivable financing agreement with St. Lawrence Pulp & Paper Corp. (St. Lawrence), a New York corporation. Under the terms of the agreement G.A.C. was to make advances to St. Lawrence, which agreed to "pledge, assign and transfer to G.A.C. all the [b]orrower's right, title and interest in and to accounts receivable * * * then owing" to St. Lawrence.

Pursuant to the agreement St. Lawrence forwarded copies of its invoices together with copies of bills of lading to G.A.C., which, upon receipt, advanced the monies to St. Lawrence at the agreed discount. . . . G.A.C. ultimately advanced $356,883.57 under the financing agreement, no part of which has been repaid. St. Lawrence is now a bankrupt.

. . .

[G.A.C. alleged that some of the invoices were fraudulent, in that they purported to represent sales that never occurred and therefore did not represent real transactions for which St. Lawrence would receive payment. G.A.C. claimed that Norwood facilitated this fraud because] the fraudulent accounts receivable described were "upon the form of bill of lading" of defendant Norwood "and were countersigned by its agent." Norwood is charged with negligence in failing to require any inspection of the quantity of goods shipped before verifying the bills of lading and in permitting a situation to occur in which the fraudulent and nonexistent accounts could be forwarded to G.A.C.

Norwood's answer alleges failure to state a claim on which relief can be granted and contributory negligence. By way of separate defense it denies any knowledge or information as to the falsity of the bills of lading or with respect to the financing agreement between St. Lawrence and G.A.C. The answer also alleges that the bills of lading involved are "uniform straight bill[s] of lading—not negotiable," as in fact they are, under Section 2 of the Federal Bills of Lading Act. 49 U.S.C.A. § 82 [now codified, as modified, at 49 U.S.C.A. § 80103].

The controversy here concerns 62 invoices and accompanying straight bills of lading forwarded to G.A.C. by St. Lawrence during 1964. Sixty of these bills concern interstate shipments of paper from St. Lawrence in Norfolk, New York, to Mohegan Converters in Hillside, New Jersey, and involve advances of $245,811.19. Each of the sixty interstate bills was on Norwood's bill of lading, and it is conceded for purposes of this motion, though denied in the answer, that the bills were signed by one of Norwood's agents.

. . .

The method by which the alleged fraudulent scheme was carried out appears for purposes of this motion to be as follows: the bankrupt St. Lawrence, as part of its facilities in Norfolk, New York, maintained a railroad siding connected with the lines of defendant carrier which had a freight office approximately 1/8th of a mile from the siding. St. Lawrence was permitted to load freight at its spur track in preparation for shipments on defendant's line. The railroad cars were sealed by St. Lawrence with seals provided by the railroad. St. Lawrence also prepared the bills of lading on blanks furnished in quadruplicate by defendant Norwood. The bills thus prepared were then presented to Norwood's agent who signed the original and one copy without inspecting the contents of the cars. No notation such as "contents of packages unknown" or "shipper's weight, load and count" was written on the bills. The signed copies were returned to St. Lawrence and forwarded with the invoices to G.A.C. which made advances on the goods described, which, as it turned out, had not been shipped.

Since sixty of the bills of lading were issued by a common carrier for the transportation of goods in interstate commerce, the issues as to these bills are controlled by the provisions of the Federal Bills of Lading Act. 49 U.S.C.A. § 81. This statute stands as "a clear expression of the determination of Congress to take the whole subject matter of such bills of lading within its control." 2 S.Williston, Sales § 406a, at 535 (rev.ed.1948); see Adams Express Co. v. Croninger, 226 U.S. 491, 33 S.Ct. 148, 57 L.Ed. 314 (1913). As such, it squarely bars the fourth claim asserted against defendant Norwood on the sixty bills representing interstate shipments.

Prior to the passage of the Federal Bills of Lading Act "the United States courts held that a carrier was not liable for the act of its agent in issuing a bill of lading for goods where no goods had in fact been received." Josephy v. Panhandle & S.F. Ry., 235 N.Y. 306, 310, 139 N.E. 277, 278 (1923); see, e.g., Clark v. Clyde S.S. Co., 148 F. 243 (S.D.N.Y.1906). The liability of carriers for acts of their agents was expanded, but not drastically, by the passage of the federal legislation which draws a sharp distinction between order bills of lading and straight bills where in fact the goods are never received for shipment by the carrier. Under § 22 of the Act, 49 U.S.C.A. § 102 [rephrased and now codified at 49 U.S.C.A. § 80113(a)], "[i]f a bill of lading has been issued by a carrier or on his behalf by an agent or employee * * *, the carrier shall be liable to * * * the holder of an order bill, who has given value in good faith, relying upon the description therein of the goods, * * * for damages caused by the nonreceipt by the carrier of all or part of the goods upon or prior to the date therein shown." However, the liability of the carrier for nonreceipt extends only to "the owner of goods covered by a straight bill,"[1] provided, of course, he also

---

1. Section 22 of the Act, 49 U.S.C.A. § 102 [as modified, now § 80113(a)], in its complete form, reads as follows:

§ 102. Liability for Nonreceipt or Misdescription of Goods

If a bill of lading has been issued by a carrier or on his behalf by an agent or employee the scope of whose actual or apparent authority includes the receiving of goods and issuing bills of lading therefor for transportation in commerce among the several States and with foreign nations, the carrier shall be liable to (a) the owner of goods covered by a straight bill subject to existing right of stoppage in transitu or (b) the holder of an order bill, who has given value in good faith, relying upon the description therein of the goods, or upon the shipment being made upon the date therein shown, for damages caused by the nonreceipt by the carrier of all or part of the goods upon or prior to the date therein shown, or their failure to correspond with the description thereof in the bill at the time of its issue.

gives value in good faith in reliance upon the description of goods contained in the bill.

It is clear that a party in the position of Norwood is not included within the narrow category of those liable on a straight bill under the federal legislation. In the first place there is no question that the straight bills of lading here involved are nonnegotiable. * * * As a consequence plaintiff G.A.C., as apparent transferee of these bills and invoices representing accounts receivable under the agreement with St. Lawrence, upon notification to the carrier of the transfer, could only "become the direct obligee of whatever obligations the carrier owed to the transferor of the bill immediately before the notification." 49 U.S.C.A. § 112 [now codified at 49 U.S.C.A. § 80106(c)]; see id. § 109. Norwood obviously owed St. Lawrence nothing because no goods in fact were received. There was therefore no outstanding obligation to G.A.C. . . .

By no stretch of the imagination does G.A.C. qualify as an "owner of goods covered by a straight bill" who can sue the carrier under § 22 of the Federal Bills of Lading Act, 49 U.S.C.A. § 102, for representing that goods in fact had been received. The reason for this is that it is completely illusory to attempt to assign an "owner" to nonexistent goods. R.Braucher, Documents of Title 23 (1958); 2 S.Williston, Sales § 419a, at 576–77 (rev.ed.1948). While the consignee is generally deemed to have title to goods shipped under a straight bill of lading, even he cannot sue the carrier for representing in a straight bill that non-existent goods had in fact been received. Martin Jessee Motors v. Reading Co., 87 F.Supp. 318 (E.D.Pa.), aff'd, 181 F.2d 766 (3d Cir.1950). The rationale applied in *Martin Jessee Motors*—that the consignee can prevail against the carrier "only by proving its title to specific property," 181 F.2d at 767—applies *a fortiori* to bar the claim of G.A.C. Plaintiff's interest in the "aggregate face value of the accounts receivable pledged as security" under no conceivable reading of the statute can be deemed an "[ownership] of goods covered by a straight bill." G.A.C. is not one of the favored few who can recover under the Federal Bills of Lading Act.

Plaintiff G.A.C. fares no better with respect to the two bills of lading representing intrastate shipments in New York. Of decisive importance, of course, are the facts that these shipments were not on Norwood's forms and were not signed by Norwood's agents. Even if they were, the carrier would escape liability. Although the awkward term "owner" in 49 U.S.C.A. § 102 [now codified at 49 U.S.C.A. § 80113(a)] has been replaced by the word "consignee" in the Uniform Commercial Code § 7–301 and the Uniform Bills of Lading Act § 23, each of which would govern the issues of liability on one of the bills of lading representing an intrastate shipment. The change is immaterial for purposes of this case. Plaintiff, perhaps an assignee, transferee or pledgee of the non-negotiable bills, though it claims not to be, is certainly not a "consignee," which is the only party protected. 2 Anderson, Uniform Commercial Code 261 n. 9 (1961); see R.Braucher,

Documents of Title 23–24 (1958). Contrast U.C.C. § 7–203. Thus, as with the sixty interstate bills, G.A.C. cannot successfully sue on the two intrastate bills.

G.A.C. cannot avoid the results dictated by the statute by casting its claim for relief in terms of common law negligence. G.A.C. was sent sixty straight interstate bills of lading by St. Lawrence. The alleged negligence consists of Norwood's permitting a situation to develop in which St. Lawrence could make untrue representations that goods had in fact been shipped under the straight bills. G.A.C. claims that it relied to its detriment upon certain statements contained in the bills. The action is based on the bills not on Norwood's negligence. "[T]he negligent or reckless language on which * * * the action is founded, language certifying the receipt of the goods, is the language of the bills—were the bills ignored, there would be nothing on which to base the action, since no representation was made apart from them." Cheasapeake & Ohio R. Co. v. State Nat'l Bank, 280 Ky. 444, 450, 133 S.W.2d 511, 514 (1939). A holding to the contrary would permit any party to circumvent the restrictions of the Federal Bills of Lading Act through the insertion of a talismanic characterization of its claim as one for "negligence." It is quite plain, however, that the declaration in 49 U.S.C.A. § 81—"bills of lading issued by any common carrier for the transportation of goods" between the states "shall be governed by this chapter"—must be taken to preclude alternative and supplementary liability under state law. The substance of the rule cannot be avoided by the form of the complaint.

   . . .

It is true that the result dictated by the federal legislation may lead to some inequities. A straight bill under the Federal Bills of Lading Act is obviously not a good security risk. The fraud of the shipper by failing to deliver goods to the carrier can result, as it did here, in misleading statements on the bills of lading, which operate to the detriment of banks and other commercial financiers making advances on the basis of the bills. Moreover, the carrier can readily prevent such a situation from arising by inserting "in the bill of lading the words, 'Shipper's weight, load, and count,' or other words of like purport" to "indicate that the goods were loaded by the shipper and the description of them made by him." 49 U.S.C.A. § 101 [now codified, as modified, at 49 U.S.C.A. § 80113(b)].

But the overriding policy considerations in the Act look the other way on the issue of liability. First, "[t]here is nothing in the statute to indicate that the mere omission of the words 'Shipper's weight, load, and count' in and of itself makes the carrier liable for damages to goods improperly loaded. The omission of the statutory words merely serves to shift upon the carrier the burden of proving that the goods were improperly loaded by the shipper, and that the damage ensued from that cause." Modern Tool Corp. v. Pennsylvania R. Co., 100 F.Supp. 595, 596–597 (D.N.J.1951); see U.C.C. § 7–301(4). According to the allegations the true culprits in this case were the shipper and its agents; there is no reason to saddle defendant Norwood with liability simply because it did not insert the "Shipper's weight, load, and count" language in the bills. In addition, practicality demands loading arrangements such as those here, where the shipper places his goods aboard and seals the railroad car which the carrier has provided. Section 21 of the Act, 49 U.S.C.A. § 101 [§ 80113(b)], anticipates that shippers are expected to do much of the counting and loading on their own sidings or spur tracks. The rapid flow of commerce might well be hindered if the carrier in every instance were charged with ascertaining whether in fact there were goods behind every one of its straight bills.

Moreover, denying security value to a straight bill of lading does not work a hardship upon banks and other commercial institutions. G.A.C., as a knowledgeable lender, is fully aware of the risks inherent in straight bills, and could well have required order bills to protect itself. It nevertheless chose to rely upon straight bills to lend money to the now bankrupt St. Lawrence at a profitable rate of interest. Wiser now, G.A.C. seeks to shift its loss to Norwood, an undoubtedly solvent defendant. The Federal Bills of Lading Act protects against this type of hindsight by requiring the lender to accept this kind of security subject to the defenses between the carrier and the shipper.

The motion of defendant Norwood ... for summary judgment is granted. . . .

QUESTIONS AND NOTES

1. The court notes that under the language of the statute, even if the plaintiff had been a buyer who, relying on the bills of lading, paid the seller, it would not have been able to recover since the Act protects only "owners" in the case of straight bills. Should a court read "owner" as including a person who would have been owner if goods actually had been loaded?

2. Should the statute be amended to protect persons in the position of G.A.C.? See UCC 7–301(1) for the position of the Code.

3. The court refers to the fact that the shipper could have avoided the problem by inserting in the bill of lading the phrase "shipper's weight, load, and count . . . ."

The section from which this language is taken, now codified at 49 U.S.C.A. § 80113, reads as follows:

80113.   Liability for nonreceipt, misdescription, and improper loading

(a) Liability for nonreceipt and misdescription. Except as provided in this section, a common carrier issuing a bill of lading is liable for damages caused by nonreceipt by the carrier of any part of the goods by the date shown in the bill or by failure of the goods to correspond with the description contained in the bill. The carrier is liable to the owner of goods transported under a nonnegotiable bill (subject to the right of stoppage in transit) or to the holder of a negotiable bill if the owner or holder gave value in good faith relying on the description of the goods in the bill or on the shipment being made on the date shown in the bill.

(b) Nonliability of carriers. A common carrier issuing a bill of lading is not liable under subsection (a) of this section

(1) when the goods are loaded by the shipper;

(2) when the bill

(A) describes the goods in terms of marks or labels, or in a statement about kind, quantity, or condition; or

(B) is qualified by "contents or condition of contents of packages unknown," "said to contain," "shipper's weight, load, and count," or words of the same meaning; and

(3) to the extent the carrier does not know whether any part of the goods were received or conform to the description.

(c) Liability for improper loading. A common carrier issuing a bill of lading is not liable for damages caused by improper loading if

(1) the shipper loads the goods; and

(2) the bill contains the words "shipper's weight, load, and count," or words of the same meaning indicating the shipper loaded the goods.

(d) Carrier's duty to determine kind, quantity, and number. (1) When bulk freight is loaded by a shipper that makes available to the common carrier adequate facilities for weighing the freight, the carrier must determine the kind and quantity of the freight within a reasonable time after receiving the written request of the shipper to make the determination. In that situation, inserting the words "shipper's weight" or words of the same meaning in the bill of lading has no effect.

(2) When goods are loaded by a common carrier, the carrier must count the packages of goods, if package freight, and determine the kind and quantity, if bulk freight. In that situation, inserting in the bill of lading or in a notice, receipt, contract, rule, or tariff, the words "shipper's weight, load, and count" or words indicating that the shipper described and loaded the goods, has no effect except for freight concealed by packages.

UCC 7–301 contains a similar provision.

Rountree v. Lydick–Barmann Co.

Texas Court of Civil Appeals, 1941.
150 S.W.2d 173.

. . .

■ SPEER, JUSTICE.

[Plaintiff, Lydick–Barmann, contracted with defendant, Rountree, for the transportation of goods from plaintiff's location in Fort Worth, Texas, to the location of Crone Co., its customer in Louisiana City, Arkansas. Defendant received the goods and issued a non-negotiable (straight) bill of lading, showing that the goods were] "consigned to Lydick–Barmann Company, destination 616 street, Louisiana City, Little Rock County, Ark. State. Notify Crone Company." The bill of lading described the merchandise, was signed by both plaintiff and defendant, acting through their respective agents, and was endorsed in blank by plaintiff. The undisputed evidence further shows that plaintiff has no office or agent at the street address in Little Rock, as given in the bill of lading. The merchandise was delivered to Crone Company. Because of this delivery by defendant, the plaintiff lost the value of its goods . . . .

We do not believe that plaintiff's right of recovery is dependent upon whether or not the bill of lading under which the shipment moved was a shipper's order billing.* It is clear that if it was a shipper's order contract, which would obligate the defendant (the carrier) not to deliver the merchandise until the endorsed bill of lading was produced and delivered to him, and delivery was made as in this case, without obtaining the bill, there would be liability. As we view it, we need not determine whether or not it was a shipper's order contract, although under one count in plaintiff's pleadings, it is claimed to be such. . . .

The undisputed facts in this case entitled plaintiff to recover, as we view the law applicable. The defendant insists that the bill of lading under which the shipment moved was a straight bill. It has all of the elements of such, except that it was on yellow . . . paper, [which is to be used for negotiable bills,] and contains the expression, "Notify Crone Co.[, which is required in negotiable bills.]" These are elements of a [negotiable] bill. They do not destroy the fact that it could be properly classed as a straight bill.

Defendant urges . . . that the term "notify Crone Co." was equivalent to the expression, "Consigned to" a named person "in care of" another, as is often used in straight bills. Our courts have held that when a bill names the consignee "in care of" another person, such other person is held to be the named agent of the consignor for delivery of the merchandise, and that delivery to that person is delivery to the consignee. See City Nat. Bank of El Paso v. El Paso & N.E.R. Co. et al., Tex.Civ.App., 225 S.W. 391, writ of error refused, affirmed by U.S. Supreme Court, as reported in 262 U.S. 695, 43 S.Ct. 640, 67 L.Ed. 1184. We have not been cited to any case, nor from an independent search have we found where any court has construed the two expressions as synonymous. It is perceivable why, if one is directed to deliver an article to another in care of one named, that delivery to the latter would be a compliance with the contract, but the same course of reasoning would not produce the same result when instructions are given to deliver to a certain person, notify another. This conclusion is emphasized

---

* I.e., a negotiable bill of lading.—Ed.

by the fact the word "notify" as used in a bill of lading is only required when a [negotiable bill is used]. In formulating the respective requisites of bills of lading, some significance must be given to the requirement that a [negotiable] bill must contain the word "notify."

For purposes of this appeal, we are construing the bill of lading in this case as a straight bill. The goods were consigned by plaintiff to itself, at Little Rock, Ark. 49 U.S.C.A. § 82 [as modified, now codified at 49 U.S.C.A. 80103] provides: "A bill in which it is stated that the goods are consigned or destined to a specified person is a straight bill." When goods are so shipped the carrier is bound by the provisions of Section 88 [§ 80110(a)], which reads: "A carrier in the absence of some lawful excuse, is bound to deliver goods upon a demand made either by the consignee named in the bill for the goods or * * *." The carrier is justified in making delivery, under 49 U.S.C.A. § 89 [§ 80110(b)] to, "(a) A person lawfully entitled to the possession of the goods, or (b) the consignee named in a straight bill for the goods." If delivery is made by the carrier under any other conditions than those provided, and the consignor suffers a loss on account thereof, the carrier is liable. Estherville Produce Co. v. Chicago, R.I. & P.R. Co., 8 Cir., 57 F.2d 50.

It is conceded by defendant that this was a straight bill of lading; that he delivered the goods to Crone Company, named in the bill as the party to be notified. In this way, defendant earnestly insists that he has performed his contract of shipment. In his brief he emphasizes the contention with many concrete, positive assertions, such as: "The contractual obligations of [defendant] in this case were in writing; were introduced in evidence by the [plaintiff], and the record abundantly demonstrates beyond question that the obligations imposed upon the [defendant] by the contract of carriage were faithfully and literally performed. * * * The [defendant] can be held liable only for the performance of the contract which was actually entered into. He may not be called upon to answer for a breach of a contract which he did not execute. He may not called upon to respond in damages because he did not do something which the [plaintiff] desired, but which was not put into the contract. The [plaintiff] must stand upon the contract as written. * * * The fact is that the parties entered into a written contract which has been fully performed." As indicated, the defendant insists that the written contract of shipment (the bill of lading) was binding alike on both the plaintiff and defendant, and since he had fully performed the contract as written, he should not be called upon to respond in damages because of a loss sustained by the plaintiff.

Defendant's contention that he had "literally" and "definitely" carried out the terms of the written contract between the parties is based upon what we believe to be an erroneous hypothesis—that delivery of the shipment to Crone Company, named as the one to be notified, was delivery to the consignee named in the bill of lading, which was the contract of shipment. Lydick–Barmann Co. (plaintiff) was the consignee in the contract. It was likewise the consignor. It was the owner of the merchandise at all times and was entitled to possession at destination. The fact that consignee had no office or place of business at Little Rock, rendering it impossible for defendant to make physical delivery of it then and there, presented no insuperable difficulty. Defendant had consignor's—consignee's—street address at Fort Worth, Texas, and when defendant found that it could not deliver the freight to the consignee, as he had promised to do, immediate notice should have been given to the consignor. It was not sufficient for defendant to choose to deliver the goods to some one else not entitled to possession.

. . .

Finding no error in the record, all assignments of error are overruled, and the judgment is affirmed.

C. SHIPMENTS UNDER RESERVATION

If the transaction does not contemplate the extension of credit, 2–310(a) states that payment is due at the time and place at which the buyer is to receive the goods even if the place of shipment is the place of delivery. This provision continues prior law and the usual trade custom under which payment is due in the buyer's city, not the seller's. The seller may arrange for an employee to travel to the buyer's place of business to receive payment, or—at much less expense—the parties may use the services of the shipping and banking industries. The remaining materials describe the way in which the typical at-a-distance cash transaction is handled.

Stated simply, the seller uses control of the bill of lading to control the goods and arranges things so that the carrier will not deliver the goods to the buyer until the price is paid. One way to do this is to obtain a negotiable bill of lading from the carrier. Under a negotiable bill the carrier will deliver only on surrender of the bill of lading. Usually the carrier will issue a negotiable bill of lading (to the order of the seller), which the seller will indorse and take to the seller's bank, which forwards the bill of lading to a bank in buyer's city. That bank will notify buyer that the bank has received the bill of lading and, when the buyer pays the price, the buyer's bank gives the bill of lading to the buyer and sends the price through the customary banking channels to the seller's bank, which credits that amount to the seller's account.

The seller may also control the delivery of the goods by shipping them under a straight bill of lading in which the goods are consigned to the seller himself or some trusted agent for the seller in the buyer's city. If a straight bill is used, a delivery order directing the carrier to deliver to the buyer (or an authorization to execute such a delivery order) ordinarily will be forwarded to a bank in the buyer's city with instructions to transfer it to the buyer upon payment.

Whether a negotiable or a straight bill is used, the buyer has, unless contracted away, the right to inspect the goods before paying for them. (See § 2–310(b)). Therefore, it will be necessary for the bank in the buyer's city, on the buyer's request, to arrange for inspection of the goods while they are still in possession of the carrier.

In cases in which the seller uses the banking system to ship goods "under reservation," the seller typically draws a draft on the buyer and forwards the draft along with the bill of lading or delivery order.

The draft may be payable to the seller or to the seller's bank. In either event, it will be indorsed so that the bank in buyer's city is in possession of a draft indorsed to it or in blank. A typical draft form is set out below.

On Sight	December 10, 2006
Pay to the Order of Hometown Bank	$5,468.75
Five Thousand Four Hundred and Sixty-eight and 75/100 dollars	
To: Buyer	
1203 Northwood Avenue	
Your City, Your State	

_____

Seller

This draft is like a check and is payable immediately when demand is made on the buyer. A draft payable on demand often is called a "sight draft" because it is payable "on sight."

Frequently the seller's bank will lend the seller the face amount of the draft as soon as the bank takes the draft and the attached documents for forwarding and collection. When the draft is paid, the bank is reimbursed.

Several provisions in Article 2 authorize the procedures just outlined. Section 2–310(b) provides that in cash transactions, "if the seller is authorized to send the goods he may ship them under reservation, and may tender the documents of title, but the buyer may inspect the goods after their arrival before payment is due unless such inspection is inconsistent with the terms of the contract (Section 2–513). . . ."

Section 2–505 is titled "Seller's Shipment Under Reservation," but the text of that section does not define "under reservation." Rather, it says that (1) procurement of a negotiable bill of lading by the seller reserves a security interest in him in the goods and (2) procurement of a non-negotiable bill of lading to himself or his nominee (other than the buyer) reserves possession of the goods as security. " 'Security interest' means an interest in personal property or fixtures which secures payment or performance of an obligation." (1–201(37) [revised 1–201(a)(35)])

The idea is that under the methods of shipment described above and referred to in 2–505, the buyer can't get possession of the goods before paying and that, therefore, the seller has a security interest in the goods to secure payment of the price. Unlike the remedy of the typical creditor with a security interest, however, the seller's remedy if the buyer doesn't pay is to refuse to deliver the goods and sue the buyer for breach of contract. See UCC 9–110 and 2–507.

Sometimes a sales contract provides that the buyer will pay "C.O.D." or "against documents." This is almost, but not quite, the same as a cash sale so far as documentary transactions go. In a cash sale the buyer is entitled to inspect the goods before payment even if the seller is entitled to ship under reservation. In the case of a C.O.D. or "against documents" transaction, the buyer has agreed to pay when the documents are exhibited, and, therefore, the buyer does not have a right to inspect the goods before paying for them. (2–513) Generally, the documents will arrive some time before the goods themselves. In the documentary cash-sale transaction, the right of inspection means that the buyer does not have to pay until the goods arrive. In an against-documents transaction, however, the buyer is obligated to pay when the documents arrive.

Sometimes sellers use a draft with attached bill of lading in credit transactions. When this is done, the draft will not be a sight draft, but will be drawn payable on some future date, either a future calendar date or a specified period after sight. This draft often is called a "time draft."

When the time draft and attached documents arrive at a bank in the buyer's city, the buyer is asked to accept the draft, and when the buyer does so (by signing the front of it, thereby "accepting" the draft) the bank surrenders the documents to the buyer. By accepting the draft, the buyer agrees to pay it according to its terms. The use of drafts in this context occurs because banks or other credit extenders may be somewhat more willing to lend on the security of an accepted draft than on the security of an open account.

D. LETTERS OF CREDIT

Particularly in international transactions, but in domestic transactions as well, sellers may decline to sell unless they have the promise of a bank to pay the price of the goods when the bank receives documents that indicate that conforming goods have been shipped. Banks provide this service through the issuance of documentary letters of credit.

A documentary letter of credit is a bank's promise to accept drafts or pay money provided there is a presentment to it of whatever documents (e.g., bill of lading, invoice, etc.) are described in the letter. In almost all cases it is written by a bank at the request of the buyer. It is directed to the seller, and it enables the seller to rely on the credit of the bank in addition to the credit of the buyer. In banking parlance the buyer is the "customer" or the "applicant," the bank promising to honor drafts is the "issuer," and the seller is the "beneficiary." The issuing bank will sometimes notify the beneficiary directly that a credit has been opened, but, if the letter is directed to a beneficiary in another country, normally the issuer will call upon a related bank in the beneficiary's country (the correspondent bank) to notify the beneficiary. The notification form is the "letter of credit," and the correspondent bank is the "notifying" or "advising" bank. Frequently the correspondent bank will be asked to "confirm" the credit. When a credit is confirmed, the correspondent bank is the "confirming bank" and its confirmation renders it liable to honor drafts drawn by the beneficiary. Under a confirmed letter of credit, the beneficiary has the right to be paid by either the issuer or the confirming bank. If the confirming bank pays under the letter of credit, it has a right of reimbursement against the issuing bank .

The advantages of letter-of-credit financing are considerable to both buyer and seller. The buyer benefits from the fact that the device is inexpensive and efficient and from the fact that the buyer is dealing with a local (issuing) bank that knows and trusts the buyer (because typically it is a bank with which the buyer regularly does business).

Frequently, the issuing bank does not demand immediate reimbursement for payments made under the credit, but rather extends the buyer credit (which may be secured by the goods covered by the documents). This leaves the buyer's working capital intact and enables the buyer to repay the issuer out of the proceeds derived from the sale of the goods. The requirement that the seller deliver specified documents before receiving payment greatly reduces the risk to the buyer, because the documents assure the buyer that the goods have been shipped and apparently conform to the contract.

The seller likewise benefits from the use of the letter of credit. Most importantly, it greatly reduces the risk of non-payment, for the seller has the promise of one or more banks, not just the promise of the buyer. In addition, a draft backed by a letter of credit is readily discountable, which means that the seller easily is able to obtain payment immediately upon shipment of the goods. Finally, banks have developed methods that permit the beneficiary to transfer the benefits of a letter of credit, and this enables the seller to use the device to finance the production of the goods.

Two legal and economic facts dominate letter-of-credit financing. The first is that the banks that issue, advise, or confirm letters of credit are financial institutions and not merchants. They deal in documents and not in merchandise. The bank's liability to the beneficiary is a direct liability, and the bank is not an agent for the customer in any regard. The matter can be summed up by stating that the letter of credit is a contract independent of the sales contract between the buyer and seller. If the terms of the letter of credit are satisfied, the issuing bank is liable to the beneficiary, notwithstanding that the seller may have breached the underlying sales contract by shipping defective goods. Conversely, nonperformance by the buyer, caused by insolvency or otherwise, does not excuse the issuer or confirming bank from performing the letter of credit contract.

Banks are isolated from the underlying sales contract for the very convincing reason that their function is only to finance the sale and not to otherwise participate in it. Therefore, letters of credit can be written inexpensively. This is the second fundamental fact of letter-of-credit financing. The inexpensiveness of the letter of credit is largely because banks are not called upon to assume any risks with respect to the performance of the sales contract. This permits them to do letter-of-credit business in a standardized, streamlined manner, for their undertaking requires only the receipt, examination, and payment against documents.

The efficiency of the work of the banks with respect to letters of credit would not be possible without universally accepted rules. As put by a leading bank lawyer:

> It is apparent that the business (letter of credit) can only be done if the letter of credit device is standardized, streamlined and made as mechanical as possible. The letter of credit, as presently conceived and used, is not a substitute for the sales contract, nor for an insurance policy, nor for the precautions which a prudent and experienced merchant ought to take. It is plain cheap food, and not a miracle drug. In concept, it could be made to be a luxury article, but in practice it is a mass production article, and unless it is to be priced out of existence, it must be a mass produced article. Mass production articles need simple, standard parts with very few trimmings. So the vital and vigorous commercial letter of credit business requires simple, standard, easily applicable rules which are internationally understood and accepted.

These rules do exist, but not as rules of law. Most of the commercial nations of the world have accepted a tabulation of customs and practices in the letter-of-credit field which has been compiled by the International Chamber of Commerce. This comprehensive tabulation is called the "Uniform Customs and Practice for Commercial Documentary Credits." American bankers adopted these rules in 1938. They were last revised in 1993, International Chamber of Commerce Publication No. 500, and they are known as "UCP 500." The UCP 500 has not been adopted by treaty or by local legislation. Nevertheless, it represents a successful effort by bankers to govern themselves and the international field by consensual regulation. As for statutory regulation, UCC Article 5 states the fundamental theories underlying letters of credit, but does not provide comprehensive regulation.

Courtaulds North America, Inc. v. North Carolina National Bank

United States Court of Appeals, Fourth Circuit, 1975.
528 F.2d 802.

■ Bryan, Senior Circuit Judge. A letter of credit with the date of March 21, 1973 was issued by the North Carolina National Bank at the request of and for the account of its customer, Adastra Knitting Mills, Inc. It made available upon the drafts of Courtaulds North America, Inc. "up to" $135,000 (later increased by $135,000) at "60 days date" to cover Adastra's purchases of acrylic yarn from Courtaulds. The life of the credit was extended in June to allow the drafts to be "drawn and negotiated on or before August 15, 1973."

Bank refused to honor a draft for $67,346.77 dated August 13, 1973 for yarn sold and delivered to Adastra. Courtaulds brought this action to recover this sum from Bank.

The defendant denied liability chiefly on the assertion that the draft did not agree with the letter's conditions, viz., that the draft be accompanied by a "Commercial invoice in triplicate stating [inter alia] that it covers * * * 100% acrylic yarn"; instead, the accompanying invoices stated that the goods were "Imported Acrylic Yarn."

Upon cross motions for summary judgment on affidavits and a stipulation of facts, the District Court held defendant Bank liable to Courtaulds for the amount of the draft, interest and costs. It concluded that the draft complied with the letter of credit when each invoice is read together with the packing lists stapled to it, for the lists stated on their faces: "Cartons marked:—100% Acrylic." After considering the insistent rigidity of the law and usage of bank credits and acceptances, we must differ with the District Judge and uphold Bank's position.

The letter of credit prescribed the terms of the drafts as follows:

"Drafts to be dated same as Bills of Lading. Draft(s) to be accompanied by:

"1. Commercial invoice in triplicate stating that it covers 100,000 lbs. 100% Acrylic Yarn, Package Dyed at $1.35 per lb., FOB Buyers Plant, Greensboro, North Carolina Land Duty Paid.

"2. Certificate stating goods will be delivered to buyers plant land duty paid.

"3. Inland Bill of Lading consigned to Adastra Knitting Mills, Inc. evidencing shipment from East Coast Port to Adastra Knitting Mills, Inc., Greensboro, North Carolina."

The shipment (the last) with which this case is concerned was made on or about August 8, 1973. On direction of Courtaulds, bills of lading of that date were prepared for the consignment to Adastra from a bonded warehouse by motor carrier. The yarn was packaged in cartons and a packing list referring to its bill of lading accompanied each carton. After the yarn was delivered to the carrier, each bill of lading with the packing list was sent to Courtaulds. There invoices for the sales were made out, and the invoices and packing lists stapled together. At the same time, Courtaulds wrote up the certificate, credit memorandum and draft called for in the letter of credit. The draft was dated August 13, 1973 and drawn on Bank by Courtaulds payable to itself.

All of these documents—the draft, the invoices and the packing lists— were sent by Courtaulds to its correspondent in Mobile for presentation to Bank and collection of the draft which for the purpose had been endorsed to the correspondent.

This was the procedure pursued on each of the prior drafts and always the draft had been honored by Bank save in the present instance. Here the draft, endorsed to Bank, and the other papers were sent to Bank on August

14. Bank received them on Thursday, August 16. Upon processing, Bank found these discrepancies between the drafts with accompanying documents and the letter of credit: (1) that the invoice did not state "100% Acrylic Yarn" but described it as "Imported Acrylic Yarn," and (2) "Draft not drawn as per terms of [letter of credit], Date [August 13] not same as Bill of Lading [August 8] and not drawn 60 days after date" [but 60 days from Bill of Lading date 8/8/73]. Finding of Fact 24. Since decision of this controversy is put on the first discrepancy we do not discuss the others.

On Monday, August 20, Bank called Adastra and asked if it would waive the discrepancies and thus allow Bank to honor the draft. In response, the president of Adastra informed Bank that it could not waive any discrepancies because a trustee in bankruptcy had been appointed for Adastra and Adastra could not do so alone. Upon word of these circumstances, Courtaulds on August 27 sent amended invoices to Bank which were received by Bank on August 27. They referred to the consignment as "100% Acrylic Yarn," and thus would have conformed to the letter of credit had it not expired. On August 29 Bank wired Courtaulds that the draft remained unaccepted because of the expiration of the letter of credit on August 15. Consequently the draft with all the original documents was returned by Bank.

During the life of the letter of credit some drafts had not been of even dates with the bills of lading, and among the large number of invoices transmitted during this period, several did not describe the goods as "100% Acrylic Yarn." As to all of these deficiencies Bank called Adastra for and received approval before paying the drafts. Every draft save the one in suit was accepted.

CONCLUSION OF LAW

The factual outline related is not in dispute, and the issue becomes one of law. It is well phrased by the District Judge in his "Discussion" in this way:

> "The only issue presented by the facts of this case is whether the documents tendered by the beneficiary to the issuer were in conformity with the terms of the letter of credit."

The letter of credit provided:

> "Except as otherwise expressly stated herein, this credit is subject to the 'Uniform Customs and Practice for Documentary Credits (1962 revision), the International Chamber of Commerce, Brochure No. 222.' " Finding of Fact 6.

Of particular pertinence, with accents added, are these injunctions of the Uniform Customs:

> "*Article 7.* Banks must examine all documents with reasonable care to ascertain that they *appear on their face* to be in accordance with the terms and conditions of the credit.

"*Article 8.* In documentary credit operations all parties concerned deal in documents and not in goods.

* * *

"If, upon receipt of the documents, the issuing bank considers that they *appear on their face* not to be in accordance with the terms and conditions of the credit, that bank must determine, on the basis of the documents alone, whether to claim that payment, acceptance or negotiation was not effected in accordance with the terms and conditions of the credit.

* * *

"*Article 9.* Banks * * * do [not] assume any liability or responsibility *for the description,* * * * quality, * * * of the goods represented thereby * * *.

* * *

"The description of the goods in the commercial *invoice* must correspond with the description in the credit. *In the remaining documents the goods may be described in general terms.*"

Also to be looked to are the North Carolina statutes, because in a diversity action, the Federal courts apply the same law as would the courts of the State of adjudication. Here applicable would be the Uniform Commercial Code—Letters of Credit, Chap. 25 G.S.N.C. Especially to be noticed are these sections:

"§ 25–5–109. Issuer's obligation to its customer."

"(1) An issuer's obligation to its customer includes good faith and observance of any general banking usage but unless other wise agreed does not include liability or responsibility

"(a) for performance of the underlying contract for sale or other transaction between the customer and the beneficiary; or

* * *

"(c) based on knowledge or lack of knowledge of any usage of any particular trade.

"(2) An issuer must examine documents with care so as to ascertain that on their face they appear to comply with the terms of the credit but unless otherwise agreed assumes no liability or responsibility for the genuineness, falsification or effect of any document which appears on such examination to be regular on its face."

In utilizing the rules of construction embodied in the letter of credit—the Uniform Customs and State statute—one must constantly recall that the drawee bank is not to be embroiled in disputes between the buyer and the seller, the beneficiary of the credit. The drawee is involved only with documents, not with merchandise. Its involvement is altogether separate and apart from the transaction between the buyer and seller; its duties and liability are governed exclusively by the terms of the letter, not the terms of the parties' contract with each other. Moreover, as the predominant authorities unequivocally declare, the beneficiary must meet the terms of the credit—and precisely—if it is to exact performance of the issuer. Failing such compliance there can be no recovery from the drawee. That is the specific failure of Courtaulds here.

Free of ineptness in wording, the letter of credit dictated that each invoice express on its face that it covered 100% acrylic yarn. Nothing less is shown to be tolerated in the trade. No substitution and no equivalent, through interpretation or logic, will serve. Harfield, Bank Credits and Acceptances (5th Ed.1974), at p. 73, commends and quotes aptly from an English case: "There is no room for documents which are almost the same, or which will do just as well." Equitable Trust Co. of N.Y. v. Dawson Partners, Ltd., 27 Lloyd's List Law Rpts. 49, 52 (1926). Although no pertinent North Carolina decision has been laid before us, in many cases elsewhere, especially in New York, we find the tenet of Harfield to be unshaken.

At trial Courtaulds prevailed on the contention that the invoices in actuality met the specifications of the letter of credit in that the packing lists attached to the invoices disclosed on their faces that the packages contained "cartons marked:—100% acrylic." On this premise it was urged that the lists were a part of the invoice since they were appended to it, and the invoices should be read as one with the lists, allowing the lists to detail the invoices. But this argument cannot be accepted. In this connection it is well to revert to the distinction made in *Uniform Customs,* supra, between the "invoice" and the "remaining documents," emphasizing that in the latter the description may be in general terms while in the invoice the goods must be described in conformity with the credit letter.

The District Judge's pat statement adeptly puts an end to this contention of Courtaulds:

> "In dealing with letters of credit, it is a custom and practice of the banking trade for a bank to only treat a document as an invoice which clearly is marked on its face as 'invoice.' " Finding of Fact 46.

This is not a pharisaical or doctrinaire persistence in the principle, but is altogether realistic in the environs of this case; it is plainly the fair and equitable measure. (The defect in description was not superficial but occurred in the statement of the *quality* of the yarn, not a frivolous concern.) The obligation of the drawee bank was graven in the credit. Indeed, there could be no departure from its words. Bank was not expected to scrutinize the collateral papers, such as the packing lists. Nor was it permitted to read into the instrument the contemplation or intention of the seller and buyer. Adherence to this rule was not only legally commanded, but it was factually ordered also, as will immediately appear.

Had Bank deviated from the stipulation of the letter and honored the draft, then at once it might have been confronted with the not improbable risk of the bankruptcy trustee's charge of liability for unwarrantably paying the draft moneys to the seller, Courtaulds, and refusal to reimburse Bank for the outlay. Contrarily, it might face a Courtaulds claim that since it had depended upon Bank's assurance of credit in shipping yarn to Adastra, Bank was responsible for the loss. In this situation Bank cannot be condemned for sticking to the letter of the letter.

Nor is this conclusion affected by the amended or substituted invoices which Courtaulds sent to Bank after the refusal of the draft. No precedent is cited to justify retroactive amendment of the invoices or extension of the credit beyond the August 15 expiry of the letter.

Finally, the trial court found that although in its prior practices Bank had pursued a strict-constructionist attitude, it had nevertheless on occasion honored drafts not within the verbatim terms of the credit letter. But it also found that in each of these instances Bank had first procured the authorization of Adastra to overlook the deficiencies. This truth is verified by the District Court in its Findings of Fact:

> "42. It is a standard practice and procedure of the banking industry and trade for a bank to attempt to obtain a waiver of discrepancies from its customer in a letter of credit transaction. This custom and practice was followed by NCNB in connection with the draft and documents received from Courtaulds.

> "43. Following this practice, NCNB had checked all previous discrepancies it discovered in Courtaulds' documents with its customer Adastra to see if Adastra would waive those discrepancies noted by NCNB. Except for the transaction in question, Adastra waived all discrepancies noted by NCNB.

> "44. It is not normal or customary for NCNB, nor is it the custom and practice in the banking trade, for a bank to notify a beneficiary or the presenter of the documents that there were any deficiencies in the draft or documents if they are waived by the customer."

This endeavor had been fruitless on the last draft because of the inability of Adastra to give its consent. Obviously the previous acceptances of truant invoices cannot be construed as a waiver in the present incident.

For these reasons, we must vacate the decision of the trial court, despite the evident close reasoning and research of the District Judge, Courtaulds North America, Inc. v. North Carolina N.B., 387 F.Supp. 92 (M.D.N.C.1975). Entry of judgment in favor of the appellant Bank on its summary motion is necessary.

Reversed and remanded for final judgment.

QUESTIONS AND NOTES

1. Problem. Bank issues a letter of credit that specifies, among other things, that the beneficiary present an invoice and a draft that refers to "Credit #53753." In due course the beneficiary presents an invoice, a draft that does not refer to any particular credit, and a letter that specifically states that the draft is being presented in connection with "Credit 53753." Is Bank obligated to honor the letter of credit?

2. Article 5 was revised in 1995, and the revision has been adopted in every jurisdiction. The rule that formerly appeared in 5–109 has been reworded and now appears in 5–108(a), (f).

United Bank Ltd. v. Cambridge Sporting Goods Corp.

New York Court of Appeals, 1976.
41 N.Y.2d 254, 392 N.Y.S.2d 265, 360 N.E.2d 943.

■ GABRIELLI, JUSTICE. On this appeal, we must decide whether fraud on the part of a seller-beneficiary of an irrevocable letter of credit may be successfully asserted as a defense against holders of drafts drawn by the seller pursuant to the credit. If we conclude that this defense may be interposed by the buyer who procured the letter of credit, we must also determine whether the courts below improperly imposed upon appellant buyer the burden of proving that respondent banks to whom the drafts were made payable by the seller-beneficiary of the letter of credit, were not holders in due course. The issues presented raise important questions concerning the application of the law of letters of credit and the rules governing proof of holder in due course status set forth in Article 3 of the Uniform Commercial Code. . . .

In April 1971 appellant Cambridge Sporting Goods Corporation (Cambridge) entered into a contract for the manufacture and sale of boxing gloves with Duke Sports (Duke), a Pakistani corporation. Duke committed itself to the manufacture of 27,936 pairs of boxing gloves at a sale price of $42,576.80; and arranged with its Pakistani bankers, United Bank Limited (United) and The Muslim Commercial Bank (Muslim), for the financing of the sale. Cambridge was requested by these banks to cover payment of the purchase price by opening an irrevocable letter of credit with its bank in New York, Manufacturers Hanover Trust Company (Manufacturers). Manufacturers issued an irrevocable letter of credit obligating it, upon the receipt of certain documents indicating shipment of the merchandise pursuant to the contract, to accept and pay, 90 days after acceptance, drafts drawn upon Manufacturers for the purchase price of the gloves.

Following confirmation of the opening of the letter of credit, Duke informed Cambridge that it would be impossible to manufacture and deliver the merchandise within the time period required by the contract, and sought an extension of time for performance until September 15, 1971, and a continuation of the letter of credit, which was due to expire on August 11. Cambridge replied on June 18 that it would not agree to a postponement of the manufacture and delivery of the gloves because of its resale commitments and, hence, it promptly advised Duke that the contract was canceled and the letter of credit should be returned. Cambridge simultaneously notified United of the contract cancellation.

Despite the cancellation of the contract, Cambridge was informed on July 17, 1971, that documents had been received at Manufacturers from United purporting to evidence a shipment of the boxing gloves under the terms of the canceled contract. The documents were accompanied by a draft, dated July 16, 1971, drawn by Duke upon Manufacturers and made payable to United, for the amount of $21,288.40, one half of the contract price of the boxing gloves. A second set of documents was received by Manufacturers from Muslim, also accompanied by a draft, dated August 20, and drawn upon Manufacturers by Duke for the remaining amount of the contract price.

An inspection of the shipments upon their arrival revealed that Duke had shipped old, unpadded, ripped and mildewed gloves rather than the new gloves to be manufactured as agreed upon. Cambridge then commenced an action against Duke in Supreme Court, New York County, joining Manufacturers as a party, and obtained a preliminary injunction prohibiting the latter from paying drafts drawn under the letter of credit. . . . Duke ultimately defaulted in the action and judgment against it was entered in the amount of the drafts, in March 1972. The present proceeding was instituted by the Pakistani banks . . . to obtain payment of the drafts on the letter of credit. The banks asserted that they were holders in due course of the drafts which had been made payable to them by Duke and, thus, were entitled to the proceeds thereof irrespective of any defenses which Cambridge had established against their transferor, Duke, in the prior action which had terminated in a default judgment. . . .

The trial court concluded that the burden of proving that the banks were not holders in due course lay with Cambridge, and directed a verdict in favor of the banks on the ground that Cambridge had not met that burden; the court stated that Cambridge failed to demonstrate that the banks themselves had participated in the seller's acts of fraud, proof of which was concededly present in the record. The Appellate Division affirmed, agreeing that while there was proof tending to establish the defenses against the seller, Cambridge had not shown that the seller's acts were "connected to the petitioners [banks] in any manner." . . .

We reverse and hold that it was improper to direct a verdict in favor of the petitioning Pakistani banks. We conclude that the defense of fraud in the transaction was established and in that circumstance the burden shifted to petitioners to prove that they were holders in due course and took the drafts for value, in good faith and without notice of any fraud on the part of Duke (§ 3–302). . . . This case does not come before us in the typical posture of a lawsuit between the bank issuing the letter of credit and presenters of drafts drawn under the credit seeking payment (see, generally, White and Summers, Uniform Commercial Code, § 18–6, pp. 619–628). Because Cambridge obtained an injunction against payment of the drafts, . . . it stands in the same position as the issuer, and, thus, the law of letters of credit governs the liability of Cambridge to the Pakistani banks. Article 5 of the Uniform Commercial Code, dealing with letters of credit, and the Uniform Customs and Practice for Documentary Credits promulgated by the International Chamber of Commerce set forth the duties and obligations of the issuer of a letter of credit.[2] A letter of credit is a commitment on the part of the issuing bank that it will pay a draft presented to it under the terms of the credit, and if it is a documentary draft, upon presentation of the required documents of title (see § 5–103). Banks issuing letters of credit deal in documents and not in goods and are not responsible for any breach of warranty or nonconformity of the goods involved in the underlying sales contract (see § 5–114, subd. [1]; Uniform Customs and Practice, General Provisions and Definitions [c] and article 9 . . . . Subdivision (2) of section 5–114, however indicates certain limited circumstances in which an issuer *may* properly refuse to honor a draft drawn under a letter of credit or a customer may enjoin an issuer from honoring such a draft.[3] Thus, where "fraud in the transaction" has been shown and the holder has not taken the draft in circumstances that would make it a holder in due course, the customer may apply to enjoin the issuer

---

2. It should be noted that the Uniform Customs and Practice controls, in lieu of Article 5 of the Code, where, unless otherwise agreed by the parties, a letter of credit is made subject to the provisions of the Uniform Customs and Practice by its terms or by agreement, course of dealing or usage of trade (§ 5–102, subd. [4]). No proof was offered that there was an agreement that the Uniform Customs and Practice should apply, nor does the credit so state (cf. Oriental Pacific [U.S.A.] v. Toronto Dominion Bank, 78 Misc.2d 819, 357 N.Y.S.2d 957). Neither do the parties otherwise contend that their rights should be resolved under the Uniform Customs and Practice. However, even if the Uniform Customs and Practice were deemed applicable to this case, it would not, in the absence of a conflict, abrogate the precode case law (now codified in § 5–114) and that authority continues to govern even where Article 5 is not controlling (see White and Summers, op. cit., pp. 613–614, 624–625). Moreover, the Uniform Customs and Practice provisions are not in conflict nor do they treat with the subject matter of section 5–114 which is dispositive of the issues presented on this appeal (see Banco Tornquist, S.A. v. American Bank & Trust Co., 71 Misc.2d 874, 875, 337 N.Y.S.2d 489; Intraworld Ind. v. Girard Trust Bank, 461 Pa. 343, 336 A.2d 316, 322; Harfield, Practice Commentary, McKinney's Cons. Laws of N.Y., Book 62½, Uniform Commercial Code, § 5–114, p. 686). Thus, we are of the opinion that the Uniform Customs and Practice, where applicable, does

not bar the relief provided for in section 5–114 of the code.

[Ed. Note: 5–102(4), adopted in New York, Alabama, and Missouri, reads as follows:

"(4) Unless otherwise agreed, this Article 5 does not apply to a letter of credit or a credit if by its terms or by agreement, course of dealing or usage of trade such letter of credit or credit is subject in whole or in part to the Uniform Customs and Practice for Commercial Documentary Credits fixed by the Thirteenth or by any subsequent Congress of the International Chamber of Commerce."]

3. Subdivision (2) of section 5–114 of the Uniform Commercial Code provides that,

"[u]nless otherwise agreed when documents appear on their face to comply with the terms of a credit but * * * there is fraud in the transaction (a) the issuer must honor the draft or demand for payment if honor is demanded by a * * * holder of the draft * * * which has taken the draft * * * under the credit and under circumstances which would make it a holder in due course (Section 3–302) * * *; and

"(b) in all other cases as against its customer, an issuer acting in good faith may honor the draft * * * despite notification from the customer of fraud, forgery or other defect not apparent on the face of the documents but a court of appropriate jurisdiction may enjoin such honor."

from paying drafts drawn under the letter of credit (see 1955 Report of N.Y.Law Rev.Comm., vol. 3, pp. 1654–1559). This rule represents a codification of precode case law most eminently articulated in the landmark case of Sztejn v. Schroder Banking Corp., 177 Misc. 719, 31 N.Y.S.2d 631, Shientag, J., where it was held that the shipment of cowhair in place of bristles amounted to more than mere breach of warranty but fraud sufficient to constitute grounds for enjoining payment of drafts to one not a holder in due course. Even prior to the *Sztejn* case, forged or fraudulently procured documents were proper grounds for avoidance of payment of drafts drawn under a letter of credit (Finkelstein, Legal Aspects of Commercial Letters of Credit, pp. 231–236–247); and cases decided after the enactment of the code have cited *Sztejn* with approval . . . .

. . . The evidentiary facts are not disputed and we hold upon the facts as established, that the shipment of old, unpadded, ripped and mildewed gloves rather than the new boxing gloves as ordered by Cambridge, constituted fraud in the transaction within the meaning of subdivision (2) of section 5–114. It should be noted that the drafters of section 5–114, in their attempt to codify the *Sztejn* case and in utilizing the term "fraud in the transaction," have eschewed a dogmatic approach and adopted a flexible standard to be applied as the circumstances of a particular situation mandate. It can be difficult to draw a precise line between cases involving breach of warranty (or a difference of opinion as to the quality of goods) and outright fraudulent practice on the part of the seller. To the extent, however, that Cambridge established that Duke was guilty of *fraud* in shipping, not merely nonconforming merchandise, but worthless fragments of boxing gloves, this case is similar to *Sztejn.*

If the petitioning banks are holders in due course they are entitled to recover the proceeds of the drafts but if such status cannot be demonstrated their petition must fail. . . .

. . .

In order to qualify as a holder in due course, a holder must have taken the instrument "without notice * * * of any defense against * * * it on the part of any person" (§ 3–302, subd. [1], par. [c]). Pursuant to subdivision (2) of section 5–114 fraud in the transaction is a valid defense to payment of drafts drawn under a letter of credit. Since the defense of fraud in the transaction was shown, the burden shifted to the banks by operation of subdivision (3) of section 3–307 to prove that they were holders in due course and took the drafts without notice of Duke's alleged fraud. . . . It was error for the trial court to direct a verdict in favor of the Pakistani banks because this determination rested upon a misallocation of the burden of proof; and we conclude that the banks have not satisfied the burden of proving that they qualified in all respects as holders in due course, by any affirmative proof. . . .

Accordingly, the order of the Appellate Division should be reversed, with costs, and the petition dismissed.

NOTE

The rule that formerly appeared in 5–114 (see footnote 3 of *Cambridge Sporting Goods*) has been modified and now appears in 5–109.

*

INDEX

References are to pages

ACCEPTANCE OF GOODS
See also, Buyer's Remedies
Actions constituting acceptance of goods, 370, 450
Buyer's action implying acceptance of goods not in buyer's possession, 450
Buyer's right revocation of, see Buyer's Remedies
Distinguished from possession, 384
Use after rejection, 380
Use after revocation of acceptance, 396, 400

ACCEPTANCE OF OFFER
See also, Contract Formation, Firm Offer
Additional terms included, effect on acceptance, 69, 78, 86, 90

ATTORNEY'S FEES
Recovery of, in Magnuson–Moss actions, 339

AUCTION SALES
Generally, 29, 211
Owner's bid, 213
Shill bidding and puffing, 213
With or without reserve, 211

BAILMENT
Generally, 200

BATTLE OF THE FORMS
Generally, 69
CISG, 85
Leases, 86
Mirror-image rule, 69, 78
Revised Article 2, 86
Terms in the box, 86, 90

BILLS OF LADING
See also Letters of Credit, Sight Drafts
Generally, 588
Carrier liability, 588, 594, 600, 606
Federal Bill of Lading Act, 593, 594
Forms, 589, 592
Negotiable bills, 588, 589
Security interest in the goods, 609
Straight bills, 588, 592
Use with carrier, 609

BLOOD TRANSFUSION
Scope of Article 2, 19

BREACH
See Buyer's Remedies, Cure; Remedies, Repudiation, Seller's Remedies, Warranty

BULK SALES
Generally, 568
Transactions constituting bulk sales, 569

BUYER IN ORDINARY COURSE
Title, 538, 543, 550

BUYER'S REMEDIES
See also, Damages, Express Warranty, Implied Warranty, Warranty Disclaimer
Breach of warranty, 300, 431
CISG, 414, 425, 430
Consequential damages, 279, 411
Contractual limitations on damages, 438, 441
Failure of essential purpose of limited remedy, 439, 441
Unconscionability, 441
Cover, 416
Cure, seller's right to, 383, 384, 396, 402, 404
Revised Article 2, 396, 407
CISG, 407
Damages for seller's breach, 415, 431, 438
Goods kept by buyer, 431
Insecurity, 491, 492
Installment contracts, right to reject, 359, 361
Lemon laws, 350, 448
Magnuson–Moss Consumer Warranty Act, 339
Notice of breach required, 432, 433, 436
Perfect-tender rule, 353, 359
Pre–Code law, 351
CISG, 358
Rejection of nonconforming goods, 351, 353, 359, 361, 370, 384
Buyer's duties on rightful rejection, 378
Good-faith limitation, 357
Installment contracts, 359, 361
Perfect-tender rule, 353, 359
Rescission distinguished, 379
Remedial promise, 419
Replevin, 408, 413
Rescission distinguished, 379
Revocation of acceptance,
Generally, 396, 402, 405
Rejection distinguished, 379

BUYER'S REMEDIES—Cont'd
Revocation of acceptance—Cont'd
    Substantial impairment of value, 396
    Use after revocation of acceptance, 400
Specific performance, 408, 412
    By agreement ex ante, 413
    CISG, 414
    Replevin, 408, 413
    Revised Article 2, 413

CARRIERS
    See also, Bills of Lading
Burden of proof, 594, 600
Carmack Amendment, 594
Carriage of Goods by Sea Act, 599
Common carrier distinguished from contract
    carrier, 598
Liability for,
    Acts of shipper, 594
    Damage in transit, 594, 600
    Fraud of seller, 600
    Improper delivery on a straight bill, 606
    Loss at sea or in the air, 599

CHOICE OF LAW
    Generally, 206
Limitations under 1–105, 37, 206
Limitations under revised 1–301, 37, 210

**CISG (Convention on Contracts for the
International Sale of Goods)**
Applicability, 28
Assurances, 512
Battle of the forms, 85
Burden of proving nonconformity, 382
Conflicting terms, 85
Contract formalities, 69
Contract modification, 114
Cover, 464
Cure, 407
Damages, 430, 455, 464
Express warranty, 267
Firm offers, 120
Implied warranty, 267
Impossibility and frustration, 533
Insecurity, 512
Modification of contract, 114
Open-price term, 172
Parol evidence, 147
Perfect-tender rule, 358
Remedies, 430, 455, 464
Replacement transactions, damages based on,
    464
Repudiation, 512
Right to reject goods, 358
Risk of loss, 205
Scope, 28
Seller's right to the price, 455
Specific performance, 415
Statute of frauds, 69
Unconscionability, 137
Varying acceptance, 85
Warranty, 267

COMMERCIAL CUSTOM
See Contract Construction

CONSEQUENTIAL DAMAGES
See Buyer's Remedies, Seller's Remedies,
    Warranty Disclaimer

CONSUMER
Magnuson–Moss Consumer Warranty Act,
    338
    Privity, 340
    Leases, 345
Parol evidence rule, 145
Privity, 311
Rights against secured creditor of seller, 550
Risk of loss, 201
Unconscionability, 136, 137
Uniform Consumer Credit Code (UCCC), 137
Warranty disclaimer,
    Revised Article 2, 284, 294
    Varying state laws, 347

CONTRACT CONSTRUCTION
    See also, Parol Evidence
Construction of terms, 140, 141, 145, 148
Parol evidence, admission of, 141
Usage of trade, 148

CONTRACT FORMATION
    See also, Acceptance of Offer, Battle of the
        Forms, CISG, Firm Offer, Statute of
        Frauds, Unconscionability
Ambiguous offers, 48
CISG, 85, 114, 69
Conflicting terms, 69, 78, 86, 90
Electronic contracting, 96
Firm offers, 117
Indefiniteness, 39, 42
Modifications, 98, 109
Offer and acceptance, 39, 42
Rolling contracts, 86, 90
Statute of frauds, 49, 57, 63
Terms in the box, 86, 90

**COURSE OF DEALING/PERFORM-
ANCE**
Supplementary terms, 148
Waiver, 98, 109

COVER
    See also Buyer's Remedies
Buyer's right, 416
CISG, 430
Leases 422

CREDIT SALES
Documentary, 587, 609

CURE
    Generally, 383, 384
After revocation of acceptance, 396, 402, 404
After time for performance expires, 394
CISG, 380
Replacement vs. repair, 366
Revised Article 2, 396, 407
Shaken-faith doctrine, 384, 389

DAMAGES
See also, Buyer's Remedies, Seller's Remedies
Actual loss as limitation, 422, 427
    CISG, 430, 455, 464
    Leases, 455, 464
Buyer's breach of contract for goods to be manufactured, 470, 471
Certainty of proof, 416
Consequential damages for breach of express warranty, 416
Contractual limitation, 438, 441
Cover, 416
    CISG 430, 464
    Leases, 464
Failure to notify buyer of repudiation, 501
Failure to notify seller of repudiation, 470
Fixed costs and overhead, recoverability of, 470
Impossibility of performance or frustration of purpose, 514, 518, 522
Liquidated damages, 475, 477, 484
    Take-or-pay contract, 477
    Leases, 487
Lost profits, 465
Repudiation, 504, 505
    CISG, 512
Requirements of proof, 498, 501, 505
Seller's duty to inform buyer of resale, 474

DELIVERY
See also Mercantile Terms, Shipment Terms
Waiver of prompt delivery, 433, 436

DISCLAIMER
See Warranty Disclaimer

DOCUMENTARY SALES
Credit sale, 587, 609

ELECTRONIC COMMERCE
Authorized, 96

ENTRUSTMENT
Rights of buyer, 550

EQUITABLE REMEDIES
See also, Remedies
Buyer's right to specific performance or replevin, See Buyer's Remedies

EXPRESS WARRANTY
See also, Implied Warranty, Warranty Disclaimer
Distinguishing "trade talk" or "puffing", 216, 219, 262
History, 215
Liability of remote sellers, 295
Privity, 295
Recovery of consequential damages for breach of, 441
Reliance, necessity of, 216, 219

FIRM OFFER
CISG, 120
Code provisions, 117

FORCE MAJEURE
Excuse for nonperformance, 517

FRAUDULENT TRANSFERS
See also, Bulk Sales
Generally, 555
Actual delivery, 564
Burden of proof, 557
Inadequate consideration, 557, 566, 567
Intent to "hinder, defraud, or delay" creditors, 566
Preferences, no presumption of fraud, 557
Retention of possession by seller, 557
Uniform Fraudulent Transfer Act, 566, 567

FRUSTRATION OF PURPOSE
See Impossibility of Performance

GOOD FAITH
Merchant, 164
Purchase by innocent third person, 539, 543, 550
Rejection, 357
Requirements under the Code, 164, 543

GOODS
Application of Article 2, 11

IMPLIED WARRANTY
See also Express Warranty, Warranty Disclaimer
Consumer expectations test, 246, 247
Fitness for particular purpose, 262, 264
Industry standards, relevance of, 235
Latent defect, 243
Liability of remote sellers, 307, 311, 321
Merchantability distinguished from fitness for purpose, 264
Non-sales transactions, 273

IMPOSSIBILITY OF PERFORMANCE
Generally, 514, 518, 522
CISG, 533
Damages, 514
Force majeure, 517
Frustration of purpose, 514, 518
Leases, 533

INTERNATIONAL SALES CONVENTION
See CISG

LETTERS OF CREDIT
Generally, 611
Fraud of seller as a defense, 619
Requirement of specificity, 613

LEMON LAWS
Remedy for consumer transactions, 350, 448

LIMITATION OF LIABILITY
Magnuson–Moss Consumer Warranty Act, 338

LIMITATION OF REMEDY
See also Unconscionability, Warranty Disclaimer
Failure of essential purpose, 495

LOST PROFITS
See Damages, Remedies

MAGNUSON–MOSS CONSUMER WARRANTY ACT
Generally, 338
Attorney's fees, 339
Disclaimer of implied warranties, 339
Leases, 345
Privity, 340
Written warranty vs. express warranty, 338

MERCANTILE TERMS
See also Delivery, Shipment Terms
As a delivery gap filler, 194, 196

MERCHANT
See also Firm Offer, Good Faith, Statute of Frauds, Unconscionability, Warranty
Battle of the forms, 69, 78
Definition, 57
Farmer as, 57
Good faith, 164
Statute of frauds, 57
Unconscionability, 123, 125
Warranty of merchantability, 231, 232, 235

MODIFICATION
CISG, 114
Oral modification, 98, 109
Waiver of requirement of writing, 89, 108

MUTUALITY OF OBLIGATION
Open-price term, 163
Output/requirements contract, 177

NOTICE
Buyer's obligation to give notice of breach, 432, 433, 436
Revised Article 2, 438
Required by standards of fair dealing, 496
Seller's obligation to notify buyer of breach, 496

OFFER
See Acceptance, Contract Formation, Firm Offer

OPEN–PRICE TERM
Generally, 161, 162
CISG, 172
Good faith, 164

OPEN–QUANTITY TERM
Indefiniteness, 171, 172

PAROL EVIDENCE
Contract formation under the UCC, 140
Enforceability of additional terms, 141, 145
Usage of trade and course of dealing, 148

PERFECT–TENDER RULE
Generally, 351
CISG, 358
Good-faith limitation, 357
Installment contracts, 359, 361

PERFORMANCE
See Buyer's Remedies, Cure, Remedies, Seller's Remedies

PRIVITY
Consequential damages, 300, 302, 311
Disclaimer of warranties, 321
Express warranties, 295
Implied warranties, 307, 311
Leases, 320
Magnuson–Moss Consumer Warranty Act, 340
Revised Article 2, 304, 324
Revocation of acceptance, 401

REAL PROPERTY
Distinguished from personal property for purposes of application of the UCC, 32

REJECTION
See also, Buyer's Remedies
Procedural requirements, 378, 379
Substantive right, 351, 353, 359, 361
Use by buyer after, 380

REMEDIES
See also, Buyer's Remedies, CISG, Seller's Remedies
Equitable requirements for specific performance, 409, 412
Pre–Code law, 413
Incidental damages, 415, 416
Lost profits, 458, 465

REPUDIATION
Generally, 497, 505
Actions constituting, 497
Anticipatory breach, 497
By seller
Buyer's duties, 505
Buyer's obligation to cover, 505
Buyer's insolvency as, 495, 496
CISG, 512
Damages
Generally, 505
Pre–Code law, 508
Diminished expectation of return performance, 491, 492
Right to demand assurances, 491, 492

REVISED ARTICLE 2
Battle of the forms, 86
Cure, 396, 407
Notice of breach, 438
Privity, 304, 324
Remedial promise, 449
Specific performance, 413, 487
Statute of frauds, 68
Warranty disclaimer, 284, 294

REVOCATION OF ACCEPTANCE OF GOODS
See Buyer's Remedies

RISK OF LOSS
See also, Shipment Terms, Statutory Terms
Applicability of the Code, 186
Bailed goods, 200
CISG, 205
Effect of breach, 201
Goods stored for buyer, 198
Pre–Code law, 186

SALE ON APPROVAL
See also Sale or Return
Creditor risk, 211

SALE OR RETURN
See also Sale on Approval
Creditor risk, 211
Risk of loss, 211

SCOPE OF ARTICLE 2
Generally, 11
Application by analogy, 29
Auctions, 29
Blood transfusions, 19
CISG, 28
Distributorships, 26
Franchises, 26
Hybrid transactions, 11, 27
Leases, 27
Real estate, 27, 32
Software, 20, 22

SECURITY INTEREST
Article 9 secured party vs. buyer, 538, 539, 543
In bill of lading, 611
Shipment under reservation, 609

SELLER'S REMEDIES
Generally, 450
Action for damages, 456, 458, 465
Action for the price, 450
CISG, 455
Obligation to notify buyer of intent to resell, 474
Right to complete manufacturing of goods, 474
Right to recover goods from insolvent buyer, 571, 579, 580, 583
Right to stop delivery or refuse delivery except for cash, 496, 497
Specially manufactured goods, 450
Specific performance, 484
Revised Article 2, 487

SHIPMENT TERMS
See also, Delivery
Generally, 187, 188
FOB, FAS and other trade terms, 188
Incoterms, 197
Risk of loss, 186

SHIPMENT UNDER RESERVATION
Seller's right to, 609

SIGHT DRAFT
In credit transactions, 610

SPECIFIC PERFORMANCE
Generally, 408, 409, 412
CISG, 414
Replevin, 413
Revised Article 2, 413, 487

STATUTE OF FRAUDS
Generally, 49, 50
Admission in court, 67
CISG, 69
Estoppel to assert, 57, 63
Leases, 69
Merchant provisions, 57
Part performance
   In general, 66
   Partial payment, 66
Quantity terms, necessity for, 173
Revised Article 2, 68

STATUTORY TERMS
Generally, 159
Delivery, 181, 182
Payment, 180
Price, 161, 164
   CISG, 172
   Open-price and other uncertain terms, 171
   Pre–Code history, 161
   Unilateral good-faith pricing, 162, 163, 164
   Variable-price terms, 163
Quantity
   Exclusive-dealing contracts, 179
   "More or less" terms, 180
   Open-quantity, 179
   Output and requirements contracts, 177
   Statute of frauds, 172
   Usage of trade, 148

TAKE–OR–PAY CONTRACTS
Enforceability, 477

THIRD PARTY RIGHTS
See also Bulk Sales, Fraudulent Transfers, Title
Bankruptcy law
   Generally, 571, 580, 583
   Limitations on avoiding powers, 578
   Statutory liens, 578
Bona fide purchaser status, 543
Bulk sales, 568
Buyer vs. Article 9 secured party, 538, 539, 543
Fraudulent transfers, 555, 557
Seller's right to recover goods from insolvent buyer as against buyer's creditors, 571, 579, 580, 583
   In bankruptcy, 571

TITLE
See also, Fraudulent Conveyances
Acquired by third parties,
By purchase from person with voidable title, 550
Goods entrusted to merchant, 550
When title passes under Code, 534

UCITA
Software transactions, 24

UCP500
Letters of credit, 613

UNCONSCIONABILITY
Generally, 123, 125
CISG, 137
Commercial transactions, 125, 135
Consumer transactions, 136, 137
Distinguished from failure of essential purpose, 441
Leases, 137
Limitation of contract terms, 122
Uniform Consumer Credit Code (UCCC), 137
Warranty disclaimer, 125, 293
See also Warranty Disclaimer

UNIFORM COMMERCIAL CODE
As a "code", 7
As federal law, 514
Historical background, 2
Philosophy concerning missing contract terms, 121
Scope of Article 2,
Generally, 11
Application to non-sales situations by analogy, 31
CISG, 28
Computer software, 20, 22
Consumer statutes, 33
Territorial limitations, 35

UNITED NATIONS CONVENTION ON CONTRACTS FOR THE INTERNATIONAL SALE OF GOODS
See CISG

WAIVER
Established by course of performance, 98, 109, 148
Relationship to no-oral-modification clauses, 98, 109

WARRANTY
See also Express Warranty, Implied Warranty, Unconscionability, Warranty Disclaimer
CISG, 227
Contractual limitation, failure of essential purpose, 438, 441
Defenses,
Assumption of the risk, 325
Contributory negligence, 325, 329, 333
Magnuson–Moss Consumer Warranty Act, 338
Privity,
Generally, 295
Express warranty, 300
Revised Article 2, 304, 324
Remedial promises under revised Article 2, 449
State warranty laws, 347
Title, warranty of, 274
CISG, 278
Disclaimer, 277
Leases, 278

WARRANTY DISCLAIMER
Generally, 307–333
"As is" clauses, 285
Conspicuousness, 279, 285
Consumer transactions, limitations in, 338, 347
Leases, 294
Magnuson–Moss Consumer Warranty Act, 338
Personal injuries, 292
Revised Article 2, 284, 294
Title, 277

†